The Iran-U.S. Claims Tribunal, concerned principally with the claims of U.S. nationals against Iran, is the most important international claims tribunal to have sat in over half a century. Its jurisprudence is bound to make a uniquely important contribution to international law and, in particular, the law relating to aliens. The series is the only complete and fully indexed report of the decisions of this unique Tribunal. These Reports are essential for all practitioners in the field of international claims, academics in private and public international law and comparative lawyers as well as all Governments and law libraries. Each volume contains a detailed consolidated index and tables of cases covering the whole series to date.

EDWARD HELGESON is a Fellow of the Lauterpacht Research Centre for International Law at the University of Cambridge.

IRAN – UNITED STATES
CLAIMS TRIBUNAL REPORTS

Volume
30

This volume may be cited as: 30 IRAN–U.S. C.T.R.–

IRAN – UNITED STATES CLAIMS TRIBUNAL REPORTS

Volume

30

EDITED
BY
EDWARD HELGESON, MA (CANTAB.), JD

CONSULTING EDITOR
SIR ELIHU LAUTERPACHT, CBE, QC
HONORARY PROFESSOR OF INTERNATIONAL LAW
UNIVERSITY OF CAMBRIDGE
BENCHER OF GRAY'S INN

A PUBLICATION OF
THE LAUTERPACHT RESEARCH CENTRE FOR INTERNATIONAL LAW,
UNIVERSITY OF CAMBRIDGE

GROTIUS PUBLICATIONS

CAMBRIDGE
UNIVERSITY PRESS

PUBLISHED BY THE PRESS SYNDICATE OF THE UNIVERSITY OF CAMBRIDGE
The Pitt Building, Trumpington Street, Cambridge, United Kingdom

CAMBRIDGE UNIVERSITY PRESS
The Edinburgh Building, Cambridge CB2 2RU, UK
40 West 20th Street, New York, NY 10011–4211, USA
10 Stamford Road, Oakleigh, Melbourne 3166, Australia
Ruiz de Alarcón 13, 28014 Madrid, Spain
Dock House, The Waterfront, Cape Town 8001, South Africa

http://www.cambridge.org

© Cambridge University Press 2001

This book is in copyright. Subject to statutory exception and to the provisions of relevant collective licensing agreements, no reproduction of any part may take place without the written permission of Cambridge University Press.

First published 2001

Printed in the United Kingdom at the University Press, Cambridge

Typeset in Baskerville 10/12.5pt   System 3b2   [CE]

A catalogue record for this book is available from the British Library

ISBN 0 521 80436 1 hardback

CONTENTS

	PAGE
Editorial Note	ix
Acknowledgments	x
Table of Cases – Volume 30	
Alphabetical	xi
According to category	xii
According to case number	xiii
Consolidated Table of Cases	
Alphabetical	xiv
According to category	xxxii
According to case number	li
According to Decision/Award number	lix
Decisions and Awards	1
Awards on Agreed Terms	
University of Southern California *v* Iran	283
Christensen, Inc. *v* Iran	292
Kidde Consultants, Inc. *v* Haydar Ghyai & Associates	302
Index	311

EDITORIAL NOTE

This series of Reports contains the texts of Decisions, Awards, Awards on Agreed Terms, Interim Awards, Interlocutory Awards, Interim and Interlocutory Awards, Selected Orders and Refusal Cases emanating from the Iran-U.S. Claims Tribunal set up under the Claims Settlement Declaration to which the Governments of Iran and the United States adhered on 19 January 1981. The present volume contains material dated during the period 1 January to 31 December 1994.

All Decisions, Awards, Interim Awards, Interlocutory Awards and Refusal Cases are printed in these Reports. Procedural Orders are printed on a selective basis from the many thousands that have been issued by the Tribunal since its inception. Also, from time to time a section of a volume may be devoted to additional documents of a procedural nature.

Awards on Agreed Terms now largely follow a standard form and are individually of little legal significance. These therefore are also printed on a selective basis, together with some relevant supporting documents. Three such Awards on Agreed Terms appear in this volume.

Each volume contains a Consolidated Index and Tables of Cases for the whole series, as well as Tables of Cases for the volume itself.

Decisions and Awards of the Tribunal are issued in numerical sequence on the basis of the date on which they are filed. The intent of these Reports is to reproduce the texts in that chronological order. This is only departed from if it is felt that a decision of particular significance should be brought forward or if there is insufficient space in a particular volume for an unusually lengthy text. Separate Opinions of individual judges follow the Decision or Award to which they refer, except when filed so late as to be unavailable for inclusion in the same volume. In such cases the absence of an Opinion is indicated by a footnote at the beginning of the case; the late-filed Opinion appears at the beginning of the first volume for which it is available.

It has been the policy of successive editors of these Reports to make no changes to the texts issued by the Tribunal. Editorial input to the texts is limited to two types. First, consistency has been sought in some small matters of style and layout, such as captions, headings and citation of Tribunal cases and decisions. Secondly, some editorial footnotes have been introduced. These are used to indicate the presence or absence of Opinions, to cross-reference previous Decisions and Awards of the Tribunal and to add other points of information for the reader. These notes are indicated by the enclosure within square brackets of both the footnote indicator and the footnote itself, and original footnotes are renumbered accordingly.

ACKNOWLEDGMENTS

This volume has been prepared within, and upon the initiative of, the Lauterpacht Research Centre for International Law of the University of Cambridge.

Special thanks are due to Mr. Timothy Walsh for his work in assembling and organising the text, and to Miss Maureen MacGlashan for her work on the Consolidated Index.

Lauterpacht Research Centre for International Law
University of Cambridge

Edward Helgeson
October 2000

TABLE OF CASES – VOLUME 30
ALPHABETICAL

Cameron Kamran Khosrowshahi *v.* Iran, *see* Khosrowshahi *v.* Iran
Catherine Etezadi *v.* Iran, *see* Etezadi *v.* Iran
Cecilia Radene Ebrahimi *v.* Iran, *see* Ebrahimi *v.* Iran
Christensen, Inc. *v.* Iran, 292
Christina Tandis Ebrahimi *v.* Iran, *see* Ebrahimi *v.* Iran
Continental Bank International *v.* Iran, *see* Continental Illinois National Bank and Trust Company of Chicago *v.* Iran
Continental Illinois National Bank and Trust Company of Chicago *v.* Iran, 3
Dadras International *v.* Iran, 104
Ebrahimi *v.* Iran, 170
Etezadi *v.* Iran, 22
Faith Lita Khosrowshahi *v.* Iran, *see* Khosrowshahi *v.* Iran
Jalal Moin *v.* Iran, *see* Moin *v.* Iran
Kevin Kayvan Khosrowshahi *v.* Iran, *see* Khosrowshahi *v.* Iran
Khatami *v.* Iran, 267
Khosrowshahi *v.* Iran, 76
Kidde Consultants, Inc. *v.* Haydar Ghyai & Associates, 302
Marcene P. Khosrowshahi *v.* Iran, *see* Khosrowshahi *v.* Iran
Mohsen Asgari Nazari *v.* Iran, *see* Nazari *v.* Iran
Moin *v.* Iran, 70
Morteza Khatami *v.* Iran, *see* Khatami *v.* Iran
Nazari *v.* Iran, 123
Per Am Construction Corporation *v.* Iran, *see* Dadras International *v.* Iran
Security Pacific National Bank *v.* Bank Markazi Iran, 13
Shahin Shaine Ebrahimi *v.* Iran, *see* Ebrahimi *v.* Iran
Susanne P. Khosrowshahi *v.* Iran, *see* Khosrowshahi *v.* Iran
Unidyne Corp. *v.* Iran, 19
University of Southern California *v.* Iran, 283
Wells Fargo Bank *v.* Iran, 8

TABLE OF CASES – VOLUME 30

ARRANGED ACCORDING TO CATEGORY: DECISIONS, AWARDS,
AWARDS ON AGREED TERMS AND ORDERS

DECISIONS

Continental Illinois National Bank and Trust Company of Chicago *v* Iran, 3
Security Pacific National Bank *v* Bank Markazi Iran, 13
Unidyne Corp. *v* Iran, 19
Wells Fargo Bank *v* Iran, 8

AWARDS

Ebrahimi *v* Iran, 170
Etezadi *v* Iran, 22
Khatami *v* Iran, 267
Khosrowshahi *v* Iran, 76
Moin *v* Iran, 70
Nazari *v* Iran, 123

AWARDS ON AGREED TERMS

Christensen, Inc. *v* Iran, 292
Kidde Consultants, Inc. *v* Haydar Ghyai & Associates, 302
University of Southern California *v* Iran, 283

ORDER

Dadras International *v* Iran, 104

TABLE OF CASES – VOLUME 30

ARRANGED ACCORDING TO CASE NUMBER

Case No.	Page
44 –	170
46 –	170
47 –	170
178 –	76
212 –	292
213 –	104
215 –	104
221 –	123
294 –	8

Case No.	Page
319 –	22
321 –	283
332 –	13
352 –	3
368 –	19
767 –	267
841 –	302
950 –	70

CONSOLIDATED TABLE OF CASES[1]

ALPHABETICAL

Abbas Ghaffari *v* National Iranian Oil Company, *see* Ghaffari (A.) *v* National Iranian Oil Company
Abboud *v* Iran, **1**, 230; **24**, 265
Abrahamian *v* Iran, **23**, 285
Abrahim Rahman Golshani *v* Iran, *see* Golshani *v* Iran
A.B.S. Worldwide Technical Services, Inc. *v* Iran, **3**, 176, 192
Accurate Machine Products Corporation *v* Iran, **19**, 374
Adams International Division of Beatrice Foods Company *v* Iran, **6**, 1
Advanced Computer Techniques Corporation *v* Iran, **2**, 33; **3**, 326
Aeromaritime, Inc. *v* Iran, **1**, 135
Aeronutronic Overseas Services, Inc. *v* Telecommunications Company of Iran, **5**, 187; **14**, 339
Aeronutronic Overseas Services, Inc. *v* The Air Force of the Islamic Republic of Iran, **1**, 483; **7**, 217; **8**, 75; **11**, 223
A.E. Staley Manufacturing Company *v* Iran, **8**, 42
AFIA *v* Iran, **8**, 236
Afrasiab Assad Bakhtiari *v* Iran, *see* Bakhtiari *v* Iran
Agrostruct International, Inc. *v* Iran State Cereals Organization, **18**, 180
AHFI Planning Associates Inc. *v* Iran, **3**, 350; **11**, 168
Ainsworth *v* Iran, **1**, 230; **4**, 26; **18**, 92; **25**, 188
Air La Carte, Inc. *v* Iran National Airlines Corporation, **1**, 163
Airlines of the Islamic Republic of Iran *v* United States, **22**, 365
Alan Craig *v* Ministry of Energy of Iran, *see* Craig *v* Ministry of Energy of Iran
Albert Berookhim and the Berookhim Partnership *v* Iran, *see* Berookhim *v* Iran
Alcan Aluminium, Limited *v* Ircable Corporation, **2**, 294
Alex Arjad *v* Iran, *see* Arjad *v* Iran
Alexander Lyons Lianosoff *v* Iran, *see* Lianosoff *v* Iran
Alfred Haber, P.A. *v* Iran, **23**, 133
Alfred L.W. Short *v* Iran, *see* Short *v* Iran
Ali Asghar *v* Iran, *see* Asghar *v* Iran
Allard *v* Iran, **23**, 413
Allen *v* Iran, **28**, 382
Allis-Chalmers Corporation *v* Iran, **4**, 39
American Bell International Inc. *v* Iran, **3**, 209; **6**, 74; **12**, 170; **14**, 173
American Cast Iron Pipe Company *v* Ahwaz Water and Sewage Board, **9**, 203
American Cyanamid Company *v* Iran, **2**, 269
American Express Company *v* Iran, **17**, 368
American Express International Banking Corp. *v* Iran, **29**, 209
American Farm Products International, Inc. *v* Cyrus Consulting Engineers, **18**, 175
American Hospital Supply Corporation *v* Iran, **7**, 269
American Housing International Inc. *v* Housing Cooperative Society, **5**, 235
American Independent Oil Company *v* National Iranian Oil Company, **3**, 372; **9**, 184
American International Group, Inc. *v* Iran, **4**, 96
American Lecithin Company *v* Iran, **10**, 365
American Motors Corporation *v* Iran, **4**, 29
AMF Inc. *v* Iran, **16**, 335
AMF Overseas Corporation, *Re*, **1**, 392

---

[1] The figures in bold type refer to the volume number.

CONSOLIDATED TABLE OF CASES (ALPHABETICAL)

Amman and Whitney *v.* Khuzestan Urban Development Organization, **5**, 115; **12**, 94
Amoco International Finance Corporation *v.* Iran, **4**, 4; **15**, 189; **25**, 314
Amoco Iran Oil Company *v.* Iran, **1**, 493; **2**, 283, 345; **3**, 297; **5**, 51; **25**, 301
Anaconda-Iran, Inc. *v.* Iran, **3**, 209; **13**, 199; **28**, 320
Andranik Khachatourians *v.* Iran, *see* Khajetoorians *v.* Iran
Anita Perry-Rohani *v.* Iran, *see* Perry-Rohani *v.* Iran
Arakel Khajetoorians *v.* Iran, *see* Khajetoorians *v.* Iran
Arco Exploration, Inc. *v.* National Iranian Oil Company, **28**, 392
Arco Iran, Inc. *v.* Iran, **3**, 372; **16**, 3; **25**, 339
Arco Seed Company *v.* Iran, **14**, 349
Ardavan Peter Samrad *v.* Iran, *see* Samrad *v.* Iran
Arensburg, *et al. v.* Ministry of Housing and Urban Development, *see* Skidmore, Owings & Merrill *v.* Ministry of Housing and Urban Development
Arik Khajetoorians *v.* Iran, *see* Khajetoorians *v.* Iran
Arjad *v.* Iran, **26**, 190
Arthur J. Fritz & Co. *v.* Sherkate Tavonie Sherkathaye Sakhtemanie, **22**, 170
Arthur Young & Company *v.* Iran, **17**, 245
Asghar *v.* Iran, **24**, 238
Assistance in Developing Educational System, Inc. *v.* Iran, **4**, 18
Asteghik Khajetoorians *v.* Iran, *see* Khajetoorians *v.* Iran
Ataollah Golpira *v.* Iran, *see* Golpira *v.* Iran
Atlantic Richfield Company *v.* Iran, **8**, 179; **28**, 401
Atomic Energy Organization of Iran *v.* National Audiovisual Center, **21**, 303
Atomic Energy Organization of Iran *v.* United States, **6**, 141; **12**, 25
August Frederick Benedix, Jr. *v.* Iran, *see* Benedix *v.* Iran
Austin Company *v.* Machine Sazi Arak, **12**, 288
Avco Corporation *v.* Iran, **19**, 200, 253

Baker International Corporation *v.* Iran, **1**, 230; **12**, 385
Bakhtiari *v.* Iran, **25**, 289
Bank Markazi Iran *v.* Barclay's Bank International, Ltd., **2**, 35
Bank Markazi Iran *v.* Continental Bank Intl. (Pacific), **8**, 371
Bank Markazi Iran *v.* European American Banking Corporation, **13**, 95
Bank Markazi Iran *v.* United States, Case No. 780, **8**, 364
Bank Markazi Iran *v.* United States, Case No. 821, **8**, 366
Bank Mellat *v.* Chase Manhattan Bank, **5**, 155
Bank Mellat *v.* Chemical Bank, New York (Cases Nos. 836, 847 and 890), **2**, 35
Bank Mellat *v.* Crocker National Bank, **2**, 246; **3**, 316, 318, 380; **5**, 57
Bank Mellat *v.* Manufacturers Hanover Trust Company, **2**, 246; **3**, 316, 318, 380; **5**, 57
Bank Mellat *v.* Morgan Guaranty Trust Company, **1**, 486
Bank Melli Iran *v.* Chase Manhattan Bank, N.A., New York, **21**, 11
Bank Melli Iran *v.* United States, **9**, 205
Bank Sepah *v.* City Bank, N.A., **2**, 30, 35
Bank Sepah *v.* Mellon Bank, N.A., **2**, 35
Bank Sepah *v.* United States, **8**, 362
Baroid International Petroleum Services, Inc. *v.* Iran, **10**, 365
Bassin, *Re*, **9**, 3
Baygell *v.* Iran, **11**, 72, 300
Bearings Inc. *v.* Iran, **19**, 374
Bechtel, Inc. *v.* Iran, **14**, 149
Behring International, Inc. *v.* Islamic Republic Iranian Air Force, **1**, 230; **3**, 173; **4**, 89; **6**, 30; **8**, 44, 238; **14**, 23; **27**, 218
Bell Industries *v.* Iran, **18**, 390
Bendix Corporation *v.* Iran, **18**, 352

Bendone-Derossi International v Iran, **1**, 178; **6**, 130; **18**, 115
Benedix v Iran, **21**, 20
Benjamin R. Isaiah v Bank Mellat, *see* Isaiah v Bank Mellat
Benny Diba and Wilfred J. Gaulin v Iran, *see* Diba and Gaulin v Iran
Berger International, Inc. v Plan & Budget Organization of Iran, *see* Louis Berger International, Inc. v Plan & Budget Organization of Iran
Berookhim v Iran, **25**, 278
Betty Laura Monemi v Iran, *see* Monemi v Iran
Betty Lou McCabe v Iran, *see* McCabe, Jr., *et al.* v Iran
B.F. Goodrich Company v Abadan Petrochemical Company, Ltd., **1**, 342
B.F. Goodrich Company v Kian Tire Manufacturing Company, **1**, 123
Bikoff and Eisenpresser v Iran, **7**, 1
Birnbaum v Iran, **14**, 147; **29**, 260
Blount Brothers Corporation v Iran (Case No. 52), **10**, 56
Blount Brothers Corporation v Iran (Case No. 53), **10**, 95
Blount Brothers Corporation v Iran (Case No. 63), **6**, 118
Blount Brothers Corporation v Iran Air, **21**, 303
Blount Brothers Corporation v Ministry of Housing and Urban Development, **2**, 268; **3**, 225
Blum Consulting Engineers, Inc. v Iran, *see* Herman Blum Consulting Engineers, Inc. v Iran
Board of Trustees of Southern Illinois University v Iran, **19**, 345
Bodnar, *Re*, **21**, 6
Boeing Company v Iran, **5**, 152; **6**, 43; **13**, 359
Borg Warner Corporation v Iran, **11**, 372
Boroumand v Iran, **29**, 59
Browne Disc, Inc. v Iran, *see* Stewart R. Browne Disc, Inc. v Iran
Bruce Vernor, Joseph Howard, Charles Petze, James Kirkendall, James Wood, Joseph Butler, James Corn, Randell Stansfield and Edward Suber, Trustees of the Tehran American School Association, and Members of the Tehran American School Association v Iran, *see* Tehran American School Association, Trustees and Members v Iran
Buckamier v Iran, **28**, 53, 307
Burton Marks and Harry Umann v Iran, *see* Marks and Umann v Iran

Cabot International Capital Corporation v Iran, **4**, 83
Cal-Maine Foods, Inc. v Iran, **6**, 52
Cameron Kamran Khosrowshahi v Iran, *see* Khosrowshahi (C.K.) v Iran
Cameron Mitchell Monemi v Iran, *see* Monemi v Iran
C and T Commodities of America, Inc. v Iran, **13**, 370
Carlson v Iran, **26**, 193
Carolina Brass, Inc. v Arya National Shipping Lines, S.A., **12**, 139
Carrier Corporation v Iran, **1**, 178; **3**, 36, 78
Cascade Overview Development Enterprises, Inc., *Re*, **1**, 127, 129, 132
Case Company v Aryan Yadak Company, *see* J.I. Case Company v Aryan Yadak Company
Case Company v Iran, *see* J.I. Case Company v Iran
Catherine Etezadi v Iran, *see* Etezadi v Iran
CBA International Development Corporation v Iran, **4**, 53; **5**, 177
CBS Inc. v Iran, **21**, 279; **25**, 131
Cecilia Radene Ebrahimi v Iran, *see* Ebrahimi (C.R.) v Iran
Chamness v Iran, **1**, 178; **25**, 172
Charles P. Stewart v Iran, *see* Stewart v Iran
Charter (Iran) Petroleum Company v National Iranian Oil Company, **3**, 372; **5**, 88
Chas. T. Main International, Inc. v Khuzestan Water and Power Authority, **1**, 337; **3**, 156; **4**, 60; **5**, 185; **8**, 41; **10**, 21; **11**, 259; **21**, 12
Chas. T. Main International, Inc. v Mahab Consulting Engineers, Inc., **3**, 270
Cherafat v Iran, **28**, 216

CONSOLIDATED TABLE OF CASES (ALPHABETICAL)

Chesapeake and Potomac Telephone Company *v.* Iran, **24**, 305
Chevron Research Company *v.* National Iranian Oil Company, **1**, 155, 334; **2**, 364; **3**, 78
Chicago Bridge & Iron Company *v.* Iran, **7**, 225; **11**, 372
Christensen, Inc. *v.* Iran, **30**, 292
Christina Tandis Ebrahimi *v.* Iran, *see* Ebrahimi (C.T.) *v.* Iran
CMI International, Inc. *v.* Ministry of Roads and Transportation, Iran, **4**, 263
Coast Survey Limited *v.* Iran, **23**, 314
Collins Systems International Inc. *v.* Islamic Republic of Iran Navy, **28**, 21, 195
Combustion Engineering, Inc. *v.* Iran, **3**, 366; **24**, 297; **26**, 60; **27**, 288
Commercial Development Center *v.* United States, **18**, 390
Commonwealth Associates, Inc. *v.* Iran, **13**, 370
Component Builders, Inc. *v.* Iran, **8**, 3, 216; **9**, 404; **23**, 3
Computer Sciences Corporation *v.* Iran, **8**, 99; **10**, 269
Consortium for International Development *v.* Iran, **26**, 244
Constantine A. Gianoplus *v.* Iran, *see* Gianoplus *v.* Iran
Continental Corporation *v.* Iran, **1**, 403
Continental Grain Export Corporation *v.* Government Trading Corporation, **3**, 319
Continental Grain Export Corporation *v.* Union of Consumers' Co-operatives for Iranian Workers (EMKAN), **11**, 292
Continental Illinois National Bank and Trust Company of Chicago *v.* Iran, **1**, 230, 232; **30**, 3
Control Data Corporation *v.* Iran, **1**, 230; **18**, 60; **21**, 303; **22**, 151
Cook Industries, Inc. *v.* Iran, **12**, 397
Cosmos Engineering, Inc. *v.* Ministry of Roads and Transportation, **13**, 179
Craig *v.* Ministry of Energy of Iran, **3**, 280
Creditcorp International, Inc., *Re*, **21**, 10
Creditcorp International, Inc. *v.* Iran Carton Company, **23**, 265
Cross Company *v.* Iran, **8**, 97
CTI-Container Leasing Corporation *v.* Starline Iran Co., **26**, 275
Cummins *v.* Iran, **14**, 21
Cyrus Petroleum Ltd. *v.* Iran, **11**, 70

Dadras International *v.* Iran, **30**, 104
Daley *v.* Iran, **18**, 232
Dallal *v.* Iran, **3**, 10; **5**, 74
Dames and Moore *v.* Iran, **4**, 212; **8**, 107
Dana Corporation *v.* Iran, **19**, 374
Dana Paul Monemi *v.* Iran, *see* Monemi *v.* Iran
Daniel, Mann, Johnson and Mendenhall *v.* Iran, **1**, 160
Daniel Purnell Delly *v.* Iran, *see* Delly (D.P.) *v.* Iran
Danielpour (M.) *v.* Iran, **22**, 118
Danielpour (S.J.) *v.* Iran, **22**, 123
David *v.* Iran, **24**, 252
David Harounian *v.* Iran, *see* Harounian *v.* Iran
David Michael Mandig *v.* Iran, *see* McCabe, Jr., *et al. v.* Iran
David Mikhael, Inc. *v.* Iran, **3**, 84; **6**, 20
Delly (D.P.) *v.* Iran, **19**, 360
Delly (S.L.J.) *v.* Iran, **19**, 360
Deloitte, Haskins and Sells *v.* Computer Services Company, **3**, 34
Department of Energy (Oak Ridge Operations) *v.* Atomic Energy Organization of Iran, **21**, 303
Department of the Environment of Iran *v.* United States, Case B-53, **5**, 105
De Soto, Inc. *v.* Iran Aircraft Industries, **14**, 349
Detroit Bank and Trust Company, *Re*, **1**, 129; **2**, 312; **3**, 3
Detroit Parts Manufacturing Company *v.* Iran, **8**, 79
Development and Resources Corporation *v.* Iran, **3**, 209; **25**, 20; **26**, 256

Diagnostic Products Corporation *v* Iran, **9**, 306
Diba and Gaulin *v* Iran, **23**, 268
Dic of Delaware, Inc. *v* Tehran Redevelopment Corporation, **1**, 154; **8**, 144; **21**, 4
Dillon *v* Ministry of Mines and Industries of Iran, *see* National Corporation for Housing Partnership *v* Ministry of Mines and Industries of Iran
Distribution International Corporation *v* Iran, **17**, 245
DoAll Dallas Company *v* Iran, **23**, 413
Donald W. David *v* Iran, *see* David *v* Iran
Dorian International Credit Co., Inc., *Re*, **21**, 10
Dorian International Credit Co., Inc. *v* Iran Carton Company, **23**, 265
Dow Chemical Company *v* Iran (Case No. 257), **6**, 38
Dow Chemical Company *v* Iran (Case No. 499), **1**, 122
Dresser Industries, Inc. *v* Iran (Cases Nos. 103-104, 107-110), **3**, 212
Dresser Industries, Inc. *v* Iran (Cases Nos. 105 and 137), **2**, 291
Dresser Industries, Inc. *v* Iran (Case No. 106), **3**, 332
Dresser Industries, Inc. *v* Iran (Case No. 466), **1**, 280, 284, 305, 320
Dresser Industries, Inc. *v* Iran (Cases Nos. 467-469 and 471), **9**, 346
Dreyco, Inc. (E.D. Allmendinger Division) *v* Iran, **8**, 13
Drucker, Jr. *v* Foreign Transaction Company, **1**, 252, 284, 305, 320; **2**, 4; **19**, 257
Duane H. Mandig, Mrs. *v* Iran, *see* McCabe, Jr., *et al. v* Iran
Du Pont de Nemours and Company *v* Iran, *see* E.I. du Pont de Nemours and Company *v* Iran

Eastman Kodak Company *v* Iran, **17**, 153; **27**, 3, 269
Eastman Kodak International Capital Company, Inc. *v* Iran, **17**, 153
Ebrahimi (C.R.) *v* Iran, **22**, 138; **30**, 170
Ebrahimi (C.T.) *v* Iran, **22**, 138; **30**, 170
Ebrahimi (M.S.) *v* Iran, **22**, 138
Ebrahimi (S.S.) *v* Iran, **22**, 138; **30**, 170
Econocorp, Inc. *v* Iran, **8**, 360
Economy Forms Corporation *v* Iran, **3**, 42; **5**, 1
Edgar Protiva *v* Iran, *see* Protiva *v* Iran
Edmund Pickup, Jr., Trustee in Bankruptcy *v* Iran, *see* Pickup, Jr. *v* Iran
Edwards *v* Iran, **23**, 290
E.I. du Pont de Nemours and Company *v* Iran, **4**, 183
Electric Heating Equipment Company *v* Iran, **19**, 374
Electronic Data Systems Corporation *v* Iran, **7**, 244
Electronic Systems International, Inc. *v* Ministry of Defence of the Islamic Republic of Iran, **22**, 339
Emanuel Too *v* Greater Modesto Insurance Associates, *see* Too *v* Greater Modesto Insurance Associates
Emory B. Washington *v* Iran, *see* Washington *v* Iran
Endo Laboratories, Inc. *v* Iran, **17**, 114; **18**, 113
Enserch Corporation *v* Iran, **8**, 66
Enserch Service Company of Iran *v* Iran, **8**, 81
E.R. Squibb and Sons, Inc. *v* Iran, **2**, 44
Eric Protiva *v* Iran, *see* Protiva *v* Iran
Esahak Saboonchian *v* Iran, *see* Saboonchian *v* Iran
Esphahanian *v* Bank Tejarat, **2**, 157, 178
Esso Africa, Inc. *v* Towlid Rowghan Refining (Public) Company, **2**, 305
Esso Europe Supply Company, Inc. *v* Towlid Rowghan Refining (Public) Company, **2**, 305
E-Systems, Inc. *v* Iran, **1**, 178, 222, 225; **2**, 51; **4**, 197
Etezadi *v* Iran, **25**, 264; **30**, 22
Etka Organization, *Re*, **19**, 185
Exxon Corporation *v* Iran, **3**, 372; **16**, 3; **23**, 401

CONSOLIDATED TABLE OF CASES (ALPHABETICAL)

Exxon Corporation *v.* National Iranian Oil Company, **17**, 3
Exxon Research and Engineering Company *v.* Iran, **15**, 3; **16**, 110

Faith Lita Khosrowshahi *v.* Iran, *see* Khosrowshahi (F.L.) *v.* Iran
Farrington *v.* Islamic Republic of Iran Airlines, **18**, 390
Fedders Corporation *v.* Iran, **13**, 97; **18**, 72
Fedders Corporation *v.* Loristan Refrigeration Industries, General Industrial Corporation, National Industries Organization of Iran, and Iran, **29**, 401
Federal Mogul International Distribution, Inc. *v.* Iran, **18**, 390
Fereydoon Ghaffari *v.* Iran, *see* Ghaffari (F.) *v.* Iran
F.H. Maloney Company *v.* Iran, **9**, 70
Figgie International Inc. (Geo. J. Meyer Manufacturing Division) *v.* Zam Zam Bottling Company, **8**, 214
First Interstate Bank of California *v.* Iran, **29**, 205
First National Bank in St. Louis *v.* Iran, **18**, 390
First National Bank of Boston *v.* Iran, **19**, 307
First National Bank of Chicago *v.* Iran, **29**, 201
First Travel Corporation *v.* Iran, **1**, 340; **9**, 360
Flexi-Van Leasing, Inc. *v.* Iran, **1**, 166, 455; **3**, 202; **5**, 138; **12**, 335; **13**, 324
Fluor Corporation *v.* Bimeh Iran, **23**, 413
Fluor Corporation *v.* Iran (Case No. 333), **1**, 121, 178; **11**, 296; **18**, 56, 68; **23**, 413
Fluor Corporation *v.* Iran (Case No. 810), **23**, 413
FMC Corporation *v.* Iran, **11**, 372; **14**, 111, 261
Ford Aerospace and Communications Corporation *v.* Iran, **2**, 281; **3**, 349; **10**, 108; **14**, 24, 255
Ford Aerospace and Communications Corporation *v.* The Air Force of the Islamic Republic of Iran, **1**, 268, 284, 305, 320; **3**, 384; **6**, 104; **8**, 284; **11**, 184; **12**, 304
Foremost McKesson, Inc. *v.* Tolidaru, **2**, 278
Foremost Tehran, Inc. *v.* Iran, **2**, 33; **3**, 361; **4**, 62; **10**, 228
Fox Geotechnical Consultants, Inc. *v.* Iran, *see* H.B. Fox Geotechnical Consultants Inc. *v.* Iran
Frederica Lincoln Riahi *v.* Iran, *see* Riahi *v.* Iran
Frederick K. Sinker *v.* Iran, *see* Sinker *v.* Iran
French American Banking Corporation *v.* Iranit, S.A., **2**, 303
Fritz & Co. *v.* Sherkate Tavonie Sherkathaye Sakhtemanie, *see* Arthur J. Fritz & Co. *v.* Sherkate Tavonie Sherkathaye Sakhtemanie
Futura Trading Inc. *v.* Khuzestan Water and Power Authority, **9**, 46
Futura Trading Inc. *v.* National Iranian Oil Company, **13**, 99

Gabay *v.* Iran, **27**, 40, 194
GAI-Tronics Corporation *v.* Iran, **19**, 374
Gaulin *v.* Iran, *see* Diba and Gaulin *v.* Iran
General Atomic Company *v.* Atomic Energy Organization of Iran, **1**, 223
General Dynamics Corporation *v.* Iran, **1**, 485; **5**, 386
General Dynamics Telephone Systems Center, Inc. *v.* Iran, **9**, 153
General Electric Company *v.* Iran (Case No. 360), **7**, 239
General Electric Company *v.* Iran (Case No. 386), **26**, 148
General Electric Company *v.* Pars Appliance Manufacturing Company, **2**, 132
General Electric Company (Space Division) *v.* Iran, **9**, 6
General Motors Corporation *v.* Iran, **2**, 33; **3**, 1; **7**, 220; **13**, 282
General Petrochemicals Corp. *v.* Iran, **27**, 196
General Tire and Rubber Company *v.* Iran Tire Manufacturing Company, **3**, 351
George Edwards *v.* Iran, *see* Edwards *v.* Iran
George Nourafchan *v.* Iran, *see* Nourafchan (G.) *v.* Iran
George W. Drucker, Jr. *v.* Foreign Transaction Company, *see* Drucker, Jr. *v.* Foreign Transaction Company
Georgetown University *v.* Iran, **23**, 413

CONSOLIDATED TABLE OF CASES (ALPHABETICAL)

Getty Iran Ltd. *v* Iran, **3**, 372; **13**, 370
Ghaffari (A.) *v* National Iranian Oil Company, **25**, 178
Ghaffari (F.) *v* Iran, **18**, 64, 79
Gianoplus *v* Iran, **11**, 217
Gibbs and Hill, Inc. *v* Iran Power Generation and Transmission Company (TAVANIR) of the Ministry of Energy of the Government of Iran, **1**, 236, 284, 305, 320
Gillette Company *v* Iran, **3**, 218
Gitty Diana Samrad *v* Iran, *see* Samrad *v* Iran
Gloria Jean Cherafat *v* Iran, *see* Cherafat *v* Iran
Glucosan (Private Joint Stock) Co., *Re*, **19**, 191
Golpira *v* Iran, **2**, 171, 178
Golshani *v* Iran, **22**, 155; **29**, 78
Goodrich Company *v* Abadan Petrochemical Company, Ltd., *see* B.F. Goodrich Company *v* Abadan Petrochemical Company Ltd.
Goodrich Company *v* Kian Tire Manufacturing Company, *see* B.F. Goodrich Company *v* Kian Tire Manufacturing Company
Goodyear Tire and Rubber Company *v* Tasmeh Melli Company, **3**, 181, 192
Gordon Williams *v* Iran, *see* Williams *v* Iran
Gould Marketing, Inc. *v* Ministry of National Defense of Iran, **3**, 147; **6**, 272; **9**, 406
Granger Associates *v* Iran, **16**, 317
Granite State Machine Company, Inc. *v* Iran, **1**, 185, 442
Grimm *v* Iran, **2**, 78
Gruen Associates, Inc. *v* Iran Housing Company, **2**, 327; **3**, 97, 124
Grune and Stratton, Inc. *v* Iran, **18**, 224
Gulf Ports Crating Company *v* Ministry of Roads and Transportation, **2**, 126

H & F Kornfeld, Inc. *v* Iran, **21**, 303
Haber, P.A. *v* Iran, *see* Alfred Haber, P.A. *v* Iran
Haddadi *v* United States, **8**, 20
Hafez Glaziery and Glass Cutting Shop *v* United States, **8**, 349
Haji-Bagherpour *v* United States, **2**, 38
Hakim *v* Iran, **24**, 269
Halliburton Company *v* Doreen/IMCO, **1**, 242, 284, 305, 320; **6**, 4
Halliburton Company *v* Iran, **9**, 310
Harnischfeger Corporation *v* Ministry of Roads and Transportation, **4**, 76; **7**, 90; **8**, 119
Harold Birnbaum *v* Iran, *see* Birnbaum *v* Iran
Haroonian *v* Iran, **2**, 226
Harounian *v* Iran, **23**, 282
Harrington and Associates, Inc. *v* Iran, **16**, 297
Harris International Telecommunications, Inc. *v* Iran, **17**, 31; **18**, 76
Harza *v* Iran, **1**, 234; **2**, 68; **4**, 59; **11**, 76
Harza Engineering Company *v* Iran, **1**, 499
H.A. Spalding, Inc. *v* Ministry of Roads and Transport, **10**, 22
Haus International, Inc. *v* Tehran Redevelopment Corporation, **3**, 87; **5**, 144; **9**, 313
Hawaiian Agronomics Company, *Re*, **1**, 138
H.B. Fox Geotechnical Consultants, Inc. *v* Iran, **18**, 70
Helali, *Re*, **1**, 134
Hemmat *v* Iran, **22**, 129
Henry F. Teichmann, Inc. *v* Hamadan Glass Company, **13**, 124
Henry Morris *v.* Iran, *see* Morris *v.* Iran
Herbach & Rademan Inc. *v* Iran, **19**, 374
Herman Blum Consulting Engineers, Inc. *v* Iran, **1**, 218; **5**, 354
Hidetomo Shinto *v* Iran, *see* Shinto *v* Iran
Highlands Insurance Company *v* Iran, **25**, 212

CONSOLIDATED TABLE OF CASES (ALPHABETICAL) xxi

Hilt v Iran, **18**, 154
Hoffland Honey Company v National Iranian Oil Company, **2**, 41
Hollyfield v Iran, **23**, 276
Homa Diba Benedix v Iran, *see* Benedix v Iran
Honeywell Information Systems, Inc. v Information Systems Iran (ISIRAN) **1**, 181
Hood Corporation v Iran, **7**, 36; **8**, 53
Hooshang Etezadi v Iran, *see* Etezadi v Iran
Hooshang Kahen v Iran, *see* Kahen v Iran
Housing and Urban Services International, Inc. v Tehran Redevelopment Corporation, *see* Haus International, Inc. v Tehran Redevelopment Corporation
Houston Contracting Company v National Iranian Oil Company, **14**, 18; **20**, 3
Howard, Needles, Tammens and Bergendoff (HNTB) v Iran, **1**, 248, 284, 305, 320; **2**, 368; **11**, 302
Howland International Company, Limited v Iran, *see* T.G. Howland International Company, Limited v Iran
Hyatt International Corporation v Iran, **9**, 72; **10**, 365

Ian L. McHarg, William W. Roberts, David A. Wallace, Thomas A. Todd v Iran, *see* McHarg, Roberts, Wallace & Todd v Iran
INA Corporation v Iran, **8**, 373
Indian Head, Inc. v Iran, **13**, 370
Industrial & Mining Bank (R.C.39), *Re*, **19**, 179
Industrial & Mining Bank (R.C.40), *Re*, **19**, 182
Industrial Equipment Co. of Houston v Iran, **19**, 374
Ingersoll-Rand Company v Iran, **18**, 390
Interaction Research Corporation v Iran, **17**, 362
Intercomp Resources Development and Engineering, Inc. v Oil Service Company of Iran, **1**, 391
Intercontinental Hotels Corporation v Iran, **7**, 249
Intercontinental Hotels Corporation and Overseas Private Investment Corporation v Iran, **7**, 249
Interfirst Bank Dallas, N.A. v Iran, **16**, 291
International Ore & Fertilizer Corporation v Razi Chemical Company Ltd., **18**, 98
International Schools Services, Inc. v Iran (Case No. 12), **10**, 6; **14**, 65, 279
International Schools Services, Inc. v Iran (Case No. 122), **1**, 156
International Schools Services, Inc. v National Iranian Copper Industries Company, **2**, 156; **3**, 316, 318; **5**, 338; **9**, 187
International Systems & Controls Corporation v Iran, **3**, 209; **12**, 239
International Systems & Controls Corporation v National Iranian Gas Company, **24**, 47
International Technical Products Corporation v Iran, **9**, 10, 206; **11**, 182
International Telephone and Telegraph Corporation v Iran, **22**, 213
Intrend International, Inc. v The Imperial Iranian Air Force, **3**, 110, 124
Iowa State University of Science and Technology v Ministry of Culture and Higher Education, **13**, 271
Iran-United States, Case A/1, **1**, 144, 189
Iran-United States, Case A/2, **1**, 101
Iran-United States, Cases A/15 (IV) & A/24, **29**, 214
Iran-United States, Case A/18, **5**, 251
Iran-United States, Case A/19, **16**, 285
Iran-United States, Case A/20, **11**, 271
Iran-United States, Case A/21, **14**, 324
Iran v Chase Manhattan Bank, **5**, 155
Iran v United States, Case No. 951, **14**, 11
Iran v United States, Case A-4, **5**, 112, 131
Iran v United States, Case A-15, **4**, 28; **5**, 112, 131; **8**, 63; **12**, 40; **13**, 173; **14**, 171, 311; **25**, 247
Iran v United States, Case A/15 IIA and IIB, **28**, 112

Iran v United States, Case A-25, **21**, 283, 302
Iran v United States, Case B-1, **4**, 57; **10**, 207; **18**, 45; **19**, 3, 273; **21**, 279; **22**, 105; **23**, 407; **27**, 282
Iran v United States, Case B-14, **23**, 413
Iran v United States, Claims of less than U.S. $250,000, **27**, 275
Iran (Civil Aviation Organization) v United States (Military Assistance Advisory Group), Case B-60, **24**, 291
Iran Brockway Company Ltd., *Re*, **17**, 331
Iran Chevron Oil Company v Iran, **3**, 372; **10**, 357
Iran Electronics Industries, *Re*, **19**, 188
Iran Helicopter Support & Renewal Company (R.C.32), *Re*, **23**, 244
Iran Helicopter Support & Renewal Company (R.C.33), *Re*, **23**, 247
Iran Helicopter Support & Renewal Company (R.C.34), *Re*, **23**, 250
Iran National Airlines Company, *Re*, **17**, 337
Iran National Airlines Company v United States, Case B-8, **17**, 187
Iran National Airlines Company v United States, Case B-9, **17**, 214
Iran National Airlines Company v United States, Case B-10, **17**, 238
Iran National Airlines Company v United States, Case B-12, **17**, 228
Iran National Airlines Company v United States, Case B-51, **17**, 200
Iran National Gas Company v United States, **17**, 183
Iran Touring and Tourism Organization v United States, **18**, 84
Iranian Customs Administration v United States, Case B-2, **13**, 155
Iranian Customs Administration v United States, Case B-3, **8**, 89
Iranian Customs Administration v United States, Case B-13, **13**, 158
Iranian Customs Administration v United States, Case B-16, **5**, 94
Iranian Customs Administration v United States, Case B-18, **13**, 161
Iranian Customs Administration v United States, Case B-20, **13**, 164
Iranian Customs Administration v United States, Case B-21, **8**, 93
Iranian Tobacco Company (R.C.26), *Re*, **21**, 8
Iranian Tobacco Company (R.C.27), *Re*, **7**, 275
Irene Boroumand v Iran, *see* Boroumand v Iran
Irving Trust Co. v Iran, **29**, 189
Isaiah v Bank Mellat, **2**, 232
Itel Corporation v Iran, **1**, 326; **28**, 159
Itel International Corporation v Social Security Organization of Iran, **7**, 31; **21**, 279; **24**, 272
ITT Industries, Inc. v Iran, **2**, 348

Jack Rankin v Iran, *see* Rankin v Iran
Jack W. Mackay v Iran Beverages Company, *see* Mackay v Iran Beverages Company
Jacqueline M. Kiaie, Jubin T. Kiaie, Julia S. Kiaie v Iran, *see* Kiaie v Iran
Jafari v. Iran, **18**, 90
Jahanger, *Re*, **1**, 128, 129, 132
Jahani, *Re*, **1**, 168
Jalal Moin v Iran, *see* Moin v Iran
James M. Saghi, Michael R. Saghi, and Allan J. Saghi v Iran, *see* Saghi v Iran
J.D. Marshall International, Inc. v Iran, **8**, 11
J.I. Case Company v Aryan Yadak Company, **14**, 349
J.I. Case Company v Iran, **3**, 62
Jimmie Barnell Leach v Iran, *see* Leach v Iran
Joan Ward Malekzadeh, Sonya Malekzadeh, Alireza Malekzadeh v Iran, *see* Malekzadeh v Iran
John Carl Warnecke and Associates v Bank Mellat, **3**, 256
John Francis Cummins v Iran, *see* Cummins v Iran
Jonathan Ainsworth v Iran, *see* Ainsworth v Iran
Joseph H. McCabe, Jr. v Iran, *see* McCabe, Jr., *et al.* v Iran

CONSOLIDATED TABLE OF CASES (ALPHABETICAL)

Joseph H. McCabe III *v.* Iran, *see* McCabe, Jr., *et al. v.* Iran
Judge N. Mangård, *Re*, *see* Mangård, *Re*
Juliette Allen *v.* Iran, *see* Allen *v.* Iran
Jurij Bodnar, *Re*, *see* Bodnar, *Re*

Kahen *v.* Iran, **18**, 289
Kaiser Engineers International, Inc. *v.* Iran, **2**, 366
Kambiz Hakim *v.* Iran, *see* Hakim *v.* Iran
Kamran Khosrowshahi *v.* Iran, *see* Khosrowshahi (F.I.) *v.* Iran
K and S Irrigation Company, *Re*, **1**, 228
Karim-Panahi *v.* United States, **28**, 225, 318
Kathleen Marie Mandig *v.* Iran, *see* McCabe, Jr., *et al. v.* Iran
Kathryn Faye Hilt *v.* Iran, *see* Hilt *v.* Iran
Katrin Zohrabegian Abrahamian *v.* Iran, *see* Abrahamian *v.* Iran
Kay Lerner *v.* Iran, **1**, 215
Kaysons International Corp. *v.* Iran, **29**, 222
Kayvan Khosrowshahi *v.* Iran, *see* Khosrowshahi (F.I.) *v.* Iran
Kem International Co. *v.* Iran, **29**, 395
Kenneth P. Yeager *v.* Iran, *see* Yeager *v.* Iran
Khajetoorians *v.* Iran, **26**, 37
Khatami *v.* Iran, **30**, 267
Khojasteh Pishdad, Mrs. *v.* Iran, *see* Pishdad *v.* Iran
Khosrowshahi (F.I.) *v.* Iran, **1**, 339; **24**, 40; **30**, 76
Khosrowshahi (N.) *v.* Iran, **17**, 266
Khubiar *v.* Iran, **11**, 180
Kiaie *v.* Iran, **14**, 307
Kianoosh Jafari *v.* Iran, *see* Jafari *v.* Iran
Kidde Consultants, Inc. *v.* Haydar Ghyai & Associates, **30**, 302
Kidde, Inc. (Walter Kidde Division) *v.* Iran National Airlines, **5**, 78
Kimberly-Clark Corporation *v.* Bank Markazi Iran, **2**, 334
Koehler *v.* Iran, **10**, 333; **11**, 285
Kornfeld, Inc. *v.* Iran, *see* H & F Kornfeld, Inc. *v.* Iran

Ladjevardi *v.* Iran, **29**, 367
Lauth *v.* Iran, **11**, 150
Lawrence *v.* Iran, **1**, 178; **25**, 190
Leach *v.* Iran, **18**, 231; **23**, 233
Lee, *Re*, **21**, 7
Leila Danesh Arfa Mahmoud *v.* Iran, *see* Mahmoud *v.* Iran
Leonard and Mavis Daley *v.* Iran, *see* Daley *v.* Iran
Levitt *v.* Iran (Case No. 209), **14**, 191
Levitt *v.* Iran (Case No. 210), **27**, 145
Lianosoff *v.* Iran, **5**, 90
Lili Tour *v.* Iran, *see* Tour *v.* Iran
Lillian Byrdine Grimm *v.* Iran, *see* Grimm *v.* Iran
Lilly Mythra Fallah Lawrence *v.* Iran, *see* Lawrence *v.* Iran
Linda J. Motamed *v.* Iran, *see* Motamed *v.* Iran
Linen, Fortinberry and Associates, Inc. *v.* Iran, **8**, 85; **19**, 62
Lischem Corporation *v.* Atomic Energy Organization of Iran, **7**, 18
Litton Systems, Inc. *v.* Iran, **12**, 126
Lockheed Corporation *v.* Iran, **11**, 363; **18**, 292; **19**, 317
Logos Development Corporation *v.* Information Systems Iran, **11**, 53
Lord Corporation *v.* Iran Helicopter Support and Renewal Company, **18**, 377
Louis Berger International *v.* Plan & Budget Organization of Iran, **14**, 349
Lowe Marschalk, Inc. *v.* Iran, **14**, 349

Luz Belen Nemazee *v* Iran, *see* Nemazee *v* Iran

M & M Productions, Inc. *v* Iran, **6**, 125
Mackay *v* Iran Beverages Company, **5**, 134
Mahmoud *v* Iran, **9**, 350
Main International, Inc. *v* Khuzestan Water and Power Authority, *see* Chas. T. Main International, Inc. *v* Khuzestan Water and Power Authority
Main International, Inc. *v* Mahab Consulting Engineers, Inc., *see* Chas. T. Main International, Inc. *v* Mahab Consulting Engineers, Inc.
Malek *v* Iran, **19**, 48; **28**, 246
Malekzadeh *v* Iran, **29**, 3
Maloney Company *v* Iran, *see* F.H. Maloney Company *v* Iran
Mangård, *Re* (Challenge Decision), **1**, 111, 509
Manuchehr Haddadi *v* United States, *see* Haddadi *v* United States
Manufacturers Hanover Trust Co. *v* Iran, **29**, 193
Marcene P. Khosrowshahi *v* Iran, *see* Khosrowshahi (F.L.) *v* Iran
Marine Midland Bank *v* Iran, **29**, 185
Marjorie Suzanne Ebrahimi *v* Iran, *see* Ebrahimi (M.S.) *v* Iran
Mark Dallal *v* Iran, *see* Dallal *v* Iran
Marks and Umann *v* Iran, **8**, 290; **9**, 69
Marshall International, Inc. *v* Iran, *see* J.D. Marshall International, Inc. *v* Iran
Mary Jane Smythe Wilson, Estate of *v* Iran, *see* McCabe, Jr., *et al. v* Iran
Mary Lou Pointon *v* Iran, *see* Pointon *v* Iran
Maxon Corporation *v* Iran, **19**, 374
McCabe, Jr., *et al. v* Iran, **23**, 413
McCollough & Company, Inc. *v.* Ministry of Post, Telegraph and Telephone, **11**, 3, 287
McHarg, Roberts, Wallace & Todd *v* Iran, **7**, 277; **13**, 286
McLaughlin Enterprises Ltd. *v* Iran, **12**, 146
Mehrdad Motamed *v* Iran, *see* Motamed *v* Iran
Mellon Bank *v* Iran, **29**, 197
Merrill Lynch & Co. Ltd. *v* Iran, **27**, 122
Michelle Danielpour *v* Iran, *see* Danielpour (M.) *v* Iran
Middle East Management and Construction Corporation *v* Iran, **9**, 340
Mikhael, Inc. *v* Iran, *see* David Mikhael, Inc. *v* Iran
Ministry of Agriculture and Rural Development of Iran *v* United States Department of Agriculture, Case B-5, **23**, 413
Ministry of Agriculture and Rural Development of Iran *v* United States Department of Agriculture, Case B-19, **23**, 413
Ministry of Defense of Iran *v* United States, Case B-15, **24**, 305
Ministry of Defense of Iran *v* United States, Case B-74, **18**, 74; **27**, 275
Ministry of Economic Affairs and Finance of Iran, *Re*, **6**, 27
Ministry of Mines and Metals and National Iranian Steel Company, *Re*, **23**, 253
Ministry of National Defence, Iran *v* Department of Defence, United States, *see* Iran *v* United States, Case B-1
Ministry of National Defence, Iran *v* United States, Cases A-3 and A-8, **27**, 256
Ministry of National Defence, Iran *v* United States, Case A-14, **4**, 74
Ministry of National Defence, Iran *v* United States, Cases B-59 and B-69, **12**, 33
Ministry of National Defence, Iran *v* United States, Case B-66, **14**, 276
Ministry of Oil of Iran *v* United States, **23**, 413
Ministry of Petroleum of the Islamic Republic of Iran *v* United States, **1**, 383
Ministry of Roads and Transportation (R.C.41), *Re*, **23**, 256
Ministry of Roads and Transportation (R.C.48), *Re*, **17**, 343
Ministry of Roads and Transportation *v* Port of Vancouver, Washington, **3**, 338
Minnesota Mining and Manufacturing Company *v* Iran, **1**, 230; **8**, 15; **17**, 294

CONSOLIDATED TABLE OF CASES (ALPHABETICAL)

Mitra Leasing Corporation *v* Iran, **18**, 62; **28**, 389
Mobasser, *Re*, **1**, 176
Mobasser *v* Iran, **10**, 177
Mobil Oil Iran Inc. *v* Iran, **3**, 372; **16**, 3; **25**, 339
Modern Film Corporation *v* Iran, **18**, 150
Mohajer-Shojaee *v* Iran, **25**, 196, 273
Mohammad Moussavi *v* United States, *see* Moussavi *v* United States
Mohsen Asgari Nazari *v* Iran, *see* Nazari *v* Iran
Moin *v* Iran, **30**, 70
Monemi *v* Iran, **28**, 232
Morgan Equipment Company *v* Iran, **3**, 7; **4**, 272
Morris *v* Iran, **2**, 241; **3**, 364
Morris Inc. *v* Iran, *see* Philip Morris Inc. *v* Iran
Morrison-Knudsen International Company, Inc. *v* Iran, **9**, 357
Morrison-Knudsen Pacific Ltd. *v* Ministry of Roads and Transportation, **3**, 76; **7**, 54
Morteza Khatami *v* Iran, *see* Khatami *v* Iran
Moshe Bassin, *Re*, *see* Bassin, *Re*
Motamed *v* Iran, **21**, 28
Motorola, Inc. *v* Iran National Airlines Corporation, **19**, 73
Moussavi *v* United States, **8**, 24
Murphy Middle East Oil Company *v* National Iranian Oil Company, **13**, 370

NAHAJA, Ministry of Defence, *Re*, **19**, 197
Nahid (Danielpour) Hemmat *v* Iran, *see* Hemmat *v* Iran
Nasrollah Khosrowshahi *v* Iran, *see* Khosrowshahi (N.) *v* Iran
Nasser Esphahanian *v* Bank Tejarat, *see* Esphahanian *v* Bank Tejarat
National Airmotive Corporation *v* Iran, **1**, 158; **3**, 91, 124
National Corporation for Housing Partnerships *v* Ministry of Mines and Industries of Iran, **3**, 87; **7**, 260
National Iranian Copper Industries Company, *Re*, **17**, 346
National Iranian Oil Company, *Re*, **17**, 334
National Training and Development Service for State and Local Government *v* Iran, **21**, 303
Navy of the Government of Iran *v* General Dynamics Corporation (Pomona Division), **14**, 251
Nazari *v* Iran, **26**, 7; **28**, 192; **30**, 123
NCR Corporation *v* Iran, **1**, 327
Near East Technological Services U.S.A., Inc. *v* Islamic Republic of Iran Air Force, **21**, 13
Nemazee *v* Iran, **25**, 153
New York Blower Company *v* Polyacryl Iran Corporation, **13**, 370
NIC Leasing, Inc. *v* Iran, **5**, 85
Nikpour *v* Iran, and Foundation for the Oppressed, **29**, 67
Ninni Ladjevardi (formerly Burgel) *v* Government of Iran, *see* Ladjevardi *v* Government of Iran
NL Industries, Inc. *v* Iran, **10**, 365
Noah A. Baygell *v* Iran, *see* Baygell *v* Iran
Norad Private Joint Stock Co. *v* United States, **19**, 374
Norman Gabay *v* Iran, *see* Gabay *v* Iran
Northern Virginia Community College *v* Iran, **18**, 66; **23**, 413
Norton Lilly & Co., Inc. *v* Iran, **6**, 147
Nourafchan (G.) *v* Iran, **23**, 307; **29**, 295
Nourafchan (R.) *v* Iran, **18**, 88
Nourafchan (Z.A.) *v* Iran, **23**, 307; **29**, 295

Ocean-Air Cargo Claims, Inc. *v* Iran (Case No. 11102), **23**, 303
Ocean-Air Cargo Claims, Inc. *v* Iran (Case No. 11429), **23**, 296
Oil Field of Texas, Inc. *v* Iran (OSCO), **1**, 347; **12**, 308
Onesco, Inc. *v* National Iranian Gas Company, **12**, 160

Opal H. Sether *v* Iran, *see* Sether *v* Iran
Orton/McCullough Crane Company *v* Iranian State Railways, **25**, 15
Otis Elevator Company *v* Iran, **14**, 283
Otis Elevator Company (New Jersey) *v* Iran, **19**, 374
Otis Engineering Corporation *v* Iran, **9**, 310
Owens-Corning Fiberglass Corporation *v* Iran, **2**, 322; **4**, 1, 280

Pan American World Airways, Inc. *v* Iran, **4**, 205
Panacaviar, S.A. *v.* Iran, **13**, 193; **14**, 100, 102; **18**, 63
Parguin Company *v* United States, **4**, 210; **13**, 261
Paridokht Kohan Haroonian *v* Iran, *see* Haroonian *v* Iran
Parsons Company *v* Iran, *see* Ralph M. Parsons Company *v* Iran
Parvin Mariam Samrad *v* Iran, *see* Samrad *v* Iran
Parviz Karim-Panahi *v* United States, *see* Karim-Panahi *v* United States
Paul Donin de Rosiere *v* Iran, *see* Panacaviar, S.A. *v* Iran
Payne *v* Iran, **12**, 3
Penwalt Corporation-Wallace & Tiernan Division *v* Iran, **19**, 374
PepsiCo, Inc. *v* Iran (Zamzam Bottling Company Azerbaijan, *et al.*), **1**, 173; **2**, 33; **13**, 3, 326
Pereira, *Re*, **21**, 3
Pereira Associates, Iran *v* Iran, *see* William L. Pereira Associates, Iran *v* Iran
Perkin Elmer Corporation *v* Iran, **19**, 374
Perry-Rohani *v* Iran, **22**, 194
Petrolane, Inc. *v* Iran, **27**, 64, 264; **28**, 3
Pfizer, Inc. *v* Iran, **2**, 90
Phelps Dodge Corp. *v* Iran, **10**, 121
Phelps Dodge International Corp. *v* Iran, **10**, 157
Phibro Corporation *v* Ministry of War-ETKA Co. Ltd., **11**, 289; **26**, 15, 254
Philip Morris Inc. *v* Iran, **1**, 220
Phillips Petroleum Company, Iran *v* Iran, **1**, 487; **2**, 1, 283; **3**, 297; **5**, 51; **21**, 79, 285
Picker International Corporation *v* Iran, **11**, 372; **12**, 306
Pickup, Jr. *v* Iran, **11**, 372
Pishdad *v* United States, **25**, 339
Plicoflex, Inc. *v* Iran, **28**, 309
Pneumo Corporation *v* Iran, **19**, 374
Pointon *v* Iran, **27**, 49
Pomeroy *v* Iran, **2**, 372; **4**, 237
Pomeroy Corporation *v* Iran, **2**, 391
Portland State University *v* Iran, **19**, 374
Powell Company *v* Iran, *see* William Powell Company *v* Iran
Procon International Inc. *v* Iran, **6**, 120
Proctor and Gamble Company *v* Iran, **3**, 186, 192
Protiva *v* Iran, **23**, 259
Puerto Rico Maritime Shipping Authority *v* Star Line Iran Company, **14**, 349

Queens Office Tower Associates *v* Iran National Airlines Corporation, **2**, 247
QuesTech, Inc. *v* Iran, **2**, 96; **4**, 72; **9**, 107

Ralph M. Parsons Company *v* Iran, **14**, 349
Ralph Wilson Farrington *v* Islamic Republic of Iran Airlines, *see* Farrington *v* Islamic Republic of Iran Airlines
Ram International Industries, Inc. *v* Air Force of the Islamic Republic of Iran, **3**, 203; **29**, 383
Ram International Industries, Inc. *v* Iran, **26**, 228
Ramin Cherafat *v* Iran, *see* Cherafat *v* Iran
Rana Nikpour *v* Iran, and Foundation for the Oppressed; *see* Nikpour *v* Iran, and Foundation for the Oppressed

CONSOLIDATED TABLE OF CASES (ALPHABETICAL)

Rankin v Iran, **17**, 135
RayGo Wagner Equipment Company v Iran Express Terminal Corporation, **2**, 141
RayGo Wagner Equipment Company v Star Line Iran Company, **1**, 411
Raymond Abboud v Iran, *see* Abboud v Iran
Raymond International (U.K.), Ltd., *Re*, **1**, 394
Raymond Joseph Khubiar v Iran, *see* Khubiar v Iran
Ray-O-Vac International Corporation v Electric Storage Battery Company Iran, **4**, 47
RCA Global Communications, Inc. v Iran, **3**, 8; **4**, 5, 9; **5**, 121; **16**, 335
Reading and Bates Corporation v International Bank of Iran, **5**, 155
Reading and Bates Corporation v Iran, **2**, 401; **4**, 199
Reading and Bates Drilling Company v Iran, **18**, 164
Reading & Bates Exploration Co. v National Iranian Oil Company, **26**, 265
Reliance Group, Inc. v Iran, **16**, 257
Reliance Group, Inc. v National Oil Company, **1**, 384
Revlon Inc. v Iran, **8**, 353
Rexnord, Inc. v Iran, **2**, 6
Reynolds Metals Company v Iran, **3**, 119, 124
Reynolds Tobacco Company v Iran, *see* R.J. Reynolds Tobacco Company v Iran
Reza Mohajer-Shojaee v Iran, *see* Mohajer-Shojaee v Iran
Reza Nemazee v Iran, *see* Nemazee v Iran
Reza Said Malek v Iran, *see* Malek v Iran
Riahi v Iran, **28**, 176
Richard D. Harza, John A. Scoville and George E. Pabich, Trustees v Iran, *see* Harza v Iran
Richard Nourafchan v Iran, *see* Nourafchan v Iran
R.J. Reynolds Tobacco Company v Iran, **1**, 119, 336; **2**, 124; **3**, 39; **4**, 2; **7**, 181; **8**, 55
Robert J. Lee, *Re*, *see* Lee, *Re*
Robert R. Schott v Iran, *see* Schott v Iran
Robin L. Allard v Iran, *see* Allard v Iran
Rockwell International Systems, Inc. v Iran, **2**, 310, 369; **23**, 150; **24**, 3
Ronald E. Chamness v Iran, *see* Chamness v Iran
Ronald Stuart Koehler v Iran, *see* Koehler v Iran
Rondu Holdings Inc. v Iran, **7**, 26
Rorer, Inc. v Toobi Company Ltd., *see* William H. Rorer, Inc. v Toobi Company Ltd.
Roxanne June Cherafat v Iran, *see* Cherafat v Iran
Roy P.M. Carlson v Iran, *see* Carlson v Iran
Rumsey Electric Company v Iran, **19**, 374

Saboonchian v Iran, **27**, 248; **28**, 51
Saghi v Iran, **14**, 3; **29**, 20
St. Regis Paper Company v Iran, **14**, 86
Samrad v Iran, **26**, 44
San Jacinto Eastern Corporation v Iran, **3**, 372; **16**, 3; **21**, 303
San Jose State University v Iran, **24**, 305
Santa Fe International Company v. Iran, **10**, 365
Santa Fe Overseas, Inc. v Iran, **10**, 365
Sara Glory Monemi v Iran, *see* Monemi v Iran
Satellite Application Project, *Re*, **17**, 340
Sayco Corporation v Iran, *see* McCabe, Jr., *et al.* v Iran
Schering Corporation v Iran, **5**, 361
Schlegel Corporation v National Iranian Copper Industries Company, **14**, 176
Schott v Iran, **24**, 203
Scott, Foresman and Company v Iran, **16**, 103
SeaCo, Inc. v Iran, **11**, 210; **22**, 370; **28**, 198
Sea-Land Service, Inc. v Iran, **1**, 335; **3**, 87; **4**, 65; **6**, 149

CONSOLIDATED TABLE OF CASES (ALPHABETICAL)

Security Pacific National Bank *v* Bank Markazi Iran, **30**, 13
Sedco, Inc. *v* Iran Marine Industrial Co., **18**, 58; **21**, 31
Sedco, Inc. *v* National Iranian Oil Company, **8**, 28; **9**, 248; **10**, 3, 180; **15**, 23; **16**, 282; **18**, 3; **21**, 31
Seismograph Service Corporation *v* National Iranian Oil Company, **22**, 3
Sether *v* Iran, **18**, 275
Shahin Shaine Ebrahimi *v* Iran, *see* Ebrahimi (S.S.) *v* Iran
Shahnaz Mohajer-Shojaee *v* Iran, *see* Mohajer-Shojaee *v* Iran
Shahram Mobasser *v* Iran, *see* Mobasser *v* Iran
Shannon and Wilson, Inc. *v* Atomic Energy Organization of Iran, **9**, 397
Sharon L. Jezl Delly *v* Iran, *see* Delly (S.L.J.) *v* Iran
Sherkate Tractor Sazi Iran (Sahami Khass), *Re*, **19**, 178
Shifflette *v* Iran, **22**, 111
Shinto *v* Iran, **1**, 178; **19**, 321
Short *v* Iran, **14**, 20; **16**, 76
Showrai, *Re*, **1**, 226
Singer Company *v* Iran (Cases Nos. 343 and 365), **8**, 18
Singer Company *v* Iran (Cases Nos. 344 and A-9), **7**, 236
Singer Company *v* Iran National Airlines Corporation, **1**, 140
Sinker *v* Iran, **18**, 390
Skidmore, Owings & Merrill *v* Ministry of Housing and Urban Development, **10**, 37
Smith International, Inc. *v* Iran, **4**, 33
Sohio-Iran Trading, Inc. *v* National Iranian Oil Company, **3**, 372; **6**, 33
Sola Tiles, Inc. *v* Iran, **14**, 223
Sonat Offshore Drilling, Inc. *v* National Iranian Oil Company, **13**, 370
Sovereign International Corporation *v* Iran (Case No. 397), **1**, 178; **25**, 229
Sovereign International Corporation *v* Iran (Case No. 398), **1**, 178; **25**, 235
Sovereign International Corporation *v* Iran (Case No. 399), **1**, 178; **25**, 241
Spalding, Inc. *v* Ministry of Roads and Transport, *see* H.A. Spalding, Inc. *v* Ministry of Roads and Transport
Sperry Corporation *v* The High State Council of Informatics of the Islamic Republic of Iran, **1**, 216
Sperry-Sun, Inc. *v* Iran, **10**, 365
Squibb and Sons, Inc. *v* Iran, *see* E.R. Squibb and Sons, Inc. *v* Iran
Staley Manufacturing Company *v* Iran, *see* A.E. Staley Manufacturing Company *v* Iran
Stanwick Corporation *v* Iran, **4**, 20; **5**, 76; **24**, 102
Starrett Housing Corporation *v* Iran, **1**, 386; **4**, 122; **7**, 119; **10**, 110; **13**, 350; **16**, 112
State University of New York College of Environmental Science and Forestry *v* Ministry of Culture and Higher Education, **13**, 277
Sterling Drug, Inc. *v* Iran, **13**, 370
Steven G. Shifflette *v* Iran, *see* Shifflette *v* Iran
Steven Joseph Danielpour *v* Iran, *see* Danielpour (S.J.) *v* Iran
Stewart *v* Iran, **24**, 116
Stewart R. Browne Disc, Inc. *v* Iran, **17**, 368
Stone and Webster Overseas Group, Inc. *v* National Petrochemical Company, **1**, 274, 284, 305, 320; **4**, 192
Stromberg-Carlson Corporation *v* Iran, **19**, 352
Sun Company, Inc. *v* National Iranian Oil Company, **28**, 394
Sundstrand Data Control, Inc. *v* Iran, **1**, 408
Suzanne P. Khosrowshahi *v* Iran, *see* Khosrowshahi (F.L.) *v* Iran
Sylvan Ginsbury, Limited *v* Iran, **21**, 303
Sylvania Technical Systems, Inc. *v* Iran, **5**, 141; **8**, 298

Tadjer-Cohen Associates, Inc. *v* Iran, **9**, 302; **18**, 59, 287; **21**, 303

CONSOLIDATED TABLE OF CASES (ALPHABETICAL) xxix

Tai, Inc. v. Iran, **29**, 411
Tavakoli v. Iran, **14**, 309
Tchacosh Company, Inc. v. Iran, **28**, 371
T.C.S.B., Inc. v. Iran, **1**, 261, 284, 305, 320; **4**, 61; **5**, 160
Technical Laboratory & Soil Mechanics of the Ministry of Roads & Transport of Iran v. Federal Highway Administration of the U.S. Department of Transportation, **24**, 305
Technology Enterprises, Inc. v. Foreign Transaction Company, **2**, 5; **5**, 118
Tehran American School Association, Trustees & Members v. Iran, **1**, 230; **19**, 365
Tehran Regional Electric Company, Re, **19**, 178
Teichmann, Inc. v. Hamadan Glass Company, *see* Henry F. Teichmann, Inc. v. Hamadan Glass Company
Telecommunication Company of Iran v. National Aeronautics and Space Administration, **5**, 357
Telecommunications Company of Iran v. United States, Case B-44, **24**, 305
Telecommunications Company of Iran v. United States, Case B-55, **23**, 320
Teledyne Farris Engineering v. Iran, **19**, 374
Teledyne Industries, Inc. v. Iran, **23**, 126
Texaco Iran Ltd. v. Iran, **3**, 372; **13**, 370
T.G. Howland International Company, Limited v. Iran, **23**, 413
The Management of Alcan Aluminium, Limited v. Ircable Corporation, *see* Alcan Aluminium, Limited v. Ircable Corporation
Theodore Lauth v. Iran, *see* Lauth v. Iran
Thomas Earl Payne v. Iran, *see* Payne v. Iran
Tidewater, Inc. v. Iran, **9**, 308
Tidewater, Inc. and Tidewater Marine Service, Inc. v. Iran, **9**, 61
Timber Purchase Company v. National Iranian Oil Company, **3**, 169
Time, Incorporated v. Iran, **7**, 8
Tippetts, Abbett, McCarthy, Stratton v. TAMS-AFFA, **6**, 219
TME International, Inc. v. Iran, **1**, 178; **24**, 121
Too v. Greater Modesto Insurance Associates, **23**, 378
Touche Ross and Company v. Iran, **3**, 59, 200, 208; **9**, 284
Tour v. Iran, **21**, 25
Training Systems Corporation v. Bank Tejarat, **13**, 331
Trans World Airlines, Inc. v. Iran, **5**, 249
Transaero, Incorporated v. Iran, **21**, 303
Transamerica ICS, Inc. v. Iran, **3**, 84; **26**, 275
Transocean Gulf Oil Company v. Iran, **3**, 372; **10**, 365
Transportation Consultants International v. Iran, *see* First Travel Corporation v. Iran
Troemner, Inc. v. Iran, **19**, 374
Trustees of Columbia University in the City of New York v. Iran, **10**, 319; **11**, 283
TRW, Inc. v. Iran, **19**, 374
Turner Entertainment Co. v. Iran, **16**, 335

Uiterwyk Corporation v. Iran, **19**, 106, 107, 171; **26**, 3, 186
Ultrasystems Incorporated v. Iran, **2**, 100, 139; **4**, 77
Unidyne Corporation v. Iran, **1**, 178; **2**, 138; **29**, 310; **30**, 19
Union Oil Company of Iran v. National Iranian Oil Company, **13**, 370
United Painting Company, Inc. v. Iran, **23**, 351
United States v. Iran, Case No. 86, **3**, 77; **25**, 327
United States v. Iran, Case A-16, **3**, 316, 318, 380; **5**, 57; **9**, 97
United States v. Iran, Case A-17, **8**, 189
United States v. Iran, Case B-24, **5**, 97
United States v. Iran, Case B-29, **6**, 12
United States v. Iran, Case B-31, **19**, 374
United States v. Iran, Case B-33, **23**, 413

United States *v* Iran, Case B-38, **25**, 327
United States *v* Iran, Case B-39, **16**, 335
United States *v* Iran, Case B-76, **25**, 327
United States *v* Iran, Case B-77, **25**, 327
United States *v* Iran, Claims of less than US $250,000, **3**, 77; **25**, 327
United States *v* Ministry of Defense of Iran, Case B-32, **27**, 275
United States (Aeroquip Corporation) *v* Iran (Civil Aviation Organization), **24**, 305
United States (Commodity Credit Corporation) *v* Iran, Case B-22, **19**, 374
United States (Department of the Air Force) *v* Iran (Iranian Air Force and the Foreign Ministry), Case B-35, **24**, 291
United States (Eberle Tanning Company) *v* Iran, **7**, 247
United States (Federal Aviation Administration) *v* Iran (Civil Aviation Organization), Case B-26, **24**, 291
United States (Food and Drug Administration of the Public Health Service) *v* Iran (Ministry of Health and Social Welfare), Case B-28, **24**, 291
United States (Shipside Packing Company, Inc.) *v* Iran, **3**, 331; **5**, 80
United States (Synalloy Corporation) *v* Iran, **7**, 258
United States (Taylor Machinery Company) *v* Iran, **5**, 150
United States (Teledyne Industries Inc.) *v* Iran, **3**, 336
United States (West Chemical Products, Inc.) *v* Iran, **5**, 148
United States Medical Export Company, Inc. *v* Iran, **8**, 83
United Technologies International, Inc., *Re*, **21**, 5
United Technologies International, Inc. *v* Iran, **13**, 254; **17**, 368
United Technologies International, Inc. *v* Iranian Air Force, **3**, 209; **7**, 209
United Technologies International, Inc. *v* Telecommunications Company of Iran, **3**, 334
Universal Enterprises, Ltd. *v* National Iranian Oil Company, **8**, 368
University of California, Santa Barbara *v* Ministry of Culture and Higher Education, **17**, 368
University of Idaho *v* Iran, **19**, 374
University of Southern California *v* Iran, **30**, 283
Upjohn Company *v* Iran, **2**, 332

Varo International Corporation *v* Iran, **25**, 3
Vernie Rodney Pointon *v* Iran, *see* Pointon *v* Iran
Vernor, Howard, Petze, Kirkendall, Wood, Butler, Corn, Stansfield and Suber, Trustees of the Tehran American School Association, and Members of the Tehran American School Association *v* Iran, *see* Tehran American School Association, Trustees and Members *v* Iran
Victor E. Pereira, *Re*, *see* Pereira, *Re*
Vivian M. Tavakoli, David Jamshid Tavakoli, & Keyvan Anthony Tavakoli *v* Iran, *see* Tavakoli *v* Iran
VSI Corporation *v* Iran, **2**, 31, 33, 260; **3**, 73, 78

W. Jack Buckamier *v* Iran, *see* Buckamier *v* Iran
W. Lloyd Holstein *v* Iran, *see* McCabe, Jr., *et al*. *v* Iran
Walter W. Arensburg, *et al*. *v* Ministry of Housing and Urban Development, *see* Skidmore, Owings & Merrill *v* Ministry of Housing and Urban Development
Warnecke and Associates *v* Bank Mellat, *see* John Carl Warnecke and Associates *v* Bank Mellat
Warner-Lambert Company *v* Iran, **1**, 230; **2**, 261
Washington *v* Iran, **19**, 374
Watkins-Johnson Company *v* Iran, **2**, 362; **22**, 218
Weatherford International Inc. *v* Iran, **17**, 368
Wells Fargo Bank *v* Iran, **30**, 8
Western Dynamics Corporation *v* Iran and Etka Organization, **8**, 49
Westinghouse Electric Corporation *v* Iran, **8**, 183; **13**, 93, 370; **14**, 104
White Consolidated Industries, Inc. *v* Iran Compressor Manufacturing Company, **14**, 349
White Westinghouse International Company *v* Bank Sepah-Iran, New York Agency, **1**, 169

Whittaker Corporation (Bermite Division) *v.* Iran, **14**, 263
Wilfred J. Gaulin *v.* Iran, *see* Diba and Gaulin *v.* Iran
William Bikoff and George Eisenpresser *v.* Iran, *see* Bikoff and Eisenpresser *v.* Iran
William H. Rorer, Inc. *v.* Toobi Company Ltd., **3**, 390
William J. Levitt *v.* Iran, *see* Levitt *v.* Iran
William L. Pereira Associates, Iran *v.* Iran, **1**, 219, 484; **5**, 198
William Powell Company *v.* Iran, **19**, 374
William R. McCabe *v.* Iran, *see* McCabe, Jr., *et al. v.* Iran
William Ray Hollyfield *v.* Iran, *see* Hollyfield *v.* Iran
Williams *v.* Iran, **17**, 269
Williams Brothers International Corporation *v.* Iran (Cases Nos. 25 and 492), **14**, 349
Williams Brothers International Corporation *v.* Iran (Cases Nos. 26 and 27), **2**, 228
Woodward-Clyde Consultants *v.* Iran, **3**, 239; **5**, 73
World Farmers Trading, Inc. *v.* Government Trading Corporation, **3**, 197; **22**, 204; **25**, 186

Xerox Corporation *v.* Iran, **7**, 223

Yeager *v.* Iran, **17**, 92
Young & Company *v.* Iran, *see* Arthur Young & Company *v.* Iran

Zaman Azar Nourafchan, George Nourafchan *v.* Iran, *see* Nourafchan *v.* Iran
Zokor International, Inc. *v.* Iran, **1**, 271, 284, 305, 320; **8**, 72

CONSOLIDATED TABLE OF CASES[1]

ARRANGED ACCORDING TO CATEGORY: DECISIONS, AWARDS, AWARDS ON AGREED TERMS, INTERIM AWARDS, INTERLOCUTORY AWARDS, INTERIM AND INTERLOCUTORY AWARDS, ORDERS AND REFUSAL CASES

DECISIONS

Ainsworth *v* Iran **25**, 188
American Bell International Inc. *v* Iran, **14**, 173
American Express International Banking Corp. *v* Government of Iran, **29**, 209
Avco Corporation *v* Iran, **19**, 253

Bank Markazi Iran *v* European American Banking Corporation, **13**, 95
Bank Melli Iran *v* Chase Manhattan Bank, N.A., New York, **21**, 11
Baygell *v* Iran, **11**, 300
Behring International, Inc. *v* Islamic Republic Iranian Air Force, **4**, 89; (Amendment to Decision), **6**, 30
Buckamier *v* Iran, **28**, 307

Cherafat *v* Iran, **28**, 216
Collins Systems International, Inc. *v* Islamic Republic of Iran Navy, **28**, 195
Component Builders, Inc. *v* Iran, **9**, 404
Continental Illinois National Bank and Trust Company of Chicago *v* Iran, **30**, 3
Control Data Corporation *v* Iran, **22**, 151

Dallal *v* Iran, **5**, 74
Dames and Moore *v* Iran, **8**, 107
Development and Resources Corporation *v* Iran, **26**, 256
Dic of Delaware, Inc. *v* Tehran Redevelopment Corporation, **21**, 4

Eastman Kodak Company *v* Iran, **27**, 269
Endo Laboratories, Inc. *v* Iran, **18**, 113
Exxon Research and Engineering Company *v* Iran, **16**, 110

Fedders Corporation *v* Iran, **13**, 97
First Interstate Bank of California *v* Iran, **29**, 205
First National Bank of Boston *v* Iran, **19**, 307
First National Bank of Chicago *v* Iran, **29**, 201
Flexi-Van Leasing, Inc. *v* Iran, **13**, 324
FMC Corporation *v* Iran, **14**, 261
Ford Aerospace & Communications Corporation *v* Air Force of the Islamic Republic of Iran, **12**, 304
Ford Aerospace & Communications Corporation *v* Iran, **14**, 255

Gabay *v* Iran, **27**, 194

Harris International Telecommunications, Inc. *v* Iran, **18**, 76
Hood Corporation *v* Iran, **8**, 53

Interfirst Bank Dallas, N. A. *v* Iran, **16**, 291
International Schools Services, Inc. *v* Iran, **14**, 279
International Technical Products Corporation *v* Iran, **11**, 182

---

[1] The figures in bold type refer to the volume number.

xxxii

CONSOLIDATED TABLE OF CASES (BY CATEGORY) xxxiii

International Telephone and Telegraph Corporation v. Iran, **22**, 213
Iran-United States, Case A/1, **1**, 144, 189
Iran-United States, Case A/2, **1**, 101
Iran-United States, Case A/18, **5**, 251
Iran-United States, Case A/19, **16**, 285
Iran-United States, Case A/20, **11**, 271
Iran-United States, Case A/21, **14**, 324
Iran v. United States, Case 951, **14**, 11
Iran v. United States, Case A-15, **8**, 63; **13**, 173
Iran v. United States, Cases A-15 (IV) & A24, **29**, 214
Iran v. United States, Case B-1, **22**, 105
Irving Trust Company v. Iran, **29**, 189

Karim-Panahi v. United States, **28**, 318
Kidde, Inc. (Walter Kidde-Division) v. Iran National Airlines, **5**, 78
Koehler v. Iran, **11**, 285

Lockheed Corporation v. Iran, **19**, 317

Mangård, Re (Challenge Decision), **1**, 111
Manufacturers Hanover Trust Co. v. Government of Iran, **29**, 193
Marine Midland Bank, N.A. v. Government of Iran, **29**, 185
McCollough & Company v. Ministry of Post Telegraph and Telephone, **11**, 287
McHarg, Roberts, Wallace & Todd v. Iran, **7**, 277
Mellon Bank N.A. v. Iran, **29**, 197
Ministry of National Defense of Iran v. United States, Cases A-3 and A-8, **27**, 256
Mohajer-Shojaee v. Iran, **25**, 273
Morris v. Iran, **3**, 364

Nazari v. Iran, **28**, 192

Panacaviar, S.A. v. Iran, **14**, 100
Parguin Company v. Iran, **4**, 210
PepsiCo, Inc. v. Iran, **13**, 328
Petrolane, Inc. v. Iran, **27**, 264
Phibro Corporation v. Ministry of War–Etka Co. Ltd., **26**, 254
Picker International Corporation v. Iran, **12**, 306

Ram International Industries, Inc. v. Air Force of Iran, **29**, 383

Saboonchian v. Iran, **28**, 51
Security Pacific National Bank v. Bank Markazi Iran, **30**, 13
Sedco, Inc. v. National Iranian Oil Company, **16**, 282

Trustees of Columbia University in the City of New York v. Iran, **11**, 283

Uiterwyk Corporation v. Iran, **19**, 171; **26**, 186
Unidyne Corporation v. Iran, **30**, 19
United States v. Iran, Case A-17, **8**, 189
United Technologies International, Inc. v. Iran, **13**, 254
Universal Enterprises, Ltd. v. National Iranian Oil Company, **8**, 368

Wells Fargo Bank v. Iran, **30**, 8
Westinghouse Electric Corporation v. Iran, **13**, 93
Woodward-Clyde Consultants v. Iran, **5**, 73
World Farmers Trading Inc. v. Government Trading Corporation, **25**, 186

AWARDS

Abboud v. Iran, **24**, 265
Aeromaritime, Inc. v. Iran, **1**, 135
Aeronutronic Overseas Services, Inc. v. The Air Force of the Islamic Republic of Iran, **11**, 223
Agrostruct International, Inc. v. Iran State Cereals Organization, **18**, 180
AHFI Planning Associates, Inc. v. Iran, **11**, 168
Ainsworth v. Iran, **18**, 92
Alcan Aluminium Limited v. Ircable Corporation, **2**, 294
Alfred Haber, P.A. v. Iran, **23**, 133
Allen v. Iran, **28**, 382
American Bell International Inc. v. Iran, **12**, 170
American Farm Products International, Inc. v. Cyrus Consulting Engineers, **18**, 175
American Housing International Inc. v. Housing Cooperative Society, **5**, 235
American International Group, Inc. v. Iran, **4**, 96
Amman & Whitney v. Khuzestan Urban Development Organization, **12**, 94
Amoco International Finance Corporation v. Iran, **15**, 189
Anaconda-Iran, Inc. v. Iran, **28**, 320
Arco Iran, Inc. v. Iran, **16**, 3
Arjad v. Iran, **26**, 190
Arthur J. Fritz & Co. v. Sherkate Tavonie Sherkathaye Sakhtemanie, **22**, 170
Arthur Young & Company v. Iran, **17**, 245
Asghar v. Iran, **24**, 238
Atomic Energy Organization of Iran v. United States, **6**, 141; **12**, 25
Austin Company v. Machine Sazi Arak, **12**, 288
Avco Corporation v. Iran, **19**, 200

Bakhtiari v. Iran, **25**, 289
Bank Mellat v. Crocker National Bank, **5**, 57
Bank Mellat v. Manufacturers Hanover Trust Company, **5**, 57
Baygell v. Iran, **11**, 72
Bechtel, Inc. v. Iran, **14**, 149
Behring International, Inc. v. Islamic Republic of Iran Air Force, **27**, 218
Bendix Corporation v. Iran, **18**, 352
Bendone-Derossi International v. Iran, **18**, 115
Benedix v. Iran, **21**, 20
Berookhim v. Iran, **25**, 278
Bikoff and Eisenpresser v. Iran, **7**, 1
Birnbaum v. Iran, **29**, 260
Blount Brothers Corporation v. Iran (Case No. 52), **10**, 56
Blount Brothers Corporation v. Iran (Case No. 53), **10**, 95
Blount Brothers Corporation v. Ministry of Housing and Urban Development, **3**, 225
Boroumand v. Iran, **29**, 59
Buckamier v. Iran, **28**, 53

Cal-Maine Foods, Inc. v. Iran, **6**, 52
Carlson v. Iran, **26**, 193
Carolina Brass, Inc. v. Arya National Shipping Lines, S.A., **12**, 139
CBA International Development Corporation v. Iran, **5**, 177
CBS Inc. v. Iran, **25**, 131
Chamness v. Iran, **25**, 172
Chas. T. Main International, Inc. v. Khuzestan Water and Power Authority, **11**, 259
Chas. T. Main International, Inc. v. Mahab Consulting Engineers, Inc., **3**, 270
CMI International, Inc. v. Ministry of Roads and Transportation, Iran, **4**, 263
Collins Systems International, Inc. v. Islamic Republic of Iran Navy, **28**, 21

CONSOLIDATED TABLE OF CASES (BY CATEGORY)　　xxxv

Combustion Engineering, Inc. *v* Iran, **26**, 60
Component Builders, Inc. *v* Iran, **23**, 3
Computer Sciences Corporation *v* Iran, **10**, 269
Consortium for International Development *v* Iran, **26**, 244
Continental Grain Export Corporation *v* Government Trading Corporation, **3**, 319
Continental Grain Export Corporation *v* Union of Consumers' Co-operatives for Iranian Workers (EMKAN), **11**, 292
Cosmos Engineering, Inc. *v* Ministry of Roads and Transportation, **13**, 179
Craig *v* Ministry of Energy of Iran, **3**, 280
Creditcorp International, Inc. *v* Iran Carton Company, **23**, 265
Cyrus Petroleum Ltd. *v* Iran, **11**, 70

Daley *v* Iran, **18**, 232
Dallal *v* Iran, **3**, 10
Dames and Moore *v* Iran, **4**, 212
Danielpour (M.) *v* Iran, **22**, 118
David *v* Iran, **24**, 252
Department of the Environment of Iran *v* United States, Case B-53, **5**, 105
Development and Resources Corporation *v* Iran, **25**, 20
Diba and Gaulin *v* Iran, **23**, 268
Dic of Delaware, Inc. *v* Tehran Redevelopment Corporation, **8**, 144
Dorian International Credit Co., Inc. *v* Iran Carton Company, **23**, 265
Dresser Industries, Inc. *v* Iran, **3**, 332
Drucker, Jr. *v* Foreign Transaction Company, **19**, 257

Eastman Kodak Company *v* Iran, **17**, 153; **27**, 3
Eastman Kodak International Capital Company, Inc. *v* Iran, **17**, 153
Ebrahimi *v* Iran, **30**, 170
Economy Forms Corporation *v* Iran, **3**, 42; **5**, 1
Edwards *v* Iran, **23**, 290
Electronic Systems International, Inc. *v* Ministry of Defence of the Islamic Republic of Iran, **22**, 339
Endo Laboratories, Inc. *v* Iran, **17**, 114
Esphahanian *v* Bank Tejarat, **2**, 157, 178
Etezadi *v* Iran, **25**, 264; **30**, 22
Exxon Corporation *v* Iran, **16**, 3
Exxon Corporation *v* National Iranian Oil Company, **17**, 3
Exxon Research and Engineering Company *v* Iran, **15**, 3

First Travel Corporation *v* Iran, **9**, 360
Flexi-Van Leasing, Inc. *v* Iran, **12**, 335
FMC Corporation *v* Iran, **14**, 111
Ford Aerospace & Communications Corporation *v* Iran, **14**, 24
Ford Aerospace & Communications Corporation *v* The Air Force of the Islamic Republic of Iran, **11**, 184
Foremost Tehran, Inc. *v* Iran, **10**, 228
French American Banking Corporation *v* Iranit, S. A., **2**, 303
Futura Trading Inc *v* Khuzestan Water and Power Authority, **9**, 46
Futura Trading Inc. *v* National Iranian Oil Company, **13**, 99

Gabay *v* Iran, **27**, 40
General Atomic Company *v* Atomic Energy Organization of Iran, **1**, 223
General Dynamics Corporation *v* Iran, **5**, 386
General Dynamics Telephone Systems Center, Inc. *v* Iran, **9**, 153
General Electric Company *v* Iran, **26**, 148
General Motors Corporation *v* Iran, **13**, 282

General Petrochemicals Corp v Iran, **27**, 96
Ghaffari v National Iranian Oil Company, **25**, 178
Gianoplus v Iran, **11**, 217
Golpira v Iran, **2**, 171, 178
Golshani v Iran, **29**, 78
Gould Marketing, Inc. v Ministry of National Defense of Iran, **6**, 272
Granite State Machine Company v Iran, **1**, 185, 442
Grimm v Iran, **2**, 78
Gruen Associates, Inc. v Iran Housing Company, **3**, 97, 124
Grune and Stratton, Inc. v Iran, **18**, 224

Haddadi v. United States, **8**, 20
Haji-Bagherpour v United States, **2**, 38
Hakim v Iran, **24**, 269
Harnischfeger Corporation v Ministry of Roads and Transportation, **7**, 90; **8**, 119
Haroonian v Iran, **2**, 226
Harounian v Iran, **23**, 282
Harrington and Associates, Inc. v Iran, **16**, 297
Harris International Telecommunications, Inc. v Iran, **17**, 31
Harza v Iran, **11**, 76
Harza Engineering Company v Iran, **1**, 499
H.A. Spalding, Inc. v Ministry of Roads and Transport, **10**, 22
Haus International, Inc. v Tehran Redevelopment Corporation, **9**, 313
Henry F. Teichmann, Inc. v Hamadan Glass Company, **13**, 124
Highlands Insurance Company v Iran, **25**, 212
Hilt v Iran, **18**, 154
Hoffland Honey Company v National Iranian Oil Company, **2**, 41
Hollyfield v Iran, **23**, 276
Hood Corporation v Iran, **7**, 36
Houston Contracting Company v National Iranian Oil Company, **20**, 3
Howard Needles Tammen & Bergendoff v Iran, **11**, 302

INA Corporation v Iran, **8**, 373
International Ore & Fertilizer Corporation v Razi Chemical Company Ltd., **18**, 98
International Schools Services, Inc. v Iran, **14**, 165
International Schools Services, Inc. v National Iranian Copper Industries Company, **9**, 187
International Systems & Controls Corporation v Iran, **12**, 239
International Systems & Controls Corporation v National Iranian Gas Company, **24**, 47
International Technical Products Corporation v Iran, **9**, 10, 206
Intrend International, Inc. v The Imperial Iranian Air Force, **3**, 110, 124
Iowa State University of Science and Technology v Ministry of Culture and Higher Education, **13**, 271
Iran v United States, Case A-15, **14**, 311
Iran v United States, Case A-15 IIA and IIB, **28**, 112
Iran v United States, Case B-1, **19**, 3, 273
Iran National Airlines Company v United States, Case B-8, **17**, 187
Iran National Airlines Company v United States, Case B-9, **17**, 214
Iran National Airlines Company v United States, Case B-10, **17**, 238
Iran National Airlines Company v United States, Case B-12, **17**, 228
Iran National Airlines Company v United States, Case B-51, **17**, 200
Iran National Gas Company v United States, **17**, 183
Iran Touring and Tourism Organization v United States, **18**, 84
Iranian Customs Administration v United States, Case B-2, **13**, 155
Iranian Customs Administration v United States, Case B-3, **8**, 89
Iranian Customs Administration v United States, Case B-13, **13**, 158

CONSOLIDATED TABLE OF CASES (BY CATEGORY)

Iranian Customs Administration v. United States, Case B-16, **5**, 94
Iranian Customs Administration v. United States, Case B-18, **13**, 161
Iranian Customs Administration v. United States, Case B-20, **13**, 164
Iranian Customs Administration v. United States, Case B-21, **8**, 93
Isaiah v. Bank Mellat, **2**, 232
Itel Corporation v. Iran, **28**, 159
Itel International Corporation v. Social Security Organization of Iran, **24**, 272

Jafari v. Iran, **18**, 90
J.I. Case Company v. Iran, **3**, 62
John Carl Warnecke and Associates v. Bank Mellat, **3**, 256

Kahen v. Iran, **18**, 289
Karim-Panahi v. United States, **28**, 225
Kaysons International Corp. v. Iran, **29**, 222
Khajetoorians v. Iran, **26**, 37
Khatami v. Iran, **30**, 267
Khosrowshahi v. Iran, **17**, 266; **30**, 76
Khubiar v. Iran, **11**, 180
Kimberly-Clark Corporation v. Bank Markazi Iran, **2**, 334
Koehler v. Iran, **10**, 333

Ladjevardi v. Iran, **29**, 367
Lauth v. Iran, **11**, 150
Leach v. Iran, **23**, 233
Levitt v. Iran (Case No. 209), **14**, 191
Levitt v. Iran (Case No. 210), **27**, 145
Lianosoff v. Iran, **5**, 90
Linen, Fortinberry and Associates, Inc. v. Iran, **19**, 62
Lischem Corporation v. Atomic Energy Organization of Iran, **7**, 18
Litton Systems, Inc. v. Iran, **12**, 126
Lockheed Corporation v. Iran, **18**, 292
Logos Development Corporation v. Information Systems Iran, **11**, 53

M & M Productions, Inc. v. Iran, **6**, 125
Mackay v. Iran Beverages Company, **5**, 134
Mahmoud v. Iran, **9**, 350
Malek v. Iran, **28**, 246
Malekzadeh v. Iran, **29**, 3
Marks and Umann v. Iran, **9**, 69
McCollough & Company v. Ministry of Post, Telegraph and Telephone, **11**, 3
McHarg, Roberts, Wallace, Todd v. Iran, **13**, 286
McLaughlin Enterprises Ltd. v. Iran, **12**, 146
Merrill Lynch & Co. Inc. v. Iran, **27**, 122
Middle East Management and Construction Corporation v. Iran, **9**, 340
Ministry of National Defence, Iran v. United States (Case A-14), **4**, 74
Ministry of National Defence, Iran v. United States (Cases B-59 and B-69), **12**, 33
Ministry of National Defence, Iran v. United States (Case B-66), **14**, 276
Minnesota Mining and Manufacturing Company v. Iran, **17**, 294
Mobasser v. Iran, **10**, 177
Mobil Oil Iran Inc. v. Iran, **16**, 3
Modern Film Corporation v. Iran, **18**, 150
Mohajer-Shojaee v. Iran, **25**, 196
Moin v. Iran, **30**, 70
Monemi v. Iran, **28**, 232
Morgan Equipment Company v. Iran, **4**, 272

Morris *v* Iran, **2**, 241
Morrison-Knudsen Pacific Ltd. *v* Ministry of Roads and Transportation, **7**, 54
Motamed *v* Iran, **21**, 28
Motorola, Inc *v* Iran National Airlines Corporation, **19**, 73
Moussavi *v* United States, **8**, 24

Nazari *v* Iran, **30**, 123
Navy of the Government of Iran *v* General Dynamics Corporation (Pomona Division), **14**, 251
Near East Technological Services U.S.A., Inc. *v* Islamic Republic of Iran Air Force, **21**, 13
Nemazee *v* Iran, **25**, 153
Nourafchan *v* Iran, **18**, 88; **29**, 295

Ocean-Air Cargo Claims, Inc. *v* Iran (Case No. 11102), **23**, 303
Ocean-Air Cargo Claims, Inc. *v* Iran (Case No. 11429), **23**, 296
Oil Field of Texas, Inc. *v* Iran, **12**, 308
Onesco, Inc. *v* National Iranian Gas Company, **12**, 160
Orton/McCullough Crane Company *v* Iranian State Railways, **25**, 15
Otis Elevator Company *v* Iran, **14**, 283

Parguin Company *v* United States, **13**, 261
Payne *v* Iran, **12**, 3
PepsiCo, Inc. *v* Iran, **13**, 3
Perry-Rohani *v* Iran, **22**, 194
Petrolane, Inc. *v* Iran, **27**, 64; **28**, 3
Phelps Dodge Corp. *v* Iran, **10**, 121
Phelps Dodge International Corp. *v* Iran, **10**, 157
Phibro Corporation *v* Ministry of War-Etka Co. Ltd., **26**, 15
Phillips Petroleum Company Iran *v* Iran, **21**, 79
Plicoflex, Inc. *v* Iran, **28**, 309
Pointon *v* Iran, **27**, 49
Pomeroy *v* Iran, **2**, 372; **4**, 237
Pomeroy Corporation *v* Iran, **2**, 391

Queens Office Tower Associates *v* Iran National Airlines Corporation, **2**, 247
Questech, Inc. *v* Iran, **9**, 107

Ram International Industries, Inc. *v* Air Force of the Islamic Republic of Iran, **3**, 203
Ram International Industries, Inc. *v* Iran, **26**, 228
Rankin *v* Iran, **17**, 135
RayGo Wagner Equipment Company *v* Iran Express Terminal Corporation, **2**, 141
RayGo Wagner Equipment Company *v* Star Line Iran Company, **1**, 411
Reading and Bates Drilling Company *v* Iran, **18**, 164
Reliance Group, Inc. *v* Iran, **16**, 257
Reliance Group, Inc. *v* National Iranian Oil Company, **1**, 384
Rexnord, Inc. *v* Iran, **2**, 6
R. J. Reynolds Tobacco Company *v* Iran, **7**, 181; **8**, 55
Rockwell International Systems, Inc. *v* Iran, **23**, 150; **24**, 3
Rondu Holdings Inc. *v* Iran, **7**, 26

Saboonchian *v* Iran, **27**, 248
Saghi *v* Iran, **29**, 20
St. Regis Paper Company *v* Iran, **14**, 86
Samrad *v* Iran, **26**, 44
San Jacinto Eastern Corporation *v* Iran, **16**, 3
Schering Corporation *v* Iran, **5**, 361
Schlegel Corporation *v* National Iranian Copper Industries Company, **14**, 176

CONSOLIDATED TABLE OF CASES (BY CATEGORY)　　　xxxix

Schott v. Iran, **24**, 203
Scott, Foresman and Company v. Iran, **16**, 103
Seaco, Inc. v. Iran, **28**, 198
Sea-Land Service, Inc. v. Iran, **6**, 149
Sedco, Inc. v. Iran Marine Industrial Company, **21**, 31
Sedco, Inc. v. National Iranian Oil Company, **15**, 23; **18**, 3; **21**, 31
Seismograph Service Corporation v. National Iranian Oil Company, **22**, 3
Sether v. Iran, **18**, 275
Shannon and Wilson v. Atomic Energy Organisation of Iran, **9**, 397
Shifflette v. Iran, **22**, 111
Shinto v. Iran, **19**, 321
Short v. Iran, **16**, 76
Skidmore, Owings & Merrill v. Ministry of Housing and Urban Development, **10**, 37
Sola Tiles, Inc. v. Iran, **14**, 223
Sovereign International Corporation v. Iran (Case No. 397), **25**, 229
Sovereign International Corporation v. Iran (Case No. 398), **25**, 235
Sovereign International Corporation v. Iran (Case No. 399), **25**, 241
Stanwick Corporation v. Iran, **24**, 102
Starrett Housing Corporation v. Iran, **16**, 112
State University of New York College of Environmental Science and Forestry v. Ministry of Culture and Higher Education, **13**, 277
Stewart v. Iran, **24**, 116
Sylvania Technical Systems, Inc. v. Iran, **8**, 298

Tchacosh Company, Inc. v. Iran, **28**, 371
T.C.S.B., Inc. v. Iran, **5**, 160
Technology Enterprises, Inc. v. Foreign Transaction Company, **5**, 118
Telecommunication Company of Iran v. National Aeronautics and Space Administration, **5**, 357
Telecommunications Company of Iran v. United States, **23**, 320
Teledyne Industries, Inc. v. Iran, **23**, 126
Time, Incorporated v. Iran, **7**, 8
Tippetts, Abbett, McCarthy, Stratton v. TAMS-AFFA, **6**, 219
TME International, Inc. v. Iran, **24**, 121
Too v. Greater Modesto Insurance Associates, **23**, 378
Touche Ross and Company v. Iran, **9**, 284
Tour v. Iran, **21**, 25
Training Systems Corporation v. Bank Tejarat, **13**, 331
Trustees of Columbia University in the City of New York v. Iran, **10**, 319

Uiterwyk Corporation v. Iran, **19**, 107; **26**, 3
Ultrasystems Incorporated v. Iran, **2**, 100; **4**, 77
Unidyne Corp. v. Iran, **29**, 310
United Painting Company, Inc. v. Iran, **23**, 351
United States v. Iran, Case A-16, **5**, 57; **9**, 97
United States v. Iran, Case B-24, **5**, 97
United States v. Iran, Case B-29, **6**, 12
United Technologies International, Inc. v. Telecommunications Company of Iran, **3**, 334

Varo International Corporation, **25**, 3

Watkins-Johnson Company v. Iran, **22**, 218
Western Dynamics Corporation v. Iran and Etka Organization, **8**, 49
White Westinghouse International Company v. Bank Sepah-Iran, New York Agency, **1**, 169
Whittaker Corporation (Bermite Division) v. Iran, **14**, 263
William L. Pereira Associates, Iran v. Iran, **5**, 198
Williams v. Iran, **17**, 269

Woodward-Clyde Consultants *v* Iran, **3**, 239
World Farmers Trading, Inc. *v* Government Trading Corporation, **3**, 197; **22**, 20

Yeager *v* Iran, **17**, 92

AWARDS ON AGREED TERMS

A.B.S. Worldwide Technical Services, Inc. *v* Iran, **3**, 176, 192
Accurate Machine Products Corporation *v* Iran, **19**, 374
Adams International Division of Beatrice Foods Company *v* Iran, **6**, 1
Advanced Computer Techniques Corporation *v* Iran, **3**, 326
Aeronutronics Overseas Services, Inc. *v* Telecommunications Company of Iran, **14**, 339
A.E. Staley Manufacturing Company *v* Iran, **8**, 42
AFIA *v* Iran, **8**, 236
Air La Carte, Inc. *v* Iran National Airlines Corporation, **1**, 163
Airlines of the Islamic Republic of Iran *v* United States, **22**, 365
Allard *v* Iran, **23**, 413
Allis-Chalmers Corporation *v* Iran, **4**, 39
American Cast Iron Pipe Company *v* Ahwaz Water and Sewage Board, **9**, 203
American Cyanamid Company *v* Iran, **2**, 269
American Express Company *v* Iran, **17**, 368
American Hospital Supply Corporation *v* Iran, **7**, 269
American Independent Oil Company *v* National Iranian Oil Company, **9**, 184
American Lecithin Company *v* Iran, **10**, 365
American Motors Corporation *v* Iran, **4**, 29
AMF Inc. *v* Iran, **16**, 335
Amoco International Finance Corporation *v* Iran, **25**, 314
Amoco Iran Oil Company *v* Iran, **25**, 301
Arco Exploration, Inc. *v* National Iranian Oil Company, **28**, 370
Arco Iran, Inc. *v* Iran, **25**, 339
Arco Seed Company *v* Iran, **14**, 349
Atlantic Richfield Company *v* Iran, **28**, 401
Atomic Energy Organization of Iran *v* National Audiovisual Center, **21**, 303

Baker International Corporation *v* Iran, **12**, 385
Bank Mellat *v* Chase Manhattan Bank, **5**, 155
Baroid International Petroleum Services, Inc. *v* Iran, **10**, 365
Bearings Inc. *v*. Iran, **19**, 374
Bell Industries *v* Iran, **18**, 390
B.F. Goodrich Company *v* Abadan Petrochemical Company, Ltd., **1**, 342
B.F. Goodrich Company *v* Kian Tire Manufacturing Company, **1**, 123
Blount Brothers Corporation *v* Iran (Case No. 63), **6**, 118
Blount Brothers Corporation *v* Iran Air, **21**, 303
Board of Trustees of Southern Illinois University *v* Iran, **19**, 345
Boeing Company *v* Iran, **13**, 359
Borg Warner Corporation *v* Iran, **11**, 372

Cabot International Capital Corporation *v* Iran, **4**, 83
C and T Commodities of America, Inc. *v* Iran, **13**, 370
Carrier Corporation *v* Iran, **3**, 36, 78
Charter (Iran) Petroleum Company *v* National Iranian Oil Company, **5**, 88
Chesapeake and Potomac Telephone Company *v* Iran, **24**, 305
Chevron Research Company *v* National Iranian Oil Company, **2**, 364; **3**, 78
Chicago Bridge & Iron Company *v* Iran, **7**, 225; **11**, 372
Christensen, Inc. *v* Iran, **30**, 292

CONSOLIDATED TABLE OF CASES (BY CATEGORY)

Coast Survey Limited v. Iran, **23**, 413
Combustion Engineering, Inc. v. Iran, **3**, 366; **24**, 297; **27**, 288
Commercial Development Center v. United States, **18**, 390
Commonwealth Associates, Inc. v. Iran, **13**, 370
Continental Corporation v. Iran, **1**, 403
Control Data Corporation v. Iran, **21**, 303
Cook Industries, Inc. v. Iran, **12**, 397
Cross Company v. Iran, **8**, 97
CTI-Container Leasing Corporation v. Starline Iran Co., **26**, 275

Dana Corporation v. Iran, **19**, 374
Daniel, Mann, Johnson and Mendenhall v. Iran, **1**, 160
David Mikhael, Inc. v. Iran, **6**, 20
Delly (D.P.) v. Iran, **19**, 360
Delly (S.L.J.) v. Iran, **19**, 360
Deloitte, Haskins and Sells v. Computer Services Company, **3**, 34
Department of Energy (Oak Ridge Operations) v. Atomic Energy Organization of Iran, **21**, 303
De Soto, Inc. v. Iran Aircraft Industries, **14**, 349
Detroit Parts Manufacturing Company v. Iran, **8**, 79
Diagnostic Products Corporation v. Iran, **9**, 306
Distribution International Corporation v. Iran, **17**, 353
DoAll Dallas Company v. Iran, **23**, 413
Dow Chemical Company v. Iran (Case No. 257), **6**, 38
Dresser Industries, Inc. v. Iran (Cases Nos. 103-104, 107-110), **3**, 212
Dresser Industries, Inc. v. Iran (Cases Nos. 105 and 137), **2**, 291
Dresser Industries, Inc. v. Iran (Cases Nos. 467-469 and 471), **9**, 346
Dreyco, Inc. (E.D. Allmendinger Division) v. Iran, **8**, 13

Econocorp, Inc. v. Iran, **8**, 360
E.I. du Pont de Nemours and Company v. Iran, **4**, 183
Electric Heating Equipment Company v. Iran, **19**, 374
Electronic Data Systems Corporation v. Iran, **7**, 244
Enserch Corporation v. Iran, **8**, 66
Enserch Service Company of Iran v. Iran, **8**, 81
E.R. Squibb and Sons, Inc. v. Iran, **2**, 44
Esso Africa, Inc. v. Towlid Rowghan Refining (Public) Company, **2**, 305
Esso Europe Supply Company, Inc. v. Towlid Rowghan Refining (Public) Company, **2**, 305
E-Systems, Inc. v. Iran, **4**, 197
Exxon Corporation v. Iran, **23**, 401

Farrington v. Islamic Republic of Iran Airlines, **18**, 390
Fedders Corp. v. Loristan Refrigeration Industries, **29**, 401
Federal Mogul International Distribution, Inc. v. Iran, **18**, 390
F.H. Maloney Company v. Iran, **9**, 70
Figgie International Inc. (Geo. J. Meyer Manufacturing Division) v. Zam Zam Bottling Company, **8**, 214
First National Bank in St. Louis v. Iran, **18**, 390
Fluor Corporation v. Bimeh Iran, **23**, 413
Fluor Corporation v. Iran (Case No. 333), **23**, 413
Fluor Corporation v. Iran (Case No. 810), **23**, 413
FMC Corporation v. Iran, **11**, 372
Foremost McKesson, Inc. v. Tolidaru, **2**, 278

GAI-Tronics Corporation v. Iran, **19**, 374
General Electric Company v. Iran, **7**, 239
General Electric Company v. Pars Appliance Manufacturing Company, **2**, 132

General Electric Company (Space Division) v. Iran, **9**, 6
General Motors Corporation v. Iran, **7**, 220
General Tire and Rubber Company v. Iran Tire Manufacturing Company, **3**, 351
Georgetown University v. Iran, **23**, 413
Getty Iran Ltd. v. Iran, **13**, 370
Gillette Company v. Iran, **3**, 218
Goodyear Tire and Rubber Company v. Tasmeh Melli Company, **3**, 181, 192
Granger Associates v. Iran, **16**, 317
Gulf Ports Crating Company v. Ministry of Roads and Transportation, **2**, 126

H & F Kornfeld, Inc. v. Iran, **21**, 303
Hafez Glaziery and Glass Cutting Shop v. United States, **8**, 349
Halliburton Company v. Doreen/IMCO, **6**, 4
Halliburton Company v. Iran, **9**, 310
Herbach & Rademan Inc. v. Iran, **19**, 374
Herman Blum Consulting Engineers, Inc. v. Iran, **5**, 354
Honeywell Information Systems, Inc. v. Information Systems Iran (ISIRAN), **1**, 181
Hyatt International Corporation v. Iran, **10**, 365

Indian Head, Inc. v. Iran, **13**, 370
Industrial Equipment Co. of Houston v. Iran, **19**, 374
Ingersoll-Rand Company v. Iran, **18**, 390
Interaction Research Corporation v. Iran, **17**, 362
Intercontinental Hotels Corporation v. Iran, **7**, 249
Inter-continental Hotels Corporation and Overseas Private Investment Corporation v. Iran, **7**, 249
International Schools Services, Inc. v. Iran, **1**, 156
Iran v. Chase Manhattan Bank, **5**, 155
Iran v. United States, Case B-1, **23**, 407; **27**, 282
Iran v. United States, Case B-14, **23**, 413
Iran v. United States, Claims of less than U.S. $250,000, **27**, 275
Iran (Civil Aviation Organization) v. United States (Military Assistance Advisory Group), Case B-60, **24**, 291
Iran Chevron Oil Company v. Iran, **10**, 357
ITT Industries, Inc. v. Iran, **2**, 348

J.D. Marshall International, Inc. v. Iran, **8**, 11
J.I. Case Company v. Aryan Yadak Company, **14**, 349

Kaiser Engineers International, Inc. v. Iran, **2**, 366
Kem International Co. v. Iran, **29**, 395
Kidde Consultants, Inc. v. Haydar Ghyai & Associates, **30**, 302

Lockheed Corporation v. Iran, **11**, 363
Lord Corporation v. Iran Helicopter Support and Renewal Company, **18**, 377
Louis Berger International, Inc. v. Plan and Budget Organization of Iran, **14**, 349
Lowe Marschalk, Inc. v. Iran, **14**, 349

Maxon Corporation v. Iran, **19**, 374
McCabe, Jr., et al. v. Iran, **23**, 413
Ministry of Agriculture and Rural Development of Iran v. United States Department of Agriculture, Case B-5, **23**, 413
Ministry of Agriculture and Rural Development of Iran v. United States Department of Agriculture, Case B-19, **23**, 413
Ministry of Defense of Iran v. United States, Case B-74, **27**, 275
Ministry of Defense of Iran v. United States, Case B-75, **24**, 305

CONSOLIDATED TABLE OF CASES (BY CATEGORY)　　　　xliii

Ministry of Oil of Iran *v.* United States, **23**, 413
Ministry of Roads and Transportation *v.* Port of Vancouver, Washington, **3**, 338
Minnesota Mining and Manufacturing Company *v.* Iran, **8**, 15
Mitra Leasing Corporation *v.* Iran, **28**, 389
Mobil Oil Inc. *v.* Iran, **25**, 339
Morris Inc. *v.* Iran, **1**, 220
Morrison-Knudsen International Company, Inc. *v.* Iran, **9**, 357
Murphy Middle East Oil Company *v.* National Iranian Oil Company, **13**, 370

National Airmotive Corporation *v.* Iran, **3**, 91, 124
National Corporation for Housing Partnerships *v.* Ministry of Mines and Industries of Iran, **7**, 260
National Training and Development Service for State and Local Government *v.* Iran, **21**, 303
NCR Corporation *v.* Iran, **1**, 217
New York Blower Company *v.* Polyacryl Iran Corporation, **13**, 370
NL Industries, Inc. *v.* Iran, **10**, 365
Norad Private Joint Stock Co. *v.* United States, **19**, 374
Northern Virginia Community College *v.* Iran, **23**, 413
Norton Lilly & Co., Inc. *v.* Iran, **6**, 147

Otis Elevator Company (New Jersey) *v.* Iran, **19**, 374
Otis Engineering Corporation *v.* Iran, **9**, 310
Owens-Corning Fiberglass Corporation *v.* Iran, **4**, 280

Pan American World Airways, Inc. *v.* Iran, **4**, 205
Penwalt Corporation–Wallace & Tiernan Division *v.* Iran, **19**, 374
Perkin Elmer Corporation *v.* Iran, **19**, 374
Pfizer, Inc. *v.* Iran, **2**, 90
Phillips Petroleum Company Iran *v.* Iran, **21**, 285
Picker International Corporation *v.* Iran, **11**, 372
Pickup, Jr. *v.* Iran, **11**, 372
Pishdad *v.* United States, **25**, 339
Pneumo Corporation *v.* Iran, **19**, 374
Portland State University *v.* Iran, **19**, 374
Procon International Inc. *v.* Iran, **6**, 120
Proctor and Gamble Company *v.* Iran, **3**, 186, 192
Puerto Rico Maritime Shipping Authority *v.* Star Line Iran Company, **14**, 349

Ralph M. Parsons Company *v.* Iran, **14**, 349
Ray-O-Vac International Corporation *v.* Electric Storage Battery Company Iran, **4**, 47
RCA Global Communications Inc. *v.* Iran, **16**, 335
Reading and Bates Corporation *v.* International Bank of Iran, **5**, 155
Reading and Bates Corporation *v.* Iran, **4**, 199
Reading & Bates Exploration Co. *v.* National Iranian Oil Company, **26**, 265
Revlon Inc. *v.* Iran, **8**, 353
Reynolds Metals Company *v.* Iran, **3**, 119, 124
Rumsey Electric Company *v.* Iran, **19**, 374

SanJacinto Eastern Corporation *v.* Iran, **21**, 303
SanJose State University *v.* Iran, **24**, 305
Santa Fe International Company *v.* Iran, **10**, 365
Santa Fe Overseas, Inc. *v.* Iran, **10**, 365
SeaCo, Inc. *v.* Iran, **22**, 370
Singer Company *v.* Iran (Cases No. 343 and 365), **8**, 18
Singer Company *v.* Iran (Cases No. 344 and A-9), **7**, 236
Singer Company *v.* Iran National Airlines Corporation, **1**, 140

Sinker v Iran, **18**, 390
Smith International, Inc. v Iran, **4**, 33
Sohio-Iran Trading, Inc. v National Iranian Oil Company, **6**, 33
Sonat Offshore Drilling, Inc. v National Iranian Oil Company, **13**, 370
Sperry Corporation v The High State Council of Informatics of the Islamic Republic of Iran, **1**, 216
Sperry-Sun, Inc. v Iran, **10**, 365
Stanwick Corporation v Iran, **4**, 20; **5**, 76
Sterling Drug, Inc. v Iran, **13**, 370
Stewart R. Browne Disc, Inc. v Iran, **17**, 368
Stone and Webster Overseas Group, Inc. v National Petrochemical Company, **4**, 192
Stromberg-Carlson Corporation v Iran, **19**, 352
Sun Company, Inc. v National Iranian Oil Company, **28**, 394
Sundstrand Data Control, Inc. v Iran, **1**, 408
Sylvan Ginsbury, Limited v Iran, **21**, 303

Tadjer-Cohen Associates, Inc. v Iran, **21**, 303
Tai, Inc. v Iran, **29**, 411
Technical Laboratory & Soil Mechanics of the Ministry of Roads & Transport of Iran v Federal Highway Administration of the U.S. Department of Transportation, **24**, 305
Tehran American School Association, Trustees and Members v Iran, **19**, 365
Telecommunications Company of Iran v United States, **24**, 305
Teledyne Farris Engineering v Iran, **19**, 374
Texaco Iran Ltd. v Iran, **13**, 370
T.G. Howland International Company, Limited v Iran, **23**, 413
Tidewater, Inc. v Iran, **9**, 308
Tidewater, Inc. and Tidewater Marine Service, Inc. v Iran, **9**, 61
Timber Purchase Company v National Iranian Oil Company, **3**, 169
Trans World Airlines, Inc. v Iran, **5**, 249
Transaero, Incorporated v Iran, **21**, 303
Transamerica ICS, Inc. v Iran, **26**, 275
Transocean Gulf Oil Company v Iran, **10**, 365
Troemner, Inc. v Iran, **19**, 374
TRW, Inc. v Iran, **19**, 374
Turner Entertainment Co. v Iran, **16**, 335

Union Oil Company of Iran v National Iranian Oil Company, **13**, 370
United States v Iran, Case No. 86, **25**, 327
United States v Iran, Case B-31, **19**, 374
United States v Iran, Case B-33, **23**, 413
United States v Iran, Case B-38, **25**, 327
United States v Iran, Case B-39, **16**, 335
United States v Iran, Case B-76, **25**, 327
United States v Iran, Case B-77, **25**, 327
United States v Iran, Claims of less than US $250,000, **25**, 327
United States v Ministry of Defense of Iran, Case B-32, **27**, 275
United States (Aeroquip Corporation) v Iran (Civil Aviation Organization), **24**, 305
United States (Commodity Credit Corporation) v Iran, Case B-22, **19**, 374
United States (Department of the Air Force) v Iran (Iranian Air Force and the Foreign Ministry), Case B-35, **24**, 291
United States (Eberle Tanning Company) v Iran, **7**, 247
United States (Federal Aviation Administration) v Iran (Civil Aviation Organization), Case B-26, **24**, 291
United States (Food and Drug Administration of the Public Health Service) v Iran (Ministry of Health and Social Welfare), Case B-28, **24**, 291

United States (Shipside Packing Company, Inc.) *v.* Iran, **5**, 80
United States (Synalloy Corporation) *v.* Iran, **7**, 258
United States (Taylor Machinery Company) *v.* Iran, **5**, 150
United States (West Chemical Products, Inc.) *v.* Iran, **5**, 148
United States Medical Export Company, Inc. *v.* Iran, **8**, 83
United Technologies International, Inc. *v.* Iran, **17**, 368
United Technologies International, Inc. *v.* Iranian Air Force, **7**, 209
University of California, Santa Barbara *v.* Ministry of Culture and Higher Education, **17**, 368
University of Idaho *v.* Iran, **19**, 374
University of Southern California *v.* Iran, **30**, 283
Upjohn Company *v.* Iran, **2**, 332

VSI Corporation *v.* Iran Aircraft Industries Corporation, **3**, 73, 78

Warner-Lambert Company *v.* Iran, **2**, 261
Washington *v.* Iran, **19**, 374
Weatherford International Inc. *v.* Iran, **17**, 368
Westinghouse Electric Corporation *v.* Iran, **8**, 183; **13**, 370
White Consolidated Industries, Inc. *v.* Iran Compressor Manufacturing Company, **14**, 349
William H. Rorer, Inc. *v.* Toobi Company Ltd., **3**, 390
William Powell Company *v.* Iran, **19**, 374
Williams Brothers International Corporation *v.* Iran (Cases Nos. 25 and 492), **14**, 349
Williams Brothers International Corporation *v.* Iran (Cases Nos. 26 and 27), **2**, 228

Xerox Corporation *v.* Iran, **7**, 223

Zokor International, Ltd. *v.* Iran, **8**, 72

INTERIM AWARDS

Aeronutronic Overseas Services, Inc. *v.* The Air Force of the Islamic Republic of Iran, **7**, 217; **8**, 75
Atlantic Richfield Company *v.* Iran, **8**, 179

Behring International, Inc. *v.* Islamic Republic Iranian Air Force, **3**, 173; **8**, 44
Bendone-Derossi International *v.* Iran, **6**, 130
Boeing Company *v.* Iran, **5**, 152; **6**, 43

CBA International Development Corporation *v.* Iran, **4**, 53

E-Systems, Inc. *v.* Iran, **2**, 51

Fluor Corporation *v.* Iran, **11**, 296
Ford Aerospace and Communications Corporation *v.* Iran, **2**, 281
Ford Aerospace and Communications Corporation *v.* The Air Force of the Islamic Republic of Iran, **3**, 384; **6**, 104

Linen, Fortinberry and Associates, Inc. *v.* Iran, **8**, 85

Panacaviar, S.A. *v.* Iran, **13**, 193

QuesTech, Inc. *v.* Iran, **2**, 96

RCA Global Communications, Inc. *v.* Iran, **4**, 5, 9; **5**, 121
Reading and Bates Corporation *v.* Iran, **2**, 401
Rockwell International Systems, Inc. *v.* Iran, **2**, 310, 369

Tadjer-Cohen Associates, Inc. *v.* Iran, **9**, 302
Touche Ross and Company *v.* Iran, **3**, 59, 200
United States (Shipside Packing Company, Inc.) *v.* Iran, **3**, 331

Watkins-Johnson Company *v.* Iran, **2**, 362

INTERLOCUTORY AWARDS

Abrahamian *v* Iran, **23**, 285
Aeronutronic Overseas Services, Inc. *v* Telecommunications Company of Iran, **5**, 187
American Bell International Inc. *v* Iran, **6**, 74
Amoco Iran Oil Company *v* Iran, **1**, 493; **3**, 297
Anaconda-Iran, Inc. *v* Iran, **13**, 199

Chas. T. Main International, Inc. *v* Khuzestan Water and Power Authority, **3**, 156; **5**, 185; **8**, 41; **10**, 21; **21**, 12
Computer Sciences Corporation *v* Iran, **8**, 99

Danielpour (S.J.) *v* Iran, **22**, 123
Dresser Industries, Inc. *v* Iran, **1**, 280, 284, 305, 320
Drucker, Jr. *v* Foreign Transaction Company, **1**, 252, 284, 305, 320

Ebrahimi (C.R.) *v* Iran, **22**, 138
Ebrahimi (C.T.) *v* Iran, **22**, 138
Ebrahimi (M.S.) *v* Iran, **22**, 138
Ebrahimi (S.S.) *v* Iran, **22**, 138

Ford Aerospace and Communications Corporation *v* The Air Force of the Islamic Republic of Iran, **1**, 268, 284, 305, 320

Gibbs and Hill, Inc. *v* Iran Power Generation and Transmission Company (TAVANIR) of the Ministry of Energy of the Government of Iran, **1**, 236, 284, 305, 320
Golshani *v.* Iran, **22**, 155
Gould Marketing, Inc. *v* Ministry of National Defense of Iran, **3**, 147

Halliburton Company *v* Doreen/IMCO, **1**, 242, 284, 305, 320
Harza *v* Iran, **2**, 68; **4**, 59
Hemmat *v* Iran, **22**, 129
Howard, Needles, Tammens and Bergendoff (HNTB) *v* Iran, **1**, 248, 284, 305, 320
Hyatt International Corporation *v* Iran, **9**, 72

International Schools Services, Inc. *v* Iran, **10**, 6
International Schools Services, Inc. *v* National Iranian Copper Industry Company, **5**, 338
Iran *v* United States, Case A-4, **5**, 131
Iran *v* United States, Case A-15, **5**, 131; **12**, 40; **25**, 247
Iran *v* United States, Case B-1, **10**, 207
Itel International Corporation *v* Social Security Organization of Iran, **7**, 31

Khosrowshahi (F.L.) *v* Iran, **24**, 40

Lawrence *v* Iran, **25**, 190

Malek *v* Iran, **19**, 48
Marks and Umann *v* Iran, **8**, 290

Nazari *v* Iran, **26**, 7
Nikpour *v* Iran, **29**, 67
Nourafchan (G.) *v* Iran, **23**, 307
Nourafchan (Z.A.) *v* Iran, **23**, 307

Oil Field of Texas, Inc. *v* Iran (OSCO), **1**, 347
Owens-Corning Fiberglass Corporation *v* Iran, **2**, 322

Phillips Petroleum Company, Iran *v* Iran, **1**, 487; **3**, 297
Protiva *v* Iran, **23**, 259
Riahi *v* Iran, **28**, 176

Saghi *v* Iran, **14**, 3

CONSOLIDATED TABLE OF CASES (BY CATEGORY) xlvii

SeaCo, Inc. *v.* Iran, **11**, 210
Sedco, Inc. *v.* National Iranian Oil Company, **9**, 248; **10**, 180
Starrett Housing Corporation *v.* Iran, **4**, 122; **7**, 119
Stone and Webster Overseas Group, Inc. *v.* National Petrochemical Company, **1**, 274, 284, 305, 320

T.C.S.B., Inc. *v.* Iran, **1**, 261, 284, 305, 320

Westinghouse Electric Corporation *v.* Iran, **14**, 104

Zokor International, Inc. *v.* Iran, **1**, 271, 284, 305, 320

INTERIM AND INTERLOCUTORY AWARDS

Behring International, Inc. *v.* Islamic Republic Iranian Air Force, **8**, 238

Component Builders, Inc. *v.* Iran, **8**, 216

ORDERS

Abboud *v.* Iran, **1**, 230
Advanced Computer Techniques Corporation *v.* Iran, **2**, 33
Aeronutronic Overseas Services, Inc. *v.* The Air Force of the Islamic Republic of Iran, **1**, 483
AHFI Planning Associates, Inc. *v.* Iran, **3**, 350
Ainsworth *v.* Iran, **1**, 230; **4**, 26
American Bell International Inc. *v.* Iran, **3**, 209
American Independent Oil Company *v.* National Iranian Oil Company, **3**, 372
Amman and Whitney *v.* Khuzestan Urban Development Organization, **5**, 115
Amoco International Finance Corporation *v.* National Iranian Oil Company, **4**, 4
Amoco Iran Oil Company *v.* Iran, **2**, 283, 345
Anaconda-Iran, Inc. *v.* Iran, **3**, 209
Arco Iran, Inc. *v.* Iran, **3**, 372
Assistance in Developing Educational System, Inc. *v.* Iran, **4**, 18

Baker International Corporation *v.* Iran, **1**, 230
Bank Markazi Iran *v.* Barclay's Bank International, Ltd., **2**, 35
Bank Markazi Iran *v.* Continental Bank Intl. (Pacific), **8**, 371
Bank Markazi Iran *v.* United States, Case No. 780, **8**, 364
Bank Markazi Iran *v.* United States, Case No. 821, **8**, 366
Bank Mellat *v.* Chemical Bank, New York (Cases Nos. 836, 847 and 890), **2**, 35
Bank Mellat *v.* Crocker National Bank, **2**, 246; **3**, 316, 318, 380
Bank Mellat *v.* Manufacturers Hanover Trust Company, **2**, 246; **3**, 316, 318, 380
Bank Mellat *v.* Morgan Guaranty Trust Company, **1**, 486
Bank Melli Iran *v.* United States, **9**, 205
Bank Sepah *v.* City Bank, N.A., **2**, 30, 35
Bank Sepah *v.* Mellon Bank, N.A., **2**, 35
Bank Sepah *v.* United States, **8**, 362
Baroid International Petroleum Services, Inc. *v.* Iran, **1**, 178
Behring International, Inc. *v.* Islamic Republic Iranian Air Force, **1**, 230; **14**, 23
Bendone-Derossi International *v.* Iran, **1**, 178
Birnbaum *v.* Iran, **14**, 147
Blount Brothers Corporation *v.* Ministry of Housing and Urban Development, **2**, 268

Carrier Corporation *v.* Iran, **1**, 178
CBS *v.* Iran, **21**, 279
Charter (Iran) Petroleum Company *v.* National Iranian Oil Company, **5**, 88
Chas. T. Main International, Inc. *v.* Khuzestan Water and Power Authority, **1**, 337; **4**, 60

xlviii   CONSOLIDATED TABLE OF CASES (BY CATEGORY)

Chevron Research Company *v* National Iranian Oil Company, **1**, 155, 334
Component Builders, Inc. *v* Iran, **8**, 3
Continental Illinois National Bank and Trust Company of Chicago *v* Iran, **1**, 230, 232
Control Data Corporation *v* Iran, **1**, 230; **18**, 60
Cummins *v* Iran, **14**, 21

Dadras International *v* Iran, **30**, 104
David Mikhael, Inc. *v* Iran, **3**, 84
Development and Resources Corporation *v* Iran, **3**, 209
Dic of Delaware, Inc. *v* Tehran Redevelopment Corporation, **1**, 154
Dow Chemical Company *v* Iran (Case 499), **1**, 122
Drucker, Jr. *v* Foreign Transaction Company, **2**, 4

E-Systems, Inc. *v* Iran, **1**, 178, 222, 225
Exxon Corporation *v* Iran, **3**, 372

Fedders Corporation *v* Iran, **18**, 72
Flexi-Van Leasing, Inc. *v* Iran, **1**, 166, 455; **3**, 202; **5**, 138
Fluor Corporation *v* Iran, **1**, 121, 178; **18**, 56, 68
Ford Aerospace and Communications Corporation *v* Iran, **3**, 349; **10**, 108
Ford Aerospace and Communications Corporation *v* The Air Force of the Islamic Republic of Iran, **8**, 284
Foremost Tehran Inc. *v* Iran, **2**, 33; **3**, 361; **4**, 62

General Dynamics Corporation *v* Iran, **1**, 485
General Motors Corporation *v* Iran, **2**, 33; **3**, 1
Getty Iran Ltd. *v* Iran, **3**, 372
Ghaffari *v* Iran, **18**, 64, 79
Gould Marketing, Inc. *v* Ministry of National Defense of Iran, **9**, 406
Gruen Associates, Inc. *v* Iran Housing Company, **2**, 327

Harnischfeger Corporation *v* Ministry of Roads and Transportation, **4**, 76
Harza *v* Iran, **1**, 234
Haus International, Inc. *v* Tehran Redevelopment Corporation, **3**, 87; **5**, 144
H.B. Fox Geotechnical Consultants, Inc. *v* Iran, **18**, 70
Herman Blum Consulting Engineers, Inc. *v* Iran, **1**, 218
Houston Contracting Company *v* National Iranian Oil Company, **14**, 18
Howard, Needles, Tammens and Bergendoff (HNTB) *v* Iran, **2**, 368

Intercomp Resources Development and Engineering, Inc. *v* Oil Service Company of Iran, **1**, 391
International Schools Services, Inc. *v* Iranian Copper Industries Company, **2**, 156; **3**, 316, 318
International Systems & Controls Corporation *v* Iran, **3**, 209
Iran *v* United States, Case A-4, **5**, 112
Iran *v* United States, Case A-15, **4**, 28; **5**, 112; **14**, 171
Iran *v* United States, Case A-25, **21**, 283, 302
Iran *v* United States, Case B-1, **4**, 57; **18**, 45; **21**, 279
Iran Chevron Oil Company *v* Iran, **3**, 372
Itel Corporation *v* Iran, **1**, 326
Itel International Corporation *v* Social Security Organization of Iran, **21**, 279

Kay Lerner *v* Iran, **1**, 215
Khosrowshahi *v* Iran, **1**, 339
Kiaie *v* Iran, **14**, 307

Leach *v.* Iran, **18**, 231

Ministry of Defense of Iran *v* United States, **18**, 74

CONSOLIDATED TABLE OF CASES (BY CATEGORY) xlix

Ministry of Petroleum of the Islamic Republic of Iran *v* United States, **1**, 383
Minnesota Mining and Manufacturing Company *v* Iran, **1**, 230
Mitra Leasing Corporation *v* Iran, **18**, 62
Mobil Oil Iran Inc. *v* Iran, **3**, 372
Morrison-Knudsen Pacific Ltd. *v* Ministry of Roads and Transportation, **3**, 76

National Airmotive Corporation *v* Iran, **1**, 158
National Corporation for Housing Partnerships *v* Ministry of Mines and Industry of Iran, **3**, 87
NIC Leasing, Inc. *v* Iran, **5**, 85
NL Industries, Inc. *v* Iran, **1**, 178
Northern Virginia Community College *v* Iran, **18**, 66

Owens-Corning Fiberglass Corporation *v* Iran, **4**, 1

Panacaviar, S.A. *v* Iran, **14**, 102; **18**, 63
Pepsico, Inc. *v* Iran (Zamzam Bottling Company Azarbaijan, et al.), **1**, 173; **2**, 33
Phibro Corporation *v* Ministry of War-ETKA Co. Ltd., **11**, 289
Phillips Petroleum Company, Iran *v* Iran, **2**, 1, 283

Questech, Inc. *v* Iran, **4**, 72

RCA Global Communications, Inc. *v* Iran, **3**, 8
R.J. Reynolds Tobacco Company *v* Iran, **1**, 119, 336; **2**, 124; **3**, 39; **4**, 2

San Jacinto Eastern Corporation *v* Iran, **3**, 372
Sea-Land Service, Inc. *v* Iran, **1**, 335; **3**, 87; **4**, 65
Sedco, Inc. *v* Iran Marine Industrial Co., **18**, 58
Sedco, Inc. *v* National Iranian Oil Company, **8**, 28, 34; **10**, 3
Short *v* Iran, **14**, 20
Sohio-Iran Trading, Inc. *v* National Iranian Oil Company, **3**, 372
Sperry-Sun, Inc. *v* Iran, **1**, 178
Starrett Housing Corporation *v* Iran, **1**, 386; **10**, 110; **13**, 350
Sylvania Technical Systems, Inc. *v* Iran, **5**, 141

Tadjer-Cohen Associates, Inc. *v* Iran, **18**, 59, 287
Tavakoli *v* Iran, **14**, 309
T.C.S.B., Inc. *v* Iran, **4**, 61
Technology Enterprises, Inc. *v* Foreign Transaction Company, **2**, 5
Tehran American School Association, Trustees and Members *v* Iran, **1**, 230
Texaco Iran Ltd. *v* Iran, **3**, 372
TME International, Inc. *v* Iran, **1**, 178
Touche Ross and Company *v* Iran, **3**, 208
Transamerica ICS, Inc. *v* Iran, **3**, 84
Transocean Gulf Oil Company *v* Iran, **3**, 372
Transportation Consultants International *v* Iran National Airlines Corporation, **1**, 340

Uiterwyk Corporation *v* Iran, **19**, 106
Ultrasystems Incorporated *v* Iran, **2**, 139
Unidyne Corporation *v* Iran, **1**, 178; **2**, 138
United States *v* Iran, Case A-16, **3**, 316, 318, 380
United States (Teledyne Industries Inc.) *v* Iran, **3**, 336
United Technologies International, Inc. *v* Iranian Air Force, **3**, 209

VSI Corporation *v* Iran, **2**, 31, 33, 260

Warner-Lambert Company *v* Iran, **1**, 230
Western Dynamics Corporation *v* Iran and Etka Organization, **1**, 178
William L. Pereira Associates, Iran *v* Iran, **1**, 219, 484

CONSOLIDATED TABLE OF CASES (BY CATEGORY)

REFUSAL CASES

AMF Overseas Corporation, Re, **1**, 392

Bassin, Re, **9**, 3
Bodnar, Re, **21**, 6

Cascade Overview Development Enterprises, Inc., Re, **1**, 127, 129, 132
Creditcorp International Inc., Re, **21**, 10

Detroit Bank and Trust Company, Re, **1**, 129; **2**, 312; **3**, 3
Dorian International Credit Co., Inc., Re, **21**, 10

Etka Organization, Re, **19**, 185

Glucosan (Private Joint Stock) Co., Re, **19**, 191

Hawaiian Agronomics Company, Re, **1**, 138
Helali, Re, **1**, 134

Industrial & Mining Bank (R.C.39), Re, **19**, 179
Industrial & Mining Bank (R.C.40), Re, **19**, 182
Iran Brockway Company Ltd., Re, **17**, 331
Iran Electronics Industries, Re, **19**, 188
Iran Helicopter Support & Renewal Company (R.C.32), Re, **23**, 244
Iran Helicopter Support & Renewal Company (R.C.33), Re, **23**, 247
Iran Helicopter Support & Renewal Company (R.C.34), Re, **23**, 250
Iran National Airlines Company, Re, **17**, 337
Iranian Tobacco Company (R.C.26), Re, **21**, 8
Iranian Tobacco Company (R.C.27), Re, **7**, 275

Jahanger, Re, **1**, 128, 129, 132
Jahani, Re, **1**, 168

K and S Irrigation Company, Re, **1**, 228

Lee, Re, **21**, 7

Ministry of Economic Affairs and Finance of Iran. Re, **6**, 27
Ministry of Mines and Metals and National Iranian Steel Company, Re, **23**, 253
Ministry of Roads and Transportation (R.C.41), Re, **23**, 256
Ministry of Roads and Transportation (R.C.48), Re, **17**, 343
Mobasser, Re, **1**, 176

NAHAJA, Ministry of Defence, Re, **19**, 197
National Iranian Copper Industries Company, Re, **17**, 346
National Iranian Oil Company, Re, **17**, 334

Pereira, Re, **21**, 3

Raymond International (U.K.), Ltd., Re, **1**, 394

Satellite Application Project, Re, **17**, 340
Sherkate Tractor Sazi Iran (Sahami Khass), Re, **19**, 176
Showrai, Re, **1**, 226

Tehran Regional Electric Company, Re, **19**, 194

United Technologies International, Inc., Re, **21**, 5

CONSOLIDATED TABLE OF CASES[1]

ARRANGED ACCORDING TO CASE NUMBER

Case No.	Page
1	**1**, 219, 484; **5**, 198
2	**4**, 96
3	**4**, 183
4	**25**, 153
5	**11**, 160
6	**1**, 236, 284, 305, 320
7	**6**, 219
8	**1**, 123, 342
10	**10**, 365
11	**10**, 365
12	**9**, 310
13	**9**, 310
14	**1**, 169
15	**2**, 31, 33, 260; **3**, 73, 78
16	**2**, 141
17	**1**, 411
18	**1**, 173; **2**, 33; **13**, 3, 328
19	**1**, 155, 334; **2**, 364; **3**, 78
20	**28**, 392
21	**28**, 394
22	**13**, 370
23	**13**, 370
24	**1**, 386; **4**, 122; **7**, 119; **10**, 110; **13**, 350; **16**, 112
25	**14**, 349
26	**2**, 228
27	**2**, 228
28	**2**, 401; **4**, 199
29	**26**, 265
30	**1**, 185, 442
31	**1**, 181
32	**7**, 223
33	**1**, 335; **3**, 87; **4**, 65; **6**, 149
34	**1**, 340; **9**, 360
35	**1**, 119, 336; **2**, 124; **3**, 39; **4**, 2; **7**, 181; **8**, 55
36	**1**, 166, 455; **3**, 202; **5**, 138; **12**, 335; **13**, 324
37	**2**, 33; **3**, 361; **4**, 62; **10**, 228
38	**5**, 361
39	**1**, 487; **2**, 1, 283; **3**, 297; **5**, 51; **21**, 79, 285
40	**2**, 372; **4**, 237
41	**2**, 391
42	**3**, 209; **7**, 209
43	**1**, 347; **12**, 308
44	**22**, 138; **30**, 170
45	**22**, 138
46	**22**, 138; **30**, 170
47	**22**, 138; **30**, 170
48	**3**, 209; **6**, 74; **12**, 170; **14**, 173
49	**3**, 147; **6**, 272; **9**, 406
50	**6**, 272; **9**, 406
51	**1**, 242, 284, 305, 320; **6**, 4
52	**10**, 56
53	**10**, 95
54	**4**, 212; **8**, 107
55	**1**, 493; **2**, 283, 345; **3**, 297; **5**, 51; **25**, 301
56	**4**, 4; **15**, 189; **25**, 314
57	**2**, 334
59	**2**, 96; **4**, 72; **9**, 107
60	**3**, 209; **25**, 20; **26**, 256
61	**10**, 37
62	**2**, 268; **3**, 225
63	**6**, 118
64	**5**, 141; **8**, 298
65	**8**, 99; **10**, 269
66	**4**, 20; **5**, 76; **24**, 102
67	**3**, 239; **5**, 73
68	**1**, 248, 284, 305, 320; **2**, 368; **11**, 302
70	**2**, 332
71	**2**, 78
72	**3**, 372; **13**, 370
73	**3**, 372; **10**, 357
74	**3**, 372; **16**, 3; **25**, 339
75	**3**, 372; **9**, 184
76	**3**, 372; **16**, 3; **21**, 303
77	**3**, 372; **5**, 88
78	**3**, 372; **10**, 365
79	**3**, 372; **6**, 33
80	**3**, 372; **13**, 370
81	**3**, 372; **16**, 3; **25**, 339
82	**7**, 1
83	**3**, 119, 124
84	**2**, 100, 139; **4**, 77
86	**3**, 77; **25**, 327

[1] The figures in bold type refer to the volume number.

li

lii CONSOLIDATED TABLE OF CASES (BY NUMBER)

Case No.	Page
87 –	**3**, 87; **7**, 260
88 –	**1**, 230; **18**, 60; **21**, 303; **22**, 151
89 –	**11**, 3, 287
90 –	**1**, 384
91 –	**2**, 294
92 –	**2**, 132
93 –	**2**, 281; **3**, 349; **10**, 108; **14**, 24, 255
94 –	**2**, 33; **3**, 1; **7**, 220; **13**, 282
95 –	**1**, 220
96 –	**4**, 83
97 –	**1**, 234; **2**, 68; **4**, 59; **11**, 76
98 –	**1**, 499
99 –	**10**, 121
100 –	**7**, 36; **8**, 53
101 –	**4**, 33
102 –	**7**, 269
103 –	**3**, 212
104 –	**3**, 212
105 –	**2**, 291
106 –	**3**, 332
107 –	**3**, 212
108 –	**3**, 212
109 –	**3**, 212
110 –	**3**, 212
111 –	**2**, 156; **3**, 316, 318; **5**, 338; **9**, 187
112 –	**3**, 319; **11**, 292
113 –	**2**, 332; **4**, 1, 280
114 –	**13**, 254; **17**, 368
115 –	**16**, 257
118 –	**29**, 367
119 –	**1**, 327
120 –	**1**, 337; **3**, 156; **4**, 60; **5**, 185; **8**, 41; **10**, 21; **11**, 259; **21**, 12
121 –	**1**, 252, 284, 305, 320; **2**, 4; **19**, 257
122 –	**1**, 156
123 –	**10**, 6; **14**, 65, 279
124 –	**3**, 256
125 –	**3**, 24
126 –	**14**, 349
127 –	**3**, 76; **7**, 54
128 –	**18**, 58; **21**, 31
129 –	**8**, 28; **9**, 248; **10**, 3, 180; **15**, 23; **16**, 282; **18**, 3; **21**, 31
130 –	**7**, 225; **11**, 372
131 –	**27**, 64, 264; **28**, 3
132 –	**2**, 6
133 –	**13**, 370
134 –	**9**, 72; **10**, 365
135 –	**10**, 157

Case No.	Page
136 –	**3**, 351
137 –	**2**, 291
138 –	**1**, 218; **5**, 354
139 –	**3**, 218
140 –	**1**, 261, 284, 305, 320; **4**, 61; **5**, 160
142 –	**4**, 29
143 –	**1**, 403
144 –	**5**, 134
145 –	**2**, 269
147 –	**26**, 228
148 –	**3**, 203; **29**, 383
149 –	**3**, 10; **5**, 74
150 –	**3**, 372; **16**, 3; **23**, 401
151 –	**2**, 305
152 –	**2**, 305
153 –	**2**, 305
154 –	**17**, 3
155 –	**15**, 3; **16**, 110
156 –	**2**, 348
157 –	**2**, 157, 178
158 –	**1**, 483; **7**, 217; **8**, 75; **11**, 223
159 –	**1**, 268, 284, 305, 320; **3**, 384; **6**, 104; **8**, 284; **11**, 184; **12**, 304
160 –	**3**, 8; **4**, 5, 9; **5**, 121; **16**, 335
161 –	**8**, 373
163 –	**29**, 185
164 –	**14**, 307
165 –	**3**, 42; **5**, 1
166 –	**7**, 8
167 –	**3**, 209; **13**, 199; **28**, 320
168 –	**22**, 118
169 –	**22**, 123
170 –	**22**, 129
171 –	**1**, 140
172 –	**2**, 247
173 –	**14**, 18; **20**, 3
174 –	**3**, 87; **5**, 144; **9**, 313
175 –	**9**, 308
176 –	**9**, 61
177 –	**4**, 39
178 –	**1**, 339; **24**, 40; **30**, 76
179 –	**3**, 350; **11**, 168
180 –	**4**, 76; **7**, 90; **8**, 119
181 –	**14**, 149
182 –	**28**, 225, 318
183 –	**5**, 90
184 –	**16**, 317
185 –	**3**, 270
186 –	**1**, 163
187 –	**17**, 269
188 –	**2**, 327; **3**, 97, 124

CONSOLIDATED TABLE OF CASES (BY NUMBER)   liii

Case No.	Page
189 –	**2**, 303
190 –	**18**, 175
192 –	**28**, 371
193 –	**19**, 48; **28**, 246
194 –	**7**, 18
195 –	**18**, 180
196 –	**18**, 150
197 –	**21**, 279; **25**, 131
198 –	**5**, 115; **12**, 94
199 –	**5**, 235
200 –	**2**, 241; **3**, 364
201 –	**6**, 1
202 –	**19**, 307
203 –	**1**, 178
204 –	**29**, 189
205 –	**1**, 216
206 –	**2**, 90
207 –	**1**, 230
208 –	**18**, 352
209 –	**14**, 191
210 –	**27**, 145
211 –	**2**, 171, 178
212 –	**30**, 292
213 –	**30**, 104
215 –	**30**, 104
217 –	**9**, 397
218 –	**4**, 18
219 –	**2**, 232
220 –	**3**, 110, 124
221 –	**26**, 7; **28**, 192; **30**, 123
222 –	**5**, 152; **6**, 43; **13**, 359
223 –	**29**, 193
226 –	**1**, 230
227 –	**17**, 153; **27**, 3, 269
228 –	**2**, 366
229 –	**2**, 366
230 –	**2**, 278
231 –	**2**, 33; **3**, 361; **4**, 62; **10**, 228
233 –	**7**, 249
236 –	**8**, 353
237 –	**9**, 350
238 –	**3**, 334
241 –	**1**, 230
242 –	**1**, 215
243 –	**2**, 33; **3**, 326
244 –	**3**, 62
245 –	**4**, 263
246 –	**8**, 368
247 –	**29**, 197
248 –	**26**, 193
249 –	**29**, 201
250 –	**13**, 97; **18**, 72; **29**, 401

Case No.	Page
251 –	**23**, 290
252 –	**1**, 230, 232
254 –	**1**, 271, 284, 305, 320; **8**, 72
255 –	**1**, 154; **8**, 144; **21**, 4
256 –	**21**, 20
257 –	**6**, 38
258 –	**9**, 357
259 –	**9**, 357
260 –	**11**, 210; **22**, 370; **28**, 198
261 –	**19**, 200, 253
262 –	**1**, 178
263 –	**12**, 160
264 –	**13**, 124
265 –	**5**, 85
267 –	**6**, 125
268 –	**24**, 203
269 –	**25**, 278
273 –	**25**, 196, 273
274 –	**28**, 232
275 –	**25**, 3
276 –	**22**, 170
277 –	**28**, 216
279 –	**3**, 176, 192
280 –	**3**, 7; **4**, 272
283 –	**1**, 485; **5**, 386
284 –	**14**, 283
285 –	**9**, 153
286 –	**14**, 263
287 –	**29**, 205
288 –	**19**, 374
289 –	**12**, 146
290 –	**25**, 289
291 –	**1**, 230; **2**, 261
292 –	**9**, 340
293 –	**1**, 274, 284, 305, 320; **4**, 192
294 –	**30**, 8
295 –	**12**, 288
298 –	**14**, 3; **29**, 20
299 –	**8**, 214
300 –	**1**, 178
302 –	**9**, 10, 206; **11**, 182
305 –	**17**, 368
307 –	**2**, 126
308 –	**3**, 366; **24**, 297; **26**, 60; **27**, 288
309 –	**25**, 178
310 –	**14**, 349
311 –	**8**, 81
312 –	**7**, 26
313 –	**27**, 248; **28**, 51
314 –	**11**, 217
315 –	**18**, 289
316 –	**23**, 259

Case No.	Page
317 –	**14**, 223
319 –	**25**, 264; **30**, 22
320 –	**8**, 97
321 –	**30**, 283
322 –	**27**, 49
324 –	**13**, 99
325 –	**9**, 46
328 –	**2**, 5; **5**, 118
332 –	**30**, 13
333 –	**1**, 121, 178; **11**, 296; **18**, 56, 68; **23**, 413
334 –	**13**, 179
335 –	**12**, 3
336 –	**1**, 178; **29**, 67
337 –	**1**, 178
338 –	**16**, 291
339 –	**16**, 335
340 –	**6**, 52
341 –	**1**, 178; **8**, 49
342 –	**1**, 408
343 –	**8**, 18
344 –	**7**, 236
345 –	**1**, 230
346 –	**3**, 280
347 –	**1**, 178; **10**, 365
348 –	**1**, 178; **10**, 365
349 –	**1**, 178; **10**, 365
350 –	**26**, 37
352 –	**1**, 178; **30**, 3
353 –	**11**, 372; **14**, 111, 261
354 –	**1**, 178; **28**, 309
355 –	**17**, 353
356 –	**1**, 178; **29**, 3
357 –	**1**, 178; **24**, 121
358 –	**1**, 230, **19**, 365
359 –	**9**, 6
360 –	**7**, 239
361 –	**11**, 372
362 –	**13**, 370
363 –	**29**, 209
364 –	**1**, 178; **17**, 368
365 –	**8**, 18
366 –	**17**, 114; **18**, 113
367 –	**29**, 222
368 –	**1**, 178; **2**, 138; **29**, 310; **30**, 19
369 –	**1**, 230; **12**, 385
370 –	**2**, 362; **22**, 218
371 –	**17**, 266
373 –	**1**, 135
374 –	**1**, 178
375 –	**1**, 178; **6**, 130; **18**, 115
377 –	**23**, 285

Case No.	Page
380 –	**1**, 178; **25**, 172
381 –	**19**, 106, 107, 171, 186
382 –	**1**, 230; **3**, 173; **4**, 89; **6**, 30; **8**, 44, 238; **14**, 23; **27**, 218
383 –	**1**, 230; **24**, 265
384 –	**14**, 349
386 –	**1**, 178; **26**, 148
387 –	**1**, 178; **3**, 36, 78
388 –	**1**, 178, 222, 225; **2**, 51; **4**, 197
389 –	**8**, 183; **13**, 93, 370; **14**, 104
390 –	**1**, 178; **25**, 190
391 –	**1**, 178; **25**, 190
392 –	**1**, 178; **25**, 190
393 –	**12**, 397
394 –	**27**, 122
395 –	**8**, 3, 216; **9**, 404; **23**, 3
396 –	**8**, 179; **28**, 401
397 –	**1**, 178; **25**, 229
398 –	**1**, 178; **25**, 235
399 –	**1**, 178; **25**, 241
400 –	**1**, 178
401 –	**1**, 178
402 –	**1**, 178
403 –	**1**, 178
404 –	**1**, 178
405 –	**1**, 178
406 –	**1**, 178
407 –	**1**, 178
408 –	**1**, 178
409 –	**17**, 31; **18**, 76
410 –	**5**, 187; **14**, 339
412 –	**23**, 307; **29**, 295
413 –	**26**, 190
414 –	**18**, 88
415 –	**23**, 307; **29**, 295
418 –	**2**, 226
420 –	**18**, 90
421 –	**29**, 411
422 –	**7**, 249
423 –	**1**, 230; **8**, 15; **17**, 294
425 –	**5**, 78
427 –	**3**, 181, 192
428 –	**2**, 38
430 –	**2**, 310, 369; **23**, 150; **24**, 3
431 –	**28**, 21, 195
433 –	**5**, 155
434 –	**5**, 249
435 –	**25**, 212
436 –	**6**, 120
437 –	**10**, 22
439 –	**3**, 209; **12**, 239
440 –	**25**, 15

CONSOLIDATED TABLE OF CASES (BY NUMBER) lv

Case No.	Page	Case No.	Page
441 –	**4**, 47	540 –	**21**, 11
442 –	**1**, 391	541 –	**21**, 11
443 –	**22**, 3	543 –	**21**, 11
444 –	**18**, 390	548 –	**21**, 11
445 –	**18**, 62; **28**, 389	556 –	**21**, 11
446 –	**8**, 66	559 –	**9**, 205
447 –	**23**, 282	569 –	**1**, 486
448 –	**13**, 331	576 –	**5**, 155
449 –	**1**, 158; **3**, 91, 124	580 –	**5**, 155
450 –	**9**, 203	582 –	**2**, 246; **3**, 316, 318, 380; **5**, 57
451 –	**26**, 275	591 –	**2**, 246; **3**, 316, 318, 380; **5**, 57
452 –	**3**, 84; **26**, 275	624 –	**11**, 70
453 –	**8**, 236	625 –	**11**, 180
454 –	**1**, 230; **4**, 26; **18**, 92; **25**, 188	626 –	**29**, 395
455 –	**26**, 244	668 –	**8**, 371
458 –	**8**, 290; **9**, 69	679 –	**13**, 95
459 –	**14**, 349	763 –	**8**, 20
461 –	**26**, 44	764 –	**3**, 197; **22**, 204; **25**, 186
462 –	**26**, 44	766 –	**4**, 210
463 –	**26**, 44	767 –	**30**, 267
464 –	**26**, 44	769 –	**12**, 126
465 –	**26**, 44	770 –	**21**, 28
466 –	**1**, 280, 284, 305, 320	771 –	**27**, 40, 194
467 –	**9**, 346	772 –	**7**, 244
468 –	**9**, 346	778 –	**2**, 35
469 –	**9**, 346	780 –	**8**, 364
471 –	**9**, 346	783 –	**2**, 35
473 –	**21**, 303	806 –	**6**, 147
474 –	**11**, 289; **26**, 15, 254	808 –	**2**, 44
476 –	**7**, 31; **21**, 279; **24**, 272	810 –	**23**, 413
477 –	**14**, 349	811 –	**23**, 413
479 –	**29**, 59	812 –	**22**, 155; **29**, 78
480 –	**3**, 59, 200, 208; **9**, 284	814 –	**22**, 339
481 –	**19**, 73	819 –	**21**, 303
482 –	**3**, 169	821 –	**8**, 366
483 –	**21**, 25	828 –	**27**, 196
484 –	**17**, 245	829 –	**11**, 363; **18**, 292; **19**, 317
485 –	**28**, 176	831 –	**22**, 194
486 –	**18**, 98	832 –	**14**, 309
487 –	**11**, 53	833 –	**11**, 372
488 –	**4**, 205	834 –	**14**, 176
489 –	**3**, 390	836 –	**2**, 35
490 –	**1**, 326; **28**, 159	841 –	**30**, 302
491 –	**13**, 370	845 –	**21**, 13
492 –	**14**, 349	847 –	**2**, 35
494 –	**24**, 47	880 –	**23**, 378
495 –	**2**, 41	890 –	**2**, 35
498 –	**13**, 193; **14**, 100, 102; **18**, 63	926 –	**3**, 84; **6**, 20
499 –	**1**, 122	928 –	**4**, 53; **5**, 177
510 –	**21**, 11	930 –	**28**, 382
534 –	**21**, 11	931 –	**13**, 370
536 –	**21**, 11	934 –	**1**, 383

CONSOLIDATED TABLE OF CASES (BY NUMBER)

Case No.	Page
940	**23**, 268
941	**28**, 53, 307
942	**8**, 349
945	**2**, 30, 35; **8**, 362
947	**10**, 177
949	**8**, 24
950	**30**, 70
951	**14**, 11
952	**24**, 269
954	**16**, 335
957	**14**, 251
965	**23**, 265
967	**29**, 260
968	**18**, 79
10001-12782	**3**, 77; **25**, 327
10026	**19**, 374
10035	**12**, 139
10043	**5**, 148
10047	**8**, 79
10059	**18**, 224
10065	**21**, 303
10066	**18**, 390
10067	**19**, 374
10087	**23**, 276
10089	**17**, 362
10105	**23**, 413
10110	**19**, 374
10126	**10**, 365
10159	**23**, 133
10163	**19**, 345
10172	**16**, 103
10173	**11**, 372; **12**, 306
10199	**17**, 92
10212	**11**, 72, 300
10216	**19**, 374
10273	**19**, 321
10296	**24**, 305
10303	**14**, 349
10335	**11**, 150
10355	**19**, 374
10398	**23**, 413
10405	**13**, 370
10415	**19**, 374
10418	**13**, 370
10425	**8**, 360
10427	**18**, 154
10457	**19**, 374
10513	**8**, 85; **19**, 62
10514	**18**, 232
10517	**10**, 319; **11**, 283
10541	**19**, 374

Case No.	Page
10547	**19**, 374
10569	**19**, 374
10605	**19**, 360
10606	**19**, 360
10633	**18**, 164
10638	**21**, 303
10645	**22**, 111
10656	**23**, 413
10706	**14**, 86
10712	**16**, 297
10719	**8**, 83
10792	**18**, 64
10812	**3**, 336; **23**, 126
10832	**14**, 147
10853	**7**, 277; **13**, 286
10854	**7**, 277; **13**, 286
10855	**7**, 277; **13**, 286
10856	**7**, 277; **13**, 286
10861	**21**, 303
10865	**5**, 150
10871	**24**, 305
10891	**19**, 374
10913	**17**, 135
10972	**19**, 374
10973	**18**, 377
11005	**14**, 349
11038	**18**, 390
11045	**22**, 213
11102	**23**, 303
11135	**14**, 20; **16**, 76
11157	**18**, 390
11244	**17**, 368
11286	**23**, 351
11294	**19**, 352
11300	**19**, 374
11377	**18**, 275
11415	**19**, 374
11429	**23**, 296
11445	**9**, 70
11485	**18**, 390
11486	**19**, 374
11491	**24**, 238
11507	**8**, 11
11539	**19**, 374
11553	**8**, 42
11590	**23**, 413
11614	**7**, 247
11653	**14**, 349
11657	**19**, 374
11697	**9**, 306
11713	**10**, 333; **11**, 285
11723	**14**, 21

CONSOLIDATED TABLE OF CASES (BY NUMBER)

Case No.		Page
11803	–	**24**, 252
11815	–	**7**, 258
11875	–	**3**, 331; **5**, 80
11887	–	**17**, 362
11961	–	**18**, 390
12118	–	**9**, 302; **18**, 59, 287; **21**, 303
12183	–	**18**, 231; **23**, 233
12257	–	**23**, 413
12384	–	**17**, 153
12438	–	**18**, 66
12458	–	**24**, 116
12567	–	**19**, 374
12701	–	**8**, 13
12713-12721	–	**23**, 413
12756	–	**18**, 70
12762	–	**23**, 413
12778	–	**19**, 374
12783	–	**13**, 261
12784	–	**25**, 339
12785	–	**19**, 374
12786-12892	–	**18**, 393; **27**, 275
A/1	–	**1**, 144, 189
A/2	–	**1**, 101
A-3	–	**27**, 256
A-4	–	**5**, 112, 131
A-8	–	**27**, 256
A-9	–	**7**, 236
A-14	–	**4**, 74
A-15	–	**4**, 28; **5**, 112, 131; **8**, 63; **12**, 40; **13**, 173; **14**, 171, 311; **25**, 247
A-15IIA and IIB	–	**28**, 112
A-15IVA and A24	–	**29**, 214
A-16	–	**3**, 316, 318, 380; **5**, 57; **9**, 97
A-17	–	**8**, 189
A/18	–	**5**, 251, 428
A/19	–	**16**, 285
A/20	–	**11**, 271
A/21	–	**14**, 324
A-24FT	–	**29**, 214
A-25	–	**21**, 283, 302
B-1	–	**4**, 57; **10**, 207; **18**, 45; **19**, 3, 273; **21**, 279; **22**, 105; **23**, 407; **27**, 282
B-2	–	**13**, 155
B-3	–	**8**, 89
B-4	–	**23**, 413
B-5	–	**23**, 413

Case No.		Page
B-7	–	**6**, 141; **12**, 25
B-8	–	**17**, 187
B-9	–	**17**, 214
B-10	–	**17**, 238
B-11	–	**22**, 365
B-12	–	**17**, 228
B-13	–	**13**, 158
B-14	–	**23**, 413
B-15	–	**24**, 305
B-16	–	**5**, 94
B-18	–	**13**, 161
B-19	–	**23**, 413
B-20	–	**13**, 164
B-21	–	**8**, 93
B-22	–	**19**, 374
B-24	–	**5**, 97
B-26	–	**24**, 291
B-27	–	**21**, 303
B-28	–	**24**, 291
B-29	–	**6**, 12
B-31	–	**19**, 374
B-32	–	**27**, 275
B-33	–	**23**, 413
B-35	–	**24**, 291
B-38	–	**25**, 327
B-39	–	**16**, 335
B-40	–	**17**, 183
B-41	–	**24**, 305
B-44	–	**24**, 305
B-47	–	**21**, 303
B-51	–	**17**, 200
B-53	–	**5**, 105
B-55	–	**23**, 320
B-56	–	**5**, 357
B-59	–	**12**, 33
B-60	–	**24**, 291
B-63	–	**18**, 84
B-65	–	**18**, 390
B-66	–	**14**, 276
B-67	–	**3**, 338
B-69	–	**12**, 33
B-71	–	**13**, 277
B-72	–	**13**, 271
B-73	–	**23**, 413
B-74	–	**18**, 74; **27**, 295
B-75	–	**24**, 305
B-76	–	**25**, 327
B-77	–	**25**, 327
R.C.1	–	**1**, 127, 129, 132
R.C.2	–	**1**, 128, 129, 132
R.C.3	–	**1**, 129; **2**, 312; **3**, 3
R.C.5	–	**21**, 3

Case No.	Page	Case No.	Page
R.C.10 –	**1**, 138	R.C.34 –	**23**, 250
R.C.11 –	**1**, 234	R.C.35 –	**17**, 331
R.C.13 –	**21**, 6	R.C.36 –	**23**, 253
R.C.14 –	**21**, 5	R.C.38 –	**19**, 176
R.C.15 –	**1**, 176	R.C.39 –	**19**, 179
R.C.16 –	**1**, 168	R.C.40 –	**19**, 182
R.C.17 –	**21**, 10	R.C.41 –	**23**, 256
R.C.18 –	**21**, 10	R.C.42 –	**17**, 334
R.C.19 –	**21**, 10	R.C.43 –	**19**, 185
R.C.20 –	**1**, 392	R.C.44 –	**17**, 337
R.C.21 –	**1**, 394	R.C.45 –	**19**, 188
R.C.24 –	**6**, 27	R.C.46 –	**19**, 191
R.C.26 –	**21**, 8	R.C.47 –	**17**, 340
R.C.27 –	**7**, 275	R.C.48 –	**17**, 343
R.C.28 –	**1**, 226	R.C.49 –	**19**, 194
R.C.29 –	**1**, 228	R.C.50 –	**17**, 346
R.C.30 –	**21**, 7	R.C.51 –	**19**, 197
R.C.32 –	**23**, 244	R.C.56 –	**9**, 3
R.C.33 –	**23**, 247		

CONSOLIDATED TABLE OF CASES[1]

ARRANGED ACCORDING TO NUMBER OF DECISION OR AWARD

DECISIONS

Decision No.	Page		Decision No.	Page
1-A2-FT	**1**, 101		42-10517-1	**11**, 283
2-REF 5-2	**21**, 3		43-11713-1	**11**, 285
3-REF 11-2	**1**, 134		44-89-3	**11**, 287
4-REF 1-FT	**1**, 127		45-A20-FT	**11**, 271
5-REF 2-FT	**1**, 128		46-10212-2	**11**, 300
6-REF 10-2	**1**, 138		47-159-3	**12**, 304
7-255-3	**21**, 4		48-10173-3	**12**, 306
8-AI-FT	**1**, 144		49-389-2	**13**, 93
9-REF 16-2	**1**, 168		50-679-2	**13**, 95
10-REF 15-3	**1**, 176		51-250-3	**13**, 97
11-REF 14-2	**21**, 5		52-A15-FT	**13**, 173
12-A1-FT	**1**, 189		53-114-3	**13**, 254
13-REF 13-2	**21**, 6		54-36-1	**13**, 324
14-REF 30-2	**21**, 7		55-18-1	**13**, 328
15-REF 28-1	**1**, 226		56-951-1	**14**, 11
16-REF 29-1	**1**, 228		57-498-1	**14**, 100
17-REF 20-FT	**1**, 392		58-48-3	**14**, 173
18-REF 21-FT	**1**, 394		59-93-1	**14**, 255
19-REF 26-1	**21**, 8		60-353-2	**14**, 261
20-REF 27-1	**7**, 275		61-123-1	**14**, 279
21-REF 17/REF 18/REF 19-3	**21**, 10		62-A21-FT	**14**, 324
22-REF 3-FT	**3**, 3		63-155-3	**16**, 110
23-REF 3-FT	**2**, 312		64-129-3	**16**, 282
24-10853/10854/10855/10856-1	**7**, 277		65-A19-FT	**16**, 285
			66-338-2	**16**, 291
25-510/534/536/540/541/543/548/556-1	**21**, 11		67-REF 35-2	**17**, 331
			68-REF 42-2	**17**, 334
26-200-1	**3**, 364		69-REF 44-2	**17**, 337
27-382-3	**4**, 89		70-REF 47-2	**17**, 340
28-766-3	**4**, 210		71-REF 48-2	**17**, 343
29-67-3	**5**, 73		72-REF 50-2	**17**, 346
30-149-1	**5**, 74		73-409-1	**18**, 76
31-425-1	**5**, 78		74-366-3	**18**, 113
32-A18-FT	**5**, 251		75-REF 38-1	**19**, 176
33-REF 24-3	**6**, 27		76-REF 39-1	**19**, 179
34-100-3	**8**, 53		77-REF 40-1	**19**, 182
35-A15-FT	**8**, 63		78-REF 43-1	**19**, 185
36-54-3	**8**, 107		79-REF 45-1	**19**, 188
37-A17-FT	**8**, 189		80-REF 46-1	**19**, 191
38-246-2	**8**, 368		81-REF 49-1	**19**, 194
39-REF 56-1	**9**, 3		82-REF 51-5	**19**, 197
40-395-3	**9**, 404		83-202-2	**19**, 307
41-302-3	**11**, 182		84-829-2	**19**, 317
			85-B1-FT	**22**, 105

[1] The figures in bold type refer to the volume number.

CONSOLIDATED TABLE OF CASES (BY AWARD NUMBER)

Decision No.	Page		Decision No.	Page
86-88-3	– **22**, 151		105-221-1	– **28**, 192
87-11045-1	– **22**, 213		106-227-2	– **28**, 216
88-REF 32-3	– **23**, 244		107-941-3	– **28**, 307
89-REF 33-3	– **23**, 247		108-182-2	– **28**, 225
90-REF 34-3	– **23**, 250		109-163-2	– **29**, 185
91-REF 36-3	– **23**, 253		110-204-2	– **29**, 189
92-REF 41-3	– **23**, 254		111-223-2	– **29**, 193
93-764-1	– **25**, 186		112-247-2	– **29**, 197
94-454-3	– **25**, 188		113-249-2	– **29**, 201
95-273-1	– **25**, 273		114-287-2	– **29**, 205
96-381-1	– **26**, 186		115-363-2	– **29**, 209
97-474-3	– **26**, 254		116-A15(IV) & A24-FT	– **29**, 214
98-60-3	– **26**, 256		118-148-2	– **29**, 383
99-771-2	– **27**, 194		119-252-3	– **30**, 3
100-A3/A8-FT	– **27**, 256		120-294-3	– **30**, 8
101-131-2	– **27**, 264		121-332-3	– **30**, 13
102-227-3	– **27**, 269		122-368-3	– **30**, 19
103-313-2	– **28**, 51			
104-431-2	– **28**, 195			

AWARDS

Award No.	Page		Award No.	Page
1-8-2	– **1**, 123		30-16-3	– **2**, 141
2-373-2	– **1**, 135		31-157-2	– **2**, 157
3-171-2	– **1**, 140		32-211-2	– **2**, 171
4-122-3	– **1**, 156		33-418-2	– **2**, 226
5-5-3	– **1**, 160		34-26/27-2	– **2**, 228
6-186-2	– **1**, 163		35-219-2	– **2**, 232
7-14-3	– **1**, 169		36-200-1	– **2**, 241
8-31-2	– **1**, 181		37-172-1	– **2**, 247
9-30-3	– **1**, 185		38-291-3	– **2**, 261
10-205-2	– **1**, 216		39-145-2	– **2**, 269
11-95-3	– **1**, 220		40-230-2	– **2**, 278
12-281-3	– **1**, 223		41-91-3	– **2**, 294
13-119-1	– **1**, 327		42-105/137-2	– **2**, 291
14-8-2	– **1**, 342		43-189-3	– **2**, 303
15-90-2	– **1**, 384		44-151/152/153-3	– **2**, 305
16-342-3	– **1**, 408		45-70-1	– **2**, 332
17-143-1	– **1**, 403		46-57-2	– **2**, 334
18-30-3	– **1**, 442		47-156-2	– **2**, 348
19-98-2	– **1**, 499		48-19-1	– **2**, 364
20-17-3	– **1**, 411		49-228/229-1	– **2**, 366
21-132-3	– **2**, 6		50-40-3	– **2**, 372
22-495-2	– **2**, 41		51-41-3	– **2**, 391
23-428-2	– **2**, 38		52-125-3	– **3**, 34
24-808-3	– **2**, 44		53-149-1	– **3**, 10
25-71-1	– **2**, 78		54-387-1	– **3**, 36
26-206-2	– **2**, 90		55-165-1	– **3**, 42
27-84-3	– **2**, 100		56-15-1	– **3**, 73
28-307-3	– **2**, 126		57-244-1	– **3**, 62
29-92-1	– **2**, 132		58-449-3	– **3**, 91

CONSOLIDATED TABLE OF CASES (BY AWARD NUMBER)

Award No.	Page		Award No.	Page
59-220-2	**3**, 110		110-144-2	**5**, 134
60-83-2	**3**, 119		111-10043-2	**5**, 148
61-188-2	**3**, 97		112-10865-2	**5**, 150
62-482-2	**3**, 169		113-433/576/580-2	**5**, 155
63-279-1	**3**, 176		114-140-2	**5**, 160
64-807-1	**3**, 186		115-928-3	**5**, 177
65-427-1	**3**, 181		116-1-3	**5**, 198
66-764-1	**3**, 197		117-119-3	**5**, 235
67-148-1	**3**, 203		118-434-3	**5**, 249
68-103/104/107/108/109/110-3	**3**, 212		119-138-1	**5**, 354
			120-B56-1	**5**, 357
69-139-3	**3**, 218		121-201-1	**6**, 1
70-185-3	**3**, 270		122-38-3	**5**, 361
71-346-3	**3**, 280		123-283-3	**5**, 386
72-124-3	**3**, 256		124-51-2	**6**, 4
73-67-3	**3**, 239		125-79-3	**6**, 33
74-62-3	**3**, 225		126-926-1	**6**, 20
75-112-1	**3**, 319		127-257-1	**6**, 38
76-243-1	**3**, 326		128-B29-1	**6**, 12
77-106-2	**3**, 332		129-63-2	**6**, 118
78-238-2	**3**, 334		130-436-1	**6**, 120
79-B67-2	**3**, 338		131-267-1	**6**, 125
80-136-1	**3**, 351		132-B7-1	**6**, 141
81-308-2	**3**, 366		133-340-3	**6**, 52
82-489-3	**3**, 390		134-806-2	**6**, 147
83-66-1	**4**, 20		135-33-1	**6**, 149
84-142-3	**4**, 29		136-49/50-2	**6**, 272
85-441-2	**4**, 47		137-312-2	**7**, 26
86-177-2	**4**, 39		138-82-2	**7**, 1
87-101-1	**4**, 33		139-166-2	**7**, 8
88-A/14-2	**4**, 74		140-194-2	**7**, 18
89-84-3	**4**, 77		141-7-2	**6**, 219
90-96-1	**4**, 83		142-100-3	**7**, 36
91-3-3	**4**, 183		143-127-3	**7**, 54
92-293-3	**4**, 192		144-180-3	**7**, 90
93-2-3	**4**, 96		145-35-3	**7**, 181
94-388-1	**4**, 197		146-42-3	**7**, 209
95-28-1	**4**, 199		147-94-1	**7**, 220
96-488-1	**4**, 205		148-130-SC	**7**, 225
97-54-3	**4**, 212		149-360-SC	**7**, 239
98-113-2	**4**, 280		150-32-SC	**7**, 223
99-245-2	**4**, 263		151-344/A9-SC	**7**, 236
100-280-2	**4**, 272		152-772-SC	**7**, 244
101-66-1	**5**, 76		153-11614-SC	**7**, 247
102-11875-1	**5**, 80		154-233/422-SC	**7**, 249
103-77-2	**5**, 88		155-11815-SC	**7**, 258
104-183-1	**5**, 90		156-102-SC	**7**, 269
105-B16-1	**5**, 94		157-87-SC	**7**, 260
106-B24-1	**5**, 97		158-11507-SC	**8**, 11
107-B53-1	**5**, 105		159-12701-SC	**8**, 13
108-A16/582/591-FT	**5**, 57		160-423-SC	**8**, 15
109-328-2	**5**, 118		161-343/365-2	**8**, 18

CONSOLIDATED TABLE OF CASES (BY AWARD NUMBER)

Award No.	Page		Award No.	Page
162-763-3	**8**, 20		213-61-1	**10**, 37
163-949-3	**8**, 24		214-134-1	**10**, 365
164-11553-1	**8**, 42		215-52-1	**10**, 56
165-341-1	**8**, 49		216-53-1	**10**, 95
166-35-3	**8**, 55		217-99-2	**10**, 121
167-446-2	**8**, 66		218-135-2	**10**, 157
168-25-3	**8**, 72		219-947-2	**10**, 177
169-10047-1	**8**, 79		220-37/231-1	**10**, 228
170-311-3	**8**, 81		221-65-1	**10**, 269
171-10719-9	**8**, 83		222-10517-1	**10**, 319
172-B3-3	**8**, 89		223-11713-1	**10**, 333
173-B21-3	**8**, 93		224-347/348/349-1	**10**, 365
174-320-1	**8**, 97		225-89-3	**11**, 3
175-180-3	**8**, 119		226-353-2	**11**, 372
176-255-3	**8**, 144		227-833-2	**11**, 372
177-389-2	**8**, 183		228-487-3	**11**, 53
178-299-1	**8**, 214		229-10173-3	**11**, 372
179-453-3	**8**, 236		230-624-1	**11**, 70
180-64-1	**8**, 298		231-10212-2	**11**, 72
181-942-2	**8**, 349		232-97-2	**11**, 76
182-236-2	**8**, 353		233-10335-3	**11**, 150
183-10425-2	**8**, 360		234-179-2	**11**, 168
184-161-1	**8**, 373		235-625-3	**11**, 180
185-359-3	**9**, 6		236-159-3	**11**, 184
186-302-3	**9**, 10		237-314-1	**11**, 217
187-325-3	**9**, 46		238-158-1	**11**, 223
188-176-2	**9**, 61		239-120-2	**11**, 259
189-458-3	**9**, 69		240-130-3	**11**, 372
190-11445-3	**9**, 70		241-361-3	**11**, 372
191-59-1	**9**, 107		242-829-1	**11**, 363
192-285-2	**9**, 153		243-112-1	**11**, 292
193-75-3	**9**, 184		244-68-2	**11**, 302
194-111-1	**9**, 187		245-335-2	**12**, 3
195-450-2	**9**, 203		246-B7-1	**12**, 25
196-302-3	**9**, 206		247-B59/B69-1	**12**, 33
197-480-1	**9**, 284		248-198-1	**12**, 94
198-11697-3	**9**, 306		249-769-1	**12**, 126
199-175-2	**9**, 308		250-369-2	**12**, 385
200-12/13-1	**9**, 310		251-393-2	**12**, 397
201-174-1	**9**, 313		252-10035-2	**12**, 139
202-292-2	**9**, 340		253-289-1	**12**, 146
203-467/468/469/471-2	**9**, 346		254-263-2	**12**, 160
204-237-2	**9**, 350		255-48-3	**12**, 170
205-258/259-1	**9**, 357		256-439-2	**12**, 239
206-34-1	**9**, 360		257-295-2	**12**, 288
207-217-2	**9**, 397		258-43-1	**12**, 308
208-73-3	**10**, 357		259-36-1	**12**, 335
209-78-3	**10**, 365		260-18-1	**13**, 3
210-10126-3	**10**, 365		261-133-2	**13**, 370
211-10/11-2	**10**, 365		262-222-1	**13**, 359
212-437-3	**10**, 22		263-324-3	**13**, 99
			264-264-1	**13**, 124

CONSOLIDATED TABLE OF CASES (BY AWARD NUMBER) lxiii

Award No.	Page		Award No.	Page
265-B2-2	**13**, 155		316-954-2	**16**, 335
266-B13-2	**13**, 158		317-339-2	**16**, 335
267-B18-2	**13**, 161		318-160-1	**16**, 335
268-B20-2	**13**, 164		319-B39-2	**16**, 335
269-72/80-3	**13**, 370		320-184-1	**16**, 317
270-389-2	**13**, 370		321-10712-3	**16**, 297
271-334-2	**13**, 179		322-154-3	**17**, 3
272-22-1	**13**, 370		323-409-1	**17**, 31
273-23-1	**13**, 370		324-10199-1	**17**, 92
274-10418-2	**13**, 370		325-366-3	**17**, 114
275-12783-3	**13**, 261		326-10913-2	**17**, 135
276-B72-2	**13**, 271		327-305-2	**17**, 368
277-B71-2	**13**, 277		328-11244-2	**17**, 368
278-362-2	**13**, 370		329-227/12384-3	**17**, 153
279-94-1	**13**, 282		330-B40-2	**17**, 183
280-491-3	**13**, 370		331-355-3	**17**, 353
281-931-3	**13**, 370		332-10089-3	**17**, 368
282-10853/10854/ 10855/10856-1	**13**, 286		333-B8-2	**17**, 187
283-448-1	**13**, 331		334-B51-2	**17**, 200
284-10405-3	**13**, 370		335-B9-2	**17**, 214
285-25/492-2	**14**, 349		336-B12-2	**17**, 228
286-10303-2	**14**, 349		337-B10-2	**17**, 238
287-384-2	**14**, 349		338-484-1	**17**, 245
288-11653-2	**14**, 349		339-114-3	**17**, 368
289-93-1	**14**, 24		340-11887-2	**17**, 362
290-123-1	**14**, 65		341-371-3	**17**, 266
291-10706-1	**14**, 86		342-187-3	**17**, 269
292-353-2	**14**, 111		343-423-3	**17**, 294
293-410-3	**14**, 339		344-364-1	**17**, 368
294-181-1	**14**, 149		345-10066-1	**18**, 390
295-834-2	**14**, 176		346-10973-2	**18**, 377
296-126-2	**14**, 349		347-B63-3	**18**, 84
297-209-1	**14**, 191		348-414-3	**18**, 88
298-317-1	**14**, 223		349-420-3	**18**, 90
299-957-1	**14**, 251		350-454-3	**18**, 92
300-459-2	**14**, 349		351-486-3	**18**, 98
301-286-1	**14**, 263		352-375-1	**18**, 115
302-B66-1	**14**, 276		353-196-2	**18**, 150
303-11005-1	**14**, 349		354-10427-2	**18**, 154
304-284-2	**14**, 283		355-10633-2	**18**, 164
305-310-2	**14**, 349		356-190-2	**18**, 175
306-A15-FT	**14**, 311		357-444-1	**18**, 390
307-477-3	**14**, 349		358-195-1	**18**, 180
308-155-3	**15**, 3		359-10059-1	**18**, 224
309-129-3	**15**, 23		360-10514-1	**18**, 232
310-56-3	**15**, 189		361-11157-2	**18**, 390
311-74/76/81/150-3	**16**, 3		362-11038-3	**18**, 390
312-11135-3	**16**, 76		363-11377-2	**18**, 275
313-10172-1	**16**, 103		364-B65-2	**18**, 390
314-24-1	**16**, 112		365-315-2	**18**, 289
315-115-3	**16**, 257		366-11961-1	**18**, 390
			367-829-2	**18**, 292

lxiv CONSOLIDATED TABLE OF CASES (BY AWARD NUMBER)

Award No.	Page		Award No.	Page
368-11485-3	**18**, 390		420-443-3	**22**, 3
369-208-2	**18**, 352		421-B11-2	**22**, 365
370-B1-FT	**19**, 3		422-260-2	**22**, 370
371-10163-2	**19**, 345		423-10645-1	**22**, 111
372-10513-2	**19**, 62		424-168-3	**22**, 118
373-481-3	**19**, 73		425-39-2	**21**, 79
374-B22-1	**19**, 374		426-276-3	**22**, 170
375-381-1	**19**, 107		427-831-3	**22**, 194
376-B31-3	**19**, 374		428-764-1	**22**, 204
377-261-3	**19**, 200		429-370-1	**22**, 218
378-173-3	**20**, 3		430-814-1	**22**, 339
379-121-2	**19**, 257		431-395-3	**23**, 3
380-12785-2	**19**, 374		432-10812-3	**23**, 126
381-10110-2	**19**, 374		433-333-1	**23**, 413
382-B1-FT	**19**, 273		434-810-1	**23**, 413
383-11486-2	**19**, 374		435-811-1	**23**, 413
384-10569-2	**19**, 374		436-150-3	**23**, 401
385-10026-2	**19**, 374		437-10159-3	**23**, 133
386-11415-2	**19**, 374		438-430-1	**23**, 150
387-10216-3	**19**, 374		439-10105 and	
388-11539-3	**19**, 374		12713-12721-1	**23**, 413
389-10541-3	**19**, 374		440-12183-1	**23**, 233
390-12567-3	**19**, 374		441-B73-2	**23**, 413
391-10355-1	**19**, 374		442-10656-1	**23**, 413
392-10415-1	**19**, 374		443-965-2	**23**, 265
393-10972-1	**19**, 374		444-940-2	**23**, 268
394-11294-1	**19**, 352		445-12257-2	**23**, 413
395-11300-1	**19**, 374		446-10087-2	**23**, 276
396-12778-1	**19**, 374		447-B4-2	**23**, 413
397-10547-2	**19**, 374		448-11590-2	**23**, 413
398-11657-2	**19**, 374		449-12762-2	**23**, 413
399-10273-3	**19**, 321		450-447-3	**23**, 282
400-10891-1	**19**, 374		451-251-2	**23**, 290
401-10067-1	**19**, 374		452-B1-FT	**23**, 407
402-288-1	**19**, 374		453-B5/B19-3	**23**, 413
403-10605/10606-3	**19**, 360		454-10398-1	**23**, 413
404-10457-1	**19**, 374		455-11429-3	**23**, 296
405-358-3	**19**, 365		456-11102-3	**23**, 303
406-845-1	**21**, 13		457-B55-1	**23**, 320
407-76-3	**21**, 303		458-11286-3	**23**, 351
408-473-1	**21**, 303		459-B14/B33-2	**23**, 413
409-10638-2	**21**, 303		460-880-2	**23**, 378
410-12118-3	**21**, 303		461-39-2	**21**, 285
411-10861-1	**21**, 303		462-10296-2	**24**, 305
412-256-2	**21**, 20		463-B26/B28/B35/	
413-483-2	**21**, 25		B60-2	**24**, 291
414-770-2	**21**, 28		464-494-3	**24**, 47
415-10065-1	**21**, 303		465-B44-2	**24**, 305
416-819-1	**21**, 303		466-B15-3	**24**, 305
417-88-3	**21**, 303		467-66-1	**24**, 102
418-B27/B47-3	**21**, 303		468-12458-2	**24**, 116
419-128/129-2	**21**, 31		469-B75-2	**24**, 305

CONSOLIDATED TABLE OF CASES (BY AWARD NUMBER)

Award No.	Page		Award No.	Page
470-B41-3	– **24**, 305		517-B32/B74/12786-	
471-10871-3	– **24**, 305		12892-3	– **27**, 275
472-308-2	– **24**, 297		518-131-2	– **27**, 64
473-357-1	– **24**, 121		519-394-1	– **27**, 122
474-268-1	– **24**, 203		520-210-3	– **27**, 145
475-11491-1	– **24**, 238		521-308-2	– **27**, 288
476-11803-1	– **24**, 252		522-828-1	– **27**, 196
477-383-2	– **24**, 265		523-382-3	– **27**, 218
478-952-2	– **24**, 269		524-313-2	– **27**, 248
479-476-2	– **24**, 272		525-B-FT	– **27**, 282
480-55-2	– **25**, 301		526-431-2	– **28**, 21
481-56-3	– **25**, 314		527-445-1	– **28**, 389
482-275-1	– **25**, 3		528-941-3	– **28**, 53
483-CLTDs/86/B38/			529-A15-FT	– **28**, 112
B76/B77/-FT	– **25**, 327		530-490-1	– **28**, 159
484-440-3	– **25**, 15		531-260-2	– **28**, 198
485-60-3	– **25**, 20		532-182-2	– **28**, 225
486-197-2	– **25**, 131		533-274-1	– **28**, 232
487-4-3	– **25**, 153		534-193-3	– **28**, 246
488-380-3	– **25**, 172		535-354-1	– **28**, 309
489-309-3	– **25**, 178		536-20-1	– **28**, 392
490-273-1	– **25**, 196		537-21-1	– **28**, 394
491-435-1	– **25**, 212		538-396-1	– **28**, 401
492-74-3	– **25**, 339		539-167-3	– **28**, 320
493-12784-1	– **25**, 339		540-192-1	– **28**, 371
494-397-1	– **25**, 229		541-930-3	– **28**, 382
495-398-1	– **25**, 235		542-626-3	– **29**, 395
496-399-1	– **25**, 241		543-356-1	– **29**, 3
497-319-1	– **25**, 264		544-298-2	– **29**, 20
498-81-3	– **25**, 339		545-479-1	– **29**, 59
499-269-1	– **25**, 278		546-812-3	– **29**, 78
500-290-3	– **25**, 289		547-203-3	– **29**, 401
501-381-1	– **26**, 3		548-367-2	– **29**, 222
502-451-2	– **26**, 275		549-967-2	– **29**, 260
503-474-3	– **26**, 15		550-412/415-3	– **29**, 295
504-350-2	– **26**, 37		551-368-3	– **29**, 310
505-461/462/463/			552-421-1	– **29**, 411
464/465-2	– **26**, 44		553-118-1	– **29**, 367
506-308-2	– **26**, 60		554-319-1	– **30**, 22
507-386-1	– **26**, 148		555-321-1	– **30**, 283
508-413-3	– **26**, 190		556-212-1	– **30**, 292
509-248-1	– **26**, 193		557-950-2	– **30**, 70
510-452-1	– **26**, 275		558-178-2	– **30**, 76
511-147-1	– **26**, 228		559-221-1	– **30**, 123
512-455-1	– **26**, 244		560-44/46/47-3	– **30**, 170
513-29-1	– **26**, 265		561-841-1	– **30**, 302
514-227-3	– **27**, 3		562-767-3	– **30**, 267
515-771-2	– **27**, 40			
516-322-1	– **27**, 49			

CONSOLIDATED TABLE OF CASES (BY AWARD NUMBER)

INTERIM AND INTERLOCUTORY AWARDS

Award No.	Page		Award No.	Page
ITL 1-6FT	**1**, 236		ITL 42-120-2	**21**, 12
ITL 2-51-FT	**1**, 242		ITL 43-476-2	**7**, 31
ITL 3-68-FT	**1**, 248		ITM 44-158-1	**7**, 217
ITL 4-121-FT	**1**, 252		ITL 45-120-2	**8**, 41
ITL 5-140-FT	**1**, 261		ITM 46-382-3	**8**, 44
ITL 6-159-FT	**1**, 268		ITM 47-158-1	**8**, 75
ITL 7-254-FT	**1**, 271		ITM 48-10513-9	**8**, 85
ITL 8-298-FT	**1**, 274		ITL 49-65-1	**8**, 99
ITL 9-466-FT	**1**, 280		ITM 50-3961	**8**, 179
ITL 10-48-FT	**1**, 347		ITM/ITL 51-395-3	**8**, 216
ITL 11-89-2	**1**, 487		ITM/ITL 52-382-3	**8**, 238
ITL 12-55-2	**1**, 493		ITL 53-458-3	**8**, 290
ITM 13-388-FT	**2**, 51		ITL 54-134-1	**9**, 72
ITL 14-97-2	**2**, 68		ITL 55-129-3	**9**, 248
ITM 15-59-1	**2**, 96		ITM 56-12118-3	**9**, 302
ITM 16-93-2	**2**, 281		ITL 57-123-1	**10**, 6
ITM 17-480-1	**2**, 310		ITL 58-120-2	**10**, 21
ITL 18-113-2	**2**, 322		ITL 59-129-3	**10**, 180
ITM 19-870-2	**2**, 362		ITL 60-B1-FT	**10**, 207
ITM 20-480-1	**2**, 369		ITL 61-260-2	**11**, 210
ITM 21-58-1	**2**, 401		ITM 62-333-1	**11**, 296
ITM 22-480-1	**3**, 59		ITL 63-A15-FT	**12**, 40
ITL 23-120-2	**3**, 156		ITM 64-498-1	**13**, 193
ITL 24-49-2	**3**, 147		ITL 65-1-167-3	**13**, 199
ITM 25-382-3	**3**, 173		ITL 66-298-2	**14**, 3
ITM 26-480-1	**3**, 200		ITL 67-389-1	**14**, 104
ITM 27-11875-1	**3**, 331		ITL 68-193-3	**19**, 48
ITM 28-159-3	**3**, 384		ITL 69-169-3	**22**, 123
ITM 29-160-1	**4**, 5		ITL 70-170-3	**22**, 129
ITM 30-160-1	**4**, 9		ITL 71-44/45/46/47-3	**22**, 138
ITM 31-928-3	**4**, 53		ITL 72-812-3	**22**, 155
ITL 32-24-1	**4**, 122		ITL 73-316-2	**23**, 259
ITL 33-A4/A15-2	**5**, 131		ITL 74-377-3	**23**, 285
ITM 34-222-1	**5**, 152		ITL 75-412/415-3	**23**, 307
ITL 35-120-2	**5**, 185		ITL 76-178-2	**24**, 40
ITL 36-410-3	**5**, 187		ITL 77-390/391/392-1	**25**, 190
ITL 37-111-FT	**5**, 338		ITL 78-A15-FT	**25**, 247
ITM 38-222-1	**6**, 43		ITL 79-221-1	**26**, 7
ITM 39-159-3	**6**, 104		ITL 80-485-1	**28**, 176
ITM 40-375-1	**6**, 130		ITL 81-336-1	**29**, 67
ITL 41-48-3	**6**, 74			

DECISIONS AND AWARDS

Continental Illinois National Bank and Trust Company of
Chicago and Continental Bank International, *Claimants*

v.

The Islamic Republic of Iran,
Bank Markazi Iran, Bank Tejarat,
Bank Mellat, Aydee Moghim Dehkordi,
Pars Felez Company, Sherkate Machinalate Omrani,
T.C.C. Trading Company, Tolito Corporation,
Techno-Way Industrial Corp., Multi-Frost Corporation Ltd.,
Sherkate Sahami Dashte Morghab, Bank Melli Iran,
Industrial Mining and Development Bank of Iran,
Parsylon Corporation, and Industrial Credit Bank,
Respondents

(Case No. 352)

Chamber Three: Arangio-Ruiz, *Chairman*; Allison, Aghahosseini, *Members*

Signed 20 *January* 1994[1]

Decision No. DEC 119-252-3

The following is the text as issued by the Tribunal:

1. On 14 January 1982 Continental Illinois National Bank and Trust Company of Chicago ("CINB") and Continental Bank International ("CBI") (together the "Claimants") brought a claim against The Islamic Republic of Iran, Bank Markazi Iran, Bank Tejarat, Bank Mellat, Aydee Moghim Dehkordi, Pars Felez Company, Sherkate Machinalate Omrani, T.C.C. Trading Company, Tolito Corporation, Techno-Way Industrial Corp., Multi-Frost Corporation Ltd., Sherkate Sahami Dashte Morghab, Bank Melli Iran, Industrial Mining and Development Bank of Iran, Parsylon Corporation and Industrial Credit Bank (the "Respondents").

2. The Statement of Claim identifies several claims which, according to the Claimants, are based on the expropriation of ownership interests in Iranian banks, unpaid bank deposits in Iranian banks, failure to pay declared dividends, overdrafts, reimbursement obligations, an unpaid letter of credit and bank guarantee, unpaid promissory notes, unpaid interest on syndicated loans and excess interest paid on Iranian deposit accounts at branches of

[1] Filed 20 January 1994.

Continental located outside the United States. The Claims are grouped in Claims of CINB (nine Claims, numbered 1 through 9) and Claims of CBI (seven Claims, numbered 1 through 7).

3. All the Claims in this Case either have been settled or withdrawn. Pursuant to their withdrawal by the Claimants, Claim No. 7 of CINB and Claim No. 3 of CBI were terminated by Orders dated 18 February 1983 and 3 May 1984 respectively. Following a settlement between the Parties all other Claims except for Claim No. 9 of CINB were terminated by Order of 14 April 1986. On 3 December 1990 the Respondents informed the Tribunal that "[that] last claim of [the] Claimant . . . ha[d] been settled." This was confirmed by the Claimants on 8 May 1991.

4. On 20 April 1992 the Tribunal advised the Parties that it "intend[ed] to terminate the proceedings in this Case in accordance with Article 34 of the Tribunal Rules unless the Respondents raise[d] justifiable objections thereto . . . [by] 11 May 1992." On 11 May 1992 the Respondents filed a letter with the Tribunal stating that they "have no objection to the termination of the Case concerning the Claims asserted by the Claimant." The Respondents added that "certain parts of the Claims asserted in Cases Nos. 683 and 645 before Chamber Two have been identified as Counterclaims in the instant Case." In the same letter the Respondents requested the Tribunal to examine these "pending [C]ounterclaims."

5. It is necessary to retrace the history of the Counterclaims in question to have a clearer view on their relationship with the Case at hand.

6. In Cases Nos. 645 and 683 Bank Markazi Iran, acting on its own behalf and on that of various agencies, filed a series of claims on 18 January 1982 against Continental[2] based on the latter's alleged failure to reimburse certain principal sums held by it for the account of the Iranian agencies and to pay interest on deposits and assets that also were held for the account of the Iranian agencies.

7. Subsequent to the Tribunal's decision in Case No. A17, *United States of America v. Islamic Republic of Iran*, Decision No. DEC 37-A17-FT (18 June 1985), *reprinted in* 8 IRAN-U.S. C.T.R. 189, Chamber Two on 24 July 1985 issued Orders in Cases Nos. 645 and 683 stating, *inter alia*, that

> 1. The Tribunal hereby informs the Parties that it intends to terminate all proceedings in th[ese] Case[s], pursuant to Article 34 of the Tribunal Rules, unless the Claimant[s] inform[ ] the Tribunal, by 2 September 1985,[3] that the present

---

[2] The Statement of Claim in Case No. 645 refers to Continental Bank International as the respondent. The Statement of Claim in Case No. 683 refers to Continental Illinois National Bank and Trust Company of Chicago as the respondent.

[3] By Order of 16 September 1985 Chamber Two extended this deadline until 1 October 1985.

Claim[s] involve[ ] . . . amounts owing and payable to [them] from Dollar Account No. 2.

2. The Tribunal reminds the Parties that if the Iranian bank claim[s] involved in the present Case[s] relate[ ] to . . . claim[s] by a United States banking institution or other private entity in another Case, then a party in such other Case may request that the Iranian bank claim[s] be decided as . . . counterclaim[s] in that other Case. Such request should be filed in the Case involving the claim brought by the United States banking institution or other private entity, not later than 1 October 1985.

8. On 1 October 1985 Bank Markazi Iran filed a letter in Cases Nos. 645 and 683 in which it stated that "none of the [Claims in the said Cases] . . . is payable from Dollar Account No. 2." At the same time, it requested the adjudication of these Claims "as [C]ounterclaims to those by the American Claimants [in Case No. 252], in accordance with paragraph 2 of the Order dated July 24, 1985."

9. On 18 November 1985 a submission signed by both Parties in the course of the month of June 1985 was filed in Cases Nos. 645 and 683 requesting "the dismissal . . . of those portions of the cases listed on Schedule 2 that pertain to the settled claims specified under each such listed case." Schedule 2 listed, *inter alia*, all Claims in Cases Nos. 645 and 683 except, on the one hand, "claims for 'Outstanding Amount' of Bank of Tehran set out in Table A1 of the Statement of Claim" in Case No. 645 and, on the other, "claims of 'Creditor Institutions' set out in Tables A and A1 of the Statement of Claim" in Case No. 683.[4]

10. On 21 November 1985 Chamber Two issued Orders in Cases Nos. 645 and 683 whereby it terminated "the arbitral proceedings in [these Cases], insofar as they relate to the portion indicated by the Parties in Schedule 2." Consequently, as of the date of that Order, the only Claims in Cases Nos. 645 and 683 that remain pending are those for U.S.$103,334.67 outstanding to Bank of Tehran and U.S.$602,962.59 outstanding to Bank Melli. *See* footnote [4], *supra*.

11. In its Orders of 27 November 1985 Chamber Two reminded the Parties that the Tribunal, in its Decision in *Case No. A-17*, has held, *inter alia*:

> Claims by Iranian banks against United States banking institutions are within the jurisdiction of the Tribunal only to the extent, if any, that they are disputes as to amounts owing from Dollar Account No. 2 for the types of debts payable out of that account which have been referred to the Tribunal in accordance with Paragraph 2(B) of the undertakings.

---

[4] Table A1 to the Statement of Claim in Case No. 645 mentions, *inter alia*, an amount of U.S.$103,334.67 outstanding to Bank of Tehran. Table A1 to the Statement of Claim in Case No. 683 contains an amount of U.S.$602,962.59 outstanding to Bank Melli.

12. Having noted Bank Markazi Iran's statement of 1 October 1985 that the Claims in Cases Nos. 645 and 683 do not involve an amount or amounts owing or payable to it from Dollar Account No. 2, Chamber Two decided in the same Orders that the Tribunal "lack[ed] jurisdiction over [those] Claim[s]." In view thereof, Chamber Two terminated the arbitral proceedings in both Cases pursuant to Article 34 of the Tribunal Rules.

13. With regard to Bank Markazi Iran's request that the remaining Claims in these Cases be adjudicated as Counterclaims in Case No. 252, Chamber Two remarked in the same Orders that its Order of 24 July 1985 required such "Counterclaim . . . [to] be filed by a Party to the Case in which the Counterclaim is sought to be filed, *and in that Case.*" (Emphasis added.) Chamber Two therefore concluded that the request filed on 1 October 1985 in Cases Nos. 645 and 683 was "made in the wrong case."

14. In considering Bank Markazi Iran's request to examine the Claims it had filed in Cases Nos. 645 and 683 that were not terminated by Chamber Two's Order of 21 November 1985 as Counterclaims in the present Case, the initial question is whether those Claims are admissible as Counterclaims in this Case. The Tribunal notes in this respect Chamber Two's Orders of 24 July 1985 requiring that the request to decide the Iranian bank claims as Counterclaims in the other Cases be filed in such other Cases not later than 1 October 1985. However, Bank Markazi Iran's requests to decide the remaining Claims in Cases Nos. 645 and 683 as Counterclaims in Case No. 252 were filed before Chamber Three in Case No. 252 several months after the October deadline set by that Order, namely on 14 January 1986.

15. Furthermore, subsequent to Bank Markazi Iran's request, Chamber Three, by Order of 3 February 1986, informed the Parties in Case No. 252 that "it intend[ed] *to terminate the arbitral proceedings in this Case* except for Claim No. 9 [of CINB] . . . unless the Parties by 28 February 1986 raise[d] justifiable grounds for objection in accordance with Article 34 of the Tribunal Rules." (Emphasis added.) Clearly, if the Respondents wanted Chamber Three to take up the remaining Claims in Cases Nos. 645 and 683 as Counterclaims in Case No. 252, they should have raised objections to such termination. Noting that no such objections were submitted by the Respondents, Chamber Three, in its Order of 11 April 1986, "terminate[d] the arbitral proceedings in this Case except for Claim No. 9 [of CINB]." The plain language of this Order indicates that the remaining Claims in Cases Nos. 645 and 683 cannot be considered in the context of Case No. 252.

16. The Tribunal also notes that for more than four and a half years the Respondents never again mentioned the existence of Counterclaims in Case No. 252. On the contrary, in several of their letters addressed to the Tribunal the Respondents themselves confirmed that the only issues that remained

outstanding in this Case concerned Claim No. 9 of CINB. In their letter filed on 1 September 1989, the Respondents wrote that

> Bank Markazi of Islamic Republic of Iran, who [sic] is carrying out settlement negotiations with the Claimant's agents in this Case, has informed us that the *only unsettled portion of the case is that related to the interest of 18 days of January 1981 on a syndicated loan made to the former Industrial and Mining Development Bank of Iran.*[5]

(Emphasis added.)

The same language appears in the Respondents' communication filed 3 September 1990. Only in their submission of 3 December 1990, when the remaining Claim No. 9 of CINB also had been settled in its entirety, did the Respondents again mention the issue of the Counterclaims.

17. In view of the above considerations, and in particular that on 11 April 1986 the Tribunal terminated all proceedings in this Case except for Claim No. 9, the Tribunal holds that the Counterclaims brought by the Respondents in Case No. 252 are inadmissible.

18. For the foregoing reasons,

THE TRIBUNAL DECIDES AS FOLLOWS:
a) The Counterclaims are not admissible.
b) The arbitral proceedings in Case No. 252 are terminated in accordance with Article 34, paragraph 2, of the Tribunal Rules.

[5] This relates to Claim No. 9 of CINB.

Wells Fargo Bank, National Association, *Claimant*

v.

The Islamic Republic of Iran,
Iran Power Generation and Transmission Co.,
Mahnakh Spinning & Weaving Co.,
Farnakh Spinning & Weaving Co.,
Bank Shahryar, Bank Melli Iran,
International Bank of Iran And Japan,
and Bank Markazi Iran, *Respondents*

(Case No. 294)

Chamber Three: Arangio-Ruiz, *Chairman*; Allison, Aghahosseini,[1] *Members*

Signed 20 *January* 1994[2]

Decision No. DEC 120-294-3

The following is the text as issued by the Tribunal:

1. On 15 January 1982 Wells Fargo Bank, National Association (the "Claimant") brought a claim against The Islamic Republic of Iran, Iran Power Generation and Transmission Co, Mahnakh Spinning & Weaving Co., Farnakh Spinning & Weaving Co., Bank Shahryar, Bank Melli Iran, International Bank of Iran and Japan and Bank Markazi Iran (the "Respondents").

2. The Statement of Claim identifies several claims which, according to the Claimant, are based on advances, loans, promissory notes, charges, reimbursement obligations and unpaid interest on syndicated loans made by the Claimant and other banks to the Respondents and excess interest paid and overpayments made by the Claimant on deposit accounts of the Respondents at branches of the Claimant located outside the United States.

3. Following a settlement between the Parties of certain portions of the Claims, the Tribunal, by Order of 24 October 1983, terminated, pursuant to Article 34, paragraph 1, of the Tribunal Rules, "the arbitral proceedings in this case, except for those items set out in paragraphs 11(a) and 12(d) of the Statement of Claim."[3] The remaining Claims also were settled in the later

---

[1] Mr. Aghahosseini's signature is accompanied by the word, "Dissenting".]
[2] Filed 20 January 1994.]
[3] In paragraph 11(a) of the Statement of Claim, the Claimant seeks the recovery of an amount of U.S.$2,550.30 from the International Bank of Iran and Japan. This sum allegedly represents late charges billed to the said Bank because it had failed to refund the Claimant timely for the

course of the proceedings. This follows from the letter of the Claimant's Counsel filed with the Tribunal on 1 May 1991 stating that "[its] client, Wells Fargo Bank, has confirmed . . . that it no longer has claims pending in connection with [this Case]."

4. On 20 April 1992 the Tribunal advised the Parties that it "intend[ed] to terminate the proceedings in this Case in accordance with Article 34 of the Tribunal Rules unless the Respondents raise[d] justifiable objections thereto . . . [by] 11 May 1992." On 11 May 1992 the Respondents filed a letter with the Tribunal stating that they "have no objection to the termination of the Case concerning the Claims asserted by the Claimant." The Respondents added that "certain parts of the Claims asserted in Cases Nos. 707 and 741 before Chamber Two have been identified as Counterclaims in the instant Case." In the same letter the Respondents requested the Tribunal to examine these "pending [C]ounterclaims."

5. It is necessary to retrace the history of the Counterclaims in question to have a clearer view on their relationship with the Case at hand.

6. In Cases Nos. 707 and 741 Bank Markazi Iran, acting on its own behalf and on that of various Iranian agencies, filed a series of claims on 18 January 1982 against Wells Fargo[4] based on the latter's alleged failure to reimburse certain principal sums held by it for the account of the Iranian agencies and to pay interest on deposits and assets which also were held for the account of the Iranian agencies.

7. On 5 September 1983 a submission signed by both Parties on 28 July 1983 was filed in Cases Nos. 707 and 741 requesting "the dismissal of portions of the cases listed on the Schedule [to the submission] that pertain to the settled claims specified under each such listed case." The Schedule indicated, *inter alia*, that "[t]he whole [of] case [No. 707 was terminated] except for certain Iranian claims as set out in Table A1 to Schedule A of the Statement of Claim, the claims being for the respective amounts of U.S.$69,310.23, U.S.$50,000.00, U.S.$47,867.03, U.S.$22,750.00, and U.S.$60,816.00." In connection with Case No. 741 the Schedule mentioned that "[t]he claim for U.S.$7,000 being a part of the total claim for

---

payment the latter had made pursuant to a number of bankers' acceptances for which it was entitled to reimbursement from the International Bank of Iran and Japan.

In paragraph 12(d) the Claimant seeks interest totalling U.S.$208,823.14 for the late payment of several syndicated loans in which it participated. These loan agreements were concluded with the Agricultural Development Bank of Iran, the Industrial Credit Bank, the Industrial and Mining Development Bank of Iran and Polyacryl Iran Corporation.

[4] The Statement of Claim in Case No. 707 refers to Wells Fargo Bank International as the respondent. The Statement of Claim in Case No. 741 refers to Wells Fargo Bank, National Association as the respondent.

U.S.$20,000.00 as set out in Table A1 to Schedule A of the Statement of Claim was terminated."[5]

8. By Orders of 6 October 1983 Chamber Two terminated the proceedings in Cases Nos. 707 and 741 pursuant to Article 34, paragraph 1, of the Tribunal Rules "insofar as they concern the above specified portion of the claim."

9. On 12 March 1984 Bank Markazi Iran filed a letter in Case No. 707 whereby it informed the Tribunal "that the claim of Bank Saderat, London Branch, against Wells Fargo for U.S.$60,816.10, referred to in Table A1 to Schedule A of the . . . Statement of Claim, has now been settled" and that "[t]herefore, Bank Markazi Iran . . . withdraw [sic] this claim against the Respondent."

10. By Order of 22 March 1984 Chamber Two terminated the proceedings in Case No. 707 pursuant to Article 34, paragraph 2 of the Tribunal Rules "insofar as the above specified portion is concerned."

11. Consequently, as of the date of that Order, the only Claims that remained pending are, on the one hand, those for the amounts of U.S.$69,310.23, U.S.$50,000.00, U.S.$47,867.03 and U.S.$22,750.00 in Case No. 707 and, on the other, the one for the balance of U.S.$13,000.00 in Case No. 741.

12. Subsequent to the Tribunal's decision in Case No. A-17, *United States of America v. Islamic Republic of Iran*, Decision No. DEC 37-A17-FT (18 June 1985), *reprinted in* 8 IRAN-U.S. C.T.R. 189, Chamber Two on 24 July 1985 issued Orders in Cases Nos. 707 and 741 stating, *inter alia*, that

> 1. The Tribunal hereby informs the Parties that it intends to terminate all proceedings in th[ese] Case[s], pursuant to Article 34 of the Tribunal Rules, unless the Claimant[s] inform[ ] the Tribunal, by 2 September 1985,[6] that the present Claim[s] involve[ ] . . . amounts owing and payable to [them] from Dollar Account No. 2.
>
> 2. The Tribunal reminds the Parties that if the Iranian bank claim[s] involved in the present Case[s] relate[ ] to . . . claim[s] by a United States banking institution or other private entity in another Case, then a party in such other Case may request that the Iranian bank claim[s] be decided as . . . counterclaim[s] in that other Case. Such request should be filed in the Case involving the claim brought by the United States banking institution or other private entity, not later than 1 October 1985.

---

[5] Table A1 to the Statement of Claim in Case No. 707 mentions, *inter alia*, an amount of U.S.$60,310.23 due to the International Bank of Iran and Japan, an amount of U.S.$50,000.00 due to Bank Iranshahr and an amount of U.S.$60,816.10 due to Bank Saderat London Branch. It does not specifically mention the amounts of U.S.$47,867.03 and U.S.$22,750.00, although it does list an amount of U.S.$376,330.08 due to the Bank of Tehran. In Table A1 to the Statement of Claim in Case No. 741 an amount of U.S.$20,000.00 is listed due to Bank Melli Iran.

[6] By Order of 16 September 1985 Chamber Two extended this deadline until 1 October 1985.

13. On 1 October 1985 Bank Markazi Iran filed a letter in Cases Nos. 707 and 741 in which it stated that "none of the [Claims in the said Cases] . . ., is payable from Dollar Account No. 2." At the same time, it requested the adjudication of these Claims "as [C]ounterclaims to those by the American Claimants [in Case No. 294], in accordance with paragraph 2 of the Order dated July 24, 1985."

14. By Orders of 26 November 1985 filed in Cases Nos. 707 and 741 Chamber Two reminded the Parties that the Tribunal, in its Decision in Case No. A-17, has held, *inter alia*

> Claims by Iranian banks against United States banking institutions are within the jurisdiction of the Tribunal only to the extent, if any, that they are disputes as to amounts owing from Dollar Account No. 2 for the types of debts payable out of that account which have been referred to the Tribunal in accordance with Paragraph 2(B) of the undertakings.

15. Having noted Bank Markazi Iran's statement of 1 October 1985 that the Claims in Cases Nos. 707 and 741 do not involve an amount or amounts owing and payable to it from Dollar Account No. 2, Chamber Two decided in the said Orders that the Tribunal "lack[ed] jurisdiction over [those] Claim[s]." In view thereof, Chamber Two terminated the arbitral proceedings in both Cases pursuant to Article 34 of the Tribunal Rules.

16. With regard to Bank Markazi Iran's request that the Claims in Cases Nos. 707 and 741 be adjudicated as Counterclaims in Case No. 294, Chamber Two remarked in the same Orders that its Orders of 24 July 1985 required such "Counterclaim . . . [to] be filed by a Party to the Case in which the Counterclaim is sought to be filed, *and in that Case*." (Emphasis added) Chamber Two therefore concluded that the request filed on 1 October 1985 in Cases Nos. 707 and 741 was "made in the wrong case."

17. In considering Bank Markazi Iran's request described in paragraph 4, *supra*, to examine the Claims it had filed in Cases Nos. 707 and 741 that were not terminated by Chamber Two's Orders of 6 October 1983 and 24 March 1984 as Counterclaims in the present Case, the initial question is whether those Claims are admissible as Counterclaims in this Case. The Tribunal notes in this respect that Chamber Two's Orders of 24 July 1985 required that the request to decide the Iranian bank claims as Counterclaims in the other Cases be filed in such other Cases not later than 1 October 1985. However, Bank Markazi Iran's requests to decide the remaining Claims in Cases Nos. 707 and 741 as Counterclaims in Case No. 294 were filed before Chamber Three in Case No. 294 several months after the October deadline set by that Order, namely on 14 January 1986.[7]

---

[7] On 14 July 1986 the Claimant objected to these requests.

18. Having noted this problem, the Tribunal observes that in order to take up the Counterclaims in the context of this Case it would, in any event, need to be established that such Counterclaims are within its jurisdiction. Although in their letter of 11 May 1992 the Respondents have requested the Tribunal "to initially determine the issues on [sic] jurisdiction," they have not put forward any arguments in support of the Tribunal's jurisdiction over the Counterclaims in question.

19. Considering that the Counterclaims do not involve an amount or amounts owing and payable from Dollar Account No. 2, if jurisdiction exists, it must be found under the Claims Settlement Declaration. According to Article II, paragraph 1, of the Claims Settlement Declaration, to be within the Tribunal's jurisdiction, a counterclaim must arise "out of the same contract, transaction or occurrence that constitutes the subject matter of . . . [the] claim." As explained in paragraph 3, *supra*, when Bank Markazi Iran filed its Counterclaims in this Case on 14 January 1986, only those Claims set out in paragraphs 11(a) and 12(d) of the Statement of Claim in Case No. 294 were still pending. It must therefore be established that Bank Markazi Iran's Counterclaims arise "out of the same contract, transaction or occurrence that constitutes the subject matter" of the Claims set out in those paragraphs.

20. The Tribunal notes that the Claims set out in paragraphs 11(a) and 12(d) of the Statement of Claim purportedly arise from loans and other banking transactions between the Claimant and the Respondents, whereas Bank Markazi Iran's Counterclaims arise out of Wells Fargo's alleged failure to transfer funds which it held in different accounts for various Iranian agencies. Bank Markazi Iran has not identified, nor has the Tribunal been able to find in the record, any specific link between the transactions forming the basis of the Claims and the account arrangements on which the Counterclaims are based.[8]

21. Consequently, the Tribunal holds that the Counterclaims do not arise out of the "same contract, transaction or occurrence" as the Claims and that, therefore, it has no jurisdiction over the Counterclaims under Article II, paragraph 1, of the Claims Settlement Declaration.

22. For the foregoing reasons,

THE TRIBUNAL DECIDES AS FOLLOWS:
a) The Counterclaims are dismissed for lack of jurisdiction.
b) The remaining arbitral proceedings in Case No. 294 are terminated in accordance with Article 34, paragraph 2, of the Tribunal Rules.

---

[8] Furthermore, as noted in footnote [4], *supra*, the Claims in Case No. 707 were brought against Wells Fargo Bank International, which is not a party to Case No. 294.

Security Pacific National Bank, *Claimant*

v.

Bank Markazi Iran, Bank Saderat Iran,
Bank Keshavarzi, Bank Maskan,
Bank Sanat Va Madan,
National Petrochemical Company,
Dopar Laboratories Co. Limited, and
The Government of Iran, *Respondents*

(Case No. 332)

Chamber Three: Arangio-Ruiz, *Chairman*; Allison, Agahosseini,[1] *Members*

Signed 20 January 1994[2]

Decision No. DEC 121-332-3

The following is the text as issued by the Tribunal:

1. On 18 January 1982 Security Pacific National Bank (the "Claimant") brought a claim against Bank Markazi Iran, Bank Saderat Iran, Bank Keshavarzi, Bank Maskan, Bank Sanat Va Madan, National Petrochemical Company, Dopar Laboratories Co. Limited and The Government of Iran (the "Respondents").

2. The Statement of Claim identifies several claims for interest pursuant to syndicated loan agreements between the Respondents and various syndicates of banking institutions of which the Claimant was a member.

3. By letter filed 19 November 1990 the Claimant informed the Tribunal that "all the claims asserted by [the Claimant] . . . in this case have been settled." The Claimant therefore requested the Tribunal to terminate the proceedings.

4. By Order of 6 December 1990 the Respondents were requested to comment by 7 January 1991 on the Claimant's submission of 19 November 1990. Having granted several extensions to this deadline, the Tribunal issued an Order on 20 April 1992 in which it stated that it "intend[ed] to terminate the proceedings in this Case in accordance with Article 34 of the Tribunal Rules unless the Respondents submit[ted the said] comments . . . invoking justifiable objections to the termination of the proceedings . . . [by] 11 May

---

[1] Mr. Aghahosseini's signature is accompanied by the word, "Dissenting".
[2] Filed 20 January 1994.

1992." On 11 May 1992 the Tribunal received the Respondent's comments. The Respondents explained therein that Bank Markazi Iran had brought certain claims against Security Pacific in other Cases before the Tribunal and requested the Tribunal to decide these Claims as Counterclaims in the present Case.

5. It is necessary to retrace the history of the Counterclaims in question to have a clearer view on their relationship with the Case at hand.

6. In Cases Nos. 689, 735 and 784 Bank Markazi Iran, acting on its own behalf and on that of various Iranian agencies, filed a series of claims on 18 and 19 January 1982 against Security Pacific[3] based on the latter's alleged failure to reimburse certain principal sums held by it for the account of the Iranian agencies and to pay interest on deposits and assets which also were held for the account of the Iranian agencies. Cases Nos. 689 and 735 were brought before Chamber Two. Case No. 784 was brought before Chamber Three.

7. On 2 September 1983 a submission signed by both Parties on 26 May 1983 was filed in Cases Nos. 689 and 735 requesting the termination of a number of Claims and the termination of portions of others, as specified in Schedules A and B to the submission. Schedule B indicated that the Claims in Cases Nos. 689 and 735 were settled "so far as [they] relate[d] to interest on [a number of] accounts" listed in the Schedule.

8. By Orders of 19 September 1983 Chamber Two terminated the proceedings in Cases Nos. 689 and 735 pursuant to Article 34, paragraph 1, of the Tribunal Rules "for the portion as specified in . . . Schedule [B]."

9. Subsequent to the Tribunal's decision in Case No. A-17, *United States of America v. Islamic Republic of Iran*, Decision No. DEC 37-A17-FT (18 June 1985), *reprinted in* 8 IRAN-U.S. C.T.R. 189, Chamber Two on 24 July 1985 issued Orders in Cases Nos. 689 and 735 stating, *inter alia*, that

> 1. The Tribunal hereby informs the Parties that it intends to terminate all proceedings in th[ese] Case[s], pursuant to Article 34 of the Tribunal Rules, unless the Claimant[s] inform[ ] the Tribunal, by 2 September 1985,[4] that the present Claim[s] involve[ ] . . . amounts owing and payable to [them] from Dollar Account No. 2.
>
> 2. The Tribunal reminds the Parties that if the Iranian bank claim[s] involved in the present Case[s] relate[ ] to . . . claim[s] by a United States banking institution or other private entity in another Case, then a party in such other Case may request

---

[3] The Statement of Claim in Case No. 689 refers to Security Pacific National Bank as the respondent. The Statement of Claim in Case No. 735 refers to Security Pacific International Bank as the respondent. The Statement of Claim in Case No. 784 refers to Security Pacific Bank as the respondent.

[4] By Orders of 16 September 1985 Chamber Two extended this deadline until 1 October 1985.

that the Iranian bank claim[s] be decided as . . . counterclaim[s] in that other Case. Such request should be filed in the Case involving the claim brought by the United States banking institution or other private entity, not later than 1 October 1985.

A similar Order was issued by Chamber Three in Case No. 784 on 10 February 1986.

10. On 1 October 1985 Bank Markazi Iran filed a letter in Cases Nos. 689 and 735 in which it stated that "none of the [Claims in the said Cases] . . ., is payable from Dollar Account No. 2." At the same time, it requested the adjudication of these Claims "as [C]ounterclaims to those by the American Claimants [in Case No. 332], in accordance with paragraph 2 of the Order dated July 24, 1985." In another letter filed on 8 April 1986 in Case No. 784 Bank Markazi Iran stated that the Claim in that Case also is not payable from Dollar Account No. 2. In the same letter, the Bank informed the Tribunal that "it intend[ed] to bring [the Claim in Case No. 784] as [a] [C]ounterclaim in Case No. 332 in accordance with the guideline provided in the Tribunal's Order of 10 [February] 1986."

11. By Orders of 26 November 1985 filed in Cases Nos. 689 and 735 Chamber Two reminded the Parties that the Tribunal has, in its Decision in Case No. A-17, held, *inter alia*:

> Claims by Iranian banks against United States banking institutions are within the jurisdiction of the Tribunal only to the extent, if any, that they are disputes as to amounts owing from Dollar Account No. 2 for the types of debts payable out of that account which have been referred to the Tribunal in accordance with Paragraph 2(B) of the undertakings.

12. Having noted Bank Markazi Iran's statement of 1 October 1985 that the Claims in Cases Nos. 689 and 735 do not involve an amount or amounts owing and payable to it from Dollar Account No. 2, Chamber Two decided in the said Orders that the Tribunal "lack[ed] jurisdiction over [those] Claim[s]." In view thereof, Chamber Two terminated the arbitral proceedings in both Cases pursuant to Article 34 of the Tribunal Rules.

13. In view of Bank Markazi Iran's letter of 8 April 1986 in Case No. 784 Chamber Three also found in its Order of 15 April 1986 that the Tribunal lacked jurisdiction over the Claim filed in the Case and therefore terminated the proceedings pursuant to Article 34 of the Tribunal Rules.

14. With regard to Bank Markazi Iran's request that the Claims in Cases Nos. 689 and 735 be adjudicated as Counterclaims in Case No. 332, Chamber Two remarked in its Orders of 26 November 1985 that its Orders of 24 July 1985 required such "Counterclaim . . . [to] be filed by a Party to the Case in which the Counterclaim is sought to be filed, *and in that Case.*"

(Emphasis added.) Chamber Two therefore concluded that the request filed on 1 October 1985 in Cases Nos. 689 and 735 was "made in the wrong case."

15. In considering Bank Markazi Iran's request described in paragraph 4, *supra*, to examine the Claims it had filed in Cases Nos. 689 and 735 that were not terminated by Chamber Two's Orders of 19 September 1983 and the Claims in Case No. 784 as Counterclaims in the present Case, the initial question is whether those Claims are admissible as Counterclaims in this Case. The Tribunal notes in this respect that Chamber Two's Orders of 24 July 1985 required that the request to decide the Iranian bank claims as Counterclaims in the other Cases be filed in such other Cases not later than 1 October 1985. However, Bank Markazi Iran's requests to decide the remaining Claims in Cases Nos. 689 and 735 as Counterclaims in Case No. 332 were filed in the latter Case several months after the October deadline set by that Order, namely on 14 January 1986. Chamber Three's Order of 10 February 1986 in Case No. 784 required the request to be made by 7 May 1986. Such request was filed timely by Bank Markazi Iran in Case No. 332 on 1 May 1986.

16. For the Tribunal to be able to take up the Counterclaims in the context of this Case, it would, in any case, need to be established that such Counterclaims are within its jurisdiction. Bank Markazi Iran developed a number of arguments in support thereof in its Statement of Counterclaim which was filed on 7 July 1986 in Case No. 332.[5] In its submission filed 19 November 1990 the Claimant argued that the Counterclaims are not within the Tribunal's jurisdiction.[6] Bank Markazi Iran replied to that submission on 11 May 1992.[7]

17. Bank Markazi Iran presents three alternative arguments in support of its position that the Tribunal has jurisdiction over the Counterclaims. First, it asserts that the Tribunal has jurisdiction on the basis of the principle of set-off. The Tribunal believes, however, that quite apart from the merits of that assertion, the Counterclaims in any event could not be set off against the Claims as the latter already have been settled in their entirety.

18. Second, Bank Markazi Iran maintains that the Tribunal's jurisdiction over the Counterclaims is grounded on Article 2 (B) of the Undertakings. With regard to this Article, Bank Markazi Iran writes as follows:

---

[5] While Bank Markazi Iran had requested Chamber Three to take up its Claims in Cases Nos. 689, 735 and 784 as Counterclaims in this Case, the Statement of Counterclaim surprisingly only refers to Case No. 735.

[6] In that submission the Claimant discussed the Counterclaims that originated from Cases Nos. 735 and 784.

[7] In its reply, which essentially is a reiteration of the Statement of Counterclaim, Bank Markazi Iran refers to Cases Nos. 735 and 689 but not to Case No. 784.

Pursuant to the Undertakings, 'In [sic] the event that within 30 days any U.S. Banking institution and the Bank Markazi are unable to agree upon the amounts owed, *either party* may refer such dispute to binding arbitration by such international arbitration panel as the parties may agree, or failing such agreement within 30 additional days after such reference, by the Iran-United States Claims Tribunal.'

Therefore, the Iran-United States Claims Tribunal is, by virtue of the Undertakings, obligated to entertain – at least as far as banking claims are concerned – the claims referred thereto by 'either party'; the Tribunal's jurisdiction over such claims is established.

19. However, in Case No. A-17 the Tribunal held that

[t]o the extent that such claims purport to be based on Paragraph 2 (B) of the Undertakings, the Tribunal determines that it has jurisdiction over such claims only to the extent, if any, that they are disputes as to amounts owing from Dollar Account No. 2, for the types of debts payable out of that account. It is evident from the text of Paragraph 2 (B) that its payment provisions deal solely with the disposition of the funds deposited in that account. Paragraph 2 (B) gives no jurisdiction over 'claims' by one bank seeking payment from another but establishes a limited jurisdiction over 'disputes', which may have been referred to the Tribunal by either Bank Markazi or the United States banking institution involved, as to 'amounts owing' from Dollar Account No. 2.

Case No. A-17, *supra*, at pp. 11-12, *reprinted in* 8 IRAN-U.S. C.T.R. at 197 (footnote omitted).

20. The Tribunal recalls that in its letters of 1 October 1985 and 8 April 1986 Bank Markazi Iran had stated that its Claims in Cases Nos. 689, 735 and 784 did not involve amounts owing and payable to it from Dollar Account No. 2. That being the case, the Tribunal concludes that it has no jurisdiction pursuant to the Undertakings over such Claims whether styled as a claim or a counterclaim.

21. Third, Bank Markazi Iran contends that its Counterclaims are within the Tribunal's jurisdiction because they meet the requirements of Article II, paragraph 1, of the Claims Settlement Declaration according to which a counterclaim must arise "out of the same contract, transaction or occurrence that constitutes the subject matter" of the claim. Bank Markazi Iran is of the opinion that this requirement is met in the present instance because "[banking] transactions are reckoned as parts of a prolonged general agreement for reciprocal transactions" in view of their "nature and type."

22. The Tribunal notes, however, that the Claims in this Case purportedly arise out of various syndicated loan agreements between the Respondents and several syndicates of banking institutions of which the Claimant was a member, whereas the Counterclaims arise out of Security Pacific's alleged

failure to transfer funds which it held in different accounts for various Iranian agencies. Bank Markazi Iran has not identified, nor has the Tribunal been able to find in the record, any specific link between the transactions forming the basis of the Claims and the account arrangements on which the Counterclaims are based.[8]

23.   Consequently, the Tribunal holds that the Counterclaims do not arise out of the "same contract, transaction or occurrence" as the Claims and that, therefore, it has no jurisdiction over the Counterclaims under Article II, paragraph 1, of the Claims Settlement Declaration.

24.   For the foregoing reasons,

THE TRIBUNAL DECIDES AS FOLLOWS:
a) The Counterclaims are dismissed for lack of jurisdiction.
b) The remaining arbitral proceedings in Case No. 332 are terminated in accordance with Article 34, paragraph 2, of the Tribunal Rules.

---

[8] Furthermore, as noted in footnote [3], *supra*, the Claims in the present Case were brought against Security Pacific National Bank, whereas the Claims in Cases No. 784 and 735 were brought against Claimants named Security Pacific Bank and Security Pacific International Bank respectively.

UNIDYNE CORPORATION, *Claimant*

v.

THE ISLAMIC REPUBLIC OF IRAN acting by and through THE NAVY OF THE ISLAMIC REPUBLIC OF IRAN, *Respondent*

(Case No. 368)

Chamber Three: Arangio-Ruiz, *Chairman*; Allison, Aghahosseini,[1] *Members*

Signed 9 *March* 1994[2]

DECISION No. DEC 122-368-3

The following is the text as issued by the Tribunal:
1. On 10 November 1993, the Tribunal filed Award No. 551-368-3 (the "Award") which decided the claims and counterclaims arising out of a contract between the parties pursuant to which the Claimant was to develop a system of scheduled "Maintenance and Material Management" for a number of the Respondent's vessels.
2. On 21 January 1994, the Agent of the Islamic Republic of Iran, on behalf of the Ministry of Defense of the Islamic Republic of Iran (the "Navy"), filed a Request for Correction of the Award and Issue of an Additional Award in Case No. 368.
3. The Request of 21 January 1994 was submitted in reliance upon Articles 36 and 37 of the Tribunal Rules. Requests under these Articles must be made "[w]ithin thirty days after the receipt of the award." The Persian version of the Award was filed on 22 December 1993. Accordingly, the Tribunal finds that the Request was timely filed. *See Hood Corporation* v. *Islamic Republic of Iran, et al.*, Decision No. DEC 34-100-3, pp. 1-2 (1 March 1985), *reprinted in* 8 IRAN-U.S. C.T.R. 53, 54.
4. The Request contains two sections. In Section A of the Request, the Agent states that

> [t]he Defense Ministry believes that the Award, particularly that part of it related to the amount of $176,304.02 which Claimant is allegedly entitled to for PMS Development Bandar Abbas, discussed in paragraphs 43 through 49 of the Award,

[1] Mr. Aghahosseini's signature is accompanied by the following statement: "The present request by the Respondent provided the Majority with yet another opportunity to set right a very grave injustice (*See* my Dissenting Opinion of 12 November 1993). It is regrettable that they, resorting to technical niceties, have failed to seize it."]
[2] Filed 9 March 1994.]

has no contractual basis in light of the facts and documentary evidence submitted in this Case by the Parties. Claimant, too, has made no claim in that respect.

5. Article 36 permits a party to request the Tribunal to correct in the award "any errors in computation, any clerical or typographical errors, or any error of similar nature." The request for correction is not made on any such grounds.

6. With regard to the request for a correction to the award concerning the amount of $176,304.02 awarded for work performed for the PMS Development at Bandar Abbas, Tribunal precedent is clear. Insofar as the request constitutes an attempt to reargue certain aspects of the Case, to disagree with the conclusions of the Tribunal in its Award, or to request the Tribunal either to review its Award or further to explain its reasons for the Award, there is no basis in the Tribunal Rules for a request of this kind on such grounds. See *Paul Donin de Rosiere, et al.* v. *Islamic Republic of Iran, et al.*, Decision No. DEC 57-498-1, para. 4 (10 Feb. 1987), *reprinted in* 14 IRAN-U.S. C.T.R. 100, 101; *Norman Gabay* v. *Islamic Republic of Iran*, Decision No. DEC 99-771-2, para. 8 (24 Sept. 1991), *reprinted in* 27 IRAN-U.S. C.T.R. 194, 195. Therefore, the Tribunal rejects the Respondent's Request for a Correction to the Award with respect to the claims for work performed at Bandar Abbas.

7. Section B of the Agent's request is for "an additional award compelling Claimant to deliver the items belonging to the Navy or the value thereof plus interest."

8. Article 37 of the Tribunal Rules permits the Tribunal to "make an additional award as to claims presented in the arbitral proceedings but omitted from the award."

9. Paragraph 31 of the Award in its enumeration of the counterclaims of the Respondent explicitly mentions "c. failure to deliver all materials."

10. Paragraphs 76-82 of the Award deal with the Parties' contentions regarding, *inter alia*, the Navy's counterclaim based on its allegation of non-completion of the contract. Paragraph 77 addresses the Navy's contention that Unidyne "failed to deliver the MRC cards, the PMS Work Centre Mannual [sic] books as well [as] the Cycle Quarterly and Weekly prepared tables" and "failed to install, deliver, test and rectify the system." The same paragraph refers to the assertion by the Navy of the gravity of Unidyne's alleged failure to complete "delivery and installation of the software and hardware." Paragraph 80 reflects the response of the Claimants to the Respondent's counterclaim based on unfinished work, that it was due to *force majeure* conditions prevailing in Iran at the time.

11. Paragraph 90 again refers to the Respondent's claim that Unidyne "refused to remit to the Navy the balance of the materials still to be delivered under the contract."

12. Paragraphs 91 *et seq.* detail the Tribunal's finding that the events in Iran in November 1979, and the Executive Orders issued by the United States imposing restrictions on dealings with Iran (the "Freeze Orders"), had the effect of barring further shipments of materials under the contract to the Navy. In Paragraph 97, the Tribunal concludes that the above situation amounted to *force majeure* for the Claimant, preventing it from continuing to "send [ ] such materials under the circumstances. . . ."

13. Paragraph 100 concludes that the Claimant should not be held liable for the non-completion of the Contract, as such non-completion resulted from circumstances beyond its control, and concluded that item *c* of Paragraph 31, (*i.e.*, the counterclaim for "failure to deliver all materials"), *inter alia*, should be dismissed.

14. By these findings, the Award dismissed on the merits the Navy's counterclaim for delivery of materials. In view of the foregoing, the Tribunal finds that the counterclaim for delivery of materials was not "omitted from the award" such that there is a basis under Article 37 for making the additional Award requested. Accordingly, the Respondent's Request for an Additional Award is rejected.

15. For the foregoing reasons:

THE TRIBUNAL DECIDES AS FOLLOWS:

> The requests filed on 21 January 1994 by the Agent of the Government of the Islamic Republic of Iran on behalf of the Ministry of Defense are denied.

CATHERINE ETEZADI, *Claimant*

v.

THE GOVERNMENT OF THE ISLAMIC REPUBLIC OF IRAN, *Respondent*

(Case No. 319)

Chamber One: Broms, *Chairman*; Noori,[1] Mosk,[2] *Members*

Signed 23 *March* 1994[3]

AWARD No. 554-319-1

The following is the text as issued by the Tribunal:

APPEARANCES

For the Claimant: Mrs. Catherine Etezadi
    Claimant
Mr. David Etezadi
Ms. Susan Etezadi
Mr. John Westberg
    Counsel
Mr. Hooshang Etezadi
    Representative

For the Respondent: Mr. Ali H. Nobari
    Agent of the Government of the
    Islamic Republic of Iran
Dr. Nasser-Ali Mansourian
Prof. Antonio Cassese
    Legal Advisers to the Agent
Prof. Paul Lagarde
Prof. Hossein Mehrpour
Legal Advisers to the Government
    of the Islamic Republic of Iran
Mr. Seyed Mohammad Jazayeri
    Attorney

---

[1] The signature of Mr. Noori is accompanied by the Statement appearing at page 44, below.]
[2] Designated as a Substitute Member under Article 13 of the Tribunal Rules. *See* Dissenting Opinion appearing at page 45, below.]
[3] Filed 23 March 1994.]

                Mr. Mehdi Mir Shafian
                    Representative of Respondent
                Mr. Nariman Ilkhani
                    Expert
                Mr. Mashallah Daneshgar
                    Witness
                Mr. Behrouz Salehpour
                    Legal Assistant to the Agent

Also Present: Mr. D. Stephen Mathias
                    Agent of the Government of the
                    United States of America
                Mrs. Mary Catherine Malin
                    Deputy Agent of the Government of
                    the United States of America.

I. PROCEEDINGS

1. Procedural History

1. On 15 January 1982, the Claimant Catherine Etezadi ("the Claimant") and her husband Hooshang Etezadi[4] together filed a Statement of Claim against The Government of the Islamic Republic of Iran ("Iran") for the alleged expropriation of a plot of land in Karaj, Iran, of a 10% interest in Shiraz Plastic Products Corporation, of the equity interest in a condominium in Tehran, and of the pension of the Claimant's husband, Hooshang Etezadi, as a retired employee of the Ministry of Foreign Affairs of Iran. In their Statement of Claim the original Claimants sought compensation in the total amount of U.S.$629,393.42.[5]

2. Iran filed its Statement of Defence on 18 January 1983.

3. In *Hooshang and Catherine Etezadi v. The Government of the Islamic Republic of Iran*, Partial Award No. 497-319-1 (15 Nov. 1990), *reprinted in* 25 IRAN-U.S. C.T.R. 264 (the "Partial Award"), the Tribunal found, *inter alia*, that Hooshang Etezadi was not a United States citizen during the relevant period of time, and therefore his Claims did not fall within the Tribunal's jurisdiction, but it went on to find that "during the relevant period Catherine Etezadi's dominant and effective nationality was that of the United States" and that she thus has standing before the Tribunal. The Tribunal also joined the remaining jurisdictional issues to the merits. (*Ibid.*, para. 21.)

4. The procedural history prior to 15 November 1990 is reflected in the Partial Award.

---

[4] Catherine and Hooshang Etezadi are referred to collectively as "the original Claimants".
[5] All references to dollars in this award are to United States dollars.

5. By its Order of 28 November 1990, the Tribunal scheduled further proceedings in this Case. Accordingly, on 25 February 1991, the remaining Claimant, Catherine Etezadi, submitted her "Statement of Claimant in Response to Order filed and dated November 28, 1990." In her submission the Claimant sought $314,696.50 as her one-half of the original Claims, with interest and costs plus expenses incurred in pursuing her Claim.

6. After having been granted six extensions, Iran filed its Hearing Memorial and Evidence on 19 March 1992. The Claimant filed her "Response and Rebuttal to Respondent's Memorial and Evidence" on 11 May 1992. After having been granted seven extensions, the Respondent filed its "Rebuttal Memorial and Evidence" on 2 April 1993. Both Parties submitted documents after the expiration of the filing deadlines established by the various scheduling Orders of the Tribunal.

7. In its Order of 19 March 1993, the Tribunal scheduled the Hearing in this Case for 20 September 1993. On 30 July 1993, the Agent of the Islamic Republic of Iran filed a letter in which he requested the Tribunal to schedule the Hearing for two days due to the complexity of the issues in this Case. On 13 August 1993, the Tribunal issued an Order in which it decided to have a two-day Hearing in this Case.

8. On 12 July 1993, the Claimant submitted a list of witnesses she would present at the Hearing. This list included one witness, Hooshang Etezadi, the Claimant's husband, who was to testify about issues within his personal knowledge concerning each of the Claimant's claims. On 16 July 1993, the Agent of the Islamic Republic of Iran filed a letter in which he stated that it was Iran's position that the Claimant's husband, Hooshang Etezadi, could not be heard as a witness by the Tribunal in this Case due to the fact that he had been a co-Claimant at the earlier stages of the proceedings and that as an owner of the properties in question he might have an interest in the outcome of this Case. On 20 August 1993, the Claimant filed her response. Iran submitted its list of witnesses on 20 August 1993. Iran's reply renewing its objection to the Claimant's witness was submitted on 27 August 1993. At the Hearing the Tribunal decided that Hooshang Etezadi could not testify as an independent witness due to his legal interest in the outcome of the Case, but could attend the Hearing as a representative of the Claimant.

9. The Hearing was held on 20 and 21 September 1993. At the Hearing, the Claimant distributed one diagram and two other documents. At the end of the Hearing, the Claimant also requested the Tribunal to permit her to file a post-hearing submission on the issue whether the Caveat in Case *A18* (the "Caveat") applies to the merits of her Claims. *See Case* No. A/18, Decision No. DEC 32-A18-FT, at 25-26 (6 Apr. 1984), *reprinted in* 5 IRAN-U.S. C.T.R. 251, 265-266.

2. *Remaining Procedural Issues*

2.1 Late Filed Documents, Late Submissions and the Claimant's Request To Be Allowed To File a Post-Hearing Submission

10. In this Case both Parties have submitted documents after the expiration of the filing deadlines established by the Tribunal's scheduling Orders. Furthermore, at the Hearing the Claimant submitted one diagram and two other new documents. At the Hearing, the Tribunal reserved until after the Hearing its decision on the admissibility of these documents. The Tribunal now turns to an examination of this issue.[6]

11. On 7 September 1993, the Claimant filed a corrected English translation of the Minutes of the Meeting of the Board of Directors of Shiraz Plastic Products Corporation, held on 14 October 1977 in California, which document was originally submitted as an exhibit to the Statement of Claim on 15 January 1982. On 16 September 1993, Iran filed its response to the Claimant's submission, including its own translation of that document. Furthermore, on 17 September 1993 Iran filed the English and Persian texts of Article 26 of the Articles of Association of Shiraz Plastic Products Corporation together with the annexed complete text of the Persian version of the same Articles.

12. It has not been the Tribunal's practice to permit the introduction of new documents in evidence prior to the Hearing unless it finds that this is justified by exceptional circumstances and unless such documents are filed not later than two months before the Hearing. The Tribunal finds that neither Party has shown the existence of exceptional circumstances which could have justified the late submission of these documents only a few days before the Hearing. Therefore, the Tribunal considers these filings inadmissible.

13. The Tribunal now turns to an examination of the documents submitted at the Hearing. At the end of the Hearing, the Claimant submitted copies of an Iranian administrative circular, No. 1069 issued on 6 July 1976 by the Ministry of Foreign Affairs, with reference to the Housing Co-operative Company for official members of the Ministry, concerning the offer of the Omran Techlar Construction Company on the construction of housing for the employees of the Ministry of Foreign Affairs, as well as copies of a Declaration by Lawrence J. Lococo rebutting the analysis of Iran's expert witness in respect of the financial condition and valuation of Shiraz Plastic Products Corporation. Iran opposed these late submissions at the Hearing.

14. The Tribunal considers that this declaration and administrative

---

[6] The Tribunal's case law on this issue is reflected in *Harris International Telecommunications Inc.* v. *The Islamic Republic of Iran*, Award No. 323-409-1, paras. 57-70 (2 Nov. 1987), *reprinted in* 17 IRAN-U.S. C.T.R. 31, 45-51.

circular No. 1069 constitute documentary evidence which must be submitted in accordance with the time limits set forth in the Tribunal's orders so that the other party is able to respond. Evidence that could have been submitted during the established time periods but which was presented late without adequate justification will normally not be accepted at the hearing, because late submissions containing facts and evidence are most likely to cause prejudice to the other Party and to disturb the arbitral process. The Tribunal notes that the Claimant has not provided any reason for the late submission of these documents. Therefore, the Tribunal considers the declaration by Lawrence J. Lococo and administrative circular No. 1069 inadmissible.

15. However, the Tribunal has found no difficulty in admitting a late submission when it contains no additional evidence. Therefore, the Tribunal considers the Claimant's diagram admissible, because the intention was to summarize the Claimant's arguments and the diagram does not contain new evidence not already submitted by the Claimant in her earlier filings, and the Respondent did not oppose the submission of that diagram at the Hearing.

16. At the end of the Hearing the Claimant also requested permission to file a post-hearing submission on the issue of the Caveat and its possible implications for this Case. However, the Tribunal decided not to permit the requested post-hearing submission in this Case, in order to preserve the fairness and orderliness of its proceedings and to avoid possible prejudice to the other Party. Furthermore, there were no exceptional circumstances to justify the permission of any post-hearing submission, and the issue of the Caveat was not raised at the Hearing for the first time in this Case. Moreover, in view of the Tribunal's findings in paras. 53-78 *infra*, there is no need for the Tribunal to address the question of the Caveat in this Case.

II. FACTS AND CONTENTIONS

1. Introduction

17. The Claimant was born in Grand Rapids, Michigan, the United States, on 19 February 1925. Thus she is a born United States citizen who upon her marriage on 4 May 1955 in Maryland, the United States, to Hooshang Etezadi, an Iranian citizen, also became an Iranian national under clause (6) of Article 976 of the Civil Code of Iran. After they were married, the Claimant and her husband moved to New York, which became their first marital domicile from 1955 to the end of 1958. In December 1958 or early in 1959 she moved to Tehran, Iran where she and her family resided and had their domicile until 1967, when she returned to the United States on 2 June 1967. Thereafter she resided in California and returned to Iran again in 1970, where she maintained her principal residence until 1974. When the Clai-

mant's husband retired from the Foreign Ministry of Iran in 1974, the Claimant moved to California, the United States together with her husband and their children, where they have since resided and had their domicile.

18. The Claimant states that pursuant to an oral agreement between her and her husband, from the time they were married everything she and her husband saved or invested was always considered to belong to both of them. In her written submissions, the Claimant explains this understanding between the spouses as being an adoption of the community property system in their matrimonial property relations. The Claimant asserts that they applied this procedure between them even when they were living in Iran, whose legal system did not contain or recognize this arrangement as such. However, the Claimant acknowledges that this joint understanding between the spouses has not been made in a written form.

19. At the Hearing, the Claimant asserted that her ownership rights to one-half of the properties in question were also to be considered as beneficial interests whose nature could be characterized as community property. Hooshang Etezadi was alleged to be the nominal owner of that one half of the properties and property rights in question, in respect of which the Claimant was alleged to be a beneficial owner.

20. To further substantiate the basis of her ownership rights and interests, the Claimant asserts that after their marriage and while working in the United States, she and her husband succeeded in accumulating joint savings of $10,000, which the Claimant states was the original capital that she and her husband transferred to and invested in Iran when they moved to that country in December 1958 or early 1959. The Claimant asserts that this capital was invested in a private enterprise in Iran and that the profits from its sale in 1967 were transferred to and invested in a motel in California, the United States, in 1967 when the Claimant and her husband returned there. However, the Claimant maintains that she and her husband had to realize their property in the United States and return to Iran in 1970. The Claimant asserts that of these funds, which she considers to have belonged to the community property or to have been jointly owned, $100,000 was transferred to Iran in 1970 and a further $50,000 in 1971. These sums allegedly were later invested in a plot of land in Karaj, Iran, in the shares of Shiraz Plastic Products Corporation, and in a condominium in one of the two apartment towers in Arya Towers Complex in the West Tehran Development area (Farahzad). The Claimant has asserted that all these investments were made out of assets that had accumulated through the couple's combined income.

21. Therefore, the Claimant contends that, due to the use of joint funds and the intention of both spouses that they have joint ownership of all the properties acquired and invested in, one-half of the property that is in her

husband's name in Iran is to be considered to be legally her property. The Claimant explained that due to practical reasons and her lack of knowledge of the Persian language and for convenience, most of the properties in question were registered under the name of her husband. The Claimant has asserted that she signed only those documents which were done in English because she did not want to sign documents she could not read. Therefore, her husband signed all the documents done in Persian. However, the Claimant emphasizes that it has always been a common understanding between herself and her husband that even if the property was registered under his name, it belonged to the sphere of community property and the Claimant owned 50% of that property. To support her assertion the Claimant also referred to affidavits filed by her. Iran disputed the evidentiary value of those affidavits. However, in view of the Tribunal's findings in paras. 60, 65, 70 and 75, *infra*, there is no need to decide the evidentiary value of those affidavits.

22. Iran argues that according to the appropriate principles of international law and conflict of laws, and also according to rules of private international law of Iran, the law to be applied to the Claimant's alleged property rights should be that of Iran. To support this argument Iran has submitted in the rebuttal filings an expert opinion from professor Paul Lagarde, who also acted as a legal adviser to the Government of the Islamic Republic of Iran at the Hearing, on the conflict of laws issues in this Case. Iran has presented further arguments in disputing the Claimant's alleged property rights on the basis of the municipal legislation. Iran argues that according to Article 966 of the Civil Code of Iran, possession, ownership and other rights to immovable and movable properties follow the laws of the country where such properties or rights exist or are located. Furthermore, if the spouses have different nationalities, then their matrimonial property relations will be subject to the law of the country of the husband. (Civil Code, Article 963.) In its rebuttal filings Iran has also submitted an expert opinion from professor Hossein Mehrpour, who also acted as a legal adviser to the Government of the Islamic Republic of Iran at the Hearing, on the matrimonial property relations between spouses in Iran. Invoking Article 1118 of the Iranian Civil Code, Iran argues that the system of community property between spouses in their matrimonial relations is not recognized in Iranian law; rather, the husband and wife are financially independent of one another. Therefore, the Claimant can be considered the owner of only those properties in Iran whose title deed has been prepared and issued in her name according to the legal requirements as set forth in the appropriate Iranian laws. Iran concludes that because all the alleged properties are in the name of the Claimant's husband and are owned by him, the Claimant has no rights to the properties and pension at issue. Iran also asserts in the alternative that the Claimant's Claims on the immovable

properties and on those which are tantamount to immovable properties should be dismissed on the basis of the Caveat.

2. *The Claimant's Property Rights in Iran*
   A. *The One Thousand Square-Meter Plot of Land in Mehrshahr, Karaj, Iran*
   23. On 26 November 1970, Hooshang Etezadi purchased a one thousand square-meter plot of land in Mehrshahr, Karaj, Iran, which before the purchase had been a part of the lands adjacent to the Pearl Palace owned by Shams Pahlavi. This plot of land, identified as lot No. 106, was subdivided from the entire tract of Hossein-Abad Afshar (also known as Mehr-Dasht), bearing the original registration number 170, and located within the Savojbalagh Tehran, Karaj Registration District. The Claimant asserts that by 1977, the purchase price had been paid off to Shams Pahlavi in 84 installments as agreed and that these payments were made by using the joint funds of the spouses. However, the deed to the plot was signed only by Hooshang Etezadi. Hooshang Etezadi acknowledged at the Hearing that he was familiar with the legal requirements set forth in Iranian legislation to establish the ownership rights to real property. On the alleged expropriation the Claimant asserts that in 1979, at the time of the Revolution in Iran, the revolutionaries took over the Pearl Palace and the adjacent lands including those portions already sold to others, of which one parcel was owned by the Etezadis.

   24. Iran asserts that the Law for Registration of Deeds and Real Estate recognizes as the owner only that person in whose name the real estate is registered. Iran maintains that if there is an intention to establish joint ownership of immovable property, it must be registered and included in the title deed accordingly. During the written proceedings Iran also submitted a letter, No. 32452 issued on 26 September 1991 by the State Organization for Registration of Deeds and Real Estate, Karaj Registration Department, which states that according to a relevant register of properties the present owner of the real property at issue is Hooshang Etezadi, in whose name it was registered before 19 January 1981. According to that register, Iran has not taken the land in question, but it is still mortgaged to the seller, Shams Pahlavi. Furthermore, at the Hearing the representatives of Iran confirmed that the land is still owned by Hooshang Etezadi. Therefore, Iran concludes that because the real property is solely in the name of and owned by Hooshang Etezadi, and the promissory notes were signed by him alone, the Claimant does not have any right to the property. Iran asserts further that the Claimant has not produced any evidence in support of the alleged expropriation of that property.

   25. Both Parties have also presented arguments on the nature of the immovable property in question. Iran has asserted that if the real property was utilized or unutilized agricultural land, or rural or urban wasteland, then no

decision has been made and no law enacted which might have affected the ownership rights to the plot of land in question. The Claimant has disputed this conclusion and asserted that the land does not belong to any of these categories.

B. *Interest in Shiraz Plastic Products Corporation*

26. In 1970 the Claimant's husband, together with other persons, founded a company, Shiraz Plastic Products Corporation (the "Corporation") in Iran. The Corporation was engaged in manufacturing plastic pipes in Shiraz, and its headquarters were located in the Techno-Frigo Building in Tehran. According to the Claimant, the Corporation employed approximately 70 employees, and its annual profits in 1977 and 1978 were approximately $1,000,000.

27. Upon investing in the shares of Shiraz Plastic Products Corporation in 1970, the Claimant's husband acquired 10% of its stock. These shares were registered solely in Hooshang Etezadi's name. The Claimant alleges that she owns one-half of the 10% equity interest in the Corporation, due to the fact that the funds invested in the Corporation were joint funds of the Etezadis and according to the joint understanding of the spouses on their property relations, these shares were considered to be owned jointly. However, the Claimant states that her name was not included on the share certificates despite their intention to be joint owners thereof.

28. The Claimant asserts that because the originals of the share certificates were placed in the Corporation's safe at its headquarters in Tehran, she has not been able to produce copies of these certificates to the Tribunal. However, in order to show indirectly her interest in the shares, the Claimant asserts that she has received her share of the profits distributed by the Corporation and that in 1977 these profits were deposited at the Bank Pars in the names of both the Claimant and her husband.

29. On the alleged expropriation of the Corporation the Claimant states that within the first six months of the founding of the Islamic Republic of Iran in 1979, Iran took over the assets of the Corporation and this caused her investment to lose its value. The Claimant further maintains that this takeover was carried out when a local, unidentified "Committee" seized control of the Corporation. The Managing Director of the Corporation was allegedly forced to resign after a conflict between him and certain workers of the Corporation, and several former clients of the Corporation were instructed to deal with an unspecified agency of Iran when paying their debts to the Corporation. The Claimant suggests that instructions given to the former clients of the Corporation have to be considered as a formal acceptance by Iran of the alleged takeover by the local "Committee". Furthermore, she asserts that no notices

or dividends have been sent to the Etezadis from the Corporation since the Revolution. She considers that these alleged acts amount to actual expropriation of the Corporation and that therefore Iran has to compensate her as a foreign national for the property taken. To support her conclusion the Claimant has also submitted a copy of the telefax including a newspaper announcement inviting the shareholders of the Corporation to convene an extraordinary session of the ordinary meeting of the shareholders in the Iranian National Industries Organizations Building. The invitation was made pursuant to the decision of the five-member board, referred to in Article 2 of the Supplementary Law on Protection and Expansion of Iranian Industries, regarding the exclusion of the Corporation from the coverage of Legal Bill No. 6738, on Designation of Temporary Managers.

30. Iran contests the Claimant's allegation that the shares have been expropriated, asserting instead that there have not been any changes in Hooshang Etezadi's shareholding, no expropriation has occurred, and no control has been exercised by instrumentalities or agencies of the Government of Iran. The supervisor of the Corporation was designated for a certain period of time, allegedly only to attend to administration and not to control the Corporation. The Corporation also had a temporary manager in 1980 due to the resignation of the former manager, Kamran Ebrahimi, in September 1979.

31. At the Hearing, when Mashallah Daneshgar, Director of the Finance Department since 1978 and former Chief Accountant (1974-1978) of Shiraz Plastic Products Corporation, was heard as Iran's witness, he asserted that the present amount of shares in the Corporation is 9000 and that Hooshang Etezadi still owns 10% of these shares. He further asserted that Hooshang Etezadi is free to use his ownership rights to these shares and to enjoy their benefits. The witness also confirmed that no expropriatory measures have been taken with respect to Hooshang Etezadi's shares of the Corporation. He added that in the register of the shareholders of the Corporation Hooshang Etezadi continues to be registered as the holder of 10% of the shares in the Corporation. The witness also disclosed that 32.5% of the shares in the Corporation were taken under governmental control. However, he confirmed that the shares of Hooshang Etezadi did not belong to the category of shares under governmental control. Furthermore, the representatives of Iran informed the Tribunal at the Hearing that Hooshang Etezadi has accrued dividends amounting to approximately 32 million Rials after deduction of taxes, which sum is freely available for him at the Corporation. Either he or his representative with a power of attorney can collect the money.

32. During his testimony Mashallah Daneshgar asserted that the reason why Hooshang Etezadi did not receive notices or dividends from the Corporation was probably due to the lack of information at the Corporation

as to how to contact him. He also asserted that the Corporation had not received any letters sent by Hooshang Etezadi. When questioned by counsel for the Claimant the witness stated that a supervisor helped to run the Corporation in early 1980, and that on 3 September 1980, a temporary manager was appointed.

33. During the written proceedings and at the Hearing both Parties presented arguments and evidence on the possible value of the Corporation and its shares.

C. *The Equity Interest in a Condominium in Tehran*

34. The Claimant asserts that she and her husband have an equity interest in a condominium in one of the two apartment towers in the Arya Towers Complex in the West Tehran Development Area (Farahzad). She also states that those apartments were allocated to employees of the Iranian Ministry of Foreign Affairs, and that the Ministry controlled the construction process. On 16 August 1976, Hooshang Etezadi made a purchase option with the Omran Techlar Construction Company Ltd. (the "Company"). On 17 August 1976, he invested in the condominium project, when he entered into Sales Agreement No. 235 with the Company and paid the down payment of Rls.1,052,750 ($15,039.29). According to the Claimant, Hooshang Etezadi made four further semi-annual principal installment payments of Rls.131,595 ($1,879.93) each, plus annual payments of Rls.245,000 ($3,300.00) as interest on the outstanding balance of the purchase price. The Claimant asserts that the total equity or principal payments amounted to Rls.1,579,130 ($22,559.00). All these funds were transferred from the joint account of the Etezadis in Bank Pars to the Company.

35. Both the option agreement and Sales Agreement No. 235, signed by Hooshang Etezadi, include a clause stating: "The deed of trust will be made out [in] the name of Mrs. Catherine M. Etezadi." The Sales Agreement states that the apartment would be delivered to the buyer on 30 June 1978. Article 4 of the Sales Agreement further states that the purchaser agrees to pay the remaining installments over a period of 12 years by 24 promissory notes. The Claimant asserts that as a result of a letter received from the Company, no further payments were made. In that letter of 24 May 1978 the Company informed the purchaser that due to unforeseen circumstances, the completion and delivery of the apartment would be delayed. Subject to *force majeure* or other unforeseen circumstances, the new date of delivery was stated to be 30 June 1979. The Company also informed its customer that it would prepare a new set of promissory notes which would be exchanged for the previous ones, and that they would be sent to the purchaser through the Ministry of Foreign Affairs if he were not in Tehran.

36. The purchaser was also informed by the same letter that the Omran Techlar Construction Company Ltd. would take responsibility for the harm caused to the purchaser of the apartment due to the delay in the construction, and that the Company would pay a penalty of 1000 Rials per day pursuant to Sections A and B of Article 6 of the Sales Agreement. The Claimant maintains that neither penalty fees nor correspondence were sent to the Claimant or her husband after the Revolution, even though the Company had their address in the United States to which they have sent other correspondence regularly. However, counsel for Iran disputed at the Hearing the relevancy of the letter of 24 May 1978, because the number of the apartment in the letter differs from that mentioned in the Sales Agreement.[7]

37. The Claimant states that she is claiming only her share of the funds advanced, plus all penalties and interest accrued thereon from the date of accrual to the present, and not the fair market value of the condominium. She alleges that the Government of Iran provided the land for the project, exercised control over the Company and expropriated the condominium.

38. Iran asserts that the Claimant's husband is the sole purchaser of the property but admits that the name of the Claimant is mentioned in the option and sales agreements, in the additional clause on the title deed. However, Iran asserts that due to the delay in construction and the failure of the purchaser to make further payments, such a title deed has not been prepared so that the ownership of the Claimant could have been established. Therefore, no expropriatory measures could have been taken by Iran concerning the apartment itself.

39. Furthermore, Iran asserts that according to the Sales Agreement each of the parties had the right to cancel the agreement without any claim against the other party and, therefore, due to the impossibility of completing the apartment in question as well as a delay in excess of six months and the purchaser's failure to make further payments, this agreement No. 235 became subject to Article 6(B) of the Sales Agreement, in addition to Article 5, and was canceled by virtue of Notice No. 12794, dated 2 July 1989. According to Article 5 of the Sales Agreement, the Omran Techlar Construction Company is allowed to withhold one-third of the monies advanced in such cases where the purchaser has failed to make the payments in due time.

40. The Omran Techlar Construction Company has requested the applicants for purchase of apartments from the Company to inform it in writing, within 10 days from the date of publication of the notice, of any change of their addresses. Such a request was made by a newspaper

---

[7] The number of the apartment in the letter of 24 May 1978 is "11031" whereas the one stipulated in the Sales Agreement is "11071".

announcement of 9 July 1985, in Daily Kayhan issue No. 12492. According to the record the Company has also twice tried (on 9 July 1989 and on 4 April 1990) to contact the Claimant's husband regarding the cancellation of the Sales Agreement and to inform him that one-third of the advance payments has been withheld and to request him to contact the finance department of the Company in order to receive his credit balance. The address used has been that of Shams Avari in Tehran. The document dated 2 July 1989 includes a clause stating that after 6 August 1989 the Company would make a decision to deposit the monies with the relevant legal authorities. The record shows that according to the information received from the Company, these termination notices were also sent to the Ministry of Foreign Affairs of Iran, whose Personnel Department later returned these documents to the Company with the note that it did not have the foreign address of the Etezadis.

41. In response to this evidence, the Claimant asserts that their address in the United States was included in the Sales Agreement, and that the Statement of Claim filed with the Tribunal in 1982 included their whereabouts. Furthermore, on the issue of promissory notes which were not paid, the Claimant responds that those notes were superseded by new promissory notes which they never actually received. However, it has been admitted that neither the Claimant nor her husband has tried to contact the Company in order to obtain further information on the situation.

42. Iran also asserts that the Claimant has failed to show either that the Omran Techlar Construction Company is an entity owned or controlled by Iran, or that Iran has had any involvement in the contractual relations between Hooshang Etezadi and the Company.

D. *The Rights to the Pension of the Claimant's Husband or to the Survivors' Pensionary Benefits*

43. The Claimant's husband, Hooshang Etezadi, joined the Ministry of Foreign Affairs of Iran in 1951 and retired from the service in April 1974. Due to his 22 years of service in the Ministry of Foreign Affairs of Iran, he was entitled to a guaranteed life pension allegedly worth $226,263. After her husband's retirement, the Claimant moved together with him and their children to the United States in 1974 and the pension was paid monthly and transferred to Hooshang Etezadi in California until May 1980. Iran asserts that the pension was discontinued by virtue of Order No. 16/23082, dated 25 August 1980, issued pursuant to the "Legal Bill on Purging the Ministries. . ." adopted by the Revolutionary Council, and that further payments were terminated. During the proceedings no copy of that Order terminating the pension has been submitted to the Tribunal by either Party. However, Iran has submitted a letter dated 26 February 1983, from the Office of Personnel and

Welfare of the Iranian Ministry of Foreign Affairs, and another letter, dated 2 July 1987, from the Director General of Administrative Affairs of the Iranian Ministry of Foreign Affairs, confirming the termination of the pension.

44. The Claimant requests her alleged one-half interest in the vested guaranteed life pension of her husband. She states that the reason for this Claim is the fact that her husband contributed from his earnings to the pension fund for 22 years. She asserts that the right of a person to receive the pension includes also the right of that person's spouse and successors to receive the same. She states that due to the fact that at the time the pension was terminated her husband was no longer in the service of the Ministry of Foreign Affairs, there cannot be any justification for the termination. The Claimant asserts that the payments of the pension were terminated by the Government of Iran without giving any notice or reason and without allowing any opportunity to respond. The Claimant further states that she and her husband also thought that by virtue of their joint understanding on the mutual ownership of their properties, the proceeds of the pension were jointly owned. Moreover, she emphasizes that she was to receive survivors' pensionary benefits upon her husband's death, and maintains that because her husband's pension was expropriated she has an interest in one-half of the full value of the pension.

45. Iran asserts that the severance of the retirement pension was based on a decision made by an administrative committee in the Ministry of Foreign Affairs after certain investigations. Iran further takes the position that the Claimant has no right to claim her alleged share of her husband's pension, since under Iranian law the right to the pension has first to be created for the Claimant's husband and then certain conditions must be met, *inter alia*, the husband has to be deceased, before the retirement pension will be converted to survivors' pensionary benefits for the wife. Iran also maintains that Hooshang Etezadi should have exhausted the appropriate administrative and legal remedies in Iran in order to contest the decision withdrawing his pension rights and to preserve these rights.

46. During the written proceedings Iran has also asserted that an abandonment of Iranian nationality results in the termination of a retirement pension as well as survivors' pensionary benefits to those persons who have received payments from the retirement fund. However, the Claimant has responded to this argument by noting that Hooshang Etezadi was purged on 25 August 1980 and that it was only after that decision he became a naturalized U.S. citizen in June of 1981 when he also became a dual national because he did not abandon his Iranian nationality.

47. According to Iran, the Claimant's Claim should be rejected because these rights to the pension benefits are exclusively owned by her husband. The

Claimant may have had a contingent right in this regard, but one which has not yet materialized as an ownership right. Therefore, Iran considers that the Claim has no legal basis.

III. JURISDICTION

48. The Tribunal has found in its Partial Award, *supra*, para. 18, that during the relevant period Catherine Etezadi's dominant and effective nationality was that of the United States, and that she does have standing before the Tribunal according to the Claims Settlement Declaration, Article II, paragraph 1 and Article VII, paragraph 1. *Ibid.*, *supra*, para. 21 (b).

49. In the Partial Award the Tribunal also decided that

> the question of whether Catherine Etezadi has a legal interest in the subject matter of the Claim, as well as the question of whether her property rights, if any, were expropriated or otherwise affected by measures taken by Iran, belongs to the merits of the Case. . . . (Partial Award, *supra*, para. 19.)

50. Iran has contested the Tribunal's jurisdiction in this Case on two grounds. As a basis for her alleged ownership interests and other property rights the Claimant has provided arguments on the joint understanding on the intended community property system between the spouses in their matrimonial relations and arguments on her beneficial ownership rights to these properties and interests. Iran asserts, firstly, that the Claimant has no legal interest in this Case because she has no proprietary interests in the properties in question. However, in view of the Tribunal's findings, paras. 60, 65, 70 and 75, *infra*, the Tribunal does not need to decide whether the Claimant has a legal interest in the properties at issue or, if so, to ascertain the nature of this interest.

51. Iran further asserts that the Claims of the Claimant are not outstanding, because Iran has neither expropriated nor taken any other measures against the Claimant's or her husband's property rights, and that the Claimant has accrued no right to the pension of Hooshang Etezadi and that she has no actualized right with respect to these pension benefits since her husband has lost his right to the pension. As an additional support to this contention, Iran also contests the evidentiary value of the Claimant's affidavits, asserting that the evidence produced by the Claimant does not meet the requirements of Article VII (2) of the Claims Settlement Declaration for ownership of claims and for continuity of such ownership during the relevant period. Iran maintains that with the exception of the Claim for the pension, the dates when the Claimant's Claims arose are uncertain and remain unspecified, and that these Claims should therefore be rejected.

52. Since these arguments cannot be separated from the merits, the Tribunal will not consider these arguments at this stage.

Therefore, the remaining jurisdictional issues are considered together with the merits.

IV. MERITS

1. Introduction

53. In order to meet her burden of proof the Claimant has to establish two distinct elements: first, that she had ownership interests in or other property rights to the properties and rights at issue and, second, that an expropriation or other measure affecting her ownership interests or other property rights, attributable to Iran, took place.

54. In this Case, the Claimant's alleged property rights are either derivative from or linked to the ownership interests and other property rights of her husband. The Tribunal notes that Hooshang Etezadi's ownership rights to the properties and rights at issue are not disputed as such.

55. Therefore, the Tribunal, turning to the second element, observes that the Claimant is alleging that her property rights at issue have been expropriated and that these acts of expropriation are attributable to Iran. The Tribunal will first examine whether the Claimant's alleged ownership interests have been expropriated.

2. The Claimant's Ownership Interests

  A. The One Thousand Square-Meter Plot of Land in Mehrshahr, Karaj, Iran

56. The Claimant contends that a one thousand square-meter plot of land in Mehrshahr,[8] Karaj, Iran, which her husband purchased from Shams Pahlavi and which before the purchase was a part of the lands adjacent to the Pearl Palace, was expropriated during the Revolution in Iran in 1979, when the "revolutionaries" took over the Pearl Palace and the adjacent lands, including those parcels sold to others, of which a portion was owned by the Etezadis.

57. However, in her written submissions the Claimant has not produced any evidence of either the alleged expropriation or how this alleged act would be attributable to Iran. The only information provided is a statement given at the Hearing by the Claimant's representative, Hooshang Etezadi, according to which he had been informed by a friend on the developments affecting the

---

[8] "Mehrdasht" has occasionally been mentioned in the file as the place where the plot of land at issue is situated, and this interchangeable local name is even reflected in the official deed of ownership attached to the Statement of Claim. However, it is clear from the record that the plot of land in question is located in an area adjacent to the Pearl Palace in the suburb of Karaj city.

real property. However, he did not want to identify the friend who had given this information to him. The Tribunal notes that because this information does not relate to Hooshang Etezadi's personal experience regarding the alleged events, but refers to what another, unidentified person has told him, the Tribunal cannot give any evidentiary value to this information.

58. The Tribunal also notes that the Claimant has not submitted any further information on the "revolutionaries" and has therefore neither established whether these "revolutionaries" in fact acted on behalf of the government, nor shown that there was a sufficient degree of Government involvement to make Iran responsible.

59. Furthermore, the Tribunal notes that the State Organization for Registration of Deeds and Real Estate in Iran has confirmed that according to the relevant register of properties the present owner of the real property at issue is Hooshang Etezadi, and that the property was registered in his name prior to 19 January 1981. According to the register, Iran has not taken the land in question. The Tribunal also notes that at the Hearing the representatives of Iran confirmed that Hooshang Etezadi still owns the real property in question. Thus, there should be no reason why he cannot use or sell this property.

60. The Tribunal concludes that, apart from her arguments, the Claimant has not provided any evidence in support of the alleged expropriation of the real property in question. Since she has not met her burden of proof in respect of this important element, this Claim is dismissed for lack of evidence.

B. *Interest in Shiraz Plastic Products Corporation*

61. The Tribunal must examine the acts of interference the Claimant complains of and determine whether any or all are attributable to the Government of Iran and whether any or all, by themselves or collectively, constitute a sufficient degree of interference to warrant a finding that an expropriation of property has occurred.

62. The Tribunal notes that 32.5% of the shares of Shiraz Plastic Products Corporation have been taken under governmental control and that the supervisor and temporary manager have been designated to the Corporation for an undisclosed period of time. It is true that under international law and the arbitral practice of this Tribunal, an expropriation or taking of property may occur through certain acts of interference by a state in the use of the property or with the enjoyment of its benefits, *see, e.g., Petrolane, Inc., et al.* v. *The Government of the Islamic Republic of Iran, et al.*, Award No. 518-131-2 (14 Aug. 1991), *reprinted in* 27 IRAN-U.S. C.T.R. 64, 96, even where legal title to the property is not affected. *See, e.g., Harold Birnbaum* v. *The Islamic Republic of Iran*, Award No. 549-967-2 (6 July 1993), para. 28, *reprinted in* 29 IRAN-U.S.

C.T.R. 260. In the Tribunal's practice the appointment of governmental managers has been regarded in some cases as a significant factor in support of a finding of a taking. On the other hand, the appointment of such managers has not, in certain cases, been found to constitute a taking. *See, e.g., Otis Elevator Company* v. *The Islamic Republic of Iran, et al.*, Award No. 304-284-2, paras. 40-44 (29 April 1987), *reprinted in* 14 IRAN-U.S. C.T.R. 283, 297; *Motorola, Inc.* v. *Iran National Airlines Corporation, et al.*, Award No. 373-481-3, para. 59 (28 June 1988), *reprinted in* 19 IRAN-U.S. C.T.R. 73, 85-86. However, the circumstances of each case and the impact of the appointment of temporary managers on the control over the company and its effects on the fundamental rights of the owners are more decisive in any finding of whether or not a taking has occurred. In this case there is not sufficient evidence that the governmental supervisor or temporary manager assumed control of the Corporation prior to 19 January 1981. Furthermore, there is no further evidence in the record to show that these acts would have had a sufficiently severe impact on the status of the Corporation and its administration to constitute an expropriation of the Corporation.

63. In any event, in order to find that an expropriation or taking had occurred, the Tribunal would have to be satisfied that there was governmental interference with Hooshang Etezadi's shareholding interest in Shiraz Plastic Products Corporation which substantially deprived Hooshang Etezadi and the Claimant of the enjoyment of their property rights and the benefit of their investment. Therefore, the Tribunal will now turn to the issue of whether the shares of the Claimant's husband have been expropriated. Hooshang Etezadi asserted at the Hearing that he had tried to contact the Corporation but had not received any reply to his letters. However, no evidence has been submitted to substantiate this assertion. Therefore, there is not sufficient evidence in the record to show that the Claimant's husband, Hooshang Etezadi, tried to exercise his ownership rights as a shareholder of the Corporation, and that these attempts were frustrated by an action attributable to the Government of Iran.

64. The Tribunal takes note of the information presented at the Hearing by the representatives of Iran that the accrued dividends, amounting to approximately 32 million Rials, are available for Hooshang Etezadi at the Corporation. The Tribunal considers that this is an additional important indication that the shares of Hooshang Etezadi have not been expropriated. Furthermore, Iran's witness, Mashallah Daneshgar, confirmed that Hooshang Etezadi still owns 10% of the shares of the Corporation and is able to exercise his ownership rights to the shares and to enjoy their benefits. The correctness of the information was confirmed by the representatives of Iran. Therefore, it appears that the property rights of Hooshang Etezadi in the Corporation have

not been affected; the shares are registered in his name, and it has been confirmed by the representatives of Iran before this Tribunal that his accrued dividends and the shares are available to him.

65. The alleged expropriation or other measures amounting to expropriation have not been proven. Therefore, the Tribunal concludes that the Claimant's Claim based on an expropriated equity interest in the shares of Shiraz Plastic Products Corporation is dismissed for lack of evidence.

C. *The Equity Interest in a Condominium in Tehran*

66. The Tribunal notes that Hooshang Etezadi signed a contract with the Omran Techlar Construction Company for the purchase of a condominium. He was the only signatory to the option and sales agreements and to the cheques, when the monies due to the Company were transferred to it. The option and sales agreements included a clause that the title deed would be prepared in the name of the Claimant. However, that title deed was never made out, and the right of the Claimant to the apartment itself was not established.

67. The funds advanced were transferred from the joint account of the Etezadis. However, even when the funds transferred to the Company have been joint funds of the spouses, the Claimant still has the burden of proof to show that these funds have been expropriated in the way she alleges, or at least that they are in the possession of a governmental entity which has not refunded the monies due to the transferor, even if requested to do so. The Tribunal notes that on the alleged expropriation there is no evidence in the record to show that the monies transferred to the Omran Techlar Construction Company would have been expropriated as such through separate measures attributable to the Government of the Islamic Republic of Iran.

68. The Tribunal now turns to the Claimant's implicit allegation that the mere possession of funds by the Company might amount to an expropriation. To prove this, the Claimant has to show a sufficient connection between the Ministry of Foreign Affairs and the Omran Techlar Construction Company to establish that the Company was under the control of the Government of the Islamic Republic of Iran. The Tribunal notes that no evidence has been provided that the Omran Techlar Construction Company was either owned or controlled by Iran before 19 January 1981. The Claimant's arguments that the apartments were intended to be used and owned by former and present officials of the Ministry of Foreign Affairs and that the land allegedly was provided by the Ministry do not substantiate such control.

69. Furthermore, there is no evidence in the record to show that the Company has acted either as a co-contractor or as an agent of the Ministry of Foreign Affairs of Iran, while entering into agreements with private citizens on

the apartments to be built. The option and sales agreements do not indicate that the seller was any other entity than the Omran Techlar Construction Company or that the Company was representing some other entity, either private or governmental. The Tribunal notes also that Hooshang Etezadi acknowledged at the Hearing that neither he nor the Claimant had tried to contact the Omran Techlar Construction Company and require new promissory notes or the refund of the monies advanced. However, on the basis of the record the Tribunal notes that the Omran Techlar Construction Company has several times expressed its wish to refund the monies due to Hooshang Etezadi. Therefore, there appears to be no reason why Hooshang Etezadi cannot obtain these monies.

70. The Tribunal consequently concludes that the Claimant has not succeeded in establishing that the monies transferred to the Omran Techlar Construction Company were expropriated, and she has thus failed to meet her burden of proof in this important element of her Claim. Therefore, the Claimant's Claim for her share of the monies transferred to the Omran Techlar Construction Company is dismissed for lack of evidence.

D. *The Alleged Beneficial Interest in the Pension of the Claimant's Husband*

71. The Tribunal notes that the Claimant's husband held various posts as a civil servant of the Iranian Ministry of Foreign Affairs between 16 February 1951 and 20 April 1974, when he retired pursuant to the provisions of Article 74 of the Civil Service Act. While working as a civil servant Hooshang Etezadi was exclusively an Iranian citizen, whose rights to a pension were provided for by the Iranian laws governing the status of civil servants. Therefore, the relations between such a retired employee and his employer continued to be governed by the appropriate Iranian laws even after his retirement. No other law than the Iranian law applicable to the relations between the retired employee and his employer may govern the pension rights of Hooshang Etezadi. Nor can these pension rights, which are based on the Iranian laws, be affected by contrary legislation or practice in the State of California, or by the oral joint understanding between the Claimant and her husband allegedly creating, for the Claimant, a beneficial interest or rights based on community property. In Iran, the rights to a pension are solely statutory rights. The transfer of these rights is not allowed under the law of Iran.

72. According to Article 70, note 1 of the Civil Service Act, the state retirement and pension system in Iran recognizes retirement pension, disability pension and survivors' pensionary benefits of heirs of employees as forms of payment from the retirement fund. According to Article 82 of the Act a distinction is made between the retirement pension and survivors' pensionary benefits of heirs of employees. The latter can be paid to the legal heirs

only after a retiree has died. Furthermore, according to Article 86, paragraph d, legal heirs include a permanent wife as long as she has not remarried. As a general rule the materialization of the derivative rights of the successors to survivors' pensionary benefits depends on the decease of the retiree, the real owner of those materialized rights. The law recognizes only a few exceptions according to which such pension payments could be made to the spouse and the children when the retiree is not deceased.

73. The Tribunal notes that according to the Civil Service Act the wife and the children of the retiree cannot have a better right in the retiree's pension than he himself enjoys. Their rights are derivative from the rights of the retiree and cannot be created or maintained separately from his status, unless there exists legislation specifically providing for an exception to this main rule. Therefore, if for any reason the rights of the retiree to a pension come to an end, the wife and children cannot obtain new or separate pension rights thereto unless such special rights have been established in the legislation. The existence of these rights in the present Case thus depends on the status of Hooshang Etezadi as an Iranian retired civil servant.

74. Hooshang Etezadi's pension was terminated on 25 August 1980 on the basis of the Legal Bill on Purging adopted by the Revolutionary Council, and a Dismissal Decree (No. 16/23082). The Tribunal notes that the decision to terminate Hooshang Etezadi's pension rights was reached before he became a naturalized U.S. citizen in June 1981 and that, therefore, he lost his rights to the pension solely as an Iranian national. In these circumstances the Tribunal concludes that it is not in a position to review internal decisions of the Iranian government. These questions are traditionally considered to belong to the domain of municipal law and are, therefore, in these circumstances, outside the competence of the Tribunal. However, the Tribunal notes that the Legal Bill on Purging includes a note stating that the Purging Committee may terminate the pension of the retiree if he is among the persons subject to purging.[9] Moreover, the same note also states that the person whose pension rights have been terminated is entitled to receive that portion of the pension which he has contributed from his salary during his employment.[10] However, the Claimant did not submit any evidence that her husband made any efforts to demand such a portion, and Hooshang Etezadi stated himself at the Hearing that he did not contact the appropriate governmental entities to request an explanation for the termination or to

---

[9] A similar provision has been included in Article 55 of the Law for Reconstructing the Manpower of the Ministries, State Agencies and Government-affiliated Institutions, enacted on 27 September 1981.

[10] The same right has been mentioned in Article 27 of the Law for Reconstructing the Manpower of the Ministries, State Agencies and Government-affiliated Institutions.

demand the monies that he considered to belong to him, when he noticed that his pension payments had been discontinued. As Hooshang Etezadi is not a Claimant in this Case the Tribunal cannot express its opinion as to whether he, in light of the existing Iranian legislation, would still be entitled to receive this particular portion of the pension. This issue will have to be decided by the competent Iranian authorities.[11] The Tribunal emphasizes that this right belongs solely to Hooshang Etezadi as a retiree and the real owner of these pension benefits.

75. Furthermore, the Tribunal notes that there is no evidence in the record that any partial pension payment was made to the Claimant by or on behalf of Iran; nor is there evidence of any agreement between the retiree and the employer which might have created independent rights for her. In addition to this, the rights which have not yet materialized, and which derive from the original legal relationship, follow the fate of the original materialized rights of the retiree. Consequently, when the statutory rights of the retiree have been terminated through the application of a special law, those rights which derive from his status also follow the fate of the original rights, and thus the Claimant's independent pension rights have not been established in this Case. The Tribunal further underlines in this context that according to the general principles of international law the creation and application of a municipal pension system belongs to the sovereign rights of the State concerned and cannot be affected by private contracts between a retiree and members of his family or by legislation in another State. Therefore, the Claimant's Claim is dismissed.

3. *Costs*

76. Both the Claimant and Iran have in their pleadings requested the Tribunal to award them the costs incurred in the proceedings in this Case.

77. In view of the circumstances of the Case, the Tribunal finds it reasonable that each Party shall bear its own costs of arbitration.

V. AWARD

78. For the foregoing reasons,

THE TRIBUNAL AWARDS AS FOLLOWS:

(a) The Claims for the alleged expropriation of a 50 per cent share of a plot of land in Karaj, Iran, of a 10 per cent interest in Shiraz Plastic

---

[11] *See, e.g.,* Article 11 of the Administrative Justice Tribunal Act, enacted on 24 January 1982 and issued in Official Gazette No. 10790 of 9 March 1982.

Products Corporation, and of the equity interest in a condominium in Tehran against the Government of the Islamic Republic of Iran are dismissed for lack of evidence.

(b) The Claim for a 50 per cent share of the terminated pension of the Claimant's husband, Hooshang Etezadi, as a retired employee of the Ministry of Foreign Affairs of Iran, against the Government of the Islamic Republic of Iran is dismissed.

(c) Each Party shall bear its own costs of arbitration.

Statement of Assadollah Noori

I concur in the present Award. However, I would like to point out that the Tribunal could and should have rejected the Claimant's claims at the earlier stages of the proceedings, for lack of jurisdiction. I am still of the opinion that the Tribunal does not have jurisdiction over the claims of Iranians with dual United States nationality. *See* my note appended to Partial Award No. 497-319-1 (15 November 1990), in *Hooshang and Catherine Etezadi* v. *The Government of the Islamic Republic of Iran, reprinted in* 25 IRAN-U.S. C.T.R. 264.

In addition, I wish, with due respect, to express my disagreement with the Tribunal's decision on the costs of arbitration (the Award, paras. 76, 77 and 78, c). I believe that the Tribunal should have granted Iran's request for legal fees and other costs, especially given that no reason or justification for apportioning the costs of arbitration can be found in this Case. The Claimant's husband, Hooshang Etezadi, was exclusively an Iranian national during the relevant period, and yet he initiated these proceedings against Iran even though he clearly had no standing to sue. The Claimant herself, in the guise of a dual Iran-United States national, has also persisted in pursuing these claims, which would belong to her husband and not to her even if they had a basis, and thereby caused Iran to sustain considerable costs and expenses, and to devote a part of its experts' limited time and manpower, in responding to these totally baseless claims. The Tribunal should therefore have obligated the Claimant to indemnify Iran for the costs and expenses incurred by it, in view of the special circumstances of this Case, Articles 38-40 of the Tribunal Rules, the settled practice of the Tribunal, and dictates of fairness and justice.

Apart from the fact that both law and equity demand it, requiring such claimants to redress the Government of Iran for its costs of arbitration would also have the salutary effect of reminding other Iranian claimants alleging to be United States nationals and seeking to pursue their inadmissible – and unfortunately, mostly spurious –claims by resorting to the vehicle of the unjust

Decision in Case No. A18, that they should not idly toy with the time and resources of the Iranian Government and the Tribunal, solely for the sake of their unlimited greed and avarice and their unwarranted obstinacy.

Dissenting Opinion of Richard M. Mosk[1]

I dissent from the award because I believe Claimant Catherine Etezadi, by virtue of her agreement with her husband and under applicable law, has a beneficial, and therefore enforceable, interest in certain assets that were held in her husband's name and that were wrongfully taken by Respondent, the Government of the Islamic Republic of Iran (hereinafter sometimes referred to as "Iran").

I agree with the majority that Claimant has not submitted sufficient evidence to establish a taking by Iran of real property or deposits for real property.

Based on the circumstances and Tribunal precedent, I conclude that Iran expropriated Shiraz Plastic Products Corporation ("Shiraz Plastics"), a private entity, in which the Etezadis had an interest. The evidence, however, makes this issue a close one. Because the question concerning Shiraz Plastics is so fact-intensive, and because there are a number of Tribunal decisions covering this issue, I do not believe it necessary to expound upon the point in great detail.

As I shall discuss, the Tribunal's decision regarding Mrs. Etezadi's rights in property, including the pension, is inconsistent with the modern and emerging view of the role and rights of the woman in the family and in society.

Procedures

The majority dwells unnecessarily on its decision to exclude some evidence submitted by Claimant after the deadline for rebuttal material. In view of the decision of the majority on the merits, none of this excluded evidence would have affected the result.

I believe that the decision to exclude this evidence was incorrect. There was no showing that the admission of the evidence was prejudicial to Respondent. Indeed, Respondent was able to reply to the evidence. Generally in judicial and arbitral proceedings, otherwise admissible and material evidence is not rejected on the basis of lack of timeliness unless there is such prejudice.

Throughout the course of this case, time limitations have not been enforced strictly. The Tribunal has granted Respondent numerous extensions that have

[1 Filed 23 March 1994.]

prolonged this case for a period exceeding a decade. Most of these extensions were granted over the objections of Claimant and without any showing of a need for such extensions. Thus, the Tribunal itself has not complied with Tribunal rules and internal guidelines concerning time limitations.

Under normal practice, rebuttal submissions should only rebut the other party's direct case. In this and many other cases, Respondent, in its rebuttal, submitted evidence that should and could have been included in its direct case. This has the effect of precluding claimants from having the opportunity to respond to, what is in effect, Respondent's principal and direct evidence and case, therefore causing prejudice to those claimants.

The Tribunal has precluded Claimant from submitting material late, even though there was no prejudice to Respondent, and despite the fact that the delayed submission was to overcome the handicap resulting from the Tribunal's failure to apply its own rules to Respondent.

Although the Iran-U.S. Claims Tribunal has many accomplishments and contributions to the development of international dispute resolution, the implementation of efficient procedures has not always been one of them. It appears that parties who have suffered the most from the inordinate delays and sometimes unequal and incorrect application of Tribunal rules have been individuals and claimants with smaller claims. Those who have helped in the operation of the United Nations Compensation Commission to deal with claims against Iraq —many of whom have had experience with the Iran U.S.-Claims Tribunal – recognized that individuals and small claimants have sometimes received inferior treatment here and therefore have taken steps to protect such parties in the newly established United Nations claims entity.

Undisputed or Established Facts

The following facts are either undisputed or established by the Tribunal's earlier award in this case, *Hooshang and Catherine Etezadi* v. *The Islamic Republic of Iran*, Award No. 497-319-1 (15 Nov. 1990), *reprinted in* 25 IRAN-U.S. C.T.R. 264.

Hooshang Etezadi, an Iranian by birth, joined the Ministry of Foreign Affairs of Iran in 1951. In order to do so, he relinquished his previously acquired United States citizenship. Such relinquishment of citizenship was a requirement only of United States law. *Id.* at para. 6, *reprinted in* 25 IRAN-U.S. C.T.R. at 266. In 1954, he was appointed as attaché to Iran's permanent delegation at the United Nations in New York.

Claimant, Catherine Etezadi, an American citizen by birth, married Hooshang Etezadi on 4 May 1955 in Maryland, but their first domicile was in New York. Mrs. Etezadi stated that upon their marriage they agreed that their interests in all assets acquired or possessed by them during their marriage would be owned by them equally and that they have reaffirmed this agreement continuously over the years, wherever they have resided. Mrs. Etezadi also stated, "[F]rom that time on we always had the understanding that everything we saved or invested in was always to be in both of our names."

Mr. Etezadi confirmed the agreement and declared that he and his wife were not only husband and wife, but "partners," and that "everything" they have owned since their marriage has been "jointly held." All of their investments came from assets accumulated through their combined income. Mrs. Etezadi worked and contributed to the marital estate. All of their assets in the United States were jointly held. For example, all bank accounts and mortgages in the United States were in their joint names. Other witnesses confirmed that the Etezadis considered all of their interests to be joint, no matter in what name title was held.

The Etezadis lived in New York until 1959, when they moved to Iran, where Mr. Etezadi continued to work in the Iranian Ministry of Foreign Affairs. In 1967, they returned to the United States, where Mr. Etezadi also worked for the Iranian Ministry of Foreign Affairs. In 1968, they purchased a home in California and there operated a motel. In 1970, the Etezadis returned to Iran, where they remained until 1974. In Iran, they maintained a joint bank account.

While in Iran, the Etezadis invested their joint monies derived from the sale of their California properties in Iranian real estate and in shares of stock in Shiraz Plastics, an Iranian entity. Because Mrs. Etezadi could not speak or read Persian and for convenience, some of these assets were held solely in Mr. Etezadi's name, but the Etezadis maintained their agreement that all such assets were jointly owned by them. This understanding was confirmed by a witness who held a power of attorney authorizing him to act regarding the Etezadis' Iranian assets.

During the years of his employment by the Iranian Ministry of Foreign Affairs, monies had been withheld from Mr. Etezadi's salary for pension rights, and those monies were allocated to a general government pension fund in Iran. In early 1974, Mr. Etezadi retired from the Iranian Ministry of Foreign Affairs, and he and his wife then moved to California, where they have been domiciled ever since. After his 22 years of Iranian Government service and his retirement, Mr. Etezadi's pension became payable in 1974, although by its terms it had "vested" in 1972. *See* Digest of Employment and Administrative Laws and Regulations, ch. 8, arts. 74-75 (as amended through 22 Sept. 1988) ("Iranian Retirement and Pension Law"). The pension monies were paid to Mr. Etezadi in California from 1974 to May of 1980 and went into the Etezadis' joint account in California. During the 1970's, on at least three occasions, Iran confirmed in writing the existence of the pension. The Etezadis stated they relied on this pension income for their maintenance.

The pension rights were for Mr. Etezadi's life, and upon his death or loss of certain rights, his family, including his wife, was entitled to pension payments.[2] There is no evidence that either Hooshang or Catherine Etezadi did anything that would under the terms of Iranian Retirement and Pension Law justify the termination of these vested pension rights. Nevertheless, after the Iranian Revolution, Iran discontinued the pension payments to Mr. Etezadi "by virtue of Order No. 16/2308 dated 25 August 1980 issued pursuant to the Legal Bill Purging Government Employees approved by the Revolutionary Council." Under this provision, a retired employee's pension can be terminated if, from the files and records, it is concluded that the retired employee collaborated with SAVAK or was unqualified or notorious for immorality or impropriety. *See* Act for Purging the Ministries and Universities and State Instrumentalities, Banks, Agencies and Companies, and for Bringing About a Favorable Environment Therein for the Growth of Revolutionary Institutions, art. 1 (dated 4 Sept. 1979) ("Legal Bill"). No ground was ever provided to Mr. Etezadi to justify termination of his pension.

Moreover, under the "Legal Bill," upon termination of his pension, Mr. Etezadi would be entitled to the return of monies he contributed to the pension. *Id.*, art. 1, note. There is no indication that he received an accounting of those contributed monies. There is no suggestion that the subject of such pension termination action – *i.e.*, of the "purging" – has any rights to a hearing or to contest the charges before those who do the "purging." According to Iran, such a former employee could appeal to the "Court of Administrative Justice," which reviews actions of government agencies.

Mr. Etezadi became an American citizen in June of 1981. As that was after the signing of the Algiers Accords, this Tribunal found him to be an exclusive Iranian national at the time of the claims and therefore ineligible to be a claimant at the Tribunal. *Hooshang and Catherine Etezadi, supra*, para. 13, *reprinted in* 25 IRAN-U.S. C.T.R. at 268-69. The Tribunal held, however, that Catherine Etezadi's dominant and effective nationality was that of the United States, and thus she was entitled to maintain her claims. *Id.* at para. 18, *reprinted in* 25 IRAN-U.S. C.T.R. at 271. These claims are for compensation

---

[2] According to the terms of the pension, even if a retired employee is "condemned to deprivation of civil rights," the spouse and children are still entitled to up to one-half of the retirement salary. Iranian Retirement and Pension Law, art. 92; *see also id.*, art. 82 ("Where a retired employee dies, four-fifths of the employee's retirement salary would be paid as pension salary to his or her legal heirs in accordance with the provisions of this law"). The only provision in the pension law disclosed to the Tribunal that would allow total termination of pension benefits – and one not applicable here – concerns the "renunciation of nationality." *Id.*, art. 97.

for the value of her one-half interest in the following: a plot of land in Iran, allegedly expropriated by the Government of Iran; an unreturned deposit in a condominium in Iran; a ten percent interest in an Iranian corporation, also allegedly expropriated by Iran; and the terminated pension, as determined by an actuary, or for the value of such a pension measured by the cost of replacement.

Applicable Law

The issue of choice-of-law with respect to marital rights in property normally arises in the context of death or divorce or, occasionally, in a claim by a creditor of the marital estate or of one of the spouses. This case is unusual in that the wife, with the husband's backing, is asserting certain beneficial rights in properties *vis-à-vis* a non-creditor third party. If there were a choice-of-law issue, the laws of several jurisdictions could be invoked.

At the time of marriage, the Etezadis were domiciled in New York; therefore, the law of New York could apply to any pre-marital or immediate post-marital agreements. *See Hague Convention on the Law Applicable to Matrimonial Property Regimes (1976)*, art. 4, in 25 Am. J. of Comp. Law 393, 395 (1977) (applicable law is that of "the State in which both spouses establish their first habitual residence after marriage"); 2 *Dicey and Morris on the Conflict of Laws* 1058-59 (L. Collins 11th ed. 1987) (Rule 154(2)) (husband's domicile upon marriage); *see also*, E. Scoles, Choice of Law in Family Transactions, 209 *Recueil des Cours* 9, 28-30 (1989), and authorities cited therein (discussing "immutability of marital rights").

The situs of the properties in issue are located in Iran, and thus Iran contends that Iranian law applies. *See* Civil Code of Iran, art. 966; *see also id.*, art. 963 ("If husband and wife are not nationals of the same country, their personal and financial relations with one another will be subject to the laws of the country of the husband").

California has been the marital domicile of the Etezadis since 1974. As such, its laws could be applied. *See* E. Scoles & P. Hay, *Conflict of Laws* § 14.4, at 468 (2d ed. 1992) ("In most instances, the state of dominant interest, as in other matters involving family and marital concerns, is the domicile of the parties").

As I shall discuss, the relevant laws of these jurisdictions that can be applied in this case are consistent. *See DIC of Delaware, et al. v. Tehran Redevelopment Corp., et al.*, Award No. 176-255-3, p. 17 (26 Apr. 1985), *reprinted in* 8 IRAN-U.S. C.T.R. 144, 156-57. The Tribunal is not restricted to applying the law of any specific place, for under Article V of the Claims Settlement Declaration, the Tribunal "shall decide all cases on the basis of respect for law, applying such choice-of-law rules and principles of commercial and international law as the

Tribunal determines to be applicable, taking into account relevant usages of the trade, contract provisions and changed circumstances."

There is not, however, a true conflict of laws, for under the law of the marital domicile at the relevant times – California – Mrs. Etezadi effectively obtained a one-half interest in the entire marital estate, including a beneficial interest in any property solely in the name of Mr. Etezadi. Under Tribunal jurisprudence, such beneficial interests are enforceable. *See infra.*

Mrs. Etezadi's Interest

Transmutation

The uncontradicted evidence establishes that the Etezadis had an agreement from the inception of their marriage, reaffirmed it throughout their marriage, and confirmed it before this Tribunal. At the time of the claim and since 1974, California has been, and now is, the marital domicile of the Etezadis. California is a community property state, *i.e.*, its law is based on the "general theory . . . that the husband and wife form a sort of partnership, and that property acquired during the marriage by the labor or skill of either belongs to both." 11 B. Witkin, *Summary of California Law, Community Property* § 1, at 374 (9th ed. 1990).

California law in effect prior to and in 1981 permitted husbands and wives by contract to agree *orally* that any and all property – including property acquired after the marriage – shall be community property, *i.e.*, to transmute the character of the property. *Id.* § 125, at 522-23.[3] This law even applied to real property and other property that might otherwise require a writing for a transfer. *Id.* As the California Supreme Court declared in *Beam v. Bank of America*, 6 Cal.3d 12, 25 (1971):

> We recognize, of course, that a husband or wife may orally transmute separate property into community property, and, even in the absence of an explicit agreement, written or oral, a court may find a transmutation of property if the circumstances clearly demonstrate that one spouse intended to effect a change in the status of his separate property. (Citations omitted.)

California permitted such an agreement to be shown by the testimony of the wife or the husband. *Id.* Moreover, the transmutation could "be shown by the very nature of the transaction or appear from the surrounding circumstances." *Allen v. Samuels*, 204 Cal.App.2d 710, 715 (1962).

---

[3] The law was changed effective 1985, *i.e.*, after this claim arose and was asserted. Cal. Civil Code § 5110.730. As of 1 January 1994, many of these sections appear in the California Family Code.

When summarizing the law of California during the relevant period at greater length, a California court, in *Estate of Sears*, 182 Cal.App.2d 525, 529-30 (1960), explained:

> There are certain principles of law, now so thoroughly established that we need not fear that we are skating on thin ice if we venture upon them. In *Woods* v. *Security-First Nat. Bank* (1956), 46 Cal.2d 697, 701, it is stated, supported by a number of citations: "It is settled that the separate property of husband or wife may be converted into community property or *vice versa* at any time by oral agreement between the spouses." The change over may be made although the title to the property may remain of record in joint tenancy (*Socol* v. *King* (1950), 36 Cal.2d 342, 345, and cases cited), or, in the case of an automobile, in the name of one or other of the spouses. (*Estate of Raphael* (1953), 115 Cal.App.2d 525, 534.) Nor is it necessary, to convert separate property into community property, that the magic words "community property" be used. As revealed in *Kenney* v. *Kenney* (1934), 220 Cal. 134, 136, it was sufficient that the parties had orally agreed ". . . that all property then owned by them or subsequently acquired was to belong to them equally or, as respondent put it, 'fifty-fifty.'" Similarly, in *Estate of Raphael* (1949), 91 Cal.App.2d 931, 936-937, the husband's statement as related by his wife that ". . . everything he had was mine, and everything I had was his; that we were partners in everything, and everything was fifty-fifty" was sufficient to alter the status of their property. *See further Estate of Raphael*, supra, 115 Cal.App.2d 525. An even broader declaration appears in *Long* v. *Long* (1948), 88 Cal.App.2d 544, 549: "It is not essential to show an express oral agreement, but the status of the property may be shown 'by the very nature of the transaction or appear from the surrounding circumstances.' (*Marvin* v. *Marvin*, 46 Cal.App.2d 551, 556.)" . . .
>
> In several of the cases cited it has been said that the status of property could be changed to that of community property by "an executed oral contract." We know of none that requires that the agreement be executed, and we read in *Estate of Raphael*, supra, 91 Cal.App.2d 931, 939: "The object of the oral agreement of transmutation was fully performed when the agreement was made for it immediately transmuted and converted the separate property of each spouse into community property, and nothing further remained to be done." (Unofficial citations omitted.)[4]

The Etezadis' conduct and agreement specifically conformed to this precedent. Thus, under California law – the law of their marital domicile – *all* of their property and investments were transmuted to community property. It does not matter whether the agreement between the Etezadis was enforceable under New York law or Iranian law because the Etezadis effectively transmuted all of their property – to the extent it was not already community

---

[4] Under California law, even if the agreement had to be "executed," this only means that "after the oral agreement, the acts or declarations of the parties must confirm and be consistent with the change in character of the property." 11 B. Witkin, *supra*, § 125, at 523.

property – to community property under the law applicable at the time. It is just as if there were an effective assignment of property rights.

Commingling

In addition, any properties acquired by the Etezadis prior to moving to California in 1968 and again in 1974 were commingled (so as not to be traceable) with funds accumulated by them while their marital domicile was in California. Thus, all such properties that might not already be considered community property became community property. 11 B. Witkin, *supra*, § 82, at 475. That property retained its community property character even though later invested in Iran, for newly acquired property assumes the status of that which it replaces. R. Leflar, L. McDougal & R. Felix, *American Conflicts Law* § 233, at 645 (4th ed. 1986); E. Scoles & P. Hay, *supra*, § 14.6, at 472.

Recognition of Community Property

Generally, property of California domiciliaries that would, if in California, be considered community property, is treated by California as community property even if it is located outside of California. Cal. Civil Code § 5110; *Rozan* v. *Rozan*, 49 Cal.2d 322, 327-28 (1957); *Ford* v. *Ford*, 276 Cal.App.2d 9, 11 (1969). Although California law cannot *directly* determine title to all properties – *e.g.*, real property in another jurisdiction – Mrs. Etezadi's interests should be recognized, especially under Tribunal jurisprudence regarding beneficial interests, as discussed *infra*.

The consequence of the transmutation and the commingling doctrines under California law is clear: "The respective interests of the husband and wife in community property during continuance of the marriage relation are present, existing and equal interests." Cal. Civil Code § 5105. By virtue of the law where Mr. and Mrs. Etezadi have been domiciled, Mrs. Etezadi has a one-half interest in all of the marital assets, wherever they are located.

Effectiveness of the Marital Agreement Under Other Law

As noted, it is not necessary to determine the validity or effect of the agreement between the Etezadis under any other law because Mrs. Etezadi obtained her interest by operation of California law. Nevertheless, the laws of other relevant jurisdictions are not inconsistent with this result.

In the absence of an agreement, there could be controversy over which law to apply to "movables" and "immovables" in connection with marital property. *See* J.H.C. Morris, *The Conflict of Laws* 410-13 (3d ed. 1984); E. Scoles & P. Hay, *supra*, §§ 14.5-14.10, at 470-81. It is widely recognized, however, that when there is an agreement between the husband and wife, it governs their respective rights. J.H.C. Morris, *supra*, at 413; E. Scoles & P. Hay, *supra*,

§ 14.15, at 489-91. "There seems no doubt but [t]hat the contract may and normally would control the marital property regime between the parties." *Id.* § 14.15, at 491.[5]

As long ago as the 13th century in Spain, in *Las Siete Partidas* 941-52 (S. Scott trans. 1931) (quoted in Juenger, *Marital Property and the Conflict of Laws: A Tale of Two Countries,* 81 Colum. L. Rev. 1061, 1065 (1981)), it was stated:

> It happens frequently that, when a husband and wife marry, they agree in what way they may hold the property which they gained together; and, after they are married, they go to dwell in some other country, where a custom, opposed to said agreement or contract which they have entered into, is practiced. . . . We decree that the contract which they made with one another shall be valid in the way which they agree upon, before or at the time when they married, and shall not be interfered with, by any contrary custom existing in the country where they went to reside.

More recently, in 2 *Dicey and Morris on the Conflict of Laws, supra,* at 1053 (Rule 153), it is stated:

> Where there is a marriage contract or settlement, the terms of the contract or settlement govern the rights of husband and wife in respect of all property within its terms which are then possessed or are afterwards acquired, notwithstanding any subsequent change of domicile.

Another authority, E. Scoles, *supra,* at 30, has noted that

> unless a State pursues the view of immutability without exception, it would seem that fully informed and consenting parties should be permitted by agreement to modify their marital property régime to meet the changing circumstances of life. Fortunately, in more and more States, married couples are being permitted to adjust their property interests after marriage as well as before. This reduces conflicts issues in most instances. (Footnotes omitted.)

American legal principles are generally in accord with these authorities, *see* 2 *Restatement (Second) of Conflict of Laws* § 258 comment d (1971); 41 *Am. Jur. 2d, Husband and Wife* § 316, at 257-58 (1968), as are recent international authorities. *See Hague Convention on the Law Applicable to Matrimonial Property Regimes (1976),* art. 3, in 25 Am. J. Comp. Law 393, 394 (1977).

Marital agreements are recognized in Iran. Dr. Hussein Mehrpour, one of Iran's legal advisors on Iranian law, in his opinion submitted to the Tribunal, asserted, in effect, that there can be an enforceable marriage contract in Iran. He declared:

---

[5] Although not universally accepted, it has been stated that the "essential validity, interpretation and effect of the marriage contract or settlement are governed by its proper law. The search for the proper law of a marriage contract or settlement is generally similar to the search for the proper law of an ordinary commercial contract." J.H.C. Morris, *supra,* at 414.

Pursuant to the Judicial High Council's approval in 1362 (1983), a circular was issued by the State Organization for Registration of Deeds to Marriage and Divorce Registries requiring them to inform the spouses, *at the time of concluding the marriage contract*, [of] certain conditions that they could stipulate under the marriage contract. If they accepted those conditions, they would be binding. These conditions mostly bind and commit the husband. One of those proposed conditions is that should the husband divorce his wife without any reason and without any fault on part of the wife, he would be required to transfer to his wife, gratis, half of the assets acquired by him during the matrimony, at the court order. This condition is brought to the attention of husband and wife at the time of con[cl]usion of [the] marriage contract. If the husband accepts it, it creates an obligation for him under the marriage contract. If he does not accept [t]his condition, the marriage contract may be concluded without including this condition, and no obligation in that respect would attach to the husband. If this condition is accepted and included in the marriage contract, should the husband divorce the wife subsequently without any fault on her part, half of the property acquired by the husband during the matrimonial ties would be transferred to the wife at the court's order. In any event, there are no provisions of law in this respect. The Judicial High Council's approval mentioned in the marriage deeds is meant only to *remind* the spouses that *they may stipulate such conditions, including the above condition, in the marriage contract. And should they accept such conditions at their own free will, they could be bound to perform it.* (Emphasis added.)

That any pre-nuptial or post-nuptial agreement could be considered oral should not matter as to its applicability in this proceeding. Iran did not raise the lack of a writing as a defense.[6] Normally the failure to assert such a defense is a waiver of it. The fact that in this proceeding both of the parties to the agreement acknowledged the agreement should preclude the application of any Statute of Frauds. Iran has not pointed to any specific statute that requires a writing for this type of agreement, and the only relevant Statute of Frauds provisions do not seem applicable. Thus, there is no indication that the agreement between the Etezadis was in consideration of marriage; the agreement is not being used in a matrimonial action; and because of the possibility of death or divorce, the agreement could have been performed within one year or, because of the possibility of divorce, within the lifetime of the parties. *See generally* 48 *N.Y. Jur. 2d, Domestic Relations* § 1251, at 60 (1985); 61 *N.Y. Jur. 2d, Statute of Frauds* § 21, at 50-51 (1987); § 40, at 95-97; § 87 at 165; 1 B. Witkin, *Summary of California Law, Contracts* § 284, at 275; § 290, at 279; § 315, at 297 (9th ed. 1987); 1 *Restatement (Second) of Contracts* § 124 comment b; § 130 comment a (1981); *see also* M. Sabi, *The Commercial Code of Iran*, in IV *Digest of Commercial Laws of the World* 11 (1982) ("Generally speaking a contract need not be reduced to a writing").

---

[6] Iran argued that there was no documentary evidence concerning the agreement, but did not assert that any such agreement was unenforceable by virtue of a legal requirement for a writing.

Even if the agreement had to be in writing, in view of the fact that the parties had relied upon it, and it has continued to be performed, it should be enforced under the part performance theory. *See* 45 *N.Y. Jur. 2d, Domestic Relations* § 141, at 461-62 (1985) (oral antenuptial agreements "became enforceable where they have been partially performed"); 1 *Restatement (Second) of Contracts, supra,* § 124 comment d; 1 B. Witkin, *supra,* §§ 312-28, at 298-309. Indeed, the Tribunal itself has recognized such a principle. *DIC of Delaware, supra,* at p. 28, *reprinted in* 8 IRAN-U.S. C.T.R. at 161.

Ordinarily, a Statute of Frauds can be invoked only by a party to the agreement or a transferee or successor to the agreement. *See* 1 B. Witkin, *supra,* § 267, at 262; 61 *N.Y. Jur. 2d, supra,* § 233, at 363; 3 S. Williston, *A Treatise on the Law of Contracts* § 530, at 746-48 (W. Jaeger 3d ed. 1960); 2 A. Corbin, *Corbin on Contracts* § 289, at 54 (1950); 1 *Restatement (Second) of Contracts, supra,* § 144 comment d ("Only parties to a contract and their transferees and successors can take advantage of the Statute of Frauds. As against others the unenforceable contract creates the same rights, powers, privileges and immunities as if it were enforceable").[7] Although in some instances it has been said that one party cannot invoke an invalid oral contract against a third party, such a concept generally applies only when one party sues a third party for inducing a breach of the oral contract. Here both parties to the contract have affirmed it. The claims against Iran are not based on an alleged breach of the oral agreement between the Etezadis; rather, the agreement only serves to establish who has certain property interests that were affected by Iran's acts. There is no good reason why Iran, as a third party, should be able to invoke in this case a Statute of Frauds or other requirement for a writing.

It is generally recognized that the Statute of Frauds does not invalidate a contract, but rather renders the contract voidable at the election of the party to the contract against whom enforcement is sought. 61 *N.Y. Jur. 2d, supra,* § 224, at 352-53; 1 B. Witkin, *supra,* § 263, at 259-60. In Iran, to the extent there was any requirement for a writing, it was evidentiary only. *See* Civil Code of Iran, art. 1310 (repealed in 1982). This Tribunal has suggested that "each forum applies its own procedural and evidentiary rules to the disputes before it, and it is arguable that the type of evidence admissible to establish a contract is a procedural or evidentiary matter." *DIC of Delaware, supra,* at p. 23, *reprinted in* 8 IRAN-U.S. C.T.R. at 161. The Tribunal received and admitted evidence of the oral agreement between the Etezadis. The Tribunal was correct in doing so. *See* 1 *Restatement (Second) of Contracts, supra,* § 143 ("The Statute of

---

[7] An exception sometimes applied to post-nuptial agreements involves the rights of creditors, *see* 2 A.Corbin, *supra,* § 291, at 60-62, and thus would not apply here.

Frauds does not make an unenforceable contract inadmissible in evidence for any purpose other than its enforcement in violation of the Statute").

It has been said that "[t]he commentators almost unanimously urge that considerations of policy indicate a restricted application of the statute of frauds, if not its total abolition." *Sunset-Sternau Food Co. v. Bonzi*, 60 Cal.2d 834, 838 n.3 (1964) (Tobriner, J.). It has been largely repealed in England. In France the application of the doctrine of *commencement de preuve* has eroded various requirements of a writing. The requirement of a writing to prove a contract is generally declining in significance. II K. Zweigert and H. Kötz, *An Introduction to Comparative Law* 59-60 (2d ed. 1987). Even "American courts have given restrictive interpretations to statute-of-fraud provisions." A. von Mehren & J. Gordley, *The Civil Law System* 935 (1977).

For these many reasons, even if the Tribunal were to ignore the rights obtained by Claimant under California law, the agreement between the Etezadis should be given effect so as to confirm Mrs. Etezadi's rights in the marital property.

Beneficial Interest

The fact that property may be in the name of only one of the spouses does not *per se* eliminate the other spouse's interest. As Professor Scoles stated in his lecture to The Hague Academy of International Law:

> Frequently, either incident to a move of the family home from a marital [community] property State to a separate property State or simply incident to convenient investment or business purposes, assets may be moved from a marital property State to a separate property State and placed in the individual name of one spouse. This may be done in good faith and with full consent of both spouses. Even so, the presumption is most likely to be that no gift of the marital interest in the asset is intended by the non-title-holding spouse. In other words, any interspousal gift of marital property must be proven by clear and convincing evidence. Consequently, absent evidence showing a gift by one spouse to the other, taking title in the name of one spouse, even when done in an individual property State, does not destroy the previously existing rights of the parties under the matrimonial régime.

E. Scoles, *supra*, at 36-37.

Iran contends it would recognize only an interest reflected by legal title. The Tribunal, however, has recognized the beneficial interest of a claimant in property in Iran in which legal title was in another. In *International Technical Products Corp., et al. v. The Islamic Republic of Iran, et al.*, Award No. 196-302-3, pp. 38-39 and n.19 (24 Oct. 1985), *reprinted in* 9 IRAN-U.S. C.T.R. 206, 232-33 and n.32, Bank Tejarat argued that "under Iranian law, the real owner of [a] building is the one who holds the title deed and that the title deed to the building in question was held by [an Iranian private joint stock company], not Claimants." The Tribunal concluded, however, that the nominal owner was beneficially owned by the claimants, who could bring their own claim under Article VII(2) of the Claims Settlement Declaration. "Bank Tejarat's argument regarding ownership of the building under Iranian law simply is irrelevant to the jurisdictional considerations dictated by the Claims Settlement Declaration." *See also Zaman Azar Nourafchan, et al. v. The Islamic Republic of Iran*, Award No. 550-412/415-3, para. 50 (19 Oct. 1993) (when claimant obtains merely a claim to land, instead of title, "interference with such a claim may constitute a proper cause of action before this Tribunal").

In *James M. Saghi v. The Islamic Republic of Iran*, Award No. 544-298-2, paras. 18-26 (22 Jan. 1993), this Tribunal recently set forth the precedent providing for the protection of beneficial ownership interests and concluded as follows:

> 24. The Tribunal's concern for beneficial interests flows naturally from the terms of the Algiers Accords, in particular, General Principle B which states the purpose of both Parties "to terminate all litigation as between the government of each party and the nationals of the other, and to bring about the settlement and termination of all such claims through binding arbitration." Articles II, paragraph 1, and VII, paragraphs 1 and 2, of the CSD [Claims Settlement Declaration] give the Tribunal jurisdiction over claims arising out of debts, contracts, expropriations or other measures affecting property rights and define the terms "national" and "claims of nationals" by reference to persons who hold "ownership interests," whether directly or indirectly. The evident purpose of these claims settlement arrangements could not be fully implemented unless the Tribunal's jurisdiction were broad enough to permit the beneficial owners of affected property interests to present their claims and have them decided on their merits by the Tribunal.

> 25. The Respondent has argued that Article 40 of the Commercial Code of Iran bars the alleged beneficial ownership. However, the issue here is not the validity *vel non* under Iranian law of beneficial ownership interests vis-à-vis the company or third parties. Rather, it is whether the Government of Iran is responsible, under international law, to beneficial owners for "expropriations and other measures affecting property rights." (Footnote omitted.)

> 26. The Tribunal's awards have recognized that beneficial ownership is both a method of exercising control over property and a compensable property interest in its own right. . . . The Tribunal concludes that the Claimants are entitled to claim compensation for the deprivation of their beneficial ownership interests. . . .

Iranian law would recognize the marital agreement. That it might not recognize the beneficial ownership in property located in Iran in the name of another is irrelevant because this Tribunal has determined that Iran agreed under the Algiers Accords that such rights are enforceable here.

Real Property and Deposit

I agree with the majority that Claimant has not been able to supply sufficient evidence to establish that the plot of land was expropriated by Iran.[8] Although Mr. and Mrs. Etezadi are entitled to the deposits on the condominium, the majority properly concludes that the evidence is not sufficient to show that the obligor is Iran or an entity controlled by Iran.

Shiraz Plastics

Whether Shiraz Plastics was expropriated is a closer question. Tribunal decisions on taking of a business are varied and have depended on the facts. The replacement of the owner's management or directors with representatives appointed by Iran generally has been a conclusive factor resulting in a holding of an expropriation as of the time when the former managers or directors were no longer able to participate in the management of the enterprise. *See Starrett Housing Corp., et al. v. The Islamic Republic of Iran, et al.*, Award No. ITL 32-24-1, pp. 51-52 (19 Dec. 1983), *reprinted in* 4 IRAN-U.S. C.T.R. 122, 155-56; *Tippetts, Abbett, McCarthy, Stratton v. TAMS-AFFA Consulting Engineers of Iran, et al.*, Award No. 141-7-2, pp. 8-12 (29 June 1984), *reprinted in* 6 IRAN-U.S. C.T.R. 219, 224-26; *Phelps Dodge Corp., et al. v. The Islamic Republic of Iran*, Award No. 217-99-2, paras. 21-23 (19 Mar. 1986), *reprinted in* 10 IRAN-U.S. C.T.R. 121, 129-131; *Thomas Earl Payne v. The Islamic Republic of Iran*, Award No. 245-335-2, paras. 20-24 (8 Aug. 1986), *reprinted in* 12 IRAN-U.S. C.T.R. 3, 9-11; *Sedco, Inc., et al. v. National Iranian Oil Co., et al.*, Award No. ITL 55-129-3, pp. 39-43 (28 Oct. 1986), *reprinted in* 9 IRAN-U.S. C.T.R. 248, 276-79. In some cases, however, the appointment of such managers has not resulted in a decision that there was a taking. *Otis Elevator Co. v. The Islamic Republic of Iran, et al.*, Award No. 304-284-2, para. 40 (29 Apr. 1987), *reprinted in* 14 IRAN-U.S. C.T.R. 283, 297; *Motorola Inc. v. Iranian National Airlines Corp., et al.*, Award No. 373-481-3, para. 59 (28 June 1988), *reprinted in* 19 IRAN-U.S. C.T.R. 73, 85-86. In still other decisions the Tribunal has found that there was not sufficient evidence to conclude that a governmental manager was appointed during the period necessary for Tribunal jurisdiction. *See, e.g., Vernie Rodney Pointon, et al. v. The Islamic Republic of Iran*, Award No. 516-322-1, paras. 34-35 (23 July 1991), *reprinted in* 27 IRAN-U.S. C.T.R. 49, 60-61.

Mrs. Etezadi's argument that Shiraz Plastics was expropriated is supported primarily by inference from a number of suggestive facts. Iran took inconsistent positions in its pleadings and failed to produce evidence to which it

---

[8] Although one can be sympathetic to Mrs. Etezadi's purported difficulty in obtaining evidence in Iran, she neglected to request Tribunal assistance in the production of evidence. *See* Tribunal Rules, art. 24(3).

presumably had access. *See* Concurring Opinion of Richard M. Mosk, *Ultrasystems, Inc. v. The Islamic Republic of Iran, et al.*, Award No. 27-84-3, p. 2 (4 Mar. 1983), *reprinted in* 2 IRAN-U.S. C.T.R. 114, 115 (access to and failure to produce relevant evidence authorizes drawing of adverse inference); *R.N. Pomeroy, et al. v. The Islamic Republic of Iran*, Award No. 50-40-3, p. 25 (8 June 1983), *reprinted in* 2 IRAN-U.S. C.T.R. 372, 384 (Tribunal to draw inferences from gaps in evidence and pleadings). Moreover, one of Iran's witnesses testified at the Hearing that a governmental manager had been appointed to run the company in September of 1980.

Determining whether sufficient evidence supports Mrs. Etezadi's claim as to Shiraz Plastics should be based on a detailed analysis of the facts in light of inferences to be drawn from the evidence before the Tribunal. I do not believe the majority has sufficiently undertaken such an analysis; nevertheless, further discourse here on these facts regarding the expropriation of Shiraz Plastics would not add to Tribunal or international jurisprudence. The choice not to engage in such a discussion should not be viewed as acquiescence in the majority's reasoning, factual statements or conclusion on this issue. Based on the record, Mrs. Etezadi is entitled to her share of the 10 percent interest in Shiraz Plastics.

Pension

The majority declares that the pensioner was Mr. Etezadi, and when Iran took away those pension rights for whatever reason, Mrs. Etezadi had no remaining rights in the pension. As I shall discuss, however, the fact remains that Iran took "measures affecting property rights" belonging to Mrs. Etezadi, and it therefore is required to compensate her. *See* Claims Settlement Declaration, Art. II(1).

As noted above, by contract the Etezadis agreed that all of their property was, in effect, community property. This agreement was reaffirmed when they moved back to California in 1974. Thus, at that time any separate property was transmuted to community property. Also, as discussed above, there were other grounds for treating their assets as community property. The California Supreme Court has stated that it has "always recognized that the community owns all pension rights attributable to employment during the marriage." *In re Marriage of Brown*, 15 Cal.3d 838, 844 (1976). Both vested and non-vested pension rights are community property. *Id.* at 844-45.

The California Supreme Court explained, *id.* at 845:

> Although some jurisdictions classify retirement pensions as gratuities, it has long been settled that under California law such benefits "do not derive from the beneficence of the employer, but are properly part of the consideration earned by

the employee." (*In re Marriage of Fithian* (1974) 10 Cal.3d 592, 596.) Since pension benefits represent a form of deferred compensation for services rendered (*In re Marriage of Jones* (1975) 13 Cal.3d 457, 461), the employee's right to such benefits is a contractual right, derived from the terms of the employment contract. Since a contractual right is not an expectancy but a chose in action, a form of property (*see* Civ. Code, § 953; *Everts v. Will S. Fawcett Co.* (1937) 24 Cal.App.2d 213, 215), we held in *Dryden v. Board of Pension Commrs.* (1936) 6 Cal.2d 575, 579, that an employee acquires a property right to pension benefits when he enters upon the performance of his employment contract. (Unofficial citations omitted.)[9]

This reasoning is widely recognized, for "[s]ince that decision, both community property and common-law property states have adopted the *Brown* reasoning." H. Foster, D. Freed and J. Brandes, *Law and the Family New York* § 17:1, at 686 (2d ed. 1986) (footnotes omitted). As one authority wrote:

> Pension (and retirement rights) are viewed as deferred compensation which will have community or separate character depending upon marital status during the period in which they accrued. The deferred compensation idea is readily applicable to pension payments dependent upon the accumulation of contributions to a pension fund of a percentage of an employee's salary either by the employer or by the employee through withholding from the salary, or by both, plus the earnings of those contributions in the fund.

W.S. McClanahan, *Community Property in the United States* § 6:21, at 365 (1982).[10]

There is no reason why Mr. Etezadi could not assign the proceeds of his pension – as any other asset – to another person who would then have rights in it. "Except where prohibited by statute, a pension granted for past services may be assigned." 70 *Corpus Juris Secundum, Pensions* § 5, at 127 (1987) (footnotes omitted).[11] Neither the majority nor Iran has pointed to any provision of law to the contrary. Thus, either by virtue of law or as an assignee, Mrs. Etezadi has enforceable rights before this Tribunal as a beneficial owner of the required pension payments. *See James M. Saghi, supra,* at paras. 24-26.

Mr. Etezadi had a vested and matured interest in the pension, *i.e.*, "a nonforfeitable right to immediate payment." W.S. McClanahan, *supra,* § 6:21,

---

[9] Pre-marital employment would reduce the community in the pension. *See* 11 B. Witkin, *supra,* § 41, at 420-22; J. Stein & J. Zuckerman, *California Community Property* § 2.45, at 2-75 (1993). Here the transmutation makes such an allocation unnecessary.

[10] The issue raised by Iran concerning federal preemption of state laws in the United States is not relevant, for the pension in question is not covered by the Federal Employee Retirement Income Security Act of 1974, Title 29 U.S.C. §§ 1001-1461 ("ERISA"), or any other law related to military pensions. Moreover, federal preemption is based on the Supremacy Clause of the United States Constitution, Article VI, and has no relevance to any choice-of-law or other issue addressed here.

[11] In order to qualify for certain tax and debtor rights in the United States, a pension may not be assignable under ERISA, but that law does not apply here.

at 366. The Iranian Retirement and Pension Law provided to the Tribunal appears to make the government obligations mandatory, with certain exceptions discussed above. *See* n.1, *supra*. There is no indication that under Iranian law the Government of Iran could terminate all pension rights at will. Here, the pension was offered by Iran as an employer. It was accepted by the employee by remaining in the employment and contributing to the pension fund. The pension is, in effect, deferred compensation. Accordingly, the pension appears to be a contractual obligation of Iran and thus not terminable at will. That a pension should be so regarded is indicated by Professor O'Connell's work on international law, in which he noted that when there is a change in sovereignty in the administration of a territory, the successor, in order to "satisfy the equities," must provide "for payment of pensions and superannuation. . . . [I]t may be suggested that the fate of pensions generally is that of debts generally." 1 D.P. O'Connell, *International Law* 391 (1970). Even if the pension were not considered a contractual obligation, Iran should not be able arbitrarily and unilaterally to deprive a former employee of all of the pension benefits after they have been earned. Surely under these circumstances, the pensioner has been denied basic rights.

Iran claims that a renunciation of Iranian citizenship causes a forfeiture of the pension. *See* Iranian Retirement and Pension Law, art. 97. Mr. Etezadi, however, has never renounced his Iranian citizenship.[12] Moreover, when the pension was terminated, Mr. Etezadi was not then even a dual national. Clearly, renunciation of citizenship was not the reason for terminating his pension. For a number of years after his retirement, Iran paid and confirmed the pension. There was no indication that Mr. Etezadi, who had left his government position years earlier, had committed any offense. No legitimate or rational reason has been provided for the termination of this vested pension. The advent of a new government does not provide justification for termination of pension rights any more than it would for the termination of any other contract or property rights. Simply passing a law authorizing the termination of vested pensions cannot validate the action. *See INA Corp.* v. *The Islamic Republic of Iran*, Award No. 184-161-1, pp. 7-8 (12 Aug. 1985), *reprinted in* 8 IRAN-U.S. C.T.R. 373, 378 (lawful nationalization still imposes obligation

---

[12] In his Concurring Opinion in *James M. Saghi, supra,* Judge Aldrich notes: "While abandonment of Iranian nationality is not, in theory, impossible under Iranian law for persons who are more than 24 years old, it requires the consent of the Iranian Council of Ministers, involves restrictions upon visits to Iran and the ownership of real property in Iran, and evidently rarely occurs in practice. *See* Article 976 of the Iranian Civil Code." *See also* Concurring Opinion of Richard M. Mosk, *Case No. A/18,* Decision No. DEC 32-A18-FT, p. 7 n.7 (6 Apr. 1984), *reprinted in* 5 IRAN-U.S. C.T.R. 269, 272 n.1. A change, if any, in Mr. Etezadi's status after 19 January 1981 would not affect the claim. *See Gruen Associates, Inc.* v. *Iran Housing Co., et al.,* Award No. 61-188-2, p. 12 (27 July 1983), *reprinted in* 3 IRAN-U.S. C.T.R. 97, 103.

to pay compensation); *Sedco, Inc. v. National Iranian Oil Co., et al.*, Award No. 309-129-3, para. 30 (2 July 1987), *reprinted in* 15 IRAN-U.S. C.T.R. 23, 34 (claimant entitled to "full value of its expropriated interest . . . regardless of whether or not the expropriation was otherwise lawful"); *see also infra*.

Although for purposes of Tribunal jurisdiction Mr. Etezadi was a national solely of Iran, and thus the Tribunal cannot decide his claim regarding the pension, the Tribunal does have jurisdiction over Mrs. Etezadi's claim to her interest in the pension and proceeds thereof. She not only has a beneficial interest in the pension by virtue of her agreement with Mr. Etezadi and by law, she also has an existing, contingent interest in the pension – *i.e.*, a right as a spouse to payments upon Mr. Etezadi's death or loss of civil rights. *See* n. 1, *supra*. Although for some purposes this interest might be considered as a mere expectancy rather than as a legally enforceable right, it may still be viewed as a property right that has a present value, which value can be determined by an actuary. *See In re Marriage of Shattuck*, 134 Cal.App.3d 683 (1982). The conclusion is inescapable that the termination of the pension was wrongful. Thus, when Iran terminated the pension, it wrongfully took Mrs. Etezadi's rights and interests in that pension.

It is true that if a husband forfeits his pension rights under the law, his wife's rights in the pension necessarily disappear regardless of any agreement between them and regardless of any contingent rights of the wife. In such an instance, the husband's acts or omissions are as a "partner" in the marriage and therefore affect the marital property. But here, it was Iran – a third party – that committed a wrongful act damaging Claimant's property rights. As a result, Iran is responsible to her under the Algiers Accords. That her right may be derivative does not make it any less a property right subject to compensation under the terms of the Algiers Accords.

Iran has also argued that Mr. Etezadi (or perhaps Mrs. Etezadi) should have pursued legal remedies in Iran, *i.e.*, they should have exhausted local or administrative remedies as a condition precedent to the right to bring a claim here. Tribunal decisions, however, have held that such exhaustion of local remedies is not a prerequisite for recovery at this Tribunal. *See, e.g., American Int'l Group, Inc., et al. v. The Islamic Republic of Iran, et al.*, Award No. 93-2-3, p. 9 (19 Dec. 1983), *reprinted in* 4 IRAN-U.S. C.T.R. 96, 101-02; *Amoco Iran Oil Co. v. The Islamic Republic of Iran, et al.*, Award No. ITL 12-55-2, pp. 3-4 (30 Dec. 1982), *reprinted in* 1 IRAN-U.S. C.T.R. 493, 495; *Rexnord Inc. v. The Islamic Republic of Iran, et al.*, Award No. 21-132-3, pp. 8-9 (10 Jan. 1983), *reprinted in* 2 IRAN-U.S. C.T.R. 6, 10; *Amoco Int'l Finance Corp. v. The Islamic Republic of Iran*, Award No. 310-56-3, para. 21 (14 July 1987), *reprinted in* 15 IRAN-U.S. C.T.R. 189, 197. These Tribunal decisions confirm the generally accepted principle that when a State agrees to arbitrate, the other party need not exhaust any administrative remedy. *See Applicability of the Obligation to Arbitrate under Section 21 of the United Nations Headquarters Agreement of 26 June 1947*, 1988 I.C.J. Reports 12 (1988); Schwebel, *Arbitration and the Exhaustion of Local Remedies Revisited*, 23 The International Lawyer 951, 952-55 (1989). Moreover, even though Mrs. Etezadi has her own rights, Iran has presented no evidence that she had an Iranian administrative remedy.

The majority suggests that an internal decision of the Iranian Government concerning a pension of an Iranian citizen is governed by municipal law and therefore is immune from scrutiny under international law and by this Tribunal. The majority's reference to "general principles of international law" to justify its conclusion lacks any supporting authority.

Paragraph 14 of the General Declaration specifically provides that claims are not barred by the act of state doctrine. This case is no different than one involving any other measure directed at an Iranian national that gives rise to a claim beneficially or indirectly owned by an American national. For example, Iran may, under its law, confiscate the property of one of its own nationals, but if an American national has a beneficial interest in that property, under Tribunal law the American national may recover for that interest.

This Tribunal has rendered awards against Iran on the ground that an Iranian law breached an obligation to a claimant. Iran itself has stated that "a State cannot plead its own law as an excuse for non-compliance with international law." Reply of the Ministry of Defense of the Islamic Republic of Iran in Case B1, at 9 (filed 29 Nov. 1982); *see also* Concurring Opinion of Charles N. Brower, *Component Builders, Inc., et al. v. The Islamic Republic of Iran*, Order in Case No. 395 (10 Jan. 1985), *reprinted in* 8 IRAN-U.S. C.T.R. 3, 9; Dissenting Opinion of Hamid Bahrami & Mohsen Mostafavi, *Case No. A-15*, Decision No. DEC 52-A15-FT, at p. 1 (24 Nov. 1986), *reprinted in* 13 IRAN-U.S. C.T.R. 177, 177-78; Draft Articles of Part Two on State Responsibility, art. 6(3), Provisionally Adopted by the International Law Commission, in *Report of the International Law Commission on the Work of Its 45th Session*, U.N. Doc. A/48/10, at 130 (1993).

Although the majority restricts its holding to pensions, there is nothing peculiar about the pension laws that would preclude this claim under international law. Here, the issue involves the termination of pension rights under an enactment and procedure that were neither part of nor pursuant to the pension law. Thus, the claim is *not* to enforce a provision of the pension law, but to assert rights based on the allegation that the "purging" action under another enactment gave rise to a claim for a measure affecting property rights. Pension rights are property rights. A beneficial interest in pension rights, including pension proceeds, is no different than such an interest in any other property and should not be treated differently.

The international law principle of the unenforceability of certain claims by a foreign state to enforce extraterritorially its laws, such as penal or revenue legislation, has no application to the instant case. *See* F.A. Mann, Prerogative Rights of Foreign States and the Conflict of Laws, 40 *Transactions of the Grotius Society* 25-28 (1955); 1 *Dicey and Morris On The Conflict of Laws* 101 (L. Collins 11th ed. 1987). This is not a case involving a state acting *jus imperii* for the purpose of *enforcing* certain laws extraterritorially. *See Computer Sciences Corp.* v. *The Islamic Republic of Iran, et al.*, Award No. 221-65-1, at pp. 55-56 (16 Apr. 1986), *reprinted in* 10 IRAN-U.S. C.T.R. 269, 312-13. As one authority has written, "if the plaintiff is a private person who enforces his own private right in his own interest, the rule does not apply, even though the claim arises in consequence of a foreign State's public laws." F.A. Mann, Conflict of Laws and Public Law, 132 *Recueil des Cours* 107, 180 (1971). Thus the majority has no basis for asserting that in this case, under international law, municipal law cannot be questioned.

Iran at the Hearing, but nowhere in its briefs, also argued that each month's pension payment was an independent obligation, and that, even assuming Mrs. Etezadi has some rights in the pension payments, the Tribunal has no jurisdiction to consider payments due after 19 January 1981 because they were not "outstanding" on that date – the date of the Algiers Accords. Claims Settlement Declaration, art. II, para. 1. Iran cites *Schering Corp.* v. *The Islamic Republic of Iran*, Award No. 122-38-3, p. 23 (13 Apr. 1984), *reprinted in* 5 IRAN-U.S. C.T.R. 361, 372-73. In that decision, involving a promissory note that did not mature until after 19 January 1981, the Tribunal concluded that no claim was outstanding at the time of the Claims Settlement Declaration. *See also Harnischfeger Corp.* v. *Ministry of Roads and Transportation, et al.*, Award No. 144-180-3, pp. 44-45 (13 July 1984), *reprinted in* 7 IRAN-U.S. C.T.R. 90, 115; *J.I. Case Co.* v. *The Islamic Republic of Iran, et al.*, Award No. 57-244-1, pp. 5-6 (15 June 1983), *reprinted in* 3 IRAN-U.S. C.T.R. 62, 65 (no jurisdiction over installment but no discussion of anticipatory breach); *cf. PepsiCo, Inc.* v. *The Islamic Republic of Iran, et al.*, Award No. 260-18-1, pp. 24-31 (11 Oct. 1986), *reprinted in* 13 IRAN-U.S. C.T.R. 3, 21-27 (jurisdiction over notes accelerated pursuant to acceleration clause); Concurring Opinion of Howard M. Holtzmann, *Shipside Packing Co. Inc.* v. *The Islamic Republic of Iran*, Award No. 102-11875-1, pp. 2-4 (12 Jan. 1984), *reprinted in* 5 IRAN-U.S. C.T.R. 80, 82-84 (storage fees due after 19 January 1981 within Tribunal jurisdiction because of storage lien).

Here, for the wrongful termination of the pension, Claimant claimed the discounted value of the pension based on life expectancy or, in the alternative, the value of a comparable retirement plan or annuity. The latter theory does not involve any payments due after 19 January 1981. But even under the former theory, Iran's reliance on *Schering* overlooks the fact that the renunciation of the pension constituted an anticipatory breach of the entire pension agreement, which agreement required payments over time, including those due at the time of the renunciation. Therefore, the whole amount of the anticipated pension, discounted to present value as of the date of the breach, becomes payable. *See Rockwell Int'l Systems, Inc. v. The Islamic Republic of Iran*, Award No. 438-430-1, para. 199 (5 Sept. 1989), *reprinted in* 23 IRAN-U.S. C.T.R. 150, 202; *Kimberly-Clark Corp. v. Bank Markazi Iran, et al.*, Award No. 46-57-2, p. 14 (25 May 1983), *reprinted in* 2 IRAN-U.S. C.T.R. 334, 341 (anticipatory breach not shown, but theory recognized); *Kaysons International Corp. v. The Islamic Republic of Iran, et al.*, Award No. 548-367-2, para. 38 (28 June 1993) (anticipatory breach not alleged, but theory recognized); *cf. Harnischfeger Corp., supra*, p. 30, *reprinted in* 7 IRAN-U.S. C.T.R. at 107 (no anticipatory breach because claimant did not treat agreement as breached).[13]

Under either one or both of Claimant's theories, the Tribunal has jurisdiction to award damages. Even if Iran's contentions were accepted, this Tribunal should still award compensation, however small, for the cessation of payments until the jurisdictional ending date, *see Foremost Tehran, Inc., et al. v. The Islamic Republic of Iran, et al.*, Award No. 220-37/231-1, pp. 31-35 (11 Apr. 1986), *reprinted in* 10 IRAN-U.S. C.T.R. 228, 250-53, or for the return of the amounts contributed by Mr. Etezadi, which return is required by the very law under which Iran terminated the payments.

The majority refers to that portion of the "Legal Bill on Purging" (which presumably was the basis for Iran's termination of the pension) that provides that the person whose pension has been terminated is entitled to receive the amount he or she contributed to the pension fund. As Mrs. Etezadi had a one-half interest in funds contributed to the pension, she would still have such an interest in such funds if and when returned and in a claim for such funds. This is another factor showing Mrs. Etezadi's interest in the pension.

Iran did not account for such contributed funds. In order to avoid the implications of Iran's failure to comply even with the terms of the "Legal Bill on Purging," the majority points to the failure by Mr. Etezadi to make a demand for those contributed funds. No such demand was necessary. Iran took an affirmative act to terminate what had been ongoing pension payments and failed to tender the amount contributed by Mr. Etezadi to the pension

---

[13] It is sometimes said that there can be no anticipatory breach of a contract that was or became unilateral. This exception has been criticized and appears not to apply in the civil law. *See* 4 A. Corbin, *Corbin on Contracts* § 962, at 864-65 (1950); at 439 (Supp. 1993). Even if the Tribunal were to accept such an exception, it would not apply here because Mr. Etezadi still had certain requirements under the pension law to maintain his eligibility for the pension – *e.g.,* Iranian nationality – even though the pension had vested.

fund. Iran did not attempt to justify its failure to comply with terms of the "Legal Bill." Under these circumstances, and under the clear terminology of the "Legal Bill" itself, the obligation arose irrespective of whether a demand was made. *See Sedco, Inc. v. Iran Marine Industrial Co., et al.*, Award No. 419-128/129-2, para. 31 (30 Mar. 1989), *reprinted in* 21 IRAN-U.S. C.T.R. 31, 45, and citations therein (demand for payment of outstanding debt unnecessary for Tribunal jurisdiction); *Mobil Oil Iran Inc., et al. v. The Islamic Republic of Iran, et al.*, Award No. 311-74/76/81/150-3, para. 46 (14 July 1987), *reprinted in* 16 IRAN-U.S. C.T.R. 3, 17 ("It suffices that a claim is ripe, so that a cause of action does exist . . ."); *Merrill Lynch & Co. Inc., et al., v. The Islamic Republic of Iran, et al.*, Award No. 519-394-1, para. 36 (19 Aug. 1991), *reprinted in* 27 IRAN-U.S. C.T.R. 122, 137 ("a debt owed and payable prior to 19 January 1981 constitutes an outstanding claim, even though payment of the debt had not been demanded prior to that date").

Although the majority, without analysis, simply concludes that Mr. Etezadi is the "real owner of these pension benefits," it did not and cannot overcome the fact that Mrs. Etezadi is the beneficial owner of one-half of the pension benefits and therefore, under Tribunal law, entitled to an award for that interest.

The "Caveat"

Iran contends that the decision establishing the rights of dual nationals with dominant and effective United States nationality to maintain a claim, *Case No. A/18*, Decision No. DEC 32-A18-FT (6 Apr. 1984), *reprinted in* 5 IRAN-U.S. C.T.R. 251, contained a "caveat" that would, in effect, bar any recovery by Mrs. Etezadi. The "caveat" is that "where the Tribunal finds jurisdiction based upon a dominant and effective nationality of the claimant, the other nationality *may* remain *relevant* to the merits of the claim." *Id.* at p. 26, *reprinted in* 5 IRAN-U.S. C.T.R. at 265-66 (emphasis added). I pointed out at that time in a concurring opinion that the Tribunal merely implied that the "use by a United States citizen of his or her Iranian nationality in a fraudulent or other inappropriate manner might adversely affect the claim by that person." Concurring Opinion of Richard M. Mosk, *supra*, at p. 7, *reprinted in* 5 IRAN-U.S. C.T.R. at 272.

Iran argues that, but for Mr. Etezadi's Iranian nationality, he would not have been able to obtain his pension, and thus Mrs. Etezadi's claims are dependent on Iranian nationality. The claim is by Mrs. Etezadi based on *her* interest – not by Mr. Etezadi.

Iran also suggests that not having a foreign spouse was a prerequisite for government employment, but Iran has presented no Iranian law, rule, or regulation supporting this contention. The only relevant section is Article

1061 of the Civil Code of Iran, which provides that "the government *can* make the marriage of *certain* government servants and officials and students supported by the government with a female foreign national dependent upon special permission." (Emphasis added.) There is no indication that such permission was *required* here or that it was not granted or would not have been granted. Based on the materials before us, a spouse has interests in the pension, and the pension in no way requires that a spouse have exclusive Iranian nationality.

Mr. Etezadi originally relinquished his United States citizenship because he was required to do so by United States law. *See Hooshang and Catherine Etezadi, supra,* para. 6, *reprinted in* 25 IRAN-U.S. C.T.R. at 266. What is of more importance here is the fact that Mrs. Etezadi did not obtain Iranian citizenship in order that her husband obtain his position and a pension or acquire property in Iran. Iranian citizenship automatically devolved upon her by virtue of her marriage. She did nothing that could be viewed as subterfuge or anything else requiring Iran's protection under the "caveat." Nor is there evidence that she did anything inappropriate in order to avoid the application of Iranian law. *See James M. Saghi, supra,* at paras. 58-60 (claimant affirmatively sought Iranian nationality to avoid limitations of Iranian law). Moreover, even if relevant to the "caveat," there is no evidence that Claimant intentionally used dual nationality to obtain benefits otherwise precluded or limited by relevant Iranian law concerning the subject matter of the claim. *See* Concurring Opinion of George H. Aldrich, *James M. Saghi, supra,* para. 3; Concurring Opinion of Richard M. Mosk, *Case No. A/18, supra,* at pp. 7-8, *reprinted in* 5 IRAN-U.S. C.T.R. at 272-73.

The argument of Iran that Mrs. Etezadi's use of her Iranian passport to enter Iran is alone enough to invoke the "caveat" would, if accepted, in effect nullify the dual nationality decision. Mrs. Etezadi obtained Iranian nationality through no voluntary act of her own. By marrying an Iranian national she automatically became an Iranian national under Iranian law, and Iranian law then compelled her to travel on that passport when entering or leaving Iran. *See Nasser Esphahanian v. Bank Tejarat,* Award No. 31-157-2, at pp. 17-18 (29 Mar. 1983), *reprinted in* 2 IRAN-U.S. C.T.R. 157, 167-68. If, as suggested by Iran, the marriage itself was the kind of act contemplated by the "caveat," then the Tribunal, by enforcing the "caveat" on such a basis, would itself be a party to a principle which on its face appears to contravene international public policy.

If, as Iran asserts, the application of the "caveat" involves equitable considerations, clearly it would be inequitable to deny pension rights when, as here, over twenty years of service have been rendered in reliance on earning a pension; contributions were made to the pension – one-half of which contributions belonged to Mrs. Etezadi; and there was no evidence of a valid or rational reason for the termination of the pension.

Conclusion

What has happened to Mr. Etezadi is unjust, but he has no recourse to this Tribunal. Mrs. Etezadi does have a right to make a claim before this Tribunal, and the law should be applied so as to be just and to recognize her rights as a woman and a wife. It has been said that "[i]n the law relating to spousal property, the policies supportive of equality of the sexes and policies promoting justness and fairness among the family participants and beneficiaries of the assets accumulated by the family unit, have particular influence on the courts, although this influence is often inarticulated." E. Scoles & P. Hay, *supra*, § 14.1, at 465.

It is widely recognized in community or marital property regimes that marriage is in part an economic and social partnership, and that after marriage anything produced by the industry of either spouse is the product of that partnership in which each has equal rights. *See* E. Scoles, *supra*, at 17-19. Here, the Etezadis exercised their rights to agree to such a partnership even before their move to California. They each contributed to their marriage partnership, and thus they each had rights in its product. When Iran wrongfully terminated the pension, it wrongfully took Mrs. Etezadi's rights in that pension. Moreover, when Iran in effect expropriated Shiraz Plastics, it deprived Mrs. Etezadi of her beneficial interest in that company.

The majority opinion basically relegates the role of the wife to an inferior position before this Tribunal, for under that opinion, unlike other claimants, she cannot obtain enforceable, beneficial rights by contracting with her husband, and her own property rights *vis-à-vis* third parties are necessarily dependent on her husband's rights.

Although theoretically the majority's opinion would apply if it were an Iranian wife who had the pension and the American husband who claimed as the beneficial owner, in reality such a situation is highly unlikely. Under Iranian law, an Iranian Moslem woman cannot marry a non-Moslem. Civil Code of Iran, art. 1059. Moreover, an Iranian woman cannot marry a foreign national without government permission. *Id.*, art. 1060. There are no such requirements imposed upon Iranian males. Iranian nationality is only imposed on a non-Iranian wife, not on a non-Iranian husband. *Id.*, art. 976(6). Thus, the situation presented in the instant case generally would arise so as to detrimentally affect a woman, but not a man.

Article II, paragraph 1, of the Claims Settlement Declaration gives the Tribunal jurisdiction over claims arising out of "expropriations or *other measures affecting property rights.*" (Emphasis added.) This phrase "has broad meaning under international law." *Harza Engineering Co. v. The Islamic Republic of Iran*, Award No. 19-98-2, p. 9 n.2 (30 Dec. 1982), *reprinted in* 1 IRAN-U.S. C.T.R. 499, 504 n.2. It does not exclude the property rights of wives. A wife's beneficial rights are no less subject to protection than those of any other beneficial owner of rights that have been protected by this Tribunal. As the applicable law validates Mrs. Etezadi's agreement with her husband, she had rights in the marital property. Because of this, she had a beneficial right in any property solely in her husband's name. Having established such a beneficial right, under Tribunal jurisprudence she is entitled to compensation for measures taken by Iran affecting these rights.

To deny Claimant her rights is contrary to the applicable law and public policy. This Tribunal should not place its imprimatur on a result not only wholly inconsistent with Tribunal precedent, but also so unjust and so contrary to the rights of women.

For the foregoing reasons, I dissent from the award.

JALAL MOIN, *Claimant*

v.

THE GOVERNMENT OF THE ISLAMIC REPUBLIC OF IRAN, *Respondent*

(Case No. 950)

Chamber Two: Skubiszewski, *Chairman*; Aldrich, Ameli,[1] *Members*

Signed 24 *May* 1994[2]

AWARD No. 557-950-2

The following is the text as issued by the Tribunal:

APPEARANCES

For the Claimant: Mr. Marvin M. David
 Attorney for Claimant
 Mr. Samad Parvin
 Co-Counsel for Claimant
 Mr. Bruce H. David
 Co-Counsel for Claimant
 Mr. Jalal Moin
 Claimant
 Mr. Amanollah Riggi
 Witness
 Mr. Massood H. Banayan
 Witness

For the Respondent: Mr. Ali H. Nobari
 Agent of the Government of the
 Islamic Republic of Iran
 Mr. Jafar Niaki
 Legal Adviser to the Agent
 Mr. Khosrow Tabasi
 Legal Adviser to the Agent
 Mr. Homayoun Rouhafzay
 Legal Adviser to the Agent

[1 Mr. Ameli's signature is accompanied by the word, "Concurring".]
[2 Filed 25 May 1994.]

Also present: Mr. D. Stephen Mathias
Agent of the United States of
America
Ms. Mary Catherine Malin
Deputy Agent of the United States
of America

I. THE PROCEEDINGS

1. The Claimant, Jalal Moin, filed a Statement of Claim against the Respondent, The Government of the Islamic Republic of Iran, on 19 January 1982, seeking compensation in the amount of approximately U.S.$22,000,000, plus interest and costs for the alleged expropriation by the Respondent of certain real estate, water rights, and financial instruments and investments in which he allegedly held a one-third interest as the result of inheritance from his father, Abolghasem Moin, who died in 1973. The Respondent objected, *inter alia*, to the jurisdiction of the Tribunal on the ground that the Claimant is exclusively a national of Iran and denied liability on the ground that the property in question had not been expropriated. The Respondent also contested the Claimant's valuation of the property.

2. By Order of 30 March 1990 the Tribunal joined "all jurisdictional issues, including the issue of the Claimant's nationality, . . . to the consideration of the merits of this Case."

3. A Hearing in this Case was held on 8 and 9 February 1994.

II. FACTS AND CONTENTIONS

4. The Tribunal shall limit itself to those facts and contentions which are necessary for the disposition of the Case.

5. The Claimant was born of Iranian parents in Iran in 1925 and thus is an Iranian national by birth. He lived the first forty years in Iran and in 1965 he entered the United States with, as he stated, "the express declaration of remaining and becoming a citizen." The Claimant became a naturalized U.S. citizen on 21 November 1972, as evidenced by a copy of his Certificate of Naturalization. He asserts that his Iranian born wife then, too, became a U.S. citizen. Two daughters were born to the marriage. The Claimant asserts that both daughters are citizens of the United States and have always resided there. The Claimant contends that he has lived continually in the United States since 1965 and that the center of both his social and business activities has been in the United States since he entered it in that year. The Claimant and his wife have owned several different houses in the New York City area

since 1972. Moin also presented evidence of his involvement in the New York City Taxi business since 1974, and he provided evidence of his activity in other business enterprises in New York City from 1970. The Claimant has further presented copies of U.S. tax returns filed jointly by him and his wife for the years 1976 through 1981.

6. The Respondent asserts that the Claimant has no standing to present a claim before this Tribunal as he has failed to prove that his U.S. nationality is dominant and effective. In particular, it argued that the Claimant never renounced his Iranian nationality, with effect in Iranian law.

7. As to his Claim, the Claimant asserts that "[his] interest was expropriated by virtue of the fact that he was a United States citizen." Both the alleged expropriation and its motivation have been denied by the Respondent. The Claimant also states that he is "unable to exercise unrestricted authority over the property." In the Statement of Claim the Claimant asserted that he was a one-third owner of the allegedly expropriated properties and rights by virtue of his and his family's inheritance of them. At the Hearing, Claimant's counsel stated that in fact the Claimant was the owner of a two-ninths part of the inheritance; the amount claimed, though, remained the same.

8. At the Hearing the Claimant presented two witnesses, Mr. Riggi and Mr. Banayan.

9. Mr. Riggi, a long-time friend of Claimant's family, testified as to the nature of the properties, most of which he had been familiar with for over sixty years. Mr. Riggi stated that in earlier years he had visited both the residential house of the Moin family in the city of Yazd and their farm and summerhouse. Mr. Riggi was also familiar with the shops the family had owned in the Bazargan area. In November 1980, Mr. Riggi left Iran. He stated that shortly before departure he passed the family house in Yazd but did not enter it. According to Mr. Riggi several men were coming out and going in. He did not recognize these men as members of the Moin family. Before leaving the country Mr. Riggi allegedly also visited the Bazargan-area shops, which were also part of the inheritance. On that occasion, Mr. Moin's cousin, a friend of Mr. Riggi, allegedly told him that the rent for the shops was being collected by the Government of Iran.

10. The other witness, Mr. Banayan, travelled to Iran in 1986 for the purpose of valuing the properties at issue in this Case. Mr. Banayan, who said that he was a real estate appraiser and broker, first visited the house in Yazd. He testified that he talked to the people then living in the house, who allegedly told him that since the Islamic Revolution the house belonged to the Foundation for the Oppressed. Mr. Banayan valued Mr. Moin's two-ninths interest in the Yazd house at U.S.$3,150,000.

11. After visiting Yazd, Mr. Banayan went to the summerhouse and the

Bazargan shopping center. At both places he asked the people occupying the properties to identify their owner. Mr. Banayan testified that both times he was told that the Foundation for the Oppressed had owned them since the Islamic Revolution. Mr. Moin's two-ninths interests in the summerhouse and the stores were each valued at approximately U.S.$2,000,000. Mr. Banayan concluded that the total value of Claimant's claim is approximately U.S.$22,000,000.

12. The Tribunal has not been presented with any documentary evidence concerning the alleged taking of the properties in question, originating either from the Claimant or from his siblings, some of whom are living in Iran and some in the United States.

13. The Respondent has first raised a jurisdictional defence to Claimant's claim. Iran notes that the Claimant has failed to give the date on which his claim arose and has not indicated the Governmental acts allegedly impairing Claimant's rights. For these reasons Iran argues that the Claimant has not actually presented a claim, and points out that the Tribunal therefore has no jurisdiction to deal with the Case.

14. On the merits, the Respondent denies that any of Claimant's property interests have been expropriated. It asserts that while some of the properties have been sold by the Claimant himself, others remain Claimant's property. To that effect the Respondent has submitted certain copies of documents that seem to establish that the Claimant, through powers of attorney, sold his share in some parcels of the relevant property before the Islamic Revolution and that he sold some as late as March 1983.

III. JURISDICTION

15. As to Claimant's nationality it is undisputed that Mr. Moin is an Iranian national by birth. There is no proof that he ever relinquished his Iranian nationality or that he otherwise lost that nationality. At the same time, Mr. Moin has shown that he has been a United States national since 1972.

16. Based on the conclusion that the Claimant was a national of Iran as well as the United States during the relevant period under consideration, the Tribunal, in accordance with the Full Tribunal's decision issued in Case No. A18, Decision No. DEC 32-A18-FT (6 Apr. 1984), *reprinted in* 5 IRAN-U.S. C.T.R. 251 (Case No. A18), must proceed to determine his dominant and effective nationality for the purpose of its jurisdiction over his Claim. In the A18 Decision the Tribunal held that it has "jurisdiction over claims against Iran by dual Iran-United States nationals where the dominant and effective nationality of the Claimant during the relevant period from the date the claim arose until 19 January 1981 was that of the United States." *Id.*, 5 IRAN-U.S.

C.T.R. at 265. Taking all the relevant factors and their evidence into consideration the Tribunal is satisfied that at all relevant times from the Iranian Revolution to 19 January 1981 Claimant's dominant and effective nationality was that of the United States. Claimant's residence and business activities were at all relevant times centered in New York, and his only financial interest in Iran evidently was his shared ownership in the properties at issue in this claim.

17. The Tribunal must also consider whether the Claimant has actually presented a claim. Indeed, certain defects or gaps in his written submissions might lead to doubts concerning the very existence of the claim. If no claim in the sense of Article II, paragraph 1, of the Claims Settlement Declaration was outstanding in the relevant period, the Tribunal would have no jurisdiction. However, in view of the statements made at the Hearing, the Tribunal is ready to admit that it was presented with a claim allegedly arising out of measures affecting the Claimant's property rights at some time during the Islamic Revolution and prior to the entry into force of the said Declaration.

IV. MERITS

18. The Claimant contends that the Government of the Islamic Republic of Iran expropriated his two-ninths interest in certain real estate and other proprietary interests. The issue here is whether certain actions for which the Respondent is responsible deprived the Claimant of his ownership.

19. In the written pleadings the Claimant has not alluded to any action by the Respondent which might constitute an expropriation or another measure affecting his property rights. In this context the Tribunal notes that Claimant's statement that he is "unable to exercise unrestricted authority over the property" might be understood as being less definite than a clear affirmation that expropriation took place. At the Hearing, the two witnesses presented by the Claimant testified that with respect to certain properties they were told that the Foundation for the Oppressed either owned the property or was collecting the rent for it. In this regard the Tribunal notes that Mr. Riggi's testimony was vague and inconclusive. He testified that when he last saw the house in Yazd in 1980, men whom he did not recognize as members of the Moin family were coming and going from it. This, in the Tribunal's view, hardly proves the alleged taking of the house. Mr. Banayan testified both on the issue of expropriation and on the value of the properties. The Tribunal notes that on the issue of the alleged expropriation Mr. Banayan only testified that in 1986 he had been told that certain properties at issue in this Case, since the beginning of the Islamic Revolution, belonged to the Foundation for the Oppressed. The Tribunal considers this to be hearsay evidence, on which it

cannot rely, unless the evidence is substantiated. Such substantiation is missing. The Tribunal is mindful of the difficulties faced by the Claimant in collecting evidence, although the Tribunal would expect that any taking of the properties in question would be indicated in some documentary evidence, for example, in contemporary correspondence. In any event, the Tribunal must base its awards on probative evidence. The question may be asked why neither the Claimant's siblings nor Mr. Banayan, when he went to Iran in 1986, were able to gather any such evidence.

20. From what has been submitted in the record and testified at the Hearing, the Tribunal must conclude that the Claimant has not shown when and by what acts the alleged expropriation of the various properties took place. As to the time, he asserted during the Hearing that it occurred sometime during the period from November 1979 to the date of the Claims Settlement Declaration. As to the expropriation acts, neither any deprivation of the Claimant's right nor the attributability of any acts to the Respondent has been proved. Accordingly, the Claim is dismissed for lack of proof.

V. COSTS

21. Each Party shall bear its own costs.

VI. AWARD

22. For the foregoing reasons,

THE TRIBUNAL AWARDS AS FOLLOWS:
   a. The Claim is hereby dismissed for lack of proof.
   b. Each of the Parties shall bear its own costs of arbitrating this Claim.

FAITH LITA KHOSROWSHAHI, SUSANNE P. KHOSROWSHAHI, MARGENE P. KHOSROWSHAHI, KEVIN KAYVAN KHOSROWSHAHI, AND CAMERON KAMRAN KHOSROWSHAHI, *Claimants*

v.

THE GOVERNMENT OF THE ISLAMIC REPUBLIC OF IRAN, THE MINISTRY OF INDUSTRIES AND MINES, THE ALBORZ INVESTMENT CORPORATION, THE KBC COMPANY, AND THE DEVELOPMENT AND INVESTMENT BANK OF IRAN *Respondents*

(Case No. 178)

Chamber Two: Ruda, *Chairman*; Aldrich, Ameli,[1] *Members*

Signed 30 *June* 1994[2]

AWARD NO. 558-178-2

The following is the text as issued by the Tribunal:

FINAL AWARD

APPEARANCES

For the Claimants: Mr. Francis X. Markey
  Attorney for Claimants
 Ms. Agnes Tabah
  Attorney for Claimants
 Ms. Faith Lita Khosrowshahi
  Claimant
 Ms. Susanne Khosrowshahi
  Claimant
 Mr. Camran Khosrowshahi
  Claimant
 Mr. Nasrollah Khosrowshahi
  Representative

[1 Mr. Ameli's signature is accompanied by the words, "Concurring as to the *dispositif*, para. 82(A), (B), (D) and (E); dissenting as to para. 82 (C) and (F). *See*, Dissenting Opinion." This Opinion is not available at present.]
[2 Filed 30 June 1994.]

Mr. Robert Reilly
  Expert Witness
Mr. William Liffers
  Witness

For the Respondents:
Mr. Ali H. Nobari
  Agent of the Government of the
  Islamic Republic of Iran
Dr. Bijan Izadi
  Deputy Agent of the Government of
  the Islamic Republic of Iran
Mr. S. Mohammadi
  Legal Adviser to the Agent of the
  Government of the Islamic Republic
  of Iran
Dr. Seyed Hossein Safaei
  Attorney for Alborz Investment
  Corporation and KBC
Dr. Mohammad Ashtari
  Attorney for Alborz Investment
  Corporation and KBC
Mr. Farhad Toupshekan
  Representative of the Respondent
Mr. Masood Amouzadeh
  Representative of the Respondent
Mr. M.S. Garrosi
  Representative of the Respondent
Mr. Abdolhossein Razavi
  Representative of the Respondent
Mr. Seyed Nasser Shajareh
  Representative of the Respondent
Mr. Antony G.P. Tracy
  Expert Witness
Mr. Grant Hyde
  Expert Witness
Mr. Abolghasem Merati
  Expert Witness
Mrs. Minoo Afshari Rad
  Representative of the Bank of
  Industries and Mines

Also present:
Mr. D. Stephen Mathias
  Agent of the United States of America
Ms. Mary Catherine Malin
  Deputy Agent of the United States
  of America

TABLE OF CONTENTS

		Para. No.
I.	INTRODUCTION	1
II.	JURISDICTIONAL AND PROCEDURAL ISSUES	5
III.	THE ALBORZ INVESTMENT CORPORATION	9
	A. Facts and Contentions	9
	1. Claimants' Alborz shares	9
	2. Alborz Dividends	21
	B. The Tribunal's Findings	23
	1. Claimants' Alborz shares	23
	2. Alborz Dividends	29
	3. Application of the Caveat to Claimants' Alborz Claim	30
	4. Valuation	34
IV.	THE KHOSROWSHAHI BROTHERS COMPANY	54
	A. Facts and Contentions	54
	B. The Tribunal's Findings	59
V.	THE DEVELOPMENT AND INVESTMENT BANK OF IRAN	60
	A. Facts and Contentions	60
	1. Claimants' DIBI shares	60
	2. DIBI Dividends	64
	B. The Tribunal's Findings	65
	1. Claimants' DIBI shares	65
	2. DIBI Dividends	68
	3. Application of the Caveat to Claimants' DIBI claim	69
	4. Valuation	74
VI.	INTEREST	80
VII.	COSTS	81
VIII.	AWARD	82

I. INTRODUCTION

1. The Claimants, Faith Lita Khosrowshahi and her four children Susanne P., Marcene P., Kevin Kayvan ("Kevin") and Cameron Kamran ("Cameron") Khosrowshahi, filed a Statement of Claim on 18 December 1981 against The Government of the Islamic Republic of Iran ("Iran"), The

Ministry of Industries and Mines, The Alborz Investment Corporation ("Alborz"), Khosrowshahi Brothers Company ("KBC"), and The Development and Investment Bank of Iran ("DIBI") (collectively "the Respondents"). As finally pleaded at the Hearing the Claimants seek U.S.$5,510,059, plus interest and costs, for the alleged expropriation of their ownership interests in Alborz, KBC, and DIBI as well as for certain allegedly unpaid dividends on their Alborz and DIBI shares.

2. The Claimants contended that they were all nationals of the United States. The Respondents argued that each of the Claimants was a national of Iran and thus ineligible to present claims against Iran before this Tribunal. Pursuant to the Full Tribunal's decision in *The Islamic Republic of Iran* v *The United States of America*, Decision No. 32-A18-FT (6 April 1984), *reprinted in* 5 IRAN-U.S. C.T.R. 251, the Tribunal addressed the issue of the Claimants' nationality in an Interlocutory Award. It held that each of the Claimants was a national of both Iran and the United States with dominant and effective United States nationality during the relevant jurisdictional period. Accordingly, the Tribunal concluded that the Claimants were nationals of the United States within the meaning of Article VII, paragraph 1 of the Claims Settlement Declaration ("CSD"). Interlocutory Award No. ITL 76-178-2 (22 Jan. 1990), *reprinted in* 24 IRAN-U.S. C.T.R. 40.

3. The Claimants allege that Iran expropriated their ownership interests in Alborz, KBC and DIBI in the Summer or Fall of 1979. The Respondents, on the other hand, argue that the Claimants' interests in Alborz were not affected by the Government measures taken prior to 19 January 1981. Denying that the Claimants ever had any ownership interest in KBC, the Respondents also argue that prior to 19 January 1981, KBC was run by managers appointed by its shareholders. Furthermore, they contend that shares in those two companies had a low or negative value at the time of the alleged expropriation. The Respondents further deny that the Claimants' DIBI shares were actually expropriated without compensation because the Government established a compensation scheme in 1980 but the Claimants chose not to make use of it. Thus, the Respondents appear to argue that the Claimants should be deemed to have waived their right to compensation by failing to take advantage of the Government's compensation offer.

4. A Hearing was held in this Case on 22 and 23 October 1992.

II. JURISDICTIONAL AND PROCEDURAL ISSUES

5. As a preliminary matter, the Respondents argue that Mrs. Khosrowshahi lacked the capacity to file a claim on behalf of her son, Cameron, who was a minor at the time the claim was filed. They contend that under the laws

of both Iran and the United States a mother cannot bring a claim on behalf of her minor child unless the father of the child is deceased or has delegated his guardianship rights to the mother. Since Mr. Khosrowshahi is alive, and there is no proof that he had earlier delegated his guardianship rights to his wife, Mrs. Khosrowshahi, Iran insists that Cameron's claim was improperly filed and should therefore be dismissed.

6. The Claimants, on the other hand, contended at the Hearing that neither the Claims Settlement Declaration nor the law of the place of their residence, *i.e.* New York, prevented the claim of a minor from being brought to arbitration before this Tribunal.

7. The Tribunal finds no bar to Cameron's claim. Neither the Claims Settlement Declaration nor the Tribunal Rules exclude minors as claimants. Moreover, the Tribunal notes that Cameron Khosrowshahi, now having reached the age of legal majority, and his father were present at the Hearing. By their presence and statements, both gave their approval to the mother's act of filing the claim in 1981 on behalf of her then minor son.

8. The Tribunal is satisfied that all of the Claims arise "out of debts, contracts . . . expropriations and other measures affecting property rights" within the meaning of Article II, paragraph 1 of the Claims Settlement Declaration.

III. THE ALBORZ INVESTMENT CORPORATION

A. Facts and Contentions

   1. Claimants' Alborz shares

9. Khosrowshahi Brothers Company was formed in 1954 as a private stock company by Mr. Haji Hassan Khosrowshahi and his six sons, including Nasrollah, Kazem, Majid and Javad Khosrowshahi. Nasrollah Khosrowshahi is Faith Lita Khosrowshahi's husband, and the father of the other Claimants. KBC initially engaged in the import, general trading and distribution of pharmaceutical products in Iran. As the company grew more successful, it diversified into a range of health, food and chemical products and began to manufacture some of its own products. In the 1960's, KBC restructured its activities and formed a number of independent but related companies to handle each different type of product. This resulted in the entire group of businesses being organized under the banner of KBC Industrial Group ("KBC Group"). While the original KBC continued to perform the import and distribution activities, its manufacturing and other activities were relinquished to other companies owned by the KBC Group.

10. In 1975, the Iranian Government enacted the "Law for Expansion of Public Ownership of Productive Units" ("Law for Expansion") which required

certain industries to sell 49% of their stock to the public. To comply with this Law, the Khosrowshahi family restructured Alborz Investment Corporation, one of the KBC Group companies, turning it into the holding company of the Alborz Industrial Group. Alborz purchased the shares of eight of the KBC Group companies and then offered 49% of its own shares to the public. The Claimants contend that by 1979, the KBC Group was composed, on the one hand, of a number of non-public companies, including the original KBC, and, on the other, of Alborz, a holding company which owned eight operating companies and whose stock was publicly traded at the Tehran Stock Exchange. The Claimants contend that at that time, the Khosrowshahi brothers and their families owned 51% of the Alborz shares.

11. The Claimants first purchased Alborz shares in November 1975, the date of Alborz's initial public offering under the Law for Expansion. In February 1977 they acquired additional shares. Although there was some initial disagreement over the total number of shares owned by the Claimants, at the Hearing the Claimants acknowledged that at the time of the alleged expropriation they collectively held 99,777.4 shares as contended by the Respondents.[3]

12. On 7 July 1979, the Government of Iran passed the "Law for Protection and Development of Industries of Iran" ("Law for Protection"), which stated that, in accordance with Bill No. 6738 (*see infra*, para. 24), "the property of [51 named individuals] shall become the ownership of the government." The Law for Protection applied to, among others, Dr. Kazem Khosrowshahi, the Claimants' brother-in-law/uncle and a 1.8% owner of Alborz stock. One month later, Iran expanded the scope of this law to include the spouses, children and, subject to the decision of a special commission, to brothers and sisters of the 51 persons originally named. Although the Law for Protection did not explicitly apply to the Claimants, they contend that in practice Iran "made no attempt to distinguish between the individual ownership interests of Dr. Kazem Khosrowshahi and other family members."

13. The Claimants further allege that Iran expropriated their interests in Alborz by its appointment of a government supervisor. On the very same day that the above Law for Protection was enacted, the Ministry of Industry and Mines issued a Decree appointing Mr. Massoud Saidi as "Official Observer for the Alborz Investment Company . . . and all of its affiliates." The Decree, issued pursuant to Bill No. 6738, explicitly empowered Mr. Saidi to "supervise all the operations of the company [and to] cosign all the documents and legal

---

[3] According to the Alborz records at the time of the alleged expropriation, Faith Lita owned 7,287.2 shares, Susanne P. and Marcene P. each owned 13,464 shares and Kevin and Cameron each owned 32,781.1 shares, collectively totalling 99,777.4 shares.

papers of the company with the officers of the company." The Decree at the same time notified "all officers and managers of Alborz Investment Company to continue their duties until new managers are appointed." Bill No. 6738 is the Act Concerning the Appointment of Provisional Directors . . . of June 16, 1979. According to the Claimants, Article 1 of the Act authorized the appropriate government ministries to "appoint" one or more persons as a director or board of directors or supervising member for the management and/or supervision over the management of the affairs of industrial or other units. Article 2 specified that the appointment of directors and "supervising members" was to be carried out by an administrative order from the related ministry. It also suspended the rights of shareholders to elect new directors pending the installment of government-appointed directors. Article 3 authorized the supervisory members to "exercise complete supervision over all the affairs of the unit concerned and especially supervision over the operation and action of the directors."

14. The Claimants assert that almost immediately upon his appointment, Mr. Saidi began to exercise his supervisorial powers. Within a week, he announced a limitation on managerial salaries. The Claimants further maintain that Mr. Saidi unilaterally altered personnel rules and required his signature on all company checks and all intercompany fund transfers. The Claimants allege that as a result, "Mr. J[avad] Khosrowshahi, as well as the rest of the Alborz Board, gradually realized that they no longer had any influence or control over Alborz's management."

15. On 9 July 1979, Mr. Javad Khosrowshahi wrote a letter to the then Prime Minister Bazargan on behalf of the Board of Directors of Alborz. In the letter he challenged the legitimacy of Mr. Saidi's appointment and his exercise of managerial authority under the terms of the Law for Protection. He also noted that Mr. Kazem Khosrowshahi owned only 1.8% of the company's shares while he exercised no managerial authority in Alborz. The letter further stated that both the Board of Directors and the managers of Alborz had been present in Iran during the Revolution and were still running the company and that Alborz remained in healthy condition and thus did not require supervision by government-appointed managers. In sum, Mr. Javad Khosrowshahi appeared to have believed at the time that the Law for Protection should not have been applied to Alborz.

16. The Claimants contend that by late July 1979, the political crisis in the country and alleged personal threats forced Mr. Javad Khosrowshahi to leave the country. Before his departure, he convened a meeting of the Alborz Board of Directors in which the Board "delegated all their rights and authorities in the management of company affairs" to four trusted company managers, namely, Ahmad Arasteh, Ali Nouri, Ali Asghar Nikafshan and Mir

Majid Hejazi. In addition, Mr. Javad Khosrowshahi issued a directive creating a "Managing Committee" for Alborz's day-to-day operations.

17. The Claimants maintain that Mr. Saidi's "constant interference . . . made it impossible for these individuals to exercise their authority and functions." They assert that Mr. Saidi continued to make unilateral decisions without the knowledge or consent of management, thereby ignoring the Khosrowshahi family's attempts to maintain managerial control of Alborz and its subsidiaries. Thus, the Claimants argue that Mr. Saidi's appointment and subsequent acts constituted a *de facto* taking of their ownership interests in Alborz.

18. The Claimants alternatively contend that if Mr. Saidi's appointment did not constitute an expropriation of their property interests in Alborz, then in any event the Government's subsequent nomination of a new Chairman and Board of Directors for Alborz should be deemed to have amounted to the expropriation of their shares. On 23 September 1979, the Ministry of Industries and Mines nominated a new Board of Directors for Alborz, with Mr. Javad Gharavi as Chairman. Four days later, at a special meeting of Alborz shareholders, the new Board was ratified by a unanimous vote. It is reflected in the minutes of that meeting that 92% of the then outstanding shares voted, either in person or by proxy. The Claimants insist that the Government's appointment of a new Board merely confirmed the *de facto* change in management that they allege had occurred by the appointment of Mr. Saidi. Furthermore, at the Hearing they rejected as unauthorized the subsequent ratification by the Claimants' alleged proxies of the Government-appointed Board.

19. The Respondents deny that Iran expropriated the Claimants' ownership interest in Alborz. First, they argue that the Claimants did not fall within the original scope of the Law for Protection (which applied in relevant part only to Kazem Khosrowshahi) or within its modified scope (which applied to Kazem's spouse and children). Moreover, although the modified scope of the Law could have extended to other Khosrowshahi brothers and sisters by decision of a commission established under the same law, it actually never was so extended and the law in any event could not have extended to the sister in law, nieces, and nephews of Kazem, as the Claimants are. Second, they maintain that under Tribunal precedent the appointment of a government supervisor and/or governmental managers is not sufficient, standing alone, to constitute an expropriation. They further insist that governmental control over Alborz became necessary to protect both employee interests and national economic interests after Alborz management had abandoned the company. Fourth, the Respondents argue that because the Claimants owned only a tiny fraction of Alborz and possessed no managerial functions, the change in

management affected neither their ownership rights nor their interests in the company. Finally, the Respondents allege that a 1985 judgment of the Islamic Revolutionary Court in Tehran ordering the expropriation of Claimants' shares in Alborz indicates that their property interests in Alborz had not been expropriated prior to that year.

20. Concerning Alborz's new Board of Directors, the Respondents maintain that it was duly elected. They have produced documents allegedly showing that the Claimants' shares were voted by proxy at the 27 September 1979 meeting. Subsequent to the Hearing, they also presented certain evidence, including statements by Messrs Ahmad Arasteh and Ali Nouri, who stated that they were present at the 27 September 1979 meeting and voted by proxy for members of the Khosrowshahi family. The Respondents, therefore, argue that the September change of control complied with the requisite corporate procedures and did thus not constitute an expropriation of the Claimants' shares in Alborz. The Claimants deny that they gave proxies to the person who allegedly voted their shares. They contend that the only individuals who held proxies to vote for them were Majid and Javad Khosrowshahi who were not in Iran on the date of the meeting. Neither party placed in evidence the proxies to which it has referred.

2. *Alborz Dividends*

21. In connection with their claim for a taking of their Alborz shares, the Claimants also allege that Alborz declared a dividend of 350 Rials per share for the fiscal year ending March 20, 1978. Although this dividend was originally to be paid as of October 23, 1978, the Claimants, among others, agreed to defer payment of those dividends until an unspecified later time because Alborz was undergoing a difficult financial period. The Claimants maintain that subsequent to the appointment of Government managers, they have repeatedly requested payment of the 1978 dividends, but to no avail.

22. The Respondents do not dispute that a dividend was declared in 1978. However, they argue that the Claimants have failed to prove that they ever demanded payment of their dividends subsequent to their agreement to defer payment and further note that the undistributed dividends were used to offset the operating losses in subsequent years. In the Respondents' view, the Claimants are thus no longer entitled to any dividends, even assuming that they ever were.

B. *The Tribunal's Findings*

1. *Claimants' Alborz shares*

23. With respect to the alleged taking of the Claimants' interests in Alborz, the Tribunal must first decide whether the Claimants' 99,777.4 shares

were expropriated with Iran's appointment of a supervisor in July 1979. The Tribunal has previously held that "a deprivation or taking of property may occur under international law through interference by a state in the use of that property or with the enjoyment of its benefits, even where legal title to the property is not affected." *Tippetts, Abbett, McCarthy and Stratton* v. *TAMS-AFFA Consulting Engineers of Iran, et al.*, Award No. 141-7-2, at 10-11 (29 June 1984), *reprinted in* 6 IRAN-U.S. C.T.R. 219, 225. The Tribunal then stated:

> [w]hile assumption of control over property by a government does not automatically and immediately justify a conclusion that the property has been taken by the government, such a conclusion is warranted whenever events demonstrate that the owner was deprived of fundamental rights of ownership and it appears that this deprivation is not merely ephemeral.

Id. at 11, 6 IRAN-U.S. C.T.R. at 225. *See also Starrett Housing Corp., et al.* v. *The Islamic Republic of Iran*, Interlocutory Award No. ITL 32-24-1 at 51 (19 Dec. 1983), *reprinted in* 4 IRAN-U.S. C.T.R. 122, 154 where the Tribunal noted:

> it is recognized in international law that measures taken by a State can interfere with property rights to such an extent that these rights are rendered so useless that they must be deemed to have been expropriated, even though the State does not purport to have expropriated them and the legal title to the property formally remains with the original owner.

24. Mr. Saidi was appointed as an "observer for Alborz . . . and all of its affiliates" pursuant to Bill number 6738. (*See supra*, para. 12.) Article 2 of the Bill states that once the government appoints new managers or directors under the Bill, "previous directors and managers will be stripped of their competence in managing" the affairs of the company and that "[t]he directive appointing a manager or board of directors, until cancellation thereof by the relevant ministry, . . . will remain in force; the manager . . . so appointed will remain in [his] position[s]; and the shareholders have no right whatsoever to choose managers in their place." Article 3 also authorizes appointees "to exercise complete supervision over all the affairs of the unit concerned and especially supervision over the operation and action of the directors." The same article provides that even observers may be granted signature authority over financial obligations of the company, as Mr. Saidi was in the present case.

25. The Tribunal has further found that the "effect [of Bill 6738] is to strip the original managers of effected [sic] companies of all authority and to deny shareholders significant rights attached to their ownership interest." *Thomas Payne* v. *The Islamic Republic of Iran*, Award No. 245-335-2, at 11 (8 Aug. 1986), *reprinted in* 12 IRAN-U.S. C.T.R. 3, 10; *see also Harold Birnbaum* v. *The Islamic Republic of Iran*, Award No. 549-967-2, para. 29 (6 July 1993), *reprinted in*

29 IRAN-U.S. C.T.R. 260. The evidence presented has satisfied the Tribunal that the authority exercised by Mr. Saidi was such as to justify a finding that the Claimants were deprived of the power to exercise their rights. Upon his appointment and assumption of duties, he immediately excluded the existing Khosrowshahi management. There is no evidence that Mr. Saidi's appointment was intended to be or in fact was temporary. The subsequent appointment of directors and chairman of the board also shows that the intention of the Government was permanent exclusion of the existing management. By effectively forcing out the existing management, Mr. Saidi deprived the Claimants, as shareholders, of their right to select by vote managers of their choice. Thus, the conclusion for the Tribunal is that the Government of Iran effectively expropriated the Claimants' shareholding interests in Alborz on 7 July 1979, the date Mr. Saidi was appointed and assumed his duties as supervisor for Alborz.

26. This finding makes it unnecessary for the Tribunal to address the Respondents' arguments that the election of a new Board of Directors subsequent to Mr. Saidi's appointment ratified the government's assumption of control. Similarly, there is no further need for the Tribunal to consider the Respondents' other assertion that a 1985 judgment by the Islamic Revolutionary Court expropriating the Claimants' shares in Alborz proves that they were not taken before that year.

27. The Respondents have also argued that the Claimants' rights as shareholders were not abrogated by the taking because they owned only a tiny fraction of Alborz shares. The Tribunal is satisfied, however, that the Claimants' rights were effectively abrogated by the terms of the Legal Bill pursuant to which Mr. Saidi was appointed, as well as by his actions.

28. Likewise, the Tribunal must reject the Respondents' denial of liability because it appointed Mr. Saidi only in accordance with Iranian law for the protection of workers and national interests jeopardized by an abandonment of Alborz by its managers. The Tribunal has previously held that "a government cannot avoid liability for compensation by showing that its actions were taken legitimately pursuant to its own laws." *See Birnbaum, supra*, para. 35; *see also American International Group, Inc. v. Islamic Republic of Iran, et al.*, Award No. 93-2-3, pp. 14-15 (19 Dec. 1983), *reprinted in* 4 IRAN-U.S. C.T.R. 96, 105. The Tribunal also has stated that "[t]he intent of the government is less important than the effects of the measures on the owner." *Tippetts, supra* at 11, 6 IRAN-U.S. C.T.R. at 225-26.

2. *Alborz Dividends*

29. From what has been submitted in the record, the Tribunal must conclude that there is no evidence that the Claimants have ever demanded

payment of the undistributed dividends. Absent evidence explaining the terms and conditions of the alleged voluntary deferment, the Claimants' allegation in this respect cannot suffice to help the Tribunal determine whether the Claimants in fact hold a compensable property interest in those dividends, much less whether it was taken. In light of this lack of evidence, the Tribunal dismisses the Claimants' claim for unpaid Alborz dividends for failure of proof.

3. Application of the Caveat to Claimants' Alborz Claim

30. Before turning to the valuation of Alborz, the Tribunal will address the "Caveat argument" advanced by the Respondents. The Respondents' position is that the Claimants are barred from seeking recovery before this Tribunal for their expropriated shares in Alborz because they purchased those shares as Iranian nationals, rather than as U.S. nationals. This argument relies on the "caveat" to the Tribunal's decision in Case A18. In that Case, the Tribunal held that "where the Tribunal finds jurisdiction based upon the dominant and effective nationality of the claimant, the other nationality may remain relevant to the merits of the claim." Case No. A18, Decision No. DEC 32-A18-FT, at 26 (6 Apr. 1984), *reprinted in* 5 IRAN-U.S. C.T.R. 251, 266. In its Interlocutory Award in the present Case, the Tribunal held:

> This jurisdictional determination of the Claimants' dominant and effective U.S. nationality remains subject to the caveat added by the Full Tribunal in its decision in Case No. A18 [5 IRAN-U.S. C.T.R. 251, 265] that 'the other nationality may remain relevant to the merits of the Claim.' The Tribunal will therefore in the further proceedings examine all circumstances of this Case also in light of this caveat, and will, for example, consider whether the Claimants used their Iranian nationality to secure benefits available under Iranian law exclusively to Iranian nationals or whether, in any other way, their conduct was such as to justify refusal of an award in their favor in the present Claims filed before the Tribunal.

Interlocutory Award No. ITL 76-178-2, *supra*, para. 16, 24 IRAN-U.S. C.T.R. at 45.

31. The Respondents contend that by not using their U.S. nationality the Claimants received a favorable tax rate on their past Alborz dividends, pursuant to Article 80, Part D (1) of the Iranian Income Tax Act. This, allegedly, was legally available only to Iranians. In support of their allegation, Respondents have submitted the affidavit of Mr. Razavi, the managing director of Alborz, which states that prior to 1978 Alborz calculated and paid the shareholders' dividend tax at the lower rate applicable to Iranian nationals residing in Iran. Attached to his affidavit are tax assessments for the years 1976 through 1978, showing that taxes were assessed at the rate applicable to Iranian nationals residing in Iran.

32. The Claimants deny that they concealed their U.S. nationality when they purchased Alborz shares and note that their stockholder cards indicate their birth in the United States and thus their U.S. nationality. The Claimants further argue that Alborz shares were freely traded, with no applicable restrictions on foreign ownership at the time they purchased their shares. The Claimants also disclaim any knowledge of a preferential tax treatment, arguing that the tax was a corporate tax withheld and paid by Alborz. Finally, the Claimants argue that Iran has failed to prove that the Claimants concealed their identity or that they received any benefit by so doing.

33. The Tribunal finds that the evidence in the record is not sufficient to support the conclusion that the Claimants concealed or otherwise abused their dual nationality when they purchased their Alborz shares. The Respondents' proffered affidavit and supporting evidence only assert that Alborz records did not reflect the American nationality of the Claimants. In a similar situation, the Tribunal found that "the mere fact that [the Claimant's] Iranian ID card number appears on his share certificate does not mean that he concealed his American nationality in order to obtain benefits available only to Iranians." *Attaollah Golpira* v. *The Islamic Republic of Iran*, Award No. 32-211-2, at 6 (29 Mar. 1983), *reprinted in* 2 IRAN-U.S. C.T.R. 171, 174. Given the lack of evidence to the contrary, the Tribunal finds no reason to deviate from its conclusion in *Golpira*. Thus, the Tribunal concludes that there is no evidence that the Claimants concealed or otherwise abused their Iranian nationality when they purchased Alborz shares or that they obtained any benefit available by law only to Iranian nationals. Moreover, as the Claimants were residing in the United States, as also indicated in their Iranian passports, their nationality was not relevant for purposes of the tax in question. Accordingly, their Alborz claim should not be barred by the caveat.

4. Valuation

Standard of Compensation

34. The Tribunal now turns to the valuation of the Claimants' expropriated shareholding interests in Alborz. The Tribunal has previously held that under the Treaty of Amity[4] a deprivation requires compensation equal to the full equivalent of the value of the interests in the property taken.[5] The Tribunal has found that the Respondents deprived the Claimants of their

---

[4] Treaty of Amity, Economic Relations, and Consular Rights Between the United States of America and Iran, *signed* 15 August 1955, *entered into force* 16 June 1957, 284 U.N.T.S. 93, T.I.A.S. No. 3853, 8 U.S.T. 900. The Tribunal has already found that the Treaty was in force at the time the claim in this case arose. *See, e.g.*, *Phelps Dodge Corp., et al.* v. *The Islamic Republic of Iran*, Award No. 217-99-2, para. 27 (19 Mar. 1986), *reprinted in* 10 IRAN-U.S. C.T.R. 121, 131-32.

[5] *Id.*, para. 28, 10 IRAN-U.S. C.T.R. 132.

ownership interests in Alborz, and consequently they are entitled to full compensation.[6] If the taken enterprise was a going concern, then the full equivalent of its value equals its fair market value.[7] Fair market value may be defined as

> the amount which a willing buyer would have paid a willing seller for the shares of a going concern, disregarding any diminution of value due to the nationalization itself or the anticipation thereof, and excluding consideration of events thereafter that might have increased or decreased the value of the shares.[8]

On the other hand, while any diminution of value caused by the expropriation of the property itself should be disregarded, "prior changes in the general political, social and economic conditions which might have affected the enterprise's business prospects as of the date the enterprise was taken should be considered." *American Int'l Group, supra*, at 18, 4 IRAN-U.S. C.T.R. at 107. In the same Award the Tribunal has also stated that the value of a going concern involves "not only the net book value of its assets but also such elements as good will and likely future profitability, had the company been allowed to continue its business under its former management." *Id.*, at 21, 4 IRAN-U.S. C.T.R. at 109.

Contentions of the Parties

35. In view of the valuation method ultimately used by the Tribunal (*see infra*, paras. 47-52), the Tribunal will only briefly summarize the Parties' main assumptions and arguments and not discuss in detail the different valuation formulae used by the Claimants and Respondents respectively.

36. The Claimants originally sought Rials 2,100 per share as compensation for their expropriated interest in Alborz. In subsequent submissions they relied on valuation analysis of several experts which gave different values of Alborz. At the Hearing, the Claimants presented and exclusively relied on the expert testimony of Mr. Robert Reilly, who arrived at a value of Rials 2,840 per share.

---

[6] In this Case, as in the *Saghi* Case, the Tribunal has used the Treaty of Amity standard of compensation without deciding whether it is applicable to claims of dual nationals whose dominant and effective nationality in the relevant period under *A18* has been that of the United States or Iran, as the case may be. *See James M. Saghi, et al. v. The Islamic Republic of Iran*, Award No. 544-298-2 (22 Jan. 1993), *reprinted in* 29 IRAN-U.S. C.T.R. 20. In neither case was that question raised or argued by the Parties.

[7] *See American Int'l Group Inc. v. The Islamic Republic of Iran*, Award No. 93-2-3, at 21-22 (19 Dec. 1983), *reprinted in* 4 IRAN-U.S. C.T.R. 96, 109; *INA Corp. v. The Islamic Republic of Iran*, Award No. 184-161-1, at 10 (12 Aug. 1985), *reprinted in* 8 IRAN-U.S. C.T.R. 373, 379; *Starrett Housing Corp. et al. v. The Islamic Republic of Iran, et al.*, Award No. 314-24-1, paras 261, 277 (14 Aug. 1987), *reprinted in* 16 IRAN-U.S. C.T.R. 112, 195, 201.

[8] *INA, supra*, at 10, 8 IRAN-U.S. C.T.R. at 380.

37. Mr. Reilly arrived at this figure by using a weighted average of three different valuation techniques: an asset accumulation approach, an income capitalization approach, and a market approach. In all three techniques Mr. Reilly assumed that Alborz was a going concern at the time of the taking. The values given by Mr. Reilly therefore include the value of Alborz's goodwill in addition to the value of its tangible assets.

38. In his asset accumulation approach Mr. Reilly first makes an upward adjustment of Alborz's book value to reflect the effects of inflation. This results in Alborz's net tangible assets being Rials 2.51 billion. Mr. Reilly then calculates that Alborz had an "intangible asset value" of Rials 2.99 billion. Adding the two figures, subtracting Alborz's long-term debt and then dividing the figure by the number of shares outstanding, yields a per share value of Rials 2,803.

39. The "income capitalization approach" is only relevant when one is doing a going-concern premise appraisal. This is because the method assigns a present value to the future stream of earnings available to the shareholders, which is not applicable in case of a liquidation. In calculating the equity value of Rials 4.3 billion, Mr. Reilly assumes that (1) Alborz's average yearly earnings will continue to be Rials 391 million, (2) inflation will remain 10% and (3) Alborz's cost of capital will remain 19.95%. The income capitalization approach results in a per share value of Rials 2,914.

40. The third and, according to Mr. Reilly, supplemental approach is the market approach. He admits that "this market approach is based upon a lot of assumptions that are not real world assumptions; so I do not rate that very heavily." Assuming that Alborz's last-traded stock price was Rials 2,005 per share in 1978 and taking a recent 1990 stock price of Rials 7,012 per share, he makes a linear extrapolation to arrive at a stock price of Rials 2,754 per share in July 1979. Based on a weighted average of the three values calculated, Mr. Reilly then concludes that Alborz's shares were worth Rials 2,840 at the date of taking.

41. The Respondents originally maintained that Alborz's shares had a book value of Rials 836 per share at the time of the taking. They later used the analysis prepared by Touche Ross to argue that the shares in fact had a negative value. At the Hearing the Respondents relied exclusively on the expert report and testimony by Mr. Anthony Tracy, a partner of Touche Ross.

42. The Touche Ross report differs fundamentally from the Reilly approach in its assumption that Alborz was no longer a viable firm at the date of taking. Although the report admits that Alborz was indeed a going concern, the valuation proposed by Touche Ross was nevertheless based upon the prospective orderly realization of assets and not on a going concern premise. The reason given by Touche Ross was that, due to Alborz's poor liquidity,

heavy debt burden and other problems, keeping Alborz as a going concern would have involved too high a measure of risk of a compulsory liquidation in the near future. Therefore, in order to avoid the drawbacks of such a forced liquidation, Touche Ross proposed an approach based on an orderly realization of assets.

43. To calculate the results of such an orderly realization, Mr. Tracy of Touche Ross discounts many of Alborz's assets to reflect the cautious view of a reasonable investor. On Alborz's liabilities side, the report does not make any adjustments noting that "the net book value appears to represent the actual amount payable in relation to the debts." The report then concludes that Alborz's liabilities exceeded the realizable value of its assets at the time of the taking. Touche Ross arrives at a net realizable value of negative Rials 620 million. Dividing this amount by the number of outstanding Alborz shares yields a negative value of Rials 417 per share.

The Tribunal's Findings

44. To resolve the conflict between the Claimants' and the Respondents' experts, the Tribunal must first determine whether Alborz was a going concern at the time of the taking. Alborz produced a wide variety of basic products including pharmaceutical, toiletries, household cleaning products, and foodstuffs. Even in the midst of the revolutionary turmoil, it can be expected that a market for these goods would have continued to exist. *Cf. Sola Tiles, Inc. v. The Islamic Republic of Iran*, Award No. 298-317-1 (22 Apr. 1987) paras. 63-64, *reprinted in* 14 IRAN-U.S. C.T.R. 223, 241-42 (finding that the Revolution had detrimentally affected the market for luxury tiles); *CBS, Inc. v. The Islamic Republic of Iran*, Award No. 486-197-2 (28 Jun. 1990) para. 52, *reprinted in* 25 IRAN-U.S. C.T.R. 131, 148-49, (finding that the Revolution had adversely affected the market for Western music in Iran).

45. An inspection of Alborz's financial statements confirms that Alborz did indeed continue to manufacture, distribute, and sell its products throughout the events of the Revolution. The financial statements in the record show that Alborz consistently increased its sales during the period beginning in 1974 and continuing through the financial year ending 20 March 1980. In fact, in the year of the taking, Alborz achieved a record sales level, exceeding the previous year's performance by more than 2 billion Rials. In that year, Alborz reported a net loss of 74 million Rials and proposed no dividend. This loss, however, appears to arise in part from adjustments for embezzlement and bad debts that can be characterized as singular events. Notwithstanding this loss it is not unreasonable to conclude that even during 1979-80 Alborz's core business remained viable.

46. The company reports issued shortly before the taking also confirm

that Alborz was a going concern. The report dated May 16, 1979, clearly indicates that Alborz did continue to operate throughout the financial year ending 20 March 1979. Despite important difficulties mentioned in this report, *i.e.* delayed delivery of raw materials, shortage of raw materials, transportation problems, and temporary closing of some production facilities, Alborz managed to meet its payroll and to continue limited production. The report states that:

> under the conditions when many companies and factories were virtually unable to pay monthly salaries to their personnel and their operations had been halted or ceased, we paid full salaries and allowances to our staff on time or with little delay and relied on ourselves without bringing any harm to [the] Corporation's repute and goodwill.

The record also shows other contemporaneous documents that indicate that Alborz remained a going concern in the months leading up to the taking. A letter written by Mr. Javad Khosrowshahi two days after Mr. Saidi's appointment stated that the company remained financially healthy and had maintained production while preserving all employee benefits. Further, the report of the government auditors who examined the 20 March 1980 financial statements does not suggest that this situation had changed. In light of all the above, the Tribunal finds that Alborz was a going concern at the time of the taking.

47. Having concluded that Alborz was a going concern at the time of the taking, the Tribunal need not respond in detail to many of the arguments raised in the Touche Ross report. These arguments are based on the assumption that the valuation of Alborz should not be made on a going concern premise. However, although Mr. Reilly's Report is based on the going concern premise, the Tribunal also has difficulty agreeing with many of the arguments advanced by him. Instead, the Tribunal finds particularly relevant the evidence relating to known trading prices of Alborz shares. Since the Tribunal's valuation precedents suppose a willing buyer and seller in order to determine the full equivalent of the property taken, a contemporaneous market price is clearly the best available evidence of the value of Alborz shares.

48. The Claimants have submitted a copy of the *Tehran Economist*, a financial news magazine, indicating that Alborz stock traded at Rials 2005 per share during the week ending October 25, 1978. The Respondents have introduced a letter from the General Secretary of the Tehran Stock Exchange stating that Alborz's last traded price before the suspension of trading of its shares in November 1978 was Rials 1850 per share. The Tribunal has consulted the Annual Report of the Tehran Stock Exchange. This report,

published in April 1979, indicates that the last trade of Alborz shares prior to their taking occurred in the month of Aban, 1357 (October or November of 1978) at a price of Rials 1850 per share. To resolve the contradiction in the evidence of the Claimants and Respondents, the Tribunal will use the Annual Report price as the basis of the valuation analysis.

49. Because the last trade in Alborz shares took place approximately eight months before the taking of the Claimants' shares in Alborz, the Tribunal finds it necessary to consider the events of the intervening period. The Tribunal is convinced that the effects of the Islamic Revolution on the value of Alborz shares cannot be ignored. It is well known that Iran's economy was disrupted and transformed by the Revolution. Although an October/November market price for Alborz would doubtless have reflected the effects of the turmoil to date, many of the most significant economic and political disruptions were yet to come in the first months of 1979. Just as those disruptions had their impact on Iran's economy as a whole, they would almost certainly have had an impact on Alborz share prices if the stock had still been trading on the market.

50. A potential investor in Alborz shares at the time of the taking would certainly have noted the events of the Revolution and weighed the resulting political and economic risks. Alborz's Annual Report for the year ending March 20, 1979 makes clear that the upheaval affected Alborz's operations adversely. As noted *supra*, para. 46, the report documents a shortage of raw materials needed for production, transportation problems, work stoppages, and temporary closures of some production facilities. Also, the 16 May 1979 report, covering the three preceding months, by Mr. Javad Khosrowshahi indicates that the above-noted problems had become more acute by mid-1979 and that the company was in an undesirable financial situation. Indeed the very fact that the Claimants, as well as some other members of the Khosrowshahi family, agreed in 1978 to defer the receipt of their declared dividends clearly indicated that Alborz was facing financial difficulties at the time.

51. However, the impact of the Revolution should not be exaggerated or reduced to broad generalizations. It can be assumed that a potential investor would be able to distinguish between investments likely to be undermined by the Revolution and those which might reasonably be expected to recover once the turmoil subsided. It is clear that Alborz, with its line of pharmaceutical, household, and personal care products, was in a better position to survive the Revolution than a concern distributing luxury tiles or western music. *See supra*, para. 44. On the other hand, the Tribunal also notes that its task is to determine the value of Alborz shares in July 1979. At that time, it was also likely that a potential willing buyer would focus more on the short-term

prospects of Alborz and the prevailing unforeseeability and instability of the market at the time. Therefore, the Tribunal finds that it must strike a fair balance, considering all the relevant factors in order to reach the fair market value which a potential willing buyer would have paid for the Alborz shares.

52. Although the evidence in this Case is not sufficient to allow the Tribunal to assign a precise value to Alborz shares at the date of the taking, the Tribunal is able to make a reasonable approximation. Based on a review of all the available evidence pertaining to valuation, the Tribunal determines that the last traded Alborz stock price of Rials 1850 per share is a reasonable starting point. In light of the above-described effects of the Revolution on Alborz, and having considered generally available information about Revolutionary conditions between the Fall of 1978 and July 7, 1979, the Tribunal concludes that it is appropriate to discount the last-traded stock price by 25%, representing a further reduction of Alborz's fair market value during the eight months immediately preceding the taking. Thus, for the purposes of compensation, the Tribunal finds that the value of each Alborz share was Rials 1387.5 at the time of the taking.

53. The Tribunal therefore awards the Claimants compensation for deprivation of their ownership interests in Alborz by the Government of the Islamic Republic of Iran as follows:

Faith Lita Khosrowshahi	IR 10,110,990	for 7,287.2 shares
Susanne P. Khosrowshahi	IR 18,681,300	for 13,464 shares
Marcene P. Khosrowshahi	IR 18,681,300	for 13,464 shares
Kevin Khosrowshahi	IR 45,483,776.25	for 32,781.1 shares
Cameron Khosrowshahi	IR 45,483,776.25	for 32,781.1 shares

Based on the exchange rate of Rials 70.475/U.S.$1 prevailing at the time of expropriation, therefore, Faith Lita is awarded $143,469.17, Susanne P. and Marcene P. are each awarded $265,076.98 and Kevin and Cameron are each awarded $645,388.80.

IV. THE KHOSROWSHAHI BROTHERS COMPANY

A. Facts and Contentions

54. As noted *supra*, KBC was organized in 1954 as a private joint stock company engaged in importing, exporting, and general trading. KBC remained a private company throughout the organization of the Alborz Group and continued to operate in conjunction with those companies, serving as the import-export arm of the Alborz Group.

55. KBC stock consisted of 1,200 bearer shares. The Claimants maintain that in late 1978, the Khosrowshahi brothers sent all 1,200 KBC bearer

shares to the Claimants and Nasrollah Khosrowshahi in the United States for safekeeping. They further maintain that as possessors of the shares, they held legal title to them all because under Article 39 of the Commercial Code of Iran, bearer shares are owned by whomever has possession of the shares "unless proven otherwise." Although initially the Claimants alleged that they owned 1,100 of the shares, they subsequently reduced that to 180 shares. Finally, at the Hearing they requested a further amendment to reduce their earlier claim to 100. They now claim for only 100 shares because the Khosrowshahi brothers allegedly agreed that each of their respective families would hold a 1/6 ownership interest in the shares. Thus, the Claimants explain, Nasrollah Khosrowshahi owns 100 shares and the Claimants own 100 shares, although the precise extent of the ownership of each individual Claimant has not been clarified. The Claimants contend that they have owned these shares continuously from early 1979 until the date of their expropriation.

56. The Claimants argue that the expropriation of their shares in Alborz constituted a *de facto* expropriation of their shares in KBC as well because KBC was "intricately tied to Alborz." Although the Claimants acknowledge that Alborz and KBC were legally distinct entities, they emphasize that the Khosrowshahi family controlled both companies and allege that there was substantial overlap in the companies' day-to-day management. In this context the Claimants further assert that the headquarters of Alborz, its operating subsidiaries and KBC were located in the same offices at 247 Naderi Avenue, Tehran.

57. As a preliminary matter, the Respondents deny that the Claimants own the KBC shares at issue. They first argue that the Claimants have failed to submit any documentary evidence proving that they actually owned the shares prior to the date of the CSD. In support of this argument, the Respondents submit the affidavit of Mr. Hossein Fathollah, the Managing Director of KBC, which states that the Claimants' names were never included among the company shareholders. In addition, they point out that the contemporaneous minutes of the KBC shareholders' meetings do not record the Claimants as shareholders.

58. In the event the Tribunal would find that the Claimants owned 100 KBC shares, the Respondents deny that Iran expropriated the Claimants' shares in KBC at the same time that it allegedly took their shares in Alborz. Noting that KBC is a separate legal entity from Alborz, they argue that the alleged expropriation of the Claimants' shares in Alborz should not necessarily result in the expropriation of their shares in KBC. Furthermore, the Respondents note that the evidence they submitted clearly demonstrates that KBC was run by managers duly appointed by its shareholders until March

1981 when the Bureau for Registration of Non-Commercial Corporations and Institutions announced the appointment of the new Directors for KBC.

B. *The Tribunal's Findings*

59. KBC was a legal entity separate from Alborz; the taking of the Claimants' shares in Alborz did, therefore, not necessarily constitute a taking of whatever shares they might have had in KBC. In the absence of well-founded evidence demonstrating that KBC and Alborz were tightly intertwined on a management and operational level, the Tribunal gives more weight to the evidence in the record showing that governmental directors were not appointed to run KBC at any time prior to 19 January 1981. The Tribunal is unconvinced that the Claimants' interest was expropriated prior to the date of the Claims Settlement Declaration. The Tribunal therefore dismisses the KBC claim for lack of jurisdiction without determining the precise nature of Claimants' interest in KBC.

V. THE DEVELOPMENT AND INVESTMENT BANK OF IRAN

A. *Facts and Contentions*
 1. *Claimants' DIBI shares*

60. DIBI was a publicly traded, joint stock bank incorporated in 1973 to provide capital for the establishment of new enterprises in Iran. The Bank's shareholders included major Iranian concerns, financial institutions, foreign banks, and certain members of the Khosrowshahi family. The Parties agree that four of the Claimants owned a combined total of 33,262 class "A" shares in DIBI, *i.e.*, Susanne P. and Marcene P. each owned 4,989 shares and Kevin and Cameron each owned 11,642 shares.

61. On 7 June 1979, the Iranian Government passed the Banks Nationalization Law, which immediately nationalized all banks in Iran and authorized the Government to "take steps to appoint directors of all banks." Pursuant to this law, the Government nationalized DIBI and appointed a new Board of Directors. The Respondents allege that the Government created a mechanism by which former bank shareholders could be compensated for their loss. According to the Respondents, Article 1 of the Legal Bill approved on June 25, 1980 announced that:

> the payment of the value of the shares of the former shareholders of the nationalized banks . . . shall be effected equivalent to the capital and reserves inserted in the banks' . . . auditing reports made on June 7, 1979, after deducting the annual losses.

62. Notwithstanding the compensation mechanism, the Claimants argue that their rights as DIBI shareholders were expropriated by the nationalization

of DIBI. They allege that from the moment of the nationalization, they have not received any official communications from or about DIBI. The Claimants contend that they have not received any communication regarding compensation and allege that they have been excluded from any compensation scheme. They have, however, submitted a copy of a letter from the Secretariat of the High Council of Banks dated 7 June 1981, which is in response to a DIBI shareholder's inquiry about the compensation scheme. The letter stated that (1) the Bank was nationalized on 7 June 1979; (2) the Islamic Revolutionary Council of Iran on 25 June 1980 had approved payment of compensation of some sort to "the previous shareholders" and (3) the "determination of the manner and date of the payment" was on the agenda of the general meeting of the High Council of Banks, but still unresolved on the date of the letter, 7 June 1981.

63. As ultimately pleaded at the Hearing, the Respondents argue that the nationalization of the Bank did not deprive the Claimants of their right to appropriate compensation because of the compensation mechanism provided for in the Legal Bill. They claim that "all the shareholders of [DIBI] including the Claimants can, in case of entitlement, directly or through their legal representatives collect the value of their shares." The Respondents have further asserted that the Claimants' DIBI claim was not outstanding on 19 January 1981 because they had not "demanded their ownership rights and interests [in DIBI] before filing the initial Statement of Claim."

2. *DIBI Dividends*

64. Finally, the Claimants maintain that DIBI declared a dividend of 90 rials per share for the fiscal year ending March 20, 1978, and that they never received this dividend. Claimants base their assertion of entitlement to the dividend upon a proposal for such payment in the auditors' report for DIBI, dated 26 May 1979. The Respondents argue that DIBI's Board of Directors never approved the dividend and that it was not paid. The Respondents therefore maintain that Claimants are not entitled to any such dividend.

B. *The Tribunal's Findings*
 1. *Claimants' DIBI shares*

65. The Tribunal concludes from the above that the Banks Nationalization Law clearly effected a compensable taking of the Claimants' DIBI shares. The Parties appear to agree with this conclusion that the Claimants' shares in DIBI were nationalized on 7 June 1979 in accordance with the Banks Nationalization Law of the same date.

66. Respondents' argument that the Claimants cannot have a claim before the Tribunal due to the existence of a compensation mechanism in Iran

cannot be accepted. The Tribunal's jurisdiction does not depend on the exhaustion of local remedies. *See, e.g., Rexnord* v. *The Islamic Republic of Iran*, Award No. 21-132-3 at 9 (10 Jan. 1983) *reprinted in* 2 IRAN-U.S. C.T.R. 6, 10. Moreover, the letter from the Secretariat of the High Council of Banks makes clear that as of 7 June 1981, no shareholders had been compensated for their DIBI shares.

67. The Tribunal must also reject Respondents' argument that this claim is not within the Tribunal's jurisdiction because the Claimants had failed to make a demand before the date of the Claims Settlement Declaration. The Tribunal has repeatedly held that no demand for such a claim is a prerequisite to a finding that the claim was outstanding at the date of the Algiers Declarations. In the present claim the Claimants do not seek to recover monies on deposit in DIBI, but, instead, seek to recover the value of their ownership interest in the Bank itself. The two cases are, therefore, markedly different. Accordingly, the Tribunal finds that the claim was outstanding and that the Banks Nationalization Law expropriated the Claimants' ownership interests in DIBI.

2. *DIBI Dividends*

68. After examining the record, the Tribunal finds no proof that the dividend payment was ever authorized by the Board of Directors. The 1979 auditors' report suggesting the payment of a dividend relied on by the Claimants is not sufficient because the payment of dividends requires the approval of the Board of Directors. Accordingly, the Claimants' claim for unpaid DIBI dividends is dismissed for lack of proof.

3. *Application of the Caveat to Claimants' DIBI Claim*

69. As with the Claimants' Alborz claim, the Tribunal first has to address the "Caveat argument" raised by the Respondents. The Respondents argue that the Claimants, by purchasing shares reserved for Iranian nationals, have abused their Iranian nationality and therefore the Tribunal should not allow the Claimants to recover the value of their DIBI shares.

70. DIBI shares were divided into categories "A" and "B". According to Article 6 of the Bank's Articles of Association:

> The stock belonging to Iranian subjects has been classified as "A category" while that owned by non-Iranian subjects as "B category." Each "B category" stock, which is transferred to Iranian subjects shall be converted by the Bank into "A category" stock, and reciprocally each "A category" stock, to be transferred to non-Iranian subjects, shall be changed by the Bank into "B category" stock.

The Notes to this Article provided that (1) the total amount of B stock could not exceed 25% of the Bank's outstanding capital and (2) except for the cases to be expressly mentioned in the Articles of Association there would be no distinction between the two categories of shares.

71. The Respondents assert that the Claimants must have concealed their U.S. nationality at the time of the purchase of "A category" shares because had the Bank been aware of Claimants' nationality, "the purchase of the shares in dispute was practically impossible."

72. The Claimants insist that they did not conceal their U.S. nationality when they purchased "A category" shares in DIBI or any time thereafter. They state that they were never asked about their nationality prior to purchasing their shares. They further argue that, at least with respect to the limitation on foreign ownership, because the 25% ceiling on foreign ownership had not been reached at the time of purchase of their shares, non-Iranians could have purchased "B category" shares just as easily as they purchased "A category" shares. With their approximately .008% of DIBI stock added to the 18.9% outstanding B stock, the 25% limit would not have been reached. Consequently, the fact that the Claimants received "A category" shares does not mean that they obtained property rights not available by law to non-Iranians.

73. An examination of the record has not convinced the Tribunal that the Claimants concealed or otherwise abused their dual nationality when purchasing "A category" shares in DIBI. It is clear from the evidence that in general foreigners were not excluded from acquiring share ownership in DIBI. Indeed, ownership of DIBI shares was open to foreign nationals, albeit within the 25% prescribed limit. The mere fact that they were issued a class of shares available only to Iranian nationals does not prove that they concealed their U.S. nationality when buying the shares. *See Golpira, supra* at 6, 2 IRAN-U.S. C.T.R. at 174. Moreover, the Respondents have not submitted any evidence demonstrating that the Claimants misrepresented or concealed their U.S. nationality. For example, the Respondents failed to submit any of the bank records concerning the way in which the shares were acquired by the Claimants as well as their representation of themselves to DIBI. *Cf. Robert R. Schott* v. *Islamic Republic of Iran, et al.*, Award No. 474-268-1 (14 March 1990) para. 43, *reprinted in* 24 IRAN-U.S. C.T.R. 203, at 218 (where there was in evidence a statement signed by the Claimants' daughter, who held the shares in dispute in her name, that if she were to surrender her Iranian nationality, she would transfer the shares to another Iranian national). It seems clear that dual nationals could not have purchased "B category" shares, as Iran would not recognize their non-Iranian nationality. Furthermore, as the Bank acknowledged at the Hearing and as the auditor's report dated 26 May 1979 suggests, the 25% limit on foreign ownership was never reached. Accordingly, the Claimants' purchase of .008% of the total shares of DIBI could well have

fallen within the permitted 25% level of foreign ownership. Furthermore, there is no evidence that the Claimants received any specific benefit by holding "A category" shares. Considering all the above circumstances, the Tribunal concludes that there is not sufficient evidence that the Claimants used their Iranian nationality at the time they acquired DIBI shares or subsequently, in order to secure benefits available under Iranian law exclusively to Iranian nationals or that in any other way their conduct was such as to justify refusal of an award in their favor with respect to this claim.

4. Valuation

74. The Claimants originally sought compensation for their DIBI shares in the amount of Rials 1600 per share. They later increased this amount to Rials 1650 per share which is the median of the known traded prices in DIBI stock during the period March 21, 1978-October 25, 1978. The Claimants have further submitted evidence showing that DIBI's last traded price was Rials 1575 per share.

75. At the Hearing, the Claimants' expert, Mr. Reilly, proposed a value of Rials 1830 per DIBI share. Mr. Reilly arrived at this amount by taking a weighted average of DIBI's last known trading price and its 1978 book value per share. According to the expert, this is a very conservative indication of the valuation, as "banks typically are valued at premiums above book value."

76. The Respondents disagree with the Claimants' valuation. At the Hearing, they argued that the government paid DIBI's former shareholders 89% of the share nominal value or Rials 890 per share. The Respondents suggested that this would be an appropriate amount of compensation for the Claimants as well.

77. As noted *supra*, para. 34, under the Treaty of Amity the Claimants are entitled to the full equivalent of their taken DIBI shares. Thus, the amount that the Government allegedly paid to other DIBI shareholders is, although relevant, not dispositive. It is the Tribunal's task to make its own determination of the value of the Claimants' DIBI shares. As in the valuation of Alborz, the Tribunal finds the evidence of DIBI's actual market prices during the year 1978 particularly relevant. *See supra*, para. 47. In that connection, the Tribunal notes that DIBI stock traded at a high of Rials 1850 per share in April and May of 1978. Its last traded price of Rials 1575 per share was in October 1978.

78. To establish a value of the DIBI shares as of 7 June 1979 the Tribunal will take the same approach as it did with the valuation of Alborz's shares. Thus, the Tribunal finds it reasonable to assume that the final price of Rials 1575 per share in October 1978 reflected the impact of revolutionary events to that date on DIBI. That price then needs to be adjusted to reflect the events

that occurred between that last-traded price and the date of the taking. As discussed above, the evidence indicates that Alborz was detrimentally affected by the events of the Revolution. *See supra*, para. 50. In the absence of evidence to the contrary, the Tribunal finds it reasonable to conclude that DIBI was also affected by these events. The decline in its share price between May and October 1978 was even sharper than the decline in the price of Alborz shares during that period. After considering all the relevant elements of this claim, the Tribunal concludes that it is fair to discount DIBI's last-traded price of Rials 1575 by 30%. This yields a per share value of Rials 1102.5 per share.

79. The Parties agree that four of the Claimants, *i.e.*, Susanne, Marcene, Kevin and Cameron, owned collectively 33,262 shares of DIBI. The Tribunal therefore awards the four Claimants compensation for deprivation of their ownership interests in DIBI by the Government of the Islamic Republic of Iran as follows:

Susanne P. Khosrowshahi	IR 5,500,372.5 for 4,989 shares
Marcene P. Khosrowshahi	IR 5,500,372.5 for 4,989 shares
Kevin Khosrowshahi	IR 12,835,305 for 11,642 shares
Cameron Khosrowshahi	IR 12,835,305 for 11,642 shares

Converted at the rate of exchange of Rials 70.475/U.S.$1, *see supra*, para. 53, Susanne P. and Marcene P. are each awarded $78,047.14 and Kevin and Cameron are each awarded $182,125.65.

VI. INTEREST

80. In order to compensate the Claimants for the damages they suffered as a result of the Respondents' failure to compensate them when their property was taken, the Tribunal considers it fair to award the Claimants simple interest at the rate of 8.6% from the dates of the deprivation of their interests.

VII. COSTS

81. Each Party shall bear its own costs of arbitration.

VIII. AWARD

82. For the foregoing reasons,

THE TRIBUNAL AWARDS AS FOLLOWS:
  A. The Claim for the expropriation of the Claimants' shares in Khosrowshahi Brothers Company is dismissed for lack of jurisdiction.

B. The Claims for the non-payment of the allegedly due dividends from the Alborz Investment Corporation and The Development and Investment Bank of Iran are dismissed for lack of proof.
C. The Respondent, the Government of the Islamic Republic of Iran, is obligated to pay the following amounts to each of the Claimants as compensation for expropriation of their shares in:
Alborz Investment Company:
- to Faith Lita Khosrowshahi, the amount of U.S.$143,469.17 (One Hundred Forty Three Thousand Four Hundred Sixty Nine United States Dollars and Seventeen Cents), plus simple interest at the rate of 8.6% per annum (365-day basis) from 7 July 1979 up to and including the date on which the Escrow Agent instructs the Depository Bank to effect payment to the Claimant out of the Security Account;
- to Susanne P. Khosrowshahi, the amount of U.S.$265,076.98 (Two Hundred Sixty Five Thousand Seventy Six United States Dollars and Ninety Eight Cents), plus simple interest at the rate of 8.6% per annum (365-day basis) from 7 July 1979 up to and including the date on which the Escrow Agent instructs the Depository Bank to effect payment to the Claimant out of the Security Account;
- to Marcene P. Khosrowshahi, the amount of U.S.$265,076.98 (Two Hundred Sixty Five Thousand Seventy Six United States Dollars and Ninety Eight Cents), plus simple interest at the rate of 8.6% per annum (365-day basis) from 7 July 1979 up to and including the date on which the Escrow Agent instructs the Depository Bank to effect payment to the Claimant out of the Security Account;
- to Kevin Kayvan Khosrowshahi, the amount of U.S.$645,388.80 (Six Hundred Forty Five Thousand Three Hundred Eighty Eight United States Dollars and Eighty Cents), plus simple interest at the rate of 8.6% per annum (365-day basis) from 7 July 1979 up to and including the date on which the Escrow Agent instructs the Depository Bank to effect payment to the Claimant out of the Security Account;
- to Cameron Kamran Khosrowshahi, the amount of U.S.$645,388.80 (Six Hundred Forty Five Thousand Three Hundred Eighty Eight United States Dollars and Eighty Cents), plus simple interest at the rate of 8.6% per annum (365-day basis) from 7 July 1979 up to and including the date on which the Escrow Agent instructs the Depository Bank to effect payment to the Claimant out of the Security Account;
and in The Development and Investment Bank of Iran:
- to Susanne P. Khosrowshahi, the amount of U.S.$78,047.14 (Seventy Eight Thousand Forty Seven United States Dollars and Fourteen

Cents), plus simple interest at the rate of 8.6% per annum (365-day basis) from 7 June 1979 up to and including the date on which the Escrow Agent instructs the Depository Bank to effect payment to the Claimant out of the Security Account;
- to Marcene P. Khosrowshahi, the amount of U.S.$78,047.14 (Seventy Eight Thousand Forty Seven United States Dollars and Fourteen Cents), plus simple interest at the rate of 8.6% per annum (365-day basis) from 7 June 1979 up to and including the date on which the Escrow Agent instructs the Depository Bank to effect payment to the Claimant out of the Security Account;
- to Kevin Kayvan Khosrowshahi, the amount of U.S.$182,125.65 (One Hundred Eighty Two Thousand One Hundred Twenty Five United States Dollars and Sixty Five Cents), plus simple interest at the rate of 8.6% per annum (365-day basis) from 7 June 1979 up to and including the date on which the Escrow Agent instructs the Depository Bank to effect payment to the Claimant out of the Security Account;
- to Cameron Kamran Khosrowshahi, the amount of U.S.$182,125.65 (One Hundred Eighty Two Thousand One Hundred Twenty Five United States Dollars and Sixty Five Cents), plus simple interest at the rate of 8.6% per annum (365-day basis) from 7 June 1979 up to and including the date on which the Escrow Agent instructs the Depository Bank to effect payment to the Claimant out of the Security Account.

D. The Claims against all other Respondents are dismissed.
E. Each Party shall bear its own costs of arbitration.
F. This Award is hereby submitted to the President of the Tribunal for notification to the Escrow Agent.

Dadras International
and Per Am Construction Corporation,
Claimants

v.

The Islamic Republic of Iran,
and Tehran Redevelopment Company, *Respondents*

(Cases Nos. 213 and 215)

Chamber Three: Arangio-Ruiz, *Chairman*; Allison,[1] Aghahosseini,[2] Members

Signed 22 *July* 1994[3]

Order

The following is the text as issued by the Tribunal:

1. Reference is made to the Request by the Agent of the Islamic Republic of Iran filed on 27 May 1994 for the reopening of the Hearing in these Cases and to the objection of the Claimants filed on 10 June 1994.

2. The Tribunal notes that the post-Hearing submission of an affidavit by Mr. Golzar and the subsequent acceptance of that affidavit into the record, as well as the evidence which was admitted by order of 23 February 1994 and through the submissions scheduled by the Tribunal, has introduced new material into the record.

3. The Tribunal notes further that it is now confronted with directly conflicting and irreconcilable statements from the two alleged signatories to the contract. The Tribunal considers that its task to determine which version of events is the more accurate can better be accomplished by observing and examining Messrs. Golzar and Dadras in each other's presence at a hearing.

4. The Tribunal hereby determines that exceptional circumstances exist such that the Hearing in these Cases should be reopened in accordance with Article 29, paragraph 2, of the Tribunal Rules, for the sole and limited purpose of hearing the testimony of Messrs. Rahman Golzar Shabestari and Aly Shahidzadeh Dadras. Because of the advanced stage of deliberations and the procedural history of these Cases, in the interests of procedural orderliness

---

[1 Mr. Allison's Dissenting Opinion to the Order of 22 July 1994 appears at page 112, below.]

[2 Mr. Aghahosseini's Concurring Opinion to the Order of 22 July 1994 appears at page 105, below.]

[3 Filed 22 July 1994.]

the Tribunal will not reopen the Hearing for any other than this very limited purpose.

5. A Hearing is scheduled to take place on 20 October 1994 at 9.30 a.m. at Parkweg 13, The Hague, The Netherlands.

6. The Parties are hereby informed that in the interests of orderliness and fairness to both Parties, the following conditions will apply at the Hearing:
  (i) The object of inquiry by the Tribunal will be the authenticity of Mr. Golzar's signatures on the Contract dated 9 September 1978 and the letter dated 27 August 1978. Questions and answers are to be confined to that subject.
  (ii) The proceedings will be confined to the subject outlined in para 6(i) above and will be limited to:
    - testimony by Mr. Golzar and Mr. Dadras;
    - cross-examination of Mr. Golzar by the Claimants and of Mr. Dadras by the Respondents;
    - examination of Mr. Golzar and Mr. Dadras by the Tribunal;
    - opening and closing remarks by Counsel for Claimants and Respondents.
  (iii) No additional witnesses, rebuttal witnesses or interested parties will be permitted to testify.
  (iv) The Parties will not be required or permitted to file additional pleadings either before or after the Hearing.

The Tribunal will consider inadmissible any document or testimony containing new material.

Concurring Opinion of Mohsen Aghahosseini to the Order of 22 July 1994[1]

The Chamber's Order of 22 July 1994 severely curtails the Parties' right, granted *inter alia* by Article 15(1) of the Tribunal Rules, to a full opportunity to present their cases and, in turn, lessens the Chamber's ability to ascertain the truth. I have, nevertheless, concurred in the Order simply to prevent the commission by the Chamber of the greater wrong of not merely curtailing but altogether dispensing with this right.

I. THE BACKGROUND

The relevant facts may first be briefly stated. As I have described

[1 Signed 12 August 1994; filed 12 August 1994.]

elsewhere,[2] the claims in the present proceedings are mainly based on the asserted breaches of a contract which, according to the Claimants, was concluded on 9 September 1978 between a Mr. Ali. S. Dadras, one of the Claimants, and a Mr. Rahman Golzar Shabestari, the then Managing Director of the Respondent TRC. The signing of this contract, the Claimants contend, took place in the presence of three individuals, namely, Messrs Mehdi Amini, Parviz Golshani, and Mohsen Farahi. Yet another individual, a Mr. Joseph Morog, who was then the TRC's chief architect, is also said to have been aware of the existence, and fully familiar with the terms, of the asserted contract.

The existence of such a contract has, on the other hand, been denied by the Respondents. Amongst a host of evidence submitted by them in this regard is a letter which bears a date subsequent to the date of the asserted contract and in which Mr. Dadras, who admits to have written the letter, pleads with Mr. Golzar to favourably consider the possibility of signing a contract with him in future. Relying on this and other pieces of evidence, they have specifically invited the Claimants to prove the authenticity of the alleged contract.

Now, although under the circumstances described, it has undoubtedly been on the Claimants to establish the existence of the challenged contract – a most essential part of their claims – they have throughout the proceedings elected not to provide the Chamber with the written or oral words of either the alleged signer of the contract, or any of those four individuals who are supposed to have intimate knowledge of it. And this in spite of the fact, now established, that, but for one, all these individuals, whose recollections would have provided the Chamber with direct evidence, live in the United States of America. Indeed, the absence of any word from any of these asserted witnesses was so conspicuous as to prompt the Members of this Chamber to repeatedly question the Claimants at the Hearing. What efforts, these Members wanted to know, had the Claimants exerted to secure the testimony of any of these individuals. In reply, nothing was said about the absence of Messrs Amini, Golshani, Farahi, and Morog. As for Mr. Golzar, the asserted signer of the contract, the representations were made that he had been approached, that he had agreed to testify in support of the Claimants' position but that "the cost of bringing him over here was beyond the capability of Mr. Dadras".

This was in January 1993, when the existence of some substantial and ongoing legal disputes between the Respondent Government and Mr. Golzar had apparently made it impractical for the said Government to either check the veracity of the Claimants' representations or otherwise seek Mr. Golzar's testimony. As stated by the Respondent Government in a subsequent submis-

---

[2] *See* Dissent to Order of 27 April 1994, filed as document No. 184.

sion, "Iran had reasons to believe that he [Mr. Golzar] would not cooperate with it to explain certain issues."

Still, and even though it was not required of the Respondents to elicit the testimonies of those whom the Claimants have named as direct witnesses to the existence of the asserted contract, the Respondents did eventually contact Mr. Golzar and, sometime after the Hearing, provided the Chamber with his sworn affidavit. In there, Mr. Golzar testifies that TRC and the Claimants have never concluded any contract, and that the signature attributed to him at the end of the asserted contract is not his.

The Claimants were then invited to comment on Mr. Golzar's affidavit. In response, they sought to challenge Mr. Golzar's general credibility, and further provided the Chamber with the testimony, for the first time, of a handwriting expert, a Mr. J. P. Osborn. The Chamber then issued its Order of 23 February 1994, under which Messrs Golzar's and Osborn's affidavits were specifically "accepted into evidence", and the Parties were invited to comment on "the relevance, materiality, and weight" of the submissions.

This led to the filing of further evidence. The Claimants offered an affidavit by a former partner of theirs who asserts that at the time he was told by Mr. Dadras that such a contract had been signed. The Respondents, on the other hand, submitted four affidavits. In the first three, Messrs Amini, Golshani, and Farahi, whom the Claimants have named as individuals exclusively present when the contract was allegedly signed, testify that the Claimants' representations are utterly false and that they know that the asserted contract between the Parties never existed. In the fourth, Mr. Morog, named by the Claimants as a witness who, having been the TRC's chief architect, has full knowledge of the existence of the contract, testifies that indeed by virtue of his position with the TRC, he does know that no such contract ever existed between the Parties.

All the affiants volunteered to appear before the Chamber and to offer themselves for further explanations.

In a most surprising reaction to these highly significant revelations, the Majority in the Chamber hastily issued the Order of 27 April 1994, under which all affidavits submitted in relation to Mr. Golzar's testimony by those with intimate knowledge of the pertinent facts were simply excluded from the evidence. This, as I stated in a Dissent to the said Order, was utterly unjustified.

The only pretext offered by the Majority for not wanting to have before them the affidavits of those who are represented by the Claimants as having first hand knowledge of the alleged transaction was that these submissions "were not in conformity" with the Order pursuant to which they were offered. This is then explained to mean that the Chamber's Order had only allowed "comments on Mr. Golzar's testimony", while the submission of affidavits goes beyond the scope of "commenting". Strangely enough, this comes from the very Majority who, in these very cases and barely two months earlier, had readily admitted into evidence an affidavit submitted by Mr. Osborn on behalf of the Claimants, even though that affidavit, too, had been submitted, as explained above, pursuant to the Chamber's earlier Order in which the Claimants had been invited to merely "comment" on Mr. Golzar's testimony!

II. THE PRESENT ORDER

The present Order is in response to the Respondents' request that the Chamber, having admitted into evidence Mr. Golzar's affidavit, convene a Hearing at which these highly significant revelations can be further explained and tested. The Order specifically recognizes the existence of "exceptional circumstances" brought about by the new developments, and grants the Respondents' request as mandated by Article 29(2) of the Tribunal Rules.

The Order goes on, however, to repeatedly warn the Parties that at the intended Hearing no witnesses other than Messrs Golzar and Dadras would be permitted to testify. This is simply an undisguised attempt to prevent from testifying, this time orally, those individuals who are supposed to have witnessed the signing of the contract, or are supposed to have otherwise direct knowledge of its existence, but who categorically deny the Claimants' assertion. Their written statements were, as already noted, hurriedly and unjustifiably excluded from the evidence. That was disturbing enough. More disturbing is the present decision not to even allow, at the intended Hearing, the oral presentation of facts by a number of witnesses who alone are privy to what came to pass. It is a decision impossible to reconcile with this forum's first and foremost duty of ascertaining the truth.

The vague and unexplained references in the Order to "the advanced stage of deliberations" and to "the interests of procedural orderliness" are hardly helpful. The fact should not be forgotten that the decision to reopen the proceedings in the present cases has already been taken, with a date set for the intended Hearing. A party's decision, if made, to devote part of its allocated time to the presentation of facts through those who are intimate with the background and whose written statements have already been disclosed to the other party, cannot affect, in the slightest, either "the advanced stage of deliberations" or "the orderliness of the proceedings". The question, the real one, is how committedly the task of ascertaining the truth is approached.

The signs are quite discouraging. Here is a Hearing set to examine Messrs

Dadras's and Golzar's contradictory versions of the central point in the present dispute: whether or not there was a contract between the two. It is Mr. Dadras's story that a number of individuals, citizens of Iran and the United States who now nearly all live outside Iran, were closely involved in every stage of the precontract negotiations and were physically present when the contract was signed. They have all declared their readiness to appear at the set Hearing, testify to the truth, and offer themselves for further examination. The Chamber, however, issues an Order warning the Parties that none of these witnesses should appear at the intended meeting. And all this despite a foremost duty to reach the facts.

III. A POINT OF LAW

And finally a few words about a point of law evidently missed in a Dissenting Opinion to the present Order by a Member of this Chamber.

In there, a lengthy review is first made of this Tribunal's past decisions to show that, in determining whether or not to reopen a case, this Tribunal has consistently relied on three factors: the justification for delay in presenting the evidence, the need for orderly proceedings, and the likelihood of prejudice to the other party.

Next, the facts related to the submission of Mr. Golzar's testimony, as seen by the writer, are examined in the light of these factors. Accusing the Respondents of a number of misdeeds, including the adoption of "dilatory tactics", the conclusion is then made that all the said factors heavily militate against the Respondents' request for a hearing.

Now all this is very odd indeed. It is odd because the decision to admit Mr. Golzar's affidavit into evidence was taken, not through the present Order, but through an Order issued over five months ago: the Order of 23 February 1994. It is very odd because that decision to admit Mr. Golzar's affidavit – to reopen the Cases after the original Hearing – was taken unanimously.

There is here – there must have been – a confusion, on a point of law, between a case in which a reopening is requested, and a case in which a reopening having already been ordered, a rehearing is asked for. This must be explained.

Under the Tribunal Rules, where there is evidence to be presented by an already admitted witness, or oral argument to be made on already admitted evidence, the right of a requesting party to a hearing, or to the reopening of a hearing, is absolute.

First, the right of a party in such a case to a hearing. This is governed by Article 15(2), which speaks of a party's automatic right to a hearing throughout the proceedings:

> If either party so requests at any stage of the proceedings, the arbitral Tribunal shall hold hearings for the presentation of evidence by witnesses, including expert witnesses, or for oral argument. . .

When held, on the other hand, a hearing may not be closed until such time as a party's right to have his witnesses heard and/or his oral arguments made is exhausted. As laid down by Article 29(1):

> The arbitral Tribunal may inquire of the parties if they have any further proof to offer or witnesses to be heard or submissions to make and, if there are none, it may declare the hearing closed.

This, then, is the position in a nutshell of a party's right to a hearing: it is an automatic right to a hearing at which his witnesses and/or oral arguments may be heard, and which may not be declared closed until his witnesses and/or oral arguments are heard.

Next, a party's right to the reopening of a hearing. It is true, of course, that here the governing rule, contained in Article 29(2), speaks not of an automatic right, but of a prior requirement of satisfying the Tribunal that a reopening is necessary:

> The arbitral Tribunal may, if it considers it necessary owing to exceptional circumstances, decide, on its own motion or upon application of a party, to reopen the hearings at any time before the award is made.

Yet a moment's reflection will readily reveal that what must be shown "necessary" is not the holding of a further hearing as such, but the admission into evidence of materials for the presentation of which the further hearing is requested. The reasons for this are manifold, one of which is the fact that a hearing, in isolation and exclusive of what is to be presented there, cannot possibly be shown to be "necessary". This point – that the required determination of the necessity of holding a hearing is made exclusively on the basis of whether or not the presentation of new materials should be allowed – is repeatedly confirmed by the Tribunal's past decisions, including the following, made nearly ten years ago:

> . . . during the interval between the close of the Hearing and the Award . . . no submission may be accepted unless the Tribunal itself determines this is "necessary owing to exceptional circumstances".[3]

It goes without saying that once such a determination is made – once submissions are accepted after the closing of a hearing – the case is necessarily reopened. This is because under the express terms of Article 29(1), a hearing

---

[3] *Dames and Moore* v. *The Islamic Republic of Iran et al.*, Decision No. 36-54-3 (23 April 1985), reprinted in 8 IRAN-U.S. C.T.R. 107.

may be closed, as we have seen, only if there are no further submissions to be made. A decision therefore by the Tribunal to allow new submissions is a decision in the first place to reopen the proceedings. And once this is done, the question of whether or not a request for a rehearing should be entertained will be governed, exclusively, by Article 15(2) of the Tribunal Rules. Under that Rule, it will be recalled, the granting of such a request is mandatory, if made by "either party at any stage of the proceedings".

This last point, too, may be summarized. A party's request for a rehearing must be justified. What requires justification, however, is not the holding of a further hearing as such, but the suggestion, necessarily implied in the request, that he be allowed to make submissions not made prior to the closing of the original hearing. Where this has already been justified – where the Tribunal has already determined that the admission of new submissions into evidence is necessary owing to exceptional circumstances – a request for oral presentation of the admitted submissions must be granted automatically. This is because, on the one hand, the admission of new evidence reopens the proceedings and hence any request for a hearing will be governed by the mandatory provision of Article 15(2) and, on the other hand, the determination referred to in Article 29(2) having already been made, a second determination to the same effect is uncalled for.

This is precisely what has happened in the present Cases. Mr. Golzar's highly material testimony was admitted into evidence well over five months ago. This was based – it must have been – on a prior determination that the admission of the testimony into evidence "was necessary owing to exceptional circumstances". Any reservation about the correctness of this determination, therefore, ought to have been indicated at that time. The determination, however, was made by the unanimous vote of all the Chamber's Members, and the admitted evidence became the subject-matter of two further rounds of pleadings.

What the present Order has done, on the other hand, is simply to grant a party's request to be allowed to orally present his already admitted evidence. Apart from being explicitly confirmed in the Tribunal Rules, a party's right to such a presentation is so fundamental to a due process of law that its acknowledgment in an Order cannot possibly form the basis of a Dissent. But then that is not the issue – though it should have been the only issue – with which the Dissenting Opinion deals. As stated before, what is done there, instead, is to first try to suggest that, in submitting the testimony after the original hearing, the Respondents were guided by "dilatory tactics". A number of cases are then reviewed to establish that this Tribunal does not reopen a case by admitting late-filed materials, unless in the exceptional circumstances in which the delay is adequately justified.

That these Cases are absolutely irrelevant to the present Order requires no proof other than the fact that a decision to admit Mr. Golzar's testimony was taken not by the present Order but by an Order issued over five months ago. That the accusation of playing "delaying tactics" is factually unfounded needs no proof other than the fact that that decision was taken unanimously.

Dissenting Opinion of Richard C. Allison to Order of 22 July 1994 Reopening Hearing

I. INTRODUCTION

1. Today this Chamber takes the step, unprecedented in the thirteen-year history of the Tribunal, of reopening a Hearing. The purpose of the reopening is to accommodate the Respondents' belated desire – first expressed nearly 16 months after the Hearing was closed – to present testimony by a witness known to the Respondents since these Claims were filed, and who was, in fact, physically present and subject to cross-examination before this Chamber prior to the Hearing the Respondents now seek to reopen.

2. The course taken today, in my view, is totally at odds with Tribunal precedent, disruptive of the orderly workings of this Chamber, and unfair to the Claimants. It is, in short, inconsistent with the fundamental precepts of fair treatment and due process embodied in Article 15(1) of the Tribunal Rules.

II. BACKGROUND

3. The impropriety of reopening the Hearing cannot be appreciated fully without an understanding of the procedural history of this matter. That history demonstrates that the proffered testimony of Mr. Rahman Golzar Shabestari ("Mr. Golzar") does not constitute newly discovered, dispositive evidence of the kind that theoretically might justify the unprecedented step of reopening a Hearing under Article 29(2) of the Tribunal Rules.

4. On 11 January 1982, the Claimants filed their Statements of Claim in these Cases alleging, *inter alia*, that the Respondents were liable for breaches of contracts that existed between Claimants and the Tehran Redevelopment Company ("TRC"), an Iranian company taken over by the Government of Iran in 1979. Attached to the Statement of Claim in Case No. 213 as Exhibits D and E were the two documents that underlie the current decision to reopen the Hearing – a letter of approval dated 27 August 1978, apparently signed by the then Managing Director of TRC, Mr. Golzar ("Letter of Approval"); and

a contract dated 9 September 1978, also apparently signed by Mr. Golzar on behalf of TRC (the "Contract").

5. In their Statement of Defence filed 9 August 1982, the Respondents argued, among other things, that the signature of Mr. Golzar on the Letter of Approval was not authentic. That signature, Respondents asserted, "is principally not conformable with the other signatures of the then Managing Director of Tehran Redevelopment Corporation." Thus, as early as August 1982 the question of the authenticity of Mr. Golzar's signature on one of the documents now at issue had been raised by Respondents. Consequently, they were on notice, at least from that date, that the testimony of Mr. Golzar might be useful to them in substantiating their affirmative defense of forgery.

6. The Claimants' reply brief in these Cases was filed on 13 August 1986. In it the Claimants noted and denied Respondents' assertion that Mr. Golzar's signature on the Letter of Approval had been forged, thereby joining issue with Respondents on this point. On 8 January 1987, Respondents submitted a "Response to the Claimant's Submission filed on 13 August 1986" in which they reiterated their allegation of forgery and expanded it to include the Contract and other related documents. These filings, once again, could only have emphasized in Respondents' minds the importance to their forgery defense of obtaining, or at least seeking, the testimony of Mr. Golzar and others alleged by Claimants to have been involved in the negotiations leading up to the Contract.

7. It is important to note that, during the period when these various pleadings were filed, Respondents had knowledge of Mr. Golzar's whereabouts and, indeed, were actually in contact with him in connection with other matters. On 19 January 1982 the Statement of Claim was filed in *Abraham Rahman Golshani v. The Government of the Islamic Republic of Iran*, Case No. 812, a case in which Mr. Golzar played a leading role.[1] Attached to the Statement of Claim in *Golshani* was an affidavit by Mr. Golzar, which had been executed in Paris. The Statement of Claim also identified the counsel in that case, the law firm of Hogan & Hartson, and provided the firm's address. Thus, as of the date the Statement of Claim was filed in *Golshani*, Respondents were apprised of the name and address of a law firm through which Mr. Golzar almost surely could have been reached.

8. Respondents' contacts with Mr. Golzar during the relevant period did not end there, however. On or about 24 November 1982, TRC sued Mr. Golzar and others in a Paris municipal court, seeking to set aside the sale by

---

[1] The claim in Case No. 812 related primarily to the Iranian Government's taking of TRC, the corporation alleged by the Claimants in the instant Cases to have breached its agreement with them.

Mr. Golzar of an apartment in Paris formerly owned by TRC. It appears from the available records that Mr. Golzar was served with process in that case, and the opinion of the court indicates that he appeared, represented by counsel, and defended himself. After the Paris court rendered a judgment in Mr. Golzar's favor in or about March 1985, TRC appealed and, it appears, subsequently served Mr. Golzar with a notice of appeal at his residence in Coral Gables, Florida. Indeed, there is no indication that the Paris litigation has yet been resolved. Thus, at least throughout the period 1982-1985, and possibly until the present, the Government of Iran (which controls TRC) has been in ongoing contact with Mr. Golzar in the Paris litigation and was informed of his home address in the United States.

9. On 23-25 April 1991, the Hearing in *Golshani* was held before this Chamber. Mr. Golzar was present at the Hearing and testified under oath on behalf of the claimant in that case. Following his direct testimony he was subjected to extensive cross-examination by several representatives of the Government of Iran. Although counsel for the Government of Iran made reference to the Contract at issue in Dadras during cross-examination of Mr. Golzar in *Golshani*, Mr. Golzar was never asked the critical question: whether he had, in fact, signed a Contract with Mr. Dadras's company in September 1978. This strategy was pursued despite the fact that Mr. Golzar was physically present, under oath, and was testifying about events related to the Dadras Contract. One can only speculate as to the motivations of Respondents' counsel in forgoing this opportunity to elicit testimony critical to the affirmative defense of forgery in Dadras; but whatever those reasons, it is clear that the Government of Iran had a timely opportunity to elicit sworn testimony from Mr. Golzar on the forgery issue had it so desired.

10. The Hearing in Dadras was held subsequently on 28-29 January 1993. Although expert testimony on the forgery issue was offered at the Hearing, neither Party presented testimony from Mr. Golzar. When questioned about the absence of Mr. Golzar, Claimants' counsel indicated that after learning of Mr. Golzar's whereabouts he had contacted Mr. Golzar and solicited his testimony, but that Mr. Golzar had expected substantial compensation for any cooperation he might provide. Respondents offered no explanation for their failure to produce evidence from Mr. Golzar or the other alleged witnesses to the signing of the Contract in support of their affirmative defense that the Contract and supporting documents had been forged.

11. On 2 March 1993, less than five weeks after the Hearing in Dadras, the Tribunal issued an Award in favor of the Government of Iran in *Golshani*. The Award was critical of Mr. Golzar's credibility, concluding that the testimony he had submitted lacked "coherence and consistency on several key aspects" and did not inspire even a "minimal degree of confidence" in the minds of the

Arbitrators. *Abraham Rahman Golshani* v. *The Government of the Islamic Republic of Iran*, Award No. 546-812-3, paras. 111, 122 (2 Mar. 1993), *reprinted in* 29 IRAN-U.S. C.T.R. 78. Judge Aghahosseini was even harsher in his concurring opinion, in which he concluded that the deed Mr. Golzar claimed to have executed (which formed a key basis for the claim) had been proven conclusively to be "a forgery," and that Mr. Golzar's affidavit was entirely unworthy of belief. Concurring Opinion of Mohsen Aghahosseini in *Abraham Rahman Golshani* v. *The Government of the Islamic Republic of Iran*, Award No. 546-812-3, pp. 1, 100-101 (2 Mar. 1993), *reprinted in* 29 IRAN-U.S. C.T.R. 78.

12. On 1 February 1994, after many months of deliberations in Dadras leading toward an Award, the Tribunal received a letter from Mr. Ali H. Nobari, the Agent for the Islamic Republic of Iran, enclosing an affidavit by Mr. Golzar. Mr. Golzar's affidavit stated that although TRC had entered into certain preliminary agreements with Mr. Dadras's company, no final contract was ever concluded. The affidavit went on to state that Mr. Golzar had never signed the Letter of Approval or the Contract "and, therefore, the signatures affixed to them as my signatures are not mine."

13. In his letter transmitting the Golzar affidavit, Mr. Nobari conceded that "Iran was mindful of seeking necessary explanations from Mr. Golzar at the first possible opportunity." He went on to explain the circumstances underlying the procurement of the affidavit as follows:

> [A]n official of the Bureau of International Legal Services of Iran (BILS) happened to meet [Mr. Golzar] in Paris. In this meeting, Mr. Golzar stated that he had not ever signed the contract in question, nor had he any recollection of the (Letter of Approval). He was subsequently shown both documents for review.

Upon the examination of the documents, he said neither of the signatures was his. Mr. Golzar was then requested to memorialize his statements in a sworn affidavit, and so he did.

14. Even given full credence, this scenario provides no excuse for Respondents' failure to seek to obtain testimony from Mr. Golzar during the prior twelve years of litigation – a period during which, as explained *supra*, Respondents were well aware of the possible materiality of Mr. Golzar's recollections and, moreover, were in contact with him and his attorneys due to the Paris litigation and the ongoing *Golshani* case. The only explanation offered in Mr. Nobari's letter is that Mr. Golzar "was Iran's adversary in Case No. 812 [*Golshani*]," and therefore "Iran had reasons to believe that he would not cooperate with it to explain certain issues."[2]

---

[2] This excuse, even if accepted, does not of course explain why no attempts were made to contact Mr. Golzar between 2 March 1993 – the date *Golshani* was decided – and early 1994.

15. Notwithstanding the Claimants' objection to the admission of the Golzar affidavit and the unpersuasive reasons advanced for the extraordinary delay in submitting it, the Chamber ultimately decided to admit the affidavit into evidence. This was accomplished by Order dated 23 February 1994, which also admitted an affidavit previously proffered by the Claimants in which the Claimants' handwriting expert opined that the signatures of Mr. Golzar on the Letter of Approval and the Contract were, in fact, genuine.

16. The same Order established a schedule for two rounds of simultaneous post-Hearing pleadings in which the Parties would comment on the "relevance, materiality and weight" of the two admitted affidavits and engage in rebuttal. Both rounds of comments were completed by 20 April 1994.

17. With that, it appeared that the record in these Cases was finally closed and that the Chamber would proceed expeditiously to evaluate all of the evidence and render a decision on the merits. Then on 27 May 1994 came Mr. Nobari's letter requesting a reopening of the Hearing.

18. In his letter – filed nearly 16 months after the Hearing in these Cases – Mr. Nobari "emphatically request[s]" that the Tribunal schedule a hearing so that oral testimony can be taken from Mr. Golzar.[3] The Claimants strongly objected to Respondents' request to reopen, pointing out that the record was already closed and that "to require Claimants to incur substantial further expense and delay because of statements obtained in 1994, long after the close of the written record and hearing, would be grossly unfair."

19. Today the Majority, with little explanation and far less justification, grants Respondents' request to reopen the Hearing in this matter. For the reasons explained below, I believe that this decision violates the Tribunal's Rules and precedents and is wholly inconsistent with the duties and obligations of this Tribunal.

III. ANALYSIS

20. The starting point for an evaluation of Respondents' request to reopen the Hearing in these Cases is, of course, the Rules of Procedure of this

---

[3] In support of his request, Mr. Nobari argued that "if an affidavit is accepted as evidence in a case while, on the other hand, the adverse party is not given the permission to orally and directly examine the said witness at the hearing session, the latter will be completely deprived of the 'full opportunity' he is supposed to be given for presenting his Case." This argument is entirely unpersuasive. First, because the Golzar affidavit supports Iran's position in these Cases, Iran is not an "adverse party" and thus would not be entitled to a hearing even under Mr. Nobari's reasoning. Second, the Claimants – who would be entitled to an opportunity to cross-examine Mr. Golzar under Mr. Nobari's reasoning – have expressly objected to the reopening of the Hearing. Finally, Mr. Nobari's argument ignores the fact that the Tribunal routinely accepts and evaluates affidavit evidence without requiring the affiant to appear and testify in person at a hearing.

Tribunal. The Rule governing the reopening of Hearings is Article 29(2), which provides as follows:

> The arbitral tribunal may, if it considers it necessary owing to exceptional circumstances, decide, on its own motion or upon application of a party, to reopen the hearings at any time before the award is made.

21. In the thirteen-year history of this Tribunal, no Chamber has ever reopened a hearing. Although such relief has been requested in several cases, in each instance it has been summarily denied.

22. The first reported case in which a request for reopening was made appears to be *Dames & Moore* v. *The Islamic Republic of Iran et al.*, Decision No. DEC 36-54-3 (23 Apr. 1985), *reprinted in* 8 IRAN-U.S. C.T.R. 107. In that case, the respondents moved to reopen the Hearing after the issuance of the Award, arguing that a key affidavit submitted by the claimant was a "mere lie," and that several important invoices were "forged." The Tribunal had no difficulty in rejecting the request, reasoning that "whatever entitlement to 'hearings for presentation of evidence by witnesses' . . . may exist prior to the rendering of any award, it thereafter is no longer extant." *Id.* at 115. The Tribunal went on to emphasize, in *dicta*, that the rule on reopening Hearings is only slightly less stringent in cases where an award has not yet been issued.

23. In later cases, the Tribunal has continued to endorse the restrictive approach to requests for reopening exhibited in *Dames & Moore*. The next case to arise was *Touche Ross and Company* v. *The Islamic Republic of Iran*, Award No. 197-480-1 (30 Oct. 1985), *reprinted in* 9 IRAN-U.S. C.T.R. 284, a case involving facts similar to those here. In *Touche Ross*, the respondent chose not to present evidence before the Hearing but subsequently moved to reopen the proceedings. The Tribunal rejected this request, stating:

> The Tribunal notes that ample opportunity was afforded to the Parties to present their respective cases before and during the hearing held on 19 October 1983. Further submissions were invited from the Parties thereafter, and both availed themselves of this opportunity. Also, as noted, both parties have filed additional submissions. The Tribunal perceives no need or justification to prolong these proceedings further.

Id. at 300.

24. To similar effect is *Development and Resources Corp.* v. *The Government of the Islamic Republic of Iran et al.*, Award No. 485-60-3 (25 June 1990), *reprinted in* 25 IRAN-U.S. C.T.R. 20. There, the respondents made a post-Hearing request for a "complementary hearing session" so that they might introduce certain new evidence. The Tribunal rejected this request, finding that the respondents

had advanced "no convincing reason" why an additional hearing was needed and that they had also failed to provide any "adequate explanation of why the documents or arguments [they] sought to advance after the final Hearing could not have been presented at or prior to the Hearing in accordance with the Tribunal's scheduling Orders." *Id.* at 24.

25. Next came *Vernie Rodney Pointon, et al.* v. *The Government of the Islamic Republic of Iran*, Award No. 516-322-1 (23 July 1991), *reprinted in* 27 IRAN-U.S. C.T.R. 49. There, the claimants moved for a reopening one month after the Hearing, arguing, *inter alia*, the need to reexamine one of the respondent's witnesses in light of inconsistencies in the record and an affidavit obtained after the Hearing that allegedly undermined the testimony of the witness. The Tribunal, citing concerns of "fairness, orderliness and possible prejudice to the other part[y]," denied claimants' request. *Id.* at 53.

26. The most recent reported case in which the reopening of a Hearing was requested is *General Petrochemicals Corp.* v. *The Islamic Republic of Iran, et al.*, Award No. 522-828-1 (21 Oct. 1991), *reprinted in* 27 IRAN-U.S. C.T.R. 196, a case that again bears a strong factual similarity to the instant matter. In that case, the claimant filed a Memorial seeking a reopening under Article 29(2) more than five months after the Hearing, arguing that its need to present new evidence constituted an "exceptional circumstance" within the meaning of the Article. The Tribunal rejected the request, relying largely on the fact that the so-called "new" evidence had in fact been available to the claimant prior to the Hearing. In reaching this result, Chamber One emphasized that the Tribunal's institutional interests weighed heavily against the granting of the claimant's request: "[T]he orderly processes of the Tribunal require that evidence be submitted in a timely manner to assure fairness and to prevent possible prejudice to other parties." *Id.* at 212.

27. In short, the Tribunal consistently has denied requests to reopen in the few prior cases in which such requests have been made. In each instance, the Tribunal looked primarily to three factors – the justification for the delay in presenting the evidence at issue, the need for orderly proceedings, and the likelihood of prejudice to the other party – to decide whether reopening was appropriate. Applying these three considerations to the facts of the instant matter, it seems to me obvious that Respondents' request should be denied. First, the justification advanced by Respondents for the delay in proffering Mr. Golzar's testimony is entirely unpersuasive. Respondents have been on notice of the possible relevance of Mr. Golzar's testimony since the earliest days of these Cases and have had knowledge of his whereabouts, and access to him, for much of the period that these Cases have been pending. Moreover, the Government of Iran had Mr. Golzar under oath, and subject to cross-examination on the very matters relevant to their forgery defense in these

Cases, during the *Golshani* Hearing. Inexplicably, its counsel failed to ask him the key question.

28. The only purported justification for the delay offered in Mr. Nobari's letter is that Mr. Golzar "was Iran's adversary" in *Golshani* and that therefore "Iran had reasons to believe that he would not cooperate with it." This explanation is patently inadequate for at least two reasons. First, all that is required by Article 15(1) and the Tribunal's precedents is that a party have a meaningful opportunity to present its case, not that it be assured of a particular result. Respondents had ample opportunity to solicit Mr. Golzar's testimony during the twelve-year period between 1982 and 1993, and the fact that they may have refrained from doing so out of concern as to his "cooperation" cannot relieve them of the burden of trying. Second, even under Respondents' theory Mr. Golzar ceased to be an "adversary" in *Golshani* on 2 March 1993, the day that the Award in that case was issued; yet Respondents nonetheless did not contact Mr. Golzar until nearly a year later and even then, according to Respondents, the encounter arose purely by chance and not through any efforts of their own. Thus, the excuse that Mr. Golzar was "Iran's adversary" simply does not hold up under scrutiny.

29. Another factor identified in the Tribunal's precedents as relevant to requests to reopen is the orderliness of the Tribunal's proceedings. This body's precedents rightly recognize that the parties that appear before it are entitled to a fair and adequate opportunity to present their cases, a dictate that was fully satisfied in the pleading and Hearing phases of these Cases. However, there is a further interest that must also be observed – namely, the protection of the procedures and efficiency of the Tribunal itself – if justice is to be served. *See, e.g., General Petrochemicals Corp.*, 27 IRAN-U.S. C.T.R. at 212. Indeed, this latter precept is inherent in the fundamental principle of equality of treatment embodied in Article 15(1) of the Tribunal's Rules. As explained by Judge Mosk more than a decade ago,

> A Tribunal having thousands of cases is far different than an international arbitration involving only one case. The claimants and respondents before this Tribunal are entitled to have cases heard and decided in a prompt, efficient and fair manner, in accordance with Tribunal rules and the law. Long delayed and expensive proceedings in which parties are not accorded equal treatment create much greater injustice than the failure to permit unlimited means and time to establish every fact in a particular case.

Concurring Opinion of Richard M. Mosk in *Ultrasystems. Inc. v. The Islamic Republic of Iran et al.*, Partial Award No. 27-84-3 (4 Mar. 1983), *reprinted in* 2 IRAN-U.S. C.T.R. 114, 123. The need for orderliness and efficiency in this

Chamber's proceedings weighs heavily against the granting of Respondents' belated request to reopen.

30. A further factor identified in the cases – prejudice to the other party – likewise speaks strongly against granting Respondents' request to reopen. The Claimants in these Cases stated in their objection to Respondents' request that the reopening of the Hearing will cause Claimants to incur "substantial further expense and delay." The element of delay is already obvious. To substantiate their contention as to expense, Claimants submitted on 26 May 1994 a "Bill of Costs" showing that the proceedings related to the Golzar affidavit had, as of that date, cost the Claimants more than $94,000 in legal fees and expenses.[4]

31. Even more fundamentally, the Claimants in these Cases, like all parties who appear before this Tribunal, have a right to expect the opposing party to present its case in the pleadings and at the Hearing, where it can be subjected to effective challenge, and not at some later time of its own choosing. Today's Order frustrates that proper expectation, and in the process creates a perverse incentive for future parties who may perceive delay as being to their strategic advantage.

32. In sum, all of the factors identified in Tribunal precedent as relevant to the possible reopening of a Hearing pursuant to Article 29(2) weigh heavily against granting Respondents' request.

33. In addition to Article 29(2), Mr. Nobari's letter also attempts to rely on Article 15(2) of the Tribunal Rules as a basis for the request to reopen. That Article provides, in pertinent part, as follows: "If either party so requests at any stage of the proceedings, the arbitral tribunal shall hold hearings for the presentation of evidence by witnesses, including expert witnesses, or for oral argument." Tribunal Rules, Article 15(2).

34. Contrary to Respondents' argument, Article 15(2) provides no basis for reopening the Hearing under the circumstances present here. As the Tribunal has held on more than one occasion,

---

[4] This sizeable amount can only be evaluated in the light of the following history of proceedings with respect to the Golzar affidavit:
  (i) In addition to the Golzar affidavit, Respondents submitted four affidavits of other persons, residing in Iran and the United States, denying the finalization of the Contract by TRC, as well as an affidavit of a handwriting expert.
  (ii) Claimants, for their part, submitted an affidavit of a witness residing in Italy supporting Professor Dadras's version of the facts and alleging that representatives of Respondents had sought, through inducements followed by threats, to obtain from him an affidavit designed to discredit Claimants' case, as well as a supplemental affidavit of their handwriting expert.
  (iii) The affidavit of Respondents' handwriting expert and the supplemental affidavit of Claimants' expert were accepted into the record. The five other affidavits were excluded from evidence by Order dated 27 April 1994.

Article 15(2) of the Tribunal Rules . . . states that a party may request a Hearing at 'any stage of the proceedings'. This provision should be interpreted, in light of the particular circumstances of each case, to mean that Hearings are to be held upon the reasonable request of a party made at an appropriate stage of the proceedings.

World Farmers Trading Inc. v. *Government Trading Corporation, et al.*, Award No. 428-764-1, para. 16 (7 July 1989), *reprinted in* 22 IRAN-U.S. C.T.R. 204, 209. Even under the most liberal reading of the cases, a request for a second Hearing made nearly 16 months after the original Hearing can hardly be considered to have been made at an "appropriate" time. *See id.* (denying request for hearing made more than 12 months after Tribunal informed parties that it would decide case on the papers); *Tchacosh Company Inc.* v. *The Government of the Islamic Republic of Iran, et al.*, Award No. 540-192-1, para. 21 (9 Dec. 1992), *reprinted in* 28 IRAN-U.S. C.T.R. 371 (denying request made more than a year after Tribunal announced that no hearing would be held).

35. Finally, it is no answer to say, as Mr. Nobari does in his letter, that reopening of the Hearing is justified by Article 15(l)'s mandate that the Tribunal ensure "that the parties are treated with equality and that at any stage of the proceedings each party is given a full opportunity of presenting his case." The key word in Article 15(1), for purposes of the instant request, is *opportunity*. As explained in the seminal treatise by Judge Holtzmann and Mr. Neuhaus,

> While, on the one hand, the arbitral tribunal must provide reasonable opportunities to each party, this does not mean that it must sacrifice all efficiency in order to accommodate unreasonable procedural demands by a party. For example, . . . [Article 15(1) of the UNCITRAL Rules] does not entitle a party to obstruct the proceedings by dilatory tactics, *such as by offering objections, amendments, or evidence on the eve of the award.*

Howard M. Holtzmann & Joseph E. Neuhaus, *A Guide To The UNCITRAL Model Law On International Commercial Arbitration* 551 (1989) (emphasis added). In this case, Respondents had more than ample opportunity to elicit Mr. Golzar's testimony in support of their forgery defense prior to the Hearing. That is all that Article 15(1) requires.

36. Indeed, far from supporting Respondents' request, Article 15(1), in my view, positively forbids it. A crucial aspect of the principle of equality of treatment embodied in that Article is that the Tribunal carry on its work in an orderly fashion and refrain from favoring either party by, for example, acceding to unreasonable procedural demands or encouraging dilatory tactics. I believe that today's Order does precisely that, and thus it is inconsistent with the fundamental precepts of Article 15(1). Whatever Mr. Golzar had to say should have been said – and presumably was – in his one-page affidavit. The

Chamber bent over backward when it took the belated Golzar affidavit into the record and permitted the Parties two additional rounds of pleadings concerning Mr. Golzar's credibility. There can be no excuse for further procedural maneuvering in these Cases.

37.   For all of the above reasons, the decision to reopen is wrong. One can only hope that this regrettable deviation from Tribunal precedent and sound principles of judicial administration will prove to be an anomaly not to be emulated in the future.[5]

---

[5] Although I disagree with the decision to reopen the Hearing in these Cases, that decision having been taken, I concur in the Order's limitation of the scope of the Hearing and its mandate that the Hearing occur on 20 October 1994.

Mohsen Asgari Nazari, *Claimant*

v.

The Government of the Islamic Republic of Iran, *Respondent*

(Case No. 221)

Chamber One: Broms, *Chairman*; Noori,[1] Holtzmann,[2] *Members*

Signed 24 *August* 1994[3]

Award No. 559-221-1

The following is the text as issued by the Tribunal:

APPEARANCES

For the Claimant: Mr. Mohsen Asgari Nazari
　　Claimant
　Mr. Donald Buckner
　Col. Thomas Irwin
　Mr. Javid Siminou
　　Witnesses
　Mr. Jonathan M. Weisgall
　　Counsel

For the Respondent: Mr. Ali H. Nobari
　　Agent of the Government of the
　　Islamic Republic of Iran
　Dr. M.H. Bordbar
　Dr. Ali Azmayesh
　Prof. B. Stern
　　Legal Advisers to the Agent

[1 The signature of Mr. Noori is accompanied by the following statement:
"I concur in the present Award. However, I would like to point out that the Tribunal could and should have rejected the Claimant's claims at the earlier stages of the proceedings for lack of jurisdiction. I am still of the opinion that the Tribunal does not have jurisdiction over the claims of Iranians with dual United States nationality. *See* my note appended to Interlocutory Award No. ITL 79-221-1 (15 January 1991), in *Mohsen Asgari Nazari* v. *The Government of the Islamic Republic of Iran, reprinted in* 26 IRAN-U.S. C.T.R. 7."]

2 [The signature of Mr. Holtzmann is accompanied by the words, "Dissenting in part, concurring in part. *See* Separate Opinion. (Signed pursuant to Article 13, para. 5 of the Tribunal Rules)." The Opinion appears at page 163, below.]

[3 Filed 24 August 1994.]

>
> Mr. Jahanbakhsh Mirzakhani
> Mr. Abass Valizadeh
> Mr. Ghassem Farshchian
> > Assistants to the Legal Advisers

Also present:
> Mr. D. Stephen Mathias
> > Agent of the Government of the
> > United States of America
> Mrs. Mary Catherine Malin
> > Deputy Agent of the Government of
> > the United States of America

I. PROCEEDINGS

1.1 Procedural History

1. On 11 January 1982, the Claimant Mohsen Asgari Nazari ("the Claimant") filed a Statement of Claim against The Government of the Islamic Republic of Iran ("Iran" or the "Respondent"). The Claimant submitted five different claims which amounted, in total, to U.S.$3,793,000.[4] First, the Claimant sought to recover $1,150,000 as compensation for money that he had allegedly advanced to Sherkat Khadamat Beinolmelali Mahat ("SKBM")[5] on behalf of the Information Systems of Iran ("ISIRAN"), a corporation allegedly owned, controlled and operated by Iran.

The Claimant asserts that when ISIRAN failed to make contractually-required payments to SKBM, he together with Mr. Hassan Asgari Pour provided SKBM with the operating funds it needed to continue to supply ISIRAN pursuant to their contract. Second, the Claimant sought $1,513,000 as compensation for the expropriation of his 33.75% interest in SKBM, allegedly taken over by Iran.[6] The Claimant also sought $2,193,750 as an indirect claim for 33.75% of $6,500,000 which he contended ISIRAN owed SKBM for services rendered under the contract. Third, the Claimant sought compensation in the amount of $858,000 arising from the alleged nationalization of his interest in Sherkat Pasandaz Va Vam Maskan Passargad ("Passargad"), a savings and home loan corporation, and of the proceeds of his purchase of shares in the said company, which were deposited in Bank Rahni Iran. Alternatively, the Claimant sought for the return of funds, amounting to

---

[4] All references to dollars in this Award are to United States dollars.
[5] SKBM is sometimes referred to as Mahat International Services.
[6] Initially, the Claimant alleged that he owned a 34% interest in SKBM; during the proceedings he corrected this to 33.75%. Moreover, the Claimant requested that the value of his shareholding interest in SKBM be determined finally at a later stage of the proceedings following an initial determination by the Tribunal of whether the Claimant's shares of SKBM had in fact been expropriated.

$660,000, that had allegedly been deposited in Bank Rahni Iran for the purchase of his shares in the corporation. Fourth, the Claimant sought compensation in the amount of $260,000 for the alleged taking of his apartment in Iran, including the contents thereof. However, the Claimant withdrew this Claim in his Hearing Memorial of 14 October 1991, due to lack of evidence. Finally, the Claimant sought $12,000 in salary and relocation benefits allegedly due to him under a contract he had with SKBM.

2. Iran filed its Statement of Defence on 3 February 1983.

3. On 15 January 1991, the Tribunal issued an interlocutory award on the question of its jurisdiction, specifically addressing the issue of the dual nationality of the Claimant. *See Mohsen Asgari Nazari v. The Government of the Islamic Republic of Iran*, Interlocutory Award No. ITL 79-221-1 (15 Jan. 1991), *reprinted in* 26 IRAN-U.S. C.T.R. 7 (the "Interlocutory Award"). The Tribunal found that the Claimant's dominant and effective nationality during the relevant period was that of the United States and decided that the Claimant thus has standing before this Tribunal under Article II, paragraph 1 and Article VII, paragraph 1 of the Claims Settlement Declaration. The Tribunal also joined the remaining jurisdictional issues to the merits of the case. (*Ibid.*, paras. 18-20, at 14.)

4. The procedural history prior to 15 January 1991 is reflected in the Interlocutory Award.

5. By its Order of 17 January 1991, the Tribunal scheduled further proceedings in this Case. Accordingly, after having been granted two extensions, on 14 October 1991 the Claimant filed a submission entitled "Claimant's Hearing Memorial, Request for Interlocutory Award or for an Extension of Time to Submit Further Evidence and for Production of Documents". In that submission the Claimant requested permission to amend his Claim by adding ISIRAN, SKBM, the Ministry of Defense, the Iranian Ground Forces, the Islamic Revolutionary Committee, Bank Rahni Iran and Passargad as new respondents. The Claimant also requested the Tribunal to order the Respondent to produce certain documents. In addition, the Claimant requested in the same submission that the issue of the alleged expropriation of SKBM be dealt with, as a preliminary question, prior to the question of its valuation. In its Order of 23 October 1991, the Tribunal invited the Respondent to comment on these requests by 23 December 1991.

6. On 6 December 1991, the Respondent submitted its comments on the Claimant's request for an interlocutory award. In that submission the Respondent concurred with the Claimant's request, arguing that certain other issues should also be decided as preliminary questions. These preliminary questions included the issues whether SKBM had been expropriated; whether the Claimant could pursue an alternative indirect contractual claim as a

shareholder despite lacking a controlling ownership interest in SKBM; whether the Claimant as a U.S. national could have purchased the shares of Passargad; whether the possession of these shares was limited solely to Iranian nationals; and, in connection with the same issue, whether the Caveat in Case A18 prevents the Claimant from pursuing this Claim. *See Case* No. A/18, Decision No. DEC 32-A18-FT, at 25-26 (6 Apr. 1984), *reprinted in* 5 IRAN-U.S. C.T.R. 251, 265-266 (the "Caveat").

7. On 19 December 1991, the Tribunal issued an Order in which it decided to bifurcate the proceedings in this Case in such a manner that it would at this stage consider all issues other than the question of the valuation of the Claimant's property rights in SKBM. The Tribunal decided to address that question at a later stage, if necessary. The Tribunal also scheduled a Hearing for 23 September 1992 and invited the Respondent to submit its comments on the Claimant's request for production of certain documents together with its Hearing Memorial and Evidence.

8. On 28 January 1992, the Claimant filed a letter in which he renewed his request to add seven additional respondents in this Case. On 5 March 1992, the Respondent filed its "Response to Claimant's Request to Add New Respondents". In that submission, Iran requested the Tribunal to reject the Claimant's request.

9. On 26 May 1992, the Respondent filed a submission entitled "Respondent's Hearing Memorial and Written Evidence". In that submission the Respondent reiterated its objection to the Claimant's request for inclusion of new respondents and argued that the Claimant's request for production of certain documents should also be rejected.

10. On 15 June 1992, the Claimant requested the Tribunal to invite the proposed additional respondents to submit their responses to the Claimant's Hearing Memorial and to reschedule the further proceedings in the Case or, as an alternative, to grant an extension of time for the Claimant's rebuttal filings.

11. On 16 June 1992, the Tribunal rendered a Decision, *Mohsen Asgari Nazari* v. *The Government of the Islamic Republic of Iran*, Decision No. DEC 105-221-1 (16 June 1992), *reprinted in* 28 IRAN-U.S. C.T.R. 192, regarding the Claimant's application to amend his Claim. Referring to Article 20 of the Tribunal Rules and the significant lapse of time involved, and emphasizing that the Tribunal had already issued Interlocutory Award No. ITL 79-22-1 in this Case and that the proposed new respondents had not had an opportunity to submit evidence during the preliminary stage of the proceedings or otherwise to participate therein, and the fact that the Claimant had not offered any justification for his delay in making this application, the Tribunal considered it inappropriate to allow the proposed amendment adding seven new respondents to the Case.

12. With regard to the Claimant's extension request the Tribunal set on 23 June 1992 a new schedule for the Parties to file their further submissions. The Tribunal also rescheduled the Hearing in this Case for 20 April 1993.

13. On 9 November 1992, after having been granted one extension, the Claimant filed a submission entitled "Claimant's Rebuttal Memorial and Evidence". On 9 March 1993, after being granted one extension, the Respondent filed a submission entitled "Respondent's Rebuttal Memorial and Evidence".

14. On 23 March 1993, the Claimant filed his list of witnesses, wherein he mentioned himself and four other persons. The Respondent did not submit any list of witnesses.

15. On 29 March 1993, the Claimant requested the Tribunal to reschedule the Hearing because one of his key witnesses would be unable to testify on the date of the Hearing as scheduled, and further because the new documents submitted in the Respondent's last filing made it impossible for the Claimant to be prepared by that time. On 29 March 1993, the Tribunal invited the Respondent to comment on the Claimant's request by 2 April 1993. On 2 April 1993, the Agent of the Islamic Republic of Iran filed the Respondent's comments on the Claimant's request. The Respondent requested that the scheduled Hearing date remain intact, but agreed that, if the Claimant deemed the testimony of his witness decisive to his case, then Iran did not object to a postponement of the Hearing for a period of no more than two months.

16. On 5 April 1993, the Tribunal cancelled the scheduled Hearing and rescheduled it for 3 December 1993. On 8 April 1993, the Agent of the Islamic Republic of Iran filed a letter in which he requested the Tribunal to reschedule the Hearing for 11 June 1993, to take the place of the Hearing already scheduled to be held then in Case No. 118. On 20 April 1993, the Tribunal issued an Order in which it did not deem it appropriate to reschedule the Hearing in this Case.

17. On 29 November 1993, the Respondent filed a letter in which it stated that the testimony of the Claimant's witnesses was irrelevant to the Case and that they should not be heard, four of them because their testimony would relate to the Claimant's denied request to file a new Claim against seven agencies and companies and the contents of such testimony would relate to the contractual rights of these entities, which are not respondents and have not participated in the proceedings in this Case; and one of them because his testimony would concern the relations between the Claimant and Mr. Asgari Pour, which is not within the jurisdiction of the Tribunal and is not at issue in this Case. The Respondent requested the Tribunal either to issue an Order that those witnesses could not be heard or to remind the Claimant that the

witnesses should not give any testimony with respect to any contractual claims. The Respondent also emphasized in the same submission that the Claimant could not be heard as a witness because of his direct interest in the outcome of this Case. On 24 November 1993, the Respondent requested the Tribunal to allocate two days for the Hearing. On 29 November 1993, the Claimant informed the Tribunal that he opposed the Respondent's request. On 30 November 1993, the Tribunal issued an Order in which the Tribunal deemed it inappropriate, in view of the proximity of the scheduled hearing date, to grant the Respondent's request or to reschedule the Hearing in this Case.

18. The Hearing was held on 3 December 1993. At the Hearing the Claimant was heard for purposes of giving information to the Tribunal. Also at the Hearing, the Respondent submitted a document entitled "Documents Submitted by the Respondent for the Ease of Reference at the Hearing".

19. On 27 December 1993, the Respondent filed its estimate of the amount of costs which Iran requests the Tribunal to award it pursuant to Articles 38-40 of the Tribunal Rules. The Respondent sought at least the amount of $17,445.00.

20. On 3 January 1994, the Claimant submitted his statement of fees and costs. The claimed costs amounted to $121,805.52.

1.2 Remaining Procedural Issues
 1.2.1 A Late Submission

21. At the Hearing, the Respondent submitted a document entitled "Documents Submitted by the Respondent for the Ease of Reference at the Hearing". The Claimant objected to the admission of this late submission. At the Hearing, the Tribunal ruled that one of the documents included in that submission was inadmissible, and reserved until after the Hearing its decision on the admissibility of the remainder of the submission. The Tribunal now turns to the examination of this issue.

22. The Tribunal considers that this submission constitutes documentary evidence which must be submitted in accordance with the time limits set forth in the Tribunal's orders, so that the other Party is able to respond. Evidence that could have been submitted during the established time periods but which was presented late without adequate justification will not be accepted at the hearing, because late submissions containing facts and evidence are most likely to cause prejudice to the other Party and to disturb the arbitral process. The Tribunal notes that the Respondent has not provided any sufficient reason for the late submission of this document. Furthermore, the documents included in that submission do not have a direct impact on the Case and do not rebut testimony given by the Claimant's witnesses at the Hearing. Therefore, the Tribunal considers the Respondent's submission inadmissible.

1.2.2 The Claimant's Request for Production of Certain Documents

23. In his Hearing Memorial filed on 14 October 1991, the Claimant requested that the Tribunal order the Respondent to produce certain documents relating to SKBM. The Tribunal invited the Respondent to submit its comments on this request together with its Hearing filings. On 26 May 1992, the Respondent submitted a memorial entitled "Respondent's Hearing Memorial and Written Evidence" wherein the Respondent asked, in commenting on the Claimant's request for production of documents, that the Tribunal reject the Claimant's request because, although the burden of proof fell on him, he had not shown that before filing his request he had tried unsuccessfully to acquire these documents directly from Iran. Furthermore, the Respondent emphasized that all the documents requested pertained to corporations which are independent of the Government and which are not respondents in this case.

24. The Tribunal notes that the requested documents mainly relate to the issues of the possible valuation of SKBM and the Claimant's equity interest in that company. Therefore, in view of the Tribunal's findings in paras. 99-140 *infra*, there is no need for the Tribunal to address the question of the possible impact of the Claimant's request upon his Claims, and the Respondent's response thereto.

II. FACTS AND CONTENTIONS

2.1 The Claimant's Claims Relating to SKBM

   2.1.1 Introduction

25. In 1975, together with three other persons, the Claimant formed an Iranian private joint stock company, SKBM, to perform computer services and other related activities mentioned in Article 2 of the Articles of Association of that company.

26. On 8 May 1975, SKBM was registered with the Office for Registration of Companies and Industrial Ownership, in Tehran. The Claimant states that a realignment of SKBM occurred at the shareholders' meeting on 16 June 1977, with the result that all the shares of SKBM were held by three individuals, who also became directors of the company, in the following amounts: Amir Hossein Amir Faiz, 57.5% (46 shares); Hassan Asgari Pour, 8.75% (7 shares); and the Claimant, Mohsen Asgari Nazari, 33.75% (27 shares). While serving with the other co-owners as a director of SKBM, the Claimant also held the position of the chief executive officer, *i.e.* managing director, from January 1976 onwards.

27. According to the Claimant, in 1976 SKBM purchased a commercial office building at No. 17 Ahar Street, Ghassr Cross Road, Koroush Kabir

Avenue, Tehran. The first and second floors of the building were used for commercial functions of SKBM and the third floor was converted to a residence, where the Claimant temporarily resided.

28. In 1976, SKBM entered into a contract with ISIRAN to provide manpower and services required by the "CALS"-project. This was a government project under the direction of ISIRAN, to computerize various agencies of the Iranian Government, including certain military agencies. ISIRAN obtained operating funds from the Iranian Armed Forces, from which it made payments to subcontractors such as SKBM. SKBM was not allowed to have any other contracts with other entities at the same time that it was performing its contract with ISIRAN. In order to fulfill the contract, SKBM recruited foreign and Iranian specialists and provided them to ISIRAN, which also controlled the daily workings of SKBM. The Claimant further states that the contract between ISIRAN and SKBM was to run until late 1980 or early 1981. Because there was an expectation that the contract would be continued, SKBM renewed its employment contracts with the expatriates it had hired for the "CALS"-project.

29. The Claimant returned to the United States in July 1978, prior to the beginning of the Islamic Revolution. The Claimant states that, due to financial difficulties, SKBM failed to make payment of $12,000 due to him in July 1978 for salary and relocation benefits to which he was entitled on the basis of his contract with the company. The Respondent contests the Claimant's alleged right to these benefits.

30. The Claimant states that in early 1978 ISIRAN began to encounter difficulties in paying its subcontractors, including SKBM, due to a shortage of funds caused by late payments from the Iranian Ground Forces. Furthermore, during the period of martial law in 1978 the Iranian banking system also began to have difficulties in functioning, and when Bank Melli, through which these payments were made, also began to experience difficulties in operating, this allegedly had a severe impact on the ability of ISIRAN to pay its subcontractors. However, SKBM as a subcontractor was instructed to continue to provide its services to ISIRAN and to ISIRAN's customers. The Claimant asserts that when no further payments were received, he and his partner, Mr. Hassan Asgari Pour, were compelled to advance their private funds to SKBM to cover its operating expenses. The Claimant alleges that by January 1979 his share of the private funds advanced to the company amounted to approximately $1,150,000. The Respondent disputes this allegation, stating that the Claimant has not provided sufficient evidence in support of his statement, and asserting at the Hearing that these funds were provided from other sources.

31. The Claimant also asserts that by January 1979 SKBM's total amount

of receivables due under contract from the Iranian Ground Forces through ISIRAN was approximately $6,500,000. The Claimant states that in December 1978, due to a lack of funds allegedly caused by these late payments from ISIRAN, SKBM did not have sufficient funds to pay its employees' salaries. The Claimant also states that the company's financial situation further deteriorated to the degree that in late January 1979, SKBM was unable to continue to provide its services to ISIRAN. Therefore, on 24 January 1979, the administration of SKBM had to issue a letter to all of its employees declaring force majeure and terminating their employment contracts as from that date due to the "current civil unrest in Iran and the inability of the company to meet its financial obligations" at that time. Attached to each letter of termination was a detailed statement of entitlements and benefits for each employee and the letter included the promise that SKBM would pay all benefits and relocation allowances upon completion of the employee's contract.

32. On or about 12 April 1979, the property of the majority shareholder of SKBM, Mr. Amir Hossein Amir Faiz, including his 57.5% share of SKBM's stock, was expropriated by the Respondent. The Claimant states in his written pleadings that the Respondent acquired control of SKBM through the said expropriation of the property of Amir Hossein Amir Faiz. The Claimant also asserts that the takeover of a majority shareholder's interest in a company results in the expropriation of the company itself. The Claimant argues that when the Respondent had full control over both SKBM and ISIRAN as a result of the expropriation the Respondent exercised this control to prevent SKBM from collecting money due to it from ISIRAN, and kept ISIRAN from paying its debts to SKBM. These acts or omissions allegedly resulted directly in a situation where the main office of SKBM was sold by a revolutionary committee to pay the local employees of SKBM. The Claimant asserts that the balance of the proceeds was given to the Foundation for the Oppressed and that as a result SKBM ceased to exist as an entity independent of the Respondent.

33. The Claimant further argues that the Respondent made it impossible for him to exercise his rights as a shareholder of SKBM. The Claimant asserts that, after he was forced to leave Iran in July 1978, he, as a U.S. citizen, was unable to return to Iran or to exercise his rights as a shareholder to protect his interest in SKBM because U.S. nationals were not at that time being granted visas to travel to Iran. The Claimant further argues that he could not designate a person in Iran to act as his agent in SKBM pursuant to a power of attorney, because the list of documents necessary for authentication of a power of attorney required that a photocopy of the so-called green card (resident permit or I-94), which he did not have as a U.S. citizen, be attached to the

application in order for the power of attorney to be recognized in Iran. Moreover, on 4 March 1980, the Revolutionary Public Prosecutor of Iran issued an order stating that powers of attorney signed in foreign countries could no longer be recognized in Iran. The Claimant also emphasizes that in any event, based on Article 121 of the Commercial Code of Iran, as amended in 1969, the Respondent as a majority shareholder could have managed the company and appointed the majority of its directors. The Claimant also states that since April or June 1979 he has not received dividends, notices of meetings or any other communications required to be sent to the shareholders of the company. Therefore, the Claimant argues, he has been deprived of his equity and creditor interests in SKBM and of all of his rights as a shareholder of the company.

34. The Claimant states that all these acts are attributable to the Respondent, because Iran is responsible for the acts which resulted in his departure from Iran, and because the Respondent did not protect his interests in Iran. The Respondent, he asserts, is liable for the takeover and sale of SKBM's building because it benefitted from and accepted the acts of the Revolutionary Committee. In particular, the Respondent's liability arises from the Respondent's acquiescence in the acts of the Revolutionary Committee and the Labor Court. Iran's failure to pay SKBM for services rendered to ISIRAN under SKBM's contract with ISIRAN, together with its acquisition of control over the company, the takeover and sale of the office building, and the confiscation of the remaining proceeds thereof, amounted in the aggregate to expropriation of SKBM and the Claimant's interest therein. The Claimant implies that the Respondent had a duty to act and prevent acts of interference with these properties or to protect the Claimant's interests in SKBM. When Iran did not act, such acts of interference became acts of State, which entailed the Respondent's liability for these acts.

35. The Claimant also states that Iran's actions were aimed at the assets of SKBM and deprived the directors and sharcholders of SKBM of their control over the company, thereby interfering with the rights of the shareholders in such a manner that they effectively amounted to an expropriation of SKBM. The Claimant further argues, in the alternative, that the acts resulting in the Government's assumption of control over SKBM and its failure to assert SKBM's claim against ISIRAN, which in turn resulted in the takeover and sale of the company's office building, constitute such an unreasonable interference in SKBM by the Respondent that it amounts to an expropriation of the company and of the Claimant's interests therein.

36. The Claimant also argues that SKBM ceased to exist as a joint stock company when the assets of Mr. Amir Hossein Amir Faiz were expropriated in April 1979, because after the Respondent took control of the company, it

did not fulfill the corporate formalities required to maintain SKBM as a valid corporation under Iranian law. The Claimant asserts that these violations of Iranian law, together with the loss of SKBM's office premises in Tehran, led to the dissolution of SKBM and the nullification of its legal personality. The Claimant states that, while he has the right to bring a direct claim for his share of the company's assets and properties, he is also entitled, in the alternative, to assert an indirect claim for 33.75% of the unpaid accounts due to SKBM from ISIRAN. As a second alternative, the Claimant asserts that he is entitled, on the basis of unjust enrichment, to 33.75% of the funds due to SKBM from ISIRAN because the Respondent has been enriched, to the detriment of the Claimant, to the extent that the Respondent caused SKBM not to collect contractual debts due to SKBM from ISIRAN, and also caused ISIRAN not to pay these debts.

37. For its part, the Respondent states that the office building of SKBM was not taken; rather, Iran asserts that SKBM's local employees filed suit before a labor tribunal to recover their salaries and wages, annual bonus and severance pay. The Respondent states that on 3 February 1979, based on the appropriate provisions of the Labor Act of Iran, the Workshop Council issued a decision in favor of these employees, which decision was served on SKBM on 3 March 1979. The decision was also confirmed by the Board for Settlement of Disputes established pursuant to the requirements of Articles 39 and 40 of the Labor Act of Iran. The decision ordered SKBM to pay Rials 13,212,348 as compensation to its 106 local employees. The Respondent further states that the employees of SKBM subsequently requested the Public Court of Tehran to enforce the decision by selling SKBM's office building, allegedly because SKBM did not voluntarily pay its debt to them. As a result of these proceedings the office building was sold for Rials 14,260,000, out of which amount debts to the local employees were satisfied. The Respondent states that the remainder of the proceeds from the sale of the building is being kept in a deposit account.

38. The Respondent further states that it has not interfered in the affairs of SKBM or altered the legal status of the company. SKBM still exists and no changes in the company's management have been announced to the Corporate and Industrial Ownership Registration Department since 16 June 1977, when Amir Hossein Amir Faiz, Hassan Asgari Pour and the Claimant were elected to the Board of Directors. The Respondent concludes that SKBM became defunct after the departure of the Claimant and the dismissal of foreign and local experts in January 1979. The Respondent argues that if SKBM was expropriated or placed under governmental control, its shares and property should be in the possession of the Foundation for the Oppressed (Bonyad-Mostazafan). However, there are no records in the office of the

Directorate of the Affairs of Shares and Companies of the Foundation for the Oppressed showing that any or all of SKBM's shares have been registered on behalf of or in the name of the Foundation, or that the company is being operated by the Foundation. Therefore, the Respondent concludes that SKBM has not been expropriated or taken under its control.

39. The Respondent also states that even if the property of Amir Hossein Amir Faiz was expropriated, SKBM did not engage in any further activities which the Respondent could have taken under its control. If one or more government-appointed managers had been designated to the company, they would have taken proper measures to pay the debts to the employees of SKBM from the company's assets and property, which was not done. Moreover, according to the Respondent, at the time of the expropriation of the property of SKBM's majority shareholder, the company did not have any other assets or property left, except its office building. The enforcement of the decision of the Labor Court did not involve any action by the Government.

40. The Respondent emphasizes that the Claimant has not submitted any evidence of an attempt on his part to travel to Iran or of acts whereby the Respondent has prevented him from returning there. In any case, the Respondent adds, the Claimant could have returned to Iran by using his Iranian passport. The Respondent also alleges that it would have been possible for the Claimant to send a legal notice and file a Statement of Claim against ISIRAN with the courts of Iran, which would not have required him to provide a power of attorney to any representative. However, the Respondent underscores that the Claimant has failed to show that an attempt to give the power of attorney to a certain person would have been frustrated or denied by the Iran Interest Section in the Embassy of Algeria in Washington or that his representative would have been barred from entering Iran or engaging in activities there.

41. The Respondent states that because SKBM still exists as an independent entity according to the registers of the Corporate and Industrial Ownership Registration Department, no dissolution or liquidation has taken place. Moreover, even if SKBM had been dissolved and been construed to be in liquidation, it could not have lost its juridical identity, because according to Article 208 of the Commercial Code of Iran, as amended in 1969, a company fully retains its legal personality until the liquidation process is completed. However, the Respondent emphasizes that the registration file of SKBM does not contain any information indicating that it has been placed in liquidation. Furthermore, the Respondent states that according to Article 199 of the Commercial Code of Iran, which regulates the situations in which a corporation may be dissolved, the decision on dissolution must be adopted either by an extraordinary general meeting of the shareholders (cf. Article 83) or by a

final judgment of the Court (cf. Article 201). The Respondent further emphasizes that any dissolution and liquidation of SKBM had to be carried out in one of these two ways. Because neither has been done, the Respondent concludes that the Claimant is not entitled to claim for his share of the funds allegedly due to SKBM.

2.1.2 *The Claim for the Funds Advanced to SKBM on Behalf of ISIRAN*

42. The Claimant states that due to financial difficulties which prevented ISIRAN from paying its subcontractors, allegedly caused by late payments to ISIRAN from the Iranian Ground Forces, he and Mr. Hassan Asgari Pour had to advance their private funds to SKBM to keep it in operation and able to fulfill its contractual obligations to the Iranian Ground Forces.

43. The Claimant states that he and his partner, Mr. Asgari Pour, opened a joint account in order to record these transfers of private funds advanced to SKBM. The Claimant has submitted a document which he states is a copy of bank records of this account. Some of the pages of that document, compiled in Persian, include the following information at the top of the page:

"Bank Shahriyar. A Public Joint Stock Corporation with capital of 5,000,000,000 Rials. Account no. 120/01/00275. Name(s) of the account holder(s): Messrs [Mohsen] Asgari [Nazari] & [Hassan] Asgari-Pour. Address: Abbasabad, the Intersection of QASR, Building No. 35, 1st floor."

The Claimant states that he advanced private funds "in the amount of one-half of each of the credits shown" in that document, and asserts that by January 1979 his share of the funds advanced amounted to approximately $1,150,000.00. The Claimant asserts that he continued to transfer funds to SKBM through this account until March 1979, because the final report required to be prepared by SKBM was delivered to ISIRAN in May 1979.

44. Three of the affidavits submitted by the Claimant make reference to the required funding of SKBM during the period when the payments through ISIRAN were not received. The affidavits of Mr. Glen Nutgrass, Mr. Donald Buckner and Col. Thomas G. Irwin include similar statements asserting that the funds required for the salary payments and the operating expenses of SKBM were provided regularly by the Claimant and Mr. Asgari Pour. The affidavit of Mr. Nutgrass also includes a statement that by January 1979, the Claimant and Mr. Asgari Pour had each advanced SKBM approximately $1,150,000. Two of these affiants, Col. Irwin and Mr. Buckner, also attended the Hearing as the Claimant's witnesses. When they were questioned on this issue, however, they were unable to confirm the specific source of the funds provided to SKBM. Furthermore, they could not confirm whether the funds were acquired as loans from local banks or were provided from the private funds of the Claimant and Mr. Asgari Pour; nor could they affirm that the

alleged funds were not repaid later. Moreover, since neither of the witnesses recognized the bank records submitted in evidence, they were unable to provide further information on this document.

45. The Claimant argues that when the Respondent expropriated the shares of the majority shareholder of SKBM and acquired control of SKBM, the company's liabilities and debts, including the alleged debt to the Claimant, were also transferred to the Respondent. As further support for this argument the Claimant refers to *Hidetomo Shinto (a claim of less than $250,000)* v. *The Islamic Republic of Iran*, Award No. 399-10273-3 (31 Oct. 1988), *reprinted in* 19 IRAN-U.S. C.T.R. 321; and he asserts that the Tribunal has already found in that Case that SKBM is a government-controlled entity, and has recognized that Iran is responsible for the debts of those companies which are under its control. Therefore, the Claimant concludes that Iran must be considered to be responsible for SKBM's debt to him.

46. The Respondent begins by disputing the Claimant's statement that the funds were transferred to SKBM. The Respondent states that Mr. Amir Faiz as the majority shareholder of the company should have approved the alleged arrangement or provided some share of the funds. Emphasizing that the only evidence provided by the Claimant was a copy of the bank records described in paragraph 43 above, the Respondent contests the evidentiary value of this document. The Respondent especially argues that the dates in the document raise suspicions because the last date in the bank records is 10 March 1979, which is eight months after the Claimant's departure from Iran; which is also more than a month after the issuance of the Labor Court award against SKBM and about one month after the alleged expropriation of SKBM by Iran. However, the Respondent emphasizes, SKBM became defunct after the Claimant's departure in 1978 or, in any case, at the latest after the dismissal of SKBM's foreign and local experts in January 1979. Furthermore, the document does not show that the transfers from this account were made for or to SKBM. The Respondent implies that this document constitutes a fraudulent attempt to recover the monies due to SKBM from ISIRAN. Therefore, the Respondent concludes, there exists no proof in the record to substantiate the Claimant's allegation that he advanced funds to SKBM.

47. In its rebuttal filings, the Respondent also submitted a document entitled the "specimen of signatures", done in connection with the opening of joint account No. 275 in Bank Shahriyar. This document lists the Claimant and Mr. Asgari Pour as the holders of this account and includes a reference to Mahat Company (SKBM), but does not include any further information on the latter.

48. As for the Claimant's alleged loan arrangement, the Respondent also argued at the Hearing that pursuant to Articles 121, 129 and 132 of the

Commercial Code of Iran, as amended in 1969, any loan to **SKBM** would have had to be accepted by the Board of Directors of that company. Furthermore, according to Article 129 of the Commercial Code, even if the Board accepts the loan, it has to inform the meeting of the shareholders of the arrangement. The Respondent emphasizes that the Claimant should have followed these formal requirements if he lent the money to the company. However, the Respondent asserts, there is no proof in the record to show that this transaction ever took place. Moreover, the Respondent states that the Claimant has not provided any information or document to show whether or how **ISIRAN** accepted this arrangement.

2.1.3 *The Claim for the Relocation Allowance and Salary*

49. The Claimant states that he is entitled to recovery of his salary and relocation benefits amounting to $12,000, which were due to him on the basis of his service contract with **SKBM** and its promise to pay these monies to him. He asserts that **SKBM** has not paid him these entitlements, even though they were due to him when he returned to the United States in July 1978. The Claimant argues that when Iran expropriated **SKBM**, it also became liable for the debts of the company; therefore, the Respondent should be liable for this debt of **SKBM** to the Claimant. The Claimant asserts that this Claim arose on or about April 1979, when the Respondent allegedly took over the assets and liabilities of **SKBM** upon expropriating the property of **SKBM**'s majority shareholder. In support of this Claim, the Claimant has only submitted an affidavit of his own asserting the entitlement and referred to *Hidetomo Shinto* v. *The Islamic Republic of Iran, supra*, stating that in that case Iran was found to be responsible to a former employee of **SKBM** for unpaid salary and relocation payments. At the Hearing, the Claimant's witnesses were also questioned on this matter, but they were not able to confirm the Claimant's statement or to give any further information or evidence on the issue.

50. The Respondent contests this Claim, stating that the Claimant has not demonstrated the existence of any contract or other evidence of a commitment to pay him the claimed salary and relocation allowance. The Respondent also disputes the relevance of the Claimant's reference to *Hidetomo Shinto* v. *The Islamic Republic of Iran, supra*, since in that case there existed an employment contract between the employer and the employee. The Respondent emphasizes that in the present Case, by contrast, the Claimant has been a shareholder and director of the company, but has not shown that he had an employment contract with **SKBM**. Therefore, the Respondent asserts, the Claimant cannot claim for the benefits due to the employees of the company. The Respondent concludes that the Claimant has not submitted any evidence in support of this Claim, and requests that the Claim be dismissed.

2.1.4 The Claim for Expropriation of an Equity Interest in SKBM

51. The Claimant first claims, as a part of his equity interest in SKBM, his share of the receivables due to SKBM. The information provided by the Claimant on the debt and on the resulting deterioration of SKBM's financial situation during 1978 and early 1979 largely appears in his written declarations concerning the contractual and financial relations between ISIRAN, the Iranian Ground Forces and SKBM. Several of his affiants have also made reference to these issues. On these grounds the Claimant states that he is entitled to claim his portion of this debt of ISIRAN to SKBM, either directly or indirectly, or, in the alternative, on the basis of unjust enrichment.

52. The Respondent disputes the Claimant's Claim concerning the SKBM receivables by stating that this question, dealt with in the Claimant's direct claim but raised in essence on behalf of SKBM, is based on the contractual relations between the aforementioned entities and, therefore, cannot be addressed in this Case because the Claimant has not included the relevant corporations among the respondents and the record does not contain the contract between these entities. The Respondent also contests the Claimant's right to raise an alternative indirect claim based on the same issue, because the Claimant's interest in SKBM was not sufficient to control the company at the time the Claim arose and therefore the Claim does not meet the requirements of the Claims Settlement Declaration for admissibility of indirect claims of shareholders.

53. The Claimant further claims his equity interest in SKBM on the basis of the effects of the expropriation of the majority interest in SKBM or, in the alternative, on the basis of unreasonable interference in SKBM, amounting to expropriation, through acts attributable to the Respondent.

54. The Claimant argues that the Respondent acquired control of SKBM upon expropriating the property of Mr. Amir Hossein Amir Faiz. Since the Iranian Ground Forces were part of the Respondent's official structure and the Respondent owned and controlled ISIRAN and because it had acquired through expropriation a majority interest in SKBM and therefore also control of SKBM, it was not in the Respondent's interest to effect the payment of the amounts due to SKBM from ISIRAN. The Claimant further argues that the Respondent made it impossible for him to exercise any influence over SKBM. These acts or omissions allegedly resulted directly in a situation where the main office of SKBM was sold by a revolutionary committee to pay the local employees of SKBM. The Claimant asserts that the balance of the proceeds was given to the Foundation for the Oppressed and that as the result SKBM ceased to exist as an entity independent of the Respondent.

55. To establish the expropriation of the property of the majority shareholder, Mr. Amir Faiz, the Claimant has submitted a copy of a decree of the

Islamic Revolutionary Court, dated 12 April 1979, issued by the Office of the General Public Prosecutor of the Islamic Republic of Iran which lists the names of those individuals whose properties were expropriated "for the benefit of the oppressed". The name of Mr. Amir Hossein Amir Faiz is listed in that document as number 181. Furthermore, on 12 April 1979, the Presiding Judge of the Religious Court added in the margin of the document a handwritten confirmation that movable and immovable properties of the persons mentioned and of their close relatives had been confiscated. As further support for his claim of expropriation, the Claimant also refers to the Case of *Hidetomo Shinto* v. *The Islamic Republic of Iran, supra*. In that Case, he states, the Tribunal found, while deciding the question of jurisdiction, that SKBM became a government-controlled entity when the shares of Mr. Amir Hossein Amir Faiz were expropriated.

56. Some of the affidavits submitted by the Claimant include references to the sale of SKBM's building and the fate of the proceeds therefrom. Mr. Glen Nutgrass, a witness for the Claimant, states in his affidavit that he heard from his Iranian colleagues at SKBM that the local revolutionary committee had sold SKBM's office building, paid the salaries of the Iranian employees and confiscated the balance. The Claimant's other witness, Mr. Donald Buckner, gives a similar statement in his affidavit and states further, without giving any date, that when he visited SKBM's office he noticed that the office building had been taken over by the revolutionary forces and that former members of SKBM's local personnel had joined them.

57. The Claimant's witness, Mr. Donald Buckner, stated at the Hearing that SKBM also had, besides its office building in Tehran, a project office in ISIRAN's corporate building in Shabnam [Avenue], Shahabbas [Street], Tehran. The premises at ISIRAN's corporate building were forcibly entered and ransacked in January 1979 by members of the local revolutionary committee. The witness states that the committee took over the entire premises of ISIRAN's corporate building in February 1979. On 21 April 1979, the furniture and files of SKBM were removed from ISIRAN's building to SKBM's office building. Furthermore, SKBM's office building was also intruded into in March or April 1979 by a number of SKBM's Iranian personnel who had joined the revolutionary forces and were accompanied by members of those forces. Mr. Buckner also stated that in April 1979 SKBM's office building was locked and Mr. Asgari Pour refused to allow him access to the premises. Therefore, he prepared the final project report for ISIRAN without having access to all necessary documents. The witness also explained that, still in March 1979, nine of SKBM's expatriate experts had to stay in Iran because at that time there were no funds left in the company to cover their travel costs.

58. As further support for the Claimant's arguments that SKBM had been expropriated together with his equity interest therein, the Claimant refers to the case law of the Tribunal and to the principles found therein.

59. The Respondent states that the office building of SKBM was not taken by the revolutionary forces as asserted by the Claimant. Rather, it was sold as the result of a legal proceeding which commenced when the local employees of the company filed a suit before "a labor tribunal" to recover their salaries and wages, annual bonus and the severance pay. The Respondent has submitted a part of the Labor Act of Iran, Article 38, paragraph 1 of which states that if a dispute between the employee and employer is not settled by reconciliation, the matter shall be referred to the local labor department, which shall refer it to the appropriate Workshop [Factory] Council within three days of the receipt of complaint.[7] The Respondent has submitted a copy of the decision of the Workshop Council, issued on 3 February 1979 in favor of these employees, together with letter No. 25133 from the Tehran Department General of Labor and Social Affairs transmitting the decision to SKBM. The Respondent states that this award was served upon SKBM on 3 March 1979.

60. Furthermore, the Respondent also states that according to Article 38, paragraph 4, of the Labor Act of Iran, the decision of the Workshop [Factory] Council may be referred to the Board for Settlement of Disputes within 10 days from the communication of the decision when it concerns, *inter alia,* wages or dismissal of a worker. The Respondent has submitted a decision of the Board for Settlement of Disputes which confirms the decision of the Workshop Council, which accordingly became final and binding. The decision of the Workshop Council ordered SKBM to pay Rials 13,212,348 as compensation to 106 locally recruited employees of SKBM.

61. The Respondent has also submitted a copy of a letter from the [Department of] Tehran Judicial Police for the Enforcement of Civil Judgments, dated 20 November 1988 and addressed to the Director of the Investigation and Restitution Bureau of the Foundation for the Oppressed, which states that according to the employees, 30% of the sums due to each employee pursuant to the decision of the Workshop Council had been received by them from the debtor company.[8]

62. The Respondent asserts that these employees requested the Public

---

[7] According to Article 38, paragraph 2, the Council shall consist of the representative of the Ministry of Labor, the representative of the employer and the representative of the workers of the factory involved.

[8] Also, all of the employees' payment requests submitted to the Enforcement Office of the Public Court of Tehran, Chamber One, state that 30% of the amounts awarded in favor of the employees should be paid to Mr. Hassan Asgari Pour.

Court of Tehran to enforce the award by selling the office building of SKBM and using the funds realized to pay the amounts awarded, allegedly because the company's representatives did not voluntarily fully satisfy them. According to evidence submitted by the Respondent, those employees sought an enforcement order from Chamber One of Tehran Public Court,[9] which was issued in the enforcement case No. 152/58.

63. The Respondent has submitted several documents to show that during the enforcement proceedings, the office building was delimited and described in oral proceedings on 3 July 1979 and 10 November 1979. Moreover, according to the Notice of Auction of 3 October 1980, SKBM's office building was sold for Rials 14,260,000, from which amount the local employees were satisfied. The Respondent has also submitted a letter from the [Department of] Tehran Judicial Police for the Enforcement of Civil Judgments, dated 20 November 1988 and addressed to the Head of the Investigation and Restitution Bureau of the Foundation for the Oppressed, which states that a sum of Rials 9,579,340 has been paid to 97 former employees of SKBM and that the remainder is being kept in a deposit fund. However, the letter also mentions that the Ministry of Finance and Economic Affairs has requested that the aforementioned balance be attached. The Respondent has also submitted a letter issued by the Head of the [Former Department of] Tehran Judicial Police for the Enforcement of Civil Judgments, issued on 19 October 1992, stating that certain amounts due the plaintiffs (the employees) have been paid and that the balance remaining, Rials 4,280,660, is being kept in deposit "to be returned to the parties winning against the company".

64. The Respondent asserts that it has not interfered in the affairs of SKBM or altered its legal status. To support this assertion, the Respondent has submitted a letter of 29 December 1991 from the Corporate and Industrial Ownership Registration Department which states that SKBM still exists and that there has not been any change in the management of the company since 16 June 1977, when Amir Hossein Amir Faiz, Hassan Asgari Pour and the Claimant were elected to the Board of Directors for a two-year term. The Respondent asserts that if SKBM had been expropriated or placed under governmental control, its shares and property would have been in the possession of the Foundation for the Oppressed. However, the letter of 26 January 1992 from the Directorate of the Affairs of Shares and Companies of the Foundation for the Oppressed, submitted by the Respondent, states that there are no records in that office showing that the company's shares, or a

---

[9] According to the record, the enforcement process has been supervised by Chamber One of Tehran Public Court. However, in one occasion, Chamber Two of the same Court has overseen the process.

portion of its shares, are registered in the Foundation's name or indicating that the company is being operated by the Foundation. Therefore, the Respondent concludes that SKBM has not been expropriated or taken under its control.

65. Furthermore, on several grounds, the Respondent contests the Claimant's reference to the Tribunal's finding in *Hidetomo Shinto* v. *The Islamic Republic of Iran, supra,* that "SKBM was a controlled entity of Iran within the provisions of Article VII, paragraph 3 of the Claims Settlement Declaration." In support of its arguments the Respondent refers to the letter from the Foundation for the Oppressed which denies, on the basis of its records, that any control has been exercised over SKBM. The Respondent also asserts that the present case fundamentally differs from the above-referenced case. Furthermore, the Respondent maintains that the finding of control by the Government over an entity does not mean as such that the Government is to be held to be responsible *vis-à-vis* third parties as shareholders, or that the entity should be deemed to have been taken.

66. The Respondent states that the Claimant's shares have not been expropriated, and that the expropriation of the property of Amir Hossein Amir Faiz has had no effect on the status of the shares of other shareholders. Furthermore, the Respondent states that the expropriation has not had any effect on the shares previously owned by Amir Faiz. The Respondent argues that although Amir Hossein Amir Faiz was convicted by the Islamic Revolutionary Court in Tehran, and a verdict was issued to confiscate his property, SKBM's registration file at the Bureau for Registration of Companies in Tehran does not include any reference to expropriation of these shares. The Respondent asserts that at least the names of the controlling entity and the managers appointed by the Government should have been included in the file, if an expropriation had occurred. The Respondent argues that because the company did not have any assets or property other than its office building at the time of the sale of the building, there was nothing left to be expropriated in SKBM. Moreover, the Respondent emphasizes that Iran has neither interfered in the affairs of SKBM nor expropriated the Claimant's alleged shares in the company.

67. The Respondent further states that the Claimant has not produced any evidence showing that the minority shareholders of SKBM were deprived of the possibilities to exercise their rights in SKBM or that they were in any way prevented from taking lawful measures with regard to the company's affairs.

2.2 The Claim for the Nationalization of an Interest in the Passargad Savings and Home Loan Company

68. The Claimant states that he owned 4,660 shares in the "Sherkat Pasandaz Va Vam Maskan Passargad" ("Passargad" or the "Company"), an

Iranian savings and home loan corporation, and that these shares were expropriated when the Company was nationalized and merged with Bank Maskan.

69. The Claimant states that he was initially informed by his business partner, Mr. Amir Faiz, of a profitable investment possibility in a newly chartered savings and home loan company, Passargad, whose purpose was to provide loans to persons intending to purchase apartments. The Claimant also stated that when he discussed the matter with Mr. Asgari Pour, the latter asked if he could also invest in the Company, to which the Claimant agreed.

70. At the Hearing, the Claimant explained that in agreeing with Mr. Amir Faiz to invest in the shares of Passargad, he and Mr. Asgari Pour originally committed themselves to purchase 50 million Rials worth of shares. However, Mr. Amir Faiz later informed them that it was only possible to purchase approximately 46 million Rials worth of shares. The Claimant states that to finance this purchase he exchanged a check worth about $100,000 and thereafter obtained two cashier's checks. The Claimant asserts in his written pleadings that the cashier's checks were used because Bank Rahni Iran required that form of payment for the shares. Therefore, he paid the alleged Rials 46,600,000 to Bank Iranian, Central Branch, and to Bank Omran, Karim-Khan Zand Branch, in order to induce these banks to issue two checks, totally in the amount of Rials 46,600,000, payable to Bank Rahni Iran. At the Hearing, the Claimant explained that after having obtained these checks he delivered them to Mr. Amir Faiz, who in turn was to deliver them to Bank Rahni Iran in order to be deposited in the account established for these payments. The Claimant states that he thereby purchased 2,330 shares of the Company's stock, worth Rials 23,300,000, on or about 8 April 1978 for himself, and that at the same time he also financed another purchase of 2,330 shares of the same Company in the name of his business partner, Hassan Asgari Pour, also worth Rials 23,300,000.

71. To prove his own purchase the Claimant has presented as evidence a copy of a document alleged to be a copy of a "Shares Purchase Receipt" (No. 1-101, 18.2.2537) which has been signed by Bank Rahni Iran. The Claimant argues that this document constitutes an acknowledgement of the receipt of the purchase price of the shares, in the form of two cashier's checks. The document acknowledges the receipt of part of one cashier's check, No. 336070, and another check, No. 201664, both dated 18.2.2537, for Rials 23,300,000. The document further states that the

> "[a]bove check(s), after clearance will be the purchase price of . . . (2,330), Ten Thousand (10,000) Rials ALEF Series Shares of PAS[S]ARGAD SAVING AND HOME LOAN CORPORATION. . . ."

The document also states that "[a]ny fund as of the date of receipt is the property of Pas[s]argad Saving and Home Loan Corporation, . . . and is only reimburs[a]ble according to the provision of the rules and regulations of Saving and Home Loan Corporations set forth by Money and Credit" Council. To prove the purchase of an additional 2,330 shares on behalf of Mr. Asgari Pour, the Claimant has provided another document, similarly entitled "Shares Purchase Receipt" (No. 1-100, dated 18.2.2537) signed by Bank Rahni Iran, which also acknowledges the receipt of part of cashier's check No. 336070, dated 18.2.2537, for Rials 23,300,000.

72. The Claimant asserts that these documents show that Bank Rahni Iran was entitled to receive, and did receive, the amount of the checks from these banks upon presentation of the documents, and that the cashier's checks were issued after he had paid the aforementioned amount to the banks. The Claimant also argues that the receipts show that the alleged purchases were made. The Claimant asserts that he did not demand a return of the checks nor did Bank Rahni Iran notify him that it did not intend to cash the checks. The Claimant further asserts that he had no means to recover these checks unless they were returned to him by Bank Rahni Iran, which never occurred.

73. The Claimant also emphasizes the fact that he and Mr. Asgari Pour had signed Passargad's Articles of Association, and states that under Iranian law only persons who have subscribed to and paid for shares of a joint stock company may approve and sign its Articles of Association. In support of this argument, the Claimant refers to Articles 16 and 17 of the Commercial Code of Iran, as amended in 1969, and asserts that these articles are to be considered as indirect evidence that payment for the shares was made.

74. The Claimant further states that later, on or about 6 July 1978, Mr. Asgari Pour, owing to his failure to reimburse the Claimant for the amount due to him for his purchase of the shares, transferred his ownership rights to the 2,330 shares purchased in his name to the Claimant by endorsing the purchase voucher in the Claimant's name. On giving the document to the Claimant, Mr. Asgari Pour explained that because he could not be sure that he would be able to pay his debt to the Claimant for the purchase of the shares, he had decided to transfer them to the Claimant in lieu of repayment.

75. At the Hearing, the Claimant asserted that he was not aware of the possible restrictions on foreign ownership of these shares. He also stated that he did not intend to enjoy the benefits of receiving home loans available to shareholders of Passargad but had bought shares only because he thought the investment would be profitable.

76. On the expropriation issue, the Claimant states that by nationalizing Passargad Iran also divested him of his rights as a shareholder in the Company. He states and produces evidence showing that Iran issued the Law

for Nationalization of Banks, which was published on 8 July 1979 in issue No. 10012 of the Official Gazette. In accordance with Article 2 of that law, new directors were appointed to manage the nationalized banks. The scope of that law was later retroactively enlarged to apply as well to all savings and home loan companies, when the Revolutionary Council of the Islamic Republic of Iran adopted the Legal Bill for Nationalization of Insurance and Credit Entities, addressed to the Ministry of Finance and Economic Affairs and published on 22 May 1980 in issue No. 10264 of the Official Gazette. Article 8 of that Bill states that

> [e]ffective from the date of enactment of the Law of Nationalization of Banks, all savings and home loan companies are covered by the said law.

The Claimant states that through this Bill the coverage of the law was expanded to include Passargad as well, and that the Company was therefore nationalized through operation of law on or about 11 June 1979.

77. The Claimant presumes in his written pleadings that after 11 June 1979, when the Government of Iran appointed directors to manage the nationalized credit enterprises, it also took such measures with respect to Passargad. Furthermore, the Claimant has produced evidence showing that by virtue of the Law for Management of Banks, issued on 25 September 1979, and also pursuant to order No. 5/3058, by the High Council of Banks, dated 27 January 1980, Passargad was consolidated with a number of other entities to form Bank Maskan.

78. The Claimant concludes that the Company has been expropriated. The Claimant asserts that by enacting and implementing the Law for Nationalization of Banks, Iran also directly expropriated his interest in the Company. He emphasizes that no compensation has been given to him, and adds that as a result of the expropriation he has been unable to exercise any of his rights as a shareholder in Passargad, and has not received any of the dividends or communications which are required by Iranian law to be paid or sent to the shareholders.

79. In his written pleadings, the Claimant has also asserted that even if Passargad had not been established as a legal entity at the time the nationalization law went into effect, Bank Rahni Iran would still have been liable for restitution of the amount paid for the purchase of the shares of stock of the company, together with interest from 8 April 1978 to the date of the payment of the Award.

80. The Respondent disputes the Claimant's arguments on the purchase of the shares, stating that these documents do not clearly establish the alleged purchases of these shares nor that any payment had been made for them. The Respondent emphasizes that the sole document in evidence in support of the

Claimant's alleged ownership of his 2,330 shares is an "A" class share purchase form which refers to checks nos. 336070 and 201664, but does not prove the actual "receipt of the amount of those checks". The Respondent also emphasizes that this form and the checks refer to the fact that once those monies are collected they will be allocated to the purchase of 2,330 Class "A" shares, and that the deposited amounts will belong to Passargad only as of the date of collection. The Respondent asserts that those documents should therefore be deemed to constitute an offer whose finality is conditional on collection of the amount of the checks, and therefore these documents *per se* do not establish that Bank Rahni Iran ever received or collected the money represented by the cashier's checks. Furthermore, the Respondent asserts that Bank Maskan, the successor to Bank Rahni Iran, "did not come across" any record evidencing that it had collected the cashier's checks allegedly received from the Claimant.[10] On this basis the Respondent concludes that the Claimant has not met his burden of proving that the alleged checks were transferred to Bank Rahni Iran or that their amounts were paid thereto.

81. On the same grounds, the Respondent also contests the Claimant's assertion that he financed the purchase of the shares of Mr. Asgari Pour. The Respondent maintains that the evidence submitted does not support the Claimant's allegation that he also paid for Mr. Asgari Pour's shares. During the oral and written pleadings, the Respondent contested the Claimant's statement that he financed both purchases of shares, and suggested instead that the documents submitted to the Tribunal as proof of the purchases are more probably to be interpreted as establishing that Mr. Asgari Pour himself financed these transactions. The Respondent also refers in this connection to the arguments made against the Claimant's alleged purchase of his own shares, and denies that any actual payment for the purchase of Mr. Asgari Pour's shares has been made by the Claimant. The Respondent concludes that on that basis, this part of the Claimant's Claim should be rejected.

82. Furthermore, the Respondent states in its written pleadings that no actual purchases of shares took place because neither Bank Rahni Iran nor its successor, Bank Maskan, has found any record evidencing that this collection took place at some later date. At the Hearing, the representatives of the Respondent stated that the mere delivery of a check was not enough to make someone a shareholder of Passargad; rather, to become a shareholder of the Company required at least both the collection and clearance of the checks and

---

[10] The Respondent also argues in its Rebuttal Memorial that even assuming, *arguendo*, that the Claimant might have issued the checks, he has submitted no evidence to show that the checks cleared, and the Respondent concludes therefore that the Claimant's alleged ownership right to the shares has not been established.

the approval of Bank Rahni Iran. However, there is no evidence in the record that these requirements were ever met.[11]

83. The Respondent contests the Claimant's allegation that the signatures on Passargad's Articles of Association should, pursuant to Articles 16 and 17 of the 1969 Amendment to the Commercial Code of Iran, be considered as evidence of payment for Passargad shares. The Respondent asserts that these legal provisions are related to subscription of the total capital of the company and to the payment of at least 35% thereof, and are not to be construed as evidence of payment of the amount of these shares or of share ownership. The Respondent further argues that the documents produced by the Claimant do not specify the total amount of the shares or the amount required to meet the obligation to pay 35% of their value in cash.

84. The Respondent also disputes the alleged transfer of the shares and states that no factual or legal transfer has been effected and that this part of the Claimant's Claim should therefore be dismissed on jurisdictional grounds. The Respondent further states and presents evidence that while these shares are transferable, their transfer is subject to certain legal requirements which have not been fulfilled.

85. The Respondent also states that the ownership of the shares of, and membership in, Passargad were specially limited to nationals of Iran. In support of these arguments, the Respondent has submitted in its rebuttal filings the Regulations of Savings and Home Loan Companies and the Articles of Association of Passargad. The Respondent cites several Articles of these Regulations and Articles of Association which contain the requirement of Iranian nationality, and concludes that according to the referred rules only Iranian nationals were entitled to purchase an equity interest in the Company and to be a member thereof. The Respondent asserts that since the acquisition of entitlements in Passargad was conditional on the possession of Iranian nationality and the Claimant must have used his Iranian nationality to obtain those benefits in the Company, he therefore should not be permitted to rely upon his other nationality in order to present a claim for recovery of those entitlements. Therefore, the Respondent concludes that the Claimant's Claim should be dismissed on the basis of the Caveat as well.

86. The Respondent also denies that Bank Rahni Iran was nationalized.

---

[11] The Respondent also states that because the monies for the shares were to be deposited into a certain account established for this purpose in Bank Rahni Iran, a working group of Bank Maskan officers was formed to clarify the issue, but in the course of their investigation they did not find any information that the monies for these purchases had been paid through or to the account designated for the collection of these payments. Therefore the Respondent maintains that it is unclear whether the shares were ever issued to the Claimant, and concludes that the Claimant has not become a shareholder of the Company.

Rather, the Respondent asserts, Bank Rahni Iran continued to operate independently as it had done prior to the issued legislation relevant to this Case. After the Law for Nationalization of Banks was promulgated Bank Rahni Iran continued to operate independently, and savings and home loan companies were merged into it. As the company was to be organized on the initiative of Bank Rahni Iran, it was the said Bank that was to receive the monies from the purchasers and to deliver the shares. The Respondent states that neither the Law for Nationalization of Banks nor the merger of Savings and Home Loan Companies, which included Passargad, into Bank Rahni Iran, had any effect on the shares of the Company. Therefore, the Respondent concludes that the status of the Claimant's shares, if he had any, was not altered.

87. The Respondent states that Article 31 of the Regulations Concerning Savings and Home Loan Companies laid down an order of preference between the different groups of creditors and holders of saving and time deposits, and shareholders, to be applied at the time of liquidation of the Company. The Claimant's alleged shares belong to the fourth and final group, whose holders are paid up to the nominal value of the shares. Pursuant to Article 32, if there is any money left after the obligatory payments are made in accordance with Article 31, the remaining amount shall be divided among the shareholders, taking into consideration the type of their shares and the amount of their savings, in the proportion they share the surplus profit of the company as mentioned in Article 23 of the Regulations. The Respondent emphasizes that the Claimant has never addressed a request to Passargad for reimbursement for the value of his alleged shares in the Company. Furthermore, Articles 74 and 75 of Passargad's Articles of Association contain provisions similar to the above mentioned Regulations, and the Respondent maintains that according to these rules, too, the Claimant was required to make a request to Passargad or to Bank Rahni Iran, as a legal successor of the Company, for the payment of his shares. In addition, the Respondent states that because the Claimant was aware of the recommendation that the former equity owners of nationalized entities contact the various newly-established banks to inquire about their nationalized interests, the Claimant should have contacted the relevant entity. The Respondent emphasizes that because the Claimant has not produced any documents to show that he did so, his Claim should not be regarded as an outstanding one. In this connection, the Respondent alleges that those shareholders who have called for their shares have been paid in accordance with the Company's existing regulations and asserts that there will be no reason to refuse payment if the Claimant contacts the entity into which Passargad was merged.

88. For his part, in response to the questions set forth at the Hearing, the

Claimant explained for the first time that Passargad was merely in formation at the time of its alleged nationalization and that it did not come fully into existence as a going concern. The Claimant further explained that after having given his cashier's checks to Mr. Amir Faiz he and Mr. Asgari Pour attended a meeting organized at the premises of the Chamber of Commerce of Iran. The Claimant stated that there were approximately 25 persons present, seven of whom, including the Claimant and Mr. Asgari Pour, signed a certain document. The Claimant stated that he did not go through the document and therefore he did not have a clear impression that by signing that document he may also have become a founder of the Company. He explained that he did not go through those documents, including the rules of Passargad, because he and Mr. Asgari Pour always trusted what Mr. Amir Faiz, who was an eminent businessman at that time in Iran and also a lawyer, told them. The Claimant did not know if the other persons signing the document also had made their purchases by delivering checks to Mr. Amir Faiz.

89. The Claimant also stated at the Hearing that Mr. Amir Faiz mentioned to him that while the Company was still in the process of formation, the shareholders' monies would be deposited in Bank Rahni Iran at 10% interest until the Company was finally established. The Claimant further stated that the checks were made out in the name of Bank Rahni Iran and that it is therefore unlikely that they were not delivered to it. However, he further stated that he never received a certificate for these shares, and that to the best of his knowledge no shares were ever issued to anyone. He confirmed that he neither received the shares nor sought to receive them after they were not submitted to him. The Claimant further stated that Passargad was not an existing operative entity before the Revolution and was only in the process of formation. The Claimant stated that he presumes that the Company was never finally established and that the shares were thus probably not issued to the investors.

90. At the Hearing, the representative of the Respondent stated, as to the establishment of Passargad, that there probably was an intention to establish a company but this intention never materialized. He further explained that the meeting of the founders was only one phase of the establishment of the Company. It remained unclear whether the process of formation was completed or Passargad ever became functional, and in any event the Claimant did not provide any proof that Passargad was finally established. Furthermore, the representatives of the Respondent stated that an investigation carried out in the offices of Bank Maskan disclosed no trace of the existence or of any activity of such a Company. Therefore, the Respondent concludes that Passargad never came into existence.

III. JURISDICTION

91. The Tribunal has found in *Mohsen Asgari Nazari* v. *The Government of the Islamic Republic of Iran*, Interlocutory Award No. ITL 79-221-1, *supra*, paras. 18-20, at 14 that during the relevant period Mohsen Asgari Nazari's dominant and effective nationality was that of the United States and that he has standing before this Tribunal under Article II, paragraph 1 and Article VII, paragraph 1 of the Claims Settlement Declaration. In that Interlocutory Award the Tribunal also joined all the remaining issues to the merits of this Case.

92. Both Parties have also submitted arguments on certain jurisdictional issues.

93. The Claimant argues that he is entitled to file an alternative indirect claim for his alleged portion of the funds owed by ISIRAN to SKBM. In support of his alleged right to file this alternative indirect Claim, the Claimant refers to several Awards in the Tribunal's case law.

94. The Respondent states that according to Article VII, paragraph 2 of the Claims Settlement Declaration and the case law of the Tribunal the Claimant is not in a position to be able to bring an indirect Claim before the Tribunal, because his equity interest in the stock of SKBM was not sufficient at the time the Claim allegedly arose to control the Corporation. The Respondent also states that the same rule should apply to the Claimant's Claim for the private funds allegedly advanced to SKBM.

95. According to Article II, paragraph 1 of the Claims Settlement Declaration, the Tribunal is established, *inter alia*, ". . .for the purpose of deciding claims of nationals of the United States against Iran. . .". Furthermore, Article VII, paragraph 2 of the Claims Settlement Declaration states that for the purposes of that agreement:

> "Claims of nationals" of Iran or the United States, as the case may be, means claims owned continuously, from the date on which the claim arose to the date on which this Agreement enters into force, by nationals of that state, including claims that are owned indirectly by such nationals through ownership of capital stock or other proprietary interests in juridical persons, provided that the ownership interests of such nationals, collectively, were sufficient at the time the claim arose to control the corporation or other entity, and provided, further, that the corporation or other entity is not itself entitled to bring a claim under the terms of this Agreement. . . .

Therefore, an indirect claim can be brought before the Tribunal in this Case only if the ownership interests in the company held by shareholders possessing United States nationality were sufficient collectively[12] to control the company

---

[12] *E.g.*, in *Richard Harza et al.*, v. *The Islamic Republic of Iran et al.*, Award No. 232-97-2 (2 May 1986), para. 29, *reprinted in* 11 IRAN-U.S. C.T.R. 76, 88, it was stated that "[w]hile Article VII,

at the time the Claim arose; and further provided that the entity in question is not itself entitled to bring the claim. SKBM is an Iranian joint stock company and, thus, not itself entitled to bring a claim under the terms of the Claims Settlement Declaration. However, the record does not establish that there were any other shareholders in the company who were U.S. nationals at the time the Claim arose. The Tribunal notes that the Claimant asserts that he held 33.75% of the stock of SKBM, but that this amount was not sufficient to control the company and thus, the requirements of Article VII, paragraph 2 of the Claims Settlement Declaration have not been satisfied. The Tribunal concludes, therefore, that the Claimant's alternative indirect claim for his share of the funds owed by ISIRAN to SKBM must be dismissed for lack of jurisdiction.

96. The Respondent has also raised several jurisdictional arguments against the Claimant's direct Claim for his share of the private funds allegedly advanced to SKBM. The Tribunal notes that many of these jurisdictional arguments also involve issues which cannot be separated from the merits. Therefore, the Tribunal decides to address these arguments together with the merits of the Claim, rather than considering them at this stage.

97. As to the Respondent's purely jurisdictional arguments concerning the Claimant's Claim for his equity interest in Passargad, the Respondent refers, *inter alia*, to Iranian municipal law on the savings and home loan companies and to Passargad's internal regulations, and states that the owners of the Company's shares have been invited to contact the related banks for their claims. On this basis, the Respondent argues that the Claimant had a duty to refer to Bank Rahni Iran or to its successor, Bank Maskan, for compensation, and since he failed to do so prior to 19 January 1981 his Claim is not outstanding. The Tribunal rejects the Respondent's argument. In the Tribunal's practice, in cases of the alleged expropriation of property rights involving equity interests in corporate stock, claimants have not been required to establish that they made a demand for compensation of their property rights before that time, in order for a claim to be "outstanding". It has been sufficient that the claim was ripe, so that a cause of action would have existed prior to that date.[13] The Tribunal notes that the cause of action in connection

---

paragraph 2 requires that the ownership interests of U.S. national owners must be sufficient collectively to control the corporation at the time the claim arose, it does not require them to bring a collective claim."

[13] *E.g.,* in *Faith Lita Khosrowshahi, et al.* v. *The Government of the Islamic Republic of Iran, et al.,* Award No. 558-178-2 (30 June 1994), at para. 67, *reprinted in* 30 IRAN-U.S. C.T.R. 176, and in *Reza Said Malek* v. *The Government of the Islamic Republic of Iran,* Award No. 534-193-3 (11 August 1992), at para. 44, *reprinted in* 28 IRAN-U.S. C.T.R. 246, the Tribunal rejected the same argument made by the Respondent in this Case, holding that claims for expropriated shares of stock in a bank, unlike claims for bank deposits, constitute outstanding claims even though no demand for payment preceded the date of the Algiers Declarations.

with this Claim finally accrued on 17 September 1980, when Passargad was merged with Bank Maskan and the alleged deprivation of the Claimant's alleged property interest occurred. Thus, the Tribunal decides that for jurisdictional purposes, the Claimant's Claim was outstanding on 19 January 1981.

98. The Respondent also argues that the Caveat applies to this Claim and does not allow the Claimant to pursue his Claim for the shares allegedly owned in Passargad before this Tribunal. Since the Respondent's arguments on this point cannot be separated from the merits, the Tribunal will not consider them at this stage. Therefore, these arguments will be addressed together with the merits, along with the remaining jurisdictional issues.

IV. MERITS

4.1 The Claim for the Funds Advanced to SKBM on Behalf of ISIRAN

99. The Tribunal notes that to succeed in this Claim, the Claimant must first establish that he advanced the alleged funds to SKBM in such a manner that a debt relationship arose between the Claimant and SKBM. He must then show that the liability for this alleged debt of SKBM to the Claimant has been transferred to Iran through acts of, or attributable to, the Respondent.

100. Thus, the Tribunal turns first to an examination of the issue whether the Claimant has shown that he advanced the alleged funds to SKBM.

101. The Tribunal notes that the document offered by the Claimant to show the alleged transfer of the funds to SKBM is a copy of the bank records of account no. 120/01/00275, jointly held by the Claimant and Mr. Asgari Pour in Bank Shahriyar. In this document most of the credit entries are cash deposits and both the credit and debit transfers bear references to certain identification numbers. However, the Claimant has not provided any further information or evidence as to what these debit transfers were and for what purposes they, or at least some of them, were made. Therefore, without any further information or evidence in the record as to the nature of the entries in that document, it is not possible to conclude whether the account was used for the purpose of the alleged advance to SKBM, or for other economic activities of its holders.

102. There is no clear evidence in the record to connect this document to SKBM, for the only reference to SKBM in this document is the address of the holders of the account. The Tribunal does note that the document containing the specimen of the holders' signatures, submitted by the Respondent, includes the note, "[r]eference: Mahat Company", but there is no further evidence or information available in the record as to the possible purpose of this reference.

103. Nor do the affidavits submitted by the Claimant give further

clarification on this question. Two of the affiants, who attended the Hearing as the Claimant's witnesses, stated that SKBM's directors somehow managed to arrange further funding for the company, but they acknowledged that they did not know the actual source of these funds. Therefore, in these circumstances the Tribunal can only conclude, on the basis of the record, that some funding was presumably provided to SKBM to enable it to continue its operations, but there is insufficient information or evidence to indicate the source of these funds. Moreover, there is no further evidence on SKBM's internal arrangements regarding the funding of its functions during the period when its debtors failed to effect their payments to the company.

104. Because the Tribunal cannot conclude, based on the foregoing, that the necessary funding for SKBM was provided by the Claimant and Mr. Asgari Pour and that those funds did not consist of bank loans and were not repaid later, the Claimant's claim is dismissed for insufficient evidence. Therefore, the Tribunal need not address the issue of whether the liability for this alleged debt has been transferred to the Respondent.

4.2 The Claim for the Relocation Allowance and Salary

105. To succeed in his Claim for the alleged relocation allowance and salary based on his employment contract with SKBM, the Claimant must first establish that he is contractually entitled to these benefits. The Tribunal notes that the Claimant's Claim is supported merely by his own declaration, where he states that those entitlements were both due and promised to him. There is no other information or any further evidence (*e.g.*, the Claimant's employment contract, a copy of a letter of termination of his employment including statements as to the salary and relocation benefits due to him, or a copy of a payment schedule of salaries, benefits and allowances paid to the Claimant prior to his departure from Iran) in the record to establish that he is entitled to those benefits, and if so, that those benefits have not been paid to him. Moreover, there is no evidence showing the amount of any benefits allegedly due to the Claimant.

106. The Tribunal thus concludes that because the Claimant has not provided any evidence in support of his alleged rights to the relocation benefits and salary, he has not met his burden of proof and his Claim for these benefits is therefore dismissed for lack of evidence.

107. The Tribunal also finds that because the Claimant has not succeeded in showing that he is entitled to these benefits, there is no need to decide the issue whether the non-payment of those benefits is due to actions attributable to the Respondent, or whether SKBM's alleged debt to the Claimant in respect of these benefits to the Claimant has been transferred to Iran as a result of acts of or attributable to the Respondent.

4.3 The Claim for the Expropriation of an Equity Interest in SKBM

108. The Tribunal notes that in support of this Claim, the Claimant has presented arguments and evidence aimed at buttressing two different theories under which the Respondent is liable for the alleged expropriation of the Claimant's equity interest in SKBM. The Claimant has argued that his equity interest was expropriated through a series of acts, allegedly attributable to the Respondent, which together or separately amounted to a taking of SKBM and the Claimant's equity interest therein. In the alternative, the Claimant has also argued that the Respondent interfered in SKBM's administration and function in such a manner that it amounted to a takeover, and that as a result the Claimant's equity interest was rendered useless and effectively (*de facto*) taken. The Claimant has also maintained, as a supplementary argument, that the Respondent is responsible for the loss of the Claimant's equity interest in SKBM on the basis of liability arising from the omission of an act, because when the Respondent acquired control of SKBM, the Respondent also assumed the duty to collect any funds owed to SKBM by ISIRAN besides the obligation to pay SKBM the same on behalf of ISIRAN. As an additional argument the Claimant has also implied that the concept of lifting the corporate veil might be applied to SKBM in such a manner that the company should be treated as liquidated, even if SKBM has not formally ceased to exist through the operation of law as asserted by the Claimant.

109. However, before addressing these questions relating to the alleged expropriation and unreasonable interference or other measures tantamount to expropriation, the Tribunal recalls that in order to meet his burden of proof the Claimant must establish two distinct elements: first, that he had ownership interests or other property rights in the properties and rights at issue and, second, that an expropriation or other measures amounting to an expropriation affecting his ownership interests or other property rights, attributable to Iran, took place.

110. As to the first element, the Tribunal notes that the evidence in the record shows that the Claimant has been a shareholder of SKBM, even if it does not clearly establish that there was no change in the shareholding interests in the company between 16 June 1977 and the date on which the Claim allegedly arose.

111. However, the threshold issue in this Claim is the second element, whether the Claimant has proven that he has been deprived of his interest in SKBM as a result of acts which, individually or collectively, would constitute *de facto* expropriation or other interference amounting to expropriation. Therefore, the Tribunal will now turn to the question of the alleged expropriation.

112. Here, the Tribunal must examine the acts of interference the

Claimant complains of and determine whether any or all of these acts are attributable to the Government of Iran and whether any or all, by themselves or collectively, constitute a sufficient degree of interference to warrant a finding that a deprivation of property has occurred. The Tribunal will first consider the different issues separately and then decide if any of these acts alone or collectively could be considered to constitute expropriation of the Claimant's property interest in SKBM.

113. The Tribunal notes that the Claimant has presented different arguments to prove expropriation referring to several acts and elements, some of which are not presented in their chronological order. Wherever possible the Tribunal chooses to address these issues in their chronological order.

114. The Tribunal first notes that there is conflicting evidence in the record on the reasons why the Claimant left Iran in July 1978. The Tribunal also observes that this was well before business activities were affected by the revolutionary developments in Iran. However, the Tribunal need not decide whether the Claimant was forced to leave Iran as implied in some of his statements and affidavits submitted during the early stages of the written proceedings, because the Claimant himself stated at the Hearing that he left Iran in July 1978 for a holiday and intended to return to Iran, and that during the holiday he also planned to recruit new foreign computer experts for SKBM. The Claimant also stated at the Hearing that he decided not to return to Iran when he was contacted by SKBM and told that there was no reason for him to return at that time, due to the company's financial situation.

115. The Claimant has also stated that the local revolutionary committee, allegedly an agency of the Government of Iran, took over the offices of SKBM in February 1979. The Claimant's witness, Mr. Donald Buckner, who stayed in Iran to finalize SKBM's final report to ISIRAN, stated that the premises of the office building were intruded upon in March or April of 1979 and that from January 1979 on, there was no access to ISIRAN's building, where SKBM's project office functioned. Later, however, on 21 April 1979, Mr. Asgari Pour refused to let the witness enter SKBM's office building in Tehran. On 3 July 1979, Mr. Asgari Pour did allow the persons sent to assess SKBM's office building to inspect the premises of the company, but stated to them that the company was closed. Without additional evidence, these facts appear to indicate that even if the premises of SKBM's office building were intruded upon, these premises remained under or were returned to the control of Mr. Asgari Pour. Therefore, the evidence in the record does not establish sufficiently that SKBM's office building in Tehran remained under the control of the intruders after their intrusion.

116. The Tribunal now turns to the issue of the sale of the office building

of SKBM. The Tribunal notes that the local employees of SKBM successfully applied to the local Workshop Council to be paid the amounts of the salaries and severance benefits due to them. According to the decision of the Workshop Council rendered on 3 February 1979, the representative of SKBM was also heard during the proceedings. The decision was confirmed by the Board for Settlement of Disputes of the Ministry of Labor and Social Affairs, and was then served on 3 March 1979 upon SKBM. The Tribunal notes that the record shows that after the decision against SKBM was confirmed, Mr. Asgari Pour paid 30% of the amounts confirmed in the decision to most of the employees on behalf of the company. This indicates that SKBM tried to meet its obligations and to satisfy, at least partially, the locally recruited employees before the execution proceedings were begun, and that Mr. Asgari Pour had control over the affairs of the company at that time.

117. When SKBM was not able to pay the full amount owed to these employees, they commenced an execution proceeding in Chamber One of Tehran Public Court. During the enforcement proceedings the office building of SKBM was valuated and finally sold on 10 March 1980. According to the record, confirmation of the transfer to the highest bidder was sought on 20 April 1980 and the transfer of the deed was effected on 1 June 1985. Therefore, the Tribunal notes that even if the enforcement proceedings were completed after the expropriation of the shares of the majority shareholder of SKBM on 12 April 1979, the cause of action for the local employees arose before the expropriation. Moreover, the evidence on the enforcement proceedings does not show any improper involvement in these proceedings by or on behalf of the Respondent, or that there was a denial of justice through lack of due process of law. The Tribunal concludes that the evidence in the present Case does not support the Claimant's allegation that the office building of SKBM was taken and sold by the local revolutionary committee. Therefore, the Tribunal finds that in the present circumstances, where the administrative and legal proceedings were conducted in order to satisfy SKBM's local employees, and because the Claimant has not shown that they were paid more than what was confirmed to be due to them and no other improper interference in the proceedings has been established, these acts cannot be considered acts of the State or acts giving rise to the liability of the Respondent.

118. However, the Tribunal notes that the remainder of these proceeds from the sale of the building, amounting to Rials 4,280,660, is still being kept in a deposit account more than ten years after the implementation of the Workshop Council's decision and the enforcement order of the Court, especially, because the last payment from these funds to the employees of the company was made on 10 February 1982. The Tribunal notes that various

municipal legal systems include a widely accepted principle that claims against entities to satisfy possible creditors are limited to a certain period of time, which quite often is a period of ten years. However, the representatives of the Respondent asserted at the Hearing that the Iranian Statute of Limitations does not include any temporal limitations upon enforcement proceedings and the record includes a letter from the Head of the [Former Department of] Tehran Judicial Police for the Enforcement of Civil Judgments, dated 19 October 1992, indicating that certain proceedings against SKBM are still pending. Therefore, the Tribunal is not prepared to conclude from that fact alone that these proceeds have been confiscated and that the Claimant has lost his possible share of these funds.

119. The evidence also indicates that at least for some time after having left Iran the Claimant was not excluded from participation in the affairs of SKBM. The Claimant himself has stated that he remained in contact with Mr. Asgari Pour on matters relating to SKBM, especially for consulting on recruitment and for SKBM's financial affairs and it is therefore clear that he continued to take part in its affairs. Thus, prior to the expropriation of the shares of Mr. Amir Faiz, no such government involvement in SKBM or change in its administration occurred which could have affected the Claimant's property interests or other rights in the company.

120. The Tribunal now turns to the question of the possible impact of the expropriation of Mr. Amir Faiz's property. The record shows that the property of Mr. Amir Faiz, SKBM's majority shareholder, was taken on 12 April 1979. According to the record, the shares of the other shareholders have not been taken; they have remained intact.

121. In the Tribunal's case law it has been established that a deprivation or taking of property may occur under international law through interference by a State in the use of that property or with the enjoyment of its benefits, even where the legal title to the property is not affected. While a government's assumption of control over property does not automatically and immediately justify a conclusion that the property has been taken by the government, thus requiring compensation under international law, such a conclusion is warranted whenever events demonstrate that the owner has been deprived of fundamental rights of ownership and it appears that this deprivation is not merely ephemeral. The intent of the government is less important than the effects of the measures on the owner, and the form of the measures of control or interference is less important than the reality of their impact. *Tippetts, Abbett, McCarthy, Stratton v. TAMS-AFFA Consulting Engineers of Iran, et al.*, Award No. 141-7-2 (29 June 1984), *reprinted in* 6 IRAN-U.S. C.T.R. 219, 225-226. Moreover, in *Starrett Housing Corporation, et al. v. The Government of the Islamic Republic of Iran, et al.*, Interlocutory Award No. ITL 32-24-1 (19 December 1983), 51-54,

reprinted in 4 IRAN-U.S. C.T.R. 122, 154, the Tribunal stated that it is recognized in international law that measures taken by a State can interfere with property rights to such an extent that these rights are rendered so useless that they must be deemed to have been expropriated, even though the State does not purport to have expropriated them and the legal title remains with the original owner.

122. Therefore, the Tribunal must address the question of the actual impact of the change in ownership of the majority share of the stock and whether the Respondent exercised the rights based on these shares in the company and, if so, how these rights were exercised. The Tribunal notes that a finding of State control over an entity for jurisdictional purposes, according to Article VII, paragraph 3 of the Claims Settlement Declaration, is different from a finding that the entity has been expropriated. To constitute expropriation, elements other than mere possibility of exercising control over the company on the basis of the change in the ownership of the majority shares must be present. According to the record in this Case, no governmental managers have been designated to SKBM. Moreover, there is no evidence that the Respondent ever used these acquired rights in SKBM or that the Respondent interfered or took part in the administration of SKBM after 12 April 1979.

123. Furthermore, the Claimant has not provided any further information showing that he or Mr. Hassan Asgari Pour was prevented from exercising their administrative functions or shareholding rights in SKBM after 12 April 1979. The minority shareholder, Mr. Asgari Pour, also appears to have represented the company after 12 April 1979. The Claimant stated at the Hearing, for example, that he communicated by phone with Mr. Asgari Pour on the affairs of SKBM until the Fall of 1979. Therefore, the record does not establish that the two minority shareholders were deprived of their right to attend to SKBM's administration.

124. The Claimant has also stated that after the Respondent expropriated the shares of Mr. Amir Faiz, the Respondent had a duty, as majority shareholder, to protect the rights of the minority shareholders and to collect the monies owed to SKBM by ISIRAN. The Claimant states that the failure to do so should be considered an omission which gives rise to liability of the Respondent towards the Claimant.

125. The Tribunal notes that in international law of State responsibility and in the case law of international tribunals, the principle that the liability of a State can arise through an act or an omission, especially when the State has had a duty to act but has failed to do so, has long since been recognized. However, before this principle can be applied there has to be sufficient evidence to establish the presence of a duty to act. This duty to act arises from

the circumstances of each case. In the present Case the existence of the alleged duty to act requires more elements than the mere change of the ownership of the majority portion of the company's shares. Moreover, possession of the shares by the government as such does not create a duty to interfere in the administration of a company. The Tribunal considers that the circumstances in this Case, and the lack of sufficient evidence of the Respondent's impact on the affairs of SKBM after the shares were expropriated, do not create a sufficient basis to find that there was an omission of an act attributable to the Respondent.

126. The Claimant has also argued that his other rights as a shareholder were violated by the Respondent. Although corporate formalities required under Iranian law may not have been complied with as to SKBM since 1979, as the Claimant states, he has not proffered evidence to show that these alleged failures were caused by acts or omissions attributable to the Respondent. Rather, it appears that SKBM became essentially inactive when it terminated all the contracts of its employees in January 1979, and as a result of this situation some of the formal requirements incumbent upon private joint stock companies were not fulfilled prior to 12 April 1979. The change in the ownership of the majority shares did not, therefore, alter the situation in the company.

127. There is no evidence in the record to substantiate the Claimant's allegation that the failure to provide information required by Iranian law to be sent to the shareholders of joint stock companies was, in light of the circumstances of this Case, the result of any interference in the administration of SKBM, or other acts attributable to the Respondent; the circumstances rather indicate that this was a result of the inactive state of the company. Therefore, there are no further elements present which would constitute an active violation of the rights of the minority shareholders.

128. The Tribunal also notes that according to the register of the Corporate and Industrial Ownership Registration Department, and in view of the appropriate rules of the Iranian Commercial Code, SKBM still exists. Therefore, the possible prerequisites for lifting the corporate veil for the benefit of the minority shareholder presuppose the presence of control exercised by the Respondent or by an entity whose acts are attributable to it. This element has not been found because there is no evidence of Iran having exercised control by virtue of its expropriation of Mr. Amir Faiz's shares in SKBM. There is no evidence either of any intention of the Respondent to utilize these shares in contravention of its legal rights, or of any failure on its part to comply with any statutory or other duty, arising from an unjust act aimed against the rights of the two minority shareholders of SKBM. Nor is there any evidence that the Respondent is culpable for proximate causation of

the Claimant's loss by virtue of Iran's possession of the majority of SKBM's shares, or as a result of any breach of duty.

129. The Tribunal recalls that any financial losses suffered by the Claimant as a shareholder of SKBM belong inherently to the risks which the promoters establishing a corporation must take into account and bear. The mere fact that both the company and the Claimant as a shareholder have sustained financial losses does not as such imply that the Claimant is entitled, as an individual shareholder, to bring a direct claim for and receive compensation for such losses. The non-payment of debts to SKBM affects the financial interests of the Claimant, but this does not mean that his rights as a shareholder have been affected. Therefore, so long as the company enjoys an independent existence the shareowner is barred from presenting a claim as an individual for debts due to the company (except in the situation where he is entitled to bring an indirect claim according to Article VII, paragraph 2 of the Claims Settlement Declaration). These questions might have had an impact upon the next stage of the proceedings, concerning valuation, had the Tribunal's findings established the need to ascertain the value of the Claimant's equity interest in SKBM. However, because it has not been found that SKBM was expropriated or subjected to other measures tantamount to expropriation, and that the Claimant's interests in SKBM would have been affected thereby, there is no need for the Tribunal to address this question any further.

130. Therefore, the Tribunal considers that the record in the present Case does not establish that any interference occurred in the affairs of SKBM other than the expropriation of the shares of Mr. Amir Faiz. The loss of the ownership of these shares did not change the actual control over the company, because there is no evidence that the Respondent ever actively utilized these shares in such a manner as to exercise, or try to exercise, the rights in the company based on these shares. No measures affecting the property rights of the Claimant as a shareholder of SKBM have been found. Nor does the Tribunal determine that these alleged acts of the Respondent do, when considered together, justify a finding of "creeping expropriation".

131. The Tribunal concludes that because the Claimant has not been able to show that there was such a degree of interference in SKBM that he was deprived of his rights as a shareholder and the company was effectively expropriated, he has failed to carry his burden of proof and this Claim must be dismissed.

4.4 The Claim for the Nationalization of an Interest in the Passargad Savings and Home Loan Company

132. The Claimant's Claim concerning his alleged interest in Passargad is based primarily on the merits on the alleged nationalization of Passargad and on its merging by the Respondent into Bank Maskan. The Claimant claims that through the nationalization of the Company he lost his rights as a shareholder including his equity interest in the Company, and that, therefore, his shares were *de facto* expropriated. In the alternative, the Claimant also states in his Hearing Memorial that if it is determined that Passargad was never established, then Bank Rahni Iran, or its successor Bank Maskan, should be found to be liable for restitution of the amount advanced to Bank Rahni Iran for the purchase of the shares of the Company at issue.

133. To successfully pursue his Claim based on nationalization of Passargad, the Claimant has first to establish that he owned an interest as a shareholder of the Company, and then to show that Passargad was expropriated in such a manner that he lost his rights as a shareholder and his equity interest therein.

134. The Tribunal will first examine whether the Claimant has shown that he owned an interest in the Company as he has alleged. The Tribunal notes that the Claimant has stated that he owned 4,660 shares in the Company, half of which were originally purchased by him and the other half of which were originally purchased for Mr. Asgari Pour through financing arranged by the Claimant, to whom Mr. Asgari Pour allegedly later transferred his ownership rights in payment of his debt to the Claimant arising from the purchase.

135. The Tribunal notes that the Claimant has not submitted a copy of a share certificate, or any provisional or other certificate, issued by Passargad or Bank Rahni Iran confirming that he owned or had rights to the stock of the Company. Therefore, the Tribunal first turns to consider the question whether the Claimant has succeeded in showing that there has been a valid purchase of these shares and that the purchaser's ownership rights to these shares have been established. The Tribunal notes that the Claimant's evidence in this regard is insufficient. The only evidence relating to the purchase of these shares consists of two substantially identical documents, both entitled "Shares Purchase Receipt", and the Parties disagree on the interpretation of these documents. The Tribunal considers that these share purchase receipts may be interpreted to show that certain amounts of money were transferred or at least intended to be transferred from the purchasers to acquire an equity interest in Passargad. However, the Tribunal notes that these receipts themselves make the actual purchase of the shares contingent upon "clearance" of the cashier's checks referred to therein. There is no evidence in the record of this Case to

show that this requirement was met. Therefore, these documents as such do not sufficiently confirm the alleged purchases.[14]

136. Furthermore, the Claimant has not been able to provide any other document showing that his ownership rights to the shares became established and that any shares in the Company were issued to him.[15] Moreover, the Claimant also confirmed at the Hearing that no shares were provided to him, and he stated that to the best of his knowledge, Passargad was never actually established as an operative Company and, therefore, probably no shares were issued to any of the investors. Therefore, the Tribunal need not consider the issue whether the transfer of Mr. Asgari Pour's shares to the Claimant was done properly so as to establish the Claimant's ownership rights to these shares.

137. The Tribunal reaches the conclusion that the Claimant has not submitted sufficient proof that he owned an interest in Passargad Savings and Home Loan Company because the Claimant has not been able to show that he ever possessed the shares which he claims to have been expropriated. Therefore, the Claimant's Claim is dismissed for lack of evidence.

138. In view of the Tribunal's conclusion that the Claimant has not succeeded in establishing that he owned shares in Passargad Savings and Home Loan Company, there is no need to decide the issues whether the Company was ever actually established, and if so, whether it was nationalized. Moreover, in view of these findings there is no need for the Tribunal to address the question of the Caveat in this Claim.

V. COSTS

139. Both Parties have requested the Tribunal to award them compensation for their costs incurred in respect of the proceedings in this Case. In view of the outcome of this Case, the Tribunal finds it reasonable to award the Respondent costs of arbitration in the amount of U.S.$5,000.00.

---

[14] Furthermore, at the Hearing the Claimant himself stated that he did not deliver these checks to Bank Rahni Iran but instead gave them to Mr. Amir Faiz, who also gave him the share purchase receipts in return for the cashier's checks and who was later to deliver them to Bank Rahni Iran in order to be deposited in the account established for these payments. However, the Claimant has not provided any evidence that Mr. Amir Faiz or any other person delivered the checks on his behalf to Bank Rahni Iran or that they were deposited to the account established for collection of payments for Passargad shares. Therefore, due to the lack of other supporting evidence or information it remains unclear what actually happened in the course of the aforementioned transactions.

[15] For instance, according to the requirements of Article 27 of the Iranian Commercial Code, as amended in 1969, the company shall give the shareholders provisional share certificates until such time as the actual shares are printed and issued.

VI. AWARD

140. For the foregoing reasons,

THE TRIBUNAL AWARDS AS FOLLOWS:
(a) The Claimant's alternative Claim against The Government of the Islamic Republic of Iran based on an indirect interest in the funds due to SKBM is dismissed for lack of jurisdiction.
(b) The Claimant's Claims against The Government of the Islamic Republic of Iran for the funds advanced to SKBM on behalf of ISIRAN, for the expropriation of an equity interest in SKBM, for the salary and relocation benefits and for the nationalization of an equity interest in Passargad Savings and Home Loan Company are dismissed for lack of evidence.
(c) Mohsen Asgari Nazari is obligated to pay to the Government of the Islamic Republic of Iran the sum of U.S.$5,000.00.

SEPARATE OPINION OF HOWARD M. HOLTZMANN, DISSENTING IN PART AND CONCURRING IN PART[1]

INTRODUCTION

The Award in this Case wrongly denies a claim for expropriation. In doing so, it ignores the realities of the business transactions that underlie the claim. Moreover, the Award fails to apply long-standing Tribunal precedents and misunderstands fundamental principles of corporation law.

While I dissent from the portions of the Award that deny the claim for expropriation, I concur in the Award's conclusions that the three other claims in this Case must be denied because the Claimant has failed to bear the burden of proving his allegations. I would, however, have written somewhat differently the descriptions and reasoning concerning these latter three claims.

I also write separately to call attention to the Tribunal's growing tendency to write Awards that are overly long and excessively detailed – a tendency that, regrettably, this Award exemplifies.

I.

The basic circumstances that underlie the expropriation claim are largely uncontested and easily understood:

[1 Signed 24 August 1994; filed 24 August 1994.]

The Claimant and two Iranian businessmen formed a joint stock corporation based in Iran, known as SKBM.[2] The majority shareholder was Mr. Amir Hossein Amir Faiz, who owned 57.5% of the outstanding shares; the Claimant owned 33.75% and the other shareholder, Mr. Hassan Asgari Pour, owned 8.75%.

During the relevant period, SKBM provided consulting and recruiting services to an entity called ISIRAN which the Tribunal has repeatedly held was owned and controlled by the Iranian government.[3] ISIRAN was SKBM's only customer, and when ISIRAN failed to pay SKBM as required by their contract SKBM lost its only source of income.

Shortly after the Islamic Revolution, Iran expropriated all of the property of SKBM's majority shareholder, Mr. Amir Faiz, including his stock in SKBM.[4] Iran was thus in the dual position of controlling both SKBM, the seller, and ISIRAN, the buyer.

It appears that at the time that Iran took the SKBM shares of Mr. Amir Faiz and thereby assumed control of that company, ISIRAN owed SKBM some U.S.$6,500,000 for services that had been rendered to it, but for which it had failed to pay. The existence of this debt to SKBM is not contested by Iran; Iran does not deny that the services were performed, nor does it submit any evidence that it paid for them. This $6,500,000 account receivable from ISIRAN was SKBM's largest asset.

Following the Islamic Revolution, ISIRAN decided that it no longer wished SKBM's services. A normal controlling shareholder of a business faced with

---

[2] The full corporate name of SKBM is Sherkat Khadamat Beinolmelali Mahat; the corporation was also sometimes referred to as Mahat International Services.

[3] ISIRAN's status as an entity owned and controlled by the Respondent is well settled. *See, e.g., Ultrasystems. Inc. v. Islamic Republic of Iran*, Award No. 27-84-3 (4 March 1983), *reprinted in* 2 IRAN-U.S. C.T.R. 100, 105; *Computer Sciences Corp. v. Islamic Republic of Iran*, Award No. 221-65-1 (16 April 1986), *reprinted in* 10 IRAN-U.S. C.T.R. 269, 281-82; *McLaughlin Enterprises. Ltd. v. Islamic Republic of Iran*, Award No. 253-289-1 (16 September 1986), *reprinted in* 12 IRAN-U.S. C.T.R. 146, 149; *Hidetomo Shinto v. Islamic Republic of Iran*, Award No. 399-10273-3 (31 October 1988), *reprinted in* 19 IRAN-U.S. C.T.R. 321, 325.

[4] As proof of this expropriation, the Claimant has submitted a declaration of a Revolutionary Court issued on 12 April 1979 stating that "[t]he moveable and immoveable property" of Amir Faiz (and certain other persons) had been "confiscated by the Islamic Republic of Iran." Doc. 60, Ex. 16. It is undisputed that just prior to this revolutionary decree Amir Faiz owned 57.5% of SKBM's stock. There is absolutely no basis upon which to conclude that Amir Faiz's SKBM holdings were somehow spared from the sweeping decree affecting all of his "moveable and immoveable property." Indeed, after examining the very same evidence in a related 1988 case, Chamber Three concluded:

"[T]he documentary evidence in the record establishes that Iran expropriated Mr. Amir Faiz'[s] shares in SKBM and that at the time of the expropriation he owned the majority of shares in the Company. It is well established in prior awards of the Tribunal that control exists where Iran has assumed a majority ownership interest in the entity at issue."

Shinto, supra note 2, at 329. The Respondent's general denial that it seized control of SKBM, therefore, is quite simply incredible.

the loss of its only customer and with few future prospects would have moved to collect the money owed to it, to wind up its affairs, and to distribute its remaining assets to all shareholders in proportion to their respective interests. Yet, Iran, the new majority owner of SKBM, took no steps to cause SKBM to collect the money owed to it by ISIRAN. By its inaction, Iran achieved a benefit for its wholly-owned entity, ISIRAN, at the expense of its partially-owned entity, SKBM. In short, Iran chose a course of keeping approximately $6,500,000 in one of its pockets in which it had a 100% interest, rather than putting that money in another of its pockets in which it had only a 57.5% interest.

By failing to collect the approximately $6,500,000 due to SKBM and to arrange an orderly liquidation of the company, Iran deprived the Claimant of the benefit of his 33.75% interest, and thereby effectively expropriated that interest.[5]

"A deprivation or taking of property," this Tribunal has observed time and again, "may occur under international law through interference by a state in the use of that property or with the enjoyment of its benefits, even when legal title to the property is not affected." *Tippetts, Abbett, McCarthy, Stratton* v. *TAMS-AFFA Consulting Engineers of Iran*, Award No. 141-7-2 (22 June 1984), *reprinted in* 6 IRAN-U.S. C.T.R. 219, 225; *see also supra*, at para. 121; *W. Jack Buckamier* v. *Islamic Republic of Iran*, Award No. 528-941-3 (6 March 1992), at p. 26, *reprinted in* 28 IRAN-U.S. C.T.R. 53; *Starrett Housing Corp.* v. *Islamic Republic of Iran*, Award No. ITL 32-24-1 (19 December 1983), *reprinted in* 4 IRAN-U.S. C.T.R. 122, 154. In the present Case, the Respondent did not issue an official decree vitiating the Claimant's legal title or dispatch Revolutionary Guards to seize his share certificates. Yet, it took from him the value of his investment just as surely as if it had resorted to such actions.

The Tribunal's jurisprudence is repeated and emphatic that Iran by seizing control of a corporation assumed the duty incumbent upon any controlling shareholder to manage the company prudently and to safeguard the investment of all shareholders. Thus, in the *Foremost* Case, this Chamber suggested that governmental management of a business enterprise following governmental assumption of majority share ownership can be said to amount to expropriation of minority share interests when "measures [are] adopted which [are] not only detrimental in their effect on [minority shareholders], but which [go] beyond the legitimate exercise by the majority of the shareholders . . . of their right to manage the company's affairs in what they

---

[5] The Claimant would, of course, have been entitled upon liquidation of SKBM to 33.75% of whatever was left of the $6,500,000 and SKBM's other assets after SKBM paid its costs and expenses and its business was wound up.

perceive[ ] to be its best interests." *Foremost Tehran, Inc.* v. *Islamic Republic of Iran*, Award No. 220-37/231-1 (10 April 1986), *reprinted in* 10 IRAN-U.S. C.T.R. 228, 248. The *Golipira* and *Schott* Cases stand for the same principle. While in *Golpira* the Tribunal held that Iran's expropriation of the holdings of the largest single shareholder of a medical company did not constitute an expropriation of the interest of the minority shareholders, it reached that conclusion only because it found that Iran had used its new controlling position to promote what could reasonably be viewed as the best interests of the company. *Ataollah Golpira* v. *The Government of Iran*, Award No. 32-211-2 (29 March 1983), *reprinted in* 2 IRAN-U.S. C.T.R. 171, 175-176. Likewise in *Schott*, this Chamber held that expropriation of the shares of a large shareholder did not amount to a taking of the claimant's minority interest only because it found that the corporate entity continued to operate for the benefit of all of its shareholders after Iran assumed effective control. *Robert R. Schott* v. *Islamic Republic of Iran*, Award No. 474-268-1 (14 March 1990), *reprinted in* 24 IRAN-U.S. C.T.R. 203, 215-216. Clearly, a State, once having seized effective control of a private enterprise, is not at liberty to use its newfound managerial power to enrich itself at the expense of minority shareholders, and at the same time to deny that in all reality a taking of their property has occurred.

The Tribunal's own precedent, set out above, is sufficient to establish the Respondent's duty as controlling shareholder in this Case. It is worth noting further, however, that the principle underlying the Tribunal's case law is also well grounded in municipal regimes of corporation law. The widespread recognition in the municipal law of many nations that controlling shareholders owe a duty of care to the corporations they control makes clear that the Tribunal's prior holdings in this regard are entirely in line with broadly accepted concepts of corporation law. The essential doctrine recognized by many nations is that a controlling shareholder may not exploit its position of control over a corporation to enrich itself at the expense of minority shareholders. *See Barcelona Traction, Light & Power Co. (Belg.* v. *Spain)*, 1970 I.C.J. 3, 35 (Judgment of 5 February 1970); *Company Law in Europe*, at pp. B82-B83, D69, 068 (R. Thomas ed. 1993); Harry G. Henn & John R. Alexander, *Laws of Corporations* 651-56 (1983); Robin Hollington, *Minority Shareholders' Rights*, at p. 2-043 (1990); Geoffrey Morse, *Company Law* 433-434, 448 (14th ed. 1991); Joachim, *The Liability of Supervisory Board Directors in German*, 25 Int'l Law. 41, 57-58, 67 (1991); Torem & Focsaneanu, *Minority Stockholders' Rights Under French Law*, 15 Bus. Law. 331 (1960).[6] A distinguished United States jurist succinctly

---

[6] In this regard, I note that Iranian law clearly prohibits directors who control a corporation from "abus[ing] their authority contrary to the company's interests for their personal gain or for another establishment in which they have [a] direct or indirect interest" and holds them liable for such breaches. *See* Commercial Code of Iran, Articles 142, 258 & 269. By all logic, the same

described the prevailing legal principle: the courts, he said, have recognized that majority shareholders have a

> responsibility to the minority and to the corporation to use their ability to control the corporation in a fair, just, and equitable manner. Majority shareholders may not use their power to control corporate activities to benefit themselves alone or in a manner detrimental to the minority. Any use to which they put the corporation or their power to control the corporation must benefit all shareholders proportionately. . . .

Jones v. *H.F. Ahmanson & Co.*, 460 P.2d 464 (Cal. 1969).

The fundamental flaw in the Award's reasoning is its failure to recognize that the moment Iran became the majority shareholder of SKBM it thereby had the duty – and the sole power – to take the necessary affirmative action to safeguard SKBM and thereby protect the interests of the minority shareholders. That duty, of course, flowed from the basic principles of corporation law recognized in the Tribunal cases and by the other authorities discussed above. The Award purports to negate that duty by stating that there is no evidence that Iran "took part in the administration of SKBM" after it became the majority shareholder. Award, *supra*, at para. 122; *see also supra* at paras. 125, 130. Again, the Award misses the central point: Iran's liability in this Case arises for the very reason that it had a duty, as controlling shareholder, to take part in the administration of SKBM in order to collect the Company's debts and safeguard the Company's assets, and yet by its own admission made no effort whatsoever to do so. This failure by Iran to act is all the more egregious because, as already noted, it controlled both the buyer and the seller and had a financial interest in leaving the seller, SKBM, to languish unattended and unpaid while permitting the buyer, ISIRAN, to keep the approximately $6,500,000 that it owed SKBM.[7]

Tribunal precedents establish that the seizure of control and subsequent neglect of a corporation's assets constitute "unreasonable [State] interference

---

prohibition should apply to a party who controls a corporation by virtue of its ouster of the previous dominant shareholder-director and corresponding assumption of his corporate powers. Certainly, although the Claimant clearly argued for liability premised on the Respondent's conduct as SKBM's controlling shareholder, the Respondent has pointed to nothing in Iranian law suggesting that Iran is out of step with other nations in this regard.

[7] Although the Respondent denies that it acted deliberately to scuttle SKBM's financial viability, its motives ultimately are irrelevant. As the Tribunal often has noted, in judging whether an expropriation has occurred, "[t]he intent of the government is less important than the effects of the measures on the owner, and the form of the measures of control or interference is less important than the reality of their impact." *Tippetts, Abbett, McCarthy, Stratton* v. *TAMS-AFFA Consulting Engineers of Iran*, Award No. 141-7-2 (29 June 1984), *reprinted in* 6 IRAN-U.S. C.T.R. 219, 225; *supra*, at para. 121; *W. Jack Buckamier* v. *Islamic Republic of Iran*, Award No. 528-941-3 (6 March 1992), at p. 26, *reprinted in* 28 IRAN-U.S. C.T.R. 53 *Phelps Dodge Corp.* v. *Islamic Republic of Iran*, Award No. 217-99-2 (19 March 1986), *reprinted in* 10 IRAN-U.S. C.T.R. 121, 130.

in the use. . . . of property" amounting to a taking. *See Colpira, supra,* at 176-177. Iran's inaction rendered the Claimant's property rights in SKM "so useless that they must be deemed to have been expropriated, even though the State does not purport to have expropriated them and the legal title to the property remains with the original owner." *Starrett Housing Corp.* v. *Islamic Republic of Iran,* Award No. ITL 32-24-1 (19 December 1983), *reprinted in* 4 IRAN-U.S. C.T.R. 122, 154. In callous disregard of both expropriation and corporation law, the Award describes the loss suffered by the Claimant as simply one of the calculated "risks which the promoters establishing a corporation must take into account and bear." *See supra,* para. 129. Here, too, the majority skirts the essential reality of this Case: the danger that a government will seize control of a corporation and cause it not to collect the debts owed it from another governmental entity is not an ordinary risk of operating a business abroad and is not one that international law requires a foreign investor to bear.

In sum, it is amply demonstrated that Iran is liable because its inaction was a breach of its duty as a controlling shareholder and that inaction deprived the Claimant of the value of his investment. Even the majority concedes that liability can stem from an omission to act as surely as from affirmative acts. As the Award correctly recognizes:

> "[I]n international law of State responsibility and in the case law of international tribunals, the principle that the liability of a State can arise through an act or an omission, especially when the State has had a duty to act but has failed to do so, has long since been recognized."

Award, *supra,* at para. 125. It is unfortunate – and unjust – that the Award does not follow this uncontested rule of law to its logical conclusion.[8]

II.

A plea for brevity must, in principle, be brief.

The lengthy Award in this case invites reconsideration of the Tribunal's practices in preparing its decisions. I write not in criticism of the draftsmen of this particular Award, but rather to point out a tendency that is growing

---

[8] The majority awards all costs against the Claimant. As noted above, I believe that the expropriation claim should have been granted, while the other claims were properly denied. Accordingly, in my view, the costs should have been apportioned between the Claimant and the Respondent in accordance with Article 40, paragraph 1 of the Tribunal Rules which provides that "the arbitral tribunal may apportion each of [the] costs between the parties if it determines that apportionment is reasonable, taking into account the circumstances of the case."

throughout the Tribunal to prepare Awards that are overly long and unnecessarily detailed.[9]

The issue is not a choice of literary style. At stake is the efficient use of the Tribunal's limited time, funds and facilities – resources which are, in my view, endangered by present practices in drafting awards. Also at stake is the usefulness of the Tribunal's Awards to readers generally, for too often the main points are obscured by a mass of needless detail. The Tribunal Rules – which in this respect are identical to the UNCITRAL Arbitration Rules – require only that "[t]he arbitral tribunal shall state the reasons upon which the award is based. . . ." Article 32, para. 3. There is no requirement in the Rules, or elsewhere, that Awards include a description of every step in the arbitral proceedings.[10] Nor is there any requirement to summarize virtually every submission of the parties on issues of fact and law.[11] Although I am aware that judicial practice in some fora favors such practices, I find no need for a profusion of detail in the arbitral process of a tribunal such as this.

I respectfully suggest that it is entirely possible – and preferable – in most Tribunal Awards to (i) shorten the description of the procedural history of the Case to include only the key events, and (ii) concentrate the description of the facts and contentions on matters that form the basis of the reasons for the decision. These steps would not only conserve the resources of the Tribunal, but also would help readers to focus on the essential elements of the case.[12]

---

[9] In contrast, it is instructive to note the brevity of the Tribunal's early Awards. For example, the first Full Tribunal Award, which decided a major issue of interpretation of the Algiers Accords, is less than three printed pages. *Iran-United States, Case A-2* (13 January 1982), *reprinted in* 1 IRAN-U.S. C.T.R. 101. The second Full Tribunal Case is reprinted in ten pages. *Iran-United States*, Case A1 (Issue II) (14 May 1982), *reprinted in* 1 IRAN-U.S. C.T.R. 144. The first Award by a chamber in a contested case is reprinted in three pages. *White Westinghouse International Company v. Bank Sepah-New York Agency*, Award No. 7-14-3 (25 June 1982), *reprinted in* 1 IRAN-U.S. C.T.R. 169. Similar brevity is found in all other Awards reprinted in the first two volumes of the Tribunal Reports.

[10] A cursory review of the Awards in the first two volumes of the Tribunal Reports shows that a number contain no procedural history at all. Where a procedural history is included it is typically limited to a single paragraph, or no more than three paragraphs, mentioning only the filing of the main pleadings and the holding of the hearing. (None of the Awards includes a detailed procedural history such as encompasses 20 paragraphs in the present Award.)

[11] The Awards in the first two volumes of the Tribunal Reports typically include very succinct statements of the main opposing contentions of the parties. None is nearly as extensive or detailed as the 29 typewritten pages devoted to "Facts and Contentions" in the present Award. *See supra*, paras. 25-90. While I recognize that some cases present more issues than others, and therefore statistical comparisons may not be entirely appropriate, nevertheless the density of detail in the present Award is in marked contrast to the earlier Awards.

[12] The instructions given by the newspaper publisher Joseph Pulitzer to his reporters are useful to drafters of arbitral awards as well: "Put things before them briefly so they will read it, clearly so they will appreciate it, picturesquely so they will remember it and, above all, accurately so they will be guided by its light." *See* William Safire & Leonard Safir, *Good Advice* 44 (1982).

SHAHIN SHAINE EBRAHIMI,
CECILIA RADENE EBRAHIMI,
CHRISTINA TANDIS EBRAHIMI
Claimants

v.

THE GOVERNMENT OF THE ISLAMIC REPUBLIC OF IRAN, *Respondent*

(Cases No. 44, 46, and 47)

Chamber Three: Arangio-Ruiz, *Chairman*; Allison,[1] Aghahosseini,[2] *Members*

Signed 12 *October* 1994[3]

AWARD No. 560-44/46/47-3

The following is the text as issued by the Tribunal:

FINAL AWARD

APPEARANCES

For the Claimants: Mr. Platt W. Davis III
                          Counsel
                      Mr. Hamid Sabi
                          Attorney for the Claimants
                      Mr. Shahin S. Ebrahimi
                      Ms. Cecilia R. Ebrahimi
                      Ms. Christina T. Ebrahimi
                          Claimants
                      Mr. Ali Ebrahimi
                      Mr. Cyrus Meshki
                          Party Witnesses
                      Mr. Mussa Siamak
                      Mr. Fariborz Ghadar

[1 Mr. Allison's signature is accompanied by the words, "Separate Opinion." The Opinion appears at page 236, below.]
[2 Mr. Aghahosseini's signature is accompanied by the words, "Dissenting with respect to certain parts to be dealt with in a Separate Opinion."]
[3 Filed 12 October 1994.]

	Mr. Robert Reilly
	Expert Witnesses
For the Respondent:	Mr. Ali H. Nobari
	Agent of the Government of the
	Islamic Republic of Iran
	Mr. Bijan Izadi
	Deputy Agent of the Government of the
	Islamic Republic of Iran
	Mr. Nozar Dabiran
	Mr. Hamid Hedayati
	Legal Advisers to the Agent
	Mr. Behrooz Salehpour
	Legal Assistant to the Agent
	Dr. Reza Shabahang
	Representative of Gostaresh Maskan Co.
	Mr. Esmaeil Bakhshi Dezfuli
	Attorney for Gostaresh Maskan Co.
	Mr. Mohammad Hossain Karimi Fard
	Mr. Hossein Fathi
	Party Witnesses
	Mr. Mostafa Goudarzi
	Mr. Yadolah Mokarami
	Mr. Antony G.P. Tracey
	Mr. Ardavan Moshiri
	Expert Witnesses
Also present:	Mr. D. Stephen Mathias
	Agent of the United States of America
	Ms. Mary Catherine Malin
	Deputy Agent of the United States
	of America
	Professor Richard A. Brealey
	Tribunal Expert
	Mrs. Suzanne S. Ebrahimi
	Mr. Albolghasem Fakharian
	Mr. Hamid Mahmoud Mazhari

TABLE OF CONTENTS

		Para.
I.	INTRODUCTION AND PROCEDURAL HISTORY	1
II.	JURISDICTION	53
III.	EXPROPRIATION	
	A. Claimants' Contentions	62

	B.	Respondent's Contentions	67
	C.	Tribunal's Findings	69
		1. Expropriation	69
		2. The A18 Caveat	80
IV.	STANDARD OF COMPENSATION AND VALUATION METHOD	
	A.	Claimants' Contentions	84
	B.	Respondent's Contentions	87
	C.	Tribunal's Findings	88
V.	VALUATION	
	A.	Claimants' Contentions	100
	B.	Respondent's Contentions	102
	C.	Tribunal's Findings	103
		1. General political, social and economic conditions	106
		2. Price adjustment receivables	108
		3. Gostaresh Blount	131
		4. Goodwill	154
		5. Value of outstanding contracts	158
		6. Other balance sheet items	161
		7. Taxes	162
		8. Minority discount	165
		9. Non-marketability discount	168
		10. Discount for unaudited accounts	171
		11. Conclusion on valuation	174
VI.	CONCLUSION	
	A.	Compensation	175
	B.	Interest	176
	C.	Costs	177
VII.	AWARD	179

I. INTRODUCTION AND PROCEDURAL HISTORY

1. Shahin Shaine Ebrahimi, Cecilia Radene Ebrahimi, and Christina Tandis Ebrahimi (collectively, the "Claimants") are the children of Ali Ebrahimi, an Iranian national, and Cecilia Louise DeFries, a United States national.[4] Claimants allege that the Government of the Islamic Republic of

---

[4] On 16 November 1981, a claim was also filed by Marjorie Suzanne Ebrahimi in connection with the alleged expropriation of certain real estate in Tehran and the personal property located therein (Case No. 45). Marjorie Suzanne Ebrahimi was Ali Ebrahimi's second wife, since 1977, following his divorce from Cecilia Louise DeFries in 1975. This claim was briefed by the Parties

Iran (the "Respondent" or the "Government") expropriated their interests in Gostaresh Maskan Company ("Gostaresh Maskan" or the "Company"), an Iranian construction firm, on 13 November 1979. According to the Claimants, the Respondent appointed successive directors to govern Gostaresh Maskan, depriving them of their "ownership and related rights" as shareholders. They seek compensation for their shares in Gostaresh Maskan, totalling 19% of the Company's outstanding stock, in the amount of approximately U.S.$20,000,000. Claimants also request interest from the date of the alleged expropriation and an award of attorneys' fees and costs.

2. Claimants submitted individual Statements of Claim on 16 November 1981, alleging that Respondent expropriated their interests in Gostaresh Maskan.

3. By Order of 17 December 1981, the Tribunal directed the Respondent to file its statement of defense in each Case by 1 March 1982. By letter of 26 February 1982, the Respondent requested a two-month extension to file the respective statements of defense. By written communication of 1 March 1982, the interim Chairman of Chamber Three granted an extension of the filing deadline until 1 April 1982. By letter of 1 April 1982, the Respondent requested a 10-day extension of the referenced filing date. On 13 April 1982, and on 14 April 1982, respectively, the Respondent filed its "Statement of Defence," including certain counterclaims, against the claim brought by Christina Tandis Ebrahimi (Case No. 47), and against the claims of Shahin Shaine Ebrahimi and Cecilia Radene Ebrahimi, respectively (Cases Nos. 44 and 46).

4. By Order of 19 April 1982, the Tribunal scheduled a pre-hearing conference for 1 October 1982. By a separate Order of 19 April 1982, the Tribunal invited each of the Claimants to file their response to the Respondent's counterclaims by 28 May 1982. On 21 May 1982, each of the Claimants filed a response to the referenced counterclaims.

5. By Order of 8 July 1982, filed on 19 July 1982, the Tribunal ordered the Parties to submit their memorials on the jurisdictional issues by 1 September 1982. On 1 September 1982, the Respondent submitted individual "Statement[s] of Defence" in which it objected to the Tribunal's jurisdiction over the claims on the ground that the Claimants are Iranian nationals.

6. By letter received on 1 September 1982, the Claimants requested that the pre-hearing conference be postponed pending a decision on the jurisdictional issue. On 9 September 1982, the Claimants filed a "Joint Memorial of

---

jointly with the present claims until it was withdrawn by Mrs. Ebrahimi on 1 June 1992. By Order of 23 June 1992, the Tribunal terminated the proceedings in Case No. 45 pursuant to Article 34(2) of the Tribunal Rules.

Claimants in Support of Jurisdiction" discussing the jurisdictional issues in each of the Claims.

7. By Order filed on 15 September 1982, the Tribunal cancelled the referenced pre-hearing conference and directed the Parties to submit their final briefs on the jurisdictional question by 29 October 1982.

8. By Order of 22 October 1982, the Tribunal indicated that it would decide the jurisdictional issue on the basis of the written submissions unless either Party filed a request for a hearing on this issue by 15 November 1982. On 29 October 1982, Respondent filed its "preliminary" memorial on jurisdiction in each of the three Cases. By letter of 11 November 1982, the Respondent made the referenced request for a hearing.

9. By Order of 16 November 1982, the Tribunal scheduled a hearing for 16 December 1982 to hear evidence on the issue of the nationality of the Claimants for purposes of the Tribunal's jurisdiction.

10. On 19 November 1982, the Agent of the United States submitted a "Memorial of the Government of the United States" on the nationality issue. By its letter of 24 November 1982, the Respondent requested that the scheduled hearing be cancelled in view of the Tribunal's acceptance of the above-mentioned Memorial of the Government of the United States "in flagrant violation of the provision [sic] of Article 15 (Note 5) of the Tribunal's provisionally adopted rules." By Order of 26 November 1982, filed on 29 November 1982, the Tribunal cancelled the referenced hearing and invited the Parties (i) to indicate by 10 December 1982 whether they would wish to comment on the Memorial filed by the U.S. Agent on 19 November 1982, and (ii) if so, to file such comments no later than 25 January 1983. By letter of 10 December 1982, filed on 13 December 1982, the Respondent informed the Tribunal that it would comment on the referenced Memorial and that it reserved the right to request a hearing. By letter of 25 January 1983, filed on 26 January 1983, the Respondent requested a 25-day extension to file these comments. By Order of 1 February 1983, filed on 4 February 1983, the Tribunal extended the Respondent's filing deadline until 21 February 1983. By letter of 21 February 1983, the Respondent requested a two-month extension to file the referenced comments. By Order of 22 March 1983, the Tribunal extended the Respondent's filing deadline until 31 May 1983, indicating that it would not grant any further extension requests without "compelling" reasons. By letter of 10 April 1983, filed on 11 April 1983, the Respondent requested that the Tribunal annul the previously indicated deadlines and issue an order to stay proceedings until the Full Tribunal decided *Case No. A18*. By letter of 6 May 1983, the Chairman of Chamber Three informed the Claimants that no further proceedings would be scheduled in these cases pending the Full Tribunal's decision in *Case No. A18*. By letter of 16

May 1983, the Respondent requested the Chairman to "nullify" the Chamber's Order of 22 March 1983, and formally to suspend the proceedings pending the Full Tribunal's decision in *Case No. A18*. By letter of 30 May 1983, the Iranian Agent informed the Chairman that he had inferred from the Order of 6 May 1983 that the proceedings had been stayed and that the Respondent had not submitted its response to the above-mentioned U.S. Memorial on that ground.

11. By Order of 28 June 1985, the Tribunal notified the Parties of the Full Tribunal's decision in *Case No. A18* and in conformity with that decision it directed the Claimants to file their written evidence, pertinent to the jurisdictional question, by 2 September 1985, with the Respondent's time limit to respond to be fixed after the Claimants' filing. By letter filed 14 October 1985, the Claimants informed the Tribunal of their intention to rely on their "Joint Memorial of Claimants in Support of Jurisdiction" which was filed on 9 September 1982. The Claimants further argued in this letter that the Respondent had had an opportunity to respond to this memorial and that, accordingly, the Chamber could rule on the jurisdictional issue without further delay. By Order of 18 October 1985, the Tribunal directed the Respondent to submit its evidence on the Claimants' nationality by 3 January 1986. By letter of 21 October 1985, the Respondent objected to the Claimants' submission of 9 September 1982, because (i) it failed to comply with the deadline of 1 September 1982, and (ii) it consisted of a joint submission for all the claims whereas no decision to consolidate those claims had been made yet. The Respondent therefore requested that additional copies be submitted in each of the claims. By Order of 16 December 1985, the Tribunal ordered the Claimants to file nine additional copies of the "Joint Memorial of Claimants in Support of Jurisdiction." By letter of 3 January 1986, the Respondent requested a six-month extension of the time limit for the submission of its evidence on jurisdiction to be calculated as of the filing by the Claimants of the nine additional copies of their "Joint Memorial." By a memorandum of 13 January 1986, the Co-Registrars of the Tribunal informed the Respondent of their receipt of twelve additional copies of the Claimants' "Joint Memorial." By letter filed on 17 January 1986, the Claimants requested that the Respondent's six-month extension request be denied on the ground that "Iran has had ample copies of this document for over three years" and that "Iran has cited no reason that it is disadvantaged by Claimant[s'] filing of the Joint Memorial in less than three weeks after receiving the Order."

12. By a separate letter filed on 17 January 1986, the Claimants requested that all the Cases (that is, including Case No. 45), and at the very least Cases Nos. 44, 46 and 47, be consolidated.

13. By Order of 20 January 1986, the Tribunal directed the Respondent to submit its response to the "Joint Memorial of Claimants in Support of Jurisdiction" by 3 April 1986. By its letter of 27 March 1986, the Respondent filed a six-month extension request for the referenced response. By Order of 4 April 1986, the Tribunal extended the time limit for the Respondent to submit its response until 3 July 1986. By letter of 2 July 1986, the Respondent filed another six-month extension request for the referenced response. By Order of 10 July 1986, the Tribunal extended the time limit for the Respondent to submit its response until 3 October 1986, adding that no further extensions would be granted "save for strong and compelling reasons." By letter of 3 October 1986, the Respondent requested "a reasonable time" for the filing of the required documents in view of (i) the fact that the relevant documentation was still scattered "in various departments and diverse places," (ii) the "Claimants' refusal in cases of this nature to provide the Respondent with information and evidence relevant to their dominant Iranian nationality," and (iii) the fact that Iran, "with its limited manpower, is presently involved in an imposed war . . . and in a number of international litigation[s]. . . ." By their letter filed on 16 December 1986, the Claimants objected to the Respondent's third extension request. They also reiterated their request for (i) an immediate ruling on the jurisdictional issue, and (ii) consolidation of, at least, Cases Nos. 44, 46, and 47. By Order of 6 February 1987, the Tribunal denied the Respondent's extension request on the ground that the offered reasons did not constitute "strong and compelling reasons." The Order further indicated the Tribunal's resolve to decide the jurisdictional issue pursuant to Article 28, para. 3 of the Tribunal Rules "as soon as its working schedule permits" on the basis of the written evidence then before it. The Order also stated that the Tribunal would "defer this course of action only if it [was] informed that settlement negotiations are ongoing and have reached a stage which would justify a postponement of the proceedings." On 23 February 1987, the Tribunal issued a "Correction to Order" in regard to its Order of 6 February 1987 so as to correct certain inaccuracies in the Persian text of the referenced Order.

14. By letter filed on 4 January 1988, the Claimants urged the Tribunal to expedite its consideration of the jurisdictional question.

15. By letter of 10 May 1988, the Respondent requested the Tribunal to issue an order directing the Claimants under Claims Nos. 44, 46 and 47 to produce documentary evidence "related to their connections with Iran, failing which it will not be possible to prepare a reply memorial." By a separate letter of the same date, which was filed in each of the Cases Nos. 44, 46 and 47, the Respondent requested that Claimants be directed to produce certain specific information or documentation in connection with each Claimant's nationality.

16. On 13 June 1988, the Respondent filed its "Respondent's Brief on Jurisdiction as to Claimant's Nationality" in Case No. 44. Under its letter of 27 June 1988, the Respondent filed an "Amendatory Addendum" to this brief so as to correct "certain errors" in the referenced document. On 3 March 1989, the Respondent filed its "Respondent's Jurisdictional Brief on Claimant's Nationality" in Cases Nos. 46 and 47.

17. On 16 June 1989, the Tribunal issued an Interlocutory Award on the jurisdictional issues in each of the Cases No. 44, No. 45, No. 46 and No. 47, holding that the dominant and effective nationality of each of the Claimants during the relevant period was that of the United States. *Shahin Shaine Ebrahimi, et al. v. The Government of the Islamic Republic of Iran*, Interlocutory Award, Award No. ITL 71-44/45/46/47-3 (16 June 1989), *reprinted in* 22 IRAN-U.S. C.T.R. 138 ("*Ebrahimi*"). The Tribunal thus concluded that Claimants could properly submit their claims for its consideration. The Iranian Member of the Chamber at that time (Mr. Parviz Ansari Moin) signed the Award indicating that he would file a Dissenting Opinion.

18. On 25 July 1989, the Tribunal issued an Order directing the Parties to submit joint legal briefs in regard to the merits of the Claims Nos. 44, 46 and 47 and directed (i) the Claimants to submit their memorial and evidence on all remaining issues no later than 24 October 1989, and (ii) the Respondent to submit its memorial and evidence within three months following receipt of the Claimants' submissions.

19. On 15 September 1989, the Iranian Member of the Chamber filed a Dissenting Opinion in Persian to the above-mentioned Interlocutory Award. The English version of this Opinion was filed on 14 November 1989. In his Opinion, Mr. Ansari concluded that the dominant and effective nationality of each of the Claimants was that of Iran, and that, accordingly, the Tribunal should have dismissed the claims for lack of jurisdiction.

20. By letter filed on 25 October 1989, the Claimants requested a "short extension" of the filing deadline for their memorial on the merits, indicating that they expected to file the requested documents on or before 27 October 1989. Claimants filed their joint Hearing Memorial on 27 October 1989.

21. By letter of 22 January 1990, referring to the Tribunal's Order of 25 July 1989, the Respondent requested a six-month extension of its filing date for its briefs on the merits. By their letter filed on 29 January 1990, the Claimants urged that the Respondent's request be denied. They added that "[n]evertheless, Claimants would not object to a two-month extension, to March 26, 1990, provided it is made clear that no further extensions will be authorized." By Order of 5 February 1990, the Tribunal extended the Respondent's filing date until 27 April 1990. The Order further fixed the Parties' filing deadlines for their rebuttal memorials as follows: (i) for the

Claimants, two months as of the Respondent's submission date; and (ii) for the Respondent, two months as of the filing of the Claimants' rebuttal memorial. The Order directed the Parties to file three originals and thirty copies of each document submitted. By its letter of 27 April 1990, the Respondent requested a six-month extension due to the "concurrence of the Now Rouz (Iranian New Year) Holidays as well as the Holy Month of Ramadan." By Order of 8 May 1990, the Tribunal extended the Respondent's filing deadline until 27 July 1990. By letter of 27 July 1990, the Respondent requested a six-month extension due to "the financial and technical dimensions of the captioned cases and the fact that the audit firm which is examining the books and other documents of G[o]staresh Maskan Co., is not able to timely prepare and submit its audit report as its preparation would require considerable time." By their letter filed on 6 August 1990, the Claimants objected to the Respondent's third extension request indicating that "Respondent has known since July 25, 1989, of its obligation to file its direct case in a timely fashion." By Order of 9 August 1990, the Tribunal extended the Respondent's filing deadline until 29 October 1990, adding that "[n]o further extension of time will be granted without specific and compelling reasons." By its letter of 29 October 1990, the Respondent announced that the Persian version of its briefs was ready for filing and requested a 30-day extension to complete the English translation thereof. By Order of 5 November 1990, the Tribunal extended the Respondent's deadline until 30 November 1990.

22. On 30 November 1990, the Respondent filed its Hearing Memorial ("Respondent's Brief and Evidence on the Remaining Issues Submitted In Compliance with the Tribunal's Order of 9 August 1990"). In its cover letter to this submission, the Respondent explained that certain photographs, attached as an exhibit to the memorial, were only submitted in nine copies rather than in thirty copies as each of the Tribunal's Orders since that of 5 February 1990 had requested. The Respondent requested that the Tribunal issue a specific order mandating it to submit additional copies if it so wished.

23. By Order of 13 December 1990, the Tribunal referred to the pertinent language in its last order (dated 5 November 1990) on the issue of the number of copies required. It also scheduled a hearing for 13 September 1991. The Order further indicated that "[t]he Tribunal does not envisage granting any extension of the two month period for each party . . . that would interfere with the Hearing date scheduled above."

24. By letter filed on 31 January 1991, the Claimants requested a two-week extension until 15 February 1991 to file their rebuttal memorial so as to complete the Persian translation thereof. By Order of 8 February 1991, the Tribunal granted the Claimants' extension request to extend the filing dead-

line for their rebuttal memorial until 15 February 1991. On 15 February 1991, Claimants filed a joint Rebuttal Memorial.

25. By letter of 12 April 1991, the Respondent requested a three-month extension of time for filing its rebuttal memorial. Respondent based its request on the ground that it had not received the Claimants' rebuttal memorial until 6 March 1991 due to "the post problems in Iran." As a result, the Respondent calculated that it had only 40 days left "to prepare, translate, bind, and file its reply with the Tribunal together with the rebuttal evidence; this was simply impossible to do within that time limit." The Respondent further pointed out that it could not meet the 15 April deadline "because of the Iranian New Year's holidays and the holy month of Ramadan (the month of fasting)." Finally, the Respondent argued that the extension requested would not affect the hearing scheduled for 13 September 1991. By their letter received by fax on 17 April 1991 and filed on 19 April 1991, the Claimants objected to the Respondent's extension request and argued that the Respondent should be given a 60-day extension at most. By Order of 23 April 1991, the Tribunal extended the Respondent's filing date for its rebuttal memorial until 15 June 1991.

26. By letter filed on 11 June 1991, the Respondent requested that the Tribunal join Cases Nos. 44, 46, and 47 to Case No. 146 (*Thomas K. Khosravi v. The Government of the Islamic Republic of Iran*) on the ground that "there was a complete connection" between the claims on the merits in these Cases. By letter, received by fax on 11 June 1991 and filed on 13 June 1991, the Claimants opposed the Respondent's proposal, arguing that it was "an obvious attempt to slow down this case and avoid its obligation to file a rebuttal case." By letter of 17 June 1991, the Respondent reiterated its request for a consolidation of Case No. 146 with Cases Nos. 44, 46 and 47 and requested the Tribunal "to set a time schedule for filing submissions in the four cases as soon as possible." By their letter, received by fax on 17 June 1991 and filed on 19 June 1991, the Claimants restated their objection to the Respondent's "dilatory tactic." By Order of 24 June 1991, the Tribunal ordered the Respondent to submit its rebuttal memorial "forthwith, but in any event no later than 19 July 1991," and it indicated that it was still considering the request for joinder of the four referenced cases. By letter of 16 July 1991, the claimant in Case No. 146 informed the Tribunal of its opposition to a consolidation of its claim with those of the Claimants. By letter of 19 July 1991, the Respondent informed the Tribunal that, absent any order on the consolidation of the four cases, it "continues to believe that it should not file the Memorial and Evidence in Rebuttal in Cases Nos. 44, 46 and 47 within the time limit set by the Tribunal (19 July 1991)." By their letter, received by fax on 23 July 1991 and filed on 24 July 1991, the Claimants reiterated their objection to a consolidation of the four claims and requested the Tribunal to

order the Respondent to file its rebuttal memorial by 1 August 1991. By Order of 26 July 1991, the Tribunal denied the Respondent's request for joinder of Case No. 146 and Cases Nos. 44, 46 and 47. The Order further directed the Respondent to submit its rebuttal memorial "forthwith, but in any event no later than 5 August 1991," and added that "[i]n view of the date of the Hearing, any submission filed after 5 August 1991 will be considered as untimely filed." On 26 July 1991, the Iranian Member of the Chamber, Mr. Mohsen Aghahosseini, filed a Dissenting Opinion to the Order of 26 July 1991. By letter of 5 August 1991, the Respondent objected to the Tribunal's Order of 26 July 1991 on the ground that it was not properly motivated and it announced that it would not file its rebuttal memorial until the Tribunal had given sufficient grounds for denying the request for joinder.

27. By their letter filed on 12 August 1991, the Claimants communicated their witness list to the Tribunal, in accordance with Article 25, para. 2 of the Tribunal Rules, with a view toward the Hearing scheduled for 13 September 1991.

28. By letter of 13 August 1991, the Respondent reiterated its objection to the Order of 26 July 1991 and it requested that the Tribunal "revise the objected Order." On 14 August 1991, the American Member of the Chamber, Mr. Richard C. Allison, filed a Concurring Opinion to the Order of 26 July 1991.

29. By Order of 21 August 1991, the Tribunal cancelled the Hearing scheduled for 13 September 1991, indicating that the new hearing date is "contemplated to be before the end of 1991."

30. By Order of 7 October 1991, the Tribunal fixed the new Hearing date at 28 January 1992. The Order further stated that "[i]n view of the rescheduling of the Hearing, the Tribunal grants the Respondent a final opportunity to submit its Memorial and evidence in rebuttal." This "final" deadline was fixed at 2 December 1991. On 2 December 1991, Respondent filed its Rebuttal Memorial.

31. Under a letter dated 3 December 1991, the Respondent submitted six copies of a document that was first submitted in a different case, as "exhibits" to its Memorial in Cases Nos. 44, 46 and 47.

32. By letter of 4 December 1991, the Respondent requested that "the duration of the scheduled hearing be increased to at least two days." By their letter received by fax and filed on 9 December 1991, the Claimants informed the Tribunal that they had no objection to a two-day hearing provided that the scheduling of the additional hearing day would not cause the Hearing to be postponed. By Order of 17 December 1991, the Tribunal granted the Respondent's request for a two-day Hearing to be held on 28 and 29 January 1992.

33. By their letters filed on 27 December 1991, the Claimants and the Respondent communicated their witness lists to the Tribunal, in accordance with Article 25, para. 2 of the Tribunal Rules. By letter received on 16 January 1992 and filed on 17 January 1992, the Claimants submitted two corrections to the English translations of two previously filed exhibits.

34. On 28 and 29 January 1992, a Hearing was held at the Tribunal (the "First Hearing").

35. Under letter received by fax on 5 March 1992, the Claimants submitted to the Tribunal six copies of the transcript of the referenced Hearing, which they had caused to be made.

36. By Order of 20 July 1992, the Tribunal decided to appoint an expert in accordance with Article 27 of the Tribunal Rules "to render a report as to certain matters relating to the valuation of Gostaresh Maskan Company as of 13 November 1979." In addition to setting forth the procedure for the appointment of the expert, the Order included a copy of the draft terms of reference for the expert.

37. By letter filed on 5 August 1992, the Claimants informed the Tribunal of their dissatisfaction with the above-mentioned Order which they believed would cause further delay in the proceedings. Accordingly, the Claimants requested that the Tribunal (i) issue an interlocutory award on all non-valuation issues "as promptly as possible," and (ii) accelerate the procedure for the appointment of an expert. On 19 August 1992, the Claimants submitted a sealed envelope containing their list of three proposed experts. On 20 August 1992, the Respondent submitted a sealed envelope containing its list of three proposed experts. In its letter filed on 20 August 1992, the Respondent objected to the Claimants' requests set forth in their 5 August 1992 letter.

38. By Order of 25 August 1992, the Tribunal, noting that the two Parties' lists did not contain any common name, requested that the Parties attempt to agree on an expert by 24 September 1992. The Order further invited the Parties to inform the Tribunal by 24 September 1992 of their objections – if any – to the filing with the Registry of the respective proposed expert lists. By letter received by fax on 24 September 1992 and filed on 30 September 1992, the Claimants informed the Tribunal of their agreement with the appointment of Professor Richard A. Brealey, one of the names that the Respondent had proposed, as the Tribunal expert for the purpose of valuing Gostaresh Maskan.

39. By Order of 5 October 1992, the Tribunal (i) informed the Parties that it had contacted Professor Richard A. Brealey in connection with his proposed appointment as the valuation expert, and (ii) invited Professor Brealey and the Parties to submit their comments on the proposed terms of reference. By letter of 16 October 1992, the Respondent filed its comments to

the above-mentioned draft terms of reference. By letter received by fax on 29 October 1992, the Claimants submitted their comments to the same draft terms of reference.

40. By Order of 14 December 1992, the Tribunal appointed Professor Richard A. Brealey as the Tribunal Expert for the purpose of valuing Gostaresh Maskan. That Order further required the Parties to provide to the Tribunal by 15 January 1993 a deposit of 55,000 pounds sterling towards the cost of retaining the Expert, with half of that amount to be paid by the Claimants and the other half to be paid by the Respondent. By Order of 20 January 1993, the Tribunal acknowledged receipt of the Claimants' share of the deposit and extended the Respondent's time limit to pay its share of the deposit until 15 February 1993.

41. By letter filed on 25 January 1993, the Claimants commented on the revised draft terms of reference set forth in the Tribunal's Order of 14 December 1992. By letter filed on 26 January 1993, the Respondent submitted the English version of its comments to these revised terms of reference. The Persian version of these comments was filed on 1 February 1993.

42. By letter of 3 February 1993, the Respondent informed the Tribunal that it had transferred its half of the deposit in respect of the Expert's fee, in the amount of 27,500 pounds sterling, to "the account of the Secretary General of [the] Iran-U.S. Claims Tribunal."

43. By Order of 4 February 1993, the Tribunal decided, upon review of the Parties' comments to the revised draft terms of reference set forth in its Order of 14 December 1992, that no further revisions were warranted. Accordingly, the Order determined the Expert's Terms of Reference.

44. Under a letter of 10 March 1993, the Expert presented his report to the Chairman of Chamber Three, Mr. Gaetano Arangio-Ruiz, indicating that "[b]efore formally accepting this report, [the Chamber] may wish to check that I have not made inappropriate assumptions on points of law, or whether there are sections of the Report that require elucidation."

45. In their letter received by fax on 24 March 1993 and filed on 26 March 1993, the Claimants requested that the Tribunal inform them of the status of the Expert's report.

46. By letter to the Expert of 2 April 1993, the Chairman of Chamber Three requested that, prior to the distribution of the report to the Parties, the Expert incorporate a comment in his report on the value of Gostaresh Maskan in the case that the claimed price adjustment receivables were due and payable, or alternatively, that they were not due and payable, in accordance with paragraph 2.D(1) of the Terms of Reference. On 14 April 1993, the Expert submitted his response to the above-mentioned letter from the Chairman and a copy of his final report (the "Expert's Report"). On 21

April 1993, the Tribunal issued an Order directing the Registry to distribute the Expert's Report to the Parties and inviting the Parties to submit their comments thereon by 18 June 1993. By their letter received by fax on 18 June 1993, the Claimants informed the Tribunal that they had sent by express delivery three originals and thirty copies of their comments on 17 June 1993. The Claimants' submission, entitled "Claimants' Comments on Report of Professor Brealey," was filed on 21 June 1993. On 18 June 1993, the Respondent filed its "Respondent's Comments in Compliance with Tribunal's Order of 21 April 1993." By their letter filed on 26 July 1993, the Claimants notified the Tribunal of certain alleged errors in the English translation of certain exhibits included in the Respondent's comments on the Expert's Report.

47. By Order of 28 July 1993, the Tribunal granted the Parties' request for a Hearing and scheduled it for 19 and 20 October 1993. By their letter received by fax on 6 August 1993 and filed on 10 August 1993, the Claimants requested that the Hearing be scheduled one week later. By Order of 12 August 1993, the Tribunal rescheduled the above-mentioned Hearing for 26 and 27 October 1993.

48. By letter filed on 24 August 1993, the Claimants submitted to the Tribunal certain portions of the Respondent's comments on the Expert's Report in Persian of which the Respondent had not submitted an English translation.

49. By letter of 23 September 1993, the Respondent submitted its witness list for the referenced Hearing. By their letter received by fax on 24 September 1993 and filed on 27 September 1993, the Claimants submitted their witness list for the Hearing.

50. By letter received by fax on 13 October 1993 and filed on 15 October 1993, the Claimants requested that the Tribunal conduct the Hearing in a manner that would allow one of their expert witnesses, Mr. Fariborz Ghadar, to be absent from the second day of the Hearing.

51. On 26 and 27 October 1993, a second Hearing in these Cases was held at the Tribunal (the "Expert Hearing").

52. On 17 November 1993, the Tribunal received a copy of the Hearing transcript that the court reporter appointed by the Tribunal had prepared (the "*Expert Hearing Transcript*").

II. JURISDICTION

53. Under the Claims Settlement Declaration, the Tribunal may exercise jurisdiction over "claims of nationals of the United States against Iran." Claims Settlement Declaration ("CSD"), Article II, para. 1. The Tribunal

determined in its Interlocutory Award that the Claimants' dominant and effective nationality during the relevant period is that of the United States and, therefore, that they may properly present claims before the Tribunal. *Ebrahimi*, 22 IRAN-U.S. C.T.R. at 144.

54. In its subsequent Hearing Memorial, the Respondent offered an argument to challenge Claimants' standing to present these Cases to the Tribunal. The Respondent contends that Claimants, being minors during the period between the acquisition of Gostaresh Maskan shares and their alleged expropriation, were not the real party in interest. The Respondent asserts that "Claimants [were] only nominal shareholders and the actual owner who had absolute powers was Mr. Ali Ebrahimi, the Claimants' father." Respondent further asserts that Ali Ebrahimi, as the legal guardian of the Claimants, arranged for the transfer of Gostaresh Maskan shares to Claimants to "achieve his initial objective of making his other properties as inviolable against his commercial liabilities" arising from Gostaresh Maskan's operations. Respondent concludes that the transfer of Gostaresh Maskan shares to Claimants lacked good faith "which is a main condition for correctness of any legal act."

55. The premise of this argument – that Ali Ebrahimi used his children as nominal shareholders if not to create, then at least to maintain, Gostaresh Maskan as a private joint stock company – is undermined by evidence submitted by Respondent's expert, Noavaran Auditors and Management Consultants ("Noavaran"), on the Company's value. The Tribunal notes first that the Company was formed, according to its Articles of Association, on 6 November 1973, some four years before Claimants acquired their shares in Gostaresh Maskan in August 1977. Moreover, the first report prepared by Noavaran lists the initial shareholders of Gostaresh Maskan as Ali Ebrahimi, Mr. Akbar Lari, and Mr. Khodadad Khosravi, holding 51%, 45%, and 4%, respectively, of the Company's stock. Mr. Ebrahimi's "initial" objective to shield his personal estate from the Company's creditors was therefore achieved as of the date the Company was organized. It thus appears that the operation of Gostaresh Maskan as a duly organized and validly existing company in good standing was neither the result of, nor conditioned on, nor in any other manner affected by, a valid stock transfer to the benefit of the Claimants. By the same token, the Tribunal sees no reason to question that Claimants had full and marketable title to their shares. In the light of the above, Respondent's assertion of an improper motive behind the transfer of Gostaresh Maskan shares to Claimants fails as a matter of fact and as a matter of law.

56. The Government of The Islamic Republic of Iran is properly named as Respondent since these Cases involve a claim of expropriation of a private

company. *See FMC Corporation v. The Ministry of National Defence, et al.*, Award No. 292-353-2, para. 74 (12 February 1987), *reprinted in* 14 IRAN-U.S. C.T.R. 111, 131 ("A claim for expropriation is . . . a claim against Iran"). Accordingly, the jurisdictional requirements of Article II, para. 1 of the Claims Settlement Declaration are satisfied in the present Case.

57. The Claims Settlement Declaration also limits the Tribunal's jurisdiction to claims that are "owned continuously, from the date on which the claim arose to [19 January 1981], by nationals [of Iran or the United States]." CSD, Article VII, para. 2. Claimants assert that they each owned shares in Gostaresh Maskan as of 26 August 1977. As evidence of their ownership, Claimants submit the minutes of a meeting of the Gostaresh Maskan Board of Directors, dated 25 August 1977, at which the Board of Directors approved the transfer by Mr. Akbar Lari of his shares in Gostaresh Maskan to "third parties." The minutes of this meeting refer to a letter from Mr. Lari describing the approved transaction. In that letter, which is dated 23 August 1977, Mr. Lari informs the Gostaresh Maskan Board of Directors of his intention to assign his shares in the Company to Claimants, in the following manner: Shahin Ebrahimi, 55 shares; Cecilia Ebrahimi, 20 shares; Christina Ebrahimi, 20 shares. These shares represented 19% of Gostaresh Maskan's outstanding stock. Assertedly, Mr. Lari transferred these shares to Claimants in exchange for 900 shares of Tamin Sakhteman Company, which they had allegedly received as a gift from their mother.

58. Claimants also offer their respective share certificates, issued by Gostaresh Maskan on 12 February 1978 upon the recapitalization of the Company, as evidence that their aggregate interest of 19% was not diluted following the recapitalization.

59. At the time of the transfer of Gostaresh Maskan shares to the Claimants, Shahin Ebrahimi was 15 years old, Cecilia Ebrahimi was 7 years old and Christina Ebrahimi was 6 years old. Respondent contends that Claimants' status as minors at that time deprives them, under the Iranian Civil Code, of certain privileges normally associated with ownership. According to Respondent, "a minor child absolutely, has not the right of interfering [with] or possessing its property and until the time that such minor child arrives at the legal age, the child's guardian shall have the absolute right to interfere in the property."

60. Nonetheless, Respondent concedes that "in various legal systems, minor children . . . have the right of ownership, and this matter is contained also in the legal system of Iran." Thus, Claimants' legal right to own shares in Gostaresh Maskan, for purposes of the Tribunal's jurisdiction under Article VII, para. 2 of the Claims Settlement Declaration, is not contested. Moreover, evidence submitted by Respondent – a "List of Shareholders Names and

Number of Shares of Gostaresh Maskan Private Co." – confirms Claimants' share ownership in the proportions claimed by them.

61. The claims in these Cases "arise out of . . . expropriation or other measures affecting property rights." CSD, Article II, para. 1. Thus, all of the nationality, standing and subject matter jurisdiction requirements of the Claims Settlement Declaration are satisfied in these Cases.

III. EXPROPRIATION

A. Claimants' Contentions

62. The Claimants trace the alleged expropriation of Gostaresh Maskan to the "Law Concerning the Appointment of Provisional Manager(s) to Supervise Productive, Industrial, Commercial, Agricultural and Services Units in the Private and Public Sectors," approved by the Islamic Revolutionary Council under No. 6738 on 16 June 1979 (26 Khordad 1358) (the "Act").[5] Pursuant to the Act, and the administrative orders implementing it, the Ministries of the Islamic Republic, acting through the Director of the Plan and Budget Organization, were empowered to appoint directors to manage private corporations if "the managers and/or owners . . . deserted [the corporation], or stopped the work, or [were] not accessible for any reason whatsoever and upon request of [the] owner[s] or directors." Act, Article 1. Government appointment of a director, according to the Act, "stripped [earlier directors] of their competence" and precluded shareholders from "appoint[ing] directors in their stead." Act, Article 2. The Act also provided that directors appointed by the Government "shall in every respect be the legal representatives of the original directors of the [corporation], and they shall have all the authorities [*sic*] necessary for managing the current and routine affairs [of the corporation]." Act, Article 3.

63. The Claimants assert that, pursuant to the Act, the Advising Minister and Director of the Plan and Budget Organization, Mr. Ezzatollah Sahabi, and the Supervisor for the Bureau of Contractors and Constructors, Mr. Heshmatollah Alaoddini, appointed Mr. Alirreza Shastfouladi as the Director of Gostaresh Maskan on 13 November 1979. The consequence of this appointment, according to the affidavit of Mr. Homayoun Amini – the then Chief Executive Officer and a Director of Gostaresh Maskan – was to

> effectively strip me, the other directors, and the other shareholders of Gostaresh Maskan of our authority. As officers and directors, we could no longer act on behalf

---

[5] In their respective Statements of Claim, the Claimants relied on a different law, *i.e.*, the "Law for the Managing and the Taking of Ownership of the Stocks in the Contracting and Consultant Engineering Entities," dated 9 March 1980 (18 Esfand 1358). *See* para. 81 and para. 83, *infra*.

of the company. As shareholders, we were deprived of the use, control and benefits of our ownership rights, particularly our right to manage the corporation.

Mr. Amini further states in his affidavit that, following the appointment of Mr. Shastfouladi, the above-mentioned Supervisor for the Bureau of Contractors and Constructors, Mr. Heshmatollah Alaoddini, told him that Mr. Shastfouladi would manage Gostaresh Maskan and that the other officers and directors should act only at Mr. Shastfouladi's direction.

64. According to Mr. Amini, the appointment of Mr. Shastfouladi was superseded by the appointment of Mohammad Javad Dormishian as Managing Director of Gostaresh Maskan later that same month. Shortly thereafter, Mr. Dormishian resigned his position as Managing Director, and the Government appointed Messrs. Dormishian, Hosseingholi Hooshmand, and Sayed Hassan Nouri as Directors of the Company. Finally, on 19 January 1980, Messrs. Dormishian, Hooshmand, and Nouri were removed as directors and Dr. Parviz Shams Towfighi was appointed as Director of Gostaresh Maskan, a position that he held for approximately eighteen months. Mr. Amini asserts that none of these successive appointments was made with the approval of Gostaresh Maskan's shareholders or elected directors. As of 1987, when Mr. Amini left Iran, Gostaresh Maskan remained under Government control.

65. The Claimants seek additional support for their claim of expropriation from the Tribunal's decision in *Blount Brothers Corporation v. Ministry of Housing and Urban Development and Gostaresh Maskan Co.*, Award No. 74-62-3 (2 September 1983), *reprinted in* 3 IRAN-U.S. C.T.R. 225 ("*Blount Brothers*"). In that Award, the Tribunal held that Gostaresh Maskan was a proper respondent because it was "an entity controlled by the Government of Iran so that the Tribunal has jurisdiction over claims against that entity." *Id.* at 231.

66. The Claimants contend that

> Gostaresh Maskan's shareholders have not been, and will not be, able to exercise the property rights associated with their ownership of stock in Gostaresh Maskan. In particular, they have been permanently deprived of their rights to vote their shares, to benefit from the company's profits, and to direct and participate in the sale of the company or the liquidation of its assets.

Accordingly, the Claimants consider that the referenced series of appointments starting from 13 November 1979, and the resulting Government interference with the Claimants' ownership rights thereafter, amounted to an expropriation of their shares within the meaning of Article II, para. 1 of the Claims Settlement Declaration. They seek compensation from the Respondent for the "full equivalent of the property taken," *i.e.*, for the value of their shares in Gostaresh Maskan on the date of the alleged expropriation. The Claimants consider that the date of the expropriation was 13 November 1979, when the first Government-appointed director was assigned to manage Gostaresh Maskan's operations.[6]

B. *Respondent's Contentions*

67. The Respondent denies that the appointment of directors to manage Gostaresh Maskan constituted an expropriation of Claimants' shares in the Company. It asserts that the appointment of directors was made only "due to excessive insistence of the existing directors and shareholders of the Company and due to [the] departure of Mr. Ali Ebrahimi, the main shareholder and director of the Company." In support of this position, Respondent refers to Article 1 of the Act which, in pertinent part, provides:

> [O]rganizations and companies . . . the managers and/or owners of which have deserted the said units . . . and upon request of [the] owner[s] or directors of the said units . . . one or more individuals may be appointed as director or board of directors or supervising members for managing or supervising over the affairs of the said units . . .

Respondent also submits the affidavit of Mr. Nasser Modaressi, who claims to have served Gostaresh Maskan as an accountant since 1975. According to Mr. Modaressi, the Company was "abandoned by its directors" in 1979 and its affairs fell into turmoil. This prompted Mr. Modaressi, "together with a number of the Company's personnel," to approach the "Plan and Budget Organization in order to have a supervisor appointed for attending to the affairs of the Company, as a result of which Mr. Ali Reza Sast Fooladi [*sic*] was appointed on 13 November 1979 as supervisor by the Plan and Budget Organization." The affidavit of Mr. Mohammad Hossein Karimi Fard, identified as a technical and executive engineer at Gostaresh Maskan since 1975, presents a substantially similar rendition of events.

68. Respondent contends that the Tribunal's decision in *Blount Brothers* does not establish the alleged expropriation of Gostaresh Maskan. According to Respondent, this holding should not dictate a finding of expropriation in the present Case because: (i) *Blount Brothers* is "devoid of the required legal firmness and is weak and shaky," given the content of Article 1 of the Act; and (ii) prior Tribunal awards are not binding in subsequent cases.

C. *The Tribunal's Findings*
1. *Expropriation*

69. In *Blount Brothers*, the Tribunal examined whether, for jurisdictional purposes, Gostaresh Maskan was an "entity controlled by the Government of

---

[6] The Claimants in their respective Statements of Claim alleged that the expropriation had occurred in early 1980. *See* note 8, *infra*.

Iran." *Blount Brothers*, 3 IRAN-U.S. C.T.R. at 231. The evidence before the Tribunal on this question included an affidavit by Mr. Ali Ebrahimi describing the seizure of Gostaresh Maskan and the Government's appointment of successive directors for the Company.

70. Contrary to the Respondent's position, *Blount Brothers* has significant precedential value in the context of the present expropriation claim. By its terms, *Blount Brothers* addressed the status of Gostaresh Maskan as a controlled entity rather than the manner in which that control was established, *i.e.*, expropriation, purchase, or otherwise. Nevertheless, the Tribunal's reliance on Mr. Ebrahimi's testimony regarding the appointment of successive directors to Gostaresh Maskan reflects its understanding of the manner in which the Company came under Government control. Thus, while *Blount Brothers* is not binding in the present Cases, the Tribunal places great weight upon its prior holding in considering the issue currently before it.

71. The present claim does not rest solely on our prior decision, however. The Respondent does not dispute that it appointed successive directors to Gostaresh Maskan, nor that these appointments had an impact on the management of the Company. Rather, it asserts that Gostaresh Maskan's elected directors and shareholders requested Government appointment of directors following Ali Ebrahimi's departure from Iran in July 1979. However, Respondent fails to support this assertion with evidence of an authorized request on behalf of Gostaresh Maskan for Government-appointed directors. Respondent's only evidence on this issue concerns the apparent petitioning by several Gostaresh Maskan employees for appointment of a Government director.

72. The Tribunal considers first that it is doubtful that the referenced requests would have satisfied the terms of the Act since Article 1 appears to refer to a request from company shareholders or directors, not employees.[7] Second, the Claimants offered evidence that the absence of Mr. Ebrahimi did not completely disrupt Gostaresh Maskan's work. Following Mr. Ebrahimi's departure from Iran in July 1979, Mr. Amini was authorized to direct the Company's activities and, in fact, continued to conduct monthly Board of

---

[7] The Tribunal notes that, during the drafting of this Award, it was suggested that the English translation of the Act that is set out above (*see* para. 62 and para. 67, *supra*), and which is substantially identical to the translations submitted by each of the Parties, was inaccurate. It was suggested that the true meaning of Article 1 was that the Iranian Government was entitled to take temporary measures for the management of certain companies *either* upon the occurrence of certain events (such as the abandonment of the company by its shareholders and/or directors), *or* upon a request by that company's shareholders or directors. Under this reading of the Article, the conditions listed above should be read as alternative rather than as cumulative requirements. The Tribunal notes that it need not rule on the definitive translation of the referenced Article as such ruling would not materially affect the Tribunal's conclusions on expropriation set out in paras. 72 through 77, *infra*.

Directors' meetings until 22 October 1979, when the last meeting of the Company's elected directors was held. Third, and more importantly, Tribunal precedent makes clear that the key issue is the objective impact of measures affecting shareholder interests, not the subjective intention behind those measures. *See Tippetts, Abbett, McCarthy, Stratton v. TAMS-AFFA Consulting Engineers of Iran, et al.*, Award No. 141-7-2 (22 June 1984), *reprinted in* 6 IRAN-U.S. C.T.R. 219, 225-226 (*"Tippetts"*) ("The intent of the government is less important than the effects of the measures on the owner, and the form of the measures of control or interference is less important than the reality of their impact"). Thus, the Respondent's contention that appointment of Government managers was necessary to stabilize Gostaresh Maskan's operations (and, presumably, to protect Gostaresh Maskan workers and Iranian interests in Gostaresh Maskan projects) does not preclude liability for expropriation. It is immaterial whether or not the alleged expropriation was justified under the Act for the purpose of finding that the Respondent has a duty to pay compensation as a matter of international law and obligations. A State may not avoid liability for compensation by showing that its actions were carried out pursuant to or in accordance with its own laws. *See American International Group, Inc., et al. v. The Islamic Republic of Iran, et al.*, Award No. 93-2-3 (19 December 1983), *reprinted in* 4 IRAN-U.S. C.T.R. 96, 105 (*"AIG"*) ("[I]t is a general principle of public international law that even in a case of lawful nationalization the former owner of the nationalized property is normally entitled to compensation for the value of the property taken"). This was recognized in *Phelps Dodge Corp., et al. v. The Islamic Republic of Iran*, Award No. 217-99-2, para. 22 (19 March 1986), *reprinted in* 10 IRAN-U.S. C.T.R. 121, 130):

> The Tribunal fully understands the reasons why the Respondent felt compelled to protect its interests through this transfer of management, and the Tribunal understands the financial, economic and social concerns that inspired the law pursuant to which it acted, but those reasons and concerns cannot relieve the Respondent of the obligation to compensate Phelps Dodge for its loss.

The Tribunal confirmed its position on this issue in *Birnbaum*, which involved the very Act under review in the present Cases:

> The Respondent's reasons and concerns for taking control of [the company] cannot relieve it from responsibility to compensate the Claimant for the taking . . . Moreover, a government cannot avoid liability for compensation by showing that its actions were taken legitimately pursuant to its own laws.

Harold Birnbaum v. The Islamic Republic of Iran, Award No. 549-967-2, para. 35 (6 July 1993), *reprinted in* 29 IRAN-U.S. C.T.R. 260, 270 (*"Birnbaum"*).

73. The Claimants have presented adequate evidence of the "reality of the impact" of the Respondent's measures affecting their ownership rights. The Claimants present the affidavit of Mr. Homayoun Amini, in which he details the appointment of successive directors to Gostaresh Maskan, commencing on 13 November 1979 with the appointment of Mr. Alirreza Shastfouladi. According to Mr. Amini, the Government's appointment of various directors to Gostaresh Maskan effectively nullified the authority of the Company's elected directors and its shareholders. Following the appointment, no further meetings of the Gostaresh Maskan shareholders or their elected directors were held. By early December 1979, the Government-appointed Director then in place, Mr. Mohamad Javad Dormishian, froze the Company's accounts and presented himself as the sole authorized representative of the Company.

74. Additional documentary evidence supports the Claimants' contention that they were deprived of their ownership rights in Gostaresh Maskan. For example, Claimants submitted the minutes of a meeting held on 26 December 1979 at the office of Mr. Alaeddini, Supervisor of Contractors' Affairs at the Plan and Budget Organization, which was attended by the Government-appointed directors of Gostaresh Maskan and representatives of the Government agencies for which the Company was carrying out construction projects. Also attending the meeting were (i) Mr. Amini, whose status at the meeting, as indicated by the minutes, was that of "Former Managing Director," and (ii) Mr. Dormishian, whom the minutes referred to as the "Government-appointed Director, Gostaresh Maskan Company."

75. The Claimants also offer an English translation of three letters, each dated 31 December 1979, from Mr. Ezzatollah Sahabi, the State Minister and Supervisor of the Plan and Budget Organization, to each of the Company's Government-appointed Directors (at that time, Mr. Dormishian, Mr. Hooshmand, and Mr. Noori) according to which they were authorized, collectively, "to appoint the Boards of Directors" of Gostaresh Maskan and its affiliated companies.

76. The Tribunal has held in previous Awards that a finding of expropriation "is warranted whenever events demonstrate that the owner was deprived of fundamental rights of ownership and it appears that this deprivation is not merely ephemeral." *Tippetts*, 6 IRAN-U.S. C.T.R. at 225. The Tribunal further held in *Tippetts* that "[a] deprivation or taking of property may occur under international law through interference by a state in the use of that property or with the enjoyment of its benefits, even where legal title to the property is not affected." *Id.* The appointment of "provisional managers" does not automatically justify a finding of expropriation. However, the Tribunal previously has held that "the appointment of managers often has been regarded as a 'highly significant indication' of a taking and thus of expropria-

tion." *Motorola, Inc.* v. *Iran National Airlines Corp., et al.*, Award No. 373-481-3, para. 58 (28 June 1988), *reprinted in* 19 IRAN-U.S. C.T.R. 73, 85 ("*Motorola*") (citing *Sedco, Inc., et al.* and *National Iranian Oil Co.*, Interlocutory Award No. ITL 55-129-3 (24 October 1985), *reprinted in* 9 IRAN-U.S. C.T.R. 248, 277-278 ("*Sedco*") (finding that appointment of managers is "a highly significant indication of expropriation because of the attendant denial of the owner's right to manage the enterprise")). Indeed, in *Payne*, the Tribunal considered the consequences of appointing directors pursuant to the Act relied upon in the present Cases and found that:

> The effect [of Legal Act No. 6738] is to strip the original managers of affected companies of all authority and to deny shareholders significant rights attached to their ownership interest . . . [T]he sum effect in this case was the deprivation of any interest of the original owners of the companies once they were made subject to provisional management by the Government.

Thomas Earl Payne v. *The Government of the Islamic Republic of Iran*, Award No. 245-335-2, para. 20 (8 August 1986), *reprinted in* 12 IRAN-U.S. C.T.R. 3, 10 ("*Payne*"). In *Birnbaum*, which involved the same Act, the Tribunal found that "[i]t is difficult to deny that once the government appointed a temporary manager under the Law of 16 June 1979 and that manager began to function, the owner was divested of the ability to participate in the management and control of his company." *Birnbaum*, at para. 29, 29 IRAN-U.S. C.T.R. at 268. *See also Starrett Housing Corporation, et al.* v. *The Government of the Islamic Republic of Iran, et al.*, Interlocutory Award No. ITL 32-24-1 (19 December 1983), *reprinted in* 4 IRAN-U.S. C.T.R. 122, 154-156 ("*Starrett*"), and *Faith Lita Khosrowshahi, et al.* v. *The Government of the Islamic Republic of Iran, et al.*, Award No. 558-178-2, paras. 23-28 (30 June 1994), *reprinted in* 30 IRAN-U.S. C.T.R. 76, 84.

77. Based on the evidence before it and the decision in *Blount Brothers*, the Tribunal finds that Respondent effectively took control of Gostaresh Maskan through the appointment of provisional managers, thereby depriving Claimants of their ownership interests in the Company.

78. As to the date of expropriation, Respondent contends that if the Tribunal defers to its prior finding in *Blount Brothers*, it must also adopt the date to which Mr. Ebrahimi attested in that Case, *i.e.*, 19 January 1980, as the date the Government seized control of Gostaresh Maskan. However, evidence offered by Claimants in the present Cases, which does not appear to have been presented in *Blount Brothers*, supports an earlier expropriation date.[8]

---

[8] In Claimants' Hearing Memorial, the expropriation is asserted to have occurred on 13 November 1979, the date of the Government's initial appointment of a director to Gostaresh

Specifically, Mr. Amini's affidavit states that the first Government-appointed Director of Gostaresh Maskan, Mr. Shastfouladi, was appointed on 13 November 1979.

79. The Tribunal previously has held that, when "the seizure of control by appointment of 'temporary' managers clearly ripens into an outright taking of title, the date of appointment presumptively should be regarded as the date of taking." *Sedco*, 9 IRAN-U.S. C.T.R. at 278. If at "the date of the government appointment of 'temporary' managers there is no reasonable prospect of return of control, a taking should conclusively be found to have occurred as of that date." *Id.* at 278-279. The Tribunal also refers to its above-mentioned finding in *Birnbaum* to the effect that the expropriation occurred on the date that the designation of the first Government-appointed director took effect. *See* para. 76, *supra*. The record shows that the Government-appointed directors took firm control of Gostaresh Maskan as of 13 November 1979. Moreover, given the circumstances in which Mr. Shastfouladi was appointed and the rapid succession of Government-appointed directors following him, relinquishment of Government control was not a reasonable prospect when Mr. Shastfouladi was appointed. *See Sedco*, 9 IRAN-U.S. C.T.R. at 279 ("[t]he Tribunal notes that Legal Bill No. 6738 does not prescribe the length of government control and does not detail 'provisions calling for judicial or administrative determination of whether the property should be returned to its original owners' "). Thus, the expropriation of the Claimants' shares in Gostaresh Maskan is deemed to have taken effect on 13 November 1979. Respondent is therefore liable to Claimants for the taking of their shares in Gostaresh Maskan as of that date.

2. *The A18 Caveat*

80. The Respondent argues that the Claims should be dismissed by application of the Caveat in *Case No. A18*.[9] Respondent states that

---

Maskan rather than "in early 1980" as they had contended in their respective Statements of Claims (*see* note 6, *supra*). This change does not alter the essence of the claim or cause delay or prejudice in the proceedings. *See* Tribunal Rule 20; Order of 15 September 1987, in *Fereydoon Ghaffari v. The Islamic Republic of Iran*, Case No. 10792, Chamber Two, *reprinted in* 18 **IRAN-U.S. C.T.R.** 64. Accordingly, Claimants' revised pleading of the date of the alleged expropriation, *i.e.*, 13 November 1979, is accepted for the purpose of assessing their claims.

[9] The Tribunal held in *Case No. A18* that in determining a claimant's dominant and effective nationality, the Tribunal is to "consider all relevant factors, including habitual residence, center of interests, family ties, participation in public life and other evidence of attachment. To this conclusion the Tribunal adds an important caveat. In cases where the Tribunal finds jurisdiction based upon a dominant and effective nationality of the claimant, the other nationality may remain relevant to the merits of the claim." *Case No. A18*, Decision No. DEC 32-A18-FT (6 April 1984), *reprinted in* 5 **IRAN-U.S. C.T.R.** 251, 265.

if ever a claim arose it would be characterized as an Iranian claim because the transfer of the alleged shares to the Claimants was made not directly but indirectly on the grounds of their being minor by their father Mr. Ali Ebrahimi who is a national of Iran and does not deny this fact.

Respondent further points out, with regard to Mr. Ali Ebrahimi, that

> [t]he only thing that never hit his imagination or that of other shareholders was the fact that his children were foreign nationals because otherwise [he] would never have taken the risk of transferring the alleged shares to his children, or indeed endangering his own property, for fear of any likely changes in the regulations concerning the ownership of shares by foreign nationals or the promulgation of laws limiting such ownership.

Moreover, Respondent asserts that the Claimants had deliberately concealed their U.S. nationality so as not to jeopardize the position of Gostaresh Maskan in public procurement procedures. In this regard, Respondent points out that "as far as the Plan and Budget Organization was concerned, its budget and the type of contracts that would have been delegated to [a company with foreign shareholders] would have been negatively affected." Accordingly, Respondent concludes that the Claimants "filed a claim against their sovereign government before this Tribunal by using their U.S. nationality for vindication of rights acquired solely under their Iranian nationality. This is a clear case of fraudulent use of nationality and abuse of right."

81. In addition, the suggestion was made that the Claimants deliberately concealed their U.S. citizenship even after the expropriation of their shares. Such non-disclosure is purportedly evidenced by the Claimants' failure to seek compensation from the local Iranian authorities under the "Law for the Managing and the Taking of Ownership of the Stocks in the Contracting and Consultant Engineering Entities," dated 9 March 1980,[10] and their decision to instead seek compensation from the Government of the Islamic Republic of Iran pursuant to an award from the Tribunal.

82. The Tribunal rejects the Respondent's contention that the Claimants' conduct implicates the A18 Caveat. The Tribunal has developed the A18 Caveat test in a number of Awards following the Full Tribunal Decision in *Case No. A18*. For instance, in *Protiva* the Tribunal, having found that the claimants' dominant and effective nationality was that of the U.S., described the A18 Caveat test as follows: "The Tribunal . . . will, for example, consider whether the Claimants used their Iranian nationality to secure benefits

---

[10] The Proviso to Article II(B) of this Law provides:
The value of the shares of foreign shareholders in the entities taken by the Government shall, upon the auditing and evaluation of each entity, be paid by the Government.

available under Iranian law exclusively to Iranian nationals or whether, in any other way, their conduct was such as to justify refusal of an award in their favor." *Edgar Protiva, et al.* v. *The Government of the Islamic Republic of Iran*, Interlocutory Award No. ITL 73-316-2, para. 18 (12 October 1989), *reprinted in* 23 IRAN-U.S. C.T.R. 259, 263. Applying this test to the present Case, the Tribunal finds that the Respondent has not provided any evidence of any benefits that would only have been available to sole Iranian nationals. The Tribunal notes, in particular, that no evidence was submitted that Gostaresh Maskan was subject to any act, rule or regulation that in any manner proscribed the issuance or transfer of stock in the Company to foreign or dual nationals. Accordingly, the Tribunal finds that the Claimants did not obtain and secure ownership of their shares in Gostaresh Maskan in a manner that would be covered by the A18 Caveat referred to above.[11]

83. The Tribunal notes that in *Saghi* it applied a broader definition of the A18 Caveat, stating that whereas

> [t]he caveat is evidently intended to apply to claims by dual nationals for benefits limited by relevant and applicable Iranian law to persons who were nationals solely of Iran[,] [t]he equitable principle expressed by this rule can, in principle, have a broader application . . . Even when a dual national's claim relates to benefits not limited by law to Iranian nationals, the Tribunal may still apply the caveat when the evidence compels the conclusion that the dual national has abused his dual nationality in such a way that he should not be allowed to recover on his claim.

James M. Saghi, et al. v. *The Islamic Republic of Iran*, Award No. 544-298-2, para. 54 (22 January 1993), *reprinted in* 29 IRAN-U.S. C.T.R. 20, 38. The Tribunal finds that there is no evidence in the present Cases that would compel such a conclusion. In particular, there are no grounds for believing that the Claimants' alleged decision not to claim compensation from the Government under the referenced "Law for the Managing and the Taking of Ownership of the Stocks in the Contracting and Consultant Engineering Entities," at a time when they could not reasonably have foreseen the creation of this Tribunal, amounts to an abuse of their dual nationality. Furthermore, based on the evidence before it, the Tribunal is satisfied that the relevant legislative act in these Cases is the Act pursuant to which the Claimants' property was expropriated (*see* para. 62, *supra*), rather than the above-mentioned law. The

---

[11] *See also Ataollah Golpira* v. *The Government of The Islamic Republic of Iran*, Award No. 32-211-2 (29 March 1983), *reprinted in* 2 IRAN-U.S. C.T.R. 171. In that case the Tribunal held, in regard to shares in an Iranian company held by a dual national (Mr. Golpira), that "[s]ince shares in the [Iranian company] were available for purchase by non-Iranians, the mere fact that Golpira's Iranian ID number appears on his share certificates does not mean that he concealed his American nationality in order to obtain benefits available only to Iranians." *Id.* at 174.

Tribunal therefore concludes that the record does not support the conclusion that the Claimants in any manner relied upon or used their Iranian nationality to obtain or secure certain benefits that they could not have enjoyed as U.S. citizens.

IV. STANDARD OF COMPENSATION AND VALUATION METHOD

A. Claimants' Contentions

84. The Claimants claim "prompt, adequate and effective compensation" as the remedy for the taking of their property rights. They point out that pursuant to Article IV, Para. 2 of the Treaty of Amity between the United States and Iran, signed on 15 August 1955,[12] the amount of the compensation must be equal to "the full equivalent of the property taken."

85. The Claimants further argue that such an amount must be equal to the fair market value of the Company as a going concern. The Claimants seek support for this position in the Tribunal's Award in *AIG*, which held that "[t]he appropriate method is to value the company as a going concern, taking into account not only the net book value of its assets but also such elements as good will and likely future profitability, had the company been allowed to continue its business under its former management." *AIG*, 4 IRAN-U.S. C.T.R. at 109; *see also Motorola*, 19 IRAN-U.S. C.T.R. at 88 ("Net book value is not an appropriate standard of compensation"). Accordingly, Claimants contend that the Tribunal must determine "the amount which a willing buyer would have paid a willing seller" for the shares of Gostaresh Maskan. *INA Corporation v. The Government of the Islamic Republic of Iran*, Award No. 184-161-1 (12 August 1985), *reprinted in* 8 IRAN-U.S. C.T.R. 373, 380 ("*INA*"). This determination is to be made without regard to "any diminution of value due to the nationali[z]ation itself or the anticipation thereof, and excluding consideration of events thereafter that might have increased or decreased the value of the shares." *Id.*

86. Claimants calculated the fair market value of Gostaresh Maskan using an asset approach. Such a valuation method yields a company value that is composed of the replacement cost of the company's tangible assets plus an amount attributable to its intangible values. In their Hearing Memorial for the Expert Hearing, Claimants also submitted a valuation of Gostaresh Maskan based on a discounted cash flow approach to provide additional support for their asset-based valuation. This method consists of discounting the cash flows

---

[12] Treaty of Amity, Economic Relations, and Consular Rights Between the United States of America and Iran, *signed* 15 August 1955, *entered into force* 16 June 1957, 284 U.N.T.S. 93, T.I.A.S. No. 3853, 8 U.S.T. 900.

which a company is expected to generate in the future at the rate of return that a reasonable investor requires from investments of comparable risk.

B. Respondent's Contentions

87. Respondent argues that the full compensation-provision of Article IV, para. 2 of the above-mentioned Treaty of Amity is of no avail to dual nationals like the Claimants who "take possession of a company's shares as Iranians, and then ask for compensation." Furthermore, while the Respondent appears to agree on the appropriateness of a fair market valuation of Gostaresh Maskan using an asset approach, it maintains that the Company was no longer a going concern at the valuation date. Respondent notes in support of its position that "[c]hanges of the government policy concerning construction works and its focusing on works related to rural areas as well as cheap housing construction works for low income classes, were greatly affecting the conditions of companies like Gostaresh Maskan Company." This, in addition to "the Company directors' negligence, failures and mismanagement before the Revolution until the date of the alleged expropriation," allegedly resulted in a situation such that by the time the first Government-appointed director arrived at Gostaresh Maskan, the Company's operations had come to a virtual standstill and its financial condition was "critical and quite negative."

C. Tribunal's Findings

88. The Tribunal believes that, while international law undoubtedly sets forth an obligation to provide compensation for property taken, international law theory and practice do not support the conclusion that the "prompt, adequate and effective" standard represents the prevailing standard of compensation. As Professor O. Schachter has pointed out, "[t]he leading European scholars – De Visscher, Lauterpacht, Rousseau –" have concluded in that sense. *See* Oscar Schachter, *International Law in Theory and Practice*, Academy of International Law, 178 Collected Courses 295 (1982) at 323. Professor Schachter has further noted, accurately, that "no international judicial or arbitral decision on compensation has adopted the 'prompt, adequate and effective' rule" as a matter of international obligation. *See* Oscar Schachter, *Compensation for Expropriation*, 78 A.J.I.L. 121, 123-127 (1984); *see also* Ian Brownlie, *Principles of Public International Law* 543-544 (Clarendon Press-Oxford 1990). Rather, customary international law favors an "appropriate" compensation standard.[13] *See* Eduardo Jimenéz de Aréchaga, *International Law in the*

---

[13] In this respect, reference is made, in particular, to Article 4 of Resolution No. 1803 (XVII) of 14 December 1962, on Permanent Sovereignty over Natural Resources (G.A. Res. 1803, 17 U.N. GAOR Supp. (No. 17) at 15, U.N. Doc. A./5217 (1962), *reprinted in* 57 Am.J.Int'l L. 710 (1963)). Article 4 states as follows:

Past Third of a Century, 159 Recueil des Cours 1, 302 (1978); Oscar Schachter, *The Question of Expropriation/Compensation in the United Nations Code in the Light of Recent State Policy and Practice*, Paper Presented at the Symposium on the Outstanding Issues in the United Nations Code of Conduct on Transnational Corporations, The Hague, 15-16 September 1989, at 3; Malcolm N. Shaw, *International Law* 521-522 (Grotius Publications Limited-Cambridge 1991); John A. Westberg, *Compensation in Cases of Expropriation and Nationalization: Awards of the Iran-United States Claims Tribunal*, 5 ICSID Review-Foreign Investment Law Journal 256, 258, 265 (1990); Pamela B. Gann, *Compensation Standard for Expropriation*, 23 Colum. J. Transnat'l L. 615, 617 (1985). The gradual emergence of this rule aims at ensuring that the amount of compensation is determined in a flexible manner, that is, taking into account the specific circumstances of each case. The prevalence of the "appropriate" compensation standard does not imply, however, that the compensation *quantum* should be always "less than full" or always "partial."

89. The Tribunal notes that the above-mentioned principles have been tested in a number of important arbitrations involving the nationalization of the oil industries of Libya and Kuwait.

90. In *TOPCO*, the sole arbitrator, Professor Dupuy, stated that "[t]he consensus by a majority of States belonging to the various representative groups indicates without the slightest doubt universal recognition of the rules . . . incorporated [in Resolution No. 1803 (XVII)], *i.e.*, with respect to nationalization and compensation the use of the rules in force in the nationalizing State, but all this in conformity with international law." *Texaco Overseas Petroleum Company and California Asiatic Oil Company v. The Government of The Libyan Arab Republic*, Award of 19 January 1977 (Dupuy, sole arb.), *reprinted in* 53 I.L.R. 389, 492 (1979) ("*TOPCO*").[14] The arbitrator went on to conclude that, given the specific circumstances of the case and, in particular, the unlawful nature of the taking, the appropriate compensation under inter-

---

(Footnote continued from p. 197)

Nationalization, expropriation or requisitioning shall be based on grounds or reasons of public utility, security or the national interest which are recognized as overriding purely individual or private interests, both domestic and foreign. In such cases the owner shall be paid appropriate compensation, in accordance with the rules in force in the State taking such measures in the exercise of its sovereignty and in accordance with international law.

[14] Professor Dupuy also considered certain later U.N. Resolutions, particularly that instrumenting the "Charter of Economic Rights and Duties of States" (Resolution 3281 (XXIX), adopted by the U.N. General Assembly on 12 December 1974). Like Resolution No. 1803 (XVII), the Charter states that "appropriate" compensation is due. Unlike Resolution No. 1803 (XVII), however, the Charter makes no reference to "international law," as a result of which the Charter was not accepted by most Western countries. On that ground, the arbitrator concluded in *TOPCO* that the "appropriate" compensation standard stated in the Charter could not be held to express a general principle of international law. *See id.* at 488, 491-93.

national law consisted of *restitutio in integrum*. *Id*. at 495-508. The arbitrator thus confirmed the view that an appropriate compensation may well be a full one.

91. In *AMINOIL*, it was held that the term "appropriate" compensation used in Resolution No. 1803 (XVII) called for a concrete interpretation, very much like related terms such as "fair," "just," "equitable," "adequate," "effective," and "prompt." The tribunal further stated that such interpretation required an inquiry "into all the circumstances relevant to the particular concrete case." *Government of Kuwait* v. *American Independent Oil Company (AMINOIL)*, Award of 24 March 1982 (Reuter, Hamed Sultan and Sir Gerald Fitzmaurice, Members), *reprinted in* 66 I.L.R. 518, 601-02 (1986), ("*AMINOIL*"). The tribunal concluded that such inquiry "does not in any way exclude a substantial indemnity." *Id*. at 602; *see also Banco Nacional de Cuba* v. *Chase Manhattan Bank*, 658 F.2d 875 (2d Cir. 1981).

92. In *LIAMCO*, the sole arbitrator, Professor Mahmassani, perceived a trend that "the rule of 'full and prior' compensation is no more imperative, and that only 'convenient and equitable' compensation is required in cases of nationalization." *Libyan American Oil Company (LIAMCO)* v. *Government of The Libyan Arab Republic*, Award of 12 April 1977 (Mahmassani, sole arb.), *reprinted in* 62 I.L.R. 140, 207 (1982) ("*LIAMCO*"). The arbitrator concluded that it is "just and reasonable to adopt the formula of 'equitable compensation' as a measure for the assessment of damages in the present dispute, with the classical formula of 'prior, adequate and effective compensation' remaining as a maximum and a practical guide for such assessment." *Id*. at 218.

93. These three awards show that the terms of the "appropriate compensation" standard or "fair compensation" standard must not be construed either to always require partial compensation or to always exclude full compensation. Regardless of the formulation of the standard, these awards reflect a consistent concern not to determine the amount of compensation rigidly, *i.e.*, without taking into account the specific circumstances of each concrete case.

94. Turning to the practice of the Tribunal, it appears that in past Awards the Tribunal has typically awarded compensation representing the full value of the expropriated property as determined by the Tribunal. In *AIG*, a case involving a lawful nationalization, the Tribunal stated explicitly that the compensation must be determined in a flexible manner in each concrete case, *i.e.*, "taking into account all relevant circumstances of the case." *AIG*, 4 IRAN-U.S. C.T.R. at 109. Also, the Tribunal rejected the respondent's argument that "modern developments in international law" required that only a "partial" compensation standard be applied. *AIG*, *Id*. at 105-106. In *Tippetts*, the Tribunal held that the claimant was entitled "under international law and general principles of law to compensation for the full value of the property of

which it was deprived." *Tippetts*, 6 IRAN-U.S. C.T.R. at 225. In *INA*, which like *AIG* involved a formal and systematic nationalization of the Iranian insurance sector, the Tribunal held that, at least as far as "large-scale nationalizations of a lawful character [are concerned], international law has undergone a gradual reappraisal, the effect of which may be to undermine the doctrinal value of any 'full' or 'adequate' (when used as identical to 'full') compensation standard." *INA*, 8 IRAN-U.S. C.T.R. at 378. The Award then determined that "international law admits compensation in an amount equal to the fair market value of the investment." *Id.* The Tribunal thus determined that the appropriate compensation in the case at issue would be the "full equivalent of the property taken." *Id.*, at 379. In his Separate Opinion to the Award in *INA* (filed 15 August 1985), Judge Lagergren considered that "'appropriate', 'equitable', 'fair' and 'just' are virtually interchangeable notions so far as standards of compensation are concerned," and that "[t]he basic thesis of 'appropriate compensation' . . . is one of inherent elasticity." Separate Opinion of Judge Lagergren in *INA Corporation* v. *The Government of the Islamic Republic of Iran*, Award No. 184-161-1 (15 August 1985), *reprinted in* 8 IRAN-U.S. C.T.R. 385, 387, 389. In *Sedco*, which like the present case involved the appointment of temporary Government managers to an Iranian company resulting in a finding that the claimant's equity interest therein had been expropriated, the Tribunal found "overwhelming . . . support" for the conclusion that in the case of a discrete expropriation (as opposed to a large-scale nationalization) of alien property, customary international law required that full compensation should be awarded for the property taken, regardless of whether the expropriation was lawful. *Sedco, Inc.* v. *National Iranian Oil Company, et al.*, Interlocutory Award No. ITL 59-129-3 (27 March 1986), *reprinted in* 10 IRAN-U.S. C.T.R. 180, at 187. *See also Sedco, Inc.* v. *National Iranian Oil Company, et al.*, Award No. 309-129-3, paras. 30-31 (7 July 1987), *reprinted in* 15 IRAN-U.S. C.T.R. 23, 34. In *Sola Tiles*, the Tribunal examined the specific nature of the "appropriate" or "fair" or "just" compensation standard which it acknowledged to be emerging in customary international law, and concluded that attempts "to invest these terms with a concrete meaning" revealed that "the distance between rhetoric and reality is narrower than might at first appear." *Sola Tiles, Inc.* v. *The Government of the Islamic Republic of Iran*, Award No. 298-317-1, para. 43 (22 April 1987), *reprinted in* 14 IRAN-U.S. C.T.R. 223, 235. Taking into account "the facts of the particular case," the Tribunal awarded full compensation for the expropriated assets as valued by the Tribunal. *Id.* at 237. Finally, the Tribunal notes that in *AMOCO* it was held that, while customary international law acknowledged that a state's sovereign right to nationalize included a general duty to compensate, "[t]he rules of customary international law relating to the determination of the nature and amount of the compensation to be paid, as well as of the conditions of its payment, are less well settled." *Amoco International Finance Corporation v. The Government of the Islamic Republic of Iran, et al.*, Partial Award No. 310-56-3, para. 117 (14 July 1987), *reprinted in* 15 IRAN-U.S. C.T.R. 189, 223 ("*Amoco*"). In that Award, the Tribunal further held that the notion of just compensation "has generally been understood as a compensation equal to the full value of the expropriated assets." *Id.* at 252.

95. Considering the scholarly opinions, arbitral practice and Tribunal precedents noted above, the Tribunal finds that once the full value of the property has been properly evaluated, the compensation to be awarded must be appropriate to reflect the pertinent facts and circumstances of each case.

96. Despite the importance of the distinction, the Tribunal need not examine here the effect of the characterization of the taking as lawful or unlawful on the available compensation. The Claimants seek compensation for *damnum emergens* only (including compensation for tangible and intangible assets and future prospects). The Claimants do not seek additional compensation for *lucrum cessans* (that is, lost profits), which claim is typically conditioned on a prior characterization of the taking as unlawful. The appropriate amount to be awarded shall therefore be determined in such a manner as to include *damnum emergens* but not *lucrum cessans*.

97. Turning to the appropriate method for valuing the property concerned, the Tribunal cannot agree with the Respondent that Gostaresh Maskan had ceased to be a going concern at the valuation date. While the record clearly shows that the Company laid-off a substantial number of employees in the months leading up to the expropriation, it also shows that at the time the first Government-appointed Director took control the Company still employed about 1,000 workers who were assigned to the Company's various construction projects, which would have produced gross revenues of approximately U.S.$190 million.[15] This allowed Mr. Parviz Shams Towfighi,

---

[15] The record includes an affidavit by Mr. Ali Ebrahimi, which was not contested by the Respondent and according to which Gostaresh Maskan was, at the time of the expropriation, involved in the following outstanding projects:
  (a) Construction of 513 residential units at SarCheshmeh for National Copper Industries;
  (b) Construction of 1,706 residential units at Bandar Shahpour for the Khuzestan Urban Development Organization ("KUDO");
  (c) Construction of 48 residential units at Tavanir for the Ministry of Water and Power;
  (d) Construction of 900 residential units at Ahwaz for the Ministry of Housing and Urban Development, Khuzestan Bureau;
  (e) Construction of 208 residential units at Ahwaz for KUDO;
  (f) Construction of 359 residential units at various locations in Ahwaz, Abadan and Andimeshk for the National Iranian Oil Company ("NIOC");
  (g) Construction of two office buildings for NIOC at Ahwaz and Abadan;
  (h) Construction of 1,262 residential units for NIOC at Isfahan;
  (i) Construction of 879 residential units for NIOC at a location to be designated in 1980; and

one of the Company's Government-appointed Directors, to state in a report to the supervising Ministry dated 12 May 1980 that Gostaresh Maskan had a "bright and promising future," provided that certain obstacles – such as the non-payment by the responsible Government agencies of the Company's price adjustment receivables – were removed. *See* para. 112 and para. 122, *infra*.

98. In regard to the valuation method, the Tribunal sees no reason to disagree with the Parties that a fair market valuation based on an asset approach is appropriate. Accordingly, the Company's value is equal to the price on which a hypothetical willing seller and a hypothetical willing buyer would agree, and that price is calculated as the sum of the replacement cost of the Company's tangible assets plus an amount reflecting its intangible values, including its goodwill, if any. This valuation model is further specified through the Terms of Reference governing the assignment of the Expert who was appointed by the Tribunal for the specific purpose of valuing Gostaresh Maskan as of 13 November 1979. *See* para. 104, *infra*.

V. VALUATION

99. The Parties' positions on the value of Gostaresh Maskan on 13 November 1979 are wide-ranging and largely contradictory.

A. *Claimants' Contentions*

100. The Claimants assert that Gostaresh Maskan was "a major construction company with significant assets and operations and with prospects for further profits and growth." They submit (i) several affidavits of their father, Mr. Ali Ebrahimi, who was the chairman of the Company's Board of Directors and one of its founders, as to the value of Gostaresh Maskan on 13 November 1979, and (ii) three valuation reports prepared by separate valuers. The information for these valuations was drawn from several sources, including Gostaresh Maskan's annual financial statements for the five years preceding the expropriation, several reports prepared by Government-appointed directors following the expropriation, a brochure which was distributed by the Company in 1980, and information included in the valuation report prepared by Noavaran, the valuation firm retained by Respondent.

101. In the opinion of Mr. Ebrahimi, who also relies on his personal knowledge of Gostaresh Maskan in valuing the Company, the Company's

(Footnote continued from p. 201)
    (j) Construction of 2,300 residential units at Parandak for the Ministry of Housing and Urban Development and the Ministry of National Defense.

value on 13 November 1979 was Rls 7,486,098,680[16] (that is, approximately, U.S.$106,412,215 million,[17] calculated on the basis of an exchange rate of Rials 70.35 per U.S. dollar). According to Mr. Mussa Siamak, whom the Claimants identify as an accountant and the former Chief Financial Officer of the Hadish Construction Company, a large Iranian construction firm, the fair market value of Gostaresh Maskan as of 13 November 1979 was Rls 5,194,339,000, or U.S.$73,835,664.[18] In the Opinion of Mr. Robert F. Reilly of Willamette Management Associates, a valuation firm retained by Claimants to comment on the Expert's valuation report, the Company's fair market value was Rls 3,984,100,000.[19] Finally, according to Mr. Fariborz Ghadar, an independent valuer who was also retained by Claimants to comment on the Expert's valuation report, the Company's value, calculated using the discounted cash flow method, ranged between Rls 3,942 million and Rls 8,322 million.

B. *Respondent's Contentions*

102. The Respondent argues that the Tribunal must reject the Claimants' valuation on the ground that it exceeds the aggregate amount requested in the Statements of Claim, thereby violating Article 18(g) and Article 20 of the Tribunal Rules.[20] Furthermore, based on its assessment of the general political, social and economic conditions prevailing in Iran at the valuation date, as well as the financial condition of Gostaresh Maskan, in particular, the Respondent has submitted its own valuation of the Company. This consists of

---

[16] This amount is composed of Rls 5,548,326,510 (representing the Company's adjusted net asset value) plus Rls 1,849,442,170 (representing the Company's goodwill, corresponding to one-third of its net worth).

[17] The aggregate claim which the Claimants indicated in their Statements of Claim was in the amount of U.S.$11,660,571.30, based on a valuation of Gostaresh Maskan at U.S.$61,371,426. In their Hearing Memorial Claimants increased their estimate of Gostaresh Maskan's value to U.S.$116,806,444, and they increased their claim accordingly. Finally, in their Rebuttal Memorial Claimants reduced the estimated value of Gostaresh Maskan to U.S.$106.4 million, and they reduced their revised claim accordingly to approximately U.S.$20,000,000.

[18] This amount is composed of Rls 3,662,593,000 (Gostaresh Maskan's net asset value) plus Rls 1,404,092,000 (goodwill).

[19] This amount includes the Company's goodwill estimated at Rls 294.9 million.

[20] Article 18 of the Tribunal Rules reads as follows, in pertinent part:
1. A party initiating recourse to arbitration before the Tribunal (the "claimant") shall do so by filing a Statement of Claim. Each Statement of Claim shall contain the following particulars:
. . .
(g) The relief or remedy sought. . . .
Article 20 of the Tribunal Rules reads as follows:
During the course of the arbitral proceedings either party may amend or supplement his claim or defence unless the arbitral tribunal considers it inappropriate to allow such amendment having regard to the delay in making it or prejudice to the other party or any other circumstances. However, a claim may not be amended in such a manner that the amended claim falls outside the jurisdiction of the arbitral tribunal.

the valuation prepared by Noavaran (the "Noavaran Report"), as expanded at the Hearing by Mr. Antony G.P. Tracey, an independent valuation expert retained by the Respondent. The Noavaran Report concludes that the value of Gostaresh Maskan, as of 13 November 1979, was negative Rls 726,104,388, or negative U.S.$10,325.34.

C. *Tribunal's Findings*

103. In regard to the Respondent's request for the rejection of the Claimants' valuation, the Tribunal refers to its Award in *Rockwell International Systems*, in which the Tribunal held:

> In exercising its discretion under Article 20 to permit amendments to claims, the Tribunal must consider whether the other party would be prejudiced by the proposed amendment, whether the other party has had an opportunity to respond to the newly-added or amended claim, and whether the proposed amendment would needlessly disrupt or delay the arbitral process. Subject to these considerations, an amendment is generally admissible if the underlying facts of a dispute, as presented in the Statement of Claim, essentially remain the basis of the dispute, and if the amendment is so closely interrelated to the initial claim that it would be contrary to judicial economy to separate the issues and litigate them separately, or possibly, in different fora.

Rockwell International Systems, Inc. v. *The Government of the Islamic Republic of Iran*, Award No. 438-430-1, para. 73 (5 September 1989), *reprinted in* 23 IRAN-U.S. C.T.R. 150, 166 ("*Rockwell*"). The Tribunal is satisfied that the Claimants' revised valuation of the Company meets the criteria laid down in *Rockwell*. Accordingly, the Respondent's request for dismissal of the valuation, and indeed of the claim, is rejected.

104. As indicated above (*see* para. 40, *supra*), by Order of 14 December 1992 the Tribunal appointed Professor Richard A. Brealey as the Tribunal Expert for the purpose of valuing Gostaresh Maskan as of 13 November 1979.[21] On 14 April 1993, the Expert submitted his valuation report (the

---

[21] The Expert's Terms of Reference are as follows, in pertinent part:
1. The Tribunal requires the assistance of the expert in determining the fair market value, as of 13 November 1979, of Gostaresh Maskan Company ("GMC"). The expert's valuation shall be made on the basis of fair market value, taking into account the tangible physical and financial assets of the undertaking and other elements, if any, including but not limited to, contractual and intellectual property rights, commercial prospects, goodwill, and likely future profitability. The effects of the very act of nationalization or effects of events that occurred subsequent to nationalization shall be excluded; however, prior changes in the general political, social, and economic conditions which might have affected GMC's business prospects as of the date it was taken shall be taken into account. *See American International Group, Inc., et al.* v. *Islamic Republic of Iran, et al.*, Award No. 93-2-3, pp. 16-21 (19 December 1983), *reprinted in* 4 IRAN-U.S. C.T.R. 96, 106-08; *Amoco International Finance Corporation* v. *The Government of the Islamic Republic of Iran, et al.*, Award No. 310-56-3, para. 264 (14 July 1987), *reprinted in* 15 IRAN-U.S. C.T.R. 189, 270.

"Original Report") in which he estimated the Company's fair market value at almost Rls 1,580 million. At the Expert Hearing, and upon review of the Parties' comments to his Report, the Expert substantially confirmed his conclusions with respect to those items on which no new information had been provided since he prepared his Report. The Expert did acknowledge, however, that his initial findings concerning those items where new or additional information was provided might have to be revisited, leading to a valuation increase or decrease as the case may be. This was the case, *inter alia*, with the valuation of the Company's interest in its subsidiary, Gostaresh Blount, as will hereafter be explained.

105. What follows are the Tribunal's findings on the critical contested issues in the valuation of Gostaresh Maskan, preceded by a brief outline of the positions of each of the Parties and the Expert.

2. For the purpose set forth above, the expert, after familiarizing itself with the documents filed by the Parties which the Tribunal, in consultation with the expert, has selected as necessary to the performance of its task, shall give its opinion as to such fair market value including:
   A. Value of fixed assets applying the appropriate index[es] and deducting actual depreciation, making such adjustments, if any, as may be appropriate in respect of (i) project expenses (vs. plant and equipment account) and (ii) allegedly fictitious transactions;
   B. Value of current assets, including but not limited to those set out below;
   C. Value of GMC's letters of credit;
   D. Value of:
      (1) accounts receivable, assuming (i) that price adjustments are applicable and, alternatively, (ii) that price adjustments are not applicable
      (2) progress payments not yet posted, including *inter alia* progress payments with respect to (i) New Town and (ii) NIOC;
   E. Value of other assets including, *inter alia*:
      (1) GE license
      (2) rights to Gypsum Mine
      (3) shares in Palayeshgar
      (4) shares in Gostaresh Blount;
   F. Value of GMC's contract backlog, taking into consideration *inter alia*:
      (1) assumptions regarding contract performance (GMC's capability, government payments)
      (2) applicability of price adjustments
      (3) status of contracts, *i.e.*, were they cancelled by 13 November 1979 or not?
   G. Value, if any, of GMC's goodwill;
   H. Effects, if any, of
      (1) doubtful debt provision
      (2) whether purchases of equipment and supplies by GMC pursuant to letters of credit were properly debited to its account by issuing banks
      (3) whether NIOC (employer supplied) materials were properly credited to NIOC
      (4) taxes applicable under Iranian law to GMC's income;
   I. Possible effect, if any such effect were deemed relevant by the Tribunal, of the Claimants' shares representing a minority interest in GMC, or the Respondent's acquisition of a controlling interest in GMC.

1. *General Political, Social and Economic Conditions*

106. The Respondent argued that in determining Gostaresh Maskan's net asset value the Expert failed to consider the prevailing social and economic conditions in Iran at the valuation date, thereby violating paragraph 1 of the Terms of Reference. The Respondent's reasoning seems to be that because of the general climate of hostility against wealthy individuals during 1979, no reasonable private purchaser would come forward and invest in a company such as Gostaresh Maskan and therefore the state of the Iranian market was such that the Company did not, and could not, have any market value.

107. The Tribunal cannot agree with this argument for the following reasons. Fair market analysis is a valuation method incorporating well-established principles of accounting and corporate finance. Its usefulness rests on the premise that like companies will be valued alike. That is, in any number of comparable cases the interaction between a hypothetical willing seller and a hypothetical willing buyer will yield a comparable result. Fair market valuation thus carries with it an inherent degree of abstract analysis. This is not to say that the "fair market" valuation of a company is conducted *in vacuo*. The Expert's Terms of Reference adequately reflected this concern as they required the Expert to perform the valuation in a manner that factored in the "prior changes in the general political, social, and economic conditions which might have affected [the Company's] business prospects as of the date it was taken." Upon review of the Expert's Report, the Tribunal is satisfied that the Expert complied with the instructions in the Terms of Reference.[22] The Tribunal further concludes that fair market valuation does not require the valuer to identify any concrete candidate buyer to substantiate his conclusions on the company's market value. To hold otherwise would mean that a company has as many fair market values as there would be more or less seriously interested buyers.[23] Moreover, it is clear that a government cannot justify non-payment (or inadequate payment) for valuable property on the ground that prospective buyers would have been lacking because of the expropriation itself or the threat thereof. Also, fair market valuation of a company is not concerned with a determination of the net worth of that company's shareholders (acting in their capacity as hypothetical sellers).[24]

---

[22] In this respect, the Tribunal notes, in particular, the Expert's analysis of the Company's goodwill and the value of its outstanding contracts. *See* para. 155 and para. 159, *infra*.

[23] It also means that the contention that there was no interested buyer for the assets concerned in a particular jurisdiction – *e.g.*, for the sole reason that the disclosure of such interest would expose such a buyer to the sweeping forces of a revolutionary movement – would be sufficient to justify the conclusion that the "fair market value" of those assets was nil.

[24] The Tribunal takes note of the Respondent's position that it was hazardous for any individual investor to enter into a large stock transaction due to the prevailing climate of hostility against any signs of affluence in Iran during at least the first months following the Islamic

This concern was reflected in the Terms of Reference's explicit requirement that the Expert value the Company itself.[25] The Tribunal finds that in this regard too the Expert complied with the Terms of Reference.

2. Price Adjustment Receivables

108. The Claimants argued that at the time of the taking, Gostaresh Maskan had outstanding claims against a number of its employers for the indexation of the nominal contract prices. These so-called price adjustment receivables ("PARs") were claimed with respect to seven construction contracts, which are referred to as: (i) New Town; (ii) Ahwaz 900; (iii) Palayeshgar; (iv) Parandak; (v) Akhgar-Gostaresh; (vi) Sarcheshmeh; and (vii) NIOC.

109. The Claimants calculated the net value of these PARs as Rls 2,342 million, whereas the Respondent valued them at Rls 824 million. Each of these valuations included an amount of almost Rls 1,554 million, net of taxes, in respect of Sarcheshmeh and NIOC, on which the Parties agreed. The Claimants sought to increase this amount by Rls 788 million (*i.e.*, Rls [2,342-1,554] million), whereas the Respondent sought to reduce it by Rls 730 million (*i.e.*, Rls [1,554-824] million). Much of the debate concerned the PARs in respect of the New Town contract, which did not contain a price adjustment clause. Of the Rls 788 million identified by the Claimants, Rls 454 million relates to the New Town contract. Relying on the same contract, the Respondent sought to reduce the aggregate value of the PARs by Rls 673 million.

110. The discussion over Gostaresh Maskan's PARs concerns three issues: (i) the legal basis for these PARs; (ii) the effect on these PARs of a possible cancellation of the underlying contracts and of any defective work claims with respect thereto; and (iii) the application of a discount, if any, to the face value of these PARs.

111. (1) *Expert's Report*. In his Report, the Expert valued these PARS at Rls 1,885 million.[26] That is, he added Rls 331 million to the value of the non-contested PARs (which were equal to Rls 1,554 million). This was his

---

Revolution. The Tribunal understands that such non-business considerations on the part of potential buyers might have made it more difficult for the shareholders in Gostaresh Maskan to sell their shares, assuming they had wanted to do so, thereby affecting their net worth. Such difficulties for the hypothetical seller are not determinative for the value of the company itself, however.

[25] *See* Terms of Reference, para. 1 ("The Tribunal requires the assistance of the expert in determining the fair market value, as of 13 November 1979, of *Gostaresh Maskan Company* ("GMC")") (*emphasis added*); the same paragraph also refers to "prior changes . . . which might have affected *GMC's* business prospects." *Id.* (*emphasis added*).

[26] *Report* paras. 12, 38, and 62.

estimated value of the disputed PARs (as opposed to Rls 788 million proposed by the Claimants, or Rls -730 million proposed by the Respondent).

112. The Expert based this valuation on the following considerations:

(a) *Legal basis for PARs*. The Expert concluded that the issue of eligibility of PARs only concerned the New Town contract.[27] Absent any price adjustment clause in that contract, the Expert concluded that it was "likely that there was authority"[28] for PARs in respect of the New Town contract on the following grounds: (i) past practice (the Respondent did not contest that Gostaresh Maskan had been paid Rls 673 million for PARs prior to the taking); (ii) the absence of any Circulars that unequivocally denied Gostaresh Maskan's PARs; (iii) the testimony at the First Hearing of Mr. Meshki, Gostaresh Maskan's counsel prior to the taking; and (iv) a May 1980 report by Mr. Towfighi, one of the Government-appointed managers running Gostaresh Maskan after the taking (*see* para. 64, *supra*), suggesting that Gostaresh Maskan was entitled to these PARs.

113. (b) *Effect on PARs of contract cancellations and "defective work" claims*. The contract-cancellation issue was raised in connection with the New Town, Ahwaz 900, and Palayeshgar contracts.[29] The Respondent argued that (i) these contracts had been cancelled, albeit subsequent to the taking, pursuant to Article 46 of the Plan & Budget Organization's General Conditions of the Contract,[30] and that (ii) this cancellation had retroactive effect within the

---

[27] *Id.* para. 42.
[28] *Id.* para. 45.
[29] *Id.* para. 47.
[30] Article 46 reads as follows, in pertinent part:

The employer may terminate the contract in the following cases:
(A) Where the contractor has caused the following cases of delay:
   (1) Delay in equipping and getting the work site ready for work in excess of half the period set forth under Paragraph (1) of Article 4 of the Contract;
   (2) Delay in beginning the implemental operations in excess of one-tenth the period set forth under Paragraph (2) of Article 6 of the Contract;
   (3) Delay in completing any of the works envisaged in the detailed implementation schedule in excess of half the period set forth under that schedule for the completion of that work in the light of the provisions of Article 31; and,
(B) Letting the work site remain unsupervised or closing down the work for over 15 days without the employer's permission or in the absence of any force majeure as provided under Article 43;
***
(D) Contractor's financial or technical incapacity to complete the works according to schedule as evaluated by the supervisory body;
***
(G) Non-performance of any of the provisions of the contract or non-compliance with the instructions of the supervisory body as regards correcting flaws or revising or amending flawed work within the time frame determined for the contractor. In such a case, the employer shall personally make good the flaws and defects on one occasion in any manner he deems expedient and shall withhold from the contractor's dues the total costs such [as

meaning of the Plan & Budget Organization's Circular of 16 October 1976.[31] Consequently, the Respondent argued that any PARs that the Claimants could have claimed in respect of these underlying contracts had been cancelled. Furthermore, the Respondent claimed a refund of approximately Rls 730 million in PARs payments which had already been made under the New Town and Ahwaz 900 (but not the Palayeshgar) contracts.[32] The Claimants argued that the New Town contract had *never* been terminated.[33] They further argued that, at any rate, the termination of any of Gostaresh Maskan's contracts subsequent to the taking was irrelevant for the purpose of valuing the Company as of 13 November 1979. The Expert noted that these three contracts appeared to have been terminated between August 1980 and April 1982 (as claimed by the Respondent) but concluded that such post-taking termination of the contracts would not operate retroactively so as to affect the PARs in respect thereof. Furthermore, the Expert found that "the documentary evidence does not indicate an accumulation of serious complaints which would have led a prospective purchaser in November 1979 to believe that cancellation of the contracts under Article 46 was likely, let alone certain."[34]

114. The "defective work" issue was raised, in particular, in connection with the Akhgar-Gostaresh and Parandak contracts, neither of which was formally cancelled. The Respondent argued that Gostaresh Maskan's inadequate performance of these contracts excluded any PARs in respect thereof. The Expert saw no conclusive evidence of any default by Gostaresh Maskan under any of these contracts that, in his judgment, could justify the non-payment of PARs in respect thereof.

115. (c) *Expert's conclusion.* In his Report, the Expert concluded that there was a legal basis for all PARs and he rejected any suggestion that these PARs would have been invalidated through the cancellation or the inadequate performance of the underlying contracts. He further concluded that the above-mentioned contract cancellations and the "defective work" claims were not foreseeable as of the valuation date. He also pointed out, however, that (i) there was a "non-zero probability of subsequent cancellation" of the contracts, and (ii) the PARs "were liable to be paid only with delay."[35] Accordingly, the

---

are] incurred along with fifteen percent of the first payment to the contractor. In case of repetition of the case set forth here, the contract shall be terminated.

[31] The Circular of 16 October 1976 states in pertinent part that "[t]he Contracts which are cancelled in [the] course of execution by the employer on the basis of Article 46 of the General Condition[s] of the Contract shall not be covered by the adjustment regulations."

[32] *Report* para. 49.
[33] *Id.* para. 52.
[34] *Id.* para. 61.
[35] *Id.* para. 62.

Expert concluded that these PARs should be discounted on the ground that (i) they might have been a subject of further disputes, and (ii) their payment might have been delayed. He indicated that he had applied a discount of 35% to the PARs in respect of the New Town contract,[36] and a discount of 25% to the other disputed PARs. Thus, the Expert arrived at a total value for all the disputed PARs of Rls 363.7 million before tax.[37] This amount includes: (i) PARs in respect of the New Town contract, valued at Rls 88.2 million,[38] and (ii) the other disputed PARs, valued at Rls 275.5 million.[39] Adding the after tax amount of Rls 331.3 million to that of the non-disputed PARs (in the net amount of Rls 1,554 million), he concluded that the aggregate net value of Gostaresh Maskan's PARs was, approximately, Rls 1,885 million.

116. (2) *Expert Hearing.* Upon review of the Parties' comments on his Report, the Expert acknowledged that the Parandak PARs had to be considered in the context of the valuation of Gostaresh Blount. Accordingly, these PARs were no longer included in the aggregate amount of Gostaresh Maskan's PARs. On the other hand, the Expert recognized additional PARs in respect of the Ahwaz 900 and NIOC contracts in the amount of Rls 128 million.[40] Furthermore, the Expert revisited his original estimate as follows.

117. (a) *Legal basis for PARs.* The Expert addressed three issues that were not discussed in his Report. First, he considered the Circulars of 24 June 1979 and 29 August 1977 which the Respondent had attached to its Comments on the Expert's Report. Second, he considered the statement made by Mr. Ali Ebrahimi during the Expert Hearing that the legal basis for Gostaresh Maskan's PARs in respect of the New Town contract was a "supplemental agreement" between the "contractors' association" (representing, *inter alia*, Gostaresh Maskan) and Khuzestan Urban Development Organization ("KUDO," Gostaresh Maskan's employer under the New Town contract), and that the only relevant Circular was that of 28 August 1979 (but only in that it contained the inflation indices used for the calculation of the

---

[36] *Id.* The Tribunal notes that in his calculation of the value of the New Town PARs the Expert actually applied a larger discount. *See* note 38, para. 120 and note 61, *infra*.

[37] *Id.* This amount corresponds to an amount of Rls 331.3 million after deduction of 8.9% tax. The Tribunal understands this tax rate to reflect the cumulative effect of a 5.5% contractor's tax, a 3.2% social security contribution, and a 0.2% training fund contribution.

[38] This amount was calculated as follows: The Expert assumed that there was a 2/3 probability that the claimed New Town PARs would be paid and a 1/3 probability that the amounts already received would have to be repaid. He thus estimated the Company's expected cash flow at [Rls 498 million x 2/3] + [Rls -673 million x 1/3] = + Rls 108 million. He then determined the net present value of this cash flow expected during the following year (applying a 20% discount rate) at Rls 88.2 million. *See Report*, para. 62; *Expert Hearing Transcript*, at 18-19.

[39] The amount of Rls 275.5 million still included the PARs in respect of the Parandak project. *See* para. 138, *infra*.

[40] *Expert Hearing Transcript* at 434.

adjustments).[41] Third, the Expert considered the meaning of the Persian word "*maghtoo*" which had been handwritten on the New Town contract at the time of signing and which was discussed by the Respondent in its Comments to the Expert's Report.[42]

118. The Expert found that neither the June 1979 Circular nor the August 1977 Circular (as commented upon by the Parties during the Expert Hearing), nor Mr. Ebrahimi's testimony,[43] nor the discussion on the "*maghtoo*" addition required him to modify his earlier conclusions. The Expert concluded, in particular with respect to the New Town PARs, that he would "continue to place a fairly heavy emphasis on the regularity with which those payments have been made."[44] He also reiterated his opinion that some discount had to be applied to the Company's PARs.

119. (b) *Cancellation and "defective work" claims*. The Expert confirmed his view that "an important issue concerns the extent to which cancellation could have been foreseen," given his finding that "[c]ancellation, when or if it occurred, was clearly after the date of taking."[45] The Expert stated that whereas "there does not appear to have been an accumulation of complaints leading up to the date of taking that would suggest that cancellation would have been regarded as certain or even probable at that date," the extent to which cancellations could have been foreseen "clearly remains an open issue."[46]

120. (c) *Discount*. The Expert appeared to acknowledge that the discounts that he had applied in his original Report (aimed at reflecting possible disputes and delays in payment and equal to at least 35% for PARs in respect of the New Town contract[47] and 25% for PARs in respect of the other contracts) might not be appropriate in an expropriation context such as that under review, in which the acquiror of the Company was also the debtor on the Company's receivables.

121. (3) *Tribunal's Findings*. The Tribunal's findings are as follows.

122. (a) *Legal basis for PARs*. Throughout the proceedings the Tribunal was provided with various data on Gostaresh Maskan's claimed entitlement to PARs. Reference is made, in particular, to (i) the past payments that Gostaresh Maskan had received before the taking (amounting to almost Rls 673 million in the case of the New Town contract), (ii) a protocol between KUDO and the

---

[41] *Id.* at 210-213.
[42] At the Expert Hearing, the Respondent reiterated its position that the word "*maghtoo*" should be construed to mean that the contract price was "fixed" in absolute terms.
[43] *Expert Hearing Transcript* at 346-348.
[44] *Id.* at 347.
[45] *Id.* at 13.
[46] *Id.*
[47] *See* note 36 and note 38, *supra*.

constructors' syndicate (representing, *inter alia*, Gostaresh Maskan) which, at the Expert Hearing, Mr. Ali Ebrahimi contended to have been executed after the signature of the New Town contract,[48] (iii) the handwritten addition of the Persian word "*maghtoo*" to the text of the New Town contract at the time of its signature, (iv) the Circular of 28 August 1979,[49] (v) the Circular of 24 June 1979,[50] (vi) the Circular of 29 August 1977,[51] (vii) a legal opinion in support of Gostaresh Maskan's claims to PARs rendered before the taking by Mr. Meshki, Gostaresh Maskan's legal counsel, (viii) the Report to the Plan & Budget Organization of 12 May 1980 that was prepared by Mr. Towfighi, the Government-appointed managing director of Gostaresh Maskan as of 19 January 1980,[52] and (ix) the reported understanding of Mr. Boroomand, managing director of KUDO, that payments should be made on Gostaresh Maskan's PARs claims, albeit through a joint account.

123. The Tribunal finds, in agreement with the Expert, that the available information suggests that Gostaresh Maskan was indeed entitled to the payment of these PARs. In reaching its conclusions, the Tribunal has given particular weight to the uncontested fact that Gostaresh Maskan received Rls 673 million (*i.e.*, almost U.S.$10 million) in PARs payments before the taking, *i.e.*, *in tempore non suspecto*. This practice, in addition to Mr. Towfighi's explicit request to the Plan & Budget Organization to pay Gostaresh Maskan's PARs without further delay, would seem to corroborate Mr. Ali Ebrahimi's testimony on the existence of an understanding (possibly instrumented by the type of protocol which he described) entitling Gostaresh Maskan to price adjustments from its employer under the New Town contract. On the other hand, the Tribunal is not persuaded by the Respondent's argument that the term "*maghtoo*" (which it first construed to mean that "the contract value is final"

---

[48] The Tribunal was not provided with a copy of this document. Nevertheless, at the Expert Hearing, Mr. Ali Ebrahimi insisted that this understanding was the sole legal basis for GM's PARs claims in respect of the New Town contract.

[49] This Circular, which like the other cited Circulars was issued by the Plan & Budget Organization, allowed for the retroactive indexation of all contracts without an explicit indexation clause which were executed before 27 January 1974. It was silent as to contracts signed after this date, such as the New Town contract, which was signed on 4 December 1974.

[50] This Circular did not contain any explicit provisions in regard to post-1974 contracts without indexation clauses either. Its relevance is limited to the fact that it abrogated the Circular of August 1977.

[51] This is the only Circular that explicitly provided for a price adjustment in respect of post-1974 contracts without indexation clauses (in particular, Article 2 thereof). This Circular was "annulled and abrogated" by the Circular of June 1979 to the extent that it related to post-1974 contracts.

[52] In his description of the "Company's Resources," Mr. Towfighi states that "the receivables of this company to be collected from government organizations, particularly in the case of adjustment, would run up to 2,596 million Rials." The report concludes with an appeal to the Plan & Budget Organization "[t]o take urgent measures for paying the adjusted value of the contracts of this Company."

and later in the proceedings explained to mean that such value was "fixed") offers conclusive evidence that the signatory parties to the New Town contract explicitly agreed to exclude any indexation of the contract price. The Tribunal understands that the price for the New Town project quoted by Gostaresh Maskan (and subsequently accepted by KUDO) was an "all-in" price for the whole project. Accordingly, in the Tribunal's view, the term "*maghtoo*" is more likely to have been added to emphasize the parties' mutual agreement that any changes in labor costs, material costs, *etc.* would not affect the "all-in" price for this project. The Tribunal believes that such a price arrangement does not in and of itself exclude any adjustment for inflation of the nominal amount of the all-in price. In view of the above, the Tribunal shares the view of the Expert that it was likely that there was authority for the payment of the PARs.

124. (b) *Cancellation and "defective work" claims.* It is well-established Tribunal precedent that while general political, social, and economic conditions that may affect a company's business prospects as of the date of taking are to be taken into account in valuing the expropriated entity, the effects of the very act of expropriation or events that occurred subsequent to expropriation shall be excluded. *See AIG*, 4 IRAN-U.S. C.T.R. at 106. Upon proof of authority for Gostaresh Maskan's PARs, they could only be directly impaired by a (i) timely, (ii) valid, and (iii) retroactive termination of the underlying contracts. The Tribunal does not believe that any of these conditions were met in the present Case. The Tribunal notes, in respect of each of these conditions, that: (i) the termination notices were sent between August 1980 and April 1982 (*i.e.*, well after the taking); for this reason alone, the Tribunal concludes that none of these terminations had a direct impact on Gostaresh Maskan's PARs as of 13 November 1979; (ii) as regards the valid termination-requirement, assuming that the Circular of 16 October 1976 was still in effect at the relevant time, it conditioned its applicability on a finding that the contractor (*i.e.*, Gostaresh Maskan) caused delay in the performance of its contractual obligations within the meaning of Article 46 of the Plan & Budget Organization's General Conditions of the Contract; there is no convincing evidence in the record that Gostaresh Maskan defaulted on the New Town contract by causing delay or any other obstacle to the completion of the project; and (iii) as regards the retroactivity requirement, it is difficult to conceive that a service agreement such as the New Town construction contract and the PARs in respect thereof could be cancelled retroactively. Accordingly, the Tribunal agrees with the Expert in this respect and holds that the Company's contracts were not timely, validly and retroactively terminated so as to have any effect on the value of the Company's PARs or the Company's eligibility thereto. Considering whether cancellations could reasonably have been anticipated by a hypothetical

prospective buyer (*i.e.*, whether cancellations were foreseeable as of 13 November 1979), the Tribunal finds that the record does not contain any conclusive evidence that the post-taking cancellation of, and the related disputes over, any of the referenced contracts were foreseeable as of the date of the taking.[53]

125. (c) *Discount*. Having established that Gostaresh Maskan could validly record the claimed PARs in its *pro forma* balance sheet as of 13 November 1979, the Tribunal must determine whether it should carry them at face value or apply a discount. The Expert proposed to discount the disputed receivables to reflect the concerns of a prospective buyer in regard to (i) the legal basis for these PARs, and (ii) possible delays in their payment (which he estimated at about one year). The Tribunal does not believe that it is appropriate in a valuation such as the present one to discount the face value of the PARs to reflect the late payment risk. The Tribunal believes that a strict application of the hypothetical seller/buyer model clearly shows that the case in which the buyer is himself indebted to the seller raises special issues. It is difficult to imagine that the hypothetical seller would be willing to accept a discounted price for his receivables merely because the buyer (who is also the debtor under those receivables) had a poor payment record or because he would announce to the seller that he would not honor the purchased receivables.[54] The logical implication would seem to be that if such a prospective buyer had systematically defaulted on all of its debts *vis-à-vis* the prospective seller in the past, the seller would have to agree to receive nothing for his receivables.[55]

---

[53] *Report* para. 61.

[54] Such refusal to pay could also result from the prospective purchaser's refusal to recognize the existence of any debt vis-à-vis the prospective seller. It bears stressing, however, that this issue arises at a juncture in the analysis at which the valuer, *e.g.*, the Tribunal, has identified the prospective purchaser as a debtor of the prospective seller on the basis of a prior inquiry into the existence of a legal basis for the receivables concerned. "Genuine" as the prospective purchaser's denial of the existence of the receivables may be, his arguments have been considered by the valuer in his inquiry into their legal basis.

[55] It is critical, as a matter of valuation theory, that regard be had to the possible interrelationship between the prospective seller and the prospective buyer. This determination of the correct premises on which the valuation will be based is not a departure from valuation orthodoxy. It is a matter of applying the fair market valuation theory correctly. Reference is made to the following example. Assume, for instance, that the prospective seller of RevCo is willing to sell the company to a prospective buyer. RevCo's assets include a receivable for 100 currency units on a third party. Before the prospective buyer will agree to pay that receivable's face value, he will want to know what the payment record is of RevCo's debtors on that type of receivable. Thus, the prospective buyer may find out that in the past these debtors typically paid one year late. Assuming that the discount rate (including inflation) is determined at, *e.g.*, 20%, the present value of the receivable will be only 80. This is what the receivable is worth at the valuation date. This value represents the maximum price that the reasonable buyer will want to pay and the minimum that the reasonable seller will accept for RevCo's receivable.

Assuming that RevCo's receivable of 100 is not on a third party but on the prospective buyer himself, and assuming, further, that the prospective buyer was on record for paying his debts to

126. The Tribunal further concludes that when discussing the expectations of the hypothetical buyer in an expropriation context, one has reached the outer limits of the hypothetical sale fiction. The Tribunal notes that these Cases do not feature a buyer who faces uncertainty over the quality of the receivables portfolio that he intends to buy. Moreover, regard should be had to the fact that Gostaresh Maskan was expropriated. That is, the valuation of Gostaresh Maskan is made following its expropriation and not in the context of a due diligence exercise in preparation for its possible acquisition by an interested buyer.[56]

127. In view of the above, the Tribunal does not believe that a discount should be applied to reflect substantiated concerns of a purchaser who is determined to hedge the risk of default. In this respect, the Tribunal does not accept the 20% discount applied by the Expert to Gostaresh Maskan's PARs owing by the expropriating debtor.[57]

128. While the Tribunal does believe that the preponderance of the evidence supports the conclusion that the PARs claims were valid and enforceable, it also believes that the degree of vagueness that has persistently marked this issue deserves to be quantified. In this respect, the Tribunal notes that the Claimants' position as to the relevance of the three Circulars mentioned above as a legal basis for Gostaresh Maskan's PARs claims remains less than crystal clear. In spite of Mr. Ali Ebrahimi's testimony at the Expert Hearing that only the indexes to the Circular of 28 August 1979 were relevant and then only for the purpose of calculating the PARs, the Claimants themselves seemed to give

---

RevCo one year late, the question is whether the prospective buyer can still demand that the face value of the receivable be reduced from 100 to 80? Under the fair market valuation theory, he cannot. For, at the relevant point in time (that is, at the time of the negotiations between the two prospective parties), the real value of the receivable, from the viewpoint of both prospective parties, is 100. This 100 is at stake during the negotiations between the parties. At that point in time, the receivable was clearly worth 100 (and not 80) to the prospective buyer. Similarly, at that given point in time, it was worth 100 to the prospective seller and he would not be willing to accept anything less than 100 from his debtor. It should be noted that fair market valuation is only concerned with "reasonable" (that is, "rational") economic actors. It is not concerned with any motives (philanthropic or otherwise) that could inspire a seller to accept anything less than the best price for his assets.

[56] *See Amoco International Finance Corporation* v. *The Government of The Islamic Republic of Iran, et al.*, Award No. 310-56-3 (14 July 1987), *reprinted in* 15 IRAN-U.S. C.T.R. 189. In that case, the Tribunal held:

[A] nationalization cannot be equated to a normal business investment or to a transaction in a free market . . . It goes without saying that the Tribunal is not in the position of a prospective investor. Rather, the Tribunal must determine *ex post facto*, the most equitable compensation required by the applicable law for a compulsory taking, excluding any speculative factor. Its first duty is to avoid any unjust enrichment or deprivation of either Party.

Id. at 257; *see also id.* at 265.

[57] At the Second Hearing, the Expert acknowledged that the propriety of discounting a debt owed by the expropriating debtor due to the risk of non-payment was "a legal issue" on which he had "no expertise." *Expert Hearing Transcript* at 344; *see also* para. 120, *supra*.

more weight to this Circular and relied on it for the purpose of establishing a legal basis for the claims. As indicated above, however (*see* note 46, *supra*), the explicit indexation authorization indicated in this Circular only relates to contracts executed before 27 January 1974. On the other hand, the Claimants never fully explained to the Tribunal to what extent the Circular of 29 August 1977 could have been relevant as a possible legal basis for Gostaresh Maskan's PARs claims, at least with respect to work performed before the issuance of the Circular of 24 June 1979.[58] Furthermore, the Tribunal cannot but wonder about the timing of the Claimants' reference to a "supplemental agreement" as the conclusive piece of evidence in the search for legal basis for the PARs.[59] Accordingly, the Tribunal agrees with the Expert that "on the evidence presented to the Tribunal any purchaser would have had some degree of unease about these payments."[60] For these reasons, the Tribunal considers that the value of Gostaresh Maskan's PARs should be discounted.

129. The Tribunal understands that the component in the Expert's discount that reflects the "unease-factor" (as opposed to the "delay-factor," *i.e.*, the time value of money) is about 20% in the case of New Town PARs,[61]

---

[58] In this respect, the Tribunal notes that (i) the Circular of 29 August 1977 was the only Circular that explicitly envisaged the possibility of the inflation adjustment of the nominal contract value of post-27 January 1974 contracts, and (ii) the temporary status reports in connection with the New Town project (which were offered in evidence by the Respondent) show that most, if not all, of the work in respect of which PARs are claimed was performed before the relevant part of the August 1977 Circular was "annulled and abrogated" by the Circular of 24 June 1979. It is unclear to the Tribunal, assuming that the June 1979 Circular did not operate retroactively, why the August 1977 Circular was not presented by the Claimants as a less peripheral piece of evidence in support of the Company's PARs claims. The Tribunal can only speculate that this was due to the fact that an argument centered on the August 1977 Circular would have revealed an inconsistency, in each of the status reports in connection with the work performed during the relevant period, with the reference therein to the Circular of 28 August 1979.

[59] Arguably, Mr. Ali Ebrahimi had indicated that this protocol was of relevance in his testimony at the First Hearing. At the Expert Hearing, however, the same witness insisted that this protocol had always been the sole legal basis for the Company's PARs claims. The Tribunal cannot but note that Mr. Ebrahimi's firm testimony on one of the Cases' most controversial issues, in addition to and in contrast with the variety of arguments which the Claimants had developed on the same issue throughout the proceedings, also appeared to have some news value to the Claimants' counsel at the Expert Hearing. The Tribunal further notes that the record does not contain any information on any efforts that the Claimants may have undertaken to provide the Tribunal with any evidence on the existence and precise content of the referenced protocol.

[60] *Report* para. 46.

[61] The Expert did not specify this figure. However, it can be derived using two pieces of information that are known: (i) in the Expert's opinion, the appropriate inflation adjustor during 1979 was 20%; and (ii) the Expert indicated to have applied a total discount of 35% to the New Town PARs. It follows from these two figures that the percentage discount for the "unease-factor" which the Expert suggested to have applied is equal to 1 - (.65 x (1 + 0.20)) = approximately .2 (or 20%). As indicated above, however (*see* note 36 and note 38, *supra*), the "unease-factor" actually applied by the Expert in his calculation of the discounted value of the New Town PARs was in the range of 35%.

and 10% in the case of other disputed PARs.[62] The Tribunal concludes that 10% represents a reasonable discount in regard to the disputed contracts other than the New Town contract. In regard to the New Town contract, however, the Tribunal considers that the degree of unease over the solidity of the legal basis for those PARs warrants the application of a higher discount. For these PARs, the Tribunal considers it reasonable to apply a 40% discount to the amount claimed by Gostaresh Maskan and a 66% discount to the refund claimed by KUDO against the Company.[63] The discounted values of the Company's PARs are calculated as follows:

(i) New Town PARs: [Rls 498 million x 60%]-[Rls 673 million x 33%] = Rls 76.7 million before tax.[64]

(ii) Other disputed contracts:[65] Rls 233.7 million x 90% = Rls 210.3 million before tax.[66]

(iii) The Tribunal considers that no discount should be applied to the value of the non-disputed PARs. The value of the PARs in respect of the NIOC and Sarcheshmeh projects is therefore Rls [1,553.5 + 106.1][67] million = Rls 1,659.6 million after tax.

130. On the basis of the above, the Tribunal determines that Gostaresh Maskan's disputed PARs could reasonably be valued at Rls (76.7 + 210.3) million = Rls 287.0 million before tax. After deduction of 8.9% tax, Gostaresh Maskan's disputed PARs are valued at Rls 261.5 million. The aggregate after tax value of Gostaresh Maskan's PARs could thus be determined at Rls (261.5 + 1,659.6) million = Rls 1,921.1 million.

---

[62] Expert Hearing Transcript at 17-18.

[63] Based on the evidence before it, the Tribunal is inclined to believe that as of the valuation date a genuine dispute existed between the Company and KUDO over the refund of Rls 673 million.

[64] This amount corresponds to Rls 69.9 million after deduction of 8.9% tax.

[65] These PARs relate to the following contracts: (i) Palayeshgar (Rls 0.4 million); (ii) Akhgar-Gostaresh (Rls 85 million); (iii) Ahwaz 900 (Rls 136.8 million); and (iv) an additional Rls 11.5 million in respect of Ahwaz 900. The latter amount is the portion related solely to the Ahwaz 900 project of the amount of Rls 128 million in respect of work that Gostaresh Maskan performed on both the Ahwaz 900 and the NIOC projects between the close of its last full fiscal year of 1358 beginning on 20 March 1979 and its expropriation on 13 November 1979 and which the Expert at the Expert Hearing acknowledged should have been added to the Company's PARs in his original Report. Absent any precise information in the record, the Tribunal has determined the referenced portion by multiplying Rls 128 million by a factor of 0.09, which is calculated as a fraction, the numerator of which is equal to the outstanding Ahwaz 900 PARs claims as of 20 March 1979 (Rls 136.8 million), and the denominator of which is equal to the NIOC PARs claims outstanding at the same date (Rls 1,594.1 million).

These PARs do not include PARs in respect of the Parandak project, which are assessed in the context of GB's valuation (*see* para. 138, *infra*).

[66] This amount corresponds to Rls 191.6 million after deduction of 8.9% tax.

[67] The amount of Rls 106.1 million represents the portion of the amount of Rls 128 million that was determined, in the manner indicated in note 62 above, to relate to the NIOC project, with a deduction of 8.9% tax.

3. *Gostaresh Blount*

131. Gostaresh Blount ("GB"), a company organized as a private joint stock company under the laws of Iran in May 1977, was a joint venture between Gostaresh Maskan and Blount Brothers Corporation (a Delaware corporation).[68] In June 1977, Gostaresh Maskan increased its 50% participation in GB to 90%. From its formation, GB was conceived by its shareholders as a special purpose vehicle that was to contribute to the completion of the Parandak project, which its shareholders had procured two months earlier.[69] According to the Claimants, one of GB's main corporate purposes was to manage the incoming and outgoing cash flows connected with this project.

132. The Tribunal notes that the information on GB submitted to it by the Parties has been fragmentary and of only an approximative degree of precision.[70] As a result, the valuation of GB's assets and liabilities evolved significantly throughout the proceedings.

133. (1) *Expert's Report.* In his Report, the Expert did not make an independent valuation of GB on the ground that he had not been provided with any reliable information that would have allowed him to determine a reasonably substantiated net asset value of GB. Instead, the Expert considered GB's impact on Gostaresh Maskan's valuation in two ways: (i) he valued Gostaresh Maskan's 90% investment in GB at cost, *i.e.*, at Rls 18 million;[71] and (ii) he added GB's PARs in regard to the Parandak contract (*i.e.*, Rls 161.258 million) to the aggregate amount of Gostaresh Maskan's PARs at 90% (*i.e.*, Rls 145.132 million). Applying a discount of 25% to the face value of the PARs in regard to the Parandak project, he valued these PARs at, approximately, Rls 99 million after tax.[72] Thus, the inclusion of these two elements increased the after tax value of Gostaresh Maskan's assets by approximately Rls 117 million. The Expert rejected the inclusion of the future income generated by the outstanding Parandak contract (calculated at,

---

[68] *See Blount Brothers Corporation*, 3 IRAN-U.S. C.T.R. at 227.

[69] This project was initiated following the award to Gostaresh Maskan and Blount Brothers by the Ministry of Housing and Urban Development of a contract for the construction of 122 residential buildings at Parandak.

[70] Reference is made, *e.g.*, to the fact that no balance sheet for GB was produced until the Parties submitted their comments on the Expert's Report. At that time, the Respondent provided a reconstructed balance sheet for the company for the fiscal year ended 20 March 1980, and the Claimants made certain adjustments based on that balance sheet.

[71] The book value of 90% of GB's registered capital of Rls 20 million equals Rls 18 million. *See Report* paras. 107-108.

[72] This Rls 99 million corresponds to Rls 109 million before tax. *See Report* para. 38 and para. 62.

approximately, Rls 355 million), on the same ground as that discussed *infra* in connection with Gostaresh Maskan's outstanding contracts.[73]

134. (2) *Claimants' position as of the Expert Hearing.* At the Expert Hearing, the Claimants emphasized that a fair market valuation on a consolidated basis of a company and its subsidiary is not tantamount to double counting of the subsidiary's assets.[74] The Claimants then presented an adjusted balance sheet for GB based on the company's balance sheet for the fiscal year ending 20 March 1980 (as reconstructed and submitted by the Respondent in its Comments to the Expert's Report). The Claimants argued that the global assessment of all of GB's assets and liabilities (as the Respondent had demanded) showed that GB's net assets should have been valued at almost Rls 962 million. Accordingly, the Claimants argued that the net value of Gostaresh Maskan's 90% interest in GB was approximately Rls 866 million (as opposed to Rls 117 million indicated in the Expert's Report). Interestingly, the Claimants proposed to increase Gostaresh Maskan's net asset value by, approximately, Rls 251 million, rather than by Rls 749 million (*i.e.*, the excess of Rls 866 million over Rls 117 million). The Tribunal understands this position to result from the Claimants' belief (contrary to the Expert's earlier conclusions in his Report) that Gostaresh Maskan's value should also be increased by 90% of (i) the value of the outstanding Parandak contract (*i.e.*, Rls. 355 million), (ii) GB's PARs in respect of the same Parandak contract, without applying a 25% discount (*i.e.*, Rls 132 million), and (iii) the annulled debt of Gostaresh Maskan *vis-à-vis* GB (in conjunction with the simultaneous annullment of GB's receivable on Gostaresh Maskan in the corresponding amount) (*i.e.*, Rls 109 million).

135. (3) *Respondent's position as of the Expert Hearing.* The Respondent indicated that, although it considered GB's liabilities to exceed its assets, it would not object to the Expert's valuation of Gostaresh Maskan's 90% interest in GB's equity at Rls 18 million.

136. (4) *Expert's amended Report as of the Expert Hearing.* At the Expert Hearing, the Expert acknowledged that the better approach to assess the impact of GB's value on Gostaresh Maskan's valuation was to start out with a valuation of GB and then to determine the share of Gostaresh Maskan in GB's net asset value. Upon review of the revised balance sheet prepared by the Claimants, the Expert determined (i) GB's equity value at, approximately, Rls 20 million, and (ii) the discounted value of GB's PARs in respect of the Parandak project at approximately Rls 110 million.[75] The only two substan-

---

[73] *Report* paras. 116-117; *see also* para. 159, *infra*.
[74] *Expert Hearing Transcript* at 57.
[75] This amount was calculated as follows: Rls 161.258 million, minus 8.9% tax, equals Rls 146.906 million, minus 25% discount, equals Rls 110.180 million (*Expert Hearing Transcript* at 345).

tive adjustments proposed by the Claimants that he was prepared to consider were (i) the inflation adjustment of GB's fixed assets (in the amount of, approximately, Rls 251 million),[76] and (ii) the annullment of the severance pay provision (in the amount of Rls 120 million).

137. (5) *Tribunal's Findings.* What follows are the Tribunal's findings on the critical items of GB's balance sheet.

138. (a) *Parandak PARs.* This issue concerns the proposed inclusion in GB's asset base of approximately Rls 161 million for PARs in connection with the Parandak project.

139. As indicated above (*see* para. 133, *supra*), the Expert determined GB's PARs in respect of the Parandak contract, after tax and discounted at 25%, at approximately Rls 110 million.

140. The Tribunal considers that the Claimants have come a long way towards demonstrating GB's entitlement to PARs in respect of the Parandak project. As indicated above, however, the Tribunal considers that these PARs must not be valued at face value. *See* paras. 128-129, *supra*. The Tribunal is not convinced that the applicable discount should be so important as to reduce the value of these receivables by one-fourth as the Expert suggested. The Tribunal determines that a discount of 10% would be more appropriate. Accordingly, the value of these PARs is determined at Rls 145.1 million before tax.

141. (b) *Value of the Outstanding Parandak Contract.* On this issue, the Expert reiterated his position that the inclusion of any value attributable to this outstanding contract over and above the value of the fixed assets necessary to complete it involved double counting, absent any evidence of an extraordinary yield.

142. As explained below in regard to the value of Gostaresh Maskan's contracts, the Tribunal agrees with the Expert on this point. *See* para. 160, *infra*. Accordingly, the Tribunal does not recognize any value for the outstanding Parandak contract.

143. (c) *Revaluation of Fixed Assets.* The Claimants proposed to adjust the book value of GB's fixed assets by analogy to the adjustment of the book value of Gostaresh Maskan's fixed assets. Thus, using the depreciation tables and price indices that the Expert used for Gostaresh Maskan's valuation, the Claimants proposed to write up GB's fixed assets by almost Rls 280 million, from Rls 154.3 million to Rls 433.2 million. At the Expert Hearing, the Respondent argued that such an adjustment grossly overstated the fixed assets' "current" value as of 13 November 1979.

144. The Expert acknowledged that the Claimants' adjustment of the

---

[76] 90% of the adjustment of Rls 278.925 million is equal to Rls 251.033 million.

fixed assets was appropriate as a matter of principle. He did not take a position on the accuracy of the calculations performed by the Claimants.

145. The Tribunal agrees with the Parties and the Expert that the book value of GB's fixed assets must be adjusted. Unlike the Respondent, the Claimants provided the Tribunal with a specific estimate of this adjustment. The Tribunal notes, however, that the Claimants' explanation of this estimate and the supporting documentation is minimal. The record does not include accurate information either on the types of assets that GB purchased, or on the date and cost of any of these purchases. The most pertinent information available in this regard is set forth in (i) a balance sheet for GB for the fiscal year ended 20 March 1978 (a document that was submitted in *Blount Brothers*, but not in these Cases), and (ii) the above-mentioned balance sheet for GB for the fiscal year ended 20 March 1980. What is certain, however, is that GB was organized four years after Gostaresh Maskan. This fact alone strongly suggests that the Claimants' calculation of GB's assets adjustment by analogy to that of Gostaresh Maskan is unlikely to justify a proportional adjustment.[77] It also suggests that the discrepancy between the book value and the adjusted value of GB's fixed assets is unlikely to be as significant as in the case of Gostaresh Maskan.[78] In the Tribunal's view, the fact that all of GB's fixed asset purchases were effected much closer to the valuation date than Gostaresh Maskan's has two consequences: (i) depreciation is unlikely to be an important factor in the calculation of the appropriate adjustment of the assets;[79] accordingly, the impact of depreciation on the value of GB's fixed assets may be ignored without creating any material distortions; and (ii) the inflation adjustment is likely to be significantly smaller than that proposed by the Claimants.

---

[77] The Tribunal notes that the Claimants' reasoning by analogy is flawed at least in the following respects:
  (i) GB's asset acquisition was not implemented in parallel with that of Gostaresh Maskan. It appears, based on the Expert's Report, that by 1978, Gostaresh Maskan (which was organized in 1973) had purchased 75% of its fixed assets (recorded as of 13 November 1979) whereas GB (which was organized in 1977) was only about to start acquiring its first fixed assets. Thus, unlike Gostaresh Maskan's fixed assets, GB's fixed assets appear to have been only one year old on average as of 13 November 1979;
  (ii) GB appears to have started writing off its fixed assets as of fiscal year 1979, whereas Gostaresh Maskan had been writing off its fixed assets since 1975. Consequently, GB's fixed assets were much less depreciated than those of Gostaresh Maskan as of the valuation date, regardless of the applicable depreciation rate; and
  (iii) the relevant depreciation rates for GB's fixed assets cannot simply be copied from Gostaresh Maskan's valuation model since no accurate information appears to be available regarding the type of assets involved.

[78] *See Report* para. 90.

[79] As indicated above, the Tribunal does not believe that, given its limited information on the nature of GB's asset base, it can reconstruct the relevant depreciation schedules with a sufficient degree of comfort as to their accuracy.

146. For these reasons, a more appropriate manner to calculate a realistic adjustment, based on the best information available, is as follows:

(i) *Balance sheet for the fiscal year ended 20 March 1978.* This balance sheet shows (i) under "Properties," an amount of Rls 66,611,052 (including almost Rls 65 million of equipment), and (ii) under "Initial pre-use costs" (*i.e.*, capitalized expenditures), an amount of Rls 59,457,390.[80] The total amount of these assets is thus Rls 126,068,442. Assuming that GB's fixed assets consisted mainly of equipment, reference can be made to the specific price index ratio that was applied by the Expert in his Report for the purpose of adjusting the book value of Gostaresh Maskan's machinery and equipment.[81] The specific price index ratio corresponds to an adjustment factor of 1.351 for assets acquired during the 1977 calendar year and of 1.210 for assets acquired during the 1978 calendar year. Assuming that GB acquired two-thirds of its fixed assets during calendar year 1977, and the remaining one-third during calendar year 1978,[82] the inflation adjustment would be calculated as follows:

(a) In regard to 1977: Rls 126 million x 2/3 = Rls 84 million; Rls 84 million x 1.351 = Rls 113.5 million (representing an adjustment of Rls 29.5 million); and

(b) In regard to 1978: Rls 126 million x 1/3 = Rls 42 million; Rls 42 million x 1.210 = Rls 50.8 million (representing an adjustment of Rls 8.8 million).

(ii) *Balance sheet for the fiscal year ended 20 March 1980.*[83] This balance sheet shows fixed assets (net of cumulative depreciation)[84] of Rls 154,359,358. The Tribunal has assumed that the additional assets purchased during fiscal year 1979 and the relevant part of fiscal year 1980 amounted to approximately Rls 154.4 million - Rls 126.1 million = Rls 28.3 million. Assuming further a weighted specific index ratio of

---

[80] To the best of the Tribunal's knowledge, no further information is available on the treatment of the capitalized expenditures item during the subsequent fiscal years.

[81] *Report* para. 90.

[82] This assumption reflects the statistical probability that there was a two-to-one chance that GB acquired all of the assets concerned during calendar year 1977 rather than during calendar year 1978 (taking into account that GB could use the last six months of 1977 and only the first three months of 1978 to purchase the referenced assets during its fiscal year 1978).

[83] The record does not include a balance sheet for the fiscal year ended 20 March 1979. As a result, it is unclear when and whether assets were acquired between 21 March 1978 and 20 March 1980.

[84] As indicated above, the Tribunal does not have sufficient information either to factor in depreciation (in instances where it has not been factored in) or to reconstruct the pre-depreciation values (in instances where depreciation was factored in). Therefore, the Tribunal has not attempted to add in any depreciation that was apparently recorded. As a result, the following calculations are likely to somewhat underestimate the value of the assets concerned.

1.131,[85] this Rls 28.3 million corresponds to an adjusted amount of Rls 32 million (representing an adjustment of Rls 3.7 million).

147. In view of the above, the Tribunal considers that the aggregate adjustment to the book value of GB's fixed assets can reasonably be estimated at Rls (29.5 + 8.8 + 3.7) million = Rls 42 million, rather than at almost Rls 280 million as the Claimants proposed.

148. (d) *Severance Pay Provision*. This item concerns the aggregate cost of termination indemnities in connection with anticipated lay-offs that the Respondent argued should be maintained on the liabilities side of GB's *pro forma* balance sheet. The Expert did not take a firm position in regard to this issue. However, he did note that rejection of the Respondent's proposed severance pay provision was "something that one may well wish to consider" depending on the conclusions of a legal review of the issue.[86]

149. The Tribunal notes as a preliminary matter that an inquiry into the appropriateness of this provision assumes that GB could not have terminated the employment agreements simply by giving the employees concerned a notice period. Clearly, the question of the appropriateness of this provision is one of law.

150. Absent a balance sheet of GB for the fiscal year ended 20 March 1979, the Tribunal has to reconstruct a *pro forma* balance sheet for GB as of 13 November 1979. In conformity with generally accepted accounting principles, the Tribunal concludes that it is appropriate to charge a severance pay provision against GB only if there was a substantial likelihood, as of 13 November 1979, that the company would lay off employees after that date and would have to pay termination indemnities. The Tribunal notes that it does not follow that because GB's balance sheet as of 20 March 1980 shows a provision, suggesting that there was a substantial likelihood that GB would have to pay termination indemnities at some point beyond 20 March 1980, the required substantial likelihood also existed on 13 November 1979. The record suggests that GB's situation (like that of Gostaresh Maskan) rapidly deteriorated after the taking of Gostaresh Maskan so that it could be argued that it was only as of 20 March 1980 that the Company would have expected to lay off many of its workers. The relevant date (13 November 1979) is more than four months before the closing date of the 1980 fiscal year. No accurate information was provided as to what happened to GB between 13 November 1979 and 20 March 1980. The Tribunal notes, in addition, that it is unclear

---

[85] This index ratio, referring to the 24-month period covering the fiscal years 1979 and 1980, represents a weighted average of the specific index ratios for the following calendar years: (i) 1978 (1.210 x 9/24); (ii) 1979, until 13 November 1979 (1.113 x 11/24); and (iii) 1979, as of 13 November 1979 (1.000 x 4/24).

[86] *Expert Hearing Transcript* at 346.

when exactly the balance sheet that purports to show GB's assets and liabilities as of March 1980 was prepared. Given that Gostaresh Maskan was expropriated on 13 November 1979, the uncontested fact is that it was prepared after the taking, when GB's board of directors and shareholders had been ousted. For these reasons, the provision in the March 1980 balance sheet deserves to be viewed with a critical eye.

151. On the other hand, given the Tribunal's information on the problems that Gostaresh Maskan had been facing throughout 1979, it seems very implausible that GB's operations were flourishing in November 1979 such that it was not anticipating any lay-offs at all. For these reasons, the Tribunal believes that there was a substantial likelihood on 13 November 1979 that GB would have to lay off some of its employees during the following months. In view also of the general accounting principle that a company's balance sheet should at all times reflect that company's financial condition in an accurate manner, the Tribunal believes that it is appropriate to record a severance pay provision in GB's *pro forma* balance sheet as of 13 November 1979.

152. The issue then becomes one of assessing the appropriate size of the provision. It is uncontested by the Parties that Iranian labor law provided for the payment of a termination indemnity corresponding to one month of salary (of the last year worked) for each year of service with the employer. In order to make a reasonable estimate of GB's aggregate cost, one would thus have to know (i) how many employees GB had on 13 November 1979,[87] and (ii) what the relevant salary and seniority was of each of these employees. The Tribunal notes that it was not provided with precise information on any of these questions. What was made available to the Tribunal is the outcome of a calculation made by the Claimants to show that the provision of Rls 120 million, reflecting GB's obligations as of 20 March 1980, corresponded to a termination indemnity of 16 months per year of service rather than only one month per year of service. The Tribunal considers that it was not provided with sufficient information to assess the reasonableness, let alone the accuracy, of the Claimants' calculation. In view of the above, the Tribunal deems it reasonable to retain one-half of the contested provision. Accordingly, the Tribunal concludes that the liabilities side of GB's *pro forma* balance sheet

---

[87] The Tribunal notes that it has been asserted throughout the proceedings that GB was merely a "book company" that was only to "receive and pay monies." *Report* para. 105 and para. 107; *see also Blount Brothers*, 3 IRAN-U.S. C.T.R. at 227. It is unclear, therefore, whether GB had executed any employment agreements itself, or whether it had on its payroll employees who strictly speaking had an employment agreement with the parent company, Gostaresh Maskan. In the latter case, the termination indemnity for laid-off employees would appear to have been due from Gostaresh Maskan.

should reflect a severance pay provision of Rls 60 million, rather than the Rls 120 million provision proposed by the Respondent or the elimination of such a provision proposed by the Claimants.

(e) *Taxes, non-marketability discount, discount for unaudited accounts.* The Tribunal concludes that GB's net asset value should not be reduced by any capital gains tax or by a non-marketability discount, or a discount for unaudited accounts. The Tribunal refers to its considerations and conclusions on each of these issues as indicated hereinafter in respect of Gostaresh Maskan. *See* paras. 164, 170, 173, *infra*.

153. *Conclusion on Gostaresh Blount.* Based on the balance sheet items discussed above, the Tribunal concludes that GB's assets can reasonably be estimated at Rls 982 million and its liabilities at Rls 726 million, yielding a net asset value of Rls 256 million. Accordingly, the value of Gostaresh Maskan's 90% interest in GB may reasonably be valued at Rls 230 million.

4. Goodwill

154. The Claimants argued that Gostaresh Maskan's balance sheet should show goodwill in the amount of Rls 1,404 million. In support of this estimate, the Claimants rely, *inter alia*, on several reports prepared under the supervision of the Company's Government-appointed directors following its expropriation. The Claimants further maintain that goodwill should be awarded to recognize the value created when a company has in place a management team, a trained staff, administrative and financial systems, and an established performance record. According to the Respondent, no value should be placed on Gostaresh Maskan's goodwill because, in its view, the Company was financially unstable and lacked any prospects for future profitability.

155. The Expert concluded that "'goodwill' does not arise from the fact that a firm's assets are expected to generate positive cash flows" and that "[e]quipment is likely to be worth more than its replacement cost if (and only if) the firm can use it to earn an abnormal rate of return – that is, a rate of return in excess of the cost of capital." Based upon his judgment of Gostaresh Maskan's business prospects as of 13 November 1979, the Expert concluded that Gostaresh Maskan was not in a position to expect such a return[88] and that it was therefore "likely that [Gostaresh Maskan's] equipment was worth less than its replacement cost and that the market value of [Gostaresh

---

[88] The Expert relied, in particular, on (i) labor unrest among GM's workforce (including the stoppage of activities on certain Khuzestan sites), (ii) the Company's liquidity shortage due to the non-payment of certain invoices, (iii) the departure of certain management staff (including Mr. Ali Ebrahimi, who left Iran in July 1979), (iv) the Company's pre-tax operating loss during the eight-month period ending on 13 November 1979, which was estimated at between Rls 10.1 million (by the Claimants) and Rls 918.2 million (by the Respondent), and (v) the general political and inflation-ridden economic climate in Iran as of November 1979.

Maskan's] equity would therefore stand at a discount to its current cost book value."[89] The Expert determined this discount at 13% of the estimated replacement value of Gostaresh Maskan's tangible assets (corresponding to an amount of Rls 240 million).[90]

156. *Tribunal's Findings.* The Tribunal shares the Expert's view that a goodwill analysis in respect of Gostaresh Maskan rests on a review of the Company's business prospects. At the Expert Hearing, the Parties went to great lengths to apprise the Tribunal of their respective assessments of the state of the Iranian economy by late 1979, in general, and of Gostaresh Maskan's likely business opportunities in that context, in particular. In this respect, the Tribunal notes the widely divergent "official" data that were provided to it regarding the inflation rate and the prevailing interest rates. As a result, the discount factors (reflecting the Company's cost of capital) proposed by the Parties to calculate the net present value of Gostaresh Maskan's expected future cash flows ranged between 12% and 45%. Depending on the source, the Tribunal was informed that Gostaresh Maskan had a bright future and that it was on the verge of bankruptcy.

157. Given the changes that accompanied the Islamic Revolution, the Tribunal considers it inappropriate to base its conclusions on goodwill on an extrapolation of the Company's past profitability record. The Tribunal is not convinced by the Claimants' valuation of Gostaresh Maskan's goodwill at Rls 1,404 million, which relied on such descriptions of Gostaresh Maskan as a "phenomenally profitable" company or as a company in which "all the ingredients for future success were in place" and which was "poised to capitalize on business opportunities." Rather, the Tribunal is satisfied that the Expert made an accurate assessment of the relevant information available. The Tribunal therefore considers that the Expert could reasonably find that Gostaresh Maskan's business prospects as of 13 November 1979 were such as to conclude that the market value of the Company was less than the replacement cost of its tangible assets, *i.e.*, that the Company had negative goodwill. The Tribunal further considers that the 13% discount for negative goodwill proposed by the Expert is reasonable. Accordingly, the net asset value of Gostaresh Maskan as determined hereafter (*see* para. 174, *infra*) is to be reduced by 13%.

5. *Value of Outstanding Contracts*

158. The Claimants valued Gostaresh Maskan's outstanding contracts at Rls 1,109 million, based on a 10% profit margin. This amount includes Rls

---

[89] *Report* para. 10.
[90] *Id.* para. 136.

738 million for Gostaresh Maskan's contracts, Rls 355 million for Gostaresh Maskan's 90% share in Gostaresh Blount's Parandak project, and Rls 16 million for Gostaresh Maskan's 50% share in the Palayeshgar project. The Claimants relied, in particular, on Gostaresh Maskan's historical earnings, its staff of 1,000 employees, contract backlog of over Rls 10 billion, shrinking competition and the government policy favoring the construction of residential housing. The Respondent placed no value on these contracts.[91]

159. The Expert was adamant that it was inappropriate to add the net present value of a company's profit margin on its outstanding contracts to the value of its tangible assets. The Expert indicated that "[t]o include in the valuation of [Gostaresh Maskan] both the value of the equipment and the cash flows that this equipment is likely to produce involves double counting."[92] The Expert further pointed out that "this does not imply that the existence of these contracts is irrelevant to the value of [Gostaresh Maskan], but only that the value of the contracts cannot be regarded as additional to that of the assets."[93] At the Expert Hearing, the Expert made it clear that he would not want to change "one iota" of this analysis.[94] The Expert reiterated his position that "we should add to the cost of the assets only the value of the abnormal cash flows (be they positive or negative) and not the value of the cash flows themselves."[95] And also, "[h]aving a backlog in itself . . . I do not believe is an indication of abnormal profits."[96] The Expert thus concluded that these intangibles should not be listed as an asset on the Company's balance sheet unless they represented abnormal expected cash flows (*i.e.*, expected cash flows in excess of the competitive level which is determined as the opportunity cost of capital). In view of the above, the Expert concluded that no value could be attributed to Gostaresh Maskan's contract backlog.

160. *Tribunal's Findings.* The Tribunal notes that the Expert, rather than valuing the aggregate outstanding contracts as an intangible asset in their own right (to be quantified by discounting the expected cash flows under those contracts), subsumed the valuation of these contracts under the valuation of goodwill.[97] The Tribunal agrees with the Expert that outstanding contracts can only affect a company's value (positively or negatively) to the extent that

---

[91] *Report* paras. 9, 12, 116.
[92] *Id.* para. 9.
[93] *Id.* para. 117.
[94] *Expert Hearing Transcript* at 359 and 361.
[95] *Id.* at 21.
[96] *Id.* at 363-64.
[97] The Expert explained that "[g]oodwill is composed of both the present value of any abnormal profits expected from the assets already in place and the present value of growth opportunities (*i.e.* the abnormal profits expected from investments to be made in the future)." *Report* para. 23.

they reflect an extraordinary (positive or negative) return. That is, such an intangible only has a recognizable value if the Company was found to outperform the market. The Tribunal is aware that previous Awards have considered the likely future profitability of an expropriated owner's property as an asset, the value of which was included straight into the company's net asset value.[98] As indicated above, however, the Tribunal believes the better approach to be that the net present value of the future cash flows to be generated by Gostaresh Maskan's outstanding contracts should only be added to its asset value to the extent that it exceeds the "normal" level of profits that a prudent investor would require given the opportunity cost of capital. The Tribunal remains unconvinced by the evidence proffered by the Claimants that Gostaresh Maskan's outstanding contracts would yield such an extraordinary return. For these reasons, the Tribunal concludes that Gostaresh Maskan's net asset value should not be increased with any value of the Company's outstanding contracts.

6. *Other Balance Sheet Items*

161. These items include: (i) undisputed current assets (Rls 1,071.2 million); (ii) other accounts receivable (Rls 153.7 million); (iii) miscellaneous working capital (Rls -118.5 million); (iv) Gostaresh Maskan's 50% interest in Palayeshgar (Rls 0); (v) fixed assets (Rls 997.7 million); (vi) gypsum mine lease arrangement, franchise and license rights (Rls 0); and (vii) undisputed liabilities (Rls 2,010.2 million). The Tribunal thus determines the aggregate net value of these items at Rls 93.9 million.

7. *Taxes*

162. The Respondent argued that Gostaresh Maskan's appreciated assets would be subject to a capital gains tax of up to Rls 2,650 million pursuant to Articles 46, 80, 116, 125 and 134 of the Direct Taxation Act of Iran of Esfand 1345 (the "DTA"). In addition, the Respondent asserted that a similar tax in

---

[98] In *AIG*, the Tribunal held that a fair market valuation of an expropriated company required the Tribunal also to consider that company's goodwill and "likely future profitability." The Tribunal indicated that these assets had to be valued taking into account such considerations as (i) the general political, social and economic climate in Iran prior to the taking, and (ii) the solidity of the past profits record that was used to project the estimated future cash flows (*AIG*, 4 IRAN-U.S. C.T.R. at 107-109). The Tribunal followed the same line of reasoning in, *inter alia*, *Phillips Petroleum Company Iran v. The Islamic Republic of Iran, et al.*, Award No. 425-39-2, paras. 159-164 (29 June 1989), *reprinted in* 21 IRAN-U.S. C.T.R. 79, 143-145; *Starrett Housing Corporation, et al. v. The Government of the Islamic Republic of Iran, et al.*, Award No. 314-24-1, paras. 337-338 (14 August 1987), *reprinted in* 16 IRAN-U.S. C.T.R. 112, 220-221; *Payne*, 12 IRAN-U.S. C.T.R. at 15-16. In none of these awards did the Tribunal condition a positive valuation of the outstanding contracts on a finding that the expected cash flows should be "abnormal" (that is, above the competitive level, as the Expert proposed).

the amount of Rls 152.5 million was due on the capital gains that allegedly accrued on the Claimants' participation in Gostaresh Maskan pursuant to the DTA's provisions on the taxation of gains arising from the disposal of shares (in particular, Articles 46, 57, 80, 116, 134 and 166 thereof). The Claimants denied that any of these taxes could validly be factored into the valuation of Gostaresh Maskan and the Claimants' interest therein.

163. The Terms of Reference instructed the Expert to consider the "[e]ffects, if any, of . . . taxes applicable under Iranian law to GMC's income."[99] In his Report, the Expert duly considered the effect of Gostaresh Maskan's estimated income taxes on the Company's net asset value. At the Expert Hearing, the Expert confirmed that he considered it inappropriate to factor in any additional tax such as a capital gains tax on any of Gostaresh Maskan's appreciated properties.

164. *Tribunal's Findings.* The assessment of a capital gains tax on Gostaresh Maskan's appreciated properties as of the valuation date assumes that one could equate the hypothetical sale of the Company with an actual transaction set in a tax jurisdiction that provides for such a tax. Regardless of whether fair market valuation theory in general, or the valuer's terms of reference in any particular case, allow for such an equation, the Tribunal notes that, as a matter of Iranian law, the mere recording of the appreciated value of an asset in the Company's *pro forma* balance sheet would not appear to trigger any sort of capital gains tax on the incremental value. Absent any taxable event within the meaning of Iranian tax law, the assessment of a capital gains tax would constitute a violation of fundamental principles of Iranian tax law. The Tribunal further understands that Iran, like most – if not all – of the world's jurisdictions honors the maxim that taxes (*i.e.*, the definition of the taxable persons, the taxable mass, the taxable event, the amount of the tax, and tax procedures) are the product of rules and regulations rather than of equity considerations. For that reason alone, the Tribunal considers that any exercise to develop a theory offering an alternative (*i.e.*, extra-statutory) basis for the tax is bound to be unsuccessful. The Tribunal further notes that it is not called upon to issue rulings on the tax implications for the contracting parties to a transaction (hypothetical or otherwise). In this respect, the Tribunal refers to its Award in *Birnbaum*. In that Award, the Tribunal held that it "has never reduced the value of assets or the compensation due [to] a Claimant for an expropriation of such assets on the ground that it caused the Claimant to realize taxable income." *Birnbaum*, at para. 128, 29 IRAN-U.S. C.T.R. at 289. In the same Award, the Tribunal further pointed out that it "must not consider as an element of value the taking itself" and that the Tribunal's

---

[99] Paragraph H(4) of the Terms of Reference (*see* para. 104, *supra*).

"consistent practice precludes any plausible argument that the taking itself somehow triggers a tax liability." *Id.* at para. 129. In view of the above, the Tribunal rejects the Respondent's argument that the valuation of an expropriated Iranian company for the purpose of determining its former shareholders' compensation must factor in a capital gains tax on the appreciated assets. These considerations equally apply to the proposed assessment of a similar tax on the net value of the Claimants' 19% interest in Gostaresh Maskan.

8. *Minority Discount*

165. The Respondent argued that the value of the Claimants' interests in Gostaresh Maskan should be reduced applying a so-called "minority discount" of 25%. This discount, according to the Respondent, reflects the fact that the Claimants' participation in Gostaresh Maskan represented only 19% of the Company's outstanding stock. The Claimants rejected the application of any minority discount.

166. In his Report, the Expert indicated that (i) if one were to analyze this question in terms of "how much would a buyer have needed to pay to induce the minority shareholders to sell?," and (ii) if the buyer "is regarded as wishing to acquire a minority holding," then it would be proper "to make some deduction for the fact that minority shareholders are in a relatively weak position, but in my judgement a discount of about 5% would be appropriate."[100] The Expert also stated that "[i]f the purchaser is regarded as buying all the shares of [Gostaresh Maskan] (which is of course what happened), then it is not clear that the minority shareholders would not be able to extract the same price as the majority shareholder."[101] At the Expert Hearing, the Expert restated that it is a critical difference whether one intended to value "a portion or the whole company."[102] The Expert did not factor in any minority discount into his calculation of Gostaresh Maskan's net asset value.[103]

---

[100] *Report* para. 13.

[101] *Report* para. 13. The Expert further pointed out that

Mr. Trac[e]y [one of the Respondent's witnesses] clearly views the prospective purchaser as acquiring *only* a minority interest in GM. In practice of course the government of Iran acquired all the shares of the claimants. If the Tribunal regarded the purchaser as acquiring the claimants['] shares as part of the purchase of the entire company rather than as an isolated purchase, Mr. Trac[e]y's argument would not apply and I would see no reason to apply any discount. *Report* para. 143.

[102] *Expert Hearing Transcript* at 436; *see also Report*, para. 12. The Expert further stated that "the problem in recognising the possible difference between a minority and majority interest is in large measure a question of what one is trying to measure, and that is a legal rather than an economic issue." *Expert Hearing Transcript* at 32.

[103] *Id.* at 436.

167. *Tribunal's Findings.* The Terms of Reference clearly instructed the Expert to determine the net asset value of Gostaresh Maskan as a company. They did not instruct him to inquire into the value of the Claimants' 19% interest in Gostaresh Maskan on the free market. The Tribunal therefore agrees with the views of the Expert on this issue. The Tribunal also notes that it held explicitly in *Birnbaum* that a minority discount cannot properly be applied to the value of a minority participation of shareholders in an expropriated company. In that Award, the Tribunal pointed out in response to the respondent's claim for a minority discount that "Tribunal precedent does not support the Respondent's position. Just as the Tribunal has never awarded surplus value for a controlling interest, it has never discounted the value of a minority interest." *Birnbaum*, at para. 147, 29 IRAN-U.S. C.T.R. at 292. In the same Award, the Tribunal held that while there could be reasons "to justify the discount of the Claimant's share . . . in the context of a valuation in view of an actual sale of shares on the open market," these reasons were "not applicable in the context of a deprivation valuation, especially in a case like this one, where the expropriating entity not only expropriated the minority share, but the whole company." *Id.* at 146. In view of the above, the Tribunal concludes that the net value of the Claimants' participation in Gostaresh Maskan must not be reduced by application of a minority discount.

9. *Non-Marketability Discount*

168. The Respondent argued that the value of the Claimants' interest in Gostaresh Maskan's net asset value should be reduced by application of a so-called "non-marketability discount" to reflect the fact that Gostaresh Maskan was a "private" or "closed" company – *i.e.*, a corporation the shares of which were not regularly traded in the market place. Thus, a non-marketability discount was advanced to reflect the absence of a liquid market for those shares. The Claimants disputed the applicability of such a discount to the value of their shares.

169. In his Report, the Expert concluded that "the fact that the shares of [Gostaresh Maskan] were not marketable . . . does not justify applying a discount to the values estimated by either party in the case."[104] He pointed out that his valuation rested on an asset replacement cost approach rather than on a discounted cash flow approach. The Expert further stated that there was no evidence that the liquidity of a stock affected the replacement value of a company's assets. The Expert indicated that "[w]hen valuing assets, it would be foolish to suggest that every dollar of equipment acquired by a private firm

---

[104] *Report* para. 13.

is immediately worth only 80 cents."[105] At the Expert Hearing, the Expert confirmed his position that "[i]f we were to discount [Gostaresh Maskan's] expected cash flows, we would indeed wish to allow for the apparent extra return that investors required from non-marketable stocks,"[106] but that in an asset valuation model no discount should be applied.

170. *Tribunal's Findings*. The Tribunal agrees with the Expert on this issue. In addition to the Expert's reasons for rejecting a non-marketability discount, it must be borne in mind that in an expropriation context such as the present, there is no prospective buyer investing in a closed company who must be offered a discount on the offered shares' face value to reflect the illiquidity of the shares. This position has been explicitly adopted by the Tribunal in *Birnbaum*. As indicated above in regard to the minority discount, the Tribunal decided in *Birnbaum* that, while there could be reasons "to justify the discount of the Claimant's share . . . in the context of a valuation, in view of an actual sale of shares on the open market," these reasons were "not applicable in the context of a deprivation valuation." *Birnbaum*, at para. 146, 29 IRAN-U.S. C.T.R. at 292. For these reasons, the Tribunal considers that no non-marketability discount should be applied to the net value of the Claimants' participation in Gostaresh Maskan.

10. Discount For Unaudited Accounts

171. An argument also was raised that Gostaresh Maskan's net asset value should be reduced by a so-called "discount for unaudited accounts" to reflect the absence, as of the expropriation date, of any audit of Gostaresh Maskan's financial statements that could have detected recording errors therein. The Claimants took issue with this argument, asserting that the lack of audited financial statements in the record resulted solely from the Respondent's decision not to submit the financial statements in their possession. The Claimants further argued that under these circumstances the application of a discount to Gostaresh Maskan's estimated net value would operate as a penalty on them for a course of action that was completely beyond their control. The Claimants concluded that, at any rate, a 15% discount was wholly arbitrary.

172. In his Report, the Expert stated that "any purchaser would have been likely to require that the accounts should be audited and would have had some qualms buying a firm whose accounts had not been audited."[107] The Expert also pointed out that (i) "there is no presumption that [Gostaresh

---

[105] *Report* para. 142.
[106] *Expert Hearing Transcript* at 29; *see also id.* at 435-436.
[107] *Report* para. 11.

Maskan's] unaudited accounts would overstate the value of the company," and (ii) the "onus of proof is on Noavaran," since "it is difficult for the claimants to bring counter-evidence" on this matter.[108] Nevertheless, the Expert proposed to apply a discount to the value of Gostaresh Maskan's net assets "to reflect the lack of protection that would be associated with the purchase of a company with unaudited accounts."[109] The Expert determined this discount at 15%.[110] At the Expert Hearing, the Expert stated that even if it is true that errors in a company's financial statements are "equally likely to be positive as negative," "auditors have the tendency to uncover extra liabilities, rather than extra assets."[111] The Expert concluded that "if I had to do it again I would be more likely to pick a lower figure than a higher figure, but I don't think it would be substantially different and I think it would be totally wrong not to apply any discount."[112]

173. *Tribunal's Findings.* The Tribunal considers it inappropriate to apply such a discount in an expropriation context on the following grounds. First, in as much as the discount is argued to accommodate the concerns of a prospective purchaser (or of the valuer for that matter), the Tribunal believes that its *rationale* is lacking. That is, one must not equate an expropriating Government with a prudent purchaser demanding protection from hidden liabilities as a condition precedent for closing an asset or stock purchase transaction. Second, in as much as the discount, or any portion thereof, aims at quantifying any remaining uncertainties over certain specific recording errors in Gostaresh Maskan's financial statements (which the Respondent alleged to have been made), the Tribunal considers that the Respondent had ample opportunity throughout the proceedings that followed the taking of the assets concerned to substantiate its claims in regard to these alleged recording errors. Clearly, the Respondent failed to produce adequate evidence that these alleged errors had in fact been committed. For these reasons, no discount should be applied to Gostaresh Maskan's net asset value to reflect the absence of audited accounts.

11. Conclusion on Valuation

174. In view of the above, the Tribunal concludes, having fully and thoroughly considered all of the evidence and arguments submitted by both Parties as well as the views of the Expert, that the net value of Gostaresh Maskan's tangible assets can reasonably be estimated at Rls 2,245.0 million.

---

[108] *Id.* para. 11.
[109] *Id.* para. 11.
[110] *Id.* para. 139.
[111] *Expert Hearing Transcript,* at 356.
[112] *Id.* at 356.

From this figure, 13% or Rls 291.9 million must be deducted for negative goodwill. The fair market value of Gostaresh Maskan is thus estimated at Rls 1,953.1 million.

VI. CONCLUSION

A. *Compensation*

175. Based on the foregoing, the Tribunal determines that the Claimants are entitled to the aggregate amount of Rls 371.1 million as compensation for the expropriation by the Respondent of their 19% ownership interest in Gostaresh Maskan. This amount is equivalent to U.S.$5,265,697.00 converted at the exchange rate of 70.475 Rials/U.S.$1. This was the exchange rate prevailing during all of 1979. *See Petrolane, Inc., et al. v. The Government of the Islamic Republic of Iran, et al.*, Award No. 518-131-2, para. 147 (14 August 1991), *reprinted in* 27 IRAN-U.S. C.T.R. 64, 115.

B. *Interest*

176. In order to compensate the Claimants for the damages they have suffered due to delayed payment, the Tribunal considers it fair to award interest at the rate of 8.60% from the date of the expropriation, 13 November 1979.

C. *Costs*

177. In their Rebuttal Memorial, filed on 15 February 1991 (*see* para. 24, *supra*), Claimants' Counsel stated that, through 31 December 1990, Claimants had incurred (i) legal fees of U.S.$117,247 and expenses of U.S.$33,656 in connection with these proceedings, and (ii) costs of U.S.$57,000 for retaining Mr. Siamak. Claimants also estimated that an additional U.S.$50,000 in legal fees plus U.S.$20,000 in expenses would be incurred.

178. Article 38 of the Tribunal Rules defines the "costs of arbitration" as including legal fees and expenses, as well as the costs of expert advice required by the Tribunal for a particular case. In view of Article 40 of the Tribunal Rules and the criteria for the award of legal fees and expenses established by the Tribunal in *Sylvania Technical Systems, Inc. v. The Government of the Islamic Republic of Iran*, Award No. 180-64-1 (27 June 1985), *reprinted in* 8 IRAN-U.S. C.T.R. 298, 323-324, the Tribunal finds it reasonable to award to the Claimants legal fees and expenses in the amount of U.S.$50,000. With respect to the costs of expert advice, the Tribunal notes that the Claimants and the Respondent each paid to the Tribunal a deposit of 27,500 pounds sterling towards the Expert's fee, for a total deposit of 54,908.04 pounds sterling (after deduction of bank charges). The Expert's fees and related expenses totalled 42,951.16 pounds sterling, leaving a balance of 11,956.88 pounds sterling on

deposit with the Tribunal. The Claimants had put forward valuations of Rls 7,486,098,680, Rls 5,194,339,000, Rls 3,984,100,000 and an amount between Rls 3,942 million and Rls 8,322 million (*see* para. 101, *supra*). The Respondent had valued the Company at Rls -726,104,388 (*see* para. 102, *supra*). In light of these claims, it is apparent that the Expert's Report performed a service for both Parties, and the Tribunal therefore considers it reasonable that each Party bear one-half of the cost of the Expert's fees and related expenses. Accordingly, the remainder of the deposit still with the Tribunal shall be divided equally between the Parties.

VII. AWARD

179. For the foregoing reasons,

THE TRIBUNAL AWARDS AS FOLLOWS:
   a. The Respondent The Government of the Islamic Republic of Iran is obligated to pay to Shahin Shaine Ebrahimi the sum of Three Million Forty-Eight Thousand Five Hundred and Sixty-One United States dollars (U.S.$3,048,561), plus simple interest at the rate of 8.60% per annum (365-day basis) from 13 November 1979 up to and including the date on which the Escrow Agent instructs the Depository Bank to effect payment out of the Security Account.
   b. The Respondent The Government of the Islamic Republic of Iran is obligated to pay to Cecilia Radene Ebrahimi the sum of One Million One Hundred and Eight Thousand Five Hundred and Sixty-Eight United States dollars (U.S.$1,108,568), plus simple interest at the rate of 8.60% per annum (365-day basis) from 13 November 1979 up to and including the date on which the Escrow Agent instructs the Depository Bank to effect payment out of the Security Account.
   c. The Respondent The Government of the Islamic Republic of Iran is obligated to pay to Christina Tandis Ebrahimi the sum of One Million One Hundred and Eight Thousand Five Hundred and Sixty-Eight United States dollars (U.S.$1,108,568), plus simple interest at the rate of 8.60% per annum (365-day basis) from 13 November 1979 up to and including the date on which the Escrow Agent instructs the Depository Bank to effect payment out of the Security Account.
   d. The Respondent The Government of the Islamic Republic of Iran is obligated to pay to Shahin Shaine Ebrahimi, Cecilia Radene Ebrahimi and Christina Tandis Ebrahimi, jointly, the aggregate sum of Fifty Thousand United States dollars (U.S.$50,000) in respect of their costs of arbitration.

e. The above-stated obligations shall be satisfied by payment out of the Security Account established pursuant to Paragraph 7 of the Declaration of the Government of the Democratic and Popular Republic of Algeria dated 19 January 1981.
f. The Secretary-General of the Tribunal shall dispose as follows of the balance of the amounts advanced by the Parties for the fees of the Expert and presently held in a special account of the Tribunal: (i) one-half jointly to the Claimants Shahin Shaine Ebrahimi, Cecilia Radene Ebrahimi and Christina Tandis Ebrahimi, and (ii) one-half to the Respondent The Government of the Islamic Republic of Iran.

This Award is hereby submitted to the President of the Tribunal for notification to the Escrow Agent.

Separate Opinion of Richard C. Allison[1]

I. INTRODUCTION

1. I concur in the result reached in the Award in these Cases in order to form the requisite majority. As set forth herein, however, there are elements of the Award's reasoning with which I cannot agree.

2. The Award properly concludes that the Claimants are entitled to receive full compensation for their 19% interest in Gostaresh Maskan Company ("Gostaresh Maskan" or the "Company"), which was expropriated by the Government of Iran on 13 November 1979. The Award, however, arrives at this correct conclusion by reliance upon the amorphous standard of "appropriate compensation," stating that

> while international law undoubtedly sets forth an obligation to provide compensation for property taken, international law theory and practice do not support the conclusion that the "prompt, adequate and effective" standard represents the prevailing standard of compensation. . . . Rather, customary international law favors an "appropriate" compensation standard. . . . The gradual emergence of this rule aims at ensuring that the amount of compensation is determined in a flexible manner, that is, taking into account the specific circumstances of each case. The prevalence of the "appropriate" compensation standard does not imply, however, that the compensation *quantum* should be always "less than full" or always "partial."

Award at para. 88.

3. I must respectfully, but profoundly, disagree with this interpretation of the law. The Award's advocacy of an ill-defined and essentially meaningless

[1 Signed 12 October 1994; filed 12 October 1994.]

standard of "appropriate" compensation is unjustifiable and out of step with the times. In today's world where nations – great and small – have come increasingly to recognize their economic interdependence and the need to inspire confidence as the basis for their development and prosperity, a "flexible" rule[2] that looks with indifference upon the deprivation of property for less than its fair value is counterproductive and backward-looking. Moreover, in this respect the Award misreads the state of customary international law as the twenty-first century approaches.[3]

II. THE CUSTOMARY INTERNATIONAL LAW STANDARD OF COMPENSATION FOR EXPROPRIATED PROPERTY

4. Contrary to the view expressed in the Award, when a State takes the property of foreign nationals, customary international law requires the payment of full compensation representing the fair market value of the expropriated property. In order to understand the current state of international law regarding the standard of compensation, a brief review of its evolution is useful.

A. *The Pre-World War II Standard*

5. Perhaps the most celebrated decision concerning compensation for expropriations is that of the Permanent Court of International Justice in *Chorzów Factory*.[4] In that case, the Court found that Poland had breached its obligation to Germany under the 15 May 1922 Geneva Convention concerning Upper Silesia. Relying upon "international practice and in particular . . . the decisions of arbitral tribunals," it stated that unlawful takings required "[r]estitution in kind, or if this is not possible, payment of a sum corresponding to the value which a restitution in kind would bear; [and] the award, if need be, of damages for loss sustained which would not be covered by restitution in

---

[2] The word "flexible" is coupled in the Award with the phrase "taking into account the specific circumstances of each case." Award at para. 88. In one sense, of course, the compensation due for a deprivation of property always must be determined with reference to the facts and circumstances of the particular case. However, the Award seems to use the word "circumstances" in the very different sense of, *inter alia*, the political and social conditions prevailing in the nationalizing State at the time of the taking. It is this approach that I believe to be wrong in theory, wrong in practice and hopelessly at odds with Tribunal precedent.

[3] The Award focuses its discussion of the correct standard of compensation upon customary international law and appears to assume *sub silencio* that customary international law is the sole source for determining the standard of compensation before this Tribunal. This approach erroneously ignores the Treaty of Amity between the United States and Iran. *See* discussion at paragraphs 40 to 47, *infra*.

[4] *Factory at Chorzów (Ger. v. Pol.)*, 1928 P.C.I.J. (ser. A) No. 17 (13 Sept. 1928).

kind or payment in place of it."[5] In contrast, in the case of a lawful expropriation, the measure of damages was "the value of the undertaking at the moment of dispossession, plus interest to the day of payment."[6] Thus, according to the principles set forth in *Chorzów Factory*, compensation amounting to no less than "the value of the undertaking" is required whether a taking is lawful or unlawful; and when the taking is unlawful additional damages may be awarded.

6. The other leading pre-World War II case on the proper standard of compensation was the decision of the Permanent Court of Arbitration in *Norwegian Shipowners' Claims*.[7] In that case, fifteen Norwegian nationals entered into contracts with shipyards in the United States for the building of ships to be used by Norway in the First World War. After the United States declared war on Germany, it adopted emergency measures authorizing the requisitioning of these ships for use in its own war effort against Germany. Having found that Norway's property had been taken, the Tribunal noted that it was not bound by certain United States legislation, "nor by any other municipal law, in so far as these provisions restricted the right of the claimants to receive immediate and full compensation, with interest from the day on which the compensation should have been fully paid *ex aequo et bono*."[8] The Tribunal then went on to award compensation equal to "the fair market value of the claimants' property."[9]

7. Many other pre-World War II decisions by international tribunals held that a state must pay full compensation for the expropriation of private property owned by foreigners.[10] For example, the U.S.-Venezuela Mixed Claims Commission held in the *Upton Case* that "[t]he right of the State, under the stress of necessity, to appropriate private property for public use is unquestioned, but always with the corresponding obligation to make just

---

[5] *Id.* at 47.
[6] *Id.*
[7] *Norwegian Shipowners' Claims (Norway v. U.S.)*, 1 R.I.A.A. 307 (30 June 1922).
[8] *Id.* at 340.
[9] *Id.*
[10] Indeed, the requirement of full compensation for the taking of property is a principle grounded in centuries of international jurisprudence. The Jay Commission in 1794 held, in *Betsey v. Great Britain*, that the measure of damages for the unlawful seizure of cargo was the "net value of the cargo at its port of destination at such time as the vessel would probably have arrived there." *Betsey (U.S.) v. Great Britain*, Moore's Arb. 4205, 4216 (19 Nov. 1794). *See also Jones (U.S.) v. Great Britain*, Moore's Arb. 3049 (1853); *Ferrer (U.S.) v. Mexico*, Moore's Arb. 2721 (4 July 1868); *British Claims in the Spanish Zone of Morocco (Spain v. U.K.)*, 2 R.I.A.A. 615 (1 May 1925); *Goldenberg Case (Ger. v. Rom.)*, 2 R.I.A.A. 901 (27 Sept. 1928); *Hatton v. United Mexican States (U.S. v. Mexico)*, 4 R.I.A.A. 329 (26 Sept. 1928); *Melczer Mining Co. v. United Mexican States (U.S. v. Mexico)*, 4 R.I.A.A. 481 (30 Apr. 1929); *Portuguese-German Arbitration*, 2 R.I.A.A. 1035 (30 June 1930); *De Sabla v. Panama (U.S. v. Pan.)*, 6 R.I.A.A. 358 (29 June 1933); *Lena Goldfields, Ltd. v. Russia* (3 Sept. 1930), *reprinted in* 36 Cornell L.Q. 42, 51-52 (1950). *See generally* J.H. Ralston, *The Law and Procedure of International Tribunals* 250-53 (rev. ed. 1926).

compensation to the owner thereof."[11] Similarly, the U.S.-Germany Mixed Claims Commission held that Germany must "make full, adequate, and complete compensation or reparation for all losses sustained by American nationals" calculated as the "reasonable market value of the property as of the time and place of taking."[12] Indeed, I am aware of no reported decision holding that compensation should be less than full.

8. Thus, there can be little doubt that in the early part of this century and before, it was generally accepted that international law required that the deprived owner be placed in as good a position as he had previously enjoyed (*i.e.*, compensated, from the Latin *compensare*, "to counterbalance") by the return of the property itself or the payment of damages equivalent to its full value.[13] In the words of this Tribunal, "'the overwhelming practice and the prevailing legal opinion' before World War II supported the view that customary international law required compensation equivalent to the full value of the property taken."[14]

B. *Post-World War II Controversy*

9. Following World War II and in particular as a result of decolonization, the spread of communism as a political and economic ideology and the desire of nations in possession of a large part of the world's petroleum reserves to wrest control of that strategic resource from the international oil companies, the traditional legal requirement of full compensation was subjected to a sustained attack. The postwar period saw a great confrontation between the Hull doctrine's[15] standard of prompt, adequate and effective compensation

---

[11] *Upton Case (U.S. v. Venez.)*, 9 R.I.A.A. 234, 236 (1905).

[12] *Administrative Decision No. III (U.S. v. Ger.)*, 7 R.I.A.A. 64, 66 (11 Dec. 1923) (emphasis omitted).

[13] This is not to say that there were no challenges to the traditional rule. The exchange between Secretary of State Hull and the Minister of Foreign Relations of Mexico in 1938 is perhaps the most famous. In that exchange, the United States insisted that property of its nationals was protected by an international standard under which Mexico was required to pay "adequate, effective and prompt" compensation. The Mexican Minister insisted that international law required only that aliens be granted national treatment and that the time and manner of payment was governed by domestic, not international, law. *See* 3 Green H. Hackworth, *Digest of International Law* 658 (1942); *see also id.* at 655-61.

It is sometimes argued that lump sum agreements are evidence of state practice accepting compensation falling short of full value. But the International Court of Justice and this Tribunal have rejected such settlements as evidence of custom. *See Barcelona Traction, Light & Power Co., Ltd. (Belg. v. Spain)*, 1970 I.C.J. Rep. 4, 40 (5 Feb. 1970) (holding that such arrangements are *sui generis* and provide no guide in other cases); *Sedco, Inc. v. National Iranian Oil Company, et al.*, Interlocutory Award No. ITL 59-129-3 (27 Mar. 1986), *reprinted in* 10 IRAN-U.S. C.T.R. 180, 185 (hereinafter "*Sedco I*") (noting that lump sum settlement agreements can be so greatly inspired by non-judicial considerations that it is extremely difficult to draw from them conclusions as to *opinio juris*).

[14] *Sedco I*, 10 IRAN-U.S. C.T.R. at 184 (footnote omitted).

[15] *See* note 13, *supra*.

versus the less exacting standard advocated by proponents of the Calvo doctrine[16] or of the so-called New International Economic Order. The newly emergent, developing States asserted permanent sovereignty over their natural resources and questioned whether the traditional standard applied with equal force to them. While natural resources such as petroleum and hard minerals provided the focal point for their argument, it was by no means confined to foreign investments in these fields. Indeed, business and personal property of every kind came to be included within its reach. The communist countries expressed an even more fundamental disagreement, reflecting an aversion to private ownership of property and favoring state control of the means of production.[17]

10. Opponents of the traditional rule used the United Nations General Assembly as a platform for their attack. Particularly notable confrontations between the States adhering to the traditional rule, on the one hand, and the communist bloc nations joined by numerous developing countries, on the other, were to be found in the debates concerning Resolution 1803 on Permanent Sovereignty over Natural Resources,[18] the Declaration on the Establishment of a New International Economic Order[19] and the Charter of Economic Rights and Duties of States.[20] However, General Assembly resolutions (including the so-called declarations of principles) are not binding legal instruments or the expression of a law-making function of the United Nations.[21] Thus, an understanding of whether such resolutions reflect the

---

[16] *See* generally Donald R. Shea, *The Calvo Clause: A Problem of Inter-American and International Law and Diplomacy* (1955).

[17] As the United States Supreme Court stated in 1964 in *Sabbatino*:

There are few if any issues in international law today on which opinion seems to be so divided as the limitations on a State's power to expropriate the property of aliens. There is, of course, authority, in international judicial and arbitral decisions, in the expressions of national governments, and among commentators for the view that a taking is improper under international law if it is not for a public purpose, is discriminatory, or is without provision for prompt, adequate, and effective compensation. However, Communist countries . . . commonly recognize no obligation on the part of the taking country. Certain representatives of the newly independent and underdeveloped countries . . . [have] argued that the traditionally articulated standards governing expropriation of property reflect "imperialist" interests and are inappropriate to the circumstances of emergent states.

Banco Nacional de Cuba v. *Sabbatino*, 376 U.S. 398, 428 (1964) (footnotes omitted). The Court noted, however, that "[w]e do not, of course, mean to say that there is no international standard in this area; we conclude only that the matter is not meet for adjudication by domestic tribunals." *Id.* at 428 n.26.

[18] G.A. Res. 1803 (1962), *reprinted in* 57 Am. J. Int'l L. 710 (1963).

[19] G.A. Res. 3201 (1974), *reprinted in* 13 I.L.M. 715 (1974).

[20] G.A. Res. 3281 (1974), *reprinted in* 14 I.L.M. 251 (1975).

[21] *See* Gaetano Arangio-Ruiz, *The Normative Role of the General Assembly of the United Nations and the Declaration of Principles of Friendly Relations*, 137 Recueil Des Cours 419, 434-518, 730 (1972 III); Stephen M. Schwebel, *The Effect of Resolutions of the U.N. General Assembly on Customary International Law*, 73 ASIL Proc. 301, 302 (1979). Of course, certain U.N. General Assembly resolutions may be

practice of States or merely the aspirations of a certain group of States requires recourse to other sources of international law,[22] including the case law.

11. During this period there were several important oil company arbitrations, including *TOPCO* and *LIAMCO*, which related to Libyan nationalizations,[23] and *AMINOIL*, which concerned a nationalization by Kuwait. These arbitrations are of special interest here because they arose in the 1970's, a time when the forces bent on undermining the traditional rule were at the peak of their influence and of their rhetoric at the United Nations and elsewhere.[24] Moreover, these arbitrations related to petroleum concessions, the quintessential natural resource adverted to in Resolution 1803. In short, the conditions were ripe to recognize the repudiation of the traditional rule in favor of an ill-defined "flexible" standard of "appropriate" compensation dependent upon the "circumstances" of the taking.

12. No matter how one reads the holdings and *dicta* of these cases, it is clear that such a repudiation did not occur. None of them held that the traditional rule had been supplanted by a nebulous and relaxed standard of compensation in international law. In *LIAMCO*, which is perceived as the most "radical" of the awards,[25] Sole Arbitrator Mahmassani, after reviewing the General Assembly Resolutions and other sources, gave the following appraisal of the state of the law in 1977:

---

persuasive evidence of practice and *opinio juris* on customary international law and treaty interpretation. Likewise, certain General Assembly resolutions may also simply reflect the design of various developing and then-communist countries, using the forum of the General Assembly and its "one-nation-one-vote" system, to alter – not reflect – the existing international regime and create a "new" international economic order. *See Government of Kuwait* v. *American Independent Oil Company (AMINOIL)* (24 Mar. 1982), *reprinted in* 66 I.L.R. 518, 600.

[22] These sources include (1) international conventions, (2) international custom, as evidence of a general practice accepted as law, (3) general principles of law recognized by civilized nations; and as subsidiary sources, (4) judicial decisions, and (5) teachings of the most highly qualified publicists of the various nations. Statute of the International Court of Justice, Art. 38(1) (1945).

[23] The other Libyan nationalization case, *BP Exploration Company*, is not entirely relevant to the present discussion in that Sole Arbitrator Lagergren ruled that *restitutio in integrum* was not an available remedy and held that the claimant was "entitled to damages arising from the wrongful act of the Respondent, to be assessed by this Tribunal in subsequent proceedings." No discussion of the damages remedy or the standard of compensation under customary international law was presented. *BP Exploration Company (Libya) Limited* v. *Government of the Libyan Arab Republic* (10 Oct. 1973 and 1 Aug. 1974), *reprinted in* 53 I.L.R. 297, 357 (hereinafter "*BP*").

[24] The United Nations debates coincided with the drive by Middle Eastern oil-producing States to replace the old concessionary system by "participation" and finally ownership, a transition that was partly accomplished by negotiation and partly by outright nationalization. This confluence of forces lent an added impetus for a time to the advocates of a New International Economic Order; however, the ultimate success of the oil-producing States may have diminished their interest in supporting what at bottom was an attempt to lessen the respect accorded to property rights by both the traditional rule of international law and their own value systems.

[25] M.H. Mendelson, *Compensation for Expropriation: The Case Law*, 79 Amer. J. Int'l L. 414, 418 (1985).

In such [a] confused state of international law, as is evident from the foregoing precedents and authoritative opinions and declarations, it appears clearly that there is no conclusive evidence of the existence of community or uniformity in principles between the domestic law of Libya and international law concerning the determination of compensation for nationalization in lieu of specific performance, and in particular concerning the problem whether or not all or part of the loss of profits (*lucrum cessans*) should be included in that compensation in addition to the damage incurred (*damnum emergens*).[26]

Arbitrator Mahmassani, citing what he considered the "practical impossibility of enforcement . . . of the remedy of *restitutio in integrum*,"[27] applied "the formula of 'equitable compensation' as a measure for the estimation of damages in the present dispute."[28] Whatever Arbitrator Mahmassani may have meant by this term, it is surely far from the outright rejection of the traditional rule that one might have expected from the most "radical" of the leading arbitral decisions during the period when the movement for a New International Economic Order ("NIEO") was at the height of its influence. Indeed, in *LIAMCO*, Arbitrator Mahmassani went on to award the claimant damages representing what he found to be the reasonable value of the property taken.[29]

13. In *TOPCO*,[30] Sole Arbitrator Dupuy examined the force and effect of the relevant U.N. Resolutions in his discussion of the current state of international law concerning sovereignty over natural resources. He noted that Article 4 of Resolution 1803 provided that in cases of nationalization, expropriation or requisition the owner shall be paid "appropriate compensation, in accordance with the rules in force in the State taking such measures in the exercise of its sovereignty and in accordance with international law."[31] Because Resolution 1803 was supported by a majority of U.N. Member States representing various shades of opinion, it seemed to Professor Dupuy that it reflected the state of customary international law. That is, Resolution 1803 reflected the "universal recognition" of the rule that nationalizations may be

---

[26] *Libyan American Oil Company (LIAMCO)* v. *Government of the Libyan Arab Republic* (12 Apr. 1977), *reprinted in* 62 I.L.R. 141, 209 (hereinafter "*LIAMCO*").

[27] *Id.* at 200. The reluctance of Arbitrators Mahmassani (*LIAMCO*) and Lagergren (*BP*) to consider *restitutio in integrum* on the ground that it would be difficult to enforce has been vigorously criticized. *See* Robert B. von Mehren & P. Nicholas Kourides, *International Arbitrations Between States And Foreign Private Parties: The Libyan Nationalization Cases*, 75 Amer. J. Int'l L. 476, 533-45 (1981).

[28] *LIAMCO*, 62 I.L.R. at 210.

[29] *Id.* at 211-15.

[30] *Texaco Overseas Petroleum Co./California Asiatic Oil Co. (TOPCO)* v. *Government of the Libyan Arab Republic* (27 Nov. 1975), *reprinted in* 53 I.L.R. 389 (hereinafter "*TOPCO*").

[31] *Id.* at 485 (quoting Resolution 1803).

undertaken using the "rules in force in the nationalizing State, but all this in conformity with international law."[32]

14. The problem, of course, is that Resolution 1803 is subject to highly contradictory interpretations. Since the term "appropriate compensation" is modified by "in accordance with international law," the search for meaning is back where it began. The United States representative at the United Nations, for example, expressed his confidence, in supporting Resolution 1803, that Article 4's requirement of "appropriate compensation . . . in accordance with international law" would be "interpreted as meaning . . . prompt, adequate and effective compensation."[33] Thus, if Resolution 1803 reflected international law, as *TOPCO* suggests, it is only because and to the extent that it required the payment of compensation "in accordance with international law" as it then existed.

15. After concluding that Resolution 1803 represented the prevailing standard of compensation, the *TOPCO* award turned to the issue of the principles of international law concerning *restitutio in integrum*. Professor Dupuy began by quoting *Chorzów Factory*'s classic formulation that:

> [R]eparation must, as far as possible, wipe out all the consequences of the illegal act and reestablish the situation which would, in all probability, have existed if that act had not been committed. Restitution in kind, or, if this is not possible, payment of a sum corresponding to the value which a restitution in kind would bear [is required]. . . .[34]

Going on to consider other international precedents and scholarly writings, Professor Dupuy ultimately held "that *restitutio in integrum* is . . . under the principles of international law, the normal sanction for non-performance of contractual obligations and that it is inapplicable only to the extent that restoration of the *status quo ante* is impossible."[35] His award ordered *restitutio in integrum* of the expropriated oil concessions.

16. In *AMINOIL*, the arbitrators likewise considered the relevant standard of compensation under international law. They observed that Article 4 of Resolution 1803 "codifie[d] positive principles" that were "not . . . contested in the present proceedings."[36] The panel then criticized both sides in the longstanding debate on the concrete interpretation of the term "appropriate compensation," noting that

---

[32] *Id.* at 492.
[33] Stephen M. Schwebel, *The Story of the U.N.'s Declaration on Permanent Sovereignty over Natural Resources*, 49 A.B.A.J. 463, 465 (1963) (quoting U.S. representative's remarks).
[34] *TOPCO*, 53 I.L.R. at 497-98 (quoting *Chorzów Factory*, 1928 P.C.I.J. (ser. A) No. 17, at 47).
[35] *Id.* at 507-08.
[36] *Government of Kuwait v. American Independent Oil Company (AMINOIL)* (24 Mar. 1982), *reprinted in* 66 I.L.R. 518, 601 (hereinafter "*AMINOIL*").

[t]here are indeed, several tendencies, all appealing to the same principle, one of which however reduces compensation almost to the status of a symbol, and the other of which assimilates the compensation due for a legitimate take-over to that due in respect of an illegitimate one. These tendencies were in mutual opposition in the United Nations when the Resolutions following No. 1803 were voted, none of which obtained unanimous acceptance, and some of which, such as the Charter of the Economic Rights and Duties of States, have been the subject of divergent interpretations. . . . The Tribunal considers that the determination of the amount of an award of "appropriate" compensation is better carried out by means of an enquiry into all the circumstances relevant to the particular concrete case, than through abstract theoretical discussion.[37]

Thus, the *AMINOIL* tribunal deftly finessed the need to pronounce itself on the theoretical meaning of "appropriate compensation" (Hull or Calvo or NIEO) and proceeded to deal on a practical basis with the elements of value present in the claim before it. Its award concluded that, considering the expropriated undertaking as a going concern, the claimant was entitled to the depreciated replacement value of the fixed assets together with compensation for loss of future profits.[38]

17. The *LIAMCO*, *TOPCO* and *AMINOIL* awards can best be understood against the background of the political and economic struggles that were raging at the time. The arbitrators, who had cases to decide, acknowledged the existence of these struggles and proceeded to render their awards without coming down decisively upon the side of either Secretary Hull or of Colonel Ghadaffi. In retrospect, it is difficult not to see these decisions as marking time as the NIEO pendulum reached its apogee and began its return toward the values embodied in the traditional rule.

C. *The Current Standard*

18. As discussed above, the middle years of this century witnessed a fundamental clash between the developing and communist countries' call for a flexible standard of "appropriate" compensation and the Western and capital-exporting countries' continued expectation of full and fair protection of foreign investments through the principle of prompt, adequate and effective compensation. But the world moves on and so does the law. Even as the heated confrontations in the United Nations and elsewhere began to subside, an interesting thing was happening. Nations of all descriptions and degrees of development – the chief actors, subjects and creators of international law – were adopting the full compensation standard in their relations with other States.

[37] *Id.* at 601-02.
[38] *Id.* at 612-13.

19. This was principally done via a burgeoning network of bilateral investment treaties ("BITs") that incorporated – in essence and often *in haec verba* – the requirement of prompt, adequate and effective compensation.[39] As of 1991, at least 195 BITs employed a compensation formula of "prompt, adequate and effective" compensation.[40] Similarly, a 1992 survey of BITs by the World Bank noted that these bilateral investment treaties evidence a trend of "each State agree[ing] not to expropriate . . . except against adequate, prompt, and effective compensation," equivalent to "the market value of the investment expropriated."[41]

20. Moreover, in 1992 the World Bank promulgated Guidelines on the Treatment of Foreign Direct Investment ("Guidelines"). Regarding compensation for expropriations, the Guidelines provide that

> [a] State may not expropriate or otherwise take in whole or in part a foreign private investment in its territory, or take measures which have similar effects, except . . . against the payment of appropriate compensation. . . . Compensation for a specific investment taken by the State will, according to the details provided below, be deemed "appropriate" if it is adequate, effective and prompt.[42]

21. While not legally binding, these Guidelines, adopted without reserva-

---

[39] While these bilateral investment treaties may or may not, in the strictest sense, create customary international law, they must at the very least be viewed as widespread evidence of state practice.

[40] *See* Mohamed I. Khalil, *Treatment of Foreign Investment in Bilateral Investment Treaties*, 7 ICSID Rev.-For. Inv. L.J. 339, 366-69 (1992). The number of such agreements continues to increase, reflecting their growing popularity as a mechanism to promote and protect foreign investment. On 15 December 1989 the European Community and sixty-nine developing countries from Africa, the Caribbean and the Pacific signed Lomé IV, which includes a joint declaration committing the contracting parties to examine existing bilateral investment agreements with a view to the negotiation of further such agreements giving particular attention to investment protection in the event of expropriation and nationalization. *See* African, Caribbean and Pacific States – European Economic Community: Final Act, Minutes and Fourth ACP-EEC Convention of Lomé, Annex LIII (15 Dec. 1989), *reprinted in* 29 I.L.M. 783, 802 (1990).

[41] World Bank Group, I *Legal Framework for the Treatment of Foreign Investment* 50 (1992). *See also* Ibrahim F.I. Shihata, *Legal Treatment of Foreign Investment: "The World Bank Guidelines"* 52 n.12 (1993).

[42] Ibrahim F.I. Shihata, *supra* note 40, at 161 (reprinting World Bank Guidelines). Similarly, the Restatement of the Foreign Relations Law of the United States, in discussing the responsibility of states under customary international law for economic injury to foreign nationals, provides that "[a] state is responsible under international law for injury resulting from: (1) a taking by the state of the property of a national of another state that (a) is not for a public purpose, or (b) is discriminatory, or (c) is not accompanied by provision for just compensation." Under the Restatement, for compensation to be "just," it "must, in the absence of exceptional circumstances, be in an amount equivalent to the value of the property taken." *Restatement (Third) of The Foreign Relations Law of the United States* § 712 (1987). The only "exceptional circumstances" suggested by the Restatement are agrarian land reforms and requisitioning of property in time of war. Moreover, the Restatement notes that "[a] departure from the general rule on the ground of such exceptional circumstances is unwarranted if . . . the property was an enterprise taken for operation as a going concern by the state." *Id.* § 712 cmt. d. For a concise summary of the standard under customary international law, *see id.* § 712, Reporters' Notes 1-2.

tion by the Development Committee representing the entire World Bank membership of 171 countries, constitute a most recent and important source for international legal principles. The Guidelines are based on a comprehensive survey of existing legal instruments and, in the words of the General Counsel of the World Bank, "attempted to maintain throughout their provisions a balanced approach which aims at the promotion of FDI [foreign direct investment] but recognizes the legitimate interests of host countries and the difficulties confronting developing host countries in particular."[43]

22. The former Soviet Union – long the champion and chief proponent of the developing world's desire for a relaxed or non-existent standard of compensation – committed itself in 1990 to the "prompt, adequate and effective" compensation formula.[44] Moreover, by 1992 the Calvo doctrine had languished and died in Argentina, the land of its birth and for a century a leading host country advocate of a national treatment standard of compensation unencumbered by international norms.[45] Mexico, no less fiercely wedded to Calvo principles than Argentina, turned its back upon them under the progressive administration of President Carlos Salinas de Gortari.[46] It would be, I submit, counterproductive, fruitless and out of step with reality to endeavor to push back the flow of events composed of a multitude of unequivocal actions by States motivated at least by their own self-interest and, presumably, by a sense of justice.

---

[43] Ibrahim F.I. Shihata, *supra* note 40, at 151.

[44] *See* Agreement for the Promotion and Reciprocal Protection of Investments, 14 Dec. 1990, Korea-U.S.S.R., Art. 5(1), *reprinted in* 30 I.L.M. 762, 766 (1991) ("Investments of investors of either Contracting Party shall not be nationalised, expropriated or subjected to measures having effect equivalent to nationalisation or expropriation . . . except for a public purpose. The expropriation shall be carried out under due process of law, on a non-discriminatory basis and shall be accompanied by prompt, adequate and effective compensation"); *see also* Law on Foreign Investments in the Russian Soviet Federated Socialist Republic, Art. 7 (4 July 1991), *reprinted in* 31 I.L.M. 408, 410 (1992) (stating that in the event of a nationalization or requisition, the foreign investor is entitled to the payment of prompt, adequate, and effective compensation).

[45] *See* Treaty Concerning the Reciprocal Encouragement and Protection of Investment, 14 Nov. 1991, Arg.-U.S., Art. IV(1), *reprinted in* 31 I.L.M. 124, 131 (1992) ("Investments shall not be expropriated or nationalized either directly or indirectly through measures tantamount to expropriation or nationalization . . . except for a public purpose; in a non-discriminatory manner; upon payment of prompt, adequate and effective compensation. . . ."). Fully as important, Argentina agreed to the submission of investment disputes to international arbitration.

[46] *See* North American Free Trade Agreement, 8-17 Dec. 1992, Can.-Mex.-U.S., Art. 1110, *reprinted in* 32 I.L.M. 612, 641-42 (1993) ("(1) No Party may directly or indirectly nationalize or expropriate an investment of an investor of another Party in its territory or take a measure tantamount to nationalization or expropriation of such an investment . . . except: (a) for a public purpose; (b) on a non-discriminatory basis; . . . and (d) on payment of compensation in accordance with paragraphs 2 through 6. (2) Compensation shall be equivalent to the fair market value of the expropriated investment immediately before the expropriation took place ('date of expropriation'), and shall not reflect any change in value occurring because the intended expropriation had become known earlier").

23. The economic and political measures taken in this area by so many nations during recent years have been reflected in the decisions of their judicial counterparts. Not the least important of these is this Tribunal. The decisions of this body have addressed the standard of compensation often and in a variety of contexts. The result has been clear. Every case decided by this Tribunal addressing the standard of compensation under customary international law has held that the standard is full compensation and none of the cases purports to award the claimants less than the full quantum of their interest in the expropriated entity.

24. The first Tribunal decision addressing the standard of compensation under customary international law was *American International Group* ("*AIG*").[47] In *AIG*, Iran argued that "appropriate" compensation was the correct standard so that only "partial" compensation should be paid, while the claimants argued that "prompt, adequate, and effective" compensation was the standard.[48] The Tribunal found that it need not resort to the specific terms of the Treaty of Amity between Iran and the United States[49] because customary international law required the award of fair market value.[50] The Tribunal concluded that "it is a general principle of public international law that even in a case of lawful nationalization the former owner of the nationalized property is normally entitled to compensation for the value of the property taken" and held that "the valuation should be made on the basis of the fair market value of the shares . . . at the date of nationalization."[51] It further held that "the appropriate method is to value the company as a going concern, taking into account not only the net book value of its assets but also such elements as good will and likely future profitability, had the company been allowed to continue its business under its former management."[52]

25. The second decision applying customary international law was *Tippetts*.[53] In the absence of any argument by the parties regarding the relevance of the Treaty of Amity, the Tribunal applied customary international

---

[47] *American International Group, Inc., et al. v. The Islamic Republic of Iran, et al.*, Award No. 93-2-3 (19 Dec. 1983), *reprinted in* 4 IRAN-U.S. C.T.R. 96.
[48] *Id.* at 105-06.
[49] Treaty of Amity, Economic Relations, and Consular Rights between the United States of America and Iran, *signed* 15 Aug. 1955, *entered into force* 16 June 1957, 284 U.N.T.S. 93, T.I.A.S. No. 3853, 8 U.S.T. 900 (hereinafter "Treaty of Amity"). Article IV, paragraph 2 of the Treaty provides that neither Party to the Treaty shall expropriate property belonging to the other's nationals without "the prompt payment of just compensation" representing "the full equivalent of the property taken." *See* Section III, *infra*.
[50] *AIG*, 4 IRAN-U.S. C.T.R. at 109.
[51] *Id.* at 105-06.
[52] *Id.* at 106.
[53] *Tippetts, Abbett, McCarthy, Stratton v. TAMS-AFFA Consulting Engineers of Iran, et al.*, Award No. 141-7-2 (29 June 1984), *reprinted in* 6 IRAN-U.S. C.T.R. 219 (hereinafter "*Tippetts*").

law, relying upon *Chorzów Factory* and *Norwegian Shipowners' Claims* in making its determination as to the correct standard of compensation.[54] It concluded that its task was to make its best judgment as to the value of the assets and liabilities of TAMS-AFFA (the expropriated entity) as of the date of the taking. The Tribunal then determined the company's fair market value and awarded the claimant U.S.$5,594,405, representing the full value of its fifty percent interest in the company.[55] Thus, *Tippetts* stands for the proposition that customary international law requires compensation equivalent to the full value of the claimant's interest in the expropriated property.[56]

26. The Award in the instant Cases cites *INA*[57] for the proposition that "at least as far as 'large-scale nationalizations of a lawful character [are concerned], international law has undergone a gradual reappraisal, the effect of which may be to undermine the doctrinal value of any "full" or "adequate" . . . compensation standard.'" But even a casual reading of *INA* reveals that this equivocal statement is nothing more than *dictum*, inasmuch as the Tribunal in *INA* found the Treaty of Amity, and not customary international law, to be dispositive. The holding of *INA* is that where there is "a *lex specialis* in the form of the Treaty of Amity, which in principle prevails over general rules" of customary international law, the Tribunal "must therefore assume that . . . the Treaty remains binding as it is drafted."[58] *INA* then cited Article IV, paragraph 2 of the Treaty of Amity and held that "the words 'the full equivalent of the property taken' entitle[ ] the Claimant to be granted compensation equal to the fair market value of its shares . . . assessed as of the date of nationalisation."[59]

27. In *Sedco*,[60] the Tribunal principally relied on the Treaty of Amity, but also considered the applicable standard under customary international law in

---

[54] *Id.* at 225.

[55] *Id.* at 225-28.

[56] *See also Sedco I*, 10 IRAN-U.S. C.T.R. at 188 ("That international law requires full compensation in cases such as that now before us is supported by the practice of this very Tribunal").

[57] *INA Corporation* v. *The Government of the Islamic Republic of Iran*, Award No. 184-161-1 (13 Aug. 1985), *reprinted in* 8 IRAN-U.S. C.T.R. 373, 378 (hereinafter "*INA*").

[58] *Id.* at 378-79.

[59] *Id.* at 379. In a Separate Opinion in *INA*, Judge Lagergren argued that "an application of current principles of international law, as encapsulated in the 'appropriate compensation' formula, would in a case of lawful large-scale nationalisations in a state undergoing a process of radical economic restructuring normally require the 'fair market value' standard to be discounted in taking account of 'all circumstances'." *Id.* at 390. Judge Holtzmann, in his Separate Opinion, pointed out that Judge Lagergren's Separate Opinion was *obiter dictum* which, while expressing his personal view, was not an opinion of the Tribunal. *Id.* at 392. Judge Holtzmann then responded with his own assessment of customary international law and concluded that while certain arbitral tribunals may have used an "appropriate" compensation standard, they in fact had awarded full compensation. *Id.* at 393, 401.

[60] *Sedco I*, 10 IRAN-U.S. C.T.R. 180.

response to the Government of Iran's argument that the Treaty simply incorporated such customary law. The Tribunal began by noting that "although the Respondents argue otherwise, it is the Tribunal's conclusion that the overwhelming practice and the prevailing legal opinion before World War II supported the view that customary international law required compensation equivalent to the full value of the property taken."[61] As to whether this standard had been eroded since that time, the Tribunal discussed at length U.N. General Assembly Resolution 1803. The Tribunal noted that commentators on this Resolution had focused mainly on its possible impact on the issue of compensation in the context of a formal, systematic, large-scale nationalization of an entire economy, industry or natural resource. With respect to discrete expropriations, the Tribunal held that:

> Opinions both of international tribunals and of legal writers overwhelmingly support the conclusion that under customary international law in a case such as here presented – a discrete expropriation of alien property – full compensation should be awarded for the property taken. This is true whether or not the expropriation itself was otherwise lawful.[62]

The Tribunal added that, "[a]s some of these opinions are expressed in the context of large-scale nationalization cases, they should *a fortiori* weigh heavily in a case such as the one here presented."[63]

28. Turning from the opinions of scholars and other arbitral panels to Tribunal precedent, the *Sedco* award noted that the conclusion that "international law requires full compensation in cases such as that now before us is supported by the practice of this very Tribunal."[64] It further noted that, whether the case involved an unlawful expropriation of a discrete entity or the lawful, large-scale nationalization of an entire industry, "[i]n practice this Tribunal has not applied 'partial' or less than 'full' compensation in any case."[65] The Tribunal then held that the claimant "must receive compensation for the full value of its expropriated interest in SEDIRAN . . . whether viewed as an application of the Treaty of Amity or, independently, of customary international law, and regardless of whether or not the expropriation was otherwise lawful."[66]

29. In *Sola Tiles* the claimant based its claim for compensation on general

---

[61] *Id.* at 184 (internal quotations omitted).
[62] *Id.* at 187.
[63] *Id.* at 187 n.24.
[64] *Id.* at 188.
[65] *Id.* at 188 n.28. The Tribunal cited *AIG* and *INA*, both of which concerned a large-scale nationalization of the Iranian insurance industry.
[66] *Id.* at 189.

principles of customary international law, citing *Chorzów Factory*.[67] However, the Tribunal found that the Treaty of Amity "must in some way form part of the legal background against which the Tribunal decides the case" and concluded that "the same standard would be required in this case by customary law as by the direct application of the Treaty itself, obviat[ing] the need to decide whether and on what footing it applies here."[68] In discussing the terms "prompt, adequate and effective," "fair," "just," and "appropriate," the Tribunal stated that, while recent arbitral and judicial opinions, including *TOPCO, Banco Nacional de Cuba*[69] and *AMINOIL*, had employed the term "appropriate" compensation, they had regularly awarded compensation equalling the full value of the property taken.[70] The Tribunal further concluded that such tribunals, applying this standard, had awarded compensation not only for physical assets, accounts receivable and cash but also for goodwill and lost future profits where the facts of the case justified such an award.[71] The Tribunal, having found that the expropriated company at issue was not a going concern, went on to award the claimant the full value of the company's physical assets, accounts receivable and cash.[72] Thus, the holding in *Sola Tiles* is that both the Treaty of Amity and customary international law require the same result: the awarding of the full value of the claimant's interest in the expropriated entity.

30. The Tribunal case that is sometimes cited by those arguing for a less-than-full compensation standard is the Partial Award in *Amoco International Finance Corporation*.[73] *Amoco* does not, however, support that proposition. The Tribunal in *Amoco* noted that "[a]s a *lex specialis* in the relations between the two countries, the Treaty [of Amity] supersedes the *lex generalis*, namely customary international law," but added that customary international law "may be useful in order to fill in possible *lacunae* of the Treaty, to ascertain the meaning of undefined terms in its text or, more generally, to aid interpretation and implementation of its provisions."[74] Having concluded that customary international law remained relevant to the interpretation of the Treaty, the Tribunal went on to consider the applicable standard of compensation under customary international law.

---

[67] *Sola Tiles, Inc. v. The Government of the Islamic Republic of Iran*, Award No. 298-317-1 (22 Apr. 1987), *reprinted in* 14 IRAN-U.S. C.T.R. 223, 234 (hereinafter "*Sola Tiles*").
[68] *Id.*
[69] *Banco Nacional de Cuba v. Chase Manhattan Bank*, 658 F.2d 875 (2d Cir. 1981).
[70] *Sola Tiles*, 14 IRAN-U.S. C.T.R. at 236.
[71] *Id.* at 237.
[72] *Id.* at 240-42.
[73] *Amoco International Finance Corporation v. The Government of the Islamic Republic of Iran, et al.*, Partial Award No. 310-56-3 (14 July 1987), *reprinted in* 15 IRAN-U.S. C.T.R. 189 (hereinafter "*Amoco*").
[74] *Id.* at 222.

31. The *Amoco* opinion began its analysis with *Chorzów Factory*. *Amoco* interpreted *Chorzów Factory* as holding that the "compensation to be paid in [the] case of a lawful expropriation (or of a taking which lacks only the payment of a fair compensation to be lawful) is limited to the value of the undertaking at the moment of the dispossession, *i.e.*, 'the just price of what was expropriated'."[75] The Tribunal then reasoned:

> Obviously the value of an expropriated enterprise does not vary according to the lawfulness or the unlawfulness of the taking. This value can not depend on the legal characterization of a fact totally foreign to the economic constituents of the undertaking, namely the conduct of the expropriating State. In the traditional language of international law it equates the *damnum emergens*, which must be compensated in any case. . . . The difference is that if the taking is lawful the value of the undertaking at the time of the dispossession is the measure and the limit of the compensation, while if it is unlawful, this value is, or may be, only a part of the reparation to be paid. In any event, even in [the] case of unlawful expropriation the damage actually sustained is the measure of the reparation, and there is no indication that "punitive damages" could be considered.[76]

The Tribunal then stated that *damnum emergens* includes corporeal properties, contractual rights, and other intangible values, including goodwill and future prospects – a definition of broad scope.[77]

32. Turning to the compensation due to the claimant, the Tribunal in *Amoco* concluded that in the case of a lawful taking, which it found the expropriation before it to be,

> the measure of . . . compensation shall be the full value of the asset taken, pursuant to Article IV, paragraph 2, of the Treaty, that is the full equivalent of the property. Compensation which would only amount to a part of this value is, therefore, excluded.[78]

Finding that "going concern" value was the proper measure of compensation on the facts before it, the Tribunal held that this encompasses

> not only the physical and financial assets of the undertaking, but also the intangible valuables which contribute to its earning power, such as contractual rights . . . as well as goodwill and commercial prospects. Although those assets are closely linked to the profitability of the concern, they cannot and must not be confused with the

---

[75] *Id.* at 247-48.
[76] *Id.* at 248.
[77] *Id.* at 249.
[78] *Id.* at 269.

financial capitalization of the revenues which might be generated by such a concern after the transfer of property resulting from the expropriation (*lucrum cessans*).[79]

33. Thus, in the case of a lawful expropriation, the Tribunal in *Amoco* found that: (1) the measure of compensation is the value of the undertaking at the time of dispossession; (2) compensation which is less than the full equivalent of the property taken is not permissible; and (3) this full value requires an award of compensation for all tangible assets and for intangible assets such as goodwill and future commercial prospects, which are distinct from "future profits." With respect to unlawful expropriations the Tribunal indicated that compensation should include (1) not only the full value of the undertaking at the time of dispossession, but also (2) all of the damages actually sustained, including the future profit that would have accrued since the date of the taking.[80] Because *Amoco* was a Partial Award, it called for further pleadings by the parties in order to arrive at the actual amount of compensation. The case was settled before the Tribunal could give the principles articulated in the Partial Award a practical application.

34. In *Phillips Petroleum Company Iran*,[81] the Tribunal took an approach somewhat different from that of *Amoco* by focusing its discussion on the text of the Treaty of Amity. Faced with an argument by the Government of Iran, citing the *dicta* of Judge Lagergren's Separate Opinion in *INA*, that the Treaty must be interpreted in light of supposed changes in customary international law, the Tribunal found that it

> need not express any view as to the asserted changes in customary international law. . . . [T]he text of the Treaty provision does not support the Respondents' argument. . . . It provides that the protection and security to be received . . . must be "most constant . . . and in no case less than that required by international law". This reference to international law . . . cannot be understood as modifying the taking and compensation requirements . . . of that [provision], which . . . completely describe the requirements for takings and compensation.[82]

---

[79] *Id.* at 270. The issue of *lucrum cessans* is irrelevant in the instant Cases, where the Claimants are not seeking lost profits.

[80] *Id.* at 248-49. In discussing the difference between future commercial prospects, which are to be compensated in lawful takings, and "future profits," which are to be paid, according to *Amoco*, only for unlawful takings, the Tribunal drew the following distinction: The former, future prospects, is an element of the company's value at the time of taking that refers to the fact that the undertaking was a "going concern" that had demonstrated a certain ability to earn revenues and was to be considered as keeping such ability for the future. The latter, future profits, relates to the amount of the earnings hypothetically accrued from the date of taking had the enterprise remained in the hands of the former owner. *Id.* at 250.

[81] *Phillips Petroleum Company Iran* v. *The Islamic Republic of Iran, et al.*, Award No. 425-39-2 (29 June 1989), *reprinted in* 21 IRAN-U.S. C.T.R. 79 (hereinafter "*Phillips*").

[82] *Id.* at 120-21.

The Tribunal continued: "Concerning the argument that treaties generally should be interpreted in the light of customary international law as it may evolve, the Tribunal has already found in the *INA* award that the Treaty of Amity as a *lex specialis* prevails in principle over general rules."[83]

35. On the issue of the significance of the lawfulness or unlawfulness of the taking, the Tribunal held that

> the lawful/unlawful taking distinction, which in customary international law flows largely from [*Chorzów Factory*], is relevant only to two possible issues: whether restitution of the property can be awarded and whether compensation can be awarded for any increase in the value of the property between the date of taking and the date of the judicial or arbitral decision awarding compensation. The *Chorzów* decision provides no basis for any assertion that a lawful taking requires less compensation than that which is equal to the value of the property on the date of taking.[84]

36. In sum, there is virtually total uniformity in the Tribunal's rulings on the standard of compensation under international law. *Every* decision rendered by this Tribunal, whether based upon the Treaty of Amity or customary international law, or both of them, has concluded that compensation must equal the full value of the expropriated property as it stood on the date of taking. Moreover, every award rendered by this Tribunal, including the Award in the instant Cases, has provided claimants what the Tribunal determined to be the full value of their interest in the property taken, regardless of whether the taking was lawful or unlawful or whether the parties relied on the Treaty of Amity or customary international law.

37. The Tribunal, of course, is not the only body that has had occasion to consider the standard of compensation under customary international law in recent years. Most notably, Tribunals of the International Centre for Settlement of Investment Disputes ("ICSID") have ruled that customary international law requires the payment of full compensation. The ICSID Tribunal in *AMCO Asia Corp. v. Republic of Indonesia*, in addressing the issue of the legal basis for the calculation of damages, concluded that "full compensation of prejudice, by awarding to the injured party the *damnum emergens* and the *lucrum cessans*, is a principle common to the main systems of municipal law, and therefore, a general principle of law which may be considered as a source of international law."[85] Similarly, in *LETCO v. Government of the Republic of Liberia*,

---

[83] *Id.* at 121.
[84] *Id.* at 122.
[85] *AMCO Asia Corp. v. Republic of Indonesia* (20 Nov. 1984), *reprinted in* 24 I.L.M. 1022, 1036-38 (1985), *partially annulled*, 25 I.L.M. 1439 (*ad hoc* Com. 1986). After the partial annulment of the first *AMCO* award, a new Tribunal was convened. That Tribunal upheld the first Tribunal's conclusion as to the applicable standard of compensation. *See AMCO Asia Corp. v. Republic of Indonesia*, paras.

the ICSID Tribunal applied Liberian law, which it found to be "in conformity with generally accepted principles of public international law," and ruled that "according to international law and, more importantly, Liberian law, LETCO is entitled to compensation for damages for both its lost investments and its foregone future profits."[86] It then awarded LETCO the full value of its investment in the expropriated forestry concession as well as its lost future profits.[87]

D. Conclusion

38. Ever since the arrival of nation States upon the scene, international law has held that when a State takes the property of aliens, compensation representing the full equivalent of the property taken is required. Whatever label is attached to this principle ("just," "adequate," "equitable" or "appropriate" compensation), international tribunals have endeavored in practice to restore, if possible, the property taken or, failing that, to award damages corresponding to the loss sustained. Although the would-be architects of a new international economic order labored assiduously in the 1960's and 1970's to eviscerate this rule, these efforts failed. Their failure is evidenced by, *inter alia*, the many actions discussed above of the very same forces that sought to undermine the standard of prompt, adequate and effective compensation.

39. To argue that this standard should be set aside in favor of "appropriate" compensation – meaning "flexible" or dependent upon the "circumstances"[88] – is not to say that a time-honored rule of law should be calibrated or adjusted to modern conditions. To the contrary, it is to say that there is, in effect, no rule and to leave the result to caprice and subjective perception.

(Footnote continued from p. 253)
176-178 (5 June 1990), *reprinted in* 5 *Int'l Arb. Rptr.* No. 11, at Sec. D (Nov. 1990); *see also* John A. Westberg, *Applicable Law, Expropriatory Takings and Compensation in Cases of Expropriation; ICSID and Iran-United States Claims Tribunal Case Law Compared*, 8 ICSID Rev.-For. Inv. L.J. 1, 5-8, 15-16 (1993).

[86] *Liberian Eastern Timber Corporation ("LETCO")* v. *Government of the Republic of Liberia* (31 Mar. 1986), *reprinted in* 26 I.L.M. 647, 658, 670 (1987), modified (as to amounts of certain costs) in *Rectification of the Award Dated 31 March 1986* (14 May 1986), *reprinted in* 26 I.L.M. 677 (1987).

[87] *Id.* at 670-77. *See also Asian Agricultural Products Limited* v. *Republic of Sri Lanka* (27 June 1990), *reprinted in* 6 ICSID Rev.-For. Inv. L.J. 526, 565 (1991); *Benvenuti & Bonfant Srl* v. *Government of the Popular Republic of the Congo* (1984), *reprinted in* 67 I.L.R. 345, 374.

[88] For example, a "circumstance" sometimes cited in the literature is the length of time the foreign investment has been in place, the argument being that the longer the period the less reason there is to provide the deprived investor with the full equivalent of the property taken. Presumably this proposition rests on the assumption that the investor will have "recovered his investment," which may or may not be correct depending on the length of time before profitability can be achieved, the extent to which earnings are reinvested to expand the business and other factors. If the encouragement of stable long-term commitments (as opposed to high return, "fly by night" capital) is considered desirable, a less salutary "special circumstance" can hardly be imagined.

III. THE TREATY OF AMITY AND THE STANDARD OF COMPENSATION FOR EXPROPRIATED PROPERTY

40. In addition to misreading the current state of customary international law, the Award further errs by failing to take into account the Treaty of Amity between the United States and Iran.

41. The Claimants in their pleadings specifically rely upon Article IV, paragraph 2 of the Treaty of Amity in arguing that they are entitled to "full" (*i.e.*, prompt, adequate and effective) compensation. That provision of the Treaty reads as follows:

> Property of nationals and companies of either High Contracting Party, including interests in property, shall receive the most constant protection and security within the territories of the other High Contracting Party, in no case less than that required by international law. Such property shall not be taken except for a public purpose, nor shall it be taken without the prompt payment of just compensation. Such compensation shall be in an effectively realizable form and shall represent the full equivalent of the property taken; and adequate provision shall have been made at or prior to the time of taking for the determination and payment thereof.

42. Under well-established principles of international law the Treaty of Amity, as a *lex specialis* in the relations between the two countries, takes precedence over the *lex generalis* of customary international law.[89] Indeed, this Tribunal has "held that the applicable law for the purpose of determining the compensation owed by the Islamic Republic of Iran for deprivations or takings of property of United States nationals during the years immediately prior to the Algiers Accords is the 1955 Treaty of Amity."[90]

43. Thus, to look to customary international law as the sole basis for determining the standard of compensation in these Cases, as the Award does, is to neglect the fundamental law governing that subject. Iran and the United

---

[89] *See INA*, 8 IRAN-U.S. C.T.R. at 378; *Phillips*, 21 IRAN-U.S. C.T.R. at 121. *See also* Vienna Convention on the Law of Treaties, 23 May 1969, Art. 26, *reprinted in* 8 I.L.M. 679 (1969) ("Every treaty in force is binding upon the parties to it and must be performed by them in good faith"); 1 Hersch Lauterpacht, *International Law: Collected Papers* 86-87 (Elihu Lauterpacht ed., 1970) ("The rights and duties of States are determined, in the first instance, by their agreement as expressed in treaties – just as in the case of individuals their rights are specifically determined by any contract which is binding upon them. When a controversy arises between two or more States with regard to a matter regulated by a treaty, it is natural that the parties should invoke and that the adjudicating agency should apply, in the first instance, the provisions of the treaty in question").

[90] *Phillips*, 21 IRAN-U.S. C.T.R. at 118 (citing *Phelps Dodge Corp., et al.* v. *The Islamic Republic of Iran*, Award No. 217-99-2 (19 Mar. 1986), *reprinted in* 10 IRAN-U.S. C.T.R. 121, 131-32; *Thomas Earl Payne* v. *The Government of the Islamic Republic of Iran*, Award No. 245-335-2 (8 Aug. 1986), *reprinted in* 12 IRAN-U.S. C.T.R. 3, 12; *Sedco I*, 10 IRAN-U.S. C.T.R. at 184-85; *Amoco*, 15 IRAN-U.S. C.T.R. at 214-22; *Starrett Housing Corporation, et al.* v. *The Government of the Islamic Republic of Iran, et al.*, Award No. 314-24-1 (14 Aug. 1987), *reprinted in* 16 IRAN-U.S. C.T.R. 112, 195).

States engaged in careful negotiations to normalize and regulate their economic relations with one another through the signing of the Treaty of Amity. The object of the Treaty was, according to the preamble, to encourage, *inter alia*, "mutually beneficial trade and investments and closer economic intercourse generally between their peoples."[91] Toward this end Iran and the United States deliberately entered into express mutual commitments on the precise point under consideration here.

44. It would be incorrect to conclude, as the Respondent suggests in these Cases, that because the Claimants are dual nationals of the United States and Iran, the Treaty of Amity somehow does not apply. Neither the text of the Treaty nor its preparatory work provides any support for a belief that it does not apply with equal force to dual nationals.[92]

45. Indeed, the Tribunal expressly applied the Treaty standard in *Saghi*,[93] a case involving, among other claimants, a dual Iran-U.S. national. There the Tribunal stated:

> The Tribunal has previously held that under the Treaty of Amity a deprivation requires compensation equal to the full equivalent of the value of the interests in the property taken. The Tribunal has found that the Respondent deprived the Claimants of their ownership interests in [the companies] N.P.I. and Novin, and consequently they are entitled to full compensation.[94]

Thus, the Tribunal ruled, without need for elaboration, that the claimants, including the dual national Allan Saghi, were entitled under the Treaty of Amity to full compensation for the expropriation of their ownership interests by the Government of Iran.[95]

46. It seems evident that there can be no justification for treating a dual Iran-U.S. national within our jurisdiction, *i.e.*, a person with dominant and effective U.S. nationality, differently from other U.S. nationals. Subject to application where appropriate of the *A18* caveat, such dual nationals enjoy exactly the same rights as other United States nationals before this Tribunal, including the protections afforded by the Treaty of Amity.

47. In sum, the Treaty of Amity, with its clear requirement of compensa-

---

[91] Treaty of Amity, 8 U.S.T. at 901.

[92] In fact, the text of the Treaty indicates precisely the opposite. Where dual Iran-U.S. nationals are not intended to enjoy the benefit of particular Treaty clauses (*e.g.*, with respect to customs and tax exemptions available to consular officers, *see id*. Art. XVII, 8 U.S.T. at 911), the Treaty specifically so states.

[93] *James M. Saghi, et al.* v. *The Islamic Republic of Iran*, Award No. 544-298-2 (22 Jan. 1993), *reprinted in* 29 IRAN-U.S. C.T.R. 20 .

[94] *Id.* at para. 79 (footnotes omitted).

[95] *See also Faith Lita Khosrowshahi, et al.* v. *The Government of the Islamic Republic of Iran*, et al., Award No. 558-178-2, para. 34 (30 June 1994), *reprinted in* 30 IRAN-U.S. C.T.R. 76 .

tion equal to "the full equivalent of the property taken," is in itself wholly dispositive on the issue of the proper standard of compensation in these Cases. But even if one were to look to customary international law, as the Award does, the conclusion would be the same – *i.e.*, that prompt, adequate and effective compensation, representing the full equivalent value of the property taken, is required.[96]

IV. THE VALUATION OF GOSTARESH MASKAN

48. Important as it is to recognize the existence of a clear standard as a guide and a goal, it would be naive to suggest that the quantification of the deprived owner's loss can always be accomplished with absolute precision, no matter what standard of compensation is adopted. The present Cases surely illustrate the point. While I would have arrived at somewhat different amounts for several elements of Gostaresh Maskan's net worth, my chief disagreements are with the Award's treatment of the elements of value discussed below.

A. *Remaining Contracts*

49. In his Report on the value of Gostaresh Maskan, the Tribunal's Expert rejects any value for the Company's remaining contracts, arguing as follows:

> Inclusion of the future income from existing contracts involves double counting. The market value of equipment is equal to the value of the income that this equipment is expected to generate. It is inappropriate both to take the value of the asset and to add to that the value of the income that this asset is expected to produce, since that income is needed to justify the value.

50. At the expertise Hearing, the Expert clarified his position on remaining contracts, but he did not change it. According to the Expert, it is

> wrong to take the replacement cost of the assets and then to take the value of the cash flows, whether from existing contracts or contracts you expect to get. . . . It is quite appropriate to take the replacement cost of the assets and then add to that the value of the abnormal profits, if any, that you expect to make from future business[,] and that would include not only cont[r]acts you've already got but contracts that you could expect to get in the future.

51. The Expert stated that contract backlog is not in itself "an indication of abnormal profits." Rather, in his view, there are several things one has to ask before one can determine the impact of a contract backlog on the share

---

[96] *See* Section II, *supra*.

price of a company, including, for example, how profitable the contract would be, the purpose of the contract (*e.g.*, to increase market share), and the like. Thus, for the Expert the question was whether the remaining contracts would produce abnormal profits, and absent such profits, the Expert maintained his position that it is wrong to value both the tangible assets and the cash flows to be generated from such assets.

52. The Award adopts the Expert's approach and therefore refuses to ascribe any value to Gostaresh Maskan's contract backlog. Notwithstanding its recognition of the long and unbroken line of Tribunal precedents awarding compensation for "the likely future profitability of an expropriated owner's property," the Award concludes that the Expert's position on the issue of the outstanding contracts represents "the better approach." Award at para. 160. On several grounds, I disagree.

53. The Tribunal has on numerous occasions included both tangible assets and intangible assets in the valuation of going concerns, like Gostaresh Maskan. As the Tribunal ruled in *Amoco*:

> Going concern value encompasses not only the physical and financial assets of the undertaking, but also the intangible valuables which contribute to its earning power, such as contractual rights (supply and delivery contracts, patent licen[s]es and so on), as well as goodwill and commercial prospects.[97]

The Tribunal in *Amoco* further observed that a nationalized asset is not only a collection of discrete tangible goods but also "intangible items . . . such as contractual rights and other valuable assets. . . . To the extent that these various components exist and have an economic value, they normally must be compensated."[98] Thus, according to *Amoco*, intangible assets such as remaining contracts constitute a "nationalized asset" and if this asset has an economic value, then it must be compensated.

54. Similarly, in *Phillips*, the Tribunal, in describing the asset valuation approach (as contrasted with the discounted cash flow method of valuation), noted that in the former one must

> first calculate[ ] the tangible assets at their depreciated replacement value, thereby adjusting book value. . . . [Then, i]n order to quantify the intangible assets including profitability of the property interest taken, an appropriate income figure is determined based on historic earnings, to which a multiple is applied, which takes into account legitimate expectations in an oil venture of this type generally and in the context of the JSA [Joint Structure Agreement] more particularly.[99]

---

[97] *Amoco*, 15 IRAN-U.S. C.T.R. at 270.
[98] *Id.* at 267.
[99] *Phillips*, 21 IRAN-U.S. C.T.R. at 124.

Further, in an important clarification, the Tribunal emphasized that

> it should clearly be understood that the Tribunal is not determining price levels and oil production quantities in order to award anticipated profits lost through breach of contract, but rather to determine what was the value of the property interests taken from the Claimant in September 1979. Those property interests constituted part of an income-producing going concern, the value of which at the time of taking, while certainly not the same as the "financial capitalization" value at that time of its anticipated future revenues, . . . nevertheless cannot be determined without taking fully into account its future income-producing prospects as they would have been perceived at that time by a buyer of those interests.[100]

55. Thus, the point, which the Award in the present Cases fails to recognize, is that Gostaresh Maskan was an income-producing going concern, and the Tribunal cannot determine the full and true value of this enterprise "without taking fully into account its future income-producing prospects."[101]

56. To similar effect is *AIG*, in which the Tribunal was unequivocal in including future profitability in the valuation of the company's intangible assets. The Tribunal determined that fair market valuation includes the "value [of] the company as a going concern, taking into account not only the net book value of its assets, but also such elements as goodwill and likely future profitability, had the company been allowed to continue its business under its former management."[102] The Tribunal further noted:

> The most important element of the compensation claimed by the Claimants for the taking of their shares in Iran America is the loss of prospective earnings. When making its own assessment of the market value to be given to these shares, the Tribunal will therefore have to conclude, *inter alia*, which assumptions could reasonably be made . . . [at the time of the taking] regarding the future life and profitability of the company in view of the relevant conditions then existing in Iran.[103]

57. Likewise, in *Starrett*,[104] the Tribunal held that

> the property interest taken by the Government of Iran must be deemed to comprise the physical property as well as the right to manage the Project and to complete the construction in accordance with the Basic Project Agreement and related agreements, and to deliver the apartments and collect the proceeds of the sales as provided in the Apartment Purchase Agreements.[105]

---

[100] *Id.* at 128-29.
[101] *Id.* at 129.
[102] *AIG*, 4 IRAN-U.S. C.T.R. at 109.
[103] *Id.* at 107.
[104] *Starrett Housing Corporation, et al. v. The Government of the Islamic Republic of Iran, et al.*, Interlocutory Award No. ITL 32-24-1 (19 Dec. 1983), *reprinted in* 4 IRAN-U.S. C.T.R. 122.
[105] *Id.* at 156-57.

58. Thus, the Tribunal has consistently awarded the value of intangibles, such as likely future profitability, in cases involving going concerns. It is also instructive to consider, by way of comparison, other Tribunal decisions not involving going concerns.

59. For example, in *Sedco*, the Tribunal found that the Government of Iran had expropriated, *inter alia*, certain oil rigs belonging to Sedco, Inc., and accordingly compensated the claimant for "the fair market value of the properties, *i.e.*, what a willing buyer and a willing seller would reasonably have agreed on as a fair price at the time of the taking in the absence of coercion on either party."[106] The claimant also sought, with respect to these rigs, compensation for the "profits lost during the period of time which would have been required to replace the converted property."[107] The Tribunal accepted the claimant's argument that compensation for property taken must include both the fair market value of the property and recovery for loss of use during the time reasonably necessary to secure a replacement.[108] Therefore, the Tribunal awarded the claimant $4,817,064 for "lost revenue damages," in addition to $26 million for the value of the rigs themselves.[109] Significantly, these damages were awarded notwithstanding the fact that only an asset expropriation, and not the expropriation of a going concern, was at issue;[110] in other words, even in that context, the Tribunal deemed it appropriate to compensate the claimant for all of the present and future losses attributable to the taking.

60. In *Sola Tiles*,[111] the Tribunal was required to rule on whether the subsidiary company (Simat), a trader in specialized luxury tiles, was a going concern. The claimant was seeking the value of Simat's tangible and intangible assets, including equity, goodwill and lost profits. The Tribunal held that Simat was not a going concern.

> Given the picture that emerges, Simat's prospects of continuing active trading after the Revolution were not . . . such as to justify treating Simat as a going concern so as to assign any value to goodwill. The decision to assign no value to Simat's goodwill suggests a similar result as to future lost profits, which also depend upon the business prospects of a going concern. In addition, Simat had the briefest past record of profitability, having shown a loss in 1976, its first year of trading, and a

---

[106] *Sedco, Inc. v. National Iranian Oil Company, et al.*, Award No. 309-129-3 (7 July 1987), *reprinted in* 15 IRAN-U.S. C.T.R. 23, 35 (hereinafter "*Sedco II*").

[107] *Id.* at 51 (internal quotations omitted).

[108] *Id.* at 53.

[109] *Id.* at 51, 53, 186.

[110] The *Sedco* case also involved a separate claim for the expropriation of the claimant's ownership interest in a related company. *See id.* at 101; *see also* text accompanying notes 64-66, *supra*.

[111] *Sola Tiles*, 14 IRAN-U.S. C.T.R. 223.

small profit the next year. Accordingly, the Tribunal assigns no value to future lost profits and therefore does not decide the question whether and to what extent lost profit can be claimed in expropriation cases in addition to the going concern value.[112]

Thus, in view of the negative impact of the revolution, and the company's checkered past earnings record, the Tribunal in *Sola Tiles* failed to perceive a value for intangibles inherent in a company whose stock in trade was a luxury item not viewed with favor by the post-revolutionary government. Nevertheless, it is important to note that the Tribunal even then awarded the claimant the "actual value of the physical assets, including inventory" plus "the total amount of accounts receivable . . . and cash expropriated."[113] *Sola Tiles* may, of course, be distinguished from the instant Cases since, as the Award holds, Gostaresh Maskan was a going concern at the time of its taking. Moreover, Gostaresh Maskan had a very positive earnings record and the Claimants have made a convincing argument that the Company had already weathered the detrimental effects of the revolution and had positive prospects for the future.

61. The foregoing examination of Tribunal precedents compels the conclusion that likely future profitability should be included as a separate element in the going concern valuation of expropriated companies. Just as *Starrett* examined "the proceeds of the sales" of apartments, just as *AIG* analyzed the "future life and profitability" of Iran America, just as *Phillips* considered the "future income-producing prospects" of the joint structure agreement, so too in these Cases should we examine the likely future profitability that Gostaresh Maskan would have enjoyed from the performance of its remaining contracts.

62. The Respondent argues that Gostaresh Maskan's remaining contracts had no value, not because of any theoretical objection such as the Expert's, but because Gostaresh Maskan was not profitable. I believe that the Tribunal should have adopted the approach taken by both the Respondent and the Claimants and made a determination of the value of the remaining contracts based on an analysis of the profits that they were likely to produce. The approach taken by the Parties comports with Tribunal precedent and the Expert's Terms of Reference, and I fail to see why we should depart from either.

63. In 1979 Gostaresh Maskan was an established income-producing going concern. Based on (i) the Company's historical earnings (averaging 30% profitability or 634 million rials per year), (ii) its staff of 1000 regular employees

---

[112] *Id.* at 241-42.
[113] *Id.* at 240.

and the available pool of additional unskilled labor, (iii) its manufacturing assets and capabilities, (iv) accelerated write-off of heavy capital expenditures, (v) shrinking competition from foreign sources, (vi) the Iranian Government's policy favoring the building of residential housing, and (vii) the Tribunal's determination in *Blount Brothers* of 10% profitability of the Parandak project,[114] it is reasonable to conclude that Gostaresh Maskan was in a position in November 1979 to reap substantial benefits from its contract backlog. Although the Award acknowledges the long line of Tribunal precedents to the contrary, it nevertheless refuses to attribute any value to the backlog. I believe that this is wrong, and that the revenues that the backlog would have been expected to provide should have been appropriately reflected in the valuation of the Company.

B. *Goodwill*

64. The Claimants placed a value of Rls 1404.1 million upon the goodwill of Gostaresh Maskan. The Respondent, through its expert, Noavaran, valued Gostaresh Maskan's goodwill at zero. The Expert assigned a negative amount of Rls 240 million[115] to the Company's goodwill; and the Award arrived at a negative figure of Rls 291.9 million. This remarkable result is largely justified on the same basis as that underlying the Award's rejection of any value for the contract backlog, *i.e.*, the supposed uncertainty of Gostaresh Maskan's business prospects attributable to the Islamic revolution. *See* Award at paras. 157, 160. Thus, under the Award, the effects of the revolution have been weighed into the balance at least twice. First, they have nullified Gostaresh Maskan's prospects as represented by its contracts in hand for future work and second, they have generated a red figure (Rls 51.9 million greater than the Expert's) for goodwill that the Award deducts directly from Gostaresh Maskan's net worth.

65. The position on goodwill taken by the Award defies sound legal principles, well-established Tribunal precedent and the weight of evidence in these Cases. In the first place, the Respondent claimed, based upon the analysis of its expert, that the value of Gostaresh Maskan's goodwill was zero; put another way, the Respondent conceded that the value of the Company's goodwill was *not less than zero*. This concession having been made, I believe that

---

[114] *Blount Brothers Corporation v. Ministry of Housing and Urban Development, et al.*, Award No. 74-62-3 (2 September 1983), *reprinted in* 3 IRAN-U.S. C.T.R. 225, 234 (hereinafter "*Blount Brothers*").

[115] The Expert valued Gostaresh Maskan's goodwill at negative Rls 240 million, and not at 13% of the tangible asset value of the Company, as the Award indicates. *See* Award at paras. 155, 157. The Expert's Report clearly stated that in his view "a discount of *240 million rials* is reasonable." Expert's Report at para. 10 (emphasis added); *see also id*. at para. 150. The Expert then went on to note that this amount was equal to 13% of his estimate of the Company's tangible asset value, which is apparently the source of the Award's erroneous reliance on the 13% figure.

the Award errs by assessing a negative goodwill figure against Gostaresh Maskan's value.

66. A further problem with the Award's approach on goodwill is that it improperly reflects the consequences of the nationalization itself. The Expert's unfavorable evaluation of Gostaresh Maskan's prospects in 1979 was based, in part, upon his perception of a liquidity problem resulting from the post-taking freeze of the Company's assets pending a government audit. This consideration was inconsistent with the Expert's Terms of Reference because those Terms – in keeping with clear Tribunal precedent – instructed the Expert to ignore the effects "of the very act of nationalization" upon Gostaresh Maskan's value. Because the freezing of Gostaresh Maskan's assets stemmed from the audit – a requirement imposed by Iranian law in cases of governmental takings – the perceived liquidity problem resulting therefrom should not have been considered by the Expert, or reflected by the Tribunal in the form of "negative goodwill."

67. Finally, the reduction for negative goodwill goes against the weight of the evidence in these Cases. As the Award correctly states, the Parties and their experts provided the Tribunal with a wide array of data and opinion supporting their respective, and very different, views concerning the opportunities and pitfalls facing Gostaresh Maskan in late 1979. The Claimants' more optimistic appraisal was supported by, *inter alia*, contemporaneous statements issued by the Government-appointed managers of Gostaresh Maskan. In light of this and other supporting evidence, it is difficult to avoid the conclusion that, at the time of its expropriation, Gostaresh Maskan possessed, and was perceived to possess, all of the elements necessary to enable it to play a significant role in fulfilling the Iranian Government's professed desire to improve upon the housing situation in the country, and to profit from its efforts.

68. In short, I believe that the evidence and the relevant law support the attribution of a positive value to Gostaresh Maskan's goodwill. *A fortiori*, the Award's attribution of negative goodwill in the amount of Rls 291.9 million is improper and unjustified.

C. *Gostaresh Blount Severance Pay Provision*

69. The final valuation issue as to which, in my view, serious errors are made in the Award concerns the assessment of the so-called "severance pay provision" of Rls 60 million against the value of Gostaresh Blount ("GB"). The post-taking balance sheet for GB submitted by the Respondent showed a liability of Rls 120 million for that company's anticipated severance pay obligation. The Claimants, relying upon the views of their expert, Mr. Siamak, argued that no severance pay reserve was appropriate. The Tribunal's Expert did not take a firm position on the issue; instead, he simply indicated

that the Tribunal "m[ight] well wish to consider" deleting the severance pay reserve from the calculation of GB's value.

70. As the Award correctly notes, the Claimants' expert testified that the Rls 120 million severance pay liability proposed by the Respondent was exaggerated by a factor of approximately 16. Award at para. 152. Although the Respondent did not challenge the accuracy of the Claimants' calculation, the Award nonetheless concludes that the evidence is insufficient to make a firm judgment on the issue and proceeds to split the difference between the Parties' positions by assessing a Rls 60 million liability against GB.

71. I disagree with both the outcome and the approach taken by the Award. The Claimants' expert, who is the former chief financial officer of a large Iranian construction company, testified at the Hearing that because the laying-off and re-hiring of daily wage laborers was a frequent and ongoing occurrence for large construction companies in Iran, such companies generally remained current on their severance pay obligations and therefore typically would not have carried any reserve at all towards future anticipated severance pay liabilities. This testimony was credible and was unrebutted by the Respondent. Accordingly, I believe that it should have been accepted by the Tribunal and that no severance pay liability should have been charged against GB.

72. In any event, there is certainly no justification for splitting the difference between the Parties' positions on the asserted severance pay liability, as the Award does. It bears repeating that this purported liability first appeared on a balance sheet for GB prepared well after the taking and submitted by the Respondent.[116] Despite having access to all of the materials capable of supporting this purported liability – a privilege the Claimants did not enjoy – the Respondent was utterly unable to justify it at the Hearing or even to rebut the testimony of the Claimants' expert that the Rls 120 million figure was grossly exaggerated. In these circumstances, it is wholly unwarranted to penalize the Claimants by assessing a Rls 60 million liability. Any gaps in the evidence on the issue should have been resolved against the Respondent, which alone had access to the relevant evidence and nonetheless failed to present it.

D. *Interest.*

73. Chamber Three of the Tribunal customarily has awarded simple interest on awards at the rate of 10% per annum on the ground that this rate

---

[116] Significantly, no severance pay reserve appeared on GB's balance sheet dated 20 March 1978 – *i.e.*, prior to the expropriation of the company. *See* discussion at paras. 145-46, 150 of Award.

fairly compensated claimants for the loss of use of the monies owed them by the Government of Iran.[117] Without either recognizing the existence of this longstanding Chamber practice or offering any rationale for departing from it, the Award sets the rate of interest in these Cases at 8.6% per annum.

74. Although I do not believe that the 8.6% rate is patently unreasonable, I do believe that legitimate questions can be raised as to its adequacy – particularly in light of the very high interest rates that prevailed during a significant portion of the period since the taking in these Cases and the fact that (in my view, erroneously) the interest is not compounded. I trust that in future cases these issues will receive a more careful and reasoned treatment than they have in this Award.

E. Conclusion

75. In sum, I believe that the Award errs in at least three significant respects in its valuation of Gostaresh Maskan. First, contrary to an unbroken string of Tribunal precedents, the Award refuses to attribute any value to Gostaresh Maskan's sizable contract backlog. Second, the Award unfairly penalizes the Claimants through its application of a negative goodwill figure unwarranted in law or fact. Finally, the Award arbitrarily deducts an alleged severance pay liability despite the lack of evidence supporting the Respondent's position. I regret that these errors in the Award have partially deprived the Claimants of that to which the Award rightly finds them to be entitled: the fair market value of their investment in Gostaresh Maskan.

* * * * *

As explained at some length in this Separate Opinion, I believe that the Award's emphasis upon a "flexible" standard of "appropriate" compensation dependent in some unspecified way upon the "circumstances" of the taking misapprehends the state of international law today. Moreover, a standard without objective norms can hardly be deemed a standard at all.

The fact that countless nations, including the former staunchest proponents of Calvo, NIEO and communist doctrine, have expressly adopted the standard of prompt, adequate and effective compensation in their relations

---

[117] *See, e.g., Unidyne Corporation* v. *The Islamic Republic of Iran,* Award No. 551-368-3 (10 Nov. 1993), *reprinted in* 29 IRAN-U.S. C.T.R. 310, 349 ; *William J. Levitt* v. *Islamic Republic of Iran, et al.,* Award No. 520-210-3 (29 Aug. 1991), *reprinted in* 27 IRAN-U.S. C.T.R. 145, 185; *McCollough & Company, Inc.* v. *The Ministry of Post, Telegraph and Telephone, et al.,* Award No. 225-89-3 (22 Apr. 1986), *reprinted in* 11 IRAN-U.S. C.T.R. 3, 26-31, 34; *Alan Craig* v. *Ministry of Energy of Iran, et al.,* Award No. 71-346-3 (2 Sept. 1983), *reprinted in* 3 IRAN-U.S. C.T.R. 280, 290; *Blount Brothers,* 3 IRAN-U.S. C.T.R. at 235.

with other States is, perhaps, the most revealing manifestation of how far we have come from the United Nations polemics of the 1960s and 1970s.

Insofar as today's Award is concerned, it is important not to lose sight of the fact that, despite its erroneous theoretical postulations, the Tribunal in these Cases does, in fact, accept the full compensation standard and endeavors, albeit imperfectly, to implement it.

MORTEZA KHATAMI, *Claimant*

v.

THE GOVERNMENT OF THE ISLAMIC REPUBLIC OF IRAN, *Respondent*

(Case No. 767)

Chamber Three: Arangio-Ruiz, *Chairman*; Allison, Aghahosseini,[1] *Members*

Signed 13 *December* 1994[2]

AWARD NO. 562-767-3

The following is the text as issued by the Tribunal:

APPEARANCES

For the Claimant: Dr. Morteza Khatami
                     Claimant
                     Mr. Dominic J. Aprile
                     Counsel

For the Respondent: Mr. Ali H. Nobari
                     Agent of the Government of the
                     Islamic Republic of Iran
                     Mr. Nozar Dabiran
                     Legal Adviser to the Agent
                     Mr. Mostafa Nadimi
                     Legal Adviser to the Agent
                     Mr. Morteza Foroutan
                     Representative, National Iranian
                     Steel Company
                     Mr. Kamal Majedi Ardekani
                     Expert Witness

Also present: Mr. D. Stephen Mathias
                     Agent of the Government of the
                     United States of America

[1 The signature of Mr. Aghahosseini is accompanied by the words, "Concurring only."]
[2 Filed 13 December 1994.]

Mrs. Mary Catherine Malin
Deputy Agent of the Government of
the United States of America

I. PROCEDURAL HISTORY

1. On 19 January 1982, the Claimant Morteza Khatami (the "Claimant") filed a Statement of Claim against the Government of the Islamic Republic of Iran ("Iran" or the "Respondent") seeking compensation for various alleged expropriations and breaches of contract in the amount of U.S.$10,310,000.00, plus interest. Specifically, the Claimant sought compensation for: (1) the balances in several accounts in Iranian banks allegedly belonging to him; (2) the alleged expropriation of certain land in Iran that he claims to have inherited; (3) the alleged expropriation of other land that he purchased in Iran; (4) unpaid salary and other benefits allegedly owed to him as a result of his employment at the University of Isfahan from 1975 to 1976; (5) air tickets and other expenses incurred through trips to Iran "to protect and take over [his] properties"; and (6) what the Claimant refers to as his wife's "Dower and Courtesy [sic] Rights."

2. The Respondent objected to, *inter alia*, the jurisdiction of the Tribunal on the ground that the Claimant is exclusively a national of Iran and that therefore his claims do not fall within the Tribunal's jurisdiction.

3. In accordance with its practice in similar cases, the Tribunal, quoting the decision of the Full Tribunal in *Case No. A18*, Decision No. DEC 32-A18-FT (6 April 1984), *reprinted in* 5 IRAN-U.S. C.T.R. 251, informed the Parties on 28 June 1985 that "it has jurisdiction over claims against Iran by dual Iran-United States nationals when the dominant and effective nationality of the Claimant during the relevant period from the date the claim arose until 19 January 1981 was that of the United States." The Tribunal ordered the Claimant to file by 2 September 1985 all evidence he wished the Tribunal to consider in determining his dominant and effective nationality. Similarly, the Tribunal requested by Order of 15 January 1986 that the Respondent file by 28 February 1986 all evidence that it wished the Tribunal to consider on the issue of the Claimant's nationality.

4. The Claimant filed a reply brief on 31 December 1985 in which he addressed, *inter alia*, the issue of nationality. After several extensions of time granted by the Tribunal, the Respondent filed a "Brief and Evidence on the Claimant's Nationality Issue" on 29 May 1990, and the Claimant filed supplemental briefs dealing with nationality and other issues on 21 November 1990 and 25 January 1991.

5. By Order of 3 December 1990, the Tribunal joined "all jurisdictional

issues, including the issue of the Claimant's nationality during the relevant period between the time the Claim allegedly arose and 19 January 1981, to the consideration of the merits in this Case."

6. In accordance with Tribunal Orders, the Claimant filed his Hearing Memorial on 31 July 1991; the Respondent filed its "Memorial and Evidence on Claimant's Nationality and other Jurisdictional Issues and Merits" on 10 June 1992; the Claimant filed his Memorial and Evidence in Rebuttal on 24 December 1992; and the Respondent filed its Memorial and Evidence in Rebuttal on 22 July 1993.

7. A Hearing was held in this Case on 30 June 1994.

II. FACTS AND CONTENTIONS

8. The Tribunal shall limit itself to those facts and contentions that are necessary for the disposition of the Case.

9. The Claimant was born in Iran to Iranian parents in either 1919 or 1925,[3] received his primary and secondary schooling in Iran and attended Tehran Medical School from 1939 until 1945. He then performed compulsory military service in the Iranian army from 1945 until 1947, after which he worked in hospitals and clinics belonging to the Anglo-Iranian Oil Company in the south of Iran until 1951. He claims to have "immigrated" to the United States in 1951 and to have been a permanent resident there ever since. According to the Claimant, his only tie to Iran was that of his "properties and . . . wealth," and his dominant and effective nationality at all relevant times was that of the United States.

10. The Claimant asserts that all of his advanced medical training and virtually all of his professional work experience has been at various hospitals in the United States, where he specialized in general surgery and thoracic and cardiovascular surgery. Between 1952 and 1975 he claims to have completed internships, fellowships and surgical residencies at a number of hospitals in the States of Massachusetts, New York, Utah, West Virginia, Illinois and New Jersey. He has submitted certificates or letters confirming his professional involvement with: the New York Polyclinic Medical School and Hospital; the Mount Vernon Hospital in New York; the Brockton Hospital in Massachusetts; the St. Michael's Medical Center in Newark, New Jersey; the St. Elizabeth Hospital in Elizabeth, New Jersey; the Newark Beth Israel Medical

---

[3] There is some lack of clarity in this regard. The Claimant's Iranian birth certificate and his American certificate of naturalization place his date of birth at 1919. However, in 1973 he applied successfully to an Iranian court to have his birth certificate "corrected" to read 1925. The corrected date, however, is hard to reconcile with certain other events in the Claimant's life, such as his attending medical school from 1939.

Center in New Jersey; and the St. James Hospital in Newark, New Jersey. The Claimant was licensed to practice medicine and surgery in New Jersey in July 1968, was certified by the American Board of Surgery in November 1971, and is also licensed to practice medicine and surgery in New York State. While in the United States, he obtained a certificate of professional proficiency in English from the University of the State of New York in 1961 and also became a Member of the American Medical Association, as evidenced by his submission of a copy of his membership card for 1972. In addition, he obtained a driver's license from the State of New Jersey, a copy of which was submitted into evidence.

11. On 18 April 1962 the Claimant married Alba Eileen Guzzo, an American national by birth, as evidenced by an extract from the office of the Registrar of Vital Statistics of the State of New Jersey. The Claimant was naturalized as an American citizen on 12 October 1971, as evidenced by his Certificate of Naturalization.

12. The Claimant contends that he returned to Iran only three times after his departure in 1951. The first visit was allegedly a three-month holiday in 1969, during which time he stayed primarily with his brother and sister. The second and third visits occurred from March 1975 until approximately June 1976, and approximately August 1976 until 21 April 1977, respectively. During these latter two periods, the Claimant took up a position at the University of Isfahan as an Assistant Professor in general surgery, allegedly at the invitation of officials from the University. The Claimant contends that this post was temporary, and that his permanent residence remained the United States. During both of these latter sojourns in Iran, his wife Alba Khatami remained behind in the United States. Between June and August 1976, the Claimant returned to his residence in New Jersey. In November 1976 the Claimant's employment with the University of Isfahan ended, and after obtaining an exit visa from Iran the Claimant returned to the United States in April 1977.

13. The Claimant has shown that he possessed American passports issued on 20 July 1976, 31 December 1982 and 26 April 1990. However, he also possessed Iranian passports issued on 14 May 1967, 16 May 1974, 22 June 1979 and 6 June 1990. The Claimant used his Iranian passports for travel to and from Iran, allegedly on the instructions of officials from the Iranian Embassy in the United States. According to the Claimant, these officials advised him that because he had been born in Iran, he was obliged to use an Iranian passport in order to enter Iran.

14. After his return to the United States from Iran in 1977, the Claimant worked at St. Francis Hospital in Pittsburgh, Pennsylvania, from May 1977 until May 1978. In July 1978 he was offered a Commission in the United

States Army. He entered the United States Army on 24 July 1978 with the rank of Major, subsequently becoming a Lieutenant Colonel, and served as an Army surgeon until he was honorably discharged on 16 July 1982 as a result of health problems.

15. The Respondent, on the other hand, while conceding that the Claimant acquired American nationality in 1971, argues that he never lost his Iranian nationality, because he failed to renounce it in accordance with the procedures prescribed by Iranian law. The Respondent further contends that the dominant and effective nationality of the Claimant at all relevant times was that of Iran.

16. The Respondent disputes the Claimant's contention that he "immigrated" to the United States in 1951, noting that he has produced no formal documentary proof to that effect. It contends that the Claimant left Iran in 1951 merely to pursue further medical studies and to gain professional experience with the ultimate intention of returning to Iran. The Respondent alleges that the Claimant returned to Iran in approximately 1972 or 1973, intending to settle permanently there. In furtherance of this goal, the Respondent argues, the Claimant bought land in order to build a medical clinic in Isfahan; corrected the date of birth on his birth certificate and identity card in order to obtain a permanent job at Isfahan University;[4] and opened bank accounts in Isfahan and Tehran. In support of the contention that the Claimant returned to Iran in about 1972, rather than in 1975 as he contends, the Respondent points to the failure of the Claimant to supply complete copies of his passports for those years, to the Deed for the properties purchased in Isfahan signed by the Claimant and dated 30 September 1972, and to the application form for a job at the University of Isfahan filled in by the Claimant in 1972. The Respondent points further to the extensive correspondence that the Claimant conducted with the Iranian Ministry of Science and Higher Education between 1969 and 1975 regarding the recognition in Iran of his American professional qualifications.

17. The Respondent contends that the ties of the Claimant to American society are weak. In this regard, the Respondent emphasizes the Claimant's own repeated expressions of loyalty to and love for Iran in letters to the then Shah, to officials of the Ministry of Science and Higher Education, and to the former Iranian Ambassador to the United States. Moreover, the Respondent contends that the Claimant's wife, Alba Khatami, acquired an Iranian passport and identity card. This latter allegation is freely admitted by the

---

[4] The Respondent contends that permanent academic staff at Isfahan University were obliged to retire at age 65, or in exceptional cases at age 70.

Claimant, who contends that this condition was "imposed" upon her by the Iranian Embassy. The Respondent further contends that the Claimant, while still married to his American spouse, contracted a second marriage to an Iranian woman on 19 August 1972 in Iran. Finally, the Respondent emphasizes that the Claimant did not obtain American citizenship until twenty years after his arrival in the United States.

18. Regarding the claims for compensation asserted by Dr. Khatami, the Tribunal notes that two of the claims set forth in the Statement of Claim – that for air travel to Iran and other expenses allegedly incurred by the Claimant "to protect . . . [his] properties," and that for "Dower and Courtesy [sic] Rights" on behalf of his wife – have not been pursued in the Claimant's subsequent pleadings or at the Hearing. Accordingly, the Tribunal regards those claims as having been abandoned.

19. The remaining claims are essentially four-fold. First, Dr. Khatami seeks compensation for the balances in several accounts in banks in Isfahan and Tehran, totaling approximately U.S.$100,000.00. The Respondent denies liability on this claim and argues, *inter alia*, that the Claimant never made a proper demand for payment of the balances.[5] Second, the Claimant seeks compensation, in the amount of U.S.$6,200,000.00, for the alleged expropriation during the 1960s of land in Iran that he claims to have inherited from his family. The Respondent counters that the Claimant has not proven his ownership of the land and that, in any event, it was not expropriated. Third, Dr. Khatami claims compensation of U.S.$3,800,000.00 for the alleged expropriation in 1980 or early 1981 of land that he purchased in Isfahan in 1972. The Respondent concedes that the property was taken by the Government of Iran but argues, *inter alia*, that the expropriation did not occur until 1984, well after the jurisdictional cut-off date under the Claims Settlement Declaration. Moreover, the Respondent maintains that monies were deposited in compensation for the taking and are available to Dr. Khatami. Finally, Dr. Khatami seeks compensation for the non-payment of salary and other benefits allegedly due to him as a result of his employment as an Assistant Professor at the University of Isfahan, in the amount of approximately U.S.$60,000.00. The Respondent, among other defenses, asserts that the University paid the Claimant all monies that he was due.

---

[5] *See Tippetts, Abbett, McCarthy, Stratton* v. *TAMS-AFFA Consulting Engineers of Iran, et al.*, Award No. 141-7-2, at 7 (29 June 1984), *reprinted in* 6 IRAN-U.S. C.T.R. 219, 223 (holding that absent a timely demand for the balance in a bank account, there is no "claim" within the meaning of Article II, para. 1 of the Claims Settlement Declaration).

III. REASONS FOR THE AWARD

A. The Claimant's Nationality And The Relevant Period

20. In order to decide whether the Tribunal has jurisdiction over Dr. Khatami's claims, it is first necessary to determine whether Dr. Khatami was a citizen of Iran, a citizen of the United States, or a citizen of both Iran and the United States during the relevant period, *i.e.*, from the time his claims arose until 19 January 1981, the date on which the Claims Settlement Declaration entered into force. According to the *A18* decision, if the Claimant was a citizen of both Iran and the United States, the Tribunal must proceed to determine the Claimant's dominant and effective nationality during that period. *See Case No. A18*, 5 IRAN-U.S. C.T.R. at 265.

21. It is undisputed that the Claimant is an Iranian national by birth. In addition, the Tribunal is satisfied that the Claimant was naturalized as a United States citizen on 12 October 1971, as evidenced by a photocopy of his Certificate of Naturalization No. 9354191. The Claimant also has produced a photocopy of the identifying pages of his American passport issued on 20 July 1976. There is no evidence in the record that the Claimant has relinquished or otherwise lost either his Iranian citizenship in accordance with Iranian law or his United States citizenship in accordance with United States law. Consequently, the Tribunal finds that from 12 October 1971 until 19 January 1981, the Claimant was a citizen of both Iran and the United States.

22. Before proceeding to examine the question of the Claimant's dominant and effective nationality, it is necessary to clarify the parameters of the relevant jurisdictional period. That task is complicated by the fact that there is some ambiguity in the pleadings regarding the dates on which several of Dr. Khatami's claims allegedly arose. It is clear, however, that his claim for compensation based upon the alleged expropriation of the property that he inherited from his family falls outside the jurisdiction of the Tribunal. Dr. Khatami's pleadings indicate that this claim arose in or about 1963, and he confirmed that date during the Hearing. Because Dr. Khatami did not become a United States citizen until 1971, the claim has not been "owned continuously" by a United States national and therefore is not within the Tribunal's jurisdiction.[6] As a result, that claim can be disregarded for purposes of determining the relevant period.

23. Dr. Khatami's remaining claims appear to have arisen no earlier than 1976. As best the Tribunal can determine, the claim involving the property

---

[6] *See* Claims Settlement Declaration, Art. VII, para. 2; *Burton Marks et al. v. The Islamic Republic of Iran*, Interlocutory Award No. ITL 53-458-3, at 7-8 (26 June 1985), *reprinted in* 8 IRAN-U.S. C.T.R. 290, 294.

Dr. Khatami purchased in Isfahan arose no earlier than 1980; his claims involving alleged deposits at various Iranian banks arose between 1977 and 1979; and his claim for salary and other benefits from Isfahan University arose in 1976, the year that his employment at the University ended. Consequently, the Tribunal concludes that the relevant period, for purposes of the inquiry into Dr. Khatami's dominant and effective nationality, is the period between 1976 and 19 January 1981.[7]

B. The Claimant's Dominant and Effective Nationality During the Relevant Period

24. In order to reach a conclusion as to the Claimant's dominant and effective nationality during the relevant period, the Tribunal must determine whether the Claimant had stronger ties with Iran or with the United States during that period. To this end, the Tribunal must consider all relevant factors, such as the Claimant's habitual residence, center of interests, family ties, participation in public life and other evidence of attachment. *See Case No. A18*, 5 IRAN-U.S. C.T.R. at 265. While the Tribunal's jurisdiction is dependent on the Claimant's dominant and effective nationality during the period between 1976 and 19 January 1981, the events and facts preceding that period remain relevant to the determination of the Claimant's dominant and effective nationality during that period. *See Reza Said Malek v. The Government of the Islamic Republic of Iran*, Interlocutory Award No. ITL 68-193-3, para. 14 (23 June 1988), *reprinted in* 19 IRAN-U.S. C.T.R. 48, 51-52. The ultimate aim of the inquiry in dual national cases is to determine whether, under the totality of the circumstances, the claimant had stronger allegiance and attachment during the relevant period to the United States or to Iran.

25. As noted above, the Claimant moved to the United States in 1951. His very long residence in the United States as an adult is a factor that suggests that by October 1971, when he acquired United States nationality, his life had become centered in the United States. Furthermore, after his initial medical training in Iran, virtually all of the Claimant's advanced professional qualifications and experience were acquired in various American hospitals. These factors suggest that, from 1951 until the early 1970s, the center of the Claimant's professional and personal life was the United States.

26. While the circumstances noted above are relevant to the determination of the Claimant's dominant and effective nationality, the Tribunal is primarily concerned with his national allegiance and attachment during the period from 1976 until 19 January 1981. With respect to that period, the

---

[7] Because of the particular circumstances upon which the Tribunal bases its conclusions on the issue of the Claimant's dominant and effective nationality, it is not necessary for the Tribunal to determine with precision the dates upon which these various claims arose.

Tribunal must take into consideration the Claimant's own utterances contained in letters written to the Shah of Iran and other Iranian officials. These statements, which appear in contemporaneous documents that the Claimant admits to having written, provide particularly important evidence of the Claimant's national allegiance and attachment during the relevant period.[8]

27. The first contemporaneous document is a June 1978 letter that the Claimant wrote to Mr. Ardeshir Zahedi, the Iranian Ambassador to the United States at that time, complaining about the termination of his employment at the University of Isfahan. In this letter the Claimant, writing about Iran, asserts that his "loyalty to [his] country and [his] love for [his] fellow countrymen should be taken for granted."

28. In a similar letter dated June 1978 and addressed to the Shah of Iran, the Claimant states that he had returned to Iran to work at Isfahan University in the mid-1970s "out of the deep and burning love [he] felt for [his] dear country." He writes that the behavior of the University officials in terminating his employment was such that he "had no alternative other than [to] leav[e] [his] homeland and return[ ] to the United States out of despair and disappointment, instead of serving [his] country which [he] love[s] so much, and which [he] wanted so much to serve." In the same letter, the Claimant even more explicitly writes:

> The purpose of submitting the present letter is to inform Your Majesty that this is how competent Iranians are *prevented from returning to their beloved homeland* and how those who at the expense of the dear nation of Iran educate abroad for years and gain knowledge and experience, *are forced to permanently reside abroad*.
>
> In any event, *if your devoted servant had the chance to be alive, I will reluctantly remain abroad only as long as it is necessary to recover emotionally, physically and financially, and then will return again after some time to my dear country,* will kiss the soil of Iran, and pray for Your Majesty and the young Crown Prince as long as I live. (emphasis added)

The Claimant ends the letter "[w]ith sincerest prayers from your devoted servant."

29. At the Hearing, the Claimant attempted to explain these statements as being motivated by the customary deference afforded to a ruling monarch whom he regarded himself as morally obliged to respect. As discussed more fully below, the Tribunal finds that although the Claimant's explanation is facially credible, it is ultimately unpersuasive. Instead, the Tribunal regards

---

[8] *See Rana Nikpour* v. *The Islamic Republic of Iran et al.*, Interlocutory Award No. ITL 81-336-1, para. 23 (18 Feb. 1993), *reprinted in* 29 IRAN-U.S. C.T.R. 67, 73 (finding the Claimant to be a dominant and effective United States national based upon, *inter alia*, a "contemporaneous evidentiary document" in which she declared her intention to remain a resident of the United States).

these utterances by the Claimant as providing highly significant and contemporaneous insight into his subjective motivations and intentions. The sentiments expressed by the Claimant suggest that even after acquiring United States nationality and taking an oath of allegiance to the United States, he continued to have primary emotional ties to Iran; and, perhaps more importantly, his statements tend to prove that given the opportunity he would have returned to Iran and lived there permanently.

30. The Claimant's contemporaneous declarations of his subjective feelings about Iran are not in themselves dispositive on the issue of dominant and effective nationality during the relevant period. This is especially true in light of the facially credible explanation from the Claimant accounting for these statements. In such a situation, the Tribunal must examine both the contemporaneous written statements and the Claimant's subsequent explanation in light of his objective behavior during the relevant time frame in order to determine which set of statements more accurately reflects the Claimant's national allegiance and attachment.

31. In making this determination, the Tribunal finds three aspects of the Claimant's objective behavior during and immediately prior to the relevant period to be particularly revealing. The first is the Claimant's acceptance of a job as an Assistant Professor at the University of Isfahan from March 1975 until November 1976. Although the Claimant alleges that this position was strictly temporary, the record suggests that the appointment of the Claimant occurred under a standard university employment contract, pursuant to which an employee would serve a two-year probationary period before becoming a permanent employee. The record indicates that the Claimant's employment was cut short by the University authorities against the wishes of the Claimant, as evidenced by his institution of complaint procedures before a board charged with hearing the employment-related complaints of government employees,[9] as well as by letters of complaint written by the Claimant. Based upon these circumstances, it appears likely that the Claimant would have continued his employment at the University of Isfahan indefinitely beyond November 1976 had the University authorities not terminated his employment against his wishes.

32. Second, in 1972 (after he had acquired United States citizenship) the Claimant purchased two plots of land in Isfahan, Iran, as evidenced by the deed of transfer and tax clearance certificates for the properties in question and title deeds showing registration in the Claimant's name. The Claimant himself asserted in his written pleadings that he had planned "to invest 12

---

[9] This was the Employment Complaints Examination Board of the State Administration and Employment Affairs Organization.

million dollars" to build a medical clinic on this land, and that the initial bank loan to finance the project had been approved. At the Hearing, the Claimant confirmed that he had in fact travelled to Iran in the early 1970s, that his intention in buying the aforementioned land had been to build a clinic, and that he had intended that it should be a home as well as a clinic. He claimed, however, that he had not intended to reside permanently in Iran, but rather to maintain a permanent residence in the United States and to "come and go" from the project in Iran. The Tribunal is not convinced by this explanation. The building of a medical clinic would have been a major project requiring financial and time commitments of Dr. Khatami that probably would have resulted in his spending significant lengths of time in Iran, such that the permanence of his residence in the United States could be questioned. Furthermore, his purchase of land and securing of the initial financing on a U.S.$12 million medical clinic, combined with his assumption of a faculty position at the University of Isfahan, strongly suggests that by 1976 the center of the Claimant's professional and economic interests had shifted back to Iran.

33. Finally, the Respondent has submitted documentation from the Ministry of Science and Higher Education in Iran consisting of correspondence conducted between the Ministry and the Claimant between 14 April 1969 and 12 July 1975 regarding his attempt to gain official recognition in Iran of the professional qualifications he had obtained in the United States. An Evaluation Certificate of Foreign Education was issued on 5 May 1969 recognizing the Claimant as a specialist in general surgery in Iran. However, the Claimant's attempt, and ultimate failure, to gain accreditation as a specialist in cardiovascular surgery continued until 1975, giving rise to an extended exchange of letters. It appears that these actions were directed toward gaining the necessary certificates to practice that specialty in Iran.

34. In particular, one letter from the Claimant to the Director General of the Secretariat of the Council for Evaluation of Foreign Academic Certificates seems to shed light on the possible aim of the Claimant in obtaining certification of his American qualifications and to reveal to some extent his general attitude toward his life in the United States. In this letter, dated July 1974, the Claimant complains about the decision of the Council not to recognize certain aspects of his American training toward the granting of a specialization in thoracic surgery. The letter states that this decision had prompted him to do an internship at Manitoba University in Canada, which was an "approved" place for such study, and laments that the Council's decision has "caused four years loss of my time." The Claimant then asks rhetorically: "Is this fair for the country [Iran] and young people?"; he goes on to request that the Council "write [him] clearly about the exact problem to

prevent the students studying abroad from wasting their time in slavery." These statements suggest that the Claimant was not professionally committed to practicing medicine in the United States, but rather, as the Respondent contends, that he viewed his professional activities in the United States as merely preparatory for practicing medicine in Iran. The statements are also consistent with the other evidence noted above regarding the Claimant's employment at the University of Isfahan and his plans to build a clinic in that city. Furthermore, the Tribunal is simply not convinced that the timing of the certification process (which extended from 1969 to 1975) or the lengths to which the Claimant went in attempting to obtain certification in thoracic and cardiovascular surgery – including moving to Manitoba, Canada, for a one-year special internship – are consistent with a decision merely to teach on a temporary basis at the University of Isfahan, as the Claimant contends.

35. The Tribunal must, of course, also weigh the Claimant's connections to the United States during the relevant period. In this regard, the Tribunal finds that the Claimant's proof of his ties to American society is less than convincing. The Tribunal considers it to be significant that although the Claimant submitted copious documentation detailing the professional and academic qualifications that he acquired in the United States, he submitted no noteworthy evidence showing his social integration into American society except for his marriage to an American-born woman in 1962.[10] No additional details or evidence of the Claimant's attachment to United States society have been provided, such as membership in clubs, societies, religious, civic or other institutions, or participation in public life. Furthermore, the quality of the English spoken and written by the Claimant is poor, as evidenced by written pleadings prepared by the Claimant without the assistance of a lawyer and as confirmed at the Hearing. The Tribunal concludes that the absence of evidence detailing the Claimant's social, civic or religious attachments to the United States constitutes a failure of proof that the Claimant immersed

---

[10] Although this is usually a significant fact, the probative value of this marriage is somewhat lessened by the Claimant's marriage to an Iranian woman in 1972 – during the course of his first marriage – as evidenced by the Claimant's Iranian identity card issued on 15 April 1975, which contains the details of this second marriage. At the Hearing, the Claimant admitted to having entered into a second marriage with an Iranian woman but contended that the marriage ceremony had taken place at the instigation of his family and that the marriage was dissolved shortly after the ceremony.

For the same reason, the Tribunal attaches less significance than might otherwise be appropriate to the fact that the Claimant's first wife did not accompany him to Iran when he accepted the position at the University of Isfahan. The significance of his first wife's failure to accompany him to Iran is further diminished by the explanation offered by the Claimant at the Hearing that she had decided not to accompany him because of her fear of travelling to Iran on an Iranian passport.

himself in American culture or integrated into American society to any significant extent.[11]

36. To be sure, the Claimant's service in the United States Army, which occurred during the last three years of the relevant jurisdictional period, is a highly significant fact pointing in favor of the Claimant's asserted status as a dominant and effective United States national. Under the particular circumstances of the present Case, however, the Tribunal concludes that Dr. Khatami's military service does not tip the balance on the nationality issue. As noted earlier, Dr. Khatami accepted a Commission as an Army surgeon shortly after his return to the United States following separation from his employment at the University of Isfahan. The Respondent suggests, and in light of the other circumstances noted above the Tribunal is inclined to agree, that Dr. Khatami's decision to become an Army surgeon seems to have been motivated less by feelings of allegiance to the United States than by necessity, *i.e.*, the need for suitable employment. Indeed, in view of the statements contained in the Claimant's June 1978 letter to the Shah, it may well be that his decision to work as an Army surgeon was part of a plan "to recover . . . financially, and then . . . return again after some time to my dear country" to carry out his private clinic project.

37. For the reasons discussed above, the Tribunal concludes that during the relevant period the Claimant's economic and social interests were centered in Iran and that, in all likelihood, he actively contemplated a permanent return to the country of his birth during that period. In this regard, the Tribunal attaches particular significance to the contemporaneous indications of the Claimant's subjective intentions contained in the letters he wrote to the Shah of Iran and other officials. The Tribunal finds that the Claimant's objective behavior prior to and during the relevant period – in particular, his

---

[11] *Cf. Zaman Azar Nourafchan v. The Islamic Republic of Iran*, Interlocutory Award No. ITL 75-412/415-3, para. 31 (15 Dec. 1989), *reprinted in* 23 IRAN-U.S. C.T.R. 307, 314 (finding claimant to be a dominant and effective United States national where he was "fully integrated into American society" and "his residence, education, professional and business life as well as family and social life were concentrated in the United States"); *Katrin Zohrabegian Abrahamian v. The Government of the Islamic Republic of Iran*, Interlocutory Award No. ITL 74-377-3, para. 10 (1 Dec. 1989), *reprinted in* 23 IRAN-U.S. C.T.R. 285, 287 (finding dominant and effective American nationality where claimant's "employment, financial obligations and family life [had become] centered in the United States"); *Nahid (Danielpour) Hemmat v. The Government of the Islamic Republic of Iran*, Interlocutory Award No. ITL 70-170-3, para. 19 (16 June 1989), *reprinted in* 22 IRAN-U.S. C.T.R. 129, 134 (finding claimant's United States nationality to be dominant where she "was fully integrated into American society"); *Reza Said Malek v. The Government of the Islamic Republic of Iran*, Interlocutory Award No. ITL 68-193-3, para. 25 (23 June 1988), *reprinted in* 19 IRAN-U.S. C.T.R. 48, 55 ("Although the Claimant never wholly severed his cultural and sentimental ties with the country of his birth, as evidenced by his marriage and his visits to Iran, his conduct since the time he settled in the United States, in 1966, demonstrates that he fully and deliberately integrated into United States society").

acceptance of a position at the University of Isfahan, his plans to build a multi-million dollar medical clinic on land that he purchased in Isfahan, and his persistent efforts to obtain recognition of his American professional qualifications in Iran – suggests that the sentiments of allegiance and devotion expressed in his letters were heartfelt. Considered in tandem with the Claimant's failure to prove that he substantially integrated himself into American culture, this leads the Tribunal to conclude that the Claimant's service in the United States Army and his lengthy residence in the United States are outweighed as indicia of dominant and effective nationality in the particular circumstances of this Case.

38. Accordingly, the Tribunal finds, based on all of the evidence before it, that the Claimant has not proven that his attachment to the United States during the period in question was dominant over his attachment to Iran. The Tribunal therefore concludes that during the relevant period the Claimant's dominant and effective nationality was not that of the United States, and that as a result the Claim of Morteza Khatami does not fall within the Tribunal's jurisdiction.

IV. AWARD

39. For the foregoing reasons,

THE TRIBUNAL DETERMINES AS FOLLOWS:
- a) The Claim of the Claimant Morteza Khatami is dismissed for lack of jurisdiction under Article II, paragraph 1, and Article VII, paragraph 1, of the Claims Settlement Declaration.
- b) Each Party shall bear its own costs of arbitration.

AWARDS ON AGREED TERMS

UNIVERSITY OF SOUTHERN CALIFORNIA, *Claimant*

v.

ISLAMIC REPUBLIC OF IRAN, ET AL., *Respondents*

(Case No. 321)

Chamber One: Broms, *Chairman*; Noori, Holtzmann, *Members*

Signed 26 *April* 1994[1]

AWARD NO. 555-321-1

The following is the text as issued by the Tribunal:

AWARD ON AGREED TERMS

1. On 8 April 1994, the Claimant, University of Southern California, and the Respondents, Ministry of Culture and High Education, Ministry of Education, National Iranian Oil Company, Atomic Energy Organization of Iran, Islamic Republic of Iran Broadcasting Organization for itself and on behalf of School of Television and Cinema, Telecommunications Company of Iran, Organization for Administration and Employment, University of Tehran, University of Shahid Beheshti (formerly, National University of Iran), University of Isfahan, University of Ferdowsi, University of Shahid Chamran (formerly, University of Jondi Shahpour), University of Kerman, University of Complex for Arts, Humanities and Letters University Complex, State Management Training Center, Alavi Foundation, Institute for Intellectual Development of Children and Young Adults, Industrial Development and Renovation Organization of Iran on behalf of Technology Inc., and The Government of the Islamic Republic of Iran (collectively "the Parties") filed with the Tribunal a Joint Request for Arbitral Award on Agreed Terms ("the Joint Request"), and attached thereto, a Settlement Agreement in Case No. 321, Chamber One, dated 11 August 1993 ("the Settlement Agreement"), signed by the representatives of the Parties. In the Joint Request the Parties explain that the Settlement Agreement "provides for full and final settlement of all disputes, differences, claims, counter-claims, and matters directly or indirectly raised out of the relationships, and matters directly or indirectly

[1 Filed 26 April 1994.]

raised or capable of arising out of the relationships, transactions, contracts, and events related to the subject matter of Case No. 321."

2. Furthermore, in the Joint Request the Parties request the Tribunal to issue, pursuant to Article 34 of the Tribunal Rules, an Arbitral Award on Agreed Terms that will record and give effect to the Settlement Agreement. Copies of both the Joint Request and the Settlement Agreement are attached and incorporated herein by reference.[2]

3. According to paragraph 1 of the Settlement Agreement,

> [t]he scope and subject matter of this Settlement Agreement is to settle and dismiss, for ever, all disputes, differences, claims, counterclaims, and matters directly or indirectly raised or capable of arising out of the relationships, transactions, contracts, and events in any manner related to the subject matter of the Statement of Claim, Counterclaims, and other submissions by the Parties in Case No. 321.

4. The Settlement Agreement also provides, *inter alia*, that

> [t]his Settlement Agreement sets forth the entire agreement between the Parties hereto, and fully supersedes any and all prior agreements and understandings between the Parties hereto pertaining to the subject matter hereof, excepting only that certain Agreement executed concurrently herewith by Claimant and National Iranian Oil Company, and the Contract and the Chair referenced therein[.] (*ibid.*, paragraph 14.)

The copy of that Agreement is also attached to the Settlement Agreement and incorporated herein by reference.

5. The Tribunal notes that the Settlement Agreement does not provide for any payment from the Security Account established pursuant to paragraph 7 of the Declaration of the Government of the Democratic and Popular Republic of Algeria dated 19 January 1981.

6. The Tribunal accepts the Settlement Agreement in accordance with Article 34, paragraph 1, of the Tribunal Rules.

7. Based on the foregoing,

THE TRIBUNAL AWARDS AS FOLLOWS:

(a) The Settlement Agreement is hereby recorded as an Award on Agreed Terms binding upon University of Southern California, Ministry of

---

[2] Paragraph 11 of the Settlement Agreement provides that the Parties should submit the Settlement Agreement to the Tribunal on or before 11 April 1994, provided however that "[i]f th[e] Settlement Agreement is not submitted on such date, or within such additional time as Parties may, through counsel, agree in writing, it shall automatically become null and void, and the Parties, without prejudicing their respective rights, will be placed in the same position as they were prior to the date of this Settlement Agreement." The Tribunal notes that the Settlement Agreement was filed with the Tribunal on 8 April 1994.

Culture and High Education, Ministry of Education, National Iranian Oil Company, Atomic Energy Organization of Iran, Islamic Republic of Iran Broadcasting Organization for itself and on behalf of School of Television and Cinema, Telecommunications Company of Iran, Organization For Administration and Employment, University of Tehran, University of Shahid Beheshti (formerly, National University of Iran), University of Isfahan, University of Ferdowsi, University of Shahid Chamran (formerly, University of Jondi Shahpour), University of Kerman, University of Complex For Arts, Humanities and Letters University Complex, State Management Training Center, Alavi Foundation, Institute For Intellectual Development of Children and Young Adults, Industrial Development and Renovation Organization of Iran on behalf of Technology Inc., and The Government of the Islamic Republic of Iran, in full and final settlement of the entire Case, each of which is bound to fulfill the conditions set forth in the Settlement Agreement.

(b) The Tribunal declares the proceedings in the Case No. 321 terminated in their entirety and with prejudice.

Joint Request for Arbitral Award on Agreed Terms[1]

Pursuant to Article 34 of the Rules of Procedure of the Iran-United States Claims Tribunal (the "Tribunal"), University of Southern California ("Claimant"), a nonprofit corporation organized and existing under the laws of California, on the one part, and Ministry of Culture and High Education, Ministry of Education, National Iranian Oil Company. Atomic Energy Organization of Iran, Islamic Republic of Iran Broadcasting Organization for itself and on behalf of School of Television and Cinema, Telecommunications Company of Iran, Organization for Administration and Employment, University of Tehran, University of Shahid Beheshti (formerly, National University of Iran), University of Isfahan, University of Ferdowsi, University of Shahid Chamran (formerly, University of Jondi Shahpour), University of Kerman, University of Complex for Arts, Humanities and Letters University Complex, State Management Training Center, Alavi Foundation, Institute for Intellectual Development of Children and Young Adults, Industrial Development and Renovation Organization of Iran on behalf of Technology Inc., and the Government of the Islamic Republic of Iran, hereinafter collectively called "Respondents," on the other part, jointly request that the Tribunal issue an

[1 Filed 8 April 1994.]

Arbitral Award on Agreed Terms that will record and give effect to the attached Settlement Agreement, which is incorporated herein by reference.

The Settlement Agreement, which was entered into on August 11, 1993, provides for full and final settlement of all disputes, differences, claims, counterclaims, and matters directly or indirectly raised out of the relationships, and matters directly or indirectly raised or capable of arising out of the relationships, transactions, contracts, and events related to the subject matter of Case No. 321

The representatives of the Parties expressly declare and warrant that they are duly empowered to sign this Joint Request, and the signing of the Joint Request by the Agent of the Islamic Republic of Iran to the Tribunal and the representatives of other Respondents. and Claimant shall signify that all necessary authorities have given their approval.

Settlement Agreement[2]

This Settlement Agreement is made and entered into this 11th day of August 1993, by and between University of Southern California ("Claimant"), a nonprofit corporation organized and existing under the laws of California, on the one part, and Ministry of Culture and High Education. Ministry of Education, National Iranian Oil Company, Atomic Energy Organization of Iran, Islamic Republic of Iran Broadcasting Organization for itself and on behalf of School of Television and Cinema, Telecommunications Company of Iran, Organization for Administration and Employment, University of Tehran, University of Shahid Beheshti (formerly, National University of Iran), University of Isfahan, University of Ferdowsi, University of Shahid Chamran (formerly, University of Jondi Shahpour), University of Kerman, University of Complex for Arts, Humanities and Letters University Complex, State Management Training Center, Alavi Foundation, Institute for Intellectual Development of Children and Young Adults, Industrial Development and Renovation Organization of Iran on behalf of Technology Inc., and the Government of the Islamic Republic of Iran, hereinafter collectively called "Respondents," on the other part. Claimant and Respondents are hereinafter collectively referred to as the "Parties."

WHEREAS, Claimant has filed a Statement of Claim with the Iran-United States Claims Tribunal ("the Tribunal") raising certain claims against the Respondents which claim was docketed by the Tribunal as Case No. 321;

[2 Filed 8 April 1994.]

Whereas, Respondents have asserted defenses and filed counterclaims in case No. 321;

WHEREAS, the Parties desire to resolve and to make full, complete, and final settlement of all their claims and disputes existing or capable of arising between them related to Case No. 321 and the claims and counterclaims filed therein;

NOW, THEREFORE, the Parties agree:

1. The scope and subject matter of this Settlement Agreement is to settle and dismiss, for ever, all disputes, differences, claims, counterclaims, and matters directly or indirectly raised or capable of arising out of the relationships, transactions, contracts and events in any manner related to the subject matter of the Statement of Claim, Counterclaims, and other submissions by the Parties in Case No. 321.

2. In consideration of the covenants and promises set forth herein, Claimant for itself and for its subsidiaries, affiliates, parents, predecessors, successors, and assigns hereby release, quitclaim, and forever discharge Respondents and their affiliates, subsidiaries, agencies, instrumentalities, predecessors, successors, and assigns, from and against any and all claims, demands, losses, damages, suits, actions and causes of action of any nature, whether in rem or in personam or otherwise, which they have ever had, now have or may have in future arising out of or in connection with Case No. 321.

3. In consideration of the covenants and promises set forth herein, Respondents for themselves and for their affiliates, subsidiaries, agencies, instrumentalities, predecessors, successors, and assigns hereby release, quitclaim, and forever discharge Claimant and its subsidiaries, affiliates, parents, predecessors, successors, and assigns from and against any and all claims, demands, losses, damages, suits, actions and causes of action of any nature, whether in rem or in personam or otherwise, which they have ever had, now have or may have in the future arising out of or in connection with Case No. 321.

4. The Parties expressly waive and relinquish all rights and benefits afforded by Section 1542 of the Civil Code of the State of California, and do so understanding and acknowledging the significance of such specific waiver of Section 1542. Section 1542 of the Civil Code of the State of California states as follows:

> A general release does not extend to claims which the creditor does not know or suspect to exist in his favor at the time of executing the release, which if known by him must have materially affected his settlement with the debtor.

Thus, notwithstanding the provisions of Section 1542, and for the purpose of implementing a full and complete release and discharge, the Parties expressly acknowledge that this Settlement Agreement is intended to include in its effect, without limitation, all claims which the Parties do not know or suspect to exist in their favor at the time of execution hereof, and that this Settlement Agreement contemplates the extinguishment of any such claim or claims.

5. Claimant shall indemnify and hold harmless Respondents, their affiliates, subsidiaries, agencies and instrumentalities, predecessors, successors, and assigns against any claim, counterclaim, action or proceeding that any or all of the Claimant, its subsidiaries, affiliates, predecessors, successors, and assigns may raise, assert, initiate or take against any or all of the Respondents, their affiliates, subsidiaries, agencies, instrumentalities, predecessors, successors, and assigns relating to, or arising out of, or capable of arising out of, the contracts, transactions, relationships, rights, or occurrences, and any matters that are the subject of the claims raised in Case No. 321.

6. Respondents shall indemnify and hold harmless Claimant, its subsidiaries, affiliates, agencies, instrumentalities, trustees, officers, parents, predecessors, successors and assigns against any claim, counterclaim, action or proceeding that any or all of the Respondents, their affiliates, subsidiaries, agencies, instrumentalities, predecessors, successors and assigns may raise, assert, initiate or take against any or all of the Claimant, its subsidiaries, affiliates, agencies, instrumentalities, trustees, officers. parents, predecessors, successors, and assigns relating to or arising out of, or capable of arising out of, the contracts, transactions, relationships, rights or occurrences and any matters that are the subject of the counterclaims raised in Case No. 321.

7. Upon the issuance of the Arbitral Award on Agreed Terms, the Parties shall not directly, indirectly, individually, or in conjunction with others at any time thereafter take or pursue any legal action or initiate or pursue arbitral or court proceedings or otherwise make any claim whatsoever against each other or any of their respective subsidiaries, affiliates, agencies, instrumentalities, trustees, officers, parents, predecessors, successors, assigns, agencies, or instrumentalities, with respect to the subject matter of the claims and counterclaims in Case No. 321.

8. Upon the issuance of the Arbitral Award on Agreed Terms, the Parties shall waive any and all claims for costs, including attorneys' fees, arising out of or related in any way to the arbitration, prosecution, or defense of any claim before any forum including the Iran-United States Claims Tribunal with respect to Case No. 321.

9. This Settlement Agreement is for the sole purpose of settling the disputes at issue in Case No. 321. Nothing in this Settlement Agreement shall be relied upon or construed as relevant to or to affect in any way any argument or position that the Parties or their subsidiaries, affiliates, agencies, instrumentalities, trustees, officers, parents, predecessors, successors, assigns

have raised or may raise concerning the jurisdiction or the merits of other cases, whether before the Tribunal or any other forum or fora. This Settlement Agreement shall not constitute a legal precedent for any person or party, and shall not be used except for the sole purpose of giving effect to its terms, and shall not prejudice or affect other rights of the Parties or the rights of any other person in other cases before the Tribunal or elsewhere.

10. The releases, waivers, transfers, undertakings, obligations, and agreements herein are self-executing upon the issuance of the Arbitral Award on Agreed Terms, and need not be authorized, evidenced, or signified by any additional document, agreement, or other writing.

11. The Parties agree to submit the Settlement Agreement on or before April 11, 1994 to the Tribunal to be recorded as an Arbitral Award on agreed Terms. If this Settlement Agreement is not submitted on such date, or within such additional time as Parties may, through counsel, agree in writing, it shall automatically become null and void, and the Parties, without prejudicing their respective rights, will be placed in the same position as they were prior to the date of this Settlement Agreement.

12. If for any reason the Award on Agreed Terms is not issued, final, and binding within 30 days of submitting of the Settlement Agreement to the Tribunal, then, unless otherwise agreed in writing by the Parties, the Tribunal shall resume jurisdiction over all claims and counterclaims in Case No. 321 and the Parties shall be placed in the same position as they had occupied prior to this Settlement Agreement as if it had not been entered into.

13. The representatives of the Parties expressly declare that they are duly empowered to sign this Settlement Agreement and that their signatures will commit their respective principals to fulfillment of their obligations under this Settlement Agreement without any limitations whatsoever. and the signing of this Settlement Agreement by Iran's Agent, other Respondents and Claimant, shall signify that all such authorities have given their approval.

14. This Settlement Agreement sets forth the entire agreement between the Parties hereto, and fully supersedes any and all prior agreements and understandings between the Parties hereto pertaining to the subject matter hereof, excepting only that certain Agreement executed concurrently herewith by Claimant and National Iranian Oil Company, and the Contract and the Chair referenced therein.

15. For the Purpose of construction and interpretation of this Settlement Agreement the entire agreement shall be read and construed as a whole without giving any specific effect to any article separately.

16. This Settlement Agreement (in four originals in each language) has been written and signed in English and Persian, and each text shall have equal validity.

IN WITNESS WHEREOF the Parties have executed and delivered this Settlement Agreement this 11th day of August 1993.

Agreement

This Agreement is entered into between the University of Southern California ("University") on the one part, and National Iranian Oil Company ("NIOC"), on the other part. The University and NIOC are in this Agreement collectively referred to as the "Parties."

WHEREAS, pursuant to the terms of the Settlement Agreement executed simultaneously herewith relating to Case No. 321 (the "Settlement Agreement") before the Iran-United States Claims Tribunal, the Parties have agreed to release each other from any claims whatsoever arising out of or in connection with Case No. 321;

WHEREAS the Parties had concluded an endowed fellowship Contract dated September 29, 1972, which under its terms the University is required to provide certain limited financial support to the Iranian students pursuing Master of Science degree in Engineering at the University (the "Contract");

WHEREAS, pursuant to the agreement between the Parties, University was paid the amount of $1,000,000 (one million U.S. dollars) for establishing a professorship chair at the University in the field of oil engineering (the "Chair");

WHEREAS the Parties desire to re-establish their scientific and educational relations based on the Contract;

NOW, THEREFORE, the Parties agree:

(1) Notwithstanding the terms of the Settlement Agreement, the rights and obligations of the Parties hereunder shall survive the execution of the Settlement Agreement.

(2) The contract will be implemented hereafter under the title of "National Iranian Oil Company Fellowships."

(3) University undertakes, as provided by the Contract, to grant hereafter the fellowships in each year commencing September 1993 at least to two Iranian students who are appropriately qualified, eligible and approved under the terms of the Contract.

(4) University undertakes that the Chair shall hereafter be operational in the name of "National Iranian oil Company."

(5) NIOC and University will undertake all reasonable steps to assure the implementation of their agreements as set forth above.

(6) Since NIOC does not have any office in New York, the University shall

forward the announcement of fellowships and all the other relevant information directly to NIOC head office in Tehran.

(7) This Agreement sets forth the entire agreement between the Parties hereto, and fully supersedes any and all prior agreements or understandings between the Parties hereto pertaining to the subject matter hereof, excepting only the Contract and the Chair.

IN WITNESS WHEREOF, the Parties hereto have executed and delivered this Agreement this 11th day of August 1993.

Christensen, Inc., *Claimant*

v.

The Islamic Republic of Iran, Oil Services Company of Iran, The Ministry of Petroleum of the Islamic Republic of Iran, The National Iranian Oil Company, *Respondents*

(Case No. 212)

Chamber One: Briner, *Chairman*; Noori, Holtzmann, *Members*

Signed 17 *May* 1994[1]

Award No. 556-212-1

The following is the text as issued by the Tribunal:

Award on Agreed Terms

1. On 11 January 1982, Christensen, Inc. ("the Claimant") filed a Statement of Claim against The Islamic Republic of Iran and The Oil Services Company of Iran ("OSCO") seeking certain amounts under several heads of recovery. In subsequent submissions, the Claimant also named as Respondents in this Case The Ministry of Petroleum of the Islamic Republic of Iran and, in connection with its claims against OSCO, The National Iranian Oil Company ("NIOC"). The Respondents filed several counter-claims against the Claimant.

2. This Case was initially referred to Chamber One. By Presidential Order No. 61 of 19 April 1988, it was transferred to Chamber Three. Subsequently, by Presidential Order No. 70 of 11 December 1989, it was transferred from Chamber Three back to Chamber One. By the same Presidential Order, Mr. Robert Briner was designated to act as Chairman of Chamber One for these proceedings, instead of Mr. Bengt Broms.

3. Pursuant to Article 34, paragraph 1, of the Tribunal Rules, a Joint Request for an Arbitral Award on Agreed Terms was filed on 4 September 1990, signed by the Agent of the Government of the Islamic Republic of Iran and NIOC on the one side, and a representative of Norton Christensen, Inc., the successor corporation to the Claimant, on the other, requesting the

[1 Filed 17 May 1994.]

Tribunal to render an Award on Agreed Terms recording and giving effect to the Settlement Agreement entered into on 16 August 1990 by Norton Christensen, Inc., on its own behalf and on behalf of its subsidiaries, parents, affiliates, predecessors, assignees, and successors, on the one side, and NIOC, on its own behalf and on behalf of its subsidiaries, affiliates, and predecessors, on the other ("the Settlement Agreement"), and that the Tribunal issue the Award on Agreed Terms upon fulfillment of the conditions set forth in the Settlement Agreement. The Tribunal understands that by signing the Joint Request, the Agent of the Government of the Islamic Republic of Iran signified the assent of his government to both the Joint Request and the Settlement Agreement. Copies of the Joint Request and the Settlement Agreement are attached hereto and incorporated by reference.

4. Article III(5) of the Settlement Agreement provides:

> Upon inspection of the equipment in Germany by NIOC representatives, NIOC will provide Claimant's German subsidiary with a signed certificate as proof of inspection that the items have been properly repaired. Claimant's German subsidiary will prepare the equipment for shipment back to Iran, C.I.F. Ahwaz. . . .

5. Article III(6) of the Settlement Agreement provides:

> Claimant's German subsidiary will present the certificate referred to in (5) above to the Tribunal, along with the shipping documents for shipment to Iran. . . . Submission to the Tribunal of the shipping documents and certificate of inspection of repairs will evidence that all conditions of this agreement have been met and will result in the issuance of the Award on Agreed Terms and the payment of the sum of U.S.$3,000,000 (three million dollars) . . . to the Claimant out of the Security Account. . . .

6. On 25 March 1994, the Tribunal received the certificate from NIOC specified in Article III(5) of the Settlement Agreement. In pertinent part, this certificate, which is dated 20 February 1994, states:

> This is to certify that the Norton Company, successor to Norton Christensen, Inc. (formerly Christensen, Inc.) . . . has fulfilled all terms of the Settlement Agreement . . . with the National Iranian Oil Company ("NIOC"). . . .
>
> Accordingly, upon the submission by Claimant of the shipping documents reflecting the shipment of the equipment referred to in the list attached hereto as Exhibit "A" . . . all conditions of the Settlement Agreement shall have been fulfilled and the Claimant shall be entitled to the disbursement of the Settlement Amount as referenced in Article III(6) of the Settlement Agreement.

Copies of both the certificate from NIOC and its Exhibit "A" are attached hereto and incorporated by reference.

7. On 25 March 1994, the Tribunal also received a series of shipping documents, consisting of bills of lading and customs invoices. Copies of these shipping documents are attached hereto and incorporated by reference.

8. In its Communication to the Parties of 6 April 1994, the Tribunal noted a number of discrepancies between the description of specified equipment on the list Exhibit A appended to the National Iranian Oil Company's 20 February 1994 certificate and the description of what appeared to be the same equipment in certain of the shipping documents referred to in para. 7, *supra*. The Tribunal went on to inform the Parties that

> [u]nless the Parties advise the Tribunal otherwise by 30 April 1994, notwithstanding the discrepancies described above, the Tribunal will assume that the equipment listed in the shipping documents submitted by the Claimant on 25 March 1994 fully satisfies the obligations of the Claimant under Article III of the 16 August 1990 Settlement Agreement between the Parties and, further, that all the documents submitted by the Claimant on 25 March 1994 satisfy in their entirety the requirements of Article III, paragraphs 5 and 6, of that Settlement Agreement, and, thus, that the Claimant has fulfilled the conditions for the issuance of the Award on Agreed Terms requested jointly by the Parties in this Case. Accordingly, after 30 April 1994, the Tribunal will issue this Award on Agreed Terms.
>
> After the issuance of the Award on Agreed Terms, the Tribunal will return to the Claimant the shipping documents the Claimant submitted to the Tribunal's Registry on 25 March 1994.

9. In response to the Tribunal's Communication to the Parties of 6 April 1994, by letter filed on 27 April 1994, the Agent of the Government of the Islamic Republic of Iran informed the Tribunal that the Respondents "have no objection to the existing discrepancies between the description of certain equipment on the list Exhibit A appended to the National Iranian Oil Company's 20 February 1994 Certificate and the description of the same equipment in the shipping documents." Concerning the Tribunal's intention to return these shipping documents to the Claimant after the issuance of the Award on Agreed Terms, the Agent noted that "[s]uch documents are evidence of the Respondents' title to the equipment and required for effecting their release from customs in Iran." Accordingly, the Agent requested the Tribunal to order "the delivery of the shipping documents to Iran upon issuance of its Award on Agreed Terms." A copy of the Agent's letter filed on 27 April 1994 is attached hereto and incorporated by reference.

10. By letter filed on 2 May 1994, the Claimant advised the Tribunal that it "has no objection to the delivery of the shipping documents to Iran upon issuance of the Tribunal's Award on Agreed Terms . . . [and] has no objection to the contents" of the letter from the Agent of the Government of the Islamic

Republic of Iran filed on 27 April 1994. A copy of the Claimant's letter filed on 2 May 1994 is attached hereto and incorporated by reference.

11. In light of the foregoing, the Tribunal is satisfied that the equipment listed in the shipping documents submitted by the Claimant on 25 March 1994 fully satisfies the obligations of the Claimant under Article III of the 16 August 1990 Settlement Agreement between the Parties and, further, that all the documents submitted by the Claimant on 25 March 1994 satisfy in their entirety the requirements of Article III, paragraphs 5 and 6, of that Settlement Agreement.

12. The Tribunal's Registry is ordered to release to the Agent of the Government of the Islamic Republic of Iran, after the issuance of the Award on Agreed Terms, the shipping documents the Claimant submitted to the Tribunal on 25 March 1994. *See* para. 7, *supra*.

13. Finding that the conditions for the issuance of an Arbitral Award on Agreed Terms are met in this Case, the Tribunal accepts the Settlement Agreement in accordance with Article 34 of the Tribunal Rules.

14. Based on the foregoing,

THE TRIBUNAL AWARDS AS FOLLOWS:

(a) The Settlement Agreement filed with the Joint Request is hereby recorded as an Award on Agreed Terms binding on all the Parties in this Case in full and final settlement of the Case in its entirety and with prejudice.

(b) The payment obligation specified in the Settlement Agreement in the amount of Three Million United States Dollars (U.S.$3,000,000) shall be satisfied by payment to Christensen, Inc. out of the Security Account established pursuant to paragraph 7 of the Declaration of the Government of the Democratic and Popular Republic of Algeria dated 19 January 1981.

(c) This Award is hereby submitted to the President of the Tribunal for the purpose of notification to the Escrow Agent.

JOINT REQUEST FOR ARBITRAL AWARD ON AGREED TERMS[1]

Pursuant to Article 34 of the Tribunal Rules, National Iranian Oil Company for itself and on behalf of its subsidiaries, affiliates and predecessors, whether or not named in Case No. 212 ("NIOC") (referred to hereinafter as "Respondent"), on the one part, and Norton Christensen, Inc. (formerly

[1 Filed 4 September 1990.]

Christensen, Inc.) (hereinafter called "Claimant"), for itself and on behalf of its parents, affiliates and subsidiaries, whether or not named in Case No. 212, on the other part, jointly request that the Iran-United States Claims Tribunal ("the Tribunal") issue an Arbitral Award on Agreed Terms upon completion of the conditions of the Settlement Agreement, that will record and give effect to the Settlement Agreement reached by the parties in Case No. 212 Chamber One.

On August 16, 1990 Claimant and Respondent entered into a Settlement Agreement, a copy of which is attached hereto, providing *inter alia:*

> Claimant's German subsidiary will present the certificate referred to in Article 111 (5) to the Tribunal, along with the shipping documents for shipment to Iran. Said shipping documents will include any replacement items required by Article 111 (2). Submission to the Tribunal of the shipping documents and certificate of inspection will evidence that all conditions of the Settlement Agreement have been met and will result in the issuance of the Award on Agreed Terms and the payment of the sum of U.S.$3,000,000 (three million dollars) (hereinafter the "Settlement Amount") to the Claimant out of the Security Account established pursuant to paragraph 7 of the Declaration of the Government of the Democratic and Popular Republic of Algeria dated January 19, 1981.

The undersigned request the Tribunal to record the attached Settlement Agreement and upon fulfilment of the conditions contained therein issue an Arbitral Award on Agreed Terms, giving effect to its terms and conditions and terminating all claims and counterclaims in Case No. 212 forever and with prejudice in the manner specified therein.

SETTLEMENT AGREEMENT[2]

This Settlement Agreement ("Agreement") is made and entered into this 16th day of August, 1990 by and between Norton Christensen, Inc. (formerly Christensen, Inc.), a company organised and existing under the laws of Utah U.S.A., which for the purpose of this Agreement represents itself, its subsidiaries, parents, affiliates, predecessors, assignees, and successors (hereinafter collectively referred to as "Claimant"), on the one part, and National Iranian Oil Company ("NIOC"), a company organised and existing under the laws of Iran, for itself and on behalf of its subsidiaries, affiliates and predecessors (hereinafter called "Respondent"), on the other part, all hereinafter collectively called the "Parties."

[2 Filed 4 September 1990.]

WHEREAS Claimant has filed certain claims in its Statement of Claim and other submissions (hereinafter referred to as the "Statement of Claim") filed with the Iran-United States Claims Tribunal (hereinafter referred to as the "Tribunal") under Case 212 against Respondent.

WHEREAS Respondent in responding to the Statement of Claim filed its Statement of Defense and Counterclaims against the Claimant.

WHEREAS the Parties have agreed to settle all their claims, disputes, and differences outstanding or capable of arising between them and/or by Claimant against Iran and/or in general all the claims and counterclaims contained in the Statement of Claim, Statements of Defense and Counterclaim, and subsequent submissions.

NOW, THEREFORE, in consideration of and under the conditions set forth herein, the parties agree as follows:

Article I

The scope and subject matters of this Settlement Agreement are:
(a) To settle, dismiss and terminate forever and with prejudice all disputes, differences, claims, counterclaims and matters directly or indirectly raised or capable of arising out of the relationships, occurrences, rights and interests related to and subject matters of the Statement of Claim and Statement of Defense and Counterclaims filed with the Tribunal, between the Parties and/or against Iran.
(b) To provide for the payment to Claimant of the Settlement Amount as defined in Article III below.
(c) To transfer to and vest in NIOC unconditionally and irrevocably, without any lien or encumbrance and without the right to any recourse, all Claimant's rights, benefits, interests in and titles to all and any properties, parts and equipments described in Appendix I hereto.

Article II

The Parties agree to submit this Settlement Agreement to the Tribunal on September 4, 1990, together with a joint motion requesting the Tribunal to record and give effect to the provisions of this Settlement Agreement as an Arbitral Award on Agreed Terms ("Award on Agreed Terms") in accordance with the terms and conditions provided herein.

Article III

In full, complete and final settlement of all disputes, differences, claims and counterclaims arising out of the rights, interests, relationships and occurrences related to the subject matters of the Statement of Claim, the Statements of Defense and Counterclaims and this Settlement Agreement, and in consideration of the covenants, premises, waivers, withdrawals, and other agreements contained herein, the parties agree as follows:

(1) Claimant authorizes NIOC to obtain possession of all equipment listed in Appendix I attached hereto which is an integral part of this agreement, including the equipment in the possession of CIPICO, an Iranian private company, within 30 days of the signing of this agreement.

(2) NIOC and Claimant's representative will inventory the equipment received from CIPICO's possession. If less than 15% of the equipment listed in Appendix I is missing Claimant's German subsidiary will replace the equipment at no additional cost to NIOC. If more than 15% is missing, the parties to this agreement will resume negotiations.

(3) Within 10 (ten) days of receipt of the equipment referred to in (1) above, by NIOC, the equipment (less diamond bits, drill collars, subs, core barrels, and other items which do not require repair) will be made available by NIOC for export and shipped to Germany at Claimant's expense.

(4) Claimant's German subsidiary will repair the equipment at Claimant's expense as soon as possible. During the time the equipment is being repaired, NIOC will send two technical representatives to Germany for training regarding said equipment. NIOC will bear all out of pocket expenses incurred regarding these representatives.

(5) Upon inspection of the equipment in Germany by NIOC representatives, NIOC will provide Claimant's German subsidiary with a signed certificate as proof of inspection that the items have been properly repaired. Claimant's German subsidiary will prepare the equipment for shipment back to Iran, C.I.F. Ahwaz. Claimant shall bear all costs and expenses for such shipment.

(6) Claimant's German subsidiary will present the certificate referred to in (5) above to the Tribunal, along with the shipping documents for shipment to Iran. Said shipping documents will include any replacement items required by (2) above. Submission to the Tribunal of the shipping documents and certificate of inspection of repairs will evidence that all conditions of this agreement have been met and will result in the issuance of the Award on Agreed Terms and the payment of the sum of U.S.$3,000,000 (three million dollars) (hereinafter the "Settlement Amount") to the Claimant out of the Security Account established pursuant to paragraph 7 of the Declaration of the Government of the Democratic and Popular Republic of Algeria dated January 19, 1981.

Article IV

Upon issuance of the Award on Agreed Terms, all titles, rights, benefits and interests of Claimant in properties claimed in Appendix I hereto shall unconditionally and irrevocably, without any lien or encumbrances and without the right to any recourse be transferred to NIOC.

Article V
(i) Upon issuance of the Award on Agreed Terms as set forth in Art. III, Claimant shall cause, without delay and with prejudice, all proceedings against Respondent and Iranian banks, companies, entities, organizations, instrumentalities, institutions and divisions, in all courts, fora or any authorities or administrative bodies to be dismissed, withdrawn and terminated and shall be barred from instituting and/or continuing with any proceedings before the Iran-United States Claims Tribunal or any other fora, authorities, or administrative bodies, whatsoever, including but not limited to any courts in the United States of America or the Islamic Republic of Iran in connection with disputes, differences, claims and matters related to and subject matters of the Statement of Claim, Statement of Defense and Counterclaim and/or this Settlement Agreement.

(ii) Upon issuance of the Award on Agreed Terms as set forth in Article III, Respondent shall cause, without delay and with prejudice, all proceedings against Claimant in all courts, fora or any authorities or administrative bodies to be dismissed, withdrawn and terminated and shall be barred from instituting and/or continuing with any proceedings before the Iran-U.S. Claims Tribunal or any other fora, authorities or administrative bodies, whatsoever, including but not limited to any courts in the United States of America or the Islamic Republic of Iran in connection with disputes, differences, claims and matters related to and subject matters of the Statement of Claim, Statement of Defense and Counterclaim, and/or this Settlement Agreement.

Article VI

In consideration of the covenants, premises, transfers, waivers and other agreements contained herein, upon the issuance of the Award on Agreed Terms by the Tribunal as set forth in Article III, Claimant and Respondent shall release and forever discharge each other, and Claimant shall release and forever discharge Iran, Iranian banks, companies, entities, organizations, instrumentalities, institutions and divisions, from any claim, rights, interests and obligations, past present or future which may be raised in connection with disputes, differences, claims and matters related to the subject matters of the

Statement of Claim, Statement of Defense and Counterclaims, and/or this Settlement Agreement.

Article VII

Upon the issuance of the Award on Agreed Terms as set forth in Article III, (i) Claimant shall indemnify and hold harmless Respondent and Iran against any claim which Claimant, its subsidiaries, parents, affiliates, assigns, transferees, successors, predecessors, agents or third persons have raised or may raise against Iran, Iranian banks, companies, entities, organizations, and institutions including Respondent, and (ii) Respondent shall indemnify and hold harmless Claimant against any claims which Respondent, its subsidiaries, affiliates, assignees, transferees, successors and agents or Iran have raised or may raise against Claimant. The foregoing indemnities and hold harmless agreements shall be limited to claims and counterclaims in connection with and under the same cause or causes of action contained or which could be contained in the Statement of Claim, Statement of Defense and Counterclaims and/or subject matters of this Settlement Agreement.

Article VIII

Upon issuance of the Award on Agreed Terms as set forth in Art. III, Claimant and Respondent shall waive any and all claims for costs (including attorney's fees) arising out of or related to the arbitration, prosecution or defense of the claims asserted before the Iran-U.S. Claims Tribunal, Iranian or United States courts or elsewhere with respect to matters involved in the Statement of Claim, Statement of Defense and Counterclaims, and/or matters which are the subject matters of this Settlement Agreement.

Article IX

Upon the issuance of the Award on Agreed Terms as set forth in Art. III the obligations, declarations, releases, waivers, withdrawals, dismissals, transfer of rights, interests, benefits and titles in properties contained and referred to in this Settlement Agreement shall become self-executing. After the issuance of the Award on Agreed Terms by the Tribunal, no further documents need to be executed in implementing the provisions of this Agreement.

Article X

This Settlement Agreement is for the sole purpose of settling the disputes at issue in Case No. 212. Nothing in this Settlement Agreement shall be relied upon or construed as relevant to or to affect in any way any argument that Iran, its agencies, instrumentalities, entities and/or Respondent or Claimant have raised, or may raise, concerning jurisdiction or the merits of this case or other cases whether before the Tribunal or any other fora.

Article XI

The Parties agree that this Settlement Agreement shall be approved and ratified by Iranian authorities. Should for any reason whatsoever they choose not to confirm this Settlement Agreement and/or if CIPICO refuses to hand over the equipment mentioned in Article III (1) to NIOC within 30 days from the date hereof, then this Settlement Agreement shall become null and void, and in that event no party to this Settlement Agreement may rely upon, cite or publish its terms or any statements made in the course of settlement discussions.

Article XII

For the purpose of construction and interpretation of this Settlement Agreement, the entire agreement shall be read and construed as a whole without giving any specific effect to any article separately.

Article XIII

The representatives of the Parties hereby expressly declare that they are duly empowered to sign this Agreement.

Article XIV

This Settlement Agreement (in four originals) has been written and signed in both languages of Persian and English and each text shall have the same equal validity. The representatives of the Parties hereto expressly declare that they are duly empowered to sign this Agreement and their signatures will commit their respective principals to fulfilment of their obligations under this agreement without any limitations except as may otherwise be contained in this Settlement Agreement.

Kidde Consultants, Inc., *Claimant*,

v.

Haydar Ghyai & Associates,
Sherkate Sahami Nowsazi Abbas Abad
Respondents

(Case No. 841)

Chamber One: Broms, *Chairman*; Noori, Duncan, *Members*

Signed 17 *October* 1994[1]

Award No. 561-841-1

The following is the text as issued by the Tribunal:

Award on Agreed Terms

1. On 1 July 1994, the Claimant, Kidde Consultants, Inc., and the Respondents, Haydar Ghyai & Associates and Sherkate Sahami Nowsazi Abbas Abad (collectively "the Parties") filed with the Tribunal a Joint Request for Arbitral Award on Agreed Terms ("the Joint Request"), and attached thereto a Settlement Agreement in Case No. 841, Chamber One dated 9 May 1994 ("the Settlement Agreement"), signed by representatives of the Parties. In the Joint Request the Parties explain that they "have entered into such Settlement Agreement settling all claims and counterclaims now existing or capable of arising in connection with Case No. 841, and any other matters related thereto." Accordingly, the Joint Request asks the Tribunal to record the Settlement Agreement as an Arbitral Award on Agreed Terms pursuant to Article 34 of the Tribunal Rules. Copies of both the Joint Request and the Settlement Agreement are attached and incorporated herein by reference.[2]

[1 Filed 17 October 1994.]
[2] Article XIII of the Settlement Agreement provides that the Parties should submit the Settlement Agreement together with the Joint Request to the Tribunal on or before 9 July 1994, provided however that the Agreement be approved and ratified by Iranian authorities as provided in Article XII, and that "[i]f th[e] Settlement Agreement is not submitted on or before July 9, 1994 or as otherwise agreed by the Parties, then it shall automatically become null and void, and the Parties, without prejudicing their respective rights will be placed in the same position as they were prior to the date of th[e] Settlement Agreement." According to Article XII, "[s]igning of the joint request by the Agent of the Islamic Republic of Iran to the Tribunal shall represent that [the] approval and ratification [by the Iranian Authorities] have been obtained." The Tribunal notes

2. By letter filed on 7 July 1994, the Agent of the Islamic Republic of Iran informed the Tribunal about a modification of Article II(ii) and submitted the corrected text of page 2 of the Settlement Agreement in both English and Persian. In addition, the Agent stated in his letter that the Parties were redrafting the letter referenced in Article X of the Settlement Agreement and that they would advise the Tribunal of the final text in due course. Pursuant to the letter of 7 July 1994, the final text of the letter referenced in Article X of the Settlement Agreement was filed by the Agent of the Islamic Republic of Iran on 26 July 1994 in both English and Persian. On 8 August 1994, a letter was filed by the counsel for the Claimant confirming that the Claimant agrees with the corrections submitted on behalf of the Respondents to the Settlement Agreement and the letter referenced in Article X thereof. Copies of all three letters are attached and incorporated herein by reference.

3. According to Article I of the Settlement Agreement,

[t]he purpose and intent of th[e] Settlement Agreement is to settle, dismiss and terminate forever and with prejudice all claims, counterclaims, disputes and differences and matters directly or indirectly raised or capable of being raised in the Case, arising out of the relationships, transactions, contracts or events in any manner related to the subject matter of the Statements of Claim, Statements of Defense and Counterclaim, and other submissions by the Parties in the Case ("the Released Claims").

4. The Settlement Agreement then provides for certain obligations, declarations, releases, waivers, indemnifications, withdrawals and dismissals. In particular, Article II, as modified by the letters of 7 July 1994 and 8 August 1994, provides, *inter alia*, that the

Claimant shall pay to the Respondents the sum of seventy thousand United States dollars (U.S.$70,000.00) ("the Settlement Amount").

(ii) The Settlement Amount shall be deposited with the Tribunal's Registry upon filing of th[e] Settlement Agreement. The Tribunal shall release the Settlement Amount to the Agent of the Islamic Republic of Iran upon delivery to the Claimant by the Registry of the letter referenced in Article X(b).

5. In addition, it is provided in Article X of the Settlement Agreement that

[w]ithin sixty days of the issuance of the Arbitral Award on Agreed Terms:

---

that the Joint Request was signed by the Agent of the Islamic Republic of Iran to the Tribunal on 29 June 1994, and that the Settlement Agreement as well as the Joint Request were filed with the Tribunal on 1 July 1994.

(a) Respondents shall deliver to the Tribunal Registry two original copies of a letter from Bank Tejarat in the form attached herewith.
(b) The Tribunal shall order the Tribunal's Registry to deliver to Claimant dual originals of the Letter of Bank Tejarat described in the preceding paragraph.

6. Finally, according to Article XI of the Settlement Agreement,

[t]he bank cheques presented by Claimant in the filings including cheques of Bank Melli Nos. 824436, 824435, 824431 and cheque of Bank Etebarat Tavoni Touzie No. 638213 are null and void. Claimant agrees that it will not present any such cheques for payment to the issuing banks or institute any legal action for their sums. Claimant hereby agrees to indemnify Respondents in connection with any such cheques against any loss that might be incurred by them or any of them that is attributable to Claimant's action in breach of this commitment.

7. The Tribunal notes that on 1 July 1994 it received from the Claimant a check [of HM Holdings, Inc.] drawn in the amount of $70,000.00 [on LaSalle National Bank, LaSalle Bank of Lisle] and payable to the order of the Agent of the Islamic Republic of Iran. On 15 September 1994, a letter was received from the counsel for the Claimant in which he informed the Tribunal that the check may be paid to the Agent of the Islamic Republic of Iran upon receipt by the Registry of the original of the letter referenced in Article X of the Settlement Agreement, and that the said letter may be delivered to the Claimant upon notice from the Agent of the Islamic Republic of Iran that the check has cleared. On 5 October 1994, the Agent of the Islamic Republic of Iran informed the Tribunal that the Settlement Amount, referred to in Article II (1) of the Settlement Agreement, has been received by the Respondents, and thereafter, the letter referenced in Article X of the Settlement Agreement was delivered to the Claimant. Copies of the letters of 15 September 1994 and 5 October 1994 are attached and incorporated herein by reference.

8. Finding that the conditions for the issuance of an Award on Agreed Terms are met in this Case, the Tribunal accepts the Settlement Agreement in accordance with Article 34, paragraph 1, of the Tribunal Rules.

9. Based on the foregoing,

THE TRIBUNAL AWARDS AS FOLLOWS:

(a) The Settlement Agreement of 1 July 1994, as modified by the Parties' letters of 7 July 1994, 26 July 1994, 8 August 1994 and 15 September 1994, is hereby recorded as an Award on Agreed Terms binding upon Kidde Consultants, Inc., Haydar Ghyai & Associates and Sherkate Sahami Nowsazi Abbas Abad, each of which is bound to fulfill the conditions set forth in the Settlement Agreement.

(b) The Tribunal declares the proceedings in Case No. 841 terminated in their entirety and with prejudice.

JOINT REQUEST FOR ARBITRAL AWARD ON AGREED TERMS[1]

Pursuant to Article 34 of the Tribunal Rules, Kidde Consultants Inc., ("Claimant"), on the one part, and Haydar Ghyai & Associates and Sherkate Sahami Nowsazi Abbas Abad ("Respondents"), on the other part, jointly request that the Tribunal issue an Arbitral Award on Agreed Terms that will record and give effect to the Settlement Agreement reached among them, a copy of which is attached hereto.

On May 9, 1994 the Parties have entered into such Settlement Agreement settling all claims and counterclaims now existing or capable of arising in connection with Case No. 841, and any other matters related thereto.

The undersigned hereby request the Tribunal to record the Settlement Agreement as an Arbitral Award on Agreed Terms, direct the payment of seventy thousand United States dollars (U.S.$70,000.00) to the Agent of the Islamic Republic of Iran upon delivery to Claimant from the Tribunal's Registry of the letter of Bank Tejarat described in Article X of the Settlement Agreement, and terminate Case No. 841 in its entirety and with prejudice.

SETTLEMENT AGREEMENT[2]

This Settlement Agreement is made this 9th day of May 1994 by and between Kidde Consultants Inc., a Delaware Corporation having a place of business in Baltimore, Maryland ("Claimant"), on the one part, and Haydar Ghyai & Associates and Sherkate Sahami Nowsazi Abbas Abad ("Respondents"), on the other part. Claimant and Respondents are hereinafter called the Parties. For the purposes of this Settlement Agreement the Parties represent themselves and their subsidiaries, parents, successors, predecessors, instrumentalities, agencies, affiliates, and their respective present and former officers, directors, employees, agents and shareholders whether or not named in the pleadings filed by the Parties in Case No. 841, Chamber One ("the Case").

Whereas Claimant has raised certain claims as contemplated in its Statement of Claim and other of Claimant's submissions filed with the Iran-

[1 Filed 1 July 1994.]
[2 Filed 1 July 1994.]

United States Claims Tribunal ("the Tribunal"), under the Case against Respondents; and

Whereas Respondents in responding to the Statement of Claim have filed Statements of Defense and Counterclaims; and

Whereas the Parties desire to resolve and to make full, complete, and final settlement of all their claims, counterclaims and disputes existing or capable of arising between them related to Case No. 841 and the claims and counterclaims filed therein:

Now, therefore, in consideration of and under the conditions set forth below, the Parties agree as follows:

Article I

The purpose and intent of this Settlement Agreement is to settle, dismiss and terminate forever and with prejudice all claims, counterclaims, disputes and differences and matters directly or indirectly raised or capable of being raised in the Case, arising out of the relationships, transactions, contracts or events in any manner related to the subject matter of the Statements of Claim, Statements of Defense and Counterclaim, and other submissions by the Parties in the Case ("the Released Claims").

Article II

(i) In consideration of the full and final settlement of all disputes, differences, claims, counterclaims, and matters directly or indirectly raised or capable of being raised in the Case, arising out of the relationships, transactions, contracts, or events in any manner related to the subject matter of the Statement of Claim, Statements of Defense and Counterclaims, and other submissions by the Parties in the Case, and in consideration of the covenants, promises, transfers, waivers, withdrawals, and other agreements set forth herein, Claimant shall pay to the Respondents the sum of seventy thousand United States dollars (U.S.$70,000.00) (the "Settlement Amount").

(ii) The Settlement Amount shall be deposited with the Tribunal's Registry upon filing of this Settlement Agreement. The Tribunal shall release the Settlement Amount to the Agent of the Islamic Republic of Iran upon delivery to the Claimant by the Registry of the letter referenced in Article X(b).

Article III

Claimant for itself and on behalf of MCA Engineering Corporation, MCA Ltd., Walter Kidde & Co. Inc., Kidde Holding Inc., and Kidde Inc., and their respective present and former officers, directors, shareholders, employees, agents, representatives, parents, subsidiaries, affiliates and successors hereby release, and forever discharge Respondents from and against the Released

Claims asserted or that could have been asserted in connection with the subject matter of the Case.

Article IV

Respondents hereby release, and forever discharge Claimant, MCA Engineering Corporation, MCA Ltd., Walter Kidde & Co. Inc., Kidde Holding Inc., and Kidde Inc., and their respective present and former officers, directors, shareholders, employees, agents, representatives, parents, subsidiaries, affiliates and successors from and against the Released Claims asserted or that could have been asserted in connection with the subject matter of the Case.

Article V

Claimant shall indemnify and hold harmless Respondents against any claim, counterclaim, action or proceeding which any or all of Claimant, MCA Engineering Corporation, MCA Ltd., Walter Kidde & Co. Inc., Kidde Holdings Inc., and Kidde Inc., and their respective present and former officers, directors, shareholders, employees, agents, representatives, parents, subsidiaries, affiliates and successors or any other persons may now or in the future raise, assert, initiate or take against any or all of Respondents with respect to the Released Claims.

Article VI

Respondents shall indemnify and hold harmless Claimant, MCA Engineering Corporation, MCA Ltd., Walter Kidde & Co. Inc., Kidde Holdings Inc., and Kidde Inc., and their respective present and former officers, directors, shareholders, employees, agents, representatives, parents, subsidiaries, affiliates and successors against any claim, counterclaim, action or proceeding which any or all of Respondents may now or in the future raise, assert, initiate or take against Claimant with respect to the Released Claims.

Article VII

(i) Upon issuance of the Award on Agreed Terms, and payment of the Settlement Amount, Claimant shall cause, without delay and with prejudice, all proceedings against Respondents in all courts, fora or any authorities or administrative bodies to be dismissed, withdrawn and terminated, and shall be barred from instituting and/or continuing with any proceedings before the Iran-United States Claims Tribunal or any other fora, authorities, or administrative bodies, whatsoever, including but not limited to any courts in the United States of America or the Islamic Republic of Iran in connection with disputes, differences, claims and any matters which are the subject matter in the Case.

(ii) Upon issuance of the Award on Agreed Terms, and payment of the Settlement Amount, Respondents shall cause, without delay and with prejudice, all proceedings against Claimant, in all courts, fora or any authorities or administrative bodies to be dismissed, withdrawn and terminated and shall be barred from instituting and/or continuing with any proceedings before the Iran-U.S. Claims Tribunal or any other fora, authorities, or administrative bodies, whatsoever, including but not limited to any courts in the United States of America or the Islamic Republic of Iran in connection with disputes, differences, claims and any matters which are the subject matter of the Case.

Article VIII
Upon issuance of the Award on Agreed Terms and payment of the Settlement Amount, the Parties shall waive any and all claims for costs, including attorneys' fees, arising out of or related in any way to the arbitration, prosecution, or defense of any claim or counterclaim before any forum, including the Iran-United States Claims Tribunal, with respect to the Case.

Article IX
Upon issuance of the Award on Agreed Terms, and payment of the Settlement Amount, the obligations, declarations, releases, waivers, withdrawals, and dismissals, referred to in this Settlement Agreement shall become self-executing. After issuance of the Award on Agreed Terms by the Tribunal and payment of the Settlement Amount, no further documents need to be executed in implementing the provisions of this Agreement.

Article X
Within sixty days of the issuance of the Arbitral Award on Agreed Terms:
(a) Respondents shall deliver to the Tribunal Registry two original copies of a letter from Bank Tejarat in the form attached herewith.
(b) The Tribunal shall order the Tribunal's Registry to deliver to Claimant dual originals of the Letter of Bank Tejarat described in the preceding paragraph.

Article XI
The bank cheques presented by Claimant in the filings including cheques of Bank Melli Nos. 824436, 824435, 824431 and cheque of Bank Etebarat Tavoni Touzie No. 638213 are null and void. Claimant agrees that it will not present any such cheques for payment to the issuing banks or institute any legal action for their sums. Claimant hereby agrees to indemnify Respondents in connection with any such cheques against any loss that might be incurred

by them or any of them that is attributable to Claimant's action in breach of this commitment.

Article XII
The Parties acknowledge that this Settlement Agreement is to be approved and ratified by the Iranian authorities within the period specified in Article XIII herein. Signing of the joint request by the Agent of the Islamic Republic of Iran to the Tribunal shall represent that such approval and ratification have been obtained. Should for any reasons whatsoever they choose not to approve this Settlement Agreement, then it shall become null and void, and in that event no party to this Settlement Agreement may rely upon, cite or publish its terms or any statements made in the course of settlement discussions.

Article XIII
The Parties agree to submit this Settlement Agreement to the Tribunal on or before July 9, 1994 together with a joint request requesting it to record and give effect to the provisions of this Settlement Agreement as an Arbitral Award on Agreed Terms, provided however that this Agreement be approved and ratified by Iranian authorities as provided in Article XII herein. If this Settlement Agreement is not submitted on or before July 9, 1994 or as otherwise agreed by the Parties, then it shall automatically become null and void, and the Parties, without prejudicing their respective rights, will be placed in the same position as they were prior to the date of this Settlement Agreement.

Article XIV
This Settlement Agreement is for the sole purpose of settling the disputes between the Parties thereto. Nothing in this Settlement Agreement shall be relied upon or construed as relevant to or to affect in any way any argument or position of the Government of Iran or the Respondents concerning the jurisdiction or the merits of the Case A/15 (I-C) before the Tribunal, or the negotiations conducted or to be conducted in that Case. This Settlement Agreement shall not constitute a legal precedent for any person or party, and shall not be used except for the sole purpose of giving effect to its terms, and shall not prejudice or affect other rights of the Parties or the rights of any other person in other cases before the Tribunal or elsewhere.

Article XV
For the purpose of construction and interpretation of the Settlement Agreement the entire Agreement shall be read and construed as a whole without giving any specific effect to any article separately.

Article XVI

The representatives of the Parties hereto expressly declare that they are duly empowered to sign this Agreement.

Article XVII

This Agreement (in four originals) has been written and signed in both languages of Persian and English and each text shall have the same and equal validity.

INDEX[1]

Abuse of judicial authority, **5**, 128
Abuse of right, **29**, 57, 183-4
Account stated, **4**, 220, 221, 228, 230-4, 236; **8**, 162-8
Acquiescence: *see* Estoppel
Acquired rights, **6**, 163
Act of State, **4**, 102, 115 n. 2; **5**, 12; **16**, 99; **17**, 100-1; **19**, 285-9, 292; **24**, 11: *see also* State responsibility
   enquiry into by international tribunal, **25**, 157, 165
Admissibility: *see under* Evidence *and* Jurisdiction of Tribunal
Admission, effect, **3**, 205 n. 2, 235, 288
Agency, **1**, 356-62, 376-81; **2**, 11, 23-4; **3**, 205; **4**, 278, 279; **6**, 159, 160, 193-5; **8**, 130, 140; **17**, 14-15, 25-30; **19**, 126, 129-32, 133-5, 138-9, 140, 152-3; **23**, 142-6, 299-300, 305-6: *see also* Evidence of, agency
   applicable law, **19**, 126
   broker distinguished, **2**, 399
   general principles of agency law, **19**, 126
Aggregation of cases: *see* Procedure, consolidation of cases
Airline practice, **9**, 360-75
Algeria, duties, **5**, 49
Algiers Declarations as changed circumstances, **1**, 208: *see also* Claims Settlement Declaration; General Declaration
Aliens, treatment of, **4**, 166, 167; **5**, 293, 383-4; **17**, 147, 181: *see also* Expropriation; Expulsion; State responsibility
   wrongful death, **2**, 81-9
Alternative forum, **6**, 49
Alternative pleading, **4**, 231, 233, 235, 236
American Arbitration Association: *see under* Arbitration rules
American law: *see* United States, law of
Appeal, **3**, 128, 364; **5**, 74: *see also* Award, correction; Award, reconsideration; Rehearing
Applicable law, **3**, 8, 14, 19, 56, 58; **4**, 5, 113-16, 174, 234, 267, 270, 292, 293; **6**, 46, 97, 98; **7**, 99, 102, 109, 113, 115, 130, 191; **8**, 105; **10**, 239, 277; **12**, 143, 273; **13**, 88-9, 229-33; **14**, 138-40, 186-7, 229-30, 245; **15**, 29, 214-24, 236-9; **16**, 20-8, 194-6, 256; **17**, 132, 142, 230-1, 239-40; **18**, 119, 361 n. 10; **19**, 29-31, 286; **21**, 68, 72; **23**, 357; **26**, 226: *see also* Choice of law
   agency, **1**, 377, 379-80; **19**, 126
   authenticity of document, **29**, 124
   contracts, **1**, 422; **2**, 27; **3**, 48, 56; **4**, 267; **6**, 236; **7**, 131; **8**, 162, 231, 232; **9**, 121, 124, 326; **10**, 216; **13**, 26; **17**, 230-1, 240; **21**, 103, 154; **22**, 243, 268-89, 324, 325; **24**, 170; **26**, 146: *see also* State contracts *below*
   corporations—
     —ownership, **17**, 328; **21**, 77 n. 30
     —pre-incorporation agreements, **2**, 154 n. 1
   date determining, **15**, 215
   diplomatic protection, **19**, 31
   disqualification of arbitrator, **20**, 203-4, 272-3
   expropriation—
     —international law, **16**, 25; **29**, 27
     —Treaty of Amity, **16**, 25, 194-5, 239; **21**, 118, 121, 125; **30**, 255-7
   expulsion, international law, **17**, 142
   general principles of commercial and international law, **16**, 21, 28, 104; **26**, 106
   general principles of law, **19**, 30; **20**, 204
   immovable property transactions, **2**, 250, 256
   international law, **16**, 28; **19**, 30-1, 286; **23**, 357

---

[1] This is a consolidated index identifying the contents of all previous volumes as well as the present volume. The figures in bold type refer to the volume number.

Applicable law (*cont.*)
 —displacement by Claims Settlement Declaration, **25**, 28
 interpretation and substance, different systems to apply, **16**, 21
 law of parties, **19**, 30; **28**, 209
 lex loci actus, **21**, 63
 marital rights, **30**, 49-56
 nationality, **2**, 166, 183, 224
 payment of cheque, **1**, 171
 pension rights, **30**, 42-3, 63
 practice of parties, **17**, 231, 240
 principles of mutual goodwill and good faith, **21**, 154
 procedure, **8**, 161; **30**, 55
 promissory notes, **21**, 44-5, 63-4
 relevance, **12**, 214
 share transfers, **19**, 272
 State contracts, **16**, 27-8; **19**, 31; **22**, 287-9: *see also* contracts *above*
 time limits, **17**, 190
 Tribunal's—
 —failure to indicate, **1**, 422
 —freedom to determine, **13**, 232; **30**, 49-50
Appointing authority
 designation, **1**, 513-14
 powers, **1**, 114-15, 117; **21**, 388, 390
Arbitral tribunal: *see* International tribunals; Tribunal
Arbitration—
 clause, jurisdiction, **25**, 26, 73-4, 141-2
 failure to comply with, **7**, 202 n. 1
 meaning, **5**, 183
 nature, **7**, 78
 objection to conduct of, **25**, 6
 waiver of right to, **7**, 202 n. 1
Arbitration rules: *see also* International Law Commission; Tribunal Rules; UNCITRAL Rules *and under* International Chamber of Commerce
American Arbitration Association, **20**, 206, 209, 245, 250, 310
American Code of Ethics for Arbitrators, **3**, 40, 296; **4**, 181; **20**, 205, 207, 208, 209, 212, 218-19, 251
Grain and Feed Trade Association, **3**, 323; **20**, 250
Inter-American Commercial Arbitration Commission, **20**, 206

International Bar Association Guidelines, **20**, 211-12, 216, 251
International Institute for the Unification of Private Law, **20**, 205
London Court of International Arbitration, **20**, 206
Netherlands Arbitration Institute, **20**, 250
UN Economic Commission for Asia and the Far East, **20**, 205
UN Economic Commission for Europe, **20**, 205
Uniform Arbitration Act, **3**, 210, 211, 295
Arbitrator—
 absence, **1**, 415-17, 425-8, 431-2, 433, 453-4; **2**, 14-16, 27-9, 343-4; **3**, 24-146, 155, 168, 209-11, 237, 238, 254, 255, 268, 269, 276, 277, 291-6, 316; **8**, 42; **19**, 116-17; **21**, 239-40; **29**, 364 n. 11
 appointment, **5**, 277 n. 1: *see also* Appointing authority
 challenge, **1**, 111-18, 509-18; **5**, 277 n. 1; **20**, 177-330; **21**, 196, 279-82, 318-402; **24**, 309-24
 —admissibility, **24**, 319, 324
 —confidentiality, **20**, 233-4
 —effect, **21**, 280, 351, 358-9
 —failure to act, **27**, 293-336
 —legal standard, **20**, 243-6, 271-82
 —procedure, **20**, 184
 —time limits: *see* Time limits, arbitrator, challenge to
 currency offence, alleged, **21**, 380-3, 395, 396-8
 disclosure obligation, **20**, 177-330 *passim*
 disqualification, **1**, 111-18, 509-18; **2**, 346, 358; **5**, 266
 —applicable law, **20**, 203-4
 —effect, **20**, 239
 —non-disclosure and, **20**, 214, 215-16, 257, 282-5; **21**, 195-6
 exceeding power, **5**, 366 n. 1; **6**, 271; **21**, 400
 failure to sign award, **1**, 204, 415-17, 424-41, 449, 452-4; **2**, 13-16, 27-8, 170, 177, 227, 343-4; **3**, 92, 108, 118, 124-9, 137, 141-6, 155, 168, 210, 211, 237, 238, 254, 255, 268, 269, 276, 277, 292-4; **4**, 111; **5**, 348; **6**, 39, 229, 230, 252; **7**, 222; **14**, 8, 10; **15**, 187-8; **16**, 112 n. 1, 237, 255-6, 282; **18**, 3-44; **19**, 107 n.

INDEX

1, 161-71; **21**, 79 n. 1, 194-8, 295; **26**, 5-6, 189; **29**, 23
—effect on validity of award: *see* Award, validity
impartiality, **1**, 115-18, 424, 427, 433, 514, 516, 518; **2**, 21, 346, 357-8; **3**, 129, 299, 303, 304, 315; **20**, 179-80, 182-3, 186; **21**, 349, 355-6, 387, 390, 398; **24**, 310-11, 316-18, 319-24
independence, **3**, 209; **20**, 179-80, 182-3, 186; **24**, 310-11, 316-18, 319-24
—European Court of Human Rights (ECHR), **20**, 218
resignation, **1**, 415-17, 426-7, 433-4, 436; **2**, 14-15; **3**, 41, 108, 117, 137-9, 144-6, 155, 168, 209-11, 237, 238, 254, 255, 268, 269, 276, 277, 291-3, 295, 375, 376; **5**, 362; **6**, 103; **7**, 56, 183; **14**, 271 n. 2; **16**, 284 n. 8; **19**, 117
rights, **19**, 167
substitute, **14**, 312, 353-4
withdrawal, **5**, 338; **20**, 329-30
witness, relationship with, **20**, 184, 185, 186, 242, 250-4, 266-7, 329
Attachment—
release, **4**, 277; **15**, 185
right of, **22**, 78
Attribution: *see* Controlled entity; State responsibility
Award—
additional, **5**, 74; **14**, 258, 280-1; **16**, 110-11, 284; **18**, 76; **25**, 187, 273-4; **28**, 51-2, 195-7; **29**, 293-4
on agreed terms: *see* Settlement
amendment, **6**, 30-2, 269, 270
arbitrary nature, alleged, **21**, 338-45
basis—
—contractual obligations, **10**, 256, 257
—legal principles, **5**, 42, 48; **21**, 338
—to be stated, **4**, 180; **5**, 129; **6**, 268-70; **21**, 215, 338
basis for legal action, **6**, 135-9; **18**, 118-19, 120-8, 130-1
bias, alleged, **21**, 332-8, 378-9
binding nature: *see* final and binding *below*
challenge to, **21**, 295-6
—withdrawal, **21**, 302
compliance, **23**, 208
contradictory, **5**, 130
contrary to fact, **5**, 46, 47
correction, **3**, 364; **4**, 111; **5**, 73, 74; **6**, 270;

8, 133-4; **11**, 284, 286, 301; **13**, 93-4; **14**, 101, 173-4, 256; **18**, 76-8, 114; **19**, 172-5, 253-5; **20**, 171; **23**, 122-5, 230-2; **25**, 187, 188-9, 273, 274-6; **26**, 186-7; **27**, 264-8; **28**, 307-8; **30**, 19-21
credibility, **5**, 267
date of receipt, **8**, 53, 134; **9**, 405; **16**, 283
declaratory, **21**, 74-5
deferred implementation, **26**, 147
delay in making, **4**, 3; **21**, 261-2, 275-8
deviation from, **18**, 79
discriminatory, **6**, 269
duty to comply with, **7**, 219
error in, **16**, 284
Escrow Agent, effect in absence of notification, **21**, 286, 288, 293
exceeding remedy sought, **6**, 232; **17**, 30
final and binding, **3**, 365; **4**, 16; **5**, 74, 252; **6**, 109; **8**, 107-18; **11**, 274, 276 n. 3; **16**, 84; **20**, 209; **21**, 293-4, 295, 301, 349, 352, 375; **22**, 208; **26**, 258-61; **29**, 23, 387-92
—proceedings in another forum and, **2**, 63, 98; **29**, 220-1
financial position of respondent, relevance, **21**, 51
Full Tribunal, powers regarding, **21**, 283-4
grounds for setting aside, **5**, 128
illegal, **5**, 41, 49; **7**, 201
insufficient reason for, **19**, 16
interim: *see* Table of Cases by Category
interlocutory: *see* Table of Cases by Category
interpretation, **3**, 364; **5**, 74; **6**, 284; **8**, 116; **12**, 304-5; **13**, 328-30; **14**, 174, 257, 261-2; **18**, 113-14; **19**, 172-3, 317-19; **25**, 187; **26**, 188, 254-5; **27**, 194-5
jurisprudential value, **6**, 115
language, **21**, 392-3
—authentic version, **21**, 293
—validity in absence of translation, **21**, 286, 288, 293-4, 295, 296-301; **27**, 267
length, **30**, 169
modification, **4**, 81; **29**, 260 n. 3
non-legalistic, **7**, 17
null compromise, **5**, 335; **6**, 271
null and void, **6**, 271; **7**, 201
—deemed by Parties as, **21**, 290, 296
—status of Award, **21**, 293-4
omission from, **16**, 284

Award (*cont.*)
  partial, **1**, 185; **2**, 44, 100; **3**, 197, 319, 366; **4**, 20, 74; **5**, 76; **6**, 141; **7**, 90, 181, 220, 225; **8**, 15, 183; **9**, 10; **11**, 363, 372 n. 2; **13**, 370 n. ; **14**, 24, 311; **15**, 189; **16**, 3; **17**, 31, 92, 153; **19**, 3, 107, 200, 273; **21**, 20
  postponement, **3**, 105
  reasons for: *see* basis *above*
  recognition, **7**, 219
  recognition and enforcement, **5**, 130; **6**, 135-9; **14**, 331, 333-6; **18**, 131-46
  reconsideration, **3**, 364, 365; **4**, 60; **5**, 74, 75; **6**, 46; **8**, 107-18; **14**, 101, 256; **18**, 76-7; **23**, 123; **25**, 186-7; **28**, 318-19
  reinstatement of case, **28**, 216-24
  rescission, **5**, 74, 75
  review: *see* reconsideration *above*
  revision, **29**, 387-92
  satisfaction of claim in another forum, **9**, 257
  supplementary, **19**, 255-6, 318, 319-20
  Tribunal's inherent power, **8**, 117, 118
  unenforceable, **6**, 271
  unjust, **7**, 17
  validity, **1**, 417-24, 433; **2**, 14-16, 27, 170, 177, 286, 289, 290, 346; **3**, 54, 124-9, 140-4, 210, 211, 295, 297-9, 302, 315, 324; **6**, 115; **7**, 162, 198; **29**, 23
  violation, **4**, 73
  void, **5**, 336
    —*ab initio*, **5**, 335
  without prejudice, **5**, 72

Bad faith, **5**, 266, 300
Bailee, **6**, 279; **8**, 270
Balance sheet, preparation of, **6**, 244
Bank guarantee: *see* Performance guarantee
Banking institutions: *see* Undertakings
Banking obligations, breach, **7**, 48
Banking practices, **1**, 170, 191, 198, 201-2, 205, 207, 210, 505-6; **2**, 168; **3**, 19, 21, 25, 27, 30; **5**, 29, 38; **6**, 167; **7**, 43; **17**, 284-5: *see also* Cheque
  waiver of defect, **17**, 285, 291-2
Bankruptcy, **2**, 151; **8**, 257-9; **9**, 15; **27**, 21-2, 34-6, 38-9
  liquidation distinguished, **2**, 10
Bill of exchange: *see* Negotiable instruments
Bill of lading, **5**, 31, 32, 39; **6**, 291
Burden of proof, **3**, 16-18, 20, 29, 65, 66, 68, 71, 107, 108, 114, 115, 252, 294, 308 n. 2; **4**, 80, 232, 251, 268, 276; **5**, 22, 23, 36, 43, 47, 173, 176, 219, 229, 231, 368, 375, 376; **6**, 66, 178, 210-12; **7**, 28, 29, 68, 80, 88, 106, 107, 116, 117, 128, 129, 190-2; **9**, 42, 57, 119, 244, 355; **10**, 216, 217, 221, 344; **11**, 275, 278, 281-2, 336-7; **12**, 153, 224, 297, 314; **13**, 23, 54-5, 58-9, 72, 112, 136, 139, 141, 153, 197; **15**, 87; **16**, 101, 106-7; **17**, 57, 68, 75, 104, 112, 142, 151, 191, 193, 204, 222, 257, 263, 285; **18**, 14, 68, 102, 105, 160, 161, 193-4, 196, 221, 228, 237, 238, 241, 263 n. 22, 264, 270-1, 324, 325, 329, 362, 369; **19**, 14, 124, 210, 220, 269, 270; **20**, 14-323, 325-7; **21**, 16, 18, 27, 29; **22**, 54, 56, 59, 88, 99, 110, 133, 171, 242, 251, 355; **23**, 168, 173, 191-3, 195, 225, 226-7, 266, 284, 293-4, 335, 337, 368; **24**, 23-4, 112, 114, 133, 152, 225, 245, 251, 258; **25**, 116, 120-1, 202, 232, 244; **27**, 52, 80; **28**, 11-12, 139, 267-8
  actori incumbit onus probandi, **1**, 209, 420, 464; **18**, 216; **29**, 92-3
  allocation, **3**, 18, 20, 70, 71; **5**, 245; **9**, 172
  authenticity of document, **2**, 119
  contract—
    —amendment, **2**, 389, 390, 399
    —breach, **2**, 382
    —existence, **30**, 106
  controlled entity status, **1**, 420-1
  dominant and effective nationality, **26**, 7 n. 1
  ei qui affirmat, non ei qui negat, incumbit probatio, **20**, 266; **29**, 123-4
  expropriation, **28**, 71; **30**, 41, 154, 160, 163
  implementation of contract, **2**, 153
  invoice or work performed, **2**, 108, 115
  modification of previous valuation, **29**, 279
  nationality of corporation, **1**, 457-8, 464, 475-7, 481-2
  payment of account, **2**, 121
  prevention of export, **28**, 9
  probandi necessitas incumbit illi qui agit, **18**, 325
  shift, **28**, 291-2; **29**, 123-4
  to support defence, **3**, 18, 20, 27 n. 2, 70, 71; **4**, 80

Calvo Clause, **18**, 246 n. 5
Canada, law of, **7**, 167
Causation
    foreseeability, **3**, 266: *see also* Frustration
    proximate cause, **2**, 42; **3**, 249, 266
Chambers: *see under* Tribunal
Changed circumstances, **3**, 52, 68, 198, 199, 309, 322, 324; **4**, 260, 268; **5**, 211; **8**, 441-4; **9**, 38-147; **11**, 33; **15**, 214, 217-19; **16**, 39; **21**, 341; **23**, 171-2, 218 n. 5
    Algiers Declarations as, **1**, 208, 241
    Claims Settlement Declaration provisions, **1**, 311
    forum selection clause and, **1**, 287-94, 308, 311-14
    in Iran, **1**, 245-6, 251, 256, 264-6, 277
    political changes, **16**, 39-40; **21**, 111-12
Charitable institutions: *see* Corporations, non-profit
Cheque, **1**, 169-72; **3**, 10-21, 24-7, 30-3, 235
    bank as drawer, **2**, 235-8
    beneficiary of, **3**, 12
    burden of proof, **3**, 19, 20
    holder in due course, **3**, 20 n. 2
    right to payment, **2**, 168-9
    signature, **3**, 20 n. 1
Choice of forum: *see* Forum selection clause
Choice of law, **4**, 234; **6**, 98
    general principles of law, **7**, 99; **8**, 140, 141; **16**, 25
Choice of law clause, **4**, 267, 268; **5**, 293; **7**, 107; **8**, 156; **10**, 63; **11**, 26; **16**, 20, 25, 26-8: *see also* Forum selection clause
    forum selection clause distinguished, **1**, 236-41, 251, 262-4, 281-2, 286-7, 299-302, 377
    interpretation and implementation distinguished, **16**, 26-8
    procedure, applicability to, **13**, 68
Civil action, alternative forum, **4**, 60
Civil Code of Iran: *see under* Iran, law of
Claimant: *see* Proper claimant
Claims: *see also* Statement of Claim
    abandonment, **5**, 171
    ambiguity, **9**, 296; **11**, 90
    amendment: *see* Statement of Claim, amendment
    for amounts larger than claims in US courts, **4**, 143

assignment, **11**, 84; **13**, 19; **15**, 183-4, 285; **16**, 301-2, 310-12; **26**, 154
barred, **7**, 116; **10**, 218
basis—
    —absence of, **22**, 353
    —alternative, **26**, 217 n. 2, 251
    —anticipatory breach of contract, **29**, 232
    —arbitration contract, **18**, 118-19
    —award of International Chamber of Commerce, **6**, 130, 131; **18**, 118-19, 120-8
    —bank account, **10**, 98, 342; **13**, 336; **26**, 251-2
    —beneficial ownership, **12**, 275-84; **29**, 25-8
    —binding contract, **4**, 230, 231; **10**, 257, 325; **22**, 115
    —confiscated equipment, **25**, 67-9
    —contractual basis, need for, **27**, 138 n. 6
    —customs charges, **13**, 157, 160, 163, 166
    —debt, **21**, 45, 75; **27**, 137
    —decline in value of dollar, **6**, 287
    —demand for payment, **24**, 219-20, 243-5, 247, 248-9; **28**, 42-3
    —different causes of action, **13**, 115-17
    —equity, **16**, 48
    —expropriation: *see* Expropriation
    —failure to establish, **6**, 127, 129
    —failure to re-export, **27**, 92-8
    —failure to secure customs clearance, **29**, 327-30
    —government interference with contractual relations, **12**, 351; **29**, 229
    —inadequacy, **29**, 350-64
    —insurance contract, **23**, 65-8, 110-22
    —intentional tort, **12**, 261-3
    —invoice, **23**, 173-89; **24**, 149-51; **25**, 39-42, 53-7, 98; **26**, 74-6, 87, 88-94, 115-18, 119-20, 132-7; **27**, 76-7, 82-5; **29**, 231, 323-7
    —latent defect, **19**, 15, 38-46
    —letter of guarantee, **13**, 157, 160, 163, 166, 167-72
    —loss of property, **24**, 151-2, 222-6; **26**, 81
    —payments made, **16**, 19, 72

Claims (*cont.*)
—performance guarantee—
——demand for payment, **25**, 100-1
——return, **19**, 212-13, 239-40; **25**, 53, 62-7, 98, 126-9
—personal injury, **17**, 140
—promissory notes, **13**, 21-7; **21**, 44-5, 46-52, 63-7
—property right, **16**, 195-6, 230-1, 238, 239; **17**, 99, 139-40, 169, 174 n. 8; **24**, 110-11; **29**, 308-9
—putative damages, **27**, 230
—relocation costs, **30**, 153
—retained monies, **27**, 76-7, 86-7, 112-15
—salary, **30**, 153
—settlement agreement, **8**, 264; **24**, 133, 153
—social security payments: *see* Social security payments
—standby letter of credit, **5**, 57-61, 66-72; **6**, 222
—statement of account, **12**, 155
—storage costs, **27**, 226-8; **29**, 343-4
—termination of contract, **26**, 76-7
—tort, **17**, 99, 139-40
—Tribunal not limited to parties' theories, **9**, 56; **12**, 184
—trust account, **27**, 228-30
—unjust enrichment, **23**, 146
—work performed, **23**, 189-200, 218-28; **25**, 57-8, 90-4; **26**, 106-8; **27**, 189, 193
between government entities, **3**, 348; **5**, 113: *see also* Claims, official
by banking institutions: *see* Undertakings
by corporation indivisible, **11**, 87
by Domestic International Sales Corporations, **7**, 186, 188, 200
by individuals, **4**, 115; **7**, 121
by Iran against US nationals, **3**, 152; **4**, 1, 75, 101-10; **5**, 15, 66, 127; **8**, 364, 366, 368, 373; **23**, 245, 248, 251, 254, 257
by Iranian banks against US banks, **8**, 362, 364, 366, 371; **9**, 36, 97-106; **16**, 293 n. 4; **17**, 253: *see also* Undertakings
by Iranian nationals against Iran, **7**, 123, 132, 171; **26**, 131
by non-profit institutions, **3**, 317 n. 1
collective, **11**, 88
continuity, **16**, 15, 104; **17**, 267; **18**, 261; **21**, 42; **22**, 10; **23**, 301; **24**, 270; **25**, 58, 138; **26**, 154; **27**, 70 n. 4; **28**, 17-19, 62, 66, 380-1; **29**, 227, 266, 306; **30**, 185: *see also* assignment *above*; Claims Settlement Declaration, Article VII, Paragraph 2; Nationality of claim, continuity
contract, arising out of, **16**, 18
courts, **4**, 142
critical date, **29**, 232-3, 378-9
damage, need for, **22**, 57-8, 182-3, 212
date arising, **10**, 48; **19**, 53, 55, 60-1, 211-12, 240; **25**, 58-9
declaratory relief, **22**, 60-1, 252-3, 335-6; **26**, 170-1
derivative, **4**, 276
direct, **5**, 297, 298, 300; **8**, 368-70; **12**, 261-4; **15**, 101; **26**, 206-12, 216-26
dismissal, **7**, 123; **9**, 344
effect of amendment to contract, **11**, 233-6, 250-5
equitable, **8**, 263
frivolous, **4**, 19; **6**, 129
indirect, **4**, 243, 244; **5**, 379; **6**, 28, 65 n. 3; **7**, 6, 7, 183, 185-7, 199, 200, 206, 207; **8**, 368-70; **9**, 233, 254-66; **10**, 61-4, 279-81; **11**, 84-9, 212-14, 311-13, 347; **12**, 251-61, 272-87; **13**, 18-19, 298-9; **14**, 179-92, 199; **15**, 195-6, 221-2; **16**, 14, 195-6, 239, 258; **17**, 115, 116, 297-8; **18**, 101, 103; **19**, 105 n. 12, 118; **22**, 10, 215; **23**, 270; **25**, 138, 175-6; **26**, 65-6, 130, 212-16; **28**, 204-5; **30**, 150-1
—on behalf of Iranian companies against Iran, **10**, 85, 279-80; **11**, 311-12, 347
—effect of expropriation, **9**, 265
—entitlement to full recovery, **10**, 63-4, 82-4
—financial losses, relevance, **30**, 160
—loss of shareholder status, **9**, 265 n. 17
—requirements, **7**, 186
—Treaty of Amity and, **15**, 34 n. 14
insurance compensation, effect, **10**, 239
insurance contract, relevance, **10**, 258; **14**, 292
interest as part of, **16**, 289-90
interest-only, **13**, 95-6
interstate nature, **5**, 291, 294-8, 334; **18**, 385-7: *see also* Diplomatic protection

INDEX

joinder: *see* Procedure, consolidation of cases
joint, **16**, 13-14; **24**, 245-7
— commingled, **24**, 247
judgment of municipal court as, **8**, 294-6; **11**, 196
larger embraces smaller, **10**, 252; **17**, 169; **22**, 42
of less than $250,000, **3**, 77; **4**, 211; **5**, 83 n. 1; **9**, 16; **16**, 104, 261-2; **18**, 24, 66, 109 n. 15, 245, 275, 383, 393-6; **19**, 345, 352, 360; **22**, 112, 213, 216-17
— as claim of owner, **11**, 284, 286, 301
— need for request for espousal, **18**, 245-6
liquidated, **8**, 263
malicious, **5**, 86, 87
multiple causes of action, **7**, 126
new, **16**, 259; **27**, 69-70
not previously filed with US courts, **4**, 143
official, **5**, 96, 99-104; **6**, 13; **12**, 36-7; **14**, 278; **17**, 183-5, 216, 229-30; **18**, 66-7, 74-5, 86; **19**, 11, 346; **23**, 337
outstanding, **3**, 65, 103, 151, 312, 313, 315, 348, 358; **4**, 95 n. 1; **5**, 82, 373; **6**, 223, 264; **7**, 42, 43, 47, 50, 52, 53, 98, 107, 115; **8**, 261; **10**, 98-101, 104-7, 325, 353; **11**, 315, 357; **12**, 122, 162; **13**, 21-7, 46, 337, 345, 347-9; **14**, 47-8, 272 n. 3; **15**, 6, 197; **16**, 16-17; **18**, 152, 166, 290, 372; **19**, 68, 138, 151; **21**, 44-5, 63-6, 152; **22**, 352; **23**, 213; **24**, 110, 243, 281-2; **26**, 110-11, 125-6; **27**, 43, 47-8, 137; **28**, 19-20, 30-4, 66-7, 197, 228, 262-5, 275-302; **29**, 265-6; **30**, 64, 96
— termination of contract, **28**, 30-3
— "whether or not filed with any court", **1**, 491-2, 497-8; **16**, 17; **30**, 98, 151
pendente lite, **5**, 113
perfected, **8**, 261
proper claimant: *see* Proper claimant
proper respondent: *see* Proper respondent
property, interest in, **16**, 195-6
reclassification, **18**, 66-7; **19**, 346
refusal to accept, **7**, 275, 276
— authority for, **19**, 177-8, 180, 183, 187, 190, 193, 195, 199
release from, **14**, 317, 320

shareholder: *see* Corporations, shareholders
subrogation, **23**, 300-1
termination, **3**, 375
third party, on behalf of, **16**, 303; **20**, 35, 39, 81, 115, 119, 136, 137
third party equipment, **27**, 98-9
time-barred, **12**, 143-5; **17**, 189-91, 202, 232, 239-42; **24**, 258; **28**, 56-8
— effect of arbitration agreement, **12**, 145
— purpose, **12**, 144
validity, duty to examine, **5**, 85
waiver, **8**, 67, 81-2; **20**, 112, 167, 168; **23**, 39, 40, 42; **24**, 154
— failure to resubmit claim, **28**, 39-40
— refusal to accept satisfaction, **28**, 19
— settlement agreement as, **28**, 67-70
— silence regarding, **28**, 122
— tacit, **11**, 251-5, 330-1, 345-6
withdrawal, **1**, 232-3, 385, 391, 486; **2**, 36-7, 246, 260; **3**, 205, 332, 333; **4**, 98 n. 1; **6**, 5, 7, 8, 11; **7**, 262; **8**, 67, 184, 186, 187, 265, 349, 353; **9**, 9, 38, 43-4; **16**, 296; **18**, 63; **28**, 376-7
Claims of nationals: *see* Nationality of Claim
Claims Settlement Declaration—
Article I, **11**, 290; **12**, 69 n. 9; **18**, 86; **25**, 259
Article II, **1**, 149, 245-6, 255, 264-6, 276-7, 288-90, 295, 349, 494, 497, 504; **2**, 199, 208-10, 212, 315; **3**, 5, 102, 151, 152, 167, 310, 312, 324; **5**, 295, 344 n. 1; **6**, 103; **10**, 35; **11**, 7, 8, 36, 215, 279, 311; **12**, 82; **13**, 180-2, 223, 224, 227, 300-1; **15**, 242; **16**, 307; **19**, 335; **25**, 259; **28**, 48, 211
— Paragraph 1, **1**, 103, 106-10, 136, 138, 168, 171, 225, 236-40, 242-7, 248, 250, 252-60, 261-7, 268-70, 271-3, 274-9, 280-3, 284-303, 305-19, 320-2, 372, 394, 395, 412, 455, 490-2, 496, 497, 503, 507-8; **2**, 9, 39-42, 55, 62-3, 66, 79-80, 82, 85-6, 88, 97, 105-6, 109-10, 112, 120 n. 1, 120 n. 2, 138, 143, 160, 296, 300-1, 312-13, 318, 320-1, 323, 324, 338, 370, 377, 378, 395, 396, 401; **3**, 3, 59, 61, 65, 66, 104, 113, 115, 116, 198, 199, 201, 231, 235, 243, 251, 252, 259, 260, 273, 286, 314, 315,

318　INDEX

Claims Settlement Declaration (*cont.*)
319, 320, 323, 335, 348, 384, 387; **4**, 6, 8, 53, 54, 95, 99, 101, 115, 142, 215, 216, 219-21, 224, 225, 229-33, 243, 247; **5**, 2, 14, 15, 69, 82, 92, 119, 120, 125, 126, 171, 173, 181, 182, 184, 194, 195, 233, 253, 268-70, 274, 278, 279, 284, 298, 342, 371, 373, 378, 388; **6**, 5, 27, 77, 79, 80, 83, 93, 100-2, 109, 112-14, 132, 135, 139, 158, 221-3, 231, 232, 235, 236, 250, 251, 255, 263, 264, 268, 270; **7**, 21, 33-5, 42, 47, 53, 66, 82, 107, 122, 132, 134, 188, 195, 218, 275; **8**, 5, 22, 27, 45-6, 51, 77, 86, 221, 224-5, 229-31, 261, 262, 264, 268, 293-7, 306, 405-6; **9**, 31-5, 36, 38 n. 18, 40, 50, 51, 88, 115-16, 135, 195, 211-12, 223, 225-6, 245, 252, 257, 293, 333-4, 400, 401; **10**, 44-5, 54, 62-3, 98, 104, 168, 233, 243, 251, 308, 311, 316, 325; **11**, 36, 55, 67, 74, 85-6, 92, 109, 151, 170-2, 188-9, 228, 241, 248, 294, 315, 317, 350, 355, 357; **12**, 100, 142-3, 150, 162, 174, 262, 273, 275, 287 n. 49, 291; **13**, 21, 27, 46, 101, 102, 132, 168-72, 203, 225, 263, 307, 322, 337, 345; **14**, 33, 48, 51, 105, 118-19, 127-8, 131, 179, 253, 272 n. 3, 277-8, 292; **15**, 198, 272, 296; **16**, 78-9, 87 n. 2, 259, 289-90; **17**, 64, 83, 98-100, 115, 119, 139, 140, 169, 184, 185, 255, 259, 260, 262; **18**, 86, 99, 100, 101, 119, 123, 128, 147, 152, 158, 166, 167, 189, 196, 208-9, 222 n. 35, 227, 282 n. 5, 290, 291, 298, 334, 355, 356, 360, 372; **19**, 30 n. 13, 203, 249, 251; **20**, 8, 9, 78; **21**, 8, 23, 29, 42, 45, 100, 102, 148, 152, 343; **22**, 187, 253, 290, 297, 351-2; **23**, 7, 128, 129, 131-2, 135, 213, 215, 237, 240, 241, 266, 369, 385; **24**, 4, 47 n. 2, 83, 110-11, 119, 220, 243; **25**, 10, 11, 17, 29, 70, 138, 142, 195, 268 n. 3, 272, 288, 297, 300; **26**, 81, 119, 125, 223; **27**, 18, 27, 58, 136, 141, 156, 235; **28**, 30, 67, 122-3, 243, 258, 262, 325-6, 354; **29**, 13, 27, 41, 65, 75, 187, 188, 191-2, 195-6; **30**, 12, 17-18, 36, 59, 64, 74, 80, 150, 183, 185, 186, 280

—Paragraph 2, **1**, 103, 106, 107, 178 n. 2, 292; **2**, 53; **3**, 348; **4**, 100; **5**, 14, 15, 96, 99-104, 352; **6**, 13, 141; **8**, 77, 91, 95, 329 n. 3; **9**, 136-7; **10**, 83-4, 85, 139-40, 309, 342, 346; **12**, 25, 36, 37; **13**, 156, 159, 162, 165, 168-72, 197, 273, 279, 284; **14**, 271 n. 2; **16**, 17; **17**, 184, 189, 201, 229-30, 239; **18**, 66, 75, 86; **19**, 11, 285, 346; **27**, 322

—Paragraph 3, **1**, 102, 103; **5**, 14, 15, 58; **8**, 91, 95, 204, 209; **10**, 46, 126, 325; **12**, 60; **13**, 180; **21**, 100; **28**, 123; **29**, 29, 217

Article III, **1**, 112, 149; **2**, 314; **14**, 353, 354; **19**, 285; **21**, 309

—Paragraph 1, **1**, 117, 431-3, 436; **2**, 301; **3**, 40, 77, 126, 139, 211, 296, 364; **7**, 204; **9**, 409; **21**, 160, 201, 203, 310, 313; **26**, 14

—Paragraph 2, **1**, 114, 130, 451 n. 4, 458, 476, 511, 516; **2**, 209, 301; **3**, 211, 296; **6**, 100; **7**, 21, 316; **8**, 275 n. 48; **11**, 84, 274, 279; **16**, 307; **26**, 258 n. 4; **27**, 317

—Paragraph 3, **1**, 2, 176, 177, 209, 230 n. 2; **2**, 301; **3**, 77; **4**, 115, 210, 211; **5**, 83 n. 1, 297; **7**, 203 n. 3, 277; **11**, 283, 285, 301; **12**, 132, 307; **13**, 263; **16**, 261; **18**, 66, 245, 383-7, 389-90

—Paragraph 4, **1**, 127-30, 176, 226-9, 394, 396; **2**, 178, 312-13, 315-16, 317-21, 338; **3**, 3, 287; **4**, 99; **5**, 79; **6**, 29, 68, 102; **8**, 369; **9**, 4; **12**, 289; **13**, 278; **16**, 304, 306-8; **21**, 3, 7, 10; **25**, 259; **27**, 69; **28**, 378-9; **29**, 116

Article IV, **8**, 266 n. 39; **18**, 148

—Paragraph 1, **2**, 56, 63; **3**, 365; **4**, 16; **5**, 74, 252; **6**, 109; **8**, 114; **9**, 406; **11**, 88; **12**, 285 n. 45; **14**, 10, 174, 317-18, 328, 333; **20**, 209; **21**, 293, 349, 352; **26**, 258; **29**, 220-1, 387

—Paragraph 2, **8**, 379; **23**, 334

—Paragraph 3, **1**, 331, 406, 465; **2**, 56, 63, 94

—Paragraph 4, **14**, 332

Article V, **1**, 198, 200, 201, 291, 294, 308, 374, 377 n. 15, 420, 422, 477; **2**, 94, 223, 237; **3**, 58; **4**, 70, 114, 234, 267; **5**, 21, 22, 233, 261, 274, 292-4; **6**, 97, 140, 161, 268, 442-3; **8**, 132 n. 10; **9**, 122,

INDEX

146, 169, 177, 330; **10**, 143, 147, 192, 312; **11**, 26, 30, 32, 50, 142, 351, 358; **12**, 21, 82; **13**, 119, 230; **14**, 9, 138-40, 186; **15**, 214, 218-20, 294 n. 12; **16**, 24-5, 39, 287-90; **18**, 119; **19**, 30; **21**, 68, 72, 104, 111, 154; **23**, 357; **26**, 106; **28**, 209; **29**, 388

Article VI, **1**, 198

—Paragraph 2, **2**, 37; **5**, 291; **7**, 221; **8**, 37, 185, 186; **9**, 62; **21**, 379

—Paragraph 3, **1**, 106, 195; **5**, 291; **6**, 68; **10**, 35

—Paragraph 4, **1**, 102, 103, 294; **2**, 59, 315, 320; **5**, 58, 252; **8**, 91, 95, 204, 209, 210; **10**, 85; **11**, 274, 275, 277; **14**, 327, 332; **16**, 289-90; **21**, 100

Article VII, **1**, 123, 137, 149, 166, 397, 503; **2**, 19, 32, 156, 208, 211, 377, 395; **3**, 2, 160; **4**, 142; **5**, 78, 268, 283, 284, 353; **7**, 221; **11**, 170, 181, 274, 276; **13**, 180, 263; **14**, 118; **18**, 208, 297; **21**, 68

—Paragraph 1, **1**, 136, 139, 223, 392, 417, 455, 456, 458, 463, 477-9, 481; **2**, 16-17, 19, 33, 105-6, 160, 209-12, 248, 301, 303, 304, 335; **3**, 46, 102, 103, 113, 161, 245, 259, 260; **4**, 1, 99, 216, 217, 264, 273; **5**, 1, 2, 18, 21, 22, 92, 126, 163, 254, 267, 269, 279, 282, 284, 338, 339, 341, 342, 352; **6**, 127, 285; **7**, 5, 20, 27-9, 41, 97, 121-3, 127-9, 185; **8**, 128, 154, 234, 261, 294, 307, 326, 370; **9**, 15, 70, 88, 116, 156, 194, 252, 291, 400; **10**, 126, 166, 238, 263 n. 9, 278-9; **11**, 86, 151, 188, 212, 271; **12**, 100, 132, 142, 162, 251, 275, 345; **13**, 18, 101, 131, 202, 306, 336; **14**, 6-8, 34, 72, 156, 179, 199, 226, 268; **15**, 5; **17**, 5, 64, 115, 162, 255; **18**, 166, 189, 237, 261, 355; **19**, 202, 203; **20**, 7; **21**, 16, 18, 22, 24, 29, 51 n. 16, 102, 103; **22**, 235; **23**, 135, 168, 262, 263, 266, 273, 283, 284; **24**, 44-5, 50, 110, 133, 218, 245-6, 255, 267, 281; **25**, 10, 28, 138, 175, 195, 200, 229, 231, 232, 235, 237, 238, 239, 241, 244, 245, 268 n. 3, 272, 281, 297; **26**, 14, 17, 18, 65, 130, 199-200, 207; **27**, 58, 70, 71, 136; **28**, 169-243, 315-16; **29**, 13, 23, 27, 65, 75, 227, 241-3, 313, 315-16, 381; **30**, 36, 280

—Paragraph 2, **1**, 136, 139, 381 n. 20, 385, 388, 392, 394, 395, 399, 456, 477, 479; **2**, 9, 55-6, 63-4, 98-9, 148, 226-7, 248, 282, 295-300, 363, 378, 396, 401; **3**, 46, 60, 273, 386; **4**, 54, 99, 101, 181, 216, 218, 243; **5**, 6, 92, 93, 129, 153, 154, 196, 271, 365, 377, 379, 388; **6**, 45, 58, 79, 80, 93, 108, 110, 115, 116, 127, 131, 263; **7**, 5, 6, 29, 66, 97, 134, 185-8, 199, 206, 218, 219; **8**, 77, 128, 159, 232-3, 261, 265 n. 38, 294, 368; **9**, 38, 132, 253, 254-66, 281, 293, 324, 325, 329 n. 12, 379; **10**, 61-3, 178, 279-81; **11**, 84, 86-9, 109, 138-41, 151, 213, 215, 246, 298-9, 311-12; **12**, 162, 174, 251, 257, 262, 273, 275, 276, 278, 283, 285 n. 45, 291, 322; **13**, 18, 193 n. 1, 300-1, 320, 323; **14**, 49, 93, 110, 179, 192, 199, 226, 244, 292; **15**, 196, 221; **16**, 13, 104, 259; **17**, 81, 139, 166, 180, 267, 297, 298; **18**, 89, 91, 95, 101, 103, 152, 158, 227, 261 n. 20; **19**, 68, 105 n. 12, 118, 269, 271; **21**, 42-3, 68; **22**, 175, 215, 351, 370 n. 1; **23**, 299, 355, 362; **24**, 255, 270, 271; **25**, 10, 28, 58, 138, 175, 201, 233, 238, 245, 268 n. 3, 283 n. 4; **26**, 56, 65, 130, 154, 200, 206, 212, 223; **27**, 70 n. 4, 71, 137, 155, 213, 216-17, 254; **28**, 62, 66, 190, 228, 371-2, 380-1; **29**, 25, 27, 227, 266, 306, 315-16; **30**, 57, 150, 160, 185, 273

—Paragraph 3, **1**, 349, 350, 356, 372, 381, 412, 413, 419, 427, 504; **2**, 20, 21, 105, 142, 143-4, 146-8, 235, 248, 295, 302, 338; **3**, 47, 102, 103, 259, 260, 273, 281; **4**, 99, 216, 218, 264, 273; **5**, 1-4, 6, 7, 13-18, 48, 135, 136, 148, 150, 164, 237, 239, 242, 378, 389; **6**, 58, 221, 285; **7**, 5, 10, 20, 42, 247, 258; **8**, 11, 13, 79, 83, 154, 221, 351, 360; **9**, 166-7, 238 n. 35, 257, 277, 306, 344, 400; **10**, 240, 242, 280-1, 341; **11**, 6, 75, 90, 151, 170, 189, 215, 294; **12**, 6, 142, 149, 162, 174, 291, 345, 346, 350 n. 13, 352, 358, 370, 372; **13**, 21, 131, 272, 278, 302, 326; **14**, 105, 129, 156-8, 167, 179, 199, 269, 292; **15**, 5; **17**, 116,

INDEX

Claims Settlement Declaration (*cont.*)
163, 166, 167, 168, 180, 184, 188, 215, 229, 272; **18**, 86, 111, 152, 166, 177, 276, 297, 382; **19**, 68, 119, 203, 325, 335, 350; **21**, 43, 67, 69-70; **22**, 175, 178, 183, 193; **23**, 135-7, 278, 281, 292, 334, 362, 363; **24**, 51, 255, 281; **26**, 13, 18, 27, 66-7, 71-2, 141, 155, 206; **28**, 61-2; **29**, 23, 25-6, 41, 91-2, 229
—Paragraph 4, **1**, 381; **2**, 302; **5**, 2, 6, 15, 16, 18; **6**, 27; **8**, 351; **9**, 93-4, 156, 231, 233 n. 30, 266, 400; **13**, 272, 278; **14**, 105; **16**, 18, 78, 105; **17**, 5, 180, 188, 215, 229; **18**, 382; **19**, 350; **23**, 334, 383, 384; **25**, 10, 28, 138, 140, 141, 216; **27**, 141
Article VIII, **1**, 138
interpretation: *see* Jurisdiction of Tribunal, interpretation of Declarations
status, **21**, 309
Class action, **2**, 300-1: *see also* Nationality of claim, shareholder claims
Co-Registrar, exceeding powers, **7**, 275, 276
Commercial law, **1**, 374, 377 n. 15, 378, 445-7; **3**, 19, 20; **4**, 101, 268, 270, 276; **5**, 394: *see also* General principles of, commercial law; International Chamber of Commerce; Iran, law of, Commercial Code; United States of America, law of, Uniform Commercial Code
Compensation: *see* Damages; Expropriation, compensation
Concurrent jurisdiction, **1**, 489, 495; **2**, 310-11, 371: *see also* Forum selection clause, jurisdiction of Tribunal
Concurring opinion: *see also* Concurring and dissenting opinion; Declaration; Dissenting opinion; Explanatory remarks; Separate opinion; Separate statement; Supplemental opinion
Aghahosseini, **30**, 105
Aldrich, **2**, 349; **3**, 348; **5**, 267; **11**, 268, 345; **14**, 320; **18**, 323; **21**, 162; **29**, 56
Allison, **23**, 130; **27**, 306
Ameli, **12**, 364; **26**, 37 n. 1
Ansari, **10**, 35; **13**, 121; **19**, 73; **24**, 47 n. 2
Bahrami, **10**, 177 n. 1
Bellet, **2**, 316

Brower, **6**, 32, 110; **8**, 5, 22, 40, 206; **9**, 280-3; **10**, 34, 363; **11**, 150 n. 1, 276; **12**, 233; **15**, 289; **16**, 60; **17**, 19, 294 n. 1; **19**, 332
Holtzmann, **1**, 227, 229, 284; **2**, 57; **3**, 55, 78, 192, 199, 325, 330; **4**, 159; **5**, 111, 144, 267; **6**, 40, 47, 133; **8**, 206; **9**, 284 n. 2, 313 n. 2, 360 n. 2; **10**, 37 n. 2, 269 n. 2; **12**, 146 n. 2; **13**, 3, 124 n. 2, 331 n. 2; **14**, 320; **16**, 237; **22**, 215; **26**, 148 n. 2
Kashani, **2**, 65; **3**, 323
Khalilian, **24**, 116 n. 1
Lagergren, **2**, 317
Mosk, **1**, 305, 363, 449; **2**, 27, 57, 114, 146, 298, 386; **3**, 277, 293, 387; **4**, 111; **5**, 230, 269; **6**, 64; **7**, 201; **10**, 81; **12**, 108, 126 n. 2
Mostafavi, **8**, 203; **10**, 103; **12**, 30; **13**, 280 n. 1
Noori, **30**, 123 n. 1
Riphagen, **5**, 273
Salans, **14**, 320
Sani, **2**, 65
Shafeiei, **2**, 65
Concurring and dissenting opinion: *see also* Concurring opinion; Declaration; Dissenting opinion; Explanatory remarks; Separate opinion; Separate statement; Supplemental opinion
Allison, **27**, 187; **28**, 292; **29**, 117
Ameli, **10**, 229 n. 1; **28**, 255 n. 21; **30**, 76 n. 1
Ansari, **8**, 203; **11**, 45, 180 n. 1, 184 n. 2; **23**, 351 n. 1; **26**, 31; **28**, 307 n. 1
Bahrami, **8**, 203; **11**, 168 n. 1; **12**, 82
Böckstiegel, **8**, 203
Brower, **9**, 241; **11**, 35, 53 n. 1, 184 n. 1; **16**, 277, 304; **17**, 173, 288; **19**, 93, 231, 304; **20**, 132; **22**, 86; **23**, 78; **24**, 85; **27**, 24
Holtzmann, **9**, 107 n. 2; **10**, 229 n. 1, 333 n. 2; **14**, 24 n. 2, 65 n. 2, 191 n. 2; **17**, 31 n. 2; **19**, 298; **23**, 217; **24**, 121 n. 2
Khalilian, **18**, 324; **21**, 62; **26**, 129; **28**, 3
Mostafavi, **9**, 107 n. 1; **10**, 269 n. 1; **13**, 329 n. 1; **14**, 86 n. 1; **17**, 31 n. 1
Noori, **18**, 128, 198, 244; **24**, 162
Confidentiality of proceedings: *see* Tribunal, confidentiality of proceedings
Confiscation: *see* Expropriation

INDEX

Conflict of laws, **3**, 48; **6**, 99 n. 1; **8**, 136, 140-1; **9**, 178; **14**, 186; **19**, 126; **21**, 63
Consolidation of cases: *see under* Procedure
Consumer law, **6**, 99
Continuity of claim: *see* Claims, continuity; Nationality of claim
Contract, **8**, 164; **19**, 15, 38-46; **29**, 321-3: *see also* Applicable Law; *Force majeure*; Forum selection clause; Lease agreements; Licence; Limitation of liability clause; Negotiable instruments; Purchase order as contract
    acceleration clause, **13**, 21-7, 46-7
    adhesion, **7**, 192
    airline tickets as, **17**, 230
    alleged bribery, **12**, 270-1, 314-15, 326
    ambiguous terms, **5**, 180, 184, 192, 195; **8**, 229-30, 306-7; **9**, 31-5, 215-17, 323-4, 367, 373; **11**, 36, 45; **13**, 235
    amendment, **11**, 166; **12**, 109-13, 116-18; **13**, 188; **16**, 37, 54, 272, 279; **18**, 195, 202-7; **19**, 226; **21**, 154
        —*ad hoc*, **16**, 37
        —conduct of parties, **18**, 195-6
        —de facto, **16**, 37, 41, 54
        —implicit acceptance, **1**, 37
        —Tribunal award as, **20**, 133
        —unilateral, **22**, 46, 97-8: *see also* Stabilization clause
    annulment, **21**, 154
    anticipatory breach, **3**, 151; **7**, 42, 53, 107, 115
    applicable law, **1**, 422; **2**, 27; **3**, 48, 56; **4**, 267; **6**, 236; **7**, 131; **8**, 162, 231, 232; **9**, 121, 124, 326; **10**, 216; **13**, 26; **17**, 230-1, 240; **21**, 103, 154; **22**, 243, 268-89, 324, 325; **24**, 170; **26**, 146
        —applicable law clause, **5**, 366
    assignment, **6**, 233; **8**, 155-60
    breach, **2**, 116-18, 382, 386-7, 399; **3**, 50, 51, 55, 57, 153, 164, 247, 261, 265, 289, 293, 294 n. 1; **4**, 232, 233 n. 1, 234, 235, 240, 252, 267; **5**, 127, 398; **6**, 63, 64, 136, 137, 139, 189, 199, 200, 203, 206, 216, 222, 285, 286, 290, 293, 294; **7**, 13, 24, 75, 79, 82, 103, 105-7, 109, 110, 113, 114, 202 n. 1, 215; **8**, 168-71, 310-12; **9**, 112-18, 157-60; **10**, 254; **12**, 151, 294, 351; **13**, 46-50, 113, 121-3, 133-4, 142, 143, 303; **14**, 200-3; **15**, 31, 234-44; **16**, 28-43, 47, 59, 64-8,

72; **17**, 77; **18**, 96, 328-31; **19**, 14-15; **22**, 56-7, 99-100, 299-310; **24**, 73-80
    —applicable law, **16**, 26
    —damage, need for, **22**, 57-8
    —justifying—
        ——repudiation of contract, **24**, 74
        ——suspension of work, **12**, 294; **22**, 309-10
    —nationalization as, **15**, 243
    —notice of, **22**, 102
    —termination for: *see* termination, for breach *below*
    —timeliness of complaint, **25**, 98
    cancellation, **14**, 269-70
    collateral, **23**, 145
    collateral promises, **6**, 197
    condition precedent, **7**, 109, 114
    contra proferentem rule: *see verba ambigua accipiuntur contra proferentem below*
    counter offer, **7**, 113
    creation of new agreement, **4**, 221; **5**, 395
    cross-termination clause, **10**, 175
    date, **23**, 42
    discharge, **2**, 251, 254
    dispute settlement provisions, **8**, 223; **21**, 105; **29**, 351-2
    disputes relating to, **19**, 341-2
    duty of reasonable efforts: *see* good faith, duty of *below*
    election, **3**, 289
    enforceability, **2**, 221, 381, 398; **3**, 13, 14, 16, 18, 27-9, 287; **6**, 62, 162; **7**, 192; **8**, 160-2, 223
    error, **8**, 133
    escalation clause, **16**, 247-9
    evidence of: *see* Evidence of, contract
    excessively onerous, **9**, 122 n. 14
    excuse, **3**, 153, 154, 264; **7**, 67, 75, 110, 193; **9**, 196-7; **18**, 302-3; **19**, 69-70
    exercise of rights under, **7**, 157, 158
    extension, **6**, 145; **13**, 338-9
    fixed-price, **24**, 172-3
    force majeure: *see* Force majeure
    formation, **3**, 47, 55, 162; **6**, 162, 176, 189, 191-3, 196, 197; **7**, 107, 109; **9**, 56; **13**, 273-5, 279-81; **17**, 126, 131, 197; **18**, 159; **19**, 69; **22**, 306-9; **23**, 340, 347 n. 5

322   INDEX

Contract (*cont.*)
    —by conduct of parties, **3**, 48, 49; **6**, 17,
      145, 191, 192, 197; **7**, 103, 113, 114;
      8, 130-1; **13**, 111-13; **22**, 307-8
    good faith, duty of, **6**, 197, 198; **7**, 160; **8**,
      133, 141-3; **9**, 122 n. 13; **14**, 140-1: *see
      also* Good faith
    guarantee, **8**, 91-2, 95-6; **13**, 157, 160,
      163, 166
    illegal, **4**, 249, 250
    implied terms, **9**, 147-9, 216-17
    impossibility: *see* Frustration
    independence, **7**, 66
    inequality of parties, **13**, 245
    interpretation, **1**, 107 n. 1, 108, 209, 213
      n. 7, 214 n. 8; **3**, 251, 261; **4**, 252, 260;
      5, 117, 128, 180, 181, 184, 192, 196,
      197, 228; **6**, 114, 115, 161, 227, 237,
      262, 277; **7**, 13, 23, 71, 72, 75, 76, 78,
      79, 86, 87, 192; **8**, 225, 231, 306-7; **9**,
      148-9, 323-4, 327-9, 367-73; **10**, 222-3,
      329; **11**, 8-11; **12**, 109-13; **13**, 214-15,
      235-6; **14**, 54, 273-5; **15**, 148, 236; **17**,
      64, 315; **18**, 312; **22**, 42, 237-9, 292-8;
      28, 43-4
      —applicable law, relevance, **22**, 293
      —circumstances at time of conclusion,
        22, 292
      —conduct of parties, **2**, 118; **3**, 288; **5**,
        232; **6**, 227, 262; **7**, 193; **12**, 103,
        200, 212; **16**, 54; **22**, 238-9
      —context, **22**, 292
      —*expressio unius exclusio alterius est*, **16**, 27
      —intention of parties, **7**, 73, 75, 79, 83;
        9, 392; **15**, 148, 152
      —preparatory works, **11**, 9-11, 45-6
      —trade usage, **9**, 367, 380-1
    legal relationship between parties, **5**, 173;
      7, 82; **8**, 130-3, 142; **9**, 326-7
    letter of credit distinguished, **13**, 102
    liability under collateral contracts, **12**, 37
    limitation of liability clause: *see* Limitation
      of liability clause
    merger of rights under separate, **7**, 34, 35
    obligations of parties in absence of, **12**,
      134
    obligations under, attempt to discharge,
      19, 80-1
    oral, **8**, 160-1; **22**, 20-1, 115
    for ownership of land, **7**, 131
    part performance, **8**, 160-1

performance, **5**, 393, 398; **6**, 85-9, 94,
  274, 290, 292-4; **7**, 110, 161; **9**, 117-18;
  12, 150-1; **18**, 302-3
  —interpretation and, **22**, 298
  —prevention, **28**, 96-103
  —progress reports, responsibility for, **9**,
    218
  —standard, **11**, 110, 114-16
  —time of the essence, **22**, 300-2
  —waiver of defects in, **6**, 87, 88
principals bound by, **6**, 72, 159
privity of, **18**, 210
pro forma invoice, **3**, 41, 49, 54; **5**, 25, 38,
  43, 46; **7**, 25
progress payments, **24**, 29-30
proper law of: *see* applicable law *above*
quantum meruit: *see* Quantum meruit
ratification by conduct of parties, **1**, 413,
  414; **2**, 145-6, 154, 380, 397; **3**, 163,
  164, 247, 248; **4**, 249, 250; **5**, 395
recovery under, **5**, 172
reformation or rectification, **2**, 117
renegotiation clause, **15**, 297; **16**, 63
repudiation, **7**, 107; **16**, 40-1, 64
required to be in writing, **7**, 13
res inter alios acta, **13**, 122
revenue actually earned, **9**, 372-5
rights under, export of property, **22**, 79
sales of goods and services between Iran
  and US, **5**, 96, 99-101, 103, 104; **13**,
  156-7, 162-3
  —educational instruction a service, **13**,
    273
scope, **19**, 70
severability of provisions, **8**, 223
stabilization clause: *see* Stabilization clause
standard inspection clause, **19**, 13-14
standby arrangement: *see* suspension *below*
State's duty to respect, **15**, 242, 294-8
sub-contractors, authorization, **24**, 30-2
  —liability for, **19**, 46-7
sub-licence, **6**, 163
subject of, **7**, 25
substitution, **3**, 274
succession to, **1**, 359-60; **15**, 60-1; **17**, 15,
  17; **20**, 7-8
superseded by Settlement Agreement, **10**,
  282-4
suspension, **10**, 168-70; **16**, 37-40, 54; **22**,
  30-2, 46, 47, 236-7; **23**, 171; **25**, 36
tax withheld, **22**, 19-20

termination, **2**, 388; **3**, 154, 155, 232, 265, 266, 289, 294; **4**, 235, 259, 260; **5**, 210, 317-19; **6**, 274; **7**, 15, 107; **8**, 313-14, 338-40; **9**, 118-20, 147-50, 196; **10**, 290; **12**, 182-5, 234-6; **13**, 187-8, 213-16, 245-52, 302; **14**, 35-9, 54, 60-1, 119-21, 140-1; **16**, 20-45, 62-3, 272; **17**, 65-8; **18**, 159-60, 331-2; **19**, 70-1, 330-1, 340-2; **20**, 49; **22**, 32-3, 46-7, 237, 298-9; **23**, 90-6; **25**, 36; **27**, 165-7: *see also Force majeure*; Frustration
— for breach, **26**, 160-1
— burden of proof, **22**, 54, 56, 99
— by agreement, **2**, 116-18
— for cause, **23**, 25, 90
— compensation for, **2**, 117
— for convenience, **23**, 26, 69, 79, 91; **25**, 96
— date, **9**, 196; **17**, 68; **19**, 70; **22**, 53, 100; **27**, 167
— for delay, **25**, 97
— invalidity distinguished, **8**, 222
— legal consequences, **9**, 120-33, 196-7; **20**, 74-5
— matter of election, **12**, 185
— non-performance, **22**, 30
— notice of, need for, **22**, 56-7; **23**, 223-4; **28**, 40
— past obligations unaffected, **9**, 201
— protection of property, **23**, 27
— right of, **22**, 21-2, 41-2, 46, 96, 248
— suspension, whether, **22**, 30-1; **25**, 39-40
— timeliness, **25**, 97, 98
— waiver of right, **13**, 251-2
third party beneficiary, **3**, 274, 278; **4**, 276; **6**, 160, 161, 193, 195, 196; **8**, 271; **9**, 401; **23**, 144, 301; **24**, 11
third party rights, **28**, 79
trade usage, **9**, 367
translation of, **1**, 317, 318; **9**, 31-5, 212-14; **13**, 181-2
ultra vires, **2**, 24
unilateral changes, **15**, 240
unjust enrichment: *see* Unjust enrichment
validity, **1**, 413, 414; **2**, 116-17, 119, 145, 155, 380-2, 397-9; **3**, 48, 162-4, 231, 245, 246, 251, 252, 278, 286-9; **4**, 249, 250; **6**, 176, 189, 192, 196; **7**, 113; **8**, 160-1, 222-3; **9**, 195, 392-4; **12**, 150, 315; **28**, 95-6; **29**, 232
value of rights under, **4**, 156
verba ambigua accipiuntuer contra proferentem, **9**, 371, 393-4
waiver of rights, **7**, 23; **13**, 251-2; **16**, 62-3, 274; **20**, 90; **29**, 327
— evidence of, **9**, 162; **11**, 233-8, 250-4, 330-1, 345-6
warranty: *see* Warranty
Contradictory assertions, **7**, 123-6, 135
Controlled entity: *see also* Evidence of, controlled entity status
Government agency carrying out acts of State and commercial acts distinguished, **1**, 421-2
independence, **21**, 71 n. 17, 72-3
Iran, **1**, 372, 389, 412, 413, 418-23, 427, 445, 475, 503; **2**, 9-10, 17-23, 26, 105, 143-4, 146-52, 165, 258-9, 302, 338; **3**, 47, 65, 103, 104, 160, 230, 231, 260, 273, 286, 323; **4**, 218; **5**, 1-23, 48-50, 71, 135, 136, 210, 237-9, 242-5, 370, 371, 378-80; **6**, 58, 59, 221, 285; **7**, 5, 10, 20, 42, 97, 188; **8**, 154-5; **9**, 15, 51, 88-96, 324-6, 343, 400; **10**, 24, 46, 62, 142-7, 166, 240-2, 281-2, 341; **11**, 55, 151, 215, 294-5; **12**, 149, 348, 372; **13**, 19, 102, 131-2, 202; **14**, 157, 179, 269; **15**, 5-6, 33, 198, 237-9; **17**, 6, 116, 119, 130, 163, 169, 174-8, 184-5, 188, 225, 298-300; **18**, 111, 158, 177; **19**, 118-19, 183, 184, 186, 187, 189, 190, 192, 193, 195, 196, 198, 199, 203, 325-9, 335-40; **21**, 43, 67-70; **22**, 178-82, 183-93; **23**, 135-7, 278-81, 333-4, 363; **24**, 281; **25**, 138-41; **26**, 153-4; **27**, 24, 71-2; **28**, 61-2
— Council for the Protection of Industries, **10**, 138-9
— critical date, **17**, 165; **22**, 171, 187; **29**, 229
— joint-stock company, **5**, 2-23
— Mostazafan Foundation, **9**, 88-96
— NIOC, **1**, 356
— private structure of organization, relevance, **6**, 58-9; **22**, 186
— Social Services Organization, **14**, 129
— subsidiary of, **19**, 119
— test for control, **5**, 6-11; **10**, 241-2;

INDEX

Controlled entity (*cont.*)
13, 19-21; **17**, 166-7, 299-300; **23**, 136, 279; **25**, 140-1
—TRC, **8**, 154-5; **9**, 325
responsibility for obligations of, bankruptcy risk, relevance, **25**, 144
substitution of State for, **17**, 167, 179; **22**, 182
United States, **1**, 106; **2**, 165; **5**, 71; **13**, 273, 278; **23**, 383-4; **27**, 141
—fiduciary responsibilities, **10**, 84
Cooperatives, **5**, 238, 239, 244 n. 1
Corporate veil, **7**, 205; **12**, 360-1, 365; **21**, 72
Corporations: *see also* Cooperatives; Evidence of, corporation
agency: *see* Agency
applicable law: *see* Applicable law, corporations
continuity of ownership: *see* Nationality of claim, continuity of ownership
control, **1**, 358, 359, 363, 381, 382, 384, 385; **4**, 101; **7**, 5, 6, 123, 134, 135, 200, 206, 207; **9**, 258-64, 281; **11**, 214; **28**, 62-5; **30**, 150-1: *see also* Controlled entity; Nationality of claim, corporations
independence, **6**, 70; **7**, 121, 130, 131; **9**, 378-9
legal personality, **6**, 70; **7**, 120, 133; **9**, 378; **28**, 65-6
nationality: *see* Nationality of claim, corporations; Nationality, corporations
non-profit, **3**, 317 n. 1; **5**, 345, 348, 350, 352; **6**, 250; **7**, 180 n. 1; **17**, 254 n. 4
—control, **5**, 349, 350
—interest of directors, **5**, 350
—jurisdiction of Tribunal, **5**, 338, 341, 343-7, 349, 351
ownership, **6**, 127; **11**, 214, 312-13; **16**, 259-60; **17**, 297-8, 325-8; **18**, 100-1, 103-9; **19**, 269; **21**, 77-8; **23**, 383
—nominal, **7**, 186
shareholders: *see also under* Nationality of claim
—assignment of shares, **15**, 101
—duties, **30**, 165-7
—rights, **2**, 352; **4**, 242, 243; **7**, 120, 122, 130-4
——to bring claim, **11**, 87
succession, **1**, 359-63, 373-6, 382, 387, 389; **13**, 334

wholly-owned subsidiary: *see* Wholly-owned subsidiary
Costs, **1**, 171, 414, 415, 447, 448, 451, 508; **2**, 12-13, 40, 146, 169, 177, 239, 244, 245, 254, 342, 385, 400; **3**, 17, 33, 58, 66, 72, 107, 108, 117, 206, 236, 253, 254, 267, 268, 275, 276, 279, 291, 294, 332, 333; **4**, 18, 19, 79, 81, 82, 110, 120, 228, 229, 271, 278; **5**, 87, 93, 96, 101, 111, 120, 137, 174, 175, 181, 230, 231, 241, 242, 360, 373, 374, 401; **6**, 18, 64, 68, 69, 129, 175, 217, 229, 283, 287, 288; **7**, 7, 16, 24, 25, 29, 30, 48, 88, 117, 198; **8**, 61, 92, 96, 134, 177, 323-4, 329-36, 384, 403; **9**, 59-60, 150-1, 168, 199, 301, 345, 377; **10**, 33, 34, 35-6, 55, 80, 103, 134, 175, 179, 256, 316, 347; **11**, 33, 34, 43-5, 52, 68, 69, 136, 137, 165, 167, 178, 179, 181, 184 n. 1, 206-7, 208, 222, 249, 250, 255, 267, 295, 344; **12**, 16, 30, 36, 38, 107, 137, 138, 145, 158, 159, 169, 231, 264, 297, 322-3, 356, 362; **13**, 35, 117, 145, 157, 160, 163, 166, 191, 269, 276, 281, 285, 309, 323, 344; **14**, 26, 49-50, 52, 80, 81-2, 93, 132, 168, 184, 211, 242, 270, 278, 279, 281, 300; **15**, 21, 184, 289; **16**, 86, 103 n. 1, 109, 235, 236, 254-5, 275, 281, 303; **17**, 18, 19, 30, 31 n. 1, 86, 113, 129, 133, 152, 172, 199, 212, 227, 237, 244, 265, 268, 290, 294 n. 1, 323-4; **18**, 87, 89, 91, 96, 102, 119, 153, 163, 173, 179, 197, 230, 243, 277, 291, 320, 372; **19**, 72, 92, 160, 229-30, 270, 331; **20**, 150-1; **21**, 19, 27, 30, 60, 61, 161; **22**, 85, 86, 116, 122, 183, 199, 255, 336, 354, 355; **23**, 74, 121, 149, 215-16, 228-30, 238, 267, 274, 284, 294, 306, 338, 389; **24**, 84, 114, 119, 201-2, 226, 247, 259, 271, 288; **25**, 13-14, 19, 109-10, 129, 150, 176, 200, 232-3, 239-40, 245-6, 288, 297; **26**, 30, 43, 127, 183, 252; **27**, 23, 31, 62, 119, 120, 121, 144, 185-6, 217, 245-6; **28**, 49, 50, 110, 215, 317, 381, 385; **29**, 55, 56, 65, 116, 117, 120-2, 240, 293, 309, 348; **30**, 162: *see also* Damages, expenses
in 'A' Cases, **27**, 257-63
auditors' fees, **9**, 133; **14**, 50
in 'B' Cases, **27**, 257-63

INDEX

in claims of less than US $250,000, **10**,
    327; **11**, 167; **13**, 309, 323; **14**, 93
damages distinguished, **23**, 228
for defending malicious claims, **5**, 86, 87
determination deferred, **9**, 44
evidence of: *see* Evidence of, costs
experts', **2**, 75, 76-7; **11**, 136, 137, 267;
    16, 236, 255; **30**, 234-5
frivolous claim, **2**, 245
lack of jurisdiction and, **2**, 43, 227, 343;
    12, 39
legal fees, **3**, 53, 58; **8**, 177, 331-5; **9**, 133,
    150-1, 242, 355, 403; **10**, 316; **14**, 49;
    17, 19; **20**, 128; **23**, 228-30, 302, 337;
    24, 155; **26**, 183; **27**, 31, 186-7
non-legal fees, **8**, 330-1, 334; **9**, 150; **20**,
    128
in official claims, **12**, 30
out-of-pocket expenses, **17**, 19
parties to pay own, **30**, 43, 44-5, 101
principle underlying, **16**, 254-5, 281
private attorney, **8**, 13, 309, 323
reasonable, **9**, 150-1, 202, 338, 377; **10**,
    81; **12**, 36, 137; **28**, 368-9
    —failure to provide information and, **2**,
        113
result of delays in proceedings, **4**, 81; **8**,
    39
translation, **18**, 197
travel expenses, **14**, 50
withdrawal of claim, **2**, 260
Counterclaims, **1**, 171, 218, 232, 233, 336,
    384, 385, 390, 485, 507, 508; **2**, 338,
    384, 400; **4**, 143, 177, 178, 214, 243; **8**,
    45-6, 383-4; **10**, 287-8; **11**, 48-50,
    108-35, 317, 341-2; **12**, 215-29, 321-2;
    16, 231-2, 303; **18**, 101, 116-20,
    128-31, 195-7, 207-8, 219-23, 304-5,
    313, 314-15, 316-17, 320, 348-51, 356,
    362; **19**, 153-4, 212-13, 249, 251-3; **21**,
    145-52; **22**, 81-3; **25**, 10-11, 12-13,
    59-61, 69-90, 149-59
admissibility, **2**, 324-6; **8**, 384; **9**, 223-4;
    13, 227, 229; **15**, 272; **21**, 146-8; **30**, 6-
    7, 11-12
    —against indirect claimant, **11**, 110
    —against third party, **11**, 109
amendment, **7**, 182; **11**, 108; **13**, 228-9;
    17, 253-4; **23**, 167-8
arising out of same contract, transaction or
    occurrence, **2**, 51, 55, 63, 324-6, 378,

379, 396; **3**, 115, 116, 152, 167, 235,
    251, 252, 260, 261, 286; **4**, 7, 243, 247;
    5, 173, 233, 400; **6**, 83, 84, 95, 100-3,
    109; **7**, 21, 82-4, 195, 196, 207, 208; **8**,
    267-9; **9**, 36-7, 135-6, 167, 225; **10**, 53-
    4, 168; **11**, 315, 316; **12**, 6-7, 291; **13**,
    134-5, 284-5, 306-7; **14**, 105-10, 118,
    119, 127; **15**, 18, 19, 100, 284-5; **16**,
    293; **17**, 259; **18**, 123, 298, 356, 360-1;
    19, 68, 78, 153, 223, 228, 249, 251,
    270; **20**, 35, 37-8; **21**, 148-9, 150; **22**,
    82, 210, 254-5, 337; **24**, 47 n. 2, 83; **25**,
    70-1, 106; **26**, 28, 81, 99-101, 215; **27**,
    141, 235-6, 239, 244-5; **28**, 325-6; **29**,
    187-8, 191-2, 200, 204, 208, 212, 237-
    9; **30**, 12, 17-18
    —bank claims, application to, **16**, 294;
        29, 187-8, 191-2, 204, 212
    —series of contracts, **25**, 71
as defence, **4**, 246; **5**, 173, 233, 400
based on
    —invalid claim, **12**, 36
    —tort, **6**, 46
    —violation of Iranian law, **6**, 84
characterization of, **6**, 46
conditional, **8**, 226
contractual waiver, **13**, 221-3, 240-4
damage, need for, **25**, 93
delay in presenting, **7**, 116; **9**, 22; **11**, 135,
    137; **17**, 57-61; **21**, 146-8
entitlement to file, **10**, 168
in excess of claim, **3**, 152
for—
    —advance payment, **15**, 94-5
    —audit, **25**, 90
    —bad oil field practices, **21**, 153-9
    —balance of down payment, **8**, 325;
        17, 82-3
    —bank guarantees—
        ——cancellation, **9**, 229-30
        ——collection, **8**, 327-8; **9**, 29; **20**,
            39-41
    —bonus payments, **15**, 87-91
    —breach of contract, **9**, 41-2, 58; **10**,
        174; **11**, 22-6, 38-9; **12**, 156-7; **13**,
        144; **14**, 50, 167; **15**, 18, 279-82,
        285-8; **18**, 305; **27**, 103; **29**, 334-45
    —breach of duty to protect goods, **8**,
        271; **27**, 241-5
    —cost of replacing goods, **13**, 142
    —costs incurred, **16**, 232

326

INDEX

Counterclaims (*cont.*)
—customs duty, **15**, 99-100; **20**, 35; **22**, 81-2
—damaged property, **11**, 19; **13**, 143
—damages and interest, **27**, 140-1
—debts, **15**, 97-8
—default, **20**, 81
—defective equipment, **24**, 153, 197-9, 287-8
—defective performance, **8**, 173-7; **9**, 133, 299; **10**, 305-6; **11**, 18-19, 121-35, 142-3, 145-9, 247-8, 342; **12**, 220-4; **13**, 143-4, 306; **15**, 85-7; **18**, 196, 220, 313; **19**, 81; **20**, 30-1, 33-5, 134-7; **21**, 159-60; **23**, 58-62, 214; **26**, 103, 118-19; **27**, 236-41; **28**, 338-87
——damage, need for, **25**, 93
——defective supervision, **12**, 224
——failure to complain, **28**, 338-87
——inadequate qualifications, **12**, 220-1
——unsatisfactory documents, **8**, 12, 221-3
—defective supervision, **12**, 224
—delay, **13**, 143; **18**, 219-20; **20**, 117; **23**, 54-8; **29**, 332-3
—deliverables, **8**, 325-6, 344-7
—double payment, **25**, 81-5
—due to excess vacations and unauthorized absences, **12**, 226
—education of Iranian children, **14**, 79
—equipment held by claimant, **14**, 52; **19**, 216-18, 223-4
—expenses, **11**, 192-3; **17**, 287; **18**, 220-1; **20**, 79-81, 82
—expired guarantees, **11**, 316-17, 341-2
—failure to deliver, **17**, 319
—goods supplied, **20**, 115-16, 169-70; **27**, 119
—improper estimates, **11**, 120-1
—improper payments, **12**, 215-18; **25**, 70-2, 78-81, 85-7
—inadequate qualifications, **12**, 220-1
—inflation-related damages, **8**, 23, 62-3; **23**, 62-3
—judgment award, **22**, 82
—legal expenses, **3**, 261, 267; **8**, 268; **9**, 230; **22**, 254-5
—liquidated damages, **8**, 177
—liquidation fees, **27**, 144

—loss of—
——operating capacity, **12**, 137
——use of land, **14**, 210
—losses—
——arising out of failure to return items sent for repair, **12**, 137
——to employees, **19**, 154
—medical insurance, **25**, 89
—non-performance, **11**, 67; **19**, 70-1; **20**, 119
—overcharges, **7**, 191
——due to excess vacations and unauthorized absences, **12**, 226
—overpayments, **10**, 304-5; **12**, 218-20, 321; **15**, 16-17; **20**, 77-8; **23**, 52-4, 116-19; **25**, 87
—payment of good performance bond, **8**, 177; **20**, 78-9, 116; **22**, 83
—performance guarantees, **24**, 275; **26**, 81: *see also* for bank guarantees *above*
—reduction of fee, **25**, 76-8
—reimbursement of
——down payment, **14**, 50; **20**, 117-18; **26**, 171-2
——escalation payments, **9**, 227
——fees, **8**, 172; **10**, 326-7
——overcharges, **13**, 35, 72-7
——overpayment, **19**, 224-5
——payments to contractors, **8**, 172-3; **9**, 26-8, 166-7; **11**, 19, 192; **20**, 33-5; **27**, 103, 140
—relief from bank guarantee, **11**, 193-4; **17**, 170-2
—rent, **16**, 232
—repayment of—
——social security payments, **17**, 262-3
——tax costs, **12**, 224-6
—return of—
——documents, **8**, 177; **11**, 19-20; **17**, 83-5
——materials, **20**, 80
——property, **14**, 126; **26**, 176-7
——unliquidated down-payment, **19**, 212-13
—salary arrears, **25**, 88; **27**, 104-5
—services, **15**, 95-6; **17**, 262; **20**, 39, 81; **22**, 82; **25**, 72-6; **26**, 82; **27**, 119
—severance pay, **15**, 87-91; **26**, 82; **27**, 104-5

INDEX

— Social Security payments: *see* Social Security payments, counterclaim for
— specific performance, **7**, 159; **9**, 26; **16**, 231-2
— standby letter of credit, **17**, 253; **24**, 275
— taxes: *see* Taxes, counterclaim for
— termination of staff contracts, **2**, 112-13
— testing costs, **20**, 32-3
— unjustifiable collection of funds in Trust Account, **8**, 272-3
— unpaid sums, **25**, 88-9; **27**, 116-18, 233-5
— unpaid taxes, **25**, 89-90
— unsatisfactory documents, **12**, 221-3
— value of —
—— leased goods, **19**, 153, 154
—— missing property, **12**, 226; **27**, 118
—— spare parts, **9**, 28-9
—— withdrawal of suit, **12**, 321-2
—— withheld documents, **26**, 103-4
—— wrongful expulsion, **9**, 16-18
implied withdrawal, **30**, 6
interest, **17**, 82-3
invalid claim as basis for, **12**, 36
jurisdiction of Tribunal, **2**, 54-60, 62-4, 65-7, 97-9, 311, 363, 371; **3**, 60, 61, 151, 152, 201, 235, 251, 261, 322, 335, 386; **4**, 7, 55, 242-5, 246 n. 1, 261; **5**, 129, 227, 229; **6**, 82-4, 93, 100-3, 108-10, 115, 116; **7**, 20, 21, 82, 84, 201, 219; **8**, 76-8, 203, 232-3, 265, 364, 366, 368, 371; **9**, 223; **10**, 287-8, 306; **11**, 109; **12**, 6-7, 106, 218, 291; **13**, 72-4, 78-83, 132-3, 144, 221-9, 284, 306-7, 342-3; **14**, 105-10; **15**, 90, 96, 272, 283-5, 288, 309; **16**, 293, 294-5, 313; **18**, 102, 116-20, 128-31, 167, 360-1, 372; **19**, 228, 249, 251-3, 310; **20**, 78; **21**, 148-52, 343-5; **25**, 70-1
— dependence on jurisdiction over main claim, **9**, 38, 87; **17**, 264; **18**, 102, 119; **21**, 18-19; **26**, 126, 215-16, 251; **28**, 314-16
— exclusive, **2**, 98; **8**, 77
— failure to prove, **9**, 223
— previous settlement, **24**, 114, 196-7, 199-200

— withdrawal of main claim, effect, **10**, 312; **12**, 264; **18**, 117
limitation on, **6**, 102; **13**, 226-7
municipal courts, **8**, 77
offset and, **10**, 309; **16**, 293; **19**, 310-16; **21**, 55, 74, 344-5; **26**, 144, 169-70; **29**, 191, 195, 199, 207, 211; **30**, 16
outstanding, **3**, 115; **10**, 102; **20**, 118; **27**, 104, 143-4; **28**, 46-7
possibility of separate pursuit, **13**, 244
preparation of, **2**, 288
proper claimant, **15**, 90, 96, 98; **19**, 153, 154; **25**, 149; **27**, 104
proper respondent, **6**, 82, 83; **7**, 126; **11**, 315; **15**, 19
relation to claim, **4**, 243, 244; **7**, 82; **9**, 312
right of, **1**, 103, 108, 219
same party, **2**, 324-6, 378; **4**, 75; **5**, 173; **7**, 21
termination of proceedings and, **30**, 6
third party, **8**, 270-1; **9**, 36-7; **15**, 98-9
time limits: *see* Time limits, counterclaims
validity, **7**, 202; **9**, 58-9
Course of dealing, **5**, 45, 46
Criminal action, alternative forum, **4**, 60
Currency, **10**, 91-4; **11**, 40-2, 50-1, 164, 184 n. 1, 206, 230; **13**, 265-6; **15**, 62-4; **16**, 274-5; **24**, 187-90
conversion, **2**, 13; **3**, 233, 250 n. 1, 288; **4**, 104 n. 1; **5**, 168, 169, 175, 214; **6**, 171; **7**, 73, 74; **8**, 17, 98, 165, 291-2, 403, 420-7; **9**, 163 n. 7, 227-8, 247, 336; **10**, 54, 78-9, 91, 345-6, 352-3; **11**, 16-17, 31-3, 35, 93 n. 8, 141, 164, 176 n. 5, 199, 206, 208, 230-1, 240-2, 340-1, 357-8; **12**, 106, 124; **13**, 190, 304, 343-4; **14**, 183, 189-90; **15**, 63-4; **16**, 223, 256, 274; **17**, 225 n. 14, 301; **18**, 162, 277, 285-6; **20**, 128-33; **24**, 180; **27**, 105
— contract provision, **11**, 32, 358; **13**, 192; **16**, 274; **17**, 319
— exchange rate changes, **5**, 11, 32-3, 41, 50, 206, 208; **11**, 32-3, 41, 50, 206, 208; **12**, 304-5; **16**, 274; **20**, 22-5, 95; **23**, 70
Currency exchange controls: *see* Foreign exchange controls
Customary international law, **2**, 179, 188, 196, 197, 210; **4**, 105, 116-18, 268; **5**, 269, 279-81, 286, 294, 300; **6**, 177, 178, 208, 209; **8**, 395-403; **9**, 273; **10**, 185,

328   INDEX

Customary international law (*cont.*)
    189; **11**, 358; **14**, 330; **15**, 222-4, 231, 246, 290; **16**, 230
  act of State, **19**, 292
  evidence of, agreed settlements, whether, **21**, 121
  export control, **28**, 144
  expropriation, **21**, 120-2, 198, 330-1; **30**, 197-8, 200, 238-44
  expulsion of aliens, **16**, 88-9; **17**, 107, 142-4; **18**, 161
  interest on damages, **17**, 22 n. 4
  jus cogens, **15**, 266
  opinio juris, **21**, 121
  protection of aliens, **17**, 147
  sovereign immunity, **28**, 133, 156, 158
  treaties and, **10**, 192, 202; **15**, 34-5; **16**, 69, 88; **17**, 264; **21**, 120-2, 330-1
Customary international practice, **3**, 19; **4**, 67, 68
Customs dues, **15**, 99-100; **20**, 35, 91-2

Damages, **1**, 387, 388, 445, 448, 452-4; **4**, 108-9; **5**, 248; **10**, 309; **12**, 22-3, 319, 333-4; **15**, 39-40, 105-7, 111, 124, 255-6, 265-9, 308; **16**, 293; **18**, 7-9, 18-19, 23, 25-6; **19**, 88, 224-5, 330-1; **21**, 55, 70, 75, 143-5, 163-4; **25**, 148; **27**, 99-101; **28**, 13-14; **29**, 279, 280-3: *see also* Expropriation, compensation
  additional costs, **11**, 231-8, 250-5
  admitted liability, **28**, 44-5
  advance payments, **2**, 107
  advertising, **14**, 204
  assigned debts, **21**, 52
  bank charges, **14**, 208; **22**, 250-1, 334-5; **23**, 205-8
  bank guarantees, **11**, 99, 175-6; **12**, 162-5
  bonds, **19**, 151-2
  breach of contract, **12**, 134-5; **15**, 73; **17**, 127-9
  breach of General Declaration, **25**, 260-2
  calculation: *see* computation *below*
  capital advances, **16**, 19, 55, 72; **19**, 127
  capital contribution, **14**, 166-7
  cargo damage settlements, **19**, 128-9
  carrying costs, **7**, 111, 112, 114
  causal link, need for, **27**, 15-17, 25
  collection expenses, **3**, 249, 253; **5**, 400
  computation, **2**, 107-11: *see also* measure *and* valuation *below*

—error in, **19**, 173-4
—need for precise criteria, **12**, 20-4; **28**, 213
conditional on return of goods, **12**, 135
consequential, **4**, 240, 277; **5**, 400; **6**, 204-6; **7**, 75; **24**, 288
consultancy fees, **16**, 312 n. 23; **19**, 71; **25**, 51-2
contract labour, **15**, 151-2
contractual obligations, **16**, 54
—foreseeable circumstances, **16**, 54-5
contractually determined, **24**, 197
conversion of currency: *see* Currency, conversion
cost adjustments, **20**, 157-9
costs of arbitration: *see* Costs
costs arising from unforeseen anomaly, **11**, 111-14
costs of delay, **9**, 160-3, 174-7; **10**, 72-4, 89-91; **20**, 56-65, 67-70, 113-14; **29**, 330
costs incurred, **19**, 134-5, 152-3; **23**, 203; **28**, 108-9; **29**, 29, 235, 430
—date, **19**, 134
customs dues, **5**, 96; **20**, 91-2
damage to financial health, **11**, 18
damaged effects, **10**, 171-2
—on damages, **12**, 24
deduction for, **7**, 114, 115; **10**, 77-8, 309; **12**, 105; **15**, 84; **16**, 293; **17**, 8, 124-5; **18**, 304, 350-1; **19**, 218, 220, 221; **21**, 74-8; **22**, 39, 337; **23**, 64, 208-10; **26**, 162; **29**, 345, 348: *see also* valuation, discounts *below*
—corrected invoice, **15**, 130, 131
—credit for work performed, **10**, 70
—debts, **12**, 23-4; **21**, 53, 61
—depreciation, **17**, 109; **28**, 3, 12-17, 107-8
—downpayment, **13**, 188; **15**, 107-8, 132-3, 149
—excess man-hours, **20**, 64, 139-41
—materials, **20**, 63
—overpayment, **15**, 63-4, 129
—payments made, **15**, 140, 144, 155
—profits from resale, **4**, 270; **19**, 145, 154, 158
—shipping costs, **17**, 109
—social security payments, **20**, 74, 87
—taxes, **2**, 324; **13**, 304; **15**, 64; **16**, 274, 276, 280; **25**, 52, 53-4, 74, 87; **30**, 228-30

—unauthorized work, **11**, 104-5
—uncompleted work, **11**, 229-30
—undelivered equipment, **11**, 192
—unliquidated advance payment, **9**, 164
—unsatisfactory performance, **18**, 335-8
—waived charges, **17**, 224-5
delivered goods, **11**, 202-4; **12**, 136; **19**, 219-20
destroyed leased equipment, **12**, 316
dispatched goods, **18**, 316
double recovery avoidance, **28**, 172, 214
escalation payments, **10**, 72-7; **22**, 15-20, 91-2
evidence of: *see* Evidence of, damages
excess taxes, **10**, 290-8
exchange losses, **10**, 174; **11**, 33, 201-2, 339; **12**, 16, 29-30; **20**, 22-5
exchange rate: *see* Currency, conversion
exemplary, **10**, 205; **11**, 44
expenses, **9**, 35, 198-9, 298; **14**, 123-4, 204, 206-7; **19**, 124-5; **27**, 183: *see also* legal fees *below*
——additional, **18**, 192-3, 214-15; **20**, 60-1, 65, 67-9, 112-14
—— need for notification, **18**, 192-3, 215
—— maintenance and repair, **1**, 19, 136; **19**, 136
—— rental payments, **19**, 135-6
—— voyage, **19**, 123-4
expropriated bank account, **12**, 213-15
expropriation: *see* Expropriation, compensation
extended overhead costs, **10**, 72, 77
facilities expenditures, **11**, 334
failure to return leased property, **10**, 254, 258; **19**, 132-5
foreseeable consequences: *see* Causation
guarantee costs, **19**, 150-1
guarding costs, **22**, 38-9, 81, 95
handling and storage, **3**, 52, 53, 56, 57
housing costs, **25**, 444-6
improper charges, **17**, 110-11
improper deductions, **15**, 83, 132
increased costs, **15**, 78-81, 129-30, 145-50; **22**, 20-1
inflation, **4**, 270; **8**, 168; **29**, 53, 277-8
injunction bond, **22**, 252; **23**, 204-5; **24**, 38-9

interim fee, **13**, 183
inventory costs, **14**, 123; **26**, 168-9
invoice claim, **9**, 19-20; **10**, 70-1, 170-4; **11**, 12-14, 20-1, 228-9, 320-30; **12**, 168, 198-213, 295; **13**, 264-6, 303-4; **14**, 39; **15**, 56-85; **17**, 15, 124-7, 188, 193-8, 201-2, 204-12, 222-7, 235-7, 242-3; **18**, 364, 367; **22**, 37-9, 59-60, 237-42, 245-7, 331-4; **26**, 162-4, 173-4, 178-9; **27**, 107-12; **28**, 36, 39-42: *see also* Claim, basis, invoice
—corrections, **15**, 62
late payments, **12**, 165-8
lease payments due, **1**, 414, 415; **2**, 259
legal basis, **18**, 332-5
legal fees, **11**, 238-42, 255-8; **14**, 205; **17**, 76-8, 91 n. 9; **19**, 125-7; **22**, 37-8, 251-2; **23**, 203-4; **24**, 37-9; **27**, 183-4; **29**, 29, 209
legitimate expectations, **16**, 54-9, 73; **17**, 76
letter of credit underfunding, **9**, 20-1
limited by amount of claim, **3**, 251; **12**, 106
liquidated, **5**, 103 n. 1; **15**, 131; **23**, 55-8, 85-6
loans, **16**, 226-31; **19**, 136-50; **27**, 18-20, 27-8, 31, 33
——equitable subrogation, **19**, 137, 143, 145, 147, 149-50, 151
——interest, **2**, 111
—— interest on, **16**, 229; **19**, 140
loss of enjoyment of property, **10**, 251; **22**, 103-4
loss suffered by third party, **28**, 12
loss of use of money, **12**, 167
losses on assets, **12**, 193-4; **17**, 107
losses on discounted goods, **26**, 165-7
losses prior to settlement, **28**, 139
lost capital transfers, **24**, 113
lost deposit, **17**, 111-12
lost earnings, **16**, 101-2; **17**, 109-10
lost fees, **8**, 170
lost opportunities, **18**, 193-4, 216
lost profits, **2**, 383-4, 387-90, 399; **3**, 233, 234; **4**, 107, 108, 118 n. 1, 260 n. 1, 268, 270; **6**, 170, 203, 204, 215, 216, 294, 295; **8**, 169-71, 319; **9**, 23-6, 123-4, 127-8, 149-50, 160, 199; **12**, 23; **14**, 45, 122-3, 142-3, 209-10; **15**, 299-304; **16**, 19, 55-8, 74, 238, 240,

INDEX

Damages (*cont.*)
  276, 277; **17**, 76; **18**, 13-15; **21**, 346 n.
  36; **22**, 40-2, 49, 60, 80-1, 95 n. 97, 99,
  102-3, 104; **23**, 202-3; **26**, 165; **27**, 25,
  36, 101; **30**, 201, 258-62
  —breach of contract, relevance, **28**,
    84-5
  —contract as measure, **16**, 74
  —contract terminated by agreement, **2**,
    110-11
  —costs and overheads distinguished,
    22, 96-7
  —*damnum emergens* and, **28**, 9 n. 17, 17,
    84-5
  —"reasonable", **22**, 40-1, 95-7
  lost property, **9**, 166, 179-80; **12**, 16; **16**,
    102 n. 16; **17**, 108-9; **18**, 194-5, 216
  lost revenue, **15**, 51-3; **26**, 169
  lost volume seller, **26**, 165
  materials, **20**, 27
  measure, **1**, 446, 447, 450, 451, 453, 454;
    3, 56-8, 106, 154, 233; **4**, 105-9, 111,
    112, 116-20, 157, 173-7, 269, 271; **5**,
    227; **6**, 65, 169, 170, 177, 204, 206,
    213-16, 244, 245, 250, 266, 268, 269,
    274, 275, 281, 285-7, 294; **7**, 162-71,
    172-5, 177; **8**, 162-71, 380-3, 387-92; **9**,
    123, 128-30, 163-4, 197-9, 247, 336-8;
    10, 64-78, 132-3, 268; **11**, 89-108,
    157-63, 174-8, 198-9, 319-41; **12**, 12-
    16, 104-6; **13**, 18; **14**, 78, 126, 203-10,
    238-42; **15**, 13-14, 34-56, 102-55,
    159-82, 248-52, 300; **16**, 54-8, 194-235,
    249 n. 15, 272-3; **17**, 108-9; **18**, 3-44,
    303-4; **19**, 88-92, 100-5, 297; **20**,
    75-6, 141-2, 145; **21**, 22, 47, 57-60,
    122-45, 164-94, 203-38; **22**, 47; **23**,
    27-31, 79-85, 100-6, 371-4; **24**,
    100-1; **25**, 147-8; **27**, 15, 17-23: *see
    also* computation *above*; valuation
    below
  —absence of evidence, **22**, 78 n. 30
  —actual benefit, **6**, 213, 215
  —actual damage, **22**, 79-80
  —actual use, **6**, 177, 213, 215, 216
  —contract provision, **2**, 106-7, 110-11,
    116-19, 399; **3**, 56, 164, 232-4, 289,
    293, 294; **4**, 234-6, 251, 260, 270;
    5, 110, 111, 234, 359, 360; **6**, 63,
    227, 275; **7**, 24, 192; **8**, 164; **9**,
    124, 147-50, 160; **10**, 64-9, 326;

  11, 177; **12**, 188, 238; **13**, 138-9;
    28, 88
  —contract terminated by agreement, **2**,
    106-11, 117-18
  —*damnum emergens*, **2**, 387 n. 1; **10**, 189;
    15, 248, 268; **30**, 201
  —equitable determination, **27**, 21
  —fair market value, **8**, 380; **12**, 22-3;
    15, 34; **16**, 201, 238, 240-1, 244-7;
    19, 102; **21**, 57, 58, 119-20, 329-30;
    25, 147; **27**, 99-101; **28**, 12-14, 16-
    17; **29**, 46; **30**, 89, 93-4, 206-7
  —fair and reasonable, **20**, 114
  —*force majeure* and breach of contract
    distinguished, **12**, 120-5, 187, 193,
    194; **15**, 13
  —going concern, **2**, 354-5; **4**, 106-8,
    118-20; **8**, 382; **12**, 21-2; **15**, 270-1;
    19, 88, 100-5; **29**, 271-3; **30**, 91-4,
    258
  —hypothetical settlement, **16**, 54
  —*lucrum cessans*, **2**, 387 n. 1; **15**, 249-51,
    258-9, 270, 305; **21**, 330
  —*Norwegian Shipowners' Claims*, **30**, 238
  —reasonable and equitable, **9**, 162; **22**,
    34, 80
  —*restitutio in integrum*, **2**, 386-7
  —service companies, **12**, 21-3
  —settling of accounts, **6**, 294
  —unpaid royalties, **2**, 340, 342
  —*Upton* case, **30**, 238-9
  —work performed, **24**, 15
  mental anguish, grief and suffering, **2**,
    78-9, 87
  method of payment, **19**, 296, 301-2
  mitigation, **3**, 52, 56, 289, 293, 294; **7**,
    108, 110, 111; **14**, 43; **17**, 128, 132; **18**,
    160; **20**, 160; **22**, 34, 36, 47, 93, 94,
    212, 243-5, 310; **23**, 207, 214; **24**, 38;
    26, 161-2; **28**, 8-9
  —international law, **22**, 244
  —Iranian law, **22**, 243-4, 324-31
  —US law, **22**, 244
  nominal, **9**, 42
  office costs, **11**, 99; **12**, 211-13
  offset: *see* deduction for *above*
  out of pocket loss, **12**, 16
  overhead costs, **14**, 124, 205-6, 219-20;
    25, 42, 118-19
  partial to avoid double recovery, **11**, 88-9,
    138-41, 313-14

INDEX

payment for equipment, **19**, 205
payments due, **20**, 13-14, 19, 27-9
performance costs, **9**, 124-7, 163-4, 201; **14**, 208-9, 218-19, 220-2; **28**, 103-8
performance withhold, **2**, 108-9; **8**, 315-17; **9**, 22, 24, 125-7, 164, 221; **11**, 14-17, 37, 174, 334; **12**, 151-3; **13**, 134-5, 183-4, 305-6; **14**, 41-2; **18**, 191-2, 211-14; **20**, 74-6, 85-7, 97-100, 145; **23**, 45-8, 49-52, 106-16; **28**, 90-1
post-contract expenses, **11**, 17-18, 38
pre-incorporation costs, **14**, 165-6
principle underlying, **16**, 254-5, 281
private attorney, **8**, 13, 309, 323
progress payment, **20**, 13-14; **23**, 31-3
provisional acceptance, **28**, 36-8
punitive, **2**, 78, 87; **10**, 205; **15**, 248
quantum meruit: *see* Quantum meruit
quasi-contract: *see* Quasi-contract
reasonable, **9**, 150-1, 202, 338, 377; **10**, 81; **12**, 36, 137; **28**, 368-9
recalculation of, **3**, 57, 114, 250, 257, 262, 264, 265, 290
reduction of, **5**, 220, 232, 234; **11**, 66-7
relocation costs, **12**, 191-3; **18**, 312; **22**, 248
rentals, **10**, 254, 258; **15**, 144-5
repair charges, **12**, 320-1; **19**, 47
—undeliverable goods, on, **19**, 213-15
repayment of loan, **13**, 21-7, 30-3
repudiation of contract, **18**, 369
restitution: *see* Restitution
result of delays in proceedings, **4**, 81; **8**, 39
return of goods, **17**, 286-7; **19**, 286-93
salaries, **11**, 96-8; **12**, 16, 190-1; **18**, 310-11; **24**, 220-1, 259-64
—definition, **25**, 79
salaries and allowances, **10**, 256, 343-5; **11**, 157-60, 166; **13**, 218-19; **14**, 77; **25**, 40-2
sales commission, **28**, 89-90
seconded staff costs, **14**, 163-5
security costs, **2**, 109-10
seizure of money, **17**, 110
services, **10**, 172, 284-8; **11**, 330-4; **12**, 168, 197-206; **15**, 151; **19**, 220-1, 225-7; **20**, 25-6; **22**, 34-7, 48, 58-9, 94, 98-9, 102, 115-16; **25**, 98; **26**, 174-6, 179
set-off: *see* deduction for *above*

Settlement Agreement, **10**, 282-3
severance pay, **24**, 221
social security premiums, **13**, 340, 342; **22**, 42-3, 50, 60; **23**, 39-42, 89 n. 13, 90
standby fee, **22**, 33-4, 92-4, 98
stock dividend, **10**, 265 n. 12
storage costs, **19**, 209-10, 215-16, 222; **26**, 168-9, 176
—between 14 November 1979 and 19 January 1981, **28**, 138-9
supplies, **10**, 172, 255
tax liability: *see* Taxes
technical service fee, **13**, 219
termination costs, **10**, 290; **11**, 160-3; **12**, 153-5, 176-97, 236-7; **13**, 189-90, 219-20, 305, 321-2, 338-9; **14**, 82-5; **17**, 31 n. 2; **19**, 210-11, 221-2; **23**, 201-2; **25**, 47-50
—in absence of contractual provision, **14**, 42-5
—accomplishment fee, **12**, 197, 237-8
—contractual profit, **14**, 53, 121-5; **22**, 60
—cost of residual office, **12**, 194-6
—demobilization expenses, **11**, 336-40
—*force majeure* and, **17**, 74-5, 87-91
—miscellaneous expenditure, **12**, 196
—overhead costs, **14**, 44-5; **25**, 50
—repatriation expenses, **10**, 172-4, 256, 288-90; **11**, 176; **13**, 190, 216-18; **14**, 77; **26**, 179-80
—security and lease of building, **17**, 75
—termination of apartment leases, **12**, 194
—termination of contract and, **8**, 164-265
—termination payments, **15**, 141-3; **22**, 60
—unamortized expenses, **22**, 39-40, 48, 60
termination of pension, **30**, 65-6
trade debts, **27**, 18
trademark fees, **10**, 255-6
translation, **18**, 197
travel expenses, **11**, 98-9; **14**, 50; **18**, 161; **19**, 71; **25**, 46-7, 117
unbilled items, **13**, 139-40
unjust enrichment: *see* Unjust enrichment
unjustified attachment, **4**, 277
unpaid rental payments, **12**, 320
unreleased deposit, **11**, 196

Damages (*cont.*)
  unsold items, **26**, 167-8
  valuation, **2**, 353-4; **4**, 116-18, 175; **10**, 132, 192-5; **12**, 11-13; **14**, 234-7; **15**, 34-5, 246-52; **16**, 69, 194-5, 238-44: *see also* computation *and* measure *above*
    —adjusted net asset value: *see* dissolution value *below*
    —assets, **15**, 155-9; **18**, 7-15, 18-20
    —book value, **16**, 243; **19**, 105; **21**, 57
    ——adjustment, **30**, 220-5
    —capitalization factor, **19**, 103
    —*Chorzów Factory*, **2**, 354; **15**, 246-7, 260, 299-304; **21**, 122, 198-9; **30**, 238, 251
    —current net book value, **21**, 57
    —customary international law, **21**, 120-2, 330-1
    —date for, **15**, 244; **16**, 201, 244; **19**, 297, 298, 299-301, 304-6; **27**, 16; **29**, 49
    —Discounted Cash Flow (DCF), **4**, 157, 176-7, 241-4; **15**, 256-65, 308; **16**, 126, 201-20; **21**, 123-4, 162-4, 199-200, 222-5, 328-30, 345-7
    ——lost profits and, **21**, 123, 199, 222-38, 246-61, 271-5, 346 n. 36, 356-8; **28**, 17 n. 31; **30**, 258-62
    —discounts, **30**, 231-3: *see also* deduction for *above*
    —dissolution value, **6**, 226; **21**, 57; **29**, 271-2
    —effect of change in political, economic and social circumstances, **29**, 53, 277-8; **30**, 89, 100-1, 206-7
    —effect of expropriating act on value, relevance, **15**, 46; **29**, 46, 53, 273; **30**, 213-14
    —expert evidence: *see* Experts, evidence of
    —goodwill, **12**, 23; **19**, 105; **30**, 225-6, 262-3
    —historical book value, **15**, 115
    —inaccurate data, **18**, 20-1
    —insured value, **15**, 39, 105, 110-11; **18**, 7, 9-10, 11, 22-3
    —international arbitral tribunals, **15**, 258
    —just, **15**, 252, 292; **16**, 195, 239; **21**, 119, 122
    —lawful expropriation, **15**, 252
  —lawfulness of taking, relevance, **15**, 246, 248-52; **16**, 69, 240; **21**, 70-2, 121-2, 198-9, 330-1; **29**, 270; **30**, 202
  —liabilities, **15**, 159-82; **18**, 16-18; **29**, 284-93
  —lost profits: *see* lost profits *above*
  —price adjustment receivables (PARs), **30**, 207-17, 220, 263-4
  —State practice, **15**, 266
  —unjust enrichment, **15**, 268-9, 308; **21**, 70-1, 73
  value of goods, **10**, 254, 258
  waiver, **8**, 60-1; **12**, 167, 317; **13**, 185
  "warehouseman's lien", **8**, 278-80
  withdrawal of claim, **16**, 296
  withheld dividends, **10**, 252, 257
  withheld taxes, **12**, 296
  work performed, **10**, 70-2; **11**, 101-3, 174-5, 190-2, 199-200, 268-70; **13**, 135-9, 267, 304; **16**, 272-4, 276, 277-80; **20**, 54-9, 61-4, 66, 69-72, 100-5, 159-61; **23**, 33-9; **28**, 42, 89
    —as measure when damages inappropriate, **12**, 134
  work permits, **11**, 99
  work-in-progress inventory, **19**, 209, 215, 221
  wrongful call on bank guarantee, **11**, 196
  wrongful death, **2**, 82-6
  wrongful expulsion, **9**, 43-4
Debt, **1**, 169-72, 185-8, 411-15, 442-8; **3**, 35, 53, 65, 72, 113, 114, 119, 169, 235, 246, 247, 249, 250; **4**, 221, 228, 231; **7**, 14, 15, 190, 191; **21**, 52, 75-6
  allocation of payments, **22**, 13, 86-90
  assignment, **3**, 274, 275; **21**, 52
  controlled entity: *see* Controlled entity, responsibility for obligations of
  evidence of, **21**, 49
  legislation providing for compensation for expropriation as basis, **28**, 260-2
  outstanding, date of becoming, **9**, 40; **21**, 44-5
  waiver of, **5**, 373
Decision: *see* Award
Declaration: *see also* Concurring and dissenting opinion; Concurring opinion; Dissenting opinion; Explanatory remarks; Separate opinion; Separate statement; Supplemental opinion

INDEX

Ameli, **13**, 40
Bahrami, **13**, 192; **14**, 8
Declaration of the Government of Algeria Concerning the Settlement of Claims by the United States and Iran (1981): *see* Claims Settlement Declaration
Declarations of Algiers: *see* Claims Settlement Declaration; General Declaration
Declaratory relief: *see* Claims, declaratory relief
Demurrage, responsibility for, **26**, 24-30, 33-6
Denial of justice, **1**, 396-402; **3**, 297
Deprivation of property, **6**, 225, 245, 256; **15**, 29-56; **26**, 108-9
Diplomatic protection, **1**, 465-7, 478-80; **2**, 161-6, 180, 196-209, 224-5; **5**, 260-3, 273, 274, 299, 302, 303, 324, 326, 331-4; **9**, 255, 256; **10**, 85; **16**, 7; **18**, 246 n. 5, 262, 279, 383-90; **19**, 31
    applicable law, **19**, 31
    national, by, **22**, 168
    nationality and, **12**, 284-6; **18**, 261 n. 20; **22**, 136; **23**, 289
    nature of relationship between State and individual, **18**, 387-8
Discontinuance: *see* Claims, withdrawal
Discount, **7**, 197
Discounted Cash Flow method: *see under* Damages, valuation
Discovery, **4**, 28, 58, 94, 95
Dispute settlement provisions: *see* Contract, dispute settlement provisions
Dissenting opinion: *see also* Concurring and dissenting opinion; Concurring opinion; Declaration; Explanatory remarks; Separate opinion; Separate statement; Supplemental opinion
    admissibility, **16**, 333
    Aghahosseini, **27**, 297; **29**, 349; **30**, 19 n. 1
    Aldrich, **1**, 320, 396; **3**, 380; **4**, 279; **9**, 356; **12**, 64; **14**, 300; **27**, 258
    Allison, **22**, 183, 200; **27**, 259; **30**, 112
    Ameli, **8**, 403; **9**, 187 n. 1; **10**, 110; **13**, 45, 351; **16**, 327; **18**, 47
    Ansari, **5**, 193, 275; **8**, 228; **10**, 5; **12**, 306 n. 1; **13**, 176; **19**, 16, 56, 333; **22**, 127, 135, 145, 160; **23**, 90, 288, 315; **25**, 112; **27**, 32

    Bahrami, **9**, 169-81; **10**, 134; **11**, 137, 300 n. 1, 346; **12**, 17, 299; **13**, 167, 177; **14**, 134, 185; **16**, 294; **19**, 16
    Brower, **8**, 284; **9**, 410-13; **10**, 224; **12**, 64, 265; **13**, 118; **16**, 86; **18**, 102
    Enayat, **1**, 104
    Holtzmann, **1**, 129, 167, 174, 178, 284, 320, 396; **2**, 33, 35, 81, 254; **3**, 17, 66, 78, 84, 87, 316, 358, 380; **4**, 12, 63, 65, 72, 206; **5**, 141; **9**, 187 n. 2; **10**, 219, 259, 351; **11**, 250; **12**, 64, 356; **13**, 345; **14**, 94, 271; **26**, 216; **27**, 259
    Kashani, **1**, 104, 241, 250, 463; **2**, 317; **5**, 1, 85, 115, 121, 275; **7**, 119
    Khalilian, **18**, 79; **24**, 40; **25**, 131 n. 1; **27**, 265
    Lagergren, **1**, 197, 241, 250; **5**, 348
    Mosk, **1**, 119, 158, 230, 232, 305, 320, 396; **2**, 124, 139, 146; **3**, 40, 41, 76, 77, 209, 318, 374, 377; **4**, 3, 28, 58, 76, 80, 93, 229; **5**, 181, 242, 374; **7**, 48; **8**, 134; **10**, 103; **30**, 45
    Mostafavi, **8**, 336; **9**, 204 n. 1, 377-96; **10**, 16, 85, 108, 328, 348; **12**, 38, 108, 324; **13**, 177, 193 n. 1, 310; **14**, 53, 212, 243, 258
    Noori, **19**, 16, 356, 370 n. 1; **22**, 257; **23**, 150 n. 1; **24**, 3; **25**, 190 n. 1, 264 n. 1, 278 n. 1; **30**, 44
    Sani, **1**, 177, 241, 250; **2**, 14, 317; **4**, 237
    Shafeiei, **1**, 104, 241, 250; **2**, 1, 178, 284, 317, 327, 345; **3**, 297; **5**, 275
Dollar Account No. 1, **8**, 198; **12**, 40-93; **14**, 316-20, 323
Dollar Account No. 2, **5**, 67-9; **8**, 197-206; **12**, 51, 54-63; **13**, 95; **16**, 293 n. 4; **30**, 16-17
Domestic International Sales Corporation, character of, **7**, 186, 187, 200, 205
Domicile, **22**, 143, 147
Drafts: *see* Negotiable instruments
Dual nationality: *see under* Nationality
Due process, **3**, 365; **30**, 156
Duress, **16**, 43; **21**, 52

Earnest money, **5**, 359, 360
Election of remedies, **4**, 233, 235, 236
Embassy, competence, **5**, 241
Enforcement: *see* Award, recognition and enforcement; Settlement, enforcement; Time limits

England, law of: *see* United Kingdom, law of
Equality: *see* Sovereign equality of States
Equity, **6**, 169, 170, 274, 294; **8**, 105, 262-3; **9**, 4-5, 197, 199, 332, 402; **10**, 173, 240; **11**, 41, 111; **12**, 197; **13**, 119-21; **14**, 188; **15**, 251, 268; **16**, 48, 221, 254, 262; **18**, 332, 348; **21**, 56, 58, 61, 105, 123, 142-3, 296, 339
Escrow Agreement (1981), **1**, 189-214; **8**, 209
  Paragraph 2, **1**, 147
  Paragraph 3, **1**, 147
  Paragraph 4, **1**, 147, 148, 206, 209, 211, 212, 214; **12**, 44, 60, 84
  Paragraph 5, **1**, 192
  purpose, **12**, 61
  Technical Clarifications, **12**, 56-7, 60, 75-6
Estoppel, **1**, 287, 315 n. 15, 318, 375, 376; **2**, 149 n. 3; **3**, 26, 27, 30, 261; **4**, 112 n. 3, 113, 235; **5**, 247, 248, 271, 274; **6**, 47-51; **7**, 47, 103, 135, 143, 162, 201; **9**, 100; **10**, 287; **11**, 229, 236; **12**, 104, 150-1, 174-5, 208-9, 228, 378; **13**, 33, 229, 253, 339; **14**, 143, 230; **15**, 196; **16**, 47, 71-2, 266; **19**, 77; **20**, 90, 153-6; **21**, 154-9, 160-1; **22**, 57, 73, 74-5, 77, 83, 99, 101, 115, 246; **25**, 99; **26**, 36; **28**, 208-10; **29**, 87-92, 176-7, 228, 232
European Community, **13**, 91-2
European Court of Human Rights, **8**, 419, 449; **10**, 251, 267; **29**, 389
Evidence, **1**, 155, 215, 226-9, 260, 306, 318, 334-6, 340, 341, 369 n. 8, 420, 421, 455-82; **10**, 87-9, 348-50: *see also* Evidence of; Procedure
  absence of challenge, **8**, 261-2; **9**, 20, 21, 126, 198, 218; **28**, 39
  adequacy, **12**, 132-3; **17**, 192-8, 202-3, 220-1, 233-4, 242-3
  admissibility, **2**, 121-3; **3**, 67, 68 n. 1, 164, 350; **4**, 70, 78, 245; **7**, 70; **14**, 20, 259; **16**, 190-1; **17**, 296-7; **19**, 113-16; **27**, 153
  affidavits, **1**, 202, 423, 462, 463, 503; **3**, 247; **5**, 245; **9**, 21; **17**, 52; **28**, 74-7; **29**, 30-3
  applicable law, **11**, 279-80
  assessment: *see* evaluation *below*
  authenticity, **2**, 35-7, 106, 118-21; **3**, 206; **4**, 80; **6**, 71; **8**, 107-18; **19**, 163-7
  availability to other parties, **3**, 350
  burden of proof: *see* Burden of proof
  claimant's statement as, **18**, 282
  computer program as, **19**, 132
  conduct of parties, **22**, 30-1, 32-3; **25**, 7; **26**, 115; **28**, 31-3
  conflicting, **6**, 280; **28**, 76
  contra proferentem, **1**, 214
  contradictory statements, **3**, 26, 69 n. 1, 249, 358, 359; **5**, 240
  costs, **22**, 34; **28**, 103-8
  credibility, **6**, 200; **18**, 247-60; **19**, 170, 227, 269
  documents, unexplained, **3**, 251
  duty to consider, **5**, 196
  duty to submit, **3**, 66, 69-71; **4**, 58; **9**, 110-11
  evaluation, **3**, 381; **4**, 60, 107-9, 119, 120, 245; **11**, 276, 277; **13**, 58; **15**, 45-51; **16**, 264; **18**, 338-47; **28**, 275-88, 290-2, 293-302, 303-6
  exclusion, **13**, 70-1
  expert: *see* Experts, evidence of
  failure to submit, **2**, 115, 152, 153, 300, 304, 355; **3**, 16-18, 20 n. 2, 21, 22, 24, 27, 53, 65, 66, 70, 71, 115, 205, 206, 247-9, 252, 382 n. 2; **4**, 70, 78, 79, 110, 225, 255, 261; **5**, 23, 33-6, 111, 226, 240, 245, 380, 383, 394; **6**, 65, 92, 96, 127, 145, 173, 178, 212, 282; **7**, 14, 15, 28, 68, 70, 79, 80, 110, 116, 128, 129; **8**, 52, 202; **9**, 29, 37, 40-2, 95, 125, 166, 180, 198 n. 13, 217, 227, 230; **10**, 175, 285; **11**, 18, 19, 26, 58, 71, 130, 156, 160, 175, 177, 178, 181, 205, 295, 327, 333, 342; **12**, 136, 137, 167, 209, 219-20, 223, 224, 226, 227, 351, 352; **13**, 154, 189, 266, 269, 302, 322; **14**, 18, 205, 206; **15**, 14; **16**, 18, 94, 247 n. 13, 272, 313; **17**, 17, 24, 263, 315-16, 319, 333, 336, 339, 342, 345, 348; **18**, 160, 297, 306, 308, 371, 372; **19**, 154, 178, 181, 184, 187, 190, 193, 196, 199, 209, 210-11, 226; **20**, 23, 62, 89, 101, 103, 105, 110, 117, 118, 119, 157, 160, 166; **21**, 26, 29; **22**, 40, 47, 60, 82, 180, 183, 211-12; **23**, 266; **25**, 13, 105, 106, 117-18, 146, 149-50; **27**, 138, 162-5, 187-93, 234; **28**, 45, 214, 228-9, 231, 315-16, 384; **29**, 231, 233, 234, 236, 242-3, 246-59

INDEX

false, **22**, 43-8; **29**, 93-116, 117-20, 123-84
— duty of party to check authenticity, **27**, 45-6
form, **20**, 148
hearsay, **3**, 68 n. 1; **12**, 371-2
inconsistent, **6**, 71; **19**, 268-9
inference, **2**, 11, 33, 115, 121, 142, 297-300, 355, 384; **3**, 21, 22, 69, 82; **4**, 81, 100, 223, 261; **5**, 245; **6**, 17, 18, 80, 145; **7**, 75, 104, 109
insufficient, **2**, 108; **8**, 163-74; **9**, 44, 58, 343, 403; **10**, 49, 50, 53, 54; **11**, 88-9; **12**, 16, 315, 316; **13**, 28-9, 33, 144, 189-90, 197, 214, 216, 217, 267, 307, 342; **14**, 130, 132; **15**, 31, 91, 150, 160, 164, 276, 279, 285; **16**, 107-9, 232; **17**, 113, 257; **18**, 96, 153, 161, 166-7 n. 5, 170, 172-3, 178-9, 194-5, 228-30, 239, 240, 241, 304, 311, 312, 313, 314, 316-17, 319, 357-8, 362, 369; **19**, 127, 148, 215, 216, 220, 221, 222, 223, 232-8; **20**, 25, 59, 61, 66, 71, 73, 78, 80, 81, 82, 104, 108, 135, 141, 147, 165; **21**, 53, 61, 152; **22**, 81, 182; **24**, 215-18, 221, 224-5, 258; **25**, 113-18, 232-3, 238-9, 244-5; **26**, 239-43; **27**, 61-2, 138-40; **28**, 169-75; **29**, 327, 342-3
interested parties, **24**, 178-81; **28**, 5-6
interpretation, **17**, 119
judicial notice: *see* Judicial notice
late submission, **10**, 101, 106, 128; **11**, 304-5; **13**, 131; **27**, 212-13; **29**, 297 n. 4, 313; **30**, 25-6, 45-6, 129
minutes, **20**, 34, 72, 125, 136-7
newspaper articles, **19**, 328, 337-9
participation in elections, **22**, 148-50
passport, **18**, 237, 260-2, 273 n. 46; **22**, 143; **23**, 135
performance of contract, **22**, 115
photocopy, **28**, 4
post-hearing submission: *see* Procedure, post-hearing submissions
presumption, **1**, 480; **5**, 196; **6**, 173, 231; **16**, 266, 279; **17**, 193, 209-10, 221-2; **18**, 308, 318; **20**, 24-5, 69
prima facie case, **2**, 238-9, 382, 399; **3**, 69, 71, 72, 288; **5**, 245, 376; **7**, 11; **9**, 28-9; **29**, 93-116, 117-20, 123-84, 235
rebuttal, right of, **29**, 5, 68
relevance, **3**, 252, 381; **4**, 95 n. 3

reliability, **20**, 19
request for, **15**, 271
return of, **4**, 60
shareholder agreements, **29**, 29-30
standard, **10**, 34; **14**, 203; **17**, 108, 191, 257; **20**, 132; **23**, 188; **29**, 117, 124
submission of invoices, **16**, 279-80
subsequent events, **10**, 263 n. 9
subsequent to decision of Tribunal, **29**, 29
tape-recorded, **8**, 38
timesheets, **20**, 59, 62, 63-4, 65, 66, 67, 72, 143-5
translation, **1**, 234, 326, 336-8, 341, 484; **2**, 139 n. 4, 368; **9**, 31-5; **13**, 54; **14**, 18; **18**, 62; **29**, 308-9
unchallenged, **12**, 168; **16**, 278
uncontroverted, **10**, 255; **12**, 295
unsigned draft, **19**, 208
validity, **12**, 380; **19**, 123-4, 243; **22**, 161
weight of, **2**, 115, 121-2, 139-40; **3**, 66, 68 n. 1, 71, 72, 381; **4**, 80, 119, 120, 245, 261; **5**, 23, 231, 375, 376; **6**, 207; **7**, 80
witnesses, **2**, 115
— compulsory attendance, **19**, 269
— credibility, **3**, 23, 24, 68
— notification, **14**, 292; **17**, 62-3
— relationship with arbitrator, **20**, 184, 185, 186, 242, 250-4, 266-7, 329
Evidence of
  acceptance of
    — letters, **20**, 17
    — services, **9**, 40
    — Settlement Agreement, **19**, 366; **22**, 152
  advance of funds, **30**, 152-3
  agency, **1**, 357, 358, 378-80; **2**, 11, 325-6; **9**, 57, 343-4; **13**, 111; **17**, 14-15; **18**, 178-9; **28**, 77-9
  amendment of Settlement Agreement, **9**, 62
  amounts claimed, **13**, 27
  approval of plans, **9**, 335
  attributability, **17**, 101-5, 144-8, 287
  authenticity of document, **29**, 93-116
  authority, **15**, 63, 66-9
  bribery, **12**, 270-2, 314-15
  capital transfer, **3**, 15, 16
  claims, interrelationship, **16**, 293
  continuity of ownership, **11**, 7
  contract, **1**, 413, 414; **3**, 48, 162, 231, 289;

336 INDEX

Evidence of (*cont.*)
  5, 43; **6**, 193, 292; **7**, 13; **8**, 160-1; **10**, 26-33; **11**, 56-7; **12**, 102; **13**, 112-13, 138-9; **22**, 115; **24**, 74-80, 87-97; **26**, 115, 135; **28**, 170-1, 172-3
  —amendment, **12**, 102-3; **15**, 120-1; **16**, 272, 277-8; **20**, 26, 34
  —authenticity, **15**, 134-6
  —breach, **13**, 22-5; **22**, 100-1; **23**, 292-4; **26**, 159, 160
  —intention to amend, **19**, 226
  —letter of credit, **13**, 111-12
  —liability, **15**, 6
  —non-operativeness, **16**, 37
  —notice under, **13**, 25-7
  —oral evidence, **9**, 368-71, 382-7; **11**, 237
  —performance, **14**, 35; **16**, 265-70; **19**, 80; **26**, 106
  —ratification, **2**, 145-6; **3**, 163, 164
  —State responsibility for, **21**, 154
  —terms, **18**, 311
contractor relationship, **13**, 121-2
contractual practice, **13**, 305-6
control of corporation, **1**, 359-61; **7**, 6; **11**, 312-13; **30**, 159, 188-91
controlled entity status, **1**, 413, 419-21; **2**, 150-2, 302; **3**, 47, 160, 230, 231, 286; **5**, 135, 242-5; **6**, 59; **7**, 10; **8**, 155; **9**, 400; **10**, 167; **11**, 215; **12**, 373-5; **14**, 157-8; **17**, 130 n. 2, 165-8, 174-8, 298-300, 333, 336, 339, 342, 345, 348; **19**, 326-7, 328-9, 337-9; **22**, 179-82, 185-93; **25**, 139-40; **29**, 41, 45: *see also* nationality of corporation *below*
  —appointment and dismissal of managers, **2**, 17-23
corporation, **26**, 31; **27**, 213-15
costs, **4**, 81; **10**, 34
  —absence of, **9**, 60, 133, 242; **10**, 102
custom and usage, **6**, 97
customary international law, **21**, 121
damages, **2**, 384, 388-90; **3**, 56, 57, 164, 231, 233, 234, 250; **4**, 269, 271; **6**, 172, 173, 205, 213, 214; **14**, 206-7
debt, **18**, 276-7; **21**, 49
delay, **20**, 64, 146
delivery of goods, **17**, 322; **18**, 228-30, 363, 367
escalation formula, **22**, 15
excess freight charges, **2**, 11-12, 25

existence of goods, **17**, 127, 131
expenses, **19**, 123-5, 140-1, 144; **20**, 39
expropriation, **1**, 420, 428 n. 6, 504-7; **4**, 105, 154, 167-9, 222, 223; **6**, 164-6, 238, 240; **10**, 303; **11**, 178, 221-2; **12**, 345-51; **13**, 302, 337-8; **14**, 298-306; **18**, 95-6; **20**, 123, 124-5; **21**, 112-16; **22**, 71-3; **27**, 60-2; **28**, 169-70, 171-2, 173-5, 212; **30**, 37-8, 39-40, 58-9, 74-5, 86-7, 154-60, 188-93
expulsion, **17**, 105-7, 144-52, 257-8
force majeure, **15**, 6-11; **17**, 286
Iran's exclusive jurisdiction, **5**, 116
liabilities, **19**, 212-13, 214-15, 219-21; **22**, 16, 39
loss of property, **24**, 227-34
mailing, **17**, 278-9, 284
marriage settlement, **30**, 53-6
mitigation of damages, **3**, 56, 294
nationality of claim, **1**, 389, 455-82; **5**, 22; **11**, 151, 188-9
nationality of corporation, **1**, 223, 224, 334, 335, 384, 385, 418, 427, 428, 455-82, 503; **2**, 9, 16-17, 31-2, 33-4, 395-6; **3**, 1; **4**, 141, 142, 216, 217, 273; **5**, 22, 23, 209, 237, 343; **6**, 127; **7**, 27-9, 65, 66, 97; **8**, 234; **9**, 13-15, 87-8, 116, 252-3, 292; **10**, 23-4, 60-1, 278-9; **11**, 7, 212, 227, 274-6, 277-82; **12**, 132, 142, 149, 161, 251, 290; **13**, 180, 202, 336; **14**, 155-6, 227-8; **15**, 4-5, 195; **16**, 15, 16; **17**, 4-5, 162; **18**, 99-101, 177-8, 208-9, 355; **19**, 202; **20**, 6-7; **21**, 16-19, 42; **22**, 174-5; **24**, 50; **25**, 25, 26, 138; **26**, 17-18, 41-3; **29**, 225-6, 244-6, 315-16
  —absence of challenge, **8**, 262; **18**, 177
nationality of person, **3**, 23 n. 1; **9**, 14-15, 353-5, 356; **12**, 6; **13**, 300; **14**, 6, 198; **18**, 236-7, 260-2; **19**, 51-2, 54-5, 57-8, 324; **21**, 21-3, 29; **22**, 42-3, 134-5, 242, 246, 262, 267-8, 272; **25**, 175, 202, 203; **26**, 38-40, 192; **28**, 62; **29**, 10-13, 14-15, 16-19, 64-5
  —dominant nationality, **25**, 203-10; **26**, 7-14; **28**, 185-91; **29**, 10-13, 14-15, 16-19, 73-4, 76-7, 379-81; **30**, 274-80
  —minor claimant, **29**, 12-13, 16-19
nature of loan, **13**, 31-2, 86-8
ordering of goods, **17**, 321-2

ownership, **9**, 233; **13**, 320; **17**, 297-8, 325-8; **18**, 100-1, 103-9
—beneficial, **29**, 28-41
payment, **8**, 19; **12**, 296-7; **17**, 193; **19**, 128, 146-7; **20**, 35; **22**, 15-16, 18-19, 86-8; **24**, 185; **28**, 38; **30**, 98
payment due, **20**, 13, 18, 20-1; **22**, 92
performance, **25**, 36-8
receipt of
—documents, **17**, 288-90
—goods, **17**, 119-24
request for transfer of funds, **10**, 100, 104-6, 342; **13**, 346-9
rescission of contract, **14**, 72-3
satisfactory performance, **9**, 221, 375, 403; **11**, 62-7, 198, 199, 204, 247; **12**, 105, 150-1, 294-5; **13**, 136-7, 303; **14**, 40-1; **16**, 268, 270, 271, 278; **17**, 6-7, 8, 68-74, 315; **18**, 169-73, 313, 320, 357-8; **29**, 345-6
service of notice, **13**, 64-7
services rendered, **19**, 221; **20**, 116; **26**, 175
settlement, **3**, 358, 359; **24**, 133-43, 175-82
shareholder status, **30**, 161-2, 184, 185-6, 223-6
shipment, **10**, 216-17, 221; **13**, 114; **18**, 311; **19**, 206-8; **28**, 41
social security payments, **20**, 14-15; **28**, 161, 163
—liability for, **2**, 112
subcontractor relationship, **3**, 273
succession, **1**, 360-3, 373-5
sums expended, **13**, 267
taking, **15**, 29-33, 54-5; **19**, 86-7; **27**, 60-1
tax liability, **3**, 107, 236; **15**, 273-5
undertaking to refund unincurred costs, **12**, 225
unlawful expulsion, **16**, 100-1, 125-6
unpaid invoices, **25**, 144-5
validity of promissory notes, **21**, 47-50
valuation, **20**, 89; **30**, 91-4
value, **19**, 88, 91, 100; **20**, 27; **29**, 46-55, 274-93
waiver of contractual entitlement, **9**, 162; **11**, 233-8, 250-4, 330-1, 345-6
work performed, **1**, 107; **20**, 59, 62, 142-3; **22**, 242-3; **28**, 88
Exchange controls: *see* Foreign exchange controls; International Monetary Fund

Exchange rates: *see* Currency, exchange rate changes
Exclusive jurisdiction: *see* Counterclaims, jurisdiction of Tribunal; Forum selection clause, jurisdiction of Tribunal
Exhaustion of local remedies, **15**, 196-7; **30**, 62-3, 97-8
Experts—
appointment, **1**, 235, 390; **2**, 70-5, 76, 355; **3**, 107, 164, 167; **4**, 91-5, 157; **5**, 185; **8**, 272 n. 45, 276 n. 51; **12**, 228; **13**, 16, 40, 142, 149-50, 175; **14**, 155; **15**, 288-9; **23**, 68; **24**, 24-8
—prerequisites, **4**, 94; **24**, 26-7
costs: *see* Costs, experts'
evidence, **1**, 202, 423, 462; **3**, 165-7; **4**, 60, 119, 120, 261; **8**, 45, 272; **11**, 5, 111-35, 264-6; **13**, 351, 354; **16**, 122-92, 196-232, 244-9, 252-3, 256; **19**, 43-244
evidence of—
—fair market value, **16**, 122-92; **30**, 206-17, 218-35, 257-8
—impartiality, **19**, 244
—need for adversary proceeding, **9**, 34
—opportunity for parties to comment, **9**, 35; **16**, 190-2
—Tribunal's obligations in respect of, **11**, 141-2; **16**, 196-200, 256
need for, **6**, 267, 269; **14**, 28
payment, **3**, 166, 167; **4**, 59, 92, 93, 95, 158; **5**, 186; **8**, 41; **10**, 21; **11**, 136, 137
terms of reference, **4**, 95, 159, 173, 175-8; **6**, 30-2; **7**, 172-7
—amendment, **6**, 31
timetable, **10**, 110-20
Tribunal's responsibility, **10**, 117
Tribunal's right to appoint, **2**, 122 n. 1
Explanatory remarks: *see also* Concurring and dissenting opinion; Concurring opinion; Declaration; Dissenting opinion; Separate opinion; Separate statement; Supplemental opinion
Aldrich, **14**, 3 n. 1, 9
Ameli, **16**, 103 n. 1, 255
Ansari, **8**, 30; **15**, 187; **18**, 3
Briner, **14**, 3 n. 1, 9
Brower, **15**, 187; **16**, 282 n. 1
Holtzmann, **16**, 237
Mangård, **15**, 187; **16**, 282 n. 1
Mostafavi, **14**, 65 n. 1, 100 n. 1, 279 n. 1
Noori, **26**, 7 n. 1

Export licence, **7**, 213; **17**, 85-6
Expropriation, **1**, 287, 375 n. 14, 387, 389, 422, 504-7; **2**, 175-7, 207, 350; **3**, 290; **4**, 105-12, 115-18, 143, 154-6, 159, 162-79, 223; **5**, 227, 371; **6**, 164-8, 178, 189, 200-3, 206, 207, 209, 215 n. 6, 216, 225, 231, 241, 250, 256, 257, 260, 268; **7**, 6, 7, 47, 48, 50, 51, 123, 125, 126, 129, 133, 134, 146, 152, 153-5, 164, 165, 168-70, 173, 256; **8**, 380-4, 385-90, 391-450; **9**, 230-41, 266-83; **10**, 130-1, 136, 170, 259-68, 302-4; **12**, 7-16, 214-15, 346-51, 370-5; **14**, 230-4; **15**, 101-87, 213-34, 297-300; **16**, 43-5, 64-9, 193-6, 237-47; **17**, 258-9; **18**, 95-6, 238; **19**, 81-7, 94-9; **20**, 123; **21**, 106, 111-22, 341; **23**, 69, 96-100, 294, 366-70; **24**, 215-18; **25**, 147-9; **27**, 91-2, 141-3: *see also* Damages; Deprivation of property; Evidence of, expropriation
   accordance with domestic law, relevance, **30**, 86
   action against specific individual, **28**, 11, 71-4
   appointment of temporary managers, **2**, 21; **14**, 297-300; **30**, 38-9, 58-9, 191-2
   appropriation of property distinguished, **23**, 25
   bankrupt company, **21**, 56-60
   breach of contract: *see* lawfulness, breach of contract *below*
   by decision of court, **12**, 318
   coercion and duress, **4**, 171
   compensation: *see* Expropriation, compensation
   conformity with domestic law, relevance, **7**, 15, 225
   constructive, **12**, 261-4, 287 n. 49; **17**, 152 n. 22
   contract rights, **4**, 163; **6**, 237, 243, 250; **15**, 220-1, 267, 269-70, 299; **16**, 231, 234-8; **21**, 106, 111-12, 119, 123-4; **24**, 82-3; **28**, 211-12, 215
      —lawfulness, determined by international law, **16**, 25
   control of corporation, **2**, 176, 349, 351, 352; **7**, 154, 159, 162; **9**, 257; **17**, 168-9; **30**, 158
   creeping, **10**, 206; **28**, 296 n. 2; **29**, 44-5; **30**, 160

date of taking, **4**, 156, 159, 164, 165, 171, 173; **9**, 240-1, 246, 265 n. 18, 278; **10**, 249-50; **12**, 11; **15**, 225-9, 290; **21**, 116-18; **28**, 259-64, 266-302; **30**, 192-3
decision reserved, **9**, 42-3
denial of access to funds, **4**, 172
deprivation of rights, **17**, 181; **22**, 71, 77-9, 103-4
discrimination, **15**, 231-2; **28**, 211
effective taking, **10**, 131, 147-52; **12**, 11
elements of, **6**, 256; **9**, 238-9, 275-9; **10**, 261-2; **15**, 223
   —insurance company's assessment, **10**, 264
   —substantive value of property, **25**, 149
   —treaty determined, **15**, 246
evidence of: *see* Evidence of, expropriation
exchange controls as, **24**, 110-11
expulsion as, **17**, 139-40
failure to protect property rights as, **2**, 79-80, 86-7
force majeure and, **21**, 107: *see also* Force majeure
forced sale, **9**, 240
formal act not required, **9**, 224-7; **10**, 259, 267
government involvement, need for, **9**, 238-9; **12**, 349; **15**, 35; **18**, 242-3; **30**, 40-1
indirect claim, effect on, **9**, 265
intent of government, **6**, 225, 256; **21**, 115; **30**, 86, 157, 190
interference with internal management, **6**, 165, 166, 199, 201, 238, 240; **7**, 162-7, 179 n. 1, 180 n. 1; **21**, 70
interference with use or enjoyment of property, **6**, 225; **10**, 243-52; **12**, 9, 319; **18**, 239-40; **19**, 85-7, 94-9; **27**, 96; **28**, 71-3, 210-11, 288, 296; **29**, 41-6; **30**, 38-9, 84-6, 157-60, 163-8
   —car parking, **28**, 290, 293
   —permanent, **28**, 288, 296 n. 2; **29**, 44, 267-70
   —taking of shares distinguished, **30**, 160, 165-6
jurisdiction of Tribunal, **4**, 101, 115; **5**, 210; **6**, 223
lawfulness, **16**, 65, 241; **27**, 143
   —breach of contract, **15**, 232, 242-6

INDEX 339

—criteria, **10**, 204-5
— determination by international law, **16**, 25; **29**, 270
lawfulness, relevance: *see* Damages, valuation, lawfulness of taking, relevance
legislation as, **24**, 215-17; **28**, 267-8
loss, need for, **21**, 56, 60
nationalization as basis of jurisdiction, **28**, 258
non-contractual, **22**, 71
pension rights, **30**, 41-3, 46-9, 59-66
public purpose, **15**, 233-4; **21**, 122
repudiation of contract as, **16**, 43-5
shares, **30**, 154-62
survival of rights and contract obligations, **6**, 242
taking of corporation and assets distinguished, **15**, 112
unlimited responsibility, **6**, 265
valuation: *see* Damages, valuation
Expropriation, compensation, **1**, 141, 171, 415, 422, 450, 451; **2**, 353-5, 383, 399; **3**, 53, 54, 106, 232-5, 264-6, 278, 279, 288-90, 293, 294; **4**, 105-9, 111, 112, 116-18, 156-7, 173-7, 223, 270, 271, 277; **5**, 109, 110, 169, 227, 248, 399, 400; **6**, 172, 225, 265, 281, 287, 290; **7**, 24, 50, 69, 71, 76, 112, 114, 165, 173; **8**, 162, 314-24, 340-2, 378-80, 393-405; **9**, 273; **10**, 4, 133-4, 184-206; **15**, 33, 34-56, 223-4, 244-71, 298-308; **16**, 33, 34-56, 68-9; **17**, 98; **21**, 70-7: *see also* Damages, valuation
agreed settlements, **21**, 121
applicable law, **8**, 415-19
basis, **19**, 302-4
BITs, **30**, 245
currency, **8**, 425-6
customary international law, **10**, 195-203, 267-8; **14**, 234; **15**, 223-4, 231; **21**, 198; **30**, 197-8, 200, 238-44
developments, **30**, 237-54
duty, **6**, 169; **9**, 219-20
failure to attempt to exercise rights, relevance, **2**, 269-70
for failure to return goods, **19**, 293-7
interest, **8**, 384, 402
interference less than expropriation, **27**, 15
liability for, **1**, 21, 106-7

measure: *see* standard *below*
request for, need for, **28**, 266-8
standard, **30**, 196-202
—adequate, **15**, 230-1
— appropriate, **8**, 386-90; **14**, 234, 237; **30**, 197-9, 201, 236-7, 247
— full equivalent, **6**, 265, 266; **10**, 184, 187-206, 267-8; **15**, 34 n. 14, 35, 269; **16**, 195, 239; **21**, 119; **29**, 46, 271-3; **30**, 88-9, 100, 199-201, 248-52
— Hull doctrine, **8**, 385-90; **30**, 239
— negotiated settlements as precedent, **8**, 399-400; **10**, 185, 196; **21**, 121
— prompt, **10**, 203 n. 36
— "prompt, adequate and effective", **30**, 197-8, 246
— UNGA Resolution 1803, **30**, 197 n. 13, 240, 242-3, 249
termination of contract by agreement, **2**, 117-18
Treaty of Amity provisions, **16**, 195, 239, 243; **21**, 120-2, 125, 329-31; **30**, 3-6, 88, 100, 196, 255-7
Tribunal practice, **30**, 247-53
World Bank Guidelines (1992), **30**, 245-6
Expulsion, **16**, 78, 83-102; **17**, 97-113, 139-51; **18**, 161-2; **23**, 233-8, 239-43; **24**, 264
in cases involving claims of less than $250,000, **9**, 18 n. 8
constructive, **16**, 87-9, 94-7
criteria, **9**, 16-18; **17**, 106-7, 142-3
global adjudication not appropriate, **17**, 97-8
juridical person, **16**, 97-8; **17**, 258
property rights affected, **17**, 99-100, 139-40
State responsibility, **17**, 100-7, 256-8
Extraterritorial effect of legislation, **8**, 258-9; **30**, 64

Fair trial, **20**, 218
Filing of claims: *see also* Time limits, filing of claims
meaning, **1**, 127, 128, 130, 132, 226, 228
FMS Trust Fund, **19**, 296, 300, 301-32
FOB (free on board), **7**, 103
Force majeure, **1**, 452; **2**, 116, 310, 369, 386, 388, 389; **3**, 52, 106, 152-4, 231; **4**, 13, 161, 165, 174, 179, 253 n. 2, 259 n. 5;

Force majeure (cont.)
  5, 210; **7**, 13; **8**, 306-10, 312; **9**, 22-6, 27, 116-25, 149-50, 157-60, 171-4, 196, 201, 294-8; **10**, 74-5, 82, 173, 174, 289; **11**, 126, 149, 338-9; **12**, 103-6, 112-15, 119, 120-5, 184-6, 205, 210-11, 235, 237; **13**, 92, 133-4, 142, 143, 147, 150, 153-4, 211-16, 245-50, 363; **14**, 35-7, 72-9, 217; **15**, 11-14, 70-3, 110, 122-3, 136-51, 211-14; **16**, 37-40, 54, 84, 269; **17**, 24, 65-8, 74, 75, 76, 77, 79, 87, 89-91, 285-6, 319; **18**, 160, 203-4, 326-31, 371, 372; **19**, 80, 85, 86, 94, 162, 224, 247; **20**, 23, 48, 75, 117, 124; **21**, 107-11, 329; **22**, 56, 116, 242, 247, 312-16, 328, 331-2, 354, 355; **23**, 47, 50, 53, 57, 58, 72 n. 44, 85-6, 89, 91-2, 95, 169-73, 185, 188-9, 190, 191-3, 196-7, 219-22, 225-6; **24**, 11-14, 60; **25**, 34-6, 115, 124-6; **27**, 79-82, 85, 115; **28**, 96-9; **29**, 221 n. 10, 225 n. 23: *see also* Frustration
  act of State as, **24**, 11
  continuing obligations, **9**, 298; **12**, 205, 211; **15**, 11-12
  contract, effect on, **21**, 107; **25**, 39-40, 99, 124-6; **27**, 167-8; **28**, 196-7
    —notice, need for, **28**, 34-5
    —provision for, **13**, 211-12, 246-8; **15**, 212; **16**, 38-9; **17**, 65-8; **29**, 336, 342-3
    —suspension, **23**, 171; **25**, 36
    —termination, **14**, 73; **23**, 25-6; **26**, 77, 80, 144-5; **28**, 31-3; **29**, 336, 342-5
  duration, **16**, 38-9
  general principle of law, **16**, 39
  liability for, **28**, 103 n. 17
    —costs incurred before *force majeure* occurred, **29**, 344-5
  losses arising, **24**, 36, 171-2; **26**, 77, 144-5, 164; **27**, 167-8, 183, 185; **28**, 43-4, 87; **29**, 327, 342-3
  Foreign exchange controls, **2**, 219, 220, 221, 239, 245, 340; **3**, 13, 32, 68 n. 2; **5**, 376 n. 1, 380, 381; **6**, 167, 178, 208-11; **7**, 44-53; **10**, 106-7, 298-302; **16**, 106, 107-9; **17**, 112; **18**, 228: *see also* International Monetary Fund, Agreement
  capital transfers, **3**, 13, 15-18, 28 n. 1, 29; **7**, 45, 46, 51, 52; **24**, 111-13
    —duty to seek approval, **24**, 111-13
  current transactions, **7**, 45, 46, 51, 52
  effect on contract, **3**, 13; **14**, 16, 18, 27-9
  as expropriation, **24**, 110-11
  justification, **5**, 382
  validity, **3**, 13; **5**, 383; **7**, 49, 50, 52; **28**, 29, 32
  in violation of treaty, **5**, 381, 383; **7**, 51, 53
Form of award: *see under* Settlement
Forum selection clause
  binding, whether, **1**, 241, 245-7, 251, 254-7, 263-7, 270, 276, 277, 285-97, 302, 305-15; **3**, 160, 198; **5**, 120; **26**, 18-19, 33, 36, 249-51
  changed circumstances and, **1**, 287-94, 308
  clear provision, need for, **9**, 216-17; **28**, 67
  jurisdiction of Tribunal, **1**, 236-319, 490, 491, 496, 497; **2**, 4, 5, 54-6, 66-7, 105-6, 138, 370, 378, 396; **3**, 61, 98, 99, 104, 113, 161, 198, 199, 246, 260, 321-5, 335, 384, 386, 387, 388 n. 2; **4**, 7, 8, 55, 143, 181, 220, 225, 230; **5**, 115-17, 119, 120, 126, 127, 130, 171, 180-4, 191-7, 210, 365, 388, 389; **6**, 5, 80-2, 93, 109, 112, 113, 115-17, 221, 222, 236, 250, 251, 255, 263, 268, 270; **7**, 33-5, 188, 218, 219; **8**, 3 n. 2, 51-2, 220-5, 228-31, 264-5, 306-7, 405-7; **9**, 31-5, 88, 115-16, 156, 170-1, 211, 293, 333; **10**, 44-5, 242-3, 277-8; **11**, 7, 35-7, 45-7, 151, 170-1, 197; **12**, 100-1, 142-3, 149-50; **13**, 21, 44, 180-2, 192, 225; **14**, 33-4, 199-200; **17**, 17, 63-4, 259-60, 300; **18**, 110, 189; **20**, 8-9; **22**, 236; **23**, 127-9, 130-2, 168-9, 371; **24**, 51-2; **25**, 17-18; **27**, 156-7; **28**, 29-30; **29**, 141, 316-17
  nullification, **21**, 105-6
  separability, **1**, 292, 308, 309; **8**, 432; **9**, 170-1
Forum shopping, **12**, 285
France, law of, **5**, 19; **7**, 166; **21**, 69 n. 12
  arbitration law, **20**, 206-7, 214-15
  Civil Code—
    —Article 524, **7**, 175 n. 1
    —Article 1131, **11**, 356
    —Article 1134, **24**, 191 n. 38
    —Article 1135, **1**, 108
    —Article 1156, **1**, 108
    —Article 1157, **1**, 107 n. 1

INDEX

—Article 1162, **1**, 213 n. 7, 214 n. 8
—Article 1184, **8**, 165
—Article 1290, **21**, 74 n. 25
—Article 1315, **1**, 209
—Articles 1372-5, **7**, 164 n. 1
—Article 1643, **19**, 38 nn. 30, 31
—Article 1644, **19**, 39
—Article 1655, **19**, 40
Code of Civil Procedure
—Article 341, **20**, 206-7
—Article 384, **1**, 233
—Article 385, **1**, 233
—Article 394, **1**, 233
—Article 395, **1**, 233
Fraud, **3**, 30; **7**, 25
Frustration, **2**, 250-3; **3**, 153, 155; **6**, 176, 177, 274, 281; **7**, 17; **8**, 340, 383; **9**, 122 n. 13, 196; **13**, 250-1; **15**, 211-13; **16**, 39; **18**, 191-2; **19**, 70, 216, 246; **22**, 299, 310-16; **24**, 14: *see also Force majeure*
fault of claimant, effect, **17**, 256-8
foreseeability and, **2**, 251, 253
requirements, **2**, 250-1
Full Tribunal: *see* Tribunal

General Assembly Resolutions
2625 (XXVIII), **8**, 445
3171 (XXVIII), **8**, 445
as source of law, **8**, 408-13
General Declaration
breach, remedies, **25**, 260-2
compliance, tribunal's powers respecting, **25**, 261
effect, **25**, 258
equitable claims, **8**, 263
General Principle A, **5**, 61, 130; **8**, 211; **12**, 45-52, 62, 64-73, 87, 89-93; **19**, 294, 303; **25**, 253, 254, 256-62, 264; **28**, 114-15
—aid to interpretation, **28**, 138
—requirement to negotiate, **12**, 62-3
General Principle B, **1**, 101, 103, 105, 106, 108, 293, 294, 309, 310, 386, 399; **2**, 55, 56, 61-2, 160, 401; **3**, 304, 305, 307, 310-13, 315; **4**, 115 n. 2, 142; **5**, 61, 153, 154, 268, 271, 284, 295, 343; **6**, 45; **7**, 122; **8**, 211, 263, 295; **9**, 137, 255; **12**, 67-70, 274-5, 322; **13**, 223, 225; **14**, 333; **16**, 310; **17**, 178, 184, 185; **18**, 86, 106, 111, 147; **21**, 68, 69 n. 12; **25**, 253, 254, 262-3; **28**, 129-32, 152-3; **29**, 27
interpretation: *see* Jurisdiction of Tribunal, interpretation of Declarations
object and purpose, **19**, 294; **28**, 149-50
Paragraph 1, **5**, 14
Paragraph 2, **2**, 147 n. 1, 209; **12**, 50
Paragraph 3, **12**, 49-50
Paragraph 4, **1**, 208; **5**, 61; **12**, 64 n. 4
Paragraphs 4-9, **12**, 48, 70-1, 73 n. 14
Paragraph 5, **1**, 208; **5**, 61-8, 206; **12**, 64 n. 4
Paragraph 6, **1**, 146, 203, 208; **5**, 61, 68; **8**, 206; **12**, 50, 55, 64 n. 4, 71 n. 12
Paragraph 7, **1**, 124, 136, 141, 146, 157, 161, 164, 172, 182, 188, 190, 199-201, 203, 205, 206, 208, 210, 211, 213, 217, 221, 328, 331, 343, 346, 404, 407, 410, 415, 427, 448; **2**, 13, 45, 91, 114, 127, 133, 147 n. 1, 169, 229, 231, 240, 262, 269, 270, 278, 280, 292, 306, 307, 333, 342, 349, 359, 365, 367, 386, 440; **3**, 35, 37, 54, 74, 79, 92, 108, 117, 120, 142, 170, 177, 182, 187, 192, 207, 213, 219, 236, 254, 268, 276, 291, 327, 340, 352, 368, 369, 391; **4**, 21, 22, 29, 30, 34, 35, 40, 48, 84, 86, 110, 184, 185, 193, 198, 200, 202, 206, 207, 229, 271, 281; **5**, 61, 69, 77, 81, 89, 149, 151, 230, 250, 355, 374; **6**, 2, 5, 19, 21, 34, 35, 39, 64, 66, 119, 121, 124, 132, 148, 175; **7**, 7, 16, 22, 24, 88, 117, 118, 198, 210, 221, 224, 228, 236, 242, 245, 248, 251, 253, 259, 263, 264, 270; **8**, 3, 14, 16, 43, 62, 74, 80, 84, 98, 178, 188, 215, 237, 279, 328, 354, 361, 384, 425; **30**, 295
Paragraph 8, **1**, 208; **5**, 61, 65 n. 4, 212; **9**, 8, 45, 60, 63, 71, 137, 168, 186, 200, 243, 301, 307, 309, 312, 339, 348, 358, 377; **10**, 55, 81, 134, 176, 258, 318, 328, 347, 358, 361, 363, 365, 366; **11**, 30, 34-5, 69, 75, 137, 165, 179, 208, 250, 267, 345, 365; **12**, 17, 38, 50, 55, 64 n. 4, 71, 77, 107, 138, 159, 169, 233, 285, 298, 324, 389, 392; **13**, 39, 40, 43, 45, 118, 146, 191, 276, 310, 345, 361; **14**, 52, 81, 168, 169, 170, 184, 212, 243, 282, 342; **15**, 22, 187; **16**, 276, 319, 322; **17**, 19, 113, 130, 288, 325, 355, 358, 363

342 INDEX

General Declaration (*cont.*)
   Paragraph 9, **1**, 208; **5**, 61; **12**, 50, 65 n. 4; **18**, 147, 174, 244, 278, 322, 374, 378; **19**, 72, 93, 161, 231, 286-8, 290-7, 303-4, 331, 346, 353, 362, 367, 368; **20**, 131; **21**, 51, 61, 161, 287, 289; **22**, 85, 117, 256, 356; **23**, 216, 377; **24**, 85, 115, 156; **25**, 111-12, 151; **26**, 128; **27**, 186; **28**, 50, 111, 130-1, 144, 370, 391, 393, 395, 397; **29**, 241, 293, 349, 397, 404, 413
   Paragraph 10, **2**, 208
   Paragraph 11, **1**, 136, 305, 490, 496; **2**, 39, 40, 79, 88, 109-10, 120 n. 1, 208; **5**, 47, 268; **7**, 153, 276; **8**, 27, 432; **9**, 195, 201 n. 2; **10**, 144, 168; **16**, 78-9, 87 n. 2; **17**, 98, 99 n. 3, 101, 256; **21**, 8, 9; **23**, 257, 361-2; **27**, 58
   Paragraph 16, **2**, 313, 315, 318, 320; **13**, 177; **14**, 329
   Paragraph 17, **1**, 102, 117, 190; **2**, 59, 313, 315, 318, 320; **5**, 58, 61, 112, 204, 209, 210; **12**, 43-5, 60, 66, 82; **14**, 329; **28**, 123; **29**, 217
   peace treaties distinguished, **5**, 284
   Point IV, **8**, 269 n. 42
   Preamble, **19**, 288
   as Treaty, **5**, 259; **19**, 286-8; **28**, 149
General principles of
   accounting, **6**, 244, 251, 269
   adjudication, **7**, 125, 126
   agency law, **19**, 126
   commercial arbitration, **6**, 135
   commercial law, **5**, 233, 394; **6**, 98; **11**, 30; **13**, 239; **15**, 29; **16**, 28; **21**, 104; **26**, 106
   common law, **23**, 144, 145
   constitutional law, **1**, 423
   contract law, **7**, 192; **15**, 81; **19**, 295; **23**, 191, 224, 225, 340; **26**, 165
   equity, **1**, 130, 133, 232, 233; **2**, 237, 254; **3**, 58, 279; **4**, 259, 268; **5**, 248, 293; **6**, 294; **11**, 41
   evidence, **13**, 71-2
   experts, use of, **16**, 199
   fairness, **3**, 30
   international arbitration practice, **11**, 274; **18**, 119, 131; **24**, 27
   international law, **1**, 109, 114, 180, 207, 212, 213, 232, 233, 289, 290-2, 294, 361, 374, 376, 377 n. 15, 402, 450, 458, 464, 475, 476, 478, 482; **2**, 194, 195, 201, 205, 207, 210, 212, 213, 223, 225, 255, 257, 353, 354, 358; **3**, 58, 69-71, 298, 312, 313, 316 n. 3; **4**, 105, 114, 155, 162, 165, 167, 172, 175, 177, 247; **5**, 3, 11, 20, 21, 48, 95, 99, 227, 233, 260, 265, 269, 270, 277, 281, 283, 286, 289, 290, 292-4, 300-4, 310, 313, 321, 322, 325, 331-5, 341, 346, 371; **6**, 98, 201 n. 1, 209, 225, 228, 243, 251, 257, 265, 270; **7**, 51 n. 3, 52, 130, 135, 153, 159, 173, 191, 192; **8**, 393-403; **10**, 155; **11**, 30; **12**, 273; **13**, 239; **14**, 9, 185, 245, 327; **16**, 25, 27, 28, 247; **17**, 142, 189, 218, 231-2, 240, 241; **18**, 246 n. 5; **19**, 295, 304; **21**, 120, 198; **22**, 80; **23**, 289; **28**, 208, 209; **29**, 14; **30**, 43, 63
   —implementation of, **10**, 149
   —stay of proceedings, **2**, 59-61
   —Vienna Convention on the Law of Treaties, codification, **12**, 61
   judicial procedure, **5**, 36
   jurisprudence, **5**, 11, 37, 40, 46, 49
   justice, **1**, 114, 158, 374, 375, 396, 400; **2**, 320, 329, 330, 356; **3**, 32, 54, 298, 302, 362; **4**, 268; **6**, 294; **17**, 23
   law, **1**, 209, 212, 232, 233, 361, 362, 374, 415, 416, 420, 421, 464, 475; **2**, 154 n. 1, 185, 186, 237, 380, 397; **3**, 32, 54, 58, 66, 278, 293, 307; **4**, 221, 231, 242, 261, 268, 270; **5**, 18, 41, 42, 129, 233, 248, 261, 293, 294, 373, 398; **6**, 90, 97, 98, 168, 225, 269, 271; **7**, 75, 120, 121, 131, 158, 163, 197; **8**, 140, 161, 162, 427; **9**, 122, 176, 402; **10**, 308; **11**, 32; **13**, 33, 211; **16**, 26-7, 66; **17**, 23; **19**, 30-1; **20**, 204, 206-8; **21**, 70, 154, 345; **22**, 297 n. 50; **23**, 86, 171, 370; **28**, 208, 209
   —absence of arbitrator, **2**, 14
   municipal law, **5**, 3, 21, 48, 261; **6**, 228, 243; **7**, 130; **10**, 143; **11**, 139
   private international law, **2**, 185, 186, 205; **3**, 47; **5**, 292, 325
   synthesis of civil and common law, **13**, 59
   trusteeship, **6**, 293
Germany, Federal Republic
   Constitutional Court, **7**, 168
   law of, **7**, 167

INDEX

343

—Civil Code, **8**, 141; **19**, 33
—Rules of Civil Procedure, **8**, 134
Good faith, **1**, 109, 206, 376, 378; **2**, 209, 223; **3**, 308; **5**, 26, 273, 277, 290; **6**, 209, 251, 270, 295; **7**, 159, 160, 178, 215; **8**, 141; **11**, 11; **15**, 233; **16**, 48, 54, 63, 72, 296, 310; **18**, 262 n. 22; **21**, 154, 155; **22**, 297; **24**, 80-2, 86-7, 96: *see also* Bad faith
Governing law: *see* Applicable law
Government, meaning, **23**, 136-7
Guarantee, **5**, 241
Guarantor, **7**, 115

Hague Convention on
  Choice of Court (1964), Article 5, **1**, 269
  Conflict of Nationality Laws (1930), **2**, 181, 196; **5**, 260, 262, 265, 266, 291
    —Article 1, **2**, 161, 224; **5**, 260, 302
    —Article 2, **5**, 302
    —Article 3, **5**, 302
    —Article 4, **2**, 161, 162, 189, 194-9, 201, 202, 205, 207, 214, 223, 224; **5**, 260, 261, 299, 300-4, 322, 323, 325-7, 331
    —Article 5, **2**, 162, 189, 195, 198, 199, 203, 205; **5**, 262, 299, 322, 325, 326
  Law Applicable to Trusts and Their Recognition, **12**, 274
  Pacific Settlement of International Disputes (1899), **29**, 388
  Pacific Settlement of International Disputes (1907), **5**, 293
Hardship, **1**, 127, 128, 130, 132, 133, 175, 300, 399; **3**, 209, 375
Hearing, postponement: *see* Postponement of hearing
Holder in due course, **7**, 99, 100, 102
Hostages, relevance, **14**, 315

Immovable property transactions, **2**, 250, 256; **7**, 131, 132: *see also* Iran, law of, immovable property
Indemnity, **13**, 120
India, arbitrator's alleged breach of currency laws, **21**, 380-3, 395, 396-8
Institute of International Law, **2**, 162, 163, 187, 199; **5**, 326, 328, 335
  Resolution of 10 September 1965, **2**, 196, 197, 200-2, 204, 207, 208, 214, 223; **5**, 266, 301, 303, 322, 324, 328, 331, 333

Interest, **1**, 170-2, 414, 415, 446-8, 450, 451, 453, 454; **2**, 169, 239, 240, 342, 343, 385, 390, 400; **3**, 33, 53, 54, 56, 57, 72, 106, 116, 117, 206, 235, 236, 251, 253, 267, 275, 279, 290, 291, 294; **4**, 110, 118, 120, 224, 228, 229, 247, 270, 271; **5**, 48, 110, 111, 169, 174, 175, 219, 226, 227, 230, 367, 374, 395, 399, 401; **6**, 18, 19, 62-5, 68, 69, 173, 178, 216, 217, 229, 283, 287; **7**, 16, 24, 74, 76, 80, 89, 101, 104, 108, 111, 112, 115, 117, 118, 183, 191, 193, 194, 198; **8**, 60-1, 168, 171, 178, 320-2, 342-4, 384; **9**, 44, 59, 198; **10**, 54, 80, 175, 189 n. 29, 252, 255, 256, 257, 264, 304, 316-18, 327, 346-7; **11**, 26-31, 34, 41-5, 52, 67-8, 69, 75, 105-7, 136, 137, 164, 165, 178, 179, 205-6, 207, 208, 242-4, 250, 254, 266, 267, 343-4; **12**, 16, 28-9, 30-2, 138, 155-7, 168-9, 229-31, 297, 298, 321, 362; **13**, 29-30, 33-5, 89-90, 95-6, 145, 191, 192, 233-8, 252-3, 268-9, 275, 308-9, 344; **14**, 46, 78, 124-6, 184; **15**, 20-1, 152, 184, 289; **16**, 48-58, 69-75, 101-2, 233-4, 236, 249-54, 275, 276, 280; **17**, 17, 20-2, 23-4, 30, 31, 79, 133-4, 199, 212, 227, 237, 244, 287-8, 322-3; **18**, 163, 173, 195, 216-19, 243, 277, 285, 304, 306, 308, 318, 319, 320, 321, 364, 367, 372; **19**, 72, 73, 92, 155-8, 172, 228-9, 238-9, 246-9; **20**, 126-8; **21**, 52, 53, 60, 161; **22**, 83-4, 116-17, 242, 251, 253-4, 255, 336, 355, 361-2; **23**, 33, 63, 64, 71-4, 121, 148, 208, 210-11, 337, 366; **24**, 113, 154-5, 201; **25**, 108-9, 110, 111, 129, 150; **26**, 36, 80, 126-7, 182-3; **27**, 22, 23, 31, 87, 105, 115, 119, 185; **29**, 55, 239, 293: *see also* Damages, interest on money borrowed
accrued, **10**, 345
applicable law, **11**, 27
  — relevance, **12**, 28; **13**, 269
bad faith not precondition, **13**, 269
calculation, **6**, 217; **7**, 193, 194; **11**, 28-30; **13**, 34
compound, **7**, 191, 192; **8**, 320; **13**, 234-5; **16**, 234-5, 251-4; **24**, 83-4; **25**, 109
  —international law, under, **16**, 253-4
contract-based, **7**, 192; **11**, 105-7, 136,

INDEX

Interest (*cont.*)
  178, 343-4; **12**, 31-2, 106; **13**, 34, 234-7, 252, 308; **14**, 160-5; **15**, 152; **21**, 76-7; **24**, 47 n. 2, 74, 83-4; **25**, 150
  —on damages, **2**, 259
  date of commencement, **9**, 44, 59, 129, 338, 377; **10**, 331; **11**, 27-31, 68; **12**, 29, 106, 108, 124, 133, 135, 169, 229-31, 233 n. 4, 297, 303, 321; **13**, 34, 145, 191, 237, 248, 269, 308-9; **15**, 20-1, 53; **16**, 234 n. 63, 280; **17**, 17-18, 20, 134, 322-3; **18**, 195, 372; **19**, 72, 92, 155-8, 228-9, 238-9, 246-9; **20**, 126; **21**, 52; **22**, 84, 252, 361-2; **23**, 86-9; **25**, 109; **26**, 164; **27**, 31, 87; **28**, 48-9; **30**, 101, 234
  on debt, **2**, 12, 27
  double recovery, avoidance, **19**, 158-9
  effect of Security Account, **8**, 321, 343-4; **11**, 30
  general principle of law, **23**, 86
  generally admitted usage, **5**, 17, 20, 128; **17**, 17, 20, 128
  lawfulness of conduct and, **11**, 150 n. 1, 164, 167
  need for consistency, **8**, 320-2; **10**, 80, 304; **11**, 31; **12**, 28, 32, 156
  non-contractual basis, **12**, 28; **13**, 237-8, 252; **14**, 78, 211, 242; **28**, 48
  principles governing, **11**, 29-31
  purpose, **11**, 29, 42; **12**, 28, 229; **13**, 269; **30**, 101, 234
  rate, **5**, 111; **8**, 61, 320-2; **9**, 129-30, 167, 202, 243, 300, 376-7; **10**, 80, 304; **11**, 27-31, 164, 206, 243; **12**, 28, 31, 137, 155-6, 229, 321; **13**, 236, 269; **16**, 234; **17**, 112, 287; **18**, 173, 195; **19**, 155, 228; **21**, 76-7; **25**, 85, 150; **26**, 182; **28**, 48-9, 88, 368; **29**, 55, 56, 239-41, 293, 330; **30**, 1, 234, 264-5
  —in official claims, **12**, 29, 31
  terminal date, **17**, 20-2
  —customary international law, **17**, 22 n. 4
  uniform rules, desirability, **16**, 292
  waiver, **28**, 48
Interim measures
  aggravation of dispute, avoidance, **8**, 277
  applicability, **8**, 182, 220
  attachment of goods, withdrawal, **3**, 7
  certificate of insurance, **8**, 281
  conservation of—
    —goods, **3**, 173-5, 331; **5**, 128; **8**, 46, 275-82; **13**, 257-8
    —rights of parties, **6**, 50; **8**, 46, 77, 227; **9**, 304; **13**, 258
  expert's expenses, **8**, 46-8
  expiry, **11**, 246
  export licence, **13**, 259-60
  full relief, **8**, 46
  ICJ and, **8**, 7 n. 4; **13**, 258
  indemnity against third party vendor claims, **8**, 280-1
  inherent power of international tribunal, **2**, 59-62; **8**, 275 n. 49
  justification for, **5**, 113; **6**, 51; **8**, 6-7, 109
    —irreparable damage, **8**, 7, 22, 108, 110, 276 n. 50; **29**, 218
  legal standards, **6**, 134, 135
  obligation to comply, **8**, 78, 87, 227
  payment of fees, **1**, 154; **21**, 4
  protection of property, **5**, 112-14, 131-3
  re-exportation of goods, **1**, 121
  rendered inapplicable, **8**, 64
  restraint of misuse of trademark, **1**, 122
  return of goods, **13**, 173-5
  revision, **8**, 48
  stay of attachment, **6**, 131-3, 140
  stay of proceedings, **1**, 222, 225; **2**, 55-7, 65-7, 98-9, 281, 282, 311, 363, 371, 402; **3**, 8, 9, 60, 61, 201, 298, 336, 337, 349, 385-8; **4**, 7, 8, 12-14, 15, 17, 55, 56, 72, 73; **5**, 121, 126-9, 130, 154; **6**, 46-51, 108-11, 115-17; **7**, 219, 277, 278; **8**, 3 n. 2, 5, 74-7, 78, 85-8, 225-7, 232-4; **9**, 131-2, 152, 304, 305; **11**, 297-9; **13**, 194-8; **14**, 48-9; **17**, 80-1, 87; **18**, 59, 288; **21**, 11; **23**, 7, 212-13: *see also* Procedure, stay of proceedings
  storage costs, **13**, 259
  substantive jurisdiction, in advance of decision on, **6**, 131; **8**, 45, 77
  withdrawal of bank guarantee, **13**, 197-8
Interlocutory Award, revision, **14**, 70-1
International Air Transport Association (IATA), **17**, 230
International Chamber of Commerce, **2**, 401, 402; **5**, 388; **6**, 130, 138; **13**, 52 n. 8; **18**, 118-19
  arbitrators, independence, **20**, 249
  confidentiality, **20**, 234
  Court of Arbitration, **6**, 135, 137

INDEX

—Internal Rules, **20**, 208, 316
——2(2), **1**, 449 n. 2
——6, **1**, 130
joinder of cases, **27**, 300 n. 5
Rules of Conciliation and Arbitration, **1**, 278; **18**, 120-5
Statute
—Article 37, **5**, 274
—Article 38, **8**, 407-8
—Article 54(3), **1**, 424
—Article 62, **3**, 298
—Article 75, **5**, 111; **6**, 46
—Article 89, **1**, 233
Uniform Customs and Practice for Documentary Credits, **1**, 170; **5**, 28, 29, 39, 46
—Article 3, **5**, 28
—Article 7, **17**, 291 n. 3
—Article 8, **17**, 284
—Article 11, **1**, 170; **17**, 286
—Article 47, **7**, 22
Uniform Rules for the Collection of Commercial Papers (1967), **1**, 443
—Article 4, **1**, 446, 447
—Article 6, **1**, 446, 447
—Article 12, **1**, 447
International Court of Justice (ICJ), **1**, 104, 110 n. 5, 290, 293, 307, 308, 313, 374, 402, 449 n. 2, 450, 457, 458, 466, 467, 475; **2**, 162, 163, 189, 196, 202-4, 208, 210, 214, 223, 245, 253, 257, 258 n. 1, 299, 352, 353, 355; **3**, 20, 28, 32 n. 1, 210, 295, 298, 299 n. 1, 302, 305 n. 1, 310 n. 2, 311 n. 4, 376; **4**, 113, 114, 116 n. 1, 173, 174; **5**, 20, 21, 113, 263, 266, 288, 309, 322-4, 329, 331-3; **6**, 108, 131, 134, 135, 211; **7**, 51 n. 3, 122, 133, 135 n. 1, 151, 152, 203; **8**, 213 n. 21, 405, 434, 449; **9**, 353; **10**, 132 n. 7, 143, 185, 191; **11**, 144; **12**, 366; **14**, 104 n. 4, 321; **15**, 216, 218; **16**, 85, 92 n. 29, 94, 196; **18**, 261 n. 20, 268, 271 n. 41, 282; **21**, 118 n. 33, 155 n. 45; **22**, 288 n. 34; **24**, 179 n. 20, 180 n. 23; **25**, 271 n. 8
stay of proceedings, **2**, 61
US Diplomatic and Consular Staff in Tehran, **2**, 84, 89 n. 1
International law: *see* Customary international law; General principles of, international law; Sources of international law; Subjects of international law
International Law Commission, **2**, 206
Draft Articles on State responsibility: *see* State responsibility, ILC Draft Articles on
International Monetary Fund, **2**, 220; **3**, 12 n. 1, 13, 14; **5**, 376 n. 1, 382, 383; **6**, 178, 211; **7**, 52, 73; **10**, 353 n. 4; **16**, 106; **24**, 111
Agreement, **3**, 14, 16, 18, 19, 28, 29; **5**, 381, 383; **6**, 178 n. 1, 208, 210; **7**, 40, 51; **10**, 106
—Article VI, **2**, 221; **3**, 13; **7**, 40, 51; **15**, 29
—Article VII, **3**, 13 n. 1; **7**, 45
—Article VIII, **2**, 220-1; **3**, 13, 14, 16, 28-30, 32; **5**, 383; **6**, 210, 211; **7**, 44
—Article XIV, **3**, 13 n. 1, 14; **6**, 210; **7**, 44, 45 n. 1
—Article XIX, **5**, 383 n. 1; **7**, 45, 46, 51, 52
—Article XXX, **3**, 29 n. 1; **6**, 211
—violation, **5**, 383
International responsibility, extension, **6**, 168
International tribunals, **1**, 310; **7**, 307; **12**, 318; **16**, 198-9; **18**, 271 n. 39
AGIP, **15**, 251
AMCO, **18**, 217 n. 28; **30**, 253
American-British Claims Commission, **1**, 132
Aminoil, **8**, 386; **12**, 187 n. 7, 234; **14**, 236-7; **15**, 232, 233, 243, 246, 251-2, 259, 270, 292, 297 n. 16, 305, 306 n. 31; **16**, 28, 65-7, 242 n. 10, 252; **18**, 223 n. 38; **21**, 121, 123, 140-1; **22**, 288 n. 34; **30**, 199, 241, 243-4
Anglo-German Commission, **2**, 185-6; **5**, 308, 318
Anglo-Greek Commission of Arbitration, **1**, 202
Anglo-Iranian Oil Company, **22**, 288 n. 34
Anglo-Italian Conciliation Commission (1952), **3**, 70; **16**, 247 n. 14
Anglo-Mexican Arbitral Commission, **2**, 194; **18**, 282
Aramco, **22**, 288 n. 34
Arbitral Commission against the German Government, **5**, 298

International tribunals (*cont.*)
  Arbitral Commission on Property Rights and Interests in Germany (1957), **2**, 59
  —Rules of Procedure, **1**, 233
  Austro-Romanian Mixed Arbitration Tribunal, **21**, 363 n. 44
  Benvenuti & Bonfant v. *Congo*, **22**, 288 n. 34
  BP (Libya) v. *Libya*, **15**, 251
  British-American Civil War Commission (1872), **2**, 181, 190; **5**, 305
  British-Mexican Commission, **2**, 187, 188; **5**, 302, 308, 309; **9**, 331; **24**, 178 n. 20, 179 n. 21
  British-US Claims Commission, **5**, 309 n. 1; **24**, 180 n. 24
  British-Venezuelan Commission, **5**, 307, 313
  Central American Court of Justice, **5**, 298
  Christian Rosing A/S 1984 v. *Air Canada*, **22**, 301 n. 53
  Colombia-United States Mixed Commission, **7**, 135 n. 2
  Ecuador-United States Court of Arbitration (*The Mechanic*), **21**, 155 n. 46
  European Commission of Human Rights, **5**, 298
  European Court of Human Rights, **5**, 298
  France-US Arbitral Tribunal, **2**, 257
  Franco-German Mixed Arbitral Tribunal, **2**, 148; **3**, 70; **16**, 247
  Franco-Italian Conciliation Commission (1948), **2**, 59-60; **5**, 263
  French-German Commission, **2**, 185-7; **5**, 308, 319
  French-Mexican Claims Commission (1928), **2**, 188; **3**, 210, 294; **5**, 316; **18**, 105
  French-Turkish Commission, **5**, 319, 320
  French-US Commission, **5**, 300 n. 1
  French-Venezuelan Mixed Commission (1902-5), **2**, 184
  German-Mexican Claims Commission, **2**, 82; **5**, 349
  German-Polish Mixed Arbitral Tribunal, **10**, 251; **21**, 155 n. 44
  German-US Mixed Claims Commission, **17**, 22 n. 4; **18**, 265 n. 28; **19**, 31 n. 14; **24**, 180 n. 23; **30**, 239
  Great Britain/Spain, Spanish Moroccan Claim, **9**, 331
  Greco-Bulgarian Commission, **5**, 308, 319

  Greco-Bulgarian Mixed Arbitral Tribunal, **3**, 311
  Hungarian-Belgian Mixed Arbitral Tribunal, **6**, 214
  Hungarian/Serbo-Croatian-Slovene Commission, **2**, 185; **5**, 308
  Imbrie, **2**, 85-6
  International Chamber of Commerce: *see* International Chamber of Commerce
  International Court of Justice: *see* International Court of Justice (ICJ)
  Italian-Mexican Claims Commission, **18**, 246 n. 5, 262
  Italian-US Conciliation Commissions, **2**, 163, 189, 197; **5**, 263, 272, 300, 303, 310, 321, 322, 324, 325, 327; **25**, 163, 165-6, 200, 206
  Italian-Venezuelan Commission, **5**, 307, 315
  Lena Goldfields, **15**, 299
  LETCO, **30**, 253-4
  LIAMCO, **15**, 251, 293 n. 8, 296 n. 15, 305, 306 n. 31; **16**, 28, 65 n. 9; **17**, 22 n. 4; **18**, 217 nn. 28, 29, 283 n. 38; **21**, 346 n. 36; **30**, 199, 241, 242, 244
  Lighthouses Arbitration between France and Greece, **15**, 251
  London Court of Arbitration, International Arbitration Rules, **1**, 130
  Lusitania cases, **2**, 82-3
  Mergé, **22**, 146
  Mexican Arbitral Commissions, **2**, 194
  Mexican Claims Commissions, **1**, 158, 180, 401, 402, 457, 475; **2**, 82, 83, 301; **3**, 70, 376; **7**, 204
  Mexican-US Claims Commission, **5**, 309 n. 1; **6**, 257; **16**, 246, 247; **17**, 104 n. 9; **18**, 105, 246 n. 5; **24**, 179 n. 23, 180 nn. 24, 25, 182 n. 6
  Mexico City Bombardment Claims, **18**, 271; **24**, 182 n. 26
  mixed arbitral tribunals, **2**, 163, 185, 189, 191, 194, 209, 214; **5**, 298, 308, 318, 321; **29**, 388-9
  North Atlantic Fisheries, **21**, 155 n. 45
  Norwegian Shipowners' Claims, **15**, 262 n. 15, 299; **19**, 30 n. 12; **30**, 238
  OPIC, **18**, 223 n. 38
  Permanent Court of Arbitration, **1**, 117, 509-11, 513, 518; **2**, 184, 190; **3**, 70; **5**,

INDEX

307, 332; **7**, 135 n. 2; **10**, 197; **16**, 247 n. 14
Pious Fund Case, **2**, 64 n. 2
Permanent Court of International Justice: *see* Permanent Court of International Justice (PCIJ)
Peru-US Arbitral Commission, **6**, 169
practice, **3**, 14, 20, 28, 31, 32, 66, 70, 85, 249, 287, 298, 302; **4**, 237; **5**, 129, 287, 293, 297, 298, 304, 331, 346, 351; **7**, 135; **10**, 149, 185; **11**, 27-30, 32, 43, 50; **12**, 275-7; **13**, 58-9; **14**, 105; **16**, 17, 27, 55, 199, 246-7, 290; **17**, 22 n. 4, 190, 218; **18**, 79, 80, 278-9, 281 n. 4; **19**, 30, 31, 171; **20**, 305; **21**, 104, 239
——acts of State, enquiry into, **25**, 157, 165
——jurisdiction, consent of parties, **22**, 296
Revere Copper, **22**, 288 n. 34
Sapphire International Petroleum Ltd v. NIOC, **15**, 251
Shufeldt Claim, **21**, 155 n. 47
Spanish Zones in Morocco, **21**, 155 n. 47
SPP (Middle East) Arbitration, **15**, 262 n. 15, 306 n. 31
Tacna-Arica Case, **18**, 271 n. 40
TOPCO, **8**, 386; **15**, 251, 293 n. 8, 296; **30**, 198-9, 241, 242, 244
Tripartite Claims Commission (US, Austria, Hungary, 1928), **5**, 307
Upper Silesian Arbitral Tribunal, **5**, 272; **23**, 387
US-Venezuelan Mixed Claims Commission, **2**, 184, 215; **5**, 306, 317; **16**, 99; **30**, 238-9
Venezuelan Arbitral Commissions (1903-5), **2**, 162, 182, 189, 190; **3**, 70, 311 n. 1; **5**, 307; **18**, 217 n. 28
Iran: *see also* Iran, law of
claims against US nationals, **1**, 101-10, 475; **4**, 75; **8**, 364, 366, 368; **14**, 278
controlled entity: *see* Controlled entity, Iran
courts—
——enforcement of judgments, **9**, 152
——jurisdiction, **5**, 130; **7**, 130-2, 137; **9**, 132, 293-4; **11**, 246, 250; **22**, 253, 256, 290; **30**, 42-3
——forum selection clause and, **9**, 194-5: *see also* Forum selection clause
——inherent and general, **5**, 128
——right to resort to, **5**, 127-9
——stay of proceedings: *see* Interim measures, stay of proceedings
——Tribunal orders and, **4**, 15
duties under international law, **6**, 111; **9**, 151-2
Foundation for the Oppressed, **9**, 88-96
French nationals in, **22**, 56
individuals' right to bring claims, **9**, 128, 383
liability for controlled entity, **2**, 26, 147 nn. 1, 2, 165, 258, 259; **4**, 72 n. 4, 248, 249; **5**, 227, 368, 371; **6**, 66; **10**, 258, 303; **21**, 67
——*proprio motu* measures, **5**, 371
Majlis' position, **1**, 236, 237, 242, 243, 246, 248, 252, 253, 255, 261, 265, 268, 269, 271, 272, 274, 275, 280, 281, 284, 291, 296, 306 n. 3, 310, 488, 490, 491, 494, 496, 497; **3**, 198, 304-9, 311, 313, 314; **5**, 119, 182 n. 1, 298; **7**, 153, 218; **19**, 288-90
misappropriation of assets, **6**, 252
responsibility for compliance with treaty obligations, **4**, 15
Workers' Councils, **5**, 369, 370, 379, 380
Iran, law of, **1**, 108, 266, 282, 291, 293, 294, 314, 315, 362, 374, 419-21, 489, 490, 495; **4**, 247; **5**, 126, 127, 333, 334, 367, 384; **6**, 160
Administration of Bank Affairs, Legal Bill concerning (1980), **28**, 259
Administrative Justice Tribunal Act (1982), **30**, 43
Administrative Regulations Pertaining to the Registration of Companies Act, Article 1, **3**, 22
agency, **1**, 266, 378-80
Apartment Purchasers Bill (1980), **4**, 146, 152
Appointment of Temporary Managers, Act for (1979), **2**, 150-2, 350, 351; **4**, 147, 153, 154; **7**, 162-5; **11**, 215; **12**, 7 n. 5; **14**, 305 n. 3; **16**, 240 n. 9; **29**, 266-70; **30**, 85-6
——Article 1, **2**, 150, 151, 350; **7**, 162; **21**, 69; **30**, 186, 189

348   INDEX

Iran law of (*cont.*)
—Article 2, **2**, 151, 350; **4**, 147; **30**, 85, 186
—Article 3, **2**, 151, 152, 350; **4**, 147; **30**, 85, 186
—Article 4, **2**, 152
—Article 5, **2**, 151, 350; **4**, 147
—Article 6, **2**, 152, 350; **4**, 147
arbitration, **3**, 210, 295; **18**, 125
Articles of Association of the Foundation for the Oppressed, Law on, **5**, 378; **9**, 88-9
authorizing Claims Settlement Declaration, **6**, 236
Banking and Monetary Law (1972), Article II(c), **7**, 44
Bankruptcy, **7**, 131, 132
Banks Nationalization Law (1979), **4**, 151; **8**, 378; **10**, 241; **19**, 53; **28**, 250-60, 264; **30**, 97-8
By-law Concerning Landed Property Ownership by Foreign Nationals (1949), **4**, 160; **6**, 183 n. 1
Civil Code, **5**, 147; **9**, 329
—Article 5, **1**, 249, 250; **5**, 182
—Article 9, **3**, 388; **4**, 114
—Article 10, **6**, 98
—Article 18, **7**, 175 n. 1
—Article 138, **9**, 393 n. 6
—Article 183, **22**, 307 n. 62
—Articles 191-4, **22**, 306 n. 61
—Article 193, **3**, 163; **8**, 161; **23**, 340
—Article 196, **6**, 72, 159, 160, 195 n. 3, 196; **24**, 11
—Article 198, **6**, 194
—Article 219, **22**, 300 n. 53
—Article 220, **6**, 99; **22**, 300 n. 53
—Article 221, **24**, 71
—Article 223, **2**, 119
—Article 224, **16**, 26
—Article 225, **16**, 26
—Article 227, **9**, 119 n. 11; **24**, 71, 171 n. 12
—Article 229, **24**, 71, 171 n. 12
—Article 230, **6**, 99; **14**, 142; **24**, 197
—Article 231, **1**, 375 n. 13; **6**, 72, 159; **18**, 210 n. 6
—Article 234, **24**, 11, 71
—Article 237, **24**, 66
—Article 239, **8**, 223
—Article 240, **8**, 223

—Article 247, **2**, 154, 380; **13**, 33; **22**, 324
—Article 248, **2**, 154, 380; **13**, 33
—Article 259, **22**, 326
—Article 261, **22**, 326
—Article 263, **22**, 326
—Article 292, **2**, 116; **4**, 232; **8**, 157
—Article 294, **21**, 74 n. 25
—Article 295, **18**, 351
—Article 301, **2**, 236
—Articles 301-6, **2**, 155; **4**, 231
—Articles 301-37, **14**, 186
—Article 303, **2**, 236, 237; **22**, 326
—Article 306, **7**, 163
—Article 308, **22**, 326
—Article 317, **22**, 326
—Articles 328-31, **6**, 99 n. 2
—Article 336, **4**, 231; **7**, 76; **9**, 402; **18**, 347
—Articles 336-7, **2**, 155; **9**, 402; **12**, 375
—Article 338, **14**, 143
—Article 340, **22**, 306 n. 61
—Article 377, **5**, 40; **22**, 317 n. 92
—Article 387, **22**, 301 n. 53
—Articles 416-21, **13**, 74-5
—Article 422, **19**, 40
—Articles 422-9, **19**, 40
—Article 424, **19**, 40
—Articles 571-606, **5**, 147; **9**, 327
—Article 575, **3**, 161
—Article 656, **1**, 379
—Article 658, **1**, 378; **6**, 194
—Article 662, **6**, 159, 160
—Article 684, **9**, 223, 224
—Article 685, **26**, 22
—Article 709, **26**, 22
—Article 744, **13**, 75
—Article 968, **1**, 378 n. 16; **22**, 289
—Article 969, **22**, 161 n. 3
—Article 976, **5**, 272 n. 1; **22**, 158; **24**, 44; **26**, 12; **29**, 57 n. 21
—Articles 976-91, **9**, 354
—Article 988, **5**, 272 n. 1, 334; **9**, 354
—Article 989, **5**, 334; **9**, 354; **28**, 266-7, 274
—Article 990, **14**, 7
—Article 998, **9**, 223, 224
—Article 1005, **22**, 150
—Article 1006, **22**, 150
—Article 1061, **30**, 66-7

INDEX

—Articles 1106-7, **2**, 85
—Article 1111, **2**, 85
—Article 1127, **2**, 85
—Article 1287, **14**, 245
—Article 1306, **5**, 43; **6**, 192, 196; **8**, 161
—Article 1310, **8**, 161; **9**, 6, 192
—Article 1324, **6**, 196
Civil Procedure Code, **8**, 77-8
    —Article 3, **16**, 26
    —Article 23, **7**, 131
    —Article 30, **21**, 74 n. 25
    —Article 35, **7**, 131, 132
    —Article 36, **7**, 131, 171
    —Article 48, **2**, 64
    —Article 57, **2**, 64
    —Article 72, **7**, 125
    —Article 127, **2**, 64; **3**, 388
    —Article 133, **27**, 300 n. 5
    —Article 146, **2**, 64
    —Article 147, **2**, 64
    —Article 225, **1**, 390
    —Article 284, **6**, 102 n. 1
    —Articles 290-8, **2**, 67; **6**, 116; **8**, 233
    —Article 298, **1**, 233; **2**, 64; **3**, 388
    —Article 322, **8**, 174
    —Article 356, **1**, 209
    —Article 508, **21**, 74 n. 25
    —Article 564, **5**, 46
    —Article 629, **1**, 329 n. 2, 405 n. 2
    —Article 630, **1**, 329 n. 2, 405 n. 2
    —Articles 632-7, **23**, 128
    —Articles 632-76, **23**, 132
    —Article 635, **1**, 240
    —Article 641, **3**, 40, 296; **7**, 204
    —Article 649, **3**, 210, 295
    —Article 657, **1**, 240, 282
    —Article 660, **1**, 425, 432; **3**, 210, 295
    —Article 662, **1**, 240
    —Article 665, **1**, 240, 282; **5**, 128; **7**, 164 n. 2
    —Article 713, **12**, 24; **13**, 252
    —Article 719, **14**, 162; **26**, 146
    —Article 728, **14**, 142
    —Article 740, **3**, 287
    —Articles 971-5, **18**, 145-6
    —Article 988, **2**, 218, 224
    —Article 989, **2**, 218, 224
Civil Responsibility Law, **6**, 99; **26**, 22
Civil Service Act
    —Article 70, **30**, 41-2
    —Article 74, **30**, 41

    —Article 82, **30**, 41-2
    —Article 86, **30**, 42
Commercial Code, **5**, 17, 147; **7**, 171; **9**, 327; **10**, 136; **21**, 44
    —Article 6, **3**, 22
    —Article 16, **30**, 144, 147
    —Article 17, **30**, 144, 147
    —Article 20, **5**, 237; **28**, 64
    —Articles 20-194, **5**, 147
    —Article 40, **10**, 239; **21**, 77; **26**, 226; **29**, 27, 137-8
    —Article 45, **2**, 176
    —Article 74, **2**, 176
    —Article 94, **5**, 18
    —Article 103, **11**, 347-8; **14**, 229, 243
    —Article 118, **2**, 154 n. 2; **3**, 287
    —Article 119, **3**, 161
    —Article 126, **2**, 23 n. 1; **13**, 69
    —Article 129, **2**, 24 n. 1; **21**, 47, 51
    —Article 131, **21**, 51
    —Article 134, **13**, 68
    —Article 135, **2**, 154 n. 2; **3**, 287
    —Article 136, **14**, 297
    —Article 141, **25**, 149
    —Article 142, **30**, 166 n. 6
    —Articles 199-231, **2**, 150
    —Article 258, **30**, 166 n. 6
    —Article 269, **30**, 166 n. 6
    —Article 313, **3**, 19
    —Article 357, **2**, 24 n. 2
    —Article 371, **22**, 317 n. 92
    —Article 382, **5**, 39
    —Article 383, **5**, 39
    —Articles 412-550, **2**, 150
    —Article 413, **14**, 302
    —Article 583, **5**, 237
    —Article 584, **28**, 64
    —Article 585, **28**, 64
    —Article 587, **5**, 4
    —Article 589, **5**, 237
    —Article 590, **5**, 2, 18; **7**, 130
    —Article 591, **5**, 2, 18; **7**, 130
conformity to international standards, **5**, 273 n. 1
Constitution, **1**, 413, 423; **3**, 308; **6**, 201; **8**, 77-8
    —Articles 1-5, **5**, 378
    —Article 31, **5**, 243
    —Article 44, **2**, 144, 150
    —Article 80, **5**, 243
    —Article 94, **5**, 378; **9**, 94

Iran, law of (*cont.*)
—Article 96, **5**, 378; **9**, 94
—Article 104, **5**, 379
—Article 107, **5**, 378; **9**, 93
—Article 139, **5**, 334 n. 1
—Article 143, **5**, 245
—Article 150, **17**, 102 n. 8
—Article 166, **5**, 129
—Principle 104, **5**, 369
—Principle 139, **3**, 305-9; **8**, 222-3
Construction Completion Bill, **4**, 146-7, 153
—Article 2, **4**, 146-7
contract, **3**, 163, 286, 287; **5**, 43; **6**, 192, 195, 196; **8**, 161; **24**, 11
Cooperative Companies Act, **22**, 184
corporations, **7**, 132, 136
Development of Petrochemical Industries Act (1965), **15**, 224, 238, 243; **21**, 154
—Article 1, **15**, 154
—Article 3, **15**, 238
Direct Taxation Act (Esfand 1345), **3**, 241; **29**, 281-91
—Article 76, **9**, 179; **10**, 283, 287; **11**, 349
—Article 283, **11**, 354 n. 12
Direct Taxation Act (Esfand 2525), **21**, 151; **25**, 106, 108
—Article 44, **21**, 73
—Article 75, **16**, 280
Duties and Authority of Temporary Managers Act (1980), **18**, 96
enforcement, **5**, 234; **9**, 177-8
Enforcement of Civil Awards Law (1977), Article 169, **18**, 145-6
foreign currency regulations, **5**, 375 n. 1; **7**, 45, 46, 52
Foreign Investments, Law on Attraction and Protection of (1955), **2**, 220, 337, 339, 340; **6**, 54, 57, 62; **7**, 40, 44; **10**, 141 n. 8, 243; **15**, 238, 243
—Article III, **10**, 243
Foreign Nationals Immovable Properties Act (1931), **4**, 160; **6**, 183 n. 1
Foreign Technical Experts Employment Law (1970), **3**, 287
General Public Code, **7**, 161
government agencies, **5**, 4, 5, 12
Government Transaction Regulations, **9**, 103 n. 8
Holding and Management of Stocks in Contracting and Consulting Engineering Firms and Institutes, Law on (1980), **3**, 230; **18**, 96
immovable property, **7**, 131, 132, 175: *see also relevant legislation*
Income Tax Act, **30**, 87
Insurance Law, **23**, 67, 120, 122
Islamic Land Reform Act (Amendment) (1986), **28**, 267-8
Islamic Workers' Councils for Manufacturing, Industrial, Agricultural and Service Units, Law Establishing, **5**, 379
Issuance of Cheques Act (Tir, 2535), Article 2, **3**, 19
Joint Stock Companies Act (1969), **5**, 12, 18, 19, 21; **7**, 130
—Article 1, **5**, 17; **7**, 131
—Article 2, **5**, 18
—Article 94, **7**, 130
—Articles 199-231, **7**, 171
Labour Code, **3**, 286; **24**, 192, 193 n. 42
—Article 33, **15**, 162; **18**, 17
—Article 38, **30**, 140
Law 7/2571 (1979): *see* Appointment of Temporary Managers, Act for (1979) *above*
Law 6738 (1979): *see* Appointment of Temporary Managers, Act for (1979) *above*
Management of the Non-Governmental Education Units Bill, **27**, 60
Maritime Act, **5**, 39
—Article 1(a), **21**, 78
—Article 52, **5**, 39 n. 1
—Article 54(6), **12**, 145 n. 8
—Article 65, **5**, 39
Mining Law of Iran (1957), Article 10, **7**, 4 n. 1
Monetary and Banking Law (1972), **29**, 138
—Article 11(c), **2**, 220; **3**, 13
—Article 42(a), **3**, 27; **13**, 88
Municipalities Act (1955), **29**, 140-1
National Divisions and the Duties of Province Governors and District Governors, Law on (1937), **5**, 3
nationality, **2**, 167, 168, 174, 218, 224; **5**, 272, 334; **9**, 354; **24**, 44
Nationalization of Insurance Corporations
—Law of (1979), **8**, 378, 417; **9**, 265 n. 17; **10**, 241

INDEX

—Paragraphs 1-2, **4**, 117, 120
Nationalization of the Iranian Oil Industry Act (1951), **3**, 309; **15**, 228, 233
Organization of Guilds Act (1971), **13**, 76 n. 26
Organizing the Distribution of Public Necessity Goods and Punishment of Hoarders and Overchargers Act and Executive Regulation (1973), **13**, 76 n. 26
Pahlavi Properties, Decree of Imam Concerning Confiscation of (1979), **4**, 168
partnership, **21**, 105 n. 21
Penal Code, **12**, 218; **13**, 76; **22**, 325
Petroleum Law (1974), **27**, 96 n. 11
Ports and Shipping Organization, Act on Permission to Establish (1960), **5**, 3
Ports and Shipping Organization, Regulation of (1970), Article 3, **6**, 195 n. 1
Prevention of Hoarding Act (1942), **13**, 76 n. 26
Protection and Development of Iranian Industries Act (1979), **2**, 152 n. 1, 302, 349, 350; **6**, 241; **7**, 50 n. 2; **9**, 273-4; **21**, 114; **24**, 206, 215-17; **29**, 140-1
—Article 1(a), **2**, 302 n. 2; **9**, 273
—Article 1(b), **9**, 273
—Article 1(c), **2**, 350; **5**, 244; **6**, 55, 58; **9**, 265, 273-4; **10**, 205-6
—Article 1(d), **9**, 274
—Article 2, **6**, 58
—Article 3, **6**, 58
—Article 15, **6**, 224
Protection of Industries and Prevention of the Closure of the Country's Factories (1964) (also referred to as Protection of Industry and Prevention of Shutdowns at the Nation's Factories, 1964), **4**, 154; **7**, 164; **10**, 129-30, 144-6
—Article 2, **10**, 130
—Article 7, **10**, 130
—Article 10, **10**, 130
Protection of Iranian Small Shareholders in Nationalized Banks and Credit Institutions (1980), **28**, 259-64
Provision of Capital for the Continuation of the Activities of Nationalized Banks and Credit Institutions (1980), Legal Bill concerning, **28**, 259
Public Accounting Law, Articles 71-9, **9**, 103 n. 8
Punishment of Merchants and Sellers Hoarding or Overcharging Act (1943), **13**, 76 n. 26
Punishment of Violators of the Organization of Guilds Act (1973), **13**, 76 n. 26
Purging the Ministries and State Institutions, Legal Bill on (1979), **30**, 42, 48, 65-6
Reconstruction of Ministries, State Agencies and Government-affiliated Institutions (1981), **30**, 42 nn. 9, 10
Registration of Deeds and Realty Act, **9**, 237-41; **29**, 131, 136, 170-1
—Article 34, **9**, 237-8, 240, 241, 245 n. 5
Registration of Property Act, Article 22, **7**, 164
Retirement and Pension Law, **30**, 48, 61
retroactivity, **22**, 20
Single Article Act (1980), **1**, 489, 495, 496; **3**, 61, 201, 303-6, 308, 309, 313, 314, 323, 324; **4**, 8; **5**, 298, 333, 334; **13**, 168, 170; **15**, 224, 228-9, 230-1, 233-4, 261, 290, 292-3; **16**, 17, 25, 43-4, 62 n. 4; **21**, 105, 114
Social Insurance Act (1960), **24**, 192, 193 n. 42
—Article 28, **17**, 261
—Article 38, **4**, 227; **10**, 313, 315
Social Security Act (1975), **24**, 192 n. 40
Social Security Law (1976), **23**, 39, 40-1; **24**, 192
Social Security Law (1978), **22**, 20-1
Social Security Organization, Law for the Formation of (1979), Article 7, **3**, 103-4
State Employment Law (1967), Article 1, **5**, 4
Statute of Limitations, **3**, 287; **5**, 128; **7**, 116; **8**, 136; **17**, 189, 216; **19**, 329-30, 340-1; **30**, 157
stay of proceedings, **3**, 388; **4**, 12, 15
Stock Companies Act, Article 40, **17**, 327-8
Tax Law, Article 85, **18**, 15
taxation, **3**, 115
Temporary Director or Directors for the

INDEX

Iran, law of (*cont.*)
 Supervision of Manufacturing, Industrial, Commercial, Agricultural and Service Units Whether in the Public or the Private Sectors, Law for the Determination of the Limits of the Duties and Authority of (1980), **12**, 9
 Treaty of Amity as part of, **4**, 114
 unjust enrichment, **6**, 168 n. 2
 Unutilized Urban Lands, Law for the Abolition of Ownership of (1979), **19**, 60; **23**, 313
 violation of, **5**, 19, 21
 Wider Share Ownership, Law on, **10**, 242
 wife's property right in husband, **2**, 85-6
Iran-United States Claims Tribunal Reports, **6**, 108 n. 1

Joint and several liability, **5**, 220-2; **7**, 82
Judgment
 in absentia, **4**, 15
 quashed, **5**, 46
Judicial independence, **8**, 78
Judicial notice, **1**, 459, 460, 480, 481; **2**, 122 n. 1, 300; **5**, 244 n. 1; **24**, 14
 in international law, **1**, 481
Judicial proceeding
 de novo, **5**, 183
 final and binding, **5**, 183
Jurisdiction of Tribunal
 in absence of agreement on implementation of General Declaration, **12**, 63
 absence of objection, **13**, 263
 account stated, **23**, 137
 act of State, review, **19**, 286, 292
 action in response to seizure of US embassy, **28**, 230-1
 admissibility, **16**, 300-3; **18**, 86
  —distinguished, **16**, 306-9
 admission, effect, **1**, 266, 318; **2**, 302
 advisory opinions, **12**, 82
 alternative, **16**, 312-13
 applicable law, **9**, 330; **11**, 30, 142; **15**, 100; **26**, 226
 assets in domestic branches of US banks, **8**, 201-2, 205-6
 availability of local remedy, **2**, 10, 165, 320; **3**, 151; **4**, 102, 115 n. 2; **7**, 10
 claims arising out of seizure of hostages, **2**, 39-40, 79, 80, 88
 Claims Settlement Declaration as basis, **9**, 157; **10**, 62, 142, 281; **12**, 273, 275; **13**, 223-6; **15**, 196, 197, 215; **16**, 289; **19**, 11; **21**, 104: *see also* Claims Settlement Declaration, Article VII
 compliance with award, **23**, 208
 consent of States, **2**, 210, 213; **3**, 298, 303, 304; **5**, 287, 288; **7**, 200
 contested by claimant, **8**, 259-66
 continuous, **14**, 332-3
 contract, breach of, **23**, 137
 counterclaims: *see* Counterclaim, jurisdiction of Tribunal
 determined by Tribunal, **8**, 6, 265; **9**, 4; **12**, 66; **17**, 333, 336, 338, 342, 345, 348
 enforcement of another tribunal's awards, **6**, 131-3; **8**, 296; **11**, 195, 197; **18**, 118, 146
 equitable discretion, **12**, 186-7, 196; **28**, 14-16
 ex aequo et bono, **12**, 82
 ex officio determination, **5**, 99
 exceeded, **13**, 145-7
 excluded issues, **6**, 227, 228
 exclusion of claims, **1**, 103, 237, 239-40, 489, 490, 495; **2**, 56-7, 62-4, 66-7, 88, 97-9, 110, 338; **3**, 60, 61, 99, 151, 198, 199, 201, 246, 260, 286, 313, 314, 321-5, 335, 348; **4**, 8, 12, 16, 55, 75, 101, 102, 142, 220, 221, 225, 230-2, 244-6; **5**, 1, 2, 15, 16, 47, 67, 96, 100, 101, 103, 116, 117, 119, 120, 126-30, 171, 182, 192-4, 196, 197, 268, 270, 388, 389; **6**, 231, 250, 255, 263, 270; **7**, 7, 33-5, 47, 124, 127, 131, 132, 135, 136, 153, 218; **8**, 224-5, 229-33, 264-6; **9**, 355; **10**, 179; **11**, 197, 201; **12**, 16, 35-6, 100-1, 142-3, 149-50, 263; **13**, 157, 160, 163, 182, 183; **16**, 17-18; **18**, 89, 91, 111, 290; **19**, 177, 180; **26**, 73-4: *see also* Claims, by Iranian banks against US banks; Forum selection clause
 —tortious character of act and, **16**, 79
 exclusive, **8**, 266; **11**, 47; **12**, 322; **13**, 306; **22**, 253
 existing contract, **22**, 115
 extension of, **5**, 13, 16
 generalized decision contrary to, **16**, 82
 IMF Agreement, alleged violation, **16**, 106
 immigration restrictions, **28**, 230-1
 insurance payment, relevance, **14**, 292

INDEX

interest, authority to award, **16**, 289-90
— inherent, **16**, 290
— uniform rules, desirability, **16**, 290
interim measures: *see* Interim measures
interpretation of Declarations, **1**, 101-10, 117, 189, 190, 509-18; **2**, 85-7; **5**, 113; **7**, 33; **9**, 253-7; **11**, 274; **12**, 43-5, 65-70, 83; **13**, 78; **16**, 289; **18**, 12
— Co-Registrars and, **3**, 8-9, 21; **17**, 332, 335, 338, 341, 344, 348; **19**, 177, 180, 183, 186, 189, 192, 195, 198
— exclusive jurisdiction, **7**, 275, 276
— Undertakings as aid, **12**, 51
interpretation of Undertakings, **8**, 206-13; **9**, 104-6; **12**, 74 n. 15
Iranian nationality of respondent, relevance, **9**, 40
liquidation proceedings not a bar, **14**, 158
matters of Iranian domestic law, **30**, 42-3, 62, 63
mediation not authorized, **12**, 82
military articles, whether covered, **19**, 290
municipal law, **8**, 258-9, 280
nationality, determination, **22**, 161
over non-government party, **5**, 66, 67; **12**, 35-6
over partnership, **9**, 292; **10**, 43
over United States nationals, **23**, 383
parity between governments, **5**, 15-17
parties' power to amend, **8**, 212-13, 297
performance guarantees, **9**, 222
political claims, **2**, 42-3
primacy, **2**, 58-9
procedural discretion, **16**, 314
proprio motu consideration, **3**, 298; **9**, 333; **14**, 61; **25**, 17; **28**, 314 n. 3
ratione materiae, **21**, 68; **26**, 126, 145
ratione personae, **21**, 67, 68; **26**, 126, 130
restricted, **5**, 6, 13, 70; **8**, 3 n. 2, 231; **9**, 378; **10**, 139; **11**, 47, 281, 349; **13**, 168-9; **22**, 296-7
settlement: *see* Settlement
Social Security payments: *see* Social Security payments
State responsibility: *see* State responsibility
taxes: *see* Taxes
threat to from parallel proceedings, **29**, 218-20
tortious acts, **23**, 237, 240 n. 2
unjust enrichment, **23**, 137

Laches, **9**, 176
Lease, **2**, 251, 254: *see also* Contract; Contract, discharge
frustration, **2**, 250-3, 256, 258
— attributability, **2**, 251, 253, 256, 258
— foreseeability, **2**, 251, 253
Lease agreements, **1**, 411-15; **2**, 250-9
Legal presumption, **6**, 72
Lender, liability, **5**, 245 n. 1
Letters of credit, **1**, 507; **5**, 28, 29, 31, 38-40, 58, 67, 68; **6**, 288; **9**, 298-9; **13**, 111-12; **17**, 31 n. 1: *see also* Claims, based on standby letters of credit *and* Jurisdiction of Tribunal
creation of special account, **2**, 127
Letters of guarantee, **5**, 96
Licence: *see also* Contract
anticipatory breach, **2**, 340, 341
breach, **2**, 340, 341
ratification, **2**, 339
termination, **2**, 341
validity, **2**, 339, 340
Limitation of liability clause, **6**, 89, 90, 94, 95-100
enforceability, **6**, 98
exceptions to, **6**, 97, 99, 100
validity, **6**, 97, 99
Liquidation: *see* Bankruptcy
Luxembourg Declaration, **13**, 91-2

Majlis position: *see* Iran, Majlis' position
Margin of appreciation, **16**, 222
Marital rights, **30**, 49-57
applicable law, **30**, 49-56
as property rights, **30**, 68-9
Materials guarantee, **17**, 316
Measures affecting property rights: *see* Expropriation; Property rights, measures affecting
Military property, **4**, 28
Minors
as claimants, **30**, 79-80, 185-6
nationality, **28**, 242; **29**, 12-13, 16-19
Misrepresentation, **5**, 247
Most favoured nation treatment (MFN), **17**, 143
Municipal institutions, respect for, **7**, 171
Municipal law, **1**, 108, 421, 422, 451, 464-6, 480, 481; **5**, 16, 19-21, 269, 270, 286, 292, 294, 302; **7**, 124, 160; **8**, 8-10, 258-9, 281-2; **14**, 331

INDEX

Municipal law *(cont.)*
  analogy to, **1**, 362, 374, 432
  effect of bribery on contract in, **12**, 270 n. 18
  incorporation of Treaty provisions in, **12**, 144-5; **15**, 219-20
  non-compliance with international obligations and, **13**, 177; **29**, 43
  obligations under, Tribunal and, **8**, 281-2; **16**, 302-3
Mutuality of commitments by Iran and US, **5**, 16
Mutually agreeable arbitration principle, **5**, 49

Naples Declaration, **13**, 92
Nationality: *see also* Naturalization
  applicable law: *see* Applicable law, nationality
  Barcelona Traction, **1**, 466-7
  corporations, **1**, 135-9, 223, 224, 384, 385, 392-402, 412, 417, 418, 455-82, 503; **2**, 9, 16; **3**, 46, 47, 63, 103, 113, 161, 202, 205 n. 2, 230, 245, 260, 272, 273; **4**, 100, 273; **5**, 2, 18, 23, 237, 342-4; **6**, 57, 80, 93; **7**, 20, 27-9, 124, 127-30, 185; **8**, 156, 220-1 n. 4, 234, 307; **9**, 194, 252-4, 258-64, 291-2, 366-7; **10**, 166; **11**, 83-4; **12**, 251; **13**, 17-18; **14**, 226-8; **16**, 15-16, 104, 259-60; **17**, 20, 21, 33, 143, 156, 248, 255, 296, 297, 304; **18**, 102, 189, 227; **20**, 6; **25**, 25-8; **29**, 225-7, 315-16: *see also* Evidence of, nationality of corporation
  Certain Norwegian Loans, **1**, 457-8
  critical date, **28**, 239-40, 253-4; **30**, 27-34
  date of acquisition, **25**, 59, 176, 202
  determination of as preliminary matter, **18**, 70, 80-3; **25**, 271
  diplomatic protection and, **12**, 284-6; **18**, 261 n. 20; **22**, 136; **23**, 289
  domicile, **22**, 143, 147
  dual nationality, **2**, 160-8, 173-5, 178-225; **5**, 251-336; **9**, 354, 356; **13**, 300; **18**, 70-1, 260-2; **24**, 42-6; **25**, 157; **26**, 7-14
  —A18 caveat, **29**, 33-41, 56-8, 63-4, 65-6, 75-7, 382; **30**, 66-8, 73-4, 87-8, 98-100, 193-6: *see also* fraudulent use *below*
  —citizenship, **5**, 267, 269, 270, 283, 285
  —dominant and effective, **2**, 161-5, 168, 173, 174, 178-82, 185-91, 195, 198, 199, 201-5, 208, 211, 212, 214, 223-5; **5**, 260, 262-6, 273-5, 283, 290, 291, 299, 304, 305, 310, 311, 315-17, 321-6, 331-3, 335; **14**, 7-8; **18**, 96; **19**, 51-61, 118; **21**, 23-4; **22**, 120-2, 125-6, 127-8, 132-4, 135-7, 142-5, 158-60, 163-8, 197-9, 200-3; **23**, 261-3, 271-3, 282-4, 285-9, 308-14, 315-17; **24**, 44-5, 218; **25**, 158-71, 182-5, 190-211, 264-72, 278-88, 289-97; **26**, 7 n. 1, 9-14, 41-3, 45-59; **28**, 185-91, 238-45; **29**, 3-41, 63-5, 72-5; **30**, 73-5, 274-80
  —equality of States and, **26**, 7 n. 1; **29**, 14, 65, 383 n. 1
  —fraudulent use, **2**, 166, 167, 225; **5**, 272; **22**, 136; **30**, 88, 98-100, 194-6: *see also* A18 caveat *above*
  —link theory, **5**, 263
  —*Mergé*, **25**, 163, 200, 206
  —pension rights, **30**, 66-8
  —rights under Treaty of Amity, **30**, 256
  Flegenheimer, **25**, 165-6
  jus sanguinis, **2**, 181, 184, 185; **5**, 274, 305; **22**, 120, 125, 131-2, 143, 158
  jus soli, **2**, 181, 184; **5**, 274, 305; **22**, 131, 143, 158
  loss of, **22**, 149; **25**, 170-1
  marriage, **14**, 56-7; **22**, 146, 150, 197; **24**, 44; **29**, 10
  minor, **28**, 242; **29**, 12-13, 16-19
  natural persons, **1**, 168, 479, 480; **2**, 16, 17, 226, 227; **3**, 286; **5**, 92, 279, 282, 292; **6**, 57; **7**, 5; **19**, 324; **21**, 25-6
  —uncertainty over, **9**, 3-5
  non-responsibility principle, **2**, 162-4, 178, 180, 181, 184, 187-91, 194-204, 207, 208, 212, 214, 215, 223; **5**, 265, 266, 290, 291, 304, 305, 309 n. 1, 310, 311, 315-17, 321, 323, 324, 326-8, 331, 333; **7**, 171
  Nottebohm, **25**, 166, 206
  partnership, **6**, 221; **10**, 43-4
  recognition, **5**, 260, 334
  religion, **22**, 165
  return of passport, effect, **18**, 237, 261
Nationality of claim, **1**, 384, 385, 392-402; **2**, 105, 297-300, 378; **3**, 39, 245, 246, 272; **4**, 101, 142, 217, 218; **5**, 209, 365; **6**, 80, 285; **7**, 97, 185, 206, 207; **9**, 255-6,

INDEX 355

366-7; **10**, 126; **12**, 259, 272-84; **16**,
239; **19**, 118: *see also* Corporations;
Evidence of, nationality of claim
beneficial ownership, **7**, 29; **11**, 85-9; **29**,
27-8, 242-6
continuity of nationality, **11**, 84
continuity of ownership, **2**, 227, 234, 235;
4, 101; **5**, 92, 93, 377; **8**, 262, 293-4; **9**,
38, 264-6; **10**, 126-7, 140-1, 239, 325,
342; **11**, 55, 188-9, 220; **12**, 100, 257-
61, 313-14; **13**, 18, 180, 202; **14**, 228-
30, 243-4; **15**, 196; **16**, 259-60, 302; **17**,
115, 255; **18**, 95, 96, 158, 166; **19**, 68;
22, 132; **25**, 28; **27**, 216-17, 254
corporations, **1**, 135-9, 455-82; **2**, 9, 10,
16; **3**, 205; **4**, 100, 101, 141, 142, 181,
216-18; **5**, 21, 163, 210, 237, 341, 342,
348, 353, 364, 365, 388; **7**, 5, 6, 9, 41,
66, 97, 122, 123, 127, 129, 134, 185,
206, 207; **8**, 156; **9**, 194, 252-4, 366-7;
10, 126; **13**, 101; **17**, 105, 272, 301,
353, 395, 396; **19**, 75-6, 117-18, 202-3;
22, 174-5; **26**, 152-3
determination as prerequisite for Award,
5, 126
shareholder claims, **2**, 297-300, 377, 378
transfer of claim to non-US nationals, **11**,
138
Nationalization: *see* Expropriation
Natural resources, **24**, 97-9
Naturalization, **2**, 192-4, 203; **9**, 353-5, 356;
26, 41, 49, 50, 51, 56: *see also*
Nationality
Negligence, **3**, 30; **5**, 398; **6**, 100; **7**, 43
Negotiable instruments, **1**, 185-8, 445-7; **5**,
373; **7**, 115; **13**, 21-7: *see also* Cheque
applicable law, **21**, 44-5, 63-4
cause of action, **21**, 44-5, 62, 63-7
common law and, **21**, 44
as contract, **21**, 77
evidence of debt, **21**, 49
guarantor, **5**, 373
loans, **21**, 50, 65-6
validity, **21**, 51-2, 66-7
Negotiated settlement: *see* Settlement
Netherlands, law of
application to Tribunal, **8**, 335 n. 8
arbitration, **20**, 207, 210, 217, 250, 274
Code of Civil Procedure
—Article 642, **1**, 331, 406
—Article 649, **5**, 128

—Articles 1029-76, **20**, 207
—Article 1033, **20**, 210, 217, 274
enforcement of arbitral award, **1**, 331, 406
Nominalism, **8**, 421, 426
Non-responsibility principle: *see under*
Nationality
November Resolution: *see* Iran, Majlis'
position
Nullification of claims: *see* Settlement
Nullified oil agreements, jurisdiction of
Tribunal, **1**, 487-98; **2**, 284-7; **3**,
298-301, 303-5, 309, 313-15; **5**, 51-3:
see also Iran, law of, Single Article Act

Odious debt, **8**, 446-7
Offset: *see* Counterclaims, offset and;
Damages, deduction for
Order—
by President, distinguished, **3**, 316
disregard, **4**, 13-16, 73
of exequatur, **6**, 133, 135, 138, 139
reasons not normally given, **14**, 21-2
validity, **2**, 346
Outstanding claims: *see* Claims, outstanding

Partnership, **3**, 161, 208; **9**, 327-33; **21**,
102-5
right of partner to bring suit, **9**, 332; **16**,
13, 15; **21**, 102-5
Passports
nationality and
—evidence of, **18**, 237, 260-2, 273 n. 46;
23, 135
—return of passport, effect, **18**, 237, 261
Patent rights, **2**, 339, 341: *see also* Licence
Pension rights
applicable law, **30**, 42-3, 63
dual nationality, relevance, **30**, 66-8
expropriation, **30**, 41-3, 46-9, 59-66
Performance guarantee, **2**, 241-5; **3**, 267; **7**,
42, 53, 121; **8**, 327-8; **9**, 22, 26, 29, 35;
12, 151-3; **23**, 363-6: *see also* Damages,
performance withhold; Materials
guarantee
cancellation, **8**, 322; **9**, 130-1, 164-5,
220-2, 242-3, 299; **12**, 106-7; **14**, 46-7,
125; **17**, 31 n. 1, 79-80, 316; **22**, 57-8,
84-5, 256, 335-6; **23**, 211-12, 217
counterclaim for, **24**, 275; **26**, 81
demand for payment, **19**, 212-13, 239-40;
25, 53, 62-7, 98, 100-1, 126-9

Performance guarantee (*cont.*)
  purpose, **22**, 57-8
  reduction, **28**, 45-6, 50
Permanent Court of International Justice
  (PCIJ), **1**, 210, 212, 213, 312, 329 n. 1,
  402, 405 n. 1; **2**, 210, 354; **3**, 20, 21, 32
  n. 1, 298 n. 1, 302 n. 4, 305 n. 1, 308 n.
  2, 310 n. 1, 313 n. 1, 314 n. 1, 315 n. 3;
  4, 115, 118, 163; **5**, 261, 287, 292-5,
  316, 342, 346 n. 1, 351; **6**, 126, 163,
  166 n. 3; **7**, 135 n. 2, 152 n. 4; **8**, 207 n.
  8, 208 n. 9, 211 n. 19, 213, 278 n. 54,
  449; **10**, 197; **11**, 27 n. 14; **14**, 234,
  321-2; **15**, 222, 246-7, 300-4; **18**, 217,
  223, 262 n. 22, 264 n. 27, 385-6; **21**,
  155 n. 46, 198; **22**, 288 n. 34, 296 n. 43,
  297 nn. 46, 47, 48
  Certain German Interests in Upper Silesia, **2**,
    147
  Mavrommatis Palestine Concessions, **2**, 149
  Revised Rules (1936), Article 69, **1**, 233
  stay of proceedings, **2**, 61
Political acts, as proximate cause, **2**, 253,
  254, 256-8
Post-hearing submissions: *see* Procedure,
  post-hearing submissions
Postponement of hearing, **2**, 124-5; **3**, 209-
  11, 316-18, 362, 375, 377, 378; **8**, 30,
  284-9; **11**, 227, 289-91
Power of attorney: *see* Representation
Precedent, **1**, 287; **2**, 185, 186, 189, 191,
  301; **9**, 169, 216; **12**, 233 n. 5; **16**, 82;
  18, 271-2, 349; **22**, 216-17, 289 n. 40;
  23, 130; **27**, 263
Preclusion, **21**, 155 n. 46, 198
  general principle of law, **21**, 154-5
Prescription, **1**, 132; **17**, 189-90, 216, 218,
  231-2
Presidential direction, **9**, 409-13
Presidential Order
  No. 1, **1**, 321, 398; **3**, 365; **7**, 205; **16**, 251,
    286-90; **21**, 312
  No. 8, **21**, 100
  No. 9, **3**, 141
  No. 10, **3**, 126, 141
  No. 12, **3**, 175
  No. 17, **5**, 112
  No. 19, **21**, 221
  No. 21, **20**, 221
  No. 27, **8**, 64
  No. 28, **8**, 64

  No. 29, **7**, 226, 236, 240, 245, 248, 250; **8**,
    64
  No. 33, **7**, 259, 262, 269; **8**, 2, 14, 16
  No. 36, **7**, 262
  No. 49, **12**, 389
  No. 50, **12**, 389
  No. 51, **14**, 174, 341, 353
  No. 52, **16**, 287
  No. 53, **14**, 354
Principles of law: *see* General principles of,
  law
Pro forma invoice: *see* Contract, pro forma
  invoice
Procedure: *see also* Time Limits; Tribunal
  Rules
  abuse, **3**, 380; **16**, 329-34
  acceleration of proceedings, **3**, 7
  agent, role, **21**, 370-1, 376, 392
  alteration of captions, **11**, 165; **18**, 279
  applicable law, **8**, 161; **30**, 55
  arbitrator, challenge to, **20**, 184, 188
  case resolution techniques, **2**, 301, 302; **3**,
    77; **5**, 298
  consolidation of cases, **2**, 379, 396; **3**, 99,
    105, 112, 213; **4**, 239-41; **12**, 99, 109,
    132, 345, 366-7; **13**, 335-6; **16**, 261-2;
    18, 58; **21**, 5; **26**, 147; **27**, 296-310
  —time limits, **4**, 241
  consolidation of issues, **3**, 154, 155; **17**,
    97-8
  date of receipt of documents, **8**, 53-4; **21**,
    361-3, 376, 379, 391
  delays, **3**, 40, 41, 55, 77, 87-9, 129, 296,
    317, 318, 376, 383; **4**, 3, 4, 46, 71, 72,
    81; **5**, 140-3, 146; **7**, 203, 204; **8**, 30-40,
    134, 284-9; **9**, 167; **10**, 15, 210; **17**, 56,
    189-91, 202, 219
  dissipation of judicial resources, **10**, 227
  duplicate proceedings, need to avoid, **8**,
    363, 365, 367, 372
  duty to abide by commitments, **8**, 29-30
  equality of parties, **9**, 172; **17**, 49; **18**, 187,
    283, 325; **20**, 6; **21**, 16; **28**, 6; **29**, 377-
    8; **30**, 121-2
  error in description of party, **9**, 50
  ex parte motion, **3**, 387
  excessive formality, **8**, 139
  failure to appear, **8**, 40; **27**, 222
  failure to provide translation, **10**, 272
  fairness to parties, **2**, 9, 123, 284, 288,
    289, 346, 356; **3**, 23, 31, 85, 88, 89,

129, 130, 257, 281, 296, 298, 301, 302, 362, 365, 374-6, 383, 388, 389; **4**, 58, 64, 65, 67, 70-2, 93-5, 214, 241, 242, 261, 279; **5**, 140; **7**, 70, 119, 120, 126, 137, 204; **9**, 322, 342, 344; **10**, 4, 5, 108, 128, 210, 324, 341; **12**, 6, 131, 225, 228, 345; **13**, 16, 101, 189, 228, 298, 317; **14**, 155, 226; **16**, 222, 258, 259; **17**, 45-52, 56-7, 59, 82, 139, 219, 296; **19**, 112-13, 238; **21**, 16; **24**, 131; **29**, 377-8

joinder of merits and—
— determination of date claim arose, **19**, 53
— interim measures, **18**, 130 n. 3
— jurisdictional issues, **29**, 10, 14, 56-7

joinder of parties, **3**, 161
joint filing of submissions, **3**, 373
judical notice, **10**, 106
late submissions, **9**, 343; **10**, 5, 128, 272-3, 324-5, 341; **12**, 324; **13**, 101, 131; **14**, 225-6, 291; **16**, 258; **17**, 45-52; **18**, 187-8, 207-8, 226-7, 231; **19**, 112-13, 238; **21**, 15-16, 101-2; **23**, 163-5, 353-5; **24**, 131; **25**, 113; **27**, 135; **29**, 29, 60, 376-8; **30**, 25-6: *see also* Evidence, late submission
— counterclaim, **17**, 57-61; **18**, 188; **24**, 131

minutes, **13**, 326 n. 4
need for—
— adversary process, **10**, 224-5
— simplification of proceedings, **10**, 219-22

notice, **1**, 232, 233, 418, 421
post-Award review, **8**, 116
post-Award submissions, **8**, 115
post-hearing submissions, 2, 9, 122, 123, 139, 345; **3**, 39, 40, 76, 87-90, 99, 116, 226, 257, 281, 302, 303, 365, 380-3; **5**, 139; **7**, 70, 74, 88; **9**, 300; **10**, 272-3; **15**, 271; **17**, 49; **28**, 324-5; **30**, 26

postponement of hearing: *see* Postponement of hearing
pre-hearing conference, **2**, 125, 327; **3**, 377, 378; **8**, 5, 133; **18**, 54-5
preliminary issues and merits, joinder, **10**, 15
— separation, **18**, 79-83
preliminary objection, **3**, 298
Procedural Guideline No. 1, **1**, 285

procedural safeguards, **1**, 215
proper party: *see* Proper claimant; Proper respondent
reliance on defence not included in Statement of Defence, **10**, 210
reliance on written record, **11**, 73
reopening of hearing, **30**, 104-22: *see also* Rehearing
reply and rejoinder, **3**, 98; **9**, 322
request for—
— further hearing, **9**, 300
— hearing, **3**, 387, 388; **25**, 276
— information, **18**, 45-7, 48-54
— production of documents, **12**, 345, 367; **13**, 17; **18**, 68-9
— rehearing, **27**, 210-13

request to—
— stay decisions, **13**, 16
— submit further statement, **3**, 362, 363
res judicata, **12**, 174, 367
stay of proceedings, **7**, 237; **9**, 254: *see also* Interim measures, stay of proceedings
submission of—
— evidence, **9**, 109-11
— Memorials, **5**, 144, 146, 147
surprise submissions, **3**, 31, 365, 381; **8**, 341
suspension of proceedings, **3**, 298; **18**, 72-3
technical imperfections, **14**, 99
third parties, absence, **28**, 326-7
translation, **19**, 169
validity, **2**, 345-7
violation of, **5**, 2, 335

Promissory notes: *see* Negotiable instruments
Proper claimant, **1**, 176, 177; **2**, 82-5, 105; **3**, 161, 246; **4**, 101, 143, 181, 210, 211; **5**, 70, 78, 79, 377; **6**, 265; **7**, 35, 120-4, 127, 129, 134-6, 171, 174, 199, 205-7; **8**, 21-2, 23; **9**, 378-9; **10**, 127; **13**, 96; **16**, 13, 15, 194, 226, 302; **17**, 5, 271; **18**, 166-7, 190-1, 209-11; **19**, 77-8; **21**, 102-6; **23**, 7-8, 142-6; **26**, 19, 130-2; **27**, 67-9, 136-7, 141: *see also* Words and phrases, *locus standi*
beneficial owner: *see* Claim, basis, beneficial ownership
claim on behalf of Iranian people, **28**, 228
existence of counterclaim, **9**, 87
joint claim, **16**, 13-14, 194

Proper claimant (cont.)
   minor, **30**, 79-80, 185-6
   percentage of share ownership, relevance, **27**, 58, 59
Proper law: *see* Applicable law
Proper respondent, **1**, 134, 219, 389, 412, 413, 418, 427, 484, 503; **2**, 24-6, 147 n. 1, 338; **3**, 53, 103, 230, 250, 275, 286, 351; **4**, 1, 75, 143; **5**, 138; **6**, 27-9, 70, 129, 174, 208 n. 1; **7**, 121, 124-6; **8**, 133-8; **9**, 244 n. 2, 323-6, 367; **10**, 242, 281; **11**, 55, 215, 247; **12**, 290; **13**, 35, 42-3, 97-8, 101, 121-2, 130, 326, 341; **14**, 26, 71, 197, 292; **15**, 197-8; **16**, 17-18, 78, 194; **17**, 5-6, 30, 52-3, 163-8, 255, 272; **18**, 230 n. 7; **19**, 77-118; **20**, 7-8; **22**, 10, 254; **23**, 362-3; **24**, 132; **27**, 156; **29**, 227-8: *see also* Controlled entity; Corporations, succession
Property rights: *see also* Iran, law of, immovable property
   beneficial ownership, **9**, 230-3; **29**, 25-8; **30**, 56-7, 66
   loans as, **27**, 28
   marital rights, **30**, 68-9
   measures affecting, **2**, 41-3, 79-80, 81-8, 207; **3**, 65, 66; **4**, 154-6, 162-5, 167-72; **6**, 260; **17**, 99-100, 139-40, 169, 174 n. 8; **23**, 369; **27**, 13, 18, 32, 61-2
   —immigration restrictions, **28**, 230-1
   —interference with contractual right, **22**, 79
   —obligation to protect, **23**, 369-71, 385-6
   —unlawful conduct, **2**, 42
   pension as, **30**, 63: *see also* pension rights
   in persons, **8**, 22, 23
   right in person, **2**, 79-80, 81-8
Proportionality, **22**, 78
Protection of goods, claimant's duty, **8**, 271
Protection of parties, **6**, 40, 41
   of claimants' own position, **9**, 5
Public order, **5**, 384; **17**, 143
Public order, protection, **7**, 165, 166, 169, 170
Purchase order as contract, **4**, 266, 267, 276; **7**, 108, 109, 113: *see also* Contract

Quantum meruit, **1**, 287, 309 n. 9; **2**, 111; **4**, 220, 221, 228, 230-6; **5**, 171; **6**, 169; **7**, 76; **8**, 162; **9**, 218, 402; **11**, 17-18; **16**, 272; **18**, 179, 348; **19**, 142, 148; **23**, 200; **26**, 201; **28**, 79-80
   contract distinguished, **4**, 232, 234; **8**, 224, 234
Quasi-contract, **3**, 278; **4**, 231, 235

Real property: *see* Immovable property transactions
Rebus sic stantibus: *see* Changed circumstances
Regular course of dealing, **7**, 113
Rehearing, **3**, 364, 365; **5**, 74: *see also* Award, reconsideration; Procedure, reopening of hearing
Representation, **1**, 176, 177
   power of attorney, **1**, 167-388
   —whether needed, **9**, 15
   proof of authority, **2**, 30, 35-7
Representative case, **2**, 285, 286, 301; **3**, 300
Request, meaning, **3**, 175, 388, 389; **4**, 15 n. 1
Respondent: *see* Proper respondent
Restitution, **1**, 287, 309 n. 9, 422, 423; **2**, 236; **3**, 57 n. 2, 293; **4**, 231; **5**, 112; **6**, 294, 295; **9**, 402; **10**, 204-5; **12**, 138, 379; **21**, 198
Rial Account, **8**, 188, 350
Rights of parties, **3**, 300-3, 387; **4**, 115
   argument to Tribunal, **3**, 19, 28, 29, 299-303, 315; **4**, 242
   defence, right of, **2**, 3, 288, 327, 330; **3**, 87, 127, 128, 130, 315; **4**, 70, 71, 241; **7**, 124-6
   prejudice to, **6**, 70
Roman law, **6**, 168
Rules of international law: *see* General principles of, international law
Rules of procedure: *see* Tribunal Rules

Sales contract, **5**, 38, 40
Security Account, **12**, 50, 54-5; **13**, 118, 119-20, 276, 345, 360, 361; **22**, 336, 356
   abuse of, **4**, 207, 208; **13**, 116-17
   currency of, **8**, 425-6; **11**, 32, 340; **16**, 274, 275-6
   disposition of interest, **1**, 189-92, 197-214
   effect on—
      —costs, **8**, 334 n. 7
      —liability, **9**, 367; **17**, 178-80
      —rate of interest, **8**, 321, 343-4

INDEX

indemnification of depositary, **1**, 196, 197; **8**, 279 n. 56
nature of, **12**, 285
payment of bank fees, **1**, 192-6
payments from, **3**, 128, 195, 196; **5**, 49; **8**, 14, 16, 43, 62, 98, 178, 188, 237, 327, 354, 361; **9**, 8, 45, 60, 63, 71, 137, 168, 186, 200, 243, 301, 307, 309, 312, 339, 348, 358, 377; **10**, 55, 81, 134, 175, 257, 258, 317-18, 328, 347, 358, 359, 361; **11**, 30, 34-5, 69, 137, 179, 207, 250, 267, 344, 365; **12**, 16, 17, 38, 72, 107, 138, 159, 169, 231, 232, 233, 298, 323, 389, 392; **13**, 36, 37, 38, 39, 40, 41, 44, 145, 191, 310; **14**, 16, 52, 81, 168, 169, 170, 184, 212, 243, 283, 342; **15**, 22, 186, 187; **16**, 235, 236, 274, 276, 319, 320; **17**, 19, 22, 113, 130, 288, 324, 355, 358, 363; **18**, 148, 174, 244, 278, 322, 373, 374; **19**, 72, 93, 161, 231, 255, 331, 346, 347, 353, 355, 362, 367, 368; **20**, 129; **21**, 61, 161, 287, 289; **22**, 85, 116, 256; **23**, 74-8, 148, 149, 216, 377; **24**, 84, 85, 115, 156; **25**, 110, 111, 151; **26**, 5, 31, 127, 128, 184; **27**, 23, 120, 121, 186; **28**, 50, 111, 369, 370, 391, 393, 401; **29**, 56, 240-1, 293, 349, 397, 404, 413; **30**, 295
—basis for, **17**, 173
—deduction from, **14**, 16-17
—deemed to be by principal debtor, **7**, 115
—deferment, **13**, 242
—unauthorized items, **3**, 82, 358, 359; **4**, 208
possible dissipation, **10**, 363
purpose, **17**, 167, 179; **18**, 147; **21**, 51; **25**, 144
repayment to, **7**, 210, 211, 214; **9**, 9
Separate opinion: *see also* Concurring and dissenting opinion; Concurring opinion; Declaration; Dissenting opinion; Explanatory remarks; Separate statement; Supplementary opinion
Aghahosseini, **28**, 303; **29**, 122
Aldrich, **1**, 200; **21**, 61; **26**, 58; **28**, 142
Allison, **28**, 142; **30**, 160, 236
Ameli, **16**, 330; **29**, 241
Ansari, **6**, 66; **8**, 65; **11**, 45, 165, 277; **13**, 244; **14**, 332; **17**, 23, 130, 290, 325; **19**, 243; **20**, 151; **22**, 109; **25**, 162

Bahrami, **8**, 65; **11**, 277; **14**, 334
Böckstiegel, **16**, 329, 333
Brower, **8**, 29; **10**, 189; **11**, 289; **13**, 240
Holtzmann, **1**, 200; **5**, 82, 101, 138; **6**, 175; **8**, 329, 391; **9**, 138-52, 200-2; **13**, 319; **14**, 82, 149 n. 2; **16**, 329; **17**, 87; **23**, 338; **24**, 156, 227, 248, 259; **25**, 201; **29**, 16; **30**, 163
Kashani, **1**, 115, 203, 329, 404; **4**, 67
Khalilian, **18**, 278; **19**, 310; **22**, 109; **23**, 389
Lagergren, **8**, 385
Mosk, **1**, 132, 200; **6**, 95
Mostafavi, **8**, 65; **11**, 255, 277, 283 n. 1, 298; **12**, 80; **14**, 81, 334
Noori, **22**, 109; **23**, 239
Sani, **1**, 452
Shafeiei, **1**, 115, 203; **2**, 356; **5**, 175; **6**, 288
Separate statement: *see also* Concurring and dissenting opinion; Concurring opinion; Declaration; Dissenting opinion; Explanatory remarks; Separate opinion; Supplementary opinion
Aldrich, **21**, 256
Böckstiegel, **26**, 5
Briner, **21**, 240
Holtzmann, **22**, 218 n. 2; **26**, 5; **29**, 221, 383 n. 2
Khalilian, **21**, 194, 245, 263
Noori, **28**, 189, 243; **29**, 14, 65, 383 n. 1
Separation of issues, **2**, 146, 285, 287; **3**, 297-301; **4**, 82; **5**, 54, 377
Services, meaning, **5**, 101, 102
Settlement, **1**, 123-6, 140-3, 156, 157, 160-5, 181-4, 216, 217, 220-1, 327-33, 342-6, 403-10; **2**, 44-50, 90-5, 126-31, 132-7, 228-31, 261-7, 269-77, 278-80, 291-3, 305-9, 332, 333, 348-61, 364, 365, 366, 367; **3**, 34-5, 36-8, 73-5, 91-6, 119-23, 169-72, 176-80, 181-5, 186-97, 212-17, 218-24, 326-30, 338-48, 351-7, 366-71, 390-4; **4**, 20-5, 29-32, 33-8, 39-46, 47-52, 83-8, 183-91, 192-6, 197-8, 199-204, 205-9, 280-5; **5**, 76-7, 80-4, 88-9, 148-9, 150-1, 155-9, 249-50, 354-6; **6**, 1-3, 4-11, 20-6, 33-7, 38-42, 118-19, 120-4, 147-8; **7**, 209-16, 220-2, 223-4, 225-35, 236-8, 239-43, 244-6, 247-8, 249-57, 258-9, 260-8, 269-74; **8**, 11-12, 13-14, 18-19, 42-3, 66-71, 72-4,

Settlement (*cont.*)
  79-80, 81-2, 83-4, 97-8, 183-8, 236-7, 249-352, 353-9; **9**, 6-9, 306-7, 308-9, 310-12, 347-9, 357-9; **10**, 357-65; **11**, 363-72; **12**, 385-404; **13**, 359-70; **14**, 339-49; **16**, 54-5, 317-35; **17**, 353-68; **18**, 377-82, 390; **19**, 345-74; **21**, 285-93; **22**, 365-79; **23**, 401-13; **24**, 291-305; **25**, 4-5, 301-39; **26**, 265-75; **27**, 275-81, 282-8; **28**, 389-91, 392-3, 394-400, 401-2; **29**, 395-400, 401-10, 411-19
  absence of financial obligations noted, **8**, 82
  agreement not to pursue claims, **6**, 36; **8**, 67
  amendment, **7**, 238; **8**, 214-15; **9**, 348; **12**, 388
  applicable law, **7**, 268
  approval of Iranian bank, **3**, 193, 194, 213, 220, 359, 360; **4**, 34
  assignment of rights, **6**, 6; **12**, 394
  authority of representative, **6**, 39-41; **7**, 221; **12**, 395; **28**, 67-70
  availability, **3**, 79
  binding nature, **6**, 22
  concurring opinion, **2**, 357, 358; **3**, 78, 358; **10**, 363-5
  conditional agreement, **7**, 213, 214, 237, 240-2, 263, 267
  conditional award, **3**, 340, 352, 358
  conditions for recording, **1**, 149-53; **3**, 78, 82, 192-4, 358
    —jurisdiction, **1**, 152
    —reasonableness, **1**, 152, 153
  confidentiality of
    —negotiations, **2**, 356
    —terms, **3**, 37, 74, 79, 80, 83, 169, 212, 339; **4**, 207, 209; **5**, 81, 82, 84, 88; **6**, 25, 34, 35; **7**, 210, 211, 222, 237; **8**, 185; **10**, 128, 358, 359; **12**, 388
  correction, request for, **22**, 151-4
  costs, waiver, **18**, 381
  currency of payment, **24**, 187-90
  default, **7**, 211
  delays in payment of award, **3**, 196
  dissent to, **3**, 37, 38, 74, 78, 177, 182, 187, 192, 194, 327, 330, 352, 360; **4**, 22, 34, 84, 198, 200, 206; **5**, 77, 82, 355; **6**, 3, 21, 121; **16**, 327; **22**, 370 n. 1
  documents, conformity, **16**, 327

effect on contract, **10**, 13-14, 17-19; **25**, 227
enforcement, **1**, 330, 331, 406, 407; **3**, 37, 38, 74, 177, 182, 187, 194, 195, 327, 330, 353, 360; **4**, 22, 34, 41, 48, 84, 198, 200, 206; **5**, 77, 82, 355; **6**, 3, 21, 121; **10**, 18
  —Security Account, **17**, 167
escrow payment, **7**, 210
exception to, **7**, 220, 226-8, 230
extinction of claims, **8**, 264
failure to—
  —agree, **16**, 54-5; **29**, 465 n. 2
  —implement, **10**, 13-14; **16**, 328
form of award, **1**, 329, 330, 405
formation of agreement, **25**, 222-7
indemnity from costs and taxes, **12**, 392-3
interdependence of terms, **6**, 121
interpretation, **10**, 283; **16**, 328; **18**, 382
  — "upon execution", **8**, 105
invitation to negotiate, **7**, 177-9
joint request for award on agreed terms as basis, **19**, 366; **22**, 152
jurisdiction of Tribunal, **1**, 161; **5**, 83, 353
modified, **6**, 120; **7**, 261; **9**, 358
null and void, **7**, 210, 211, 213, 214
payment to Iranian bank, **3**, 192
performance, **7**, 213, 214
precedential value, **6**, 122, 124
prejudicial to one party, **6**, 40
ratification, **7**, 222, 240; **8**, 19, 185, 186
reach, **7**, 215; **8**, 105, 270-1, 282; **10**, 46-53, 282-3
  —damages for, **8**, 105-6
reasons omitted, **17**, 259
reciprocal obligations of parties, **3**, 75, 80, 177, 182, 194, 195, 327, 330, 353, 360; **4**, 22, 34, 84, 198, 200, 206; **5**, 77, 82, 355; **6**, 3, 21, 121; **7**, 220; **8**, 66, 97
release from liability, **8**, 214; **12**, 387, 388, 392, 393; **18**, 380-1
request for, need for agreement, **25**, 5
revocation, **7**, 214
separate opinion, **18**, 382-90; **21**, 293, 294
signature of parties, **4**, 22, 23, 39; **29**, 397
standards for acceptance by Tribunal, **3**, 78, 82, 358; **4**, 208
status, **5**, 353

suspension of—
  —contract rights, **8**, 105; **10**, 13-14
  —proceedings, **7**, 237; **18**, 380
terms of attempted settlement not admission, **14**, 77
third party claims, **6**, 24
waiver of claims, **8**, 81-2
withdrawal, **3**, 99
withdrawal of claims, **9**, 9; **14**, 343
without payment from Security Account, **7**, 236
without prejudice, **1**, 161; **5**, 159
Shareholder claims: *see* Corporations, shareholders; Nationality of claims, shareholder claims
Social security payments, **3**, 248, 249; **7**, 69; **9**, 132; **10**, 54, 78, 313-16; **13**, 340-3; **17**, 31 n. 1, 259-64; **20**, 28; **24**, 156-61, 190-6, 200-1, 287; **25**, 42-4; **28**, 48
  clearance certificate, **20**, 13-14, 15, 28, 85, 95-7, 99, 156-8; **24**, 144-8, 157-8, 159
  contractual obligation, whether, **9**, 167, 177, 225-6; **15**, 18, 93-4, 221-3; **24**, 157, 159; **26**, 181
  counterclaim for, **3**, 116, 167, 236; **4**, 246-8; **5**, 233, 234; **6**, 84, 85, 90, 91, 96, 174; **7**, 87; **8**, 326, 347-8; **9**, 135-6, 167, 177, 299-300; **10**, 313-16; **11**, 26, 39, 51-2, 67, 172, 184 n. 1, 204-5, 248-9, 317-19, 349-55; **12**, 157, 233 n. 5; **13**, 182-3, 307, 342-3; **14**, 79-80, 168, 281; **15**, 19-20, 91-4; **17**, 83, 262-3; **18**, 167, 197, 221-3, 297-8, 349-50; **20**, 35-6, 82, 118-19; **22**, 254, 337; **23**, 62, 215; **25**, 90, 94, 101; **26**, 83-4, 97-8, 99, 143-4, 180; **27**, 103-4, 119; **29**, 348
  effect of contract on, **6**, 91, 92; **12**, 157
  indemnity, request for, **23**, 213
  payment, evidence of, **20**, 14-15, 28, 161, 163
  withhold, liability for, **22**, 20; **26**, 77-80, 88, 94-7, 137-43
Sole jurisdiction: *see* Forum selection clause, jurisdiction of Tribunal
Sources of international law, **2**, 84, 196; **4**, 114; **5**, 233, 332; **8**, 397-401, 407-9: *see also* Customary international law; General principles of, international law; Treaties

international tribunals, **15**, 223; **17**, 142; **18**, 216
State practice, **15**, 223; **16**, 310-12; **17**, 142
UN General Assembly Resolutions and Declarations, **10**, 185-6, 198-200; **15**, 223
writings of scholars, **17**, 142; **18**, 216
Sovereign equality of States, **5**, 263, 266, 304, 311, 312, 327, 331
  dual nationality and, **26**, 7 n. 1; **29**, 14, 65, 383 n. 1
Sovereign immunity, **1**, 107, 207; **2**, 149, 212, 259; **4**, 115 n. 2; **5**, 6, 7, 10, 16, 117
  customary international law confirming US law, **28**, 133, 156, 158
  lien on property of foreign government and, **28**, 130, 154-8
  restrictive theory, **28**, 155-6
  waiver, **28**, 156-7
Sovereignty, **1**, 105, 106, 192, 210, 212, 213, 516; **2**, 183, 188, 205, 206, 210, 224, 353 n. 1; **3**, 298, 308 n. 2, 312-14; **5**, 11; **7**, 47, 135, 170; **8**, 340; **12**, 19, 22, 49, 287, 314, 315, 330, 337
Soviet Union, law of, **5**, 19
Speculative reasoning, **6**, 71
Stabilization clause, **9**, 178; **15**, 239-41, 243, 294, 297; **16**, 27, 64-8; **21**, 140-1, 162-3: *see also* State contracts
  whether binding on government, **15**, 240-1; **16**, 65-8
  —conditions, **16**, 66-7
State—
  government as synonym, **23**, 136-7
  "political subdivision", **23**, 384
State contracts: *see also* Stabilization clause
  applicable law, **16**, 27-8; **19**, 30-1; **22**, 287-9
  evidence of, **21**, 154
State organ, **9**, 238-9
State practice, **15**, 223; **16**, 310-12; **17**, 142
  arbitral award, enforcement, **18**, 124-7, 131-46
  expropriation, compensation, **15**, 266
State responsibility: *see also* Act of State; Aliens, treatment of; Expulsion; Public order, protection
  abusive practice, **2**, 188, 189; **6**, 210

State responsibility (*cont.*)
  acts and omissions of—
    —bank, **9**, 238-9
    —controlled entity, **1**, 421-2; **12**, 352, 364, 366; **15**, 237-9; **17**, 178-9; **21**, 67-73; **25**, 144; **27**, 96 n. 11
    —judiciary, **2**, 64
    —officials, **6**, 202, 203; **27**, 13-14
    —overthrown government, **16**, 84-5
    —revolutionary movement and, **2**, 88-9; **17**, 102-5; **23**, 361-2; **24**, 119, 152, 234-6
      ——individuals, **18**, 266-73
      ——organ not formally recognised, **17**, 103-5
      ——which becomes government, **16**, 84-5, 98-100; **17**, 101-3, 143-4, 147
  attribution, **3**, 153; **4**, 143, 165-7, 171, 173; **5**, 12; **6**, 79, 83-6, 94-5, 99-102, 166, 201, 203; **7**, 152, 173; **10**, 75; **17**, 100-5, 110-11, 141, 147, 256-7; **18**, 162, 178-9; **21**, 110-11, 112 n. 26; **23**, 387, 396; **26**, 108-9; **27**, 92
  due diligence, **2**, 78-9, 81, 84, 89
  duty to act, need for, **30**, 158-9
  for effect of acts, **6**, 207; **17**, 147; **23**, 387
  enforcement of contracts, **2**, 220, 221
  expropriation, **15**, 246-7; **16**, 43; **21**, 70-3
  expulsion, **17**, 100-7, 256-8
  ILC Draft Articles on, **9**, 238; **16**, 83, 99, 100, 141, 143, 147-8; **17**, 100-1, 111, 141, 143, 147-8; **20**, 205 n. 4; **21**, 112 n. 26; **23**, 386; **24**, 234
  international obligations, **8**, 8-9; **9**, 142 n. 7; **18**, 288
  lawful measures, **2**, 257, 258; **7**, 166, 169
  legal obligations of previous government, **21**, 111
  minimum standard, **23**, 386
  for nationals, **7**, 124
  non-discrimination, **23**, 387, 388
  omission, **30**, 168
  protection of—
    —aliens, **7**, 169; **17**, 111, 143
    —foreign investments, **7**, 151, 152, 159, 160
    —property, **23**, 385-6, 392-6
  reach of contract, **22**, 288 n. 34
  termination of contract, **17**, 148
  treaty obligations, **3**, 388; **6**, 111; **8**, 78
  unjust enrichment, **2**, 237; **8**, 390

visa acknowledgment, **23**, 382
State-controlled entity: *see* Controlled entity
Statement of claim, **1**, 134; **6**, 60, 62, 70; **8**, 136; **9**, 401; **10**, 12; **17**, 183 n. 3, 253-4; **19**, 53; **24**, 271; **28**, 193-4, 378-80
  amendment, **1**, 173, 174 n. 2, 176, 177, 392-402; **2**, 338; **3**, 11, 30, 31, 81, 82, 358, 359; **4**, 1, 101; **5**, 30, 377; **6**, 28, 29, 60, 63, 68; **8**, 126, 134-40, 297; **9**, 127; **10**, 12, 14-15, 16-17; **11**, 17; **12**, 6, 18-21, 131, 289-90, 346 n. 9; **13**, 17, 97-8; **14**, 26, 90-3, 94-9, 148, 310; **16**, 304, 312; **17**, 53-7, 138-9, 253-4; **18**, 64-5; **19**, 53; **23**, 165-7, 382, 397; **24**, 270-1; **26**, 150-1, 239; **28**, 58-60, 169, 377-9; **29**, 264-5
    —time limits: *see* Time limits, amendment of claim
  failure to include specific plea, **13**, 142, 148-50
  preparation, **4**, 26
  specificity, need for, **19**, 76-7
  time limits: *see* Time limits
  video tapes, **4**, 26
Statement of counterclaim, **7**, 88
Statement of defence, **1**, 166; **5**, 138, 139
  act of State, whether, **17**, 172
  amendment, **3**, 116
  clarification, **8**, 269 n. 41
  failure to file, **2**, 1-3; **3**, 374, 375
  preparation, **2**, 288
  summary nature, **3**, 378
  time limits: *see* Time limits, statement of defence
Stay of proceedings: *see* Interim measures, stay of proceedings; Procedure, stay of proceedings
Stock certificates, to be delivered, **10**, 253
Subcontractor, **3**, 273, 274, 278, 279; **5**, 166
Subjects of international law, individuals, right to bring claims, **18**, 283
Subrogation, **10**, 133
Succession: *see* Contract; Corporations
Summary enforcement procedures: *see* Arbitral award, basis for legal action
Supplemental opinion
  Allison, **29**, 364
  Arangio-Ruiz, **29**, 364
Sweden
  arbitration, **7**, 204
  law of, RB 13:5(2), Grade 139, **1**, 233

INDEX

Switzerland
law of—
—Code of Obligations, **7**, 191; **20**, 228; **21**, 75 n. 25, 103
—company law, **20**, 242
——resignation of director, **8**, 20, 230

Taking: *see* Expropriation
Taxes, **2**, 324; **7**, 69; **10**, 290-8; **13**, 304; **15**, 64; **16**, 274, 276, 280; **21**, 733-75; **24**, 200-1; **25**, 52, 53-4, 74, 87, 99; **29**, 284-93; **30**, 228-30: *see also* Customs dues; Social Security payments
  applicability, **3**, 115
  contract liability, **10**, 294-8; **11**, 94-6, 244-5; **18**, 221-3; **28**, 47-8
  contract tax, **3**, 114
  counterclaim for, **15**, 272-9; **23**, 62, 68, 69; **25**, 89-90
    —jurisdiction of Tribunal, **2**, 113; **3**, 115, 167, 236, 252, 288; **4**, 246-8; **5**, 233, 234; **6**, 84, 85, 90, 96; **9**, 37-8, 134, 167, 177, 225-6; **10**, 54, 102, 287, 306-13, 346; **11**, 26, 39, 51-2, 172, 245, 248, 317-19, 349-56; **12**, 157-8, 233 n. 5; **13**, 182, 192, 307, 343; **14**, 50-1, 168, 210; **15**, 279; **17**, 263, 319; **18**, 196-7, 221-3, 349-50; **19**, 154; **20**, 36-8, 119; **21**, 45-6, 150-2; **22**, 254, 337; **25**, 89-90, 94; **26**, 97-8, 99, 180-1; **27**, 103-4, 119; **28**, 48
    —taxes outstanding on expropriated property, **11**, 318
  deductibility, **3**, 114, 235, 262, 264, 288; **15**, 14; **22**, 19-20
  effect of contract on, **6**, 91, 92
  enforcement of laws relating to, **5**, 233, 234; **9**, 152 n. 21; **10**, 312-13, 346
  income tax, **3**, 288
  indemnity, request for, **23**, 213
  production of receipts, **3**, 368
  reimbursement, **11**, 95-6; **20**, 90-1, 114-15
  release from liability, **14**, 47-8
Technical Agreement with De Nederlandsche Bank NV (1981), **1**, 192-9, 204-12; **12**, 55; **13**, 43-4, 59 n. 14
  Appendix I, **1**, 204, 207
  Paragraph 1, **1**, 196, 198; **3**, 196; **6**, 66; **8**, 279 n. 56

Paragraph 3, **1**, 193, 194
Technical Arrangement between Banque Centrale d'Algérie, Bank of England and Federal Reserve Bank of New York, **8**, 209 n. 2; **12**, 53, 78 n. 16, 192-9, 204-12: *see also* Dollar Account No. 1; Dollar Account No. 2
Paragraph 7, **5**, 68, 69
Paragraph 10, **1**, 193
Time limits: *see also* Procedure
  amendment of claim, **2**, 338; **3**, 11, 30, 31; **6**, 60, 68; **8**, 134-40; **12**, 20; **14**, 93; **16**, 303, 304, 306-9; **17**, 53-7, 296; **22**, 215, 216-17, 234; **28**, 378-9
  arbitrator, challenge to, **20**, 234, 237; **21**, 348, 349, 352, 355, 360-4, 375-7, 379, 391-4, 399-402
  consolidation of cases, **4**, 241
  contractual, **17**, 189-90, 217, 232, 240-1
  correction of award, **5**, 73; **30**, 19
  counterclaims, **2**, 113, 268, 283, 286-9, 347; **3**, 116, 226, 253; **4**, 182; **5**, 400; **9**, 37-8, 227; **11**, 205; **12**, 100, 123, 225, 227-9; **17**, 57-61, 252-3, 296; **18**, 188; **20**, 6; **22**, 234-5; **24**, 131, 275; **26**, 102-3, 151-2; **27**, 154-5; **30**, 6, 11, 16
  enforcement, **3**, 85, 379
  exceptions, **2**, 315, 320
  extension, **1**, 119, 120, 173-5, 230, 231, 320-5, 483; **2**, 3, 125, 283-90, 311, 327-31, 345-7; **3**, 41, 60, 85, 89, 90, 200, 301-3, 372-5, 377-9; **4**, 13, 17, 59, 63-7, 71-3, 76; **5**, 139, 140; **8**, 28, 39, 361; **9**, 348; **13**, 310-17; **18**, 56-7, 60-1, 73; **21**, 12
    —justification for, **3**, 84; **18**, 56-7
    —when imposed by Award, **2**, 283
  failure to meet, **1**, 132, 133, 171, 226-9, 334-6, 391, 485; **2**, 3, 123, 312, 313, 317, 318, 320, 321; **3**, 85, 90, 116, 226, 253, 380, 382; **4**, 3, 61, 64, 67, 73, 76, 143, 182, 214, 227; **5**, 400; **7**, 116, 117, 182; **11**, 181, 182, 287; **15**, 20; **21**, 7
    —delay by Registrar, **28**, 57
    —delay in mail, **1**, 127, 129-31, 226-9
    —excused, **2**, 317
    —failure of courier, **1**, 128-31; **2**, 313, 318; **3**, 5; **4**, 76; **21**, 3
  failure to set, **1**, 158, 159, 178-80; **4**, 66; **5**, 141-3
  fairness to parties, **28**, 61, 379

Time limits (*cont.*)
  filing of claim, **8**, 369; **9**, 4; **28**, 56-7
  filing of documents, **12**, 131-2; **17**, 98; **22**, 234
  filing of Settlement Agreement, amendment, **9**, 62, 71, 348
  implied modification, **8**, 185, 186
  interest, claim for, **17**, 50-1
  new claim, **16**, 259
  notification of costs, **13**, 299; **16**, 258; **17**, 50-1
  payments from Security Account, effect on, **17**, 367
  request for hearing, **22**, 208-9
  request for interpretation and correction of Award, **9**, 405
  request for revision of Award, **4**, 11, 182; **22**, 208
  statement of defence, **2**, 283, 286-9; **3**, 85, 89, 253, 374, 375
  statutes of limitations and, **3**, 287; **5**, 128; **7**, 116; **8**, 136; **16**, 306; **17**, 189-90, 216, 231, 240; **19**, 329-30, 340-1; **30**, 157
  submission of evidence, **17**, 52; **28**, 249-50
  Undertakings: *see* Undertakings, time limits
Trade law, **3**, 54; **5**, 394
Trade practice, **5**, 32, 33; **13**, 232-3; **16**, 25, 48
  applicable law, **16**, 27
Transfer of cases, **7**, 183, 200, 205
Transfer of documents, **3**, 108, 119, 120
Translation: *see* Award, language; Evidence, translation
Treaties: *see also* Treaties (and analogous instruments)
  customary international law and, **10**, 192, 202; **15**, 34-5; **16**, 69, 88; **17**, 264; **21**, 120-2, 330-1
  interpretation: *see* Treaty interpretation
  obligations. municipal law and, **19**, 287-8
  pre-existing obligations, effect on, **19**, 286-7
  reservations, **19**, 287-8
  right to invoke, **10**, 148, 150, 192
  termination—
    —evidence of, **15**, 218
    —parties' rights and, **10**, 191 n. 9; **15**, 218
  validity—
    —duress or fraud, **15**, 214-15

  —*jus cogens*, **15**, 216
  —violation of internal laws, **3**, 303-9
Treaties (and analogous instruments)
  Agreement between US and Egypt Concerning Claims of Nationals of the United States (1976), **5**, 283, 285, 329
  Agreement Providing for Determination of Amount of Claims Against Germany, US-Germany (1922), **2**, 83
  Amity, Economic Relations and Consular Rights, Iran-US (1955), **1**, 313, 365, 501; **2**, 84, 161, 257, 353; **4**, 103-5, 109, 112-17, 155, 156, 174, 179; **5**, 381-3; **6**, 151, 168, 178, 200, 201 n. 1, 208; **7**, 41, 47, 50, 51; **8**, 378-9, 428-50; **9**, 272-3; **10**, 106, 267; **15**, 29, 34-5, 214; **16**, 249; **17**, 143, 147; **18**, 161; **23**, 395; **26**, 227
  applicability, indirect claim, **15**, 34 n. 14
  —Article II, **4**, 174 n. 2; **6**, 168; **16**, 88, 89; **17**, 107
  —Article III(1), **21**, 71 n. 17
  —Article IV, **2**, 353, 388; **4**, 102, 112, 114 n. 1, 116, 174 n. 2, 234 n. 10; **6**, 168, 200 n. 2, 225 n. 1; **7**, 40, 46, 51; **8**, 379, 404; **10**, 131-3, 148, 184, 192-6, 203, 204 n. 38; **12**, 12; **15**, 34 n. 14, 219-22, 230, 231, 246, 252, 290, 292, 298; **16**, 88 n. 5, 195 n. 29, 239, 241; **17**, 107; **21**, 118, 161; **29**, 271; **30**, 196
  —Article V, **6**, 183 n. 1; **16**, 88 n. 5
  —Article VII, **3**, 28 n. 1; **5**, 382; **6**, 211, 212; **7**, 40, 46, 47
  —Article XVII, **5**, 270
  —Article XX, **4**, 174 n. 2
  —Article XXI, **8**, 405
  —Article XXIII, **4**, 112, 113; **10**, 131, 190; **15**, 218
  —and customary international law, **9**, 273; **10**, 151, 184, 192; **14**, 234; **15**, 214, 300; **16**, 69 n. 19, 88-9, 238 n. 5; **21**, 125
  —expropriation, applicable law, **16**, 25, 68-9, 194-5, 239; **21**, 118-19, 121, 125; **30**, 255-7
  —expulsion and, **16**, 88; **17**, 107, 143
  —"interests in property", **16**, 195-6; **21**, 118-19
  —source of law, **10**, 132, 150, 184; **17**, 143

—termination or breach, **4**, 112-14; **5**, 381, 383; **15**, 218
—validity, **7**, 8, 379, 431-51; **10**, 149, 190-1; **17**, 143
—whether binding, **5**, 381
Claims Settlement Declaration: *see* Claims Settlement Declaration
Convention on the Elimination of All Forms of Discrimination Against Women, **5**, 273 n. 1
Convention on the Recognition and Enforcement of Foreign Arbitral Awards (1958) (New York), **2**, 60; **6**, 137 n. 2; **18**, 138-9
Convention on the Recognition and Enforcement of Foreign Judgments (1983), **5**, 233; **18**, 138-9
Convention on the Settlement of Matters Arising out of the War and Occupation (1952), **5**, 272, 298
Draft Articles on Sovereign Immunity of States and State Properties, **5**, 11 n. 1
Draft Articles on State Responsibility, **5**, 12; **12**, 318 n. 4; **16**, 83, 84, 99, 100
Draft Code of Conduct for Transnational Corporations, **10**, 204 n. 39
Draft Convention on Arbitral Procedure, **3**, 301 n. 1
Draft Convention on the International Responsibility of States for Injuries to Aliens, **10**, 259 n. 6
Draft Convention on the Protection of Foreign Property (1967), **4**, 118 n. 2, 174
Draft Convention on Recognition and Enforcement of Foreign Judgments in Civil and Commercial Matters, **9**, 152 n. 21
European Convention on Foreign Money Liabilities (1967), **8**, 424
European Convention on International Commercial Arbitration (1961), **1**, 292 n. 24
Federal Republic of Germany-Iran, Double Taxation Agreement, **16**, 223
General Convention providing a Uniform Law for Bills of Exchange (1930), **13**, 32-3, 69; **21**, 63 n. 2
General Declaration: *see* General Declaration

Geneva Convention providing a Uniform Law for Cheques (1931), **2**, 168, 235; **3**, 19: *see also* European Convention on International Commercial Arbitration *above*
Germany-US, Treaty of Peace of Berlin (1921), **2**, 80, 83, 84
Hague Conventions: *see* Hague Conventions on
Hague Rules: *see* International Convention for the Unification of Certain Rules Relating to Bills of Lading (1924) (amended 1968 and 1979) *below*
Harvard Draft Convention on the International Responsibility of States for Injuries to Aliens (1961), **2**, 84, 89, 351, 352, 388; **4**, 115, 118 n. 2, 162, 166 n. 1, 173; **7**, 51
Harvard Draft Convention on the Responsibility of States (1929), **2**, 196, 197, 205; **5**, 326
Human Rights of Individuals who are not Citizens of the Country in which they live, Draft Declaration, **16**, 88-9
International Convention for the Unification of Certain Rules Relating to Bills of Lading (1924) (amended 1968 and 1979), **12**, 143-5
International Monetary Fund Agreement: *see* International Monetary Fund, Agreement
New York Convention on the Recognition and Enforcement of Foreign Arbitral Awards, **18**, 136 n. 21, 138-9
Seoul Declaration on the Progressive Development of Principles of Public International Law Relating to a New International Economic Order, **14**, 235
Treaty of Neuilly, **3**, 311; **5**, 320
Treaty of Paris, France-Great Britain (1814), **2**, 181; **5**, 304, 312
Treaty of Peace, UN and Italy, **2**, 206; **5**, 310, 326
Treaty of Rome, **13**, 92
Treaty of Versailles (1919), **2**, 80, 83, 84, 186
Treaty of Washington, Great Britain-US (1871), **2**, 181, 190; **5**, 305
UN Charter, **3**, 24 n. 1
—Article 51, **2**, 258 n. 1
UN Charter of Economic Rights and

366 INDEX

Treaties (and analogous instruments) (*cont.*)
  Duties of States, **4**, 105, 106, 114 n. 1; **5**, 11; **7**, 170; **10**, 185, 198; **15**, 223
  UN Convention on Contracts for the International Sale of Goods, **5**, 45; **13**, 50; **19**, 34; **22**, 244, 245 n. 18, 318 n. 92, 329
  UN Convention on the Recognition and Enforcement of Foreign Arbitral Awards, **14**, 327 n. 8
  UN Declaration on the Establishment of a New Economic Order, **10**, 185, 198
  UN Declaration on the Human Rights of Individuals who are not Nationals of the Country in which they live, **14**, 20
  UN Declaration on Inadmissibility of Intervention into Domestic Affairs of States, **8**, 445
  UN Declaration on Permanent Sovereignty over Natural Resources (1962), **4**, 114 n. 1; **10**, 186, 198, 204 n. 38; **14**, 235; **15**, 242, 294 n. 12
  UN Declaration on Principles of Friendly Relations, **3**, 8, 445
  Universal Declaration of Human Rights, **5**, 273 n. 1
  US-Iran Guaranty of Private Investments (1957), **10**, 141, 148, 151-2
  US-Mexican Claims Convention (1868), **2**, 83
  US-Mexican General Claims Convention (1923), **2**, 80, 83
  US-Mexican Special Claims Convention (1923), **2**, 80
  US-Poland Agreement (1960), Article 3, **1**, 466 n. 1
  Vienna Convention: *see* Vienna Convention on the Law of Treaties
  Warsaw Convention for the Unification of Certain Rules Relating to International Carriage by Air, **17**, 230 n. 5
Treaty interpretation, **1**, 101-10, 190-2, 198-201, 205, 207-13, 288, 289, 292-5, 307, 308, 310; **2**, 160-8, 178-215, 311, 315, 320, 363, 371, 402; **3**, 305; **5**, 2, 67, 83, 253, 259, 271, 273, 277, 294, 329-33, 341-6, 351; **6**, 168; **7**, 33; **8**, 92, 95, 207-13, 295; **10**, 140; **14**, 328-30; **18**, 123: *see also* Contract, interpretation; Jurisdiction of Tribunal, interpretation of Declarations; Vienna Convention on the Law of Treaties (1969)
aids, **2**, 161-4, 179-215; **3**, 310; **5**, 262, 281, 290, 291, 329; **8**, 211; **19**, 288; **28**, 138
  —context, **17**, 166; **28**, 151
  —judicial precedents, **5**, 262, 271, 304-28, 331, 332
  —negotiating history, **1**, 245, 246, 255, 256, 265, 266, 276, 277, 284-6, 310-12, 477; **2**, 161, 165, 196-8, 201, 202, 210, 212; **3**, 303, 304, 305-11, 313-15; **5**, 261, 300, 301, 304; **10**, 193; **12**, 75-6; **13**, 168, 329; **16**, 239; **19**, 288-90; **21**, 118
  —subsequent practice, **2**, 149; **5**, 71, 268, 271, 289, 332, 346, 347, 353; **8**, 201, 407, 440, 447-50; **9**, 104-5, 411-13; **18**, 384; **19**, 294, 304; **21**, 28, 120-1, 129, 151
  —writings of scholars, **5**, 262, 264, 328
ambiguity, effect, **2**, 317; **5**, 287, 289, 290; **11**, 87
applicable law, **12**, 82
associated agreements, **12**, 51
good faith, **6**, 251, 270; **12**, 60-1; **14**, 330; **16**, 310
guidelines—
  —clear language required to vary existing rule, **10**, 313
  —*contra proferentem* rule: *see verba ambigua accipiuntur contra proferentem below*
  —effectiveness, **6**, 251; **12**, 46, 68 n. 7; **14**, 330-1; **25**, 258
  —*eiusdem generis*, **2**, 79, 86-7
  —equilibrium to be maintained, **12**, 54-5, 79-80
  —*expressio unius est exclusio alterius*, **8**, 264; **12**, 59, 78; **13**, 252; **16**, 307
  —flexible, **1**, 199 n. 1, 309 n. 8
  —*generalia specialibus non derogant*, **13**, 88; **14**, 329
  —intention of parties, **1**, 103-5, 107-10, 190, 191, 198, 201, 205-7, 210, 211, 213, 245, 246, 255, 256, 265, 266, 276, 277, 284-6, 311, 312, 489, 491, 492, 495, 497, 498, 516; **2**, 166, 210, 211, 213, 223, 315, 316, 320; **3**, 303-5, 307-10, 312-15; **5**, 14, 260, 267, 270, 272, 280, 281, 288, 329, 352; **6**, 270; **7**, 33

INDEX

—language, structure and purpose, **12**, 74
—object and purpose, **5**, 261, 268, 270, 271, 281, 284, 285; **8**, 200-1; **18**, 387; **19**, 287, 294; **28**, 149-50
—*obligatio tertio non contrahitur*, **13**, 43
—ordinary meaning, **2**, 55, 63; **8**, 207-8; **10**, 193-5; **12**, 46; **14**, 329; **18**, 123-4; **19**, 287; **25**, 258; **28**, 150
—*pacta tertiis nec nocent nec prosunt*, **13**, 43
—plain language, **28**, 152
—reasonableness, **10**, 83
—restrictive, **1**, 192, 198, 211-13, 309 n. 8, 480; **2**, 80, 179, 211, 223; **3**, 309, 312, 313; **5**, 13, 93, 95, 99, 126, 281, 287, 288, 330, 351; **7**, 135; **11**, 87; **13**, 168-9
—*specialia derogant generalibus*, **1**, 104, 410 n. 3; **15**, 222; **21**, 121, 125
—*ut res magis valeat quam pereat*, **1**, 292 n. 25; **12**, 46, 68 n. 7, 89; **25**, 258
—*verba ambigua accipiuntur contra proferentem*, **2**, 211; **5**, 281, 286, 288, 330; **9**, 255; **10**, 329, 331
international claims practice, **10**, 83
lacunae, **12**, 54, 58-60; **21**, 330
pacta sunt servanda, **1**, 114, 210; **9**, 140; **13**, 231-3; **15**, 294 n. 10
—State's duty to respect contracts distinguished, **15**, 242-3
phrases—
—"control", **2**, 16-22, 147-52; **17**, 166-7, 178-9
—"property rights", **2**, 82-5
preamble, status, **12**, 46-8, 67-8
procès-verbaux, **2**, 198
rebus sic stantibus: *see* Changed circumstances
reciprocity, **1**, 106, 107; **8**, 432-41
terms, meaning, **3**, 311, 314, 315; **5**, 4, 260, 267, 268, 270, 280, 281, 284, 285, 289, 290
Tribunal: *see also* International tribunals
absence of arbitrator: *see* Arbitrator, absence
applicable law, **20**, 204
arbitrary action, **6**, 232
authority of President, **5**, 51, 52; **9**, 409-13
Chambers: *see also* Full Tribunal *below*
—assignment of cases to, **3**, 92, 126, 141, 237, 254, 268, 276, 292
—authority, **5**, 47, 53
—composition, **9**, 409-13
—independence, **5**, 251; **16**, 290
claims: *see* Claims
competence, **5**, 127; **6**, 52
confidentiality of proceedings, **1**, 424, 428-31, 441, 449; **2**, 29, 343, 357; **19**, 106, 167, 170; **21**, 365-6, 387, 394; **29**, 364-6
dicta, **4**, 178, 180
disclosure of documents, **21**, 354, 372-4, 389
discretion, **3**, 192, 207, 212, 234, 316, 339, 362, 382 n. 1; **4**, 12, 224; **5**, 262; **7**, 116; **15**, 148
duty to—
—act in informed way, **18**, 111
—apply principles of law, **9**, 146
—avoid entering into execution of Award, **13**, 40
—avoid excessive technicality, **8**, 139
—avoid unjust enrichment, **15**, 257
—clarify aim, **7**, 121, 126
—clarify requests, **5**, 147
—determine legitimate expectation, **16**, 54
—enforce law of Iran, **9**, 177
—examine jurisdiction, **9**, 34, 332
—execute Algiers Declarations, **8**, 65
—exercise equitable discretion, **16**, 221
—fill omissions in UNCITRAL rules, **11**, 278
—give reasoned decision, **10**, 330
—implement international law, **7**, 171
—respect laws of Iran, **7**, 136
—respect legal facts, **5**, 12
—respond to arguments, **5**, 289
—settle disputes, **14**, 64; **18**, 106, 146-7
equity and, **18**, 334
exceeding powers, **5**, 335
expeditious conduct of business, **7**, 204; **8**, 288
expenses, **1**, 107, 108
Full Tribunal: *see also* Chambers *above*
—binding nature of finding, **11**, 197
—preemption by Chamber, **10**, 85-6
—relinquishment of cases to, **21**, 98, 100-2
—residual authority, **21**, 283-4

368

INDEX

Tribunal (*cont.*)
 functus officio rule (*dessaisissement de juge*), **3**, 177, 182, 187, 195, 196, 330 n. 3
 impartiality, **5**, 36, 41, 42, 49, 86; **6**, 41, 251, 252, 270, 271
 inherent powers, **5**, 129; **6**, 108; **7**, 219; **8**, 117, 118; **25**, 187; **28**, 221-3; **29**, 383, 387-90
 —interim measures, **2**, 59-62
 international character, **5**, 261, 284, 294-7, 299; **9**, 177, 330
 interstate nature, **18**, 385
 juge d'instruction, **2**, 285, 286, 346; **3**, 300; **5**, 54
 jurisdiction: *see* Jurisdiction of Tribunal
 majority decision, **2**, 29, 114, 123, 146, 390; **3**, 55, 199, 210, 211, 277, 293, 295, 325; **4**, 82, 111, 159; **5**, 269, 277 n. 1; **8**, 143; **9**, 140, 409-13; **10**, 96; **18**, 47-8
 moral issues, **13**, 117, 119 n. 3
 neutrality, **5**, 15, 16, 24, 49
 not bound by parties' legal theories, **13**, 101; **17**, 50
 obligation to comply with decisions of, **9**, 394
 powers—
  —to investigate, **2**, 115, 122 n. 1, 284, 285; **3**, 88, 89
  —to secure compliance with General Declaration, **25**, 261
 precedent, effect: *see* Precedent
 President—
  —absence, **21**, 282
  —appointment, **21**, 201-3, 309-17
  —powers, **21**, 311-12
 quorum, **1**, 117
 refusal of claims, responsibility for, **19**, 178, 181, 183, 184, 185, 193, 195, 199
 statements contrary to fact, **5**, 36, 37
 suspension of proceedings, **7**, 281, 289, 301-2; **8**, 64
 ultra petitio, **13**, 41, 43
 ultra vires conduct, **3**, 125-9, 140-4, 146, 297-301, 302 n. 2, 315, 324; **5**, 335, 336; **6**, 252, 271; **13**, 41, 43; **18**, 48
 workload, **4**, 68, 69, 71; **7**, 203; **8**, 415 n. 23
Tribunal Rules
 Article 1, **19**, 314
 Article 2, **1**, 127, 128, 130, 226, 228, 337, 398; **7**, 275; **8**, 54 n. 4, 134, 361, 370, 376, 379, 391; **11**, 183, 287; **13**, 54; **17**, 332, 335, 338, 341, 344, 347; **19**, 180, 183, 186, 189, 192, 195, 198; **21**, 3; **23**, 245, 248, 251, 254, 257; **25**, 237, 274; **28**, 57
 Article 4, **1**, 167; **2**, 36; **28**, 219-20, 223-4
 Article 5, **9**, 407
 Article 6, **1**, 113, 511-14
 Article 7, **1**, 113
 Article 8, **1**, 113
 Article 9, **1**, 113, 114; **20**, 179, 203, 204-6, 220, 221, 222, 273, 276, 278-9, 282-3, 285, 324; **21**, 391; **24**, 310, 312, 314, 316, 317, 318
 Articles 9-12, **21**, 312; **24**, 309, 311, 312, 316, 323, 324
 Article 10, **1**, 112-15, 509, 512, 514, 516-18; **3**, 209; **20**, 183, 184, 220, 233, 241, 273, 278-9, 282, 315; **21**, 318, 355, 390, 391, 395; **24**, 324
 Articles 10-12, **20**, 206-8
 Article 11, **1**, 112-15, 509, 512, 516, 517; **20**, 183, 184, 187, 188, 234, 266, 315; **21**, 318, 348, 350, 352, 360, 375, 379, 391, 392, 393, 395, 399; **24**, 319, 320; **27**, 297, 312
 Article 12, **1**, 112-15, 509, 512-14, 516-18; **20**, 181, 183; **27**, 297
 Article 13, **3**, 126, 139, 209 n. 4, 215; **9**, 409-13; **10**, 96; **14**, 271 n. 2, 312, 353, 354; **16**, 284; **19**, 106, 117, 162, 164, 167-9, 170; **21**, 282, 393; **23**, 234; **26**, 5, 150, 189; **27**, 293-336; **30**, 22 n. 2
 —Amendment to, **7**, 56, 92; **14**, 271 n. 2
 Article 14, **3**, 209 n. 4, 316 n. 3; **4**, 214; **5**, 362; **7**, 56, 183; **20**, 238
 Article 15, **1**, 167, 306; **2**, 54, 59 n. 1, 122 n. 1; **3**, 88, 362, 372, 387, 389; **4**, 64, 70, 95; **7**, 126; **8**, 115-16; **10**, 109; **13**, 130; **14**, 71; **17**, 45; **18**, 111, 283; **21**, 282, 393; **22**, 209; **25**, 187, 276; **27**, 308 n. 5; **28**, 6, 380; **29**, 370
 Article 15(1), **30**, 105, 112, 121-2
 Article 15(2), **30**, 109-11, 120-1
 Article 17, **1**, 234; **2**, 368; **4**, 206; **8**, 54; **10**, 272; **13**, 54; **17**, 62; **21**, 10, 293; **28**, 384
 Article 18, **1**, 134, 167, 396; **3**, 378; **4**, 26; **7**, 88; **9**, 109; **17**, 254; **19**, 313, 314; **21**, 6, 10

INDEX

—advisory, **9**, 109
Article 19, **1**, 120, 159, 167, 171, 175, 179, 498; **2**, 268, 289; **3**, 116, 226, 253, 374, 377, 378; **4**, 143, 182, 227; **5**, 400; **6**, 83, 101; **7**, 88, 116; **8**, 428-9; **9**, 38, 167, 168, 227; **10**, 108, 308, 310; **11**, 135; **12**, 100; **13**, 83 n. 31, 225, 228; **14**, 281; **15**, 20; **17**, 57, 60-1, 254; **19**, 313, 314; **21**, 146, 147; **23**, 188, 353, 354; **24**, 131; **25**, 13; **26**, 151-2; **27**, 154
Article 19(2), **2**, 36
Article 19(3), **2**, 70-1, 113
Article 20, **1**, 309 n. 9, 393, 395, 399-401; **2**, 338; **3**, 11, 31; **4**, 101; **5**, 378; **6**, 28, 60, 63, 68, 70, 102; **8**, 137, 297 n. 16; **9**, 127; **10**, 12, 16-17; **11**, 17, 108; **12**, 6, 20, 100, 131, 289; **13**, 97, 228; **14**, 26, 90, 95, 148, 308, 310; **16**, 302, 306, 310; **17**, 55, 138, 254; **18**, 64; **19**, 53, 60, 76; **22**, 216, 234; **23**, 166, 382, 397; **24**, 131, 270-1; **26**, 150, 239; **28**, 58-60, 169, 192-4, 377, 379; **29**, 269
Article 21, **1**, 284, 285, 292, 294, 308, 320, 334, 335; **7**, 136; **8**, 44; **13**, 162; **17**, 184; **18**, 80-1, 231
Article 22, **3**, 382 n. 1; **17**, 45; **18**, 187; **29**, 377
Article 23, **17**, 45
Article 24, **1**, 323, 464, 477; **2**, 300, 389; **3**, 20, 294; **4**, 58, 80, 268; **5**, 22; **6**, 210; **9**, 244; **11**, 274, 327; **13**, 54-5; **16**, 106-7; **17**, 47, 263, 285; **18**, 105, 111, 325; **20**, 87; **24**, 23; **25**, 275 n. 6; **27**, 52; **28**, 249, 287-8
Article 24(3), **2**, 122; **30**, 58 n. 8
Article 25, **1**, 306, 458, 484, 485; **2**, 122; **3**, 381; **5**, 59 n. 1; **11**, 274, 276, 278, 281; **13**, 326 n. 4; **14**, 197-8, 200, 291; **17**, 52, 62-3; **19**, 113-15; **23**, 342; **25**, 7; **27**, 153; **29**, 245, 259, 313
Article 25(2), **30**, 180, 181
Article 25(6), **2**, 122
Article 26, **1**, 154, 390; **2**, 65-6, 370, 371, 402; **3**, 60, 175; **4**, 7, 58; **5**, 128; **6**, 140; **8**, 47, 65, 218, 275, 278 n. 55, 280; **13**, 176, 177, 196, 257, 258-9; **16**, 197 n. 37; **18**, 122 n. 3; **21**, 4
Article 26(1), **2**, 60-1
Article 27, **1**, 235; **4**, 95, 158; **8**, 276 n. 31; **9**, 34-5; **13**, 351; **16**, 190, 198, 245; **24**, 24, 26

Article 28, **1**, 324; **3**, 85, 363, 382 n. 2; **8**, 40; **10**, 179; **11**, 181; **17**, 46, 254; **18**, 89, 187; **23**, 265, 283, 286; **25**, 230, 236; **26**, 191; **29**, 377
Article 29, **2**, 101, 122; **8**, 115-16; **27**, 52, 210-13
Article 29(2), **30**, 104-5, 108-11, 112, 116-22
Article 30, **9**, 410, 412; **25**, 6
Article 31, **1**, 200 n. 2, 323, 424, 429, 449 n. 1; **2**, 29, 121; **3**, 55; **4**, 82, 159; **9**, 410; **12**, 233 n. 2, 268 n. 9; **16**, 238 n. 4, 334; **18**, 47; **19**, 106, 167, 170; **21**, 256, 349, 366, 367-8, 387, 394; **23**, 218 n. 4; **29**, 364
Article 32, **1**, 330, 331, 406, 420, 422, 449, 452, 454; **2**, 333, 365, 367; **3**, 37, 74, 79, 83, 109, 118, 155, 168, 169, 212, 238, 255, 269, 293, 294, 339, 365; **4**, 180, 198, 206, 209; **5**, 81, 84, 252; **6**, 34, 109, 268; **7**, 183, 210, 222; **8**, 114, 185; **9**, 400; **10**, 152, 358; **12**, 21, 119 n. 4, 388, 394; **14**, 10, 174; **15**, 187; **16**, 256; **19**, 163; **21**, 338, 349, 352, 375; **26**, 6, 189, 259, 260; **29**, 23, 387, 397, 402, 413
Article 32(1), **2**, 101
Article 32(3), **30**, 169
Article 33, **16**, 256; **18**, 334
Article 34, **1**, 140, 149, 150-3, 156, 160, 161, 163, 182-4, 216, 220, 221, 328-31, 342, 343, 404-6, 409; **2**, 45, 126, 133, 134, 229, 262, 269, 279, 292, 306, 333, 348, 356, 357, 364, 367; **3**, 35, 37, 38, 74, 75, 78, 92, 119, 141, 169, 176, 181, 182, 187, 192, 194-6, 213, 219, 327, 328, 330, 338, 352, 353, 360, 390-2; **4**, 21, 22, 29, 30, 33, 34, 42, 47, 49, 83, 85, 86, 183, 185, 193, 194, 197-201, 205, 206, 282; **5**, 74, 76, 77, 80, 82, 149, 151, 156, 250, 355; **6**, 2, 3, 5, 21, 23, 34, 39, 121, 147; **7**, 210, 221, 224, 227, 236, 237, 242, 245, 248, 250, 253, 259, 262, 264, 269; **8**, 12, 14, 16, 18, 43, 67, 73, 80, 82, 84, 97, 184, 186, 187, 215, 237, 349, 354, 361; **9**, 8, 63, 71, 185, 204, 205, 307, 309, 312, 348, 358; **10**, 358, 359; **11**, 365; **12**, 394; **13**, 361; **14**, 342; **16**, 294, 317, 319, 320; **17**, 61, 355, 362, 363; **18**, 63, 93-4, 377, 378; **19**, 310, 345, 346, 352, 353,

Tribunal Rules (*cont.*)
354, 361, 362, 367; **21**, 296-9, 302; **22**, 208, 365, 366, 372, 373; **23**, 403, 407, 409; **25**, 5; **26**, 252; **27**, 275, 282, 284; **28**, 222, 316-17, 376, 381, 389, 390, 393, 394, 401, 402; **29**, 188, 192, 196, 200, 204, 208, 213; **30**, 284, 295, 302
Article 34(1), **2**, 90; **30**, 8-9, 10, 14, 15, 284, 292
Article 34(2), **30**, 7, 10, 12, 18, 173 n. 4
Article 35, **3**, 364; **4**, 60; **5**, 74; **8**, 115; **9**, 405, 406; **11**, 182-3, 274, 287; **12**, 305, 307, 388; **13**, 327-8; **14**, 70 n. 6, 101-2, 173-5, 256-7, 261-2; **16**, 282-4; **19**, 171-3, 318; **22**, 208; **25**, 187; **26**, 186-7, 188, 258, 260; **27**, 195, 270-1
Article 36, **3**, 364; **4**, 60, 81, 82, 111; **5**, 73, 74; **6**, 269; **8**, 117 n. 11, 133; **9**, 405, 406; **11**, 182-3, 274, 283-4, 285-6, 300; **12**, 306; **13**, 93-4; **14**, 70 n. 6, 101, 173-5, 256; **16**, 282-4; **18**, 76-7, 114; **19**, 171-5, 253, 255; **20**, 171; **21**, 293; **22**, 153, 208; **23**, 122-5, 230, 231; **25**, 187, 188, 275; **26**, 186-7, 258, 261; **27**, 195, 264-5, 268, 271; **28**, 308; **29**, 387; **30**, 19, 20
Article 37, **3**, 364; **4**, 18; **5**, 73, 74; **8**, 53, 116-17; **9**, 406; **11**, 182-3; **13**, 324, 327; **14**, 70 n. 6, 257-8, 280-1; **16**, 110, 282-4; **18**, 76-7; **19**, 253, 256, 318, 319-20; **22**, 208; **25**, 187, 274; **26**, 258, 267; **27**, 195, 271; **28**, 51, 196; **29**, 294, 387; **30**, 19, 20-1
Article 38, **1**, 414, 447, 451; **2**, 113, 259, 385, 400; **3**, 33, 58, 71, 253, 275, 291; **4**, 79; **5**, 231; **7**, 47, 88, 197; **8**, 330; **9**, 60, 242; **10**, 34, 35, 316; **11**, 43; **14**, 282; **16**, 111; **25**, 109, 176; **26**, 183, 260; **27**, 260, 263
Article 38(1), **2**, 12
Article 40, **1**, 414, 447, 451, 508; **2**, 113, 245, 259, 385, 400; **3**, 33, 58, 71, 253, 275, 391; **4**, 79; **6**, 217; **7**, 47, 197; **8**, 330, 331; **9**, 60; **10**, 34, 35, 103; **11**, 43; **12**, 38-9; **16**, 254, 281; **21**, 19; **23**, 229; **25**, 109, 176; **26**, 183, 260; **27**, 260; **29**, 120; **30**, 234
Article 40(1), **2**, 40; **30**, 168 n. 8
Article 40(2), **2**, 12
Article 41(2), **2**, 75, 76; **3**, 166; **4**, 92, 93, 158; **5**, 186; **8**, 41, 47, 331; **10**, 21, 35

interpretation, **16**, 295
—*travaux préparatoires*, **27**, 317-22, 324, 332
Introductory Rules, Article 3, **1**, 431
parties' agreement on, **5**, 268
Section II, **21**, 309
violation, **4**, 81; **6**, 70
Tribunal Staff Rules
Article 1, **16**, 331, 332
Article 9, **16**, 331

UNCITRAL Rules, **20**, 210, 235 n. 4, 247-8; **27**, 293-336: *see also* Tribunal Rules
travaux préparatoires, **20**, 247, 315
UNCTAD, **8**, 409
Undertakings, **12**, 50-2
interpretation, Tribunal's jurisdiction, **8**, 206-13; **9**, 104-6
object and purpose, **12**, 50, 73 n. 4
Paragraph 1, **12**, 50
Paragraph 2, **6**, 66
Paragraph 2(A), **5**, 67; **10**, 83; **12**, 55, 72
Paragraph 2(B), **1**, 137 n. 1; **2**, 312-21; **3**, 3-6, 381; **5**, 58, 61, 67-70, 71; **8**, 197-206; **9**, 97-106; **12**, 55, 72, 77; **16**, 293 n. 4, 294; **29**, 187, 191, 195, 199-200, 203-4, 207-8, 212; **30**, 16-17
—ambiguity, **8**, 198-200, 205
procedural requirements, **2**, 313, 319; **3**, 5, 6
time limits, **2**, 313-19; **3**, 5, 6
Undue influence, **21**, 52
Unequal bargaining power, **3**, 320, 325
Unilateral commitments, binding nature, **14**, 321-3
United Kingdom
arbitration law, **20**, 213-14, 242 n. 18
interest on debt, **2**, 12, 27
United Kingdom, law of
Misrepresentation Act 1967, **3**, 30
Oil and Undersea Pipeline Act 1975, **7**, 168
Sale of Goods Act 1979, **19**, 32 n. 16, 33
United Nations, **7**, 170, 171
Charter, Article 11, **10**, 186 n. 19
resolutions, effect, **30**, 240-1
Security Council Resolution 598 of 20 July 1987, **19**, 293
United States
courts—
—expropriation, **14**, 236

INDEX

— injunction, **3**, 267
— John Doe action, **3**, 15, 25
— jurisdiction, **9**, 136-7
— stay of proceedings, **5**, 154, 344 n. 1
— termination of claims, **2**, 62; **9**, 136-7
—— need to contest lien and, **28**, 129-30, 152-3
duty to examine validity of claims, **5**, 85
Foreign Claims Settlement Commission, **5**, 350; **10**, 140; **12**, 23; **18**, 273 n. 46
nationality of corporation, proof, **1**, 456-74
United States, law of, **1**, 459, 460, 464, 467-74, 479-81
Agricultural Foreign Investment Disclosure Act (1978), **1**, 472
antitrust, **13**, 83-6
arbitration, **3**, 210, 211, 295; **20**, 207, 215, 216, 243-4, 253-4, 274-5, 278, 305-14
Arbitration Act, **20**, 309, 310-11, 312-13
Arms Export Control Act, **19**, 289-93
Atomic Energy Act 1954, **28**, 134
Bankruptcy Act, **8**, 257-9; **19**, 118
California—
— Civil Code, **14**, 229; **30**, 50-2
— Code of Civil Procedure, **6**, 102
— Constitution, **7**, 204
— marital rights, **30**, 49-56
Carriage of Goods by Sea Act, **12**, 145
citizenship, **5**, 270
Code of Ethics for Arbitrators in Commercial Disputes, **7**, 180 n. 1, 204
Code of Federal Regulations, **7**, 192; **11**, 176; **17**, 217
Code of Judicial Conduct, **20**, 275, 278, 310
Code (USC), **7**, 10, 122; **17**, 22 n. 4, 217-18; **25**, 204 n. 11
Constitution, **5**, 296
— Article II(2), **3**, 307 n. 1
— Article VI, **4**, 114
contract, **3**, 163; **6**, 196, 274
corporations, **7**, 205; **21**, 77
Domestic International Sales Corporation, **3**, 40; **7**, 186, 205
Executive Order of 14 November 1979 (freezing Iranian assets), **7**, 192; **13**, 52 n. 7; **19**, 288, 289-93; **23**, 206-7
Executive Order 12205 of 7 April 1980, **29**, 340

Executive Order 12211 of 17 April 1980, **17**, 190-1, 233; **23**, 391
Executive Order 12281, **28**, 125, 126-7, 129, 151
Executive Order 12294 of 24 February 1981, **12**, 287
Executive Orders Prohibiting Transactions with Iran, **2**, 249, 251, 255 n. 1; **5**, 60, 61; **6**, 28; **13**, 28; **19**, 216-17, 247; **29**, 340-2
— disposal of blocked property, **19**, 217-18
Export on Administration Act 1979, **28**, 134
extraterritorial effect, **8**, 258-9
Federal Communications Act (1934), **1**, 468
Federal Rules of Civil Procedure—
— Rule 13(a), **6**, 101; **13**, 78-83
— Rule 15, **8**, 136 n. 3; **16**, 311 n. 19
— Rule 17, **16**, 310-11
— Rule 41, **1**, 233
Foreign Corrupt Practices Act, **12**, 218
Foreign Sovereign Immunities Act (1976), **2**, 148-9; **10**, 205 n. 40; **28**, 130, 157-8
government agencies, **5**, 8-11
Immigration and Nationality Acts, **2**, 222; **5**, 100, 102; **22**, 149; **25**, 64 n. 5, 169-71; **26**, 41, 49, 50, 51
International Claims Settlement Act, **5**, 346 n. 1
International Investment Survey Act (1976), **1**, 460
Iranian Assets Control Regulations, **2**, 248, 251, 252, 255 n. 1; **5**, 14 n. 1, 60; **13**, 52 n. 7, 90; **24**, 39
Merchant Marine Acts (1920 and 1936), **1**, 471
military equipment, export, **19**, 289-93
non-profit corporations, **5**, 345; **10**, 325
Nuclear Non-Proliferation Act 1978, **28**, 134
offset, **21**, 74 n. 25
partnership, **3**, 161
receivership, **21**, 69
Restatement of Agency (Second), **19**, 126, 135 n. 14; **23**, 146 n. 9
Restatement of Conflict of Laws (Second), **7**, 99 n. 1; **30**, 53
Restatement of Foreign Relations Law (Revised) (Draft) (1986), **10**, 202 n. 35

United States, law of (*cont.*)
  Restatement of Foreign Relations Law (Second) (1965), **2**, 84; **5**, 297; **7**, 169; **8**, 135, 397-9; **9**, 142 n. 7; **18**, 388
  Restatement of Foreign Relations Law (Second) (Revised) (Tentative Final Draft) (1985), **8**, 11, 40
  Restatement of Foreign Relations Law (Third), **19**, 56 n. 6; **23**, 387
  Restatement of the Law of Contracts, **13**, 50-1; **24**, 86
  Restatement of the Law of Contracts (Second), 3-56; **28**, 209; **30**, 54, 55
  Restatement of the Law of Restitution, **12**, 379
  Restatement of Trusts (Second), **10**, 239 n. 6
  Rules for the ICC Court of Arbitration, **7**, 204
  Securities Act (1933), **2**, 148 n. 1
  Shipping Act (1916), **1**, 471
  Statute of Limitations, **17**, 216-19, 231, 240
  Tax Reform Act (1984), **7**, 205
  Tentative Final Draft Restatement, Foreign Relations Law (Revised) (1985), **9**, 275
  Treasury Regulations, **5**, 14; **25**, 256-62, 263; **28**, 124-5, 127-37
  Uniform Commercial Code, **4**, 268; **5**, 45; **7**, 99, 102, 109, 113, 114; **8**, 140
    —$1-105, **22**, 287 n. 33
    —$1-106, **3**, 57 n. 2
    —$1-201, **3**, 20 n. 2
    —$2-204, **3**, 48
    —$2-206, **3**, 50
    —$2-207, **3**, 49
    —$2-208, **13**, 51-2
    —$2-235, **13**, 51
    —$2-240, **7**, 109 n. 2
    —$2-301(a), **12**, 300 n. 4
    —$2-313, **19**, 31, 32
    —$2-319, **7**, 100 n. 2
    —$2-325, **7**, 109
    —$2-504, **7**, 100 n. 2
    —$2-509, **7**, 100
    —$2-602, **7**, 101 n. 1
    —$2-609, **22**, 318 n. 92
    —$2-612, **13**, 50 n. 4
    —$2-703, **7**, 110 n. 1; **13**, 50 n. 4
    —$2-706, **7**, 110 n. 1, 111, 114 n. 1; **22**, 245 n. 18
    —$2-708, **7**, 111; **26**, 165
    —$2-709, **3**, 52, 56
    —$2-710, **3**, 52, 56; **7**, 111
    —$2-714, **19**, 33, 39 n. 35
    —$3-122, **7**, 115; **21**, 44
    —$3-302, **2**, 235; **3**, 20 n. 2; **7**, 99
    —$3-305, **3**, 20 n. 2; **7**, 99, 100 n. 1
    —$3-307, **3**, 20
    —$3-309, **3**, 51
    —$3-413, **2**, 168; **3**, 19
    —$3-506, **3**, 20 n. 2
    —$3-507, **2**, 169
  Uniform Partnership Act, **11**, 313, 348
Unjust enrichment, **1**, 287, 309 n. 9; **2**, 155, 234-9; **3**, 30-2, 278, 279; **4**, 231, 232, 278, 279; **5**, 171, 172; **6**, 168, 169, 172, 177, 213, 215; **8**, 60, 390; **9**, 56-8, 401, 402-3; **10**, 107, 171; **11**, 238, 335-6, 351; **12**, 352-6, 363, 375-80; **13**, 101, 115, 116, 117, 119 n. 3, 120; **14**, 180-9; **15**, 257, 268-9, 308; **16**, 19; **18**, 222, 309-10, 323-4, 347; **19**, 139, 142, 146, 148, 150, 152, 295; **21**, 70-1, 73; **22**, 354; **23**, 146; **26**, 26-7, 251; **28**, 16, 85-7, 205-8, 215
Unlawful acts, **6**, 169

Valuation: *see* Damages, valuation
Video tapes: *see* Statement of claim, video tapes
Vienna Convention on the Law of Treaties (1969), **1**, 190, 205, 209, 289; **5**, 281, 351, 353; **8**, 443; **9**, 256; **12**, 68 n. 7, 82
  Article 2, **19**, 287
  Article 12, **1**, 200
  Article 19, **19**, 287-8
  Article 26, **1**, 109; **12**, 61; **13**, 231
  Article 27, **1**, 490, 495; **3**, 304, 305
  Article 31, **1**, 109, 198, 200, 211, 288, 307; **2**, 160, 161, 209, 210; **3**, 305 n. 1, 310, 312 n. 1; **5**, 83, 259, 260, 265, 273, 279, 281, 289, 290, 329-32, 341, 346; **8**, 92, 95, 201 n. 12, 207, 295, 440, 447; **10**, 193 n. 12; **11**, 87; **12**, 46, 51, 74, 89, 273; **13**, 168; **14**, 328; **16**, 310; **18**, 123, 385; **19**, 287, 294, 304; **25**, 258, 259; **28**, 129, 151 n. 7
  Article 31(1), **2**, 82, 147
  Article 31(3), **2**, 149
  Article 32, **1**, 109, 211 n. 3, 288, 307; **2**,

INDEX

160; **3**, 305 n. 1, 310; **5**, 259, 279, 280; **11**, 46; **13**, 168; **15**, 221; **19**, 288
Article 33, **11**, 8, 9, 36, 46; **12**, 82; **22**, 295
Article 34, **13**, 43-4
Article 45, **4**, 112 n. 3, 113
Article 46, **1**, 490, 495; **3**, 304-6
Article 47, **1**, 489, 495; **3**, 304, 306
Article 49, **15**, 215
Article 51, **15**, 215
Article 52, **15**, 215
Article 53, **15**, 216
Article 54, **4**, 112 n. 3; **10**, 191
Article 60, **2**, 257
Article 62, **1**, 314; **4**, 112 n. 3; **8**, 443-4; **9**, 122; **15**, 217
Article 65, **4**, 112 n. 3; **8**, 444; **10**, 191
Article 67, **4**, 112 n. 3; **10**, 191
Article 70, **10**, 191 n. 9
Visa, suspension, **23**, 382, 385, 390-2

Warranty
  breach, **19**, 12-14, 31-8
  implied, **19**, 31 n. 16
  testing to confirm specifications distinguished, **19**, 14
Wholly-owned subsidiary, **7**, 206: *see also under* Nationality of claim, corporations
Withdrawal of action: *see* Claims, withdrawal
Witnesses: *see* Evidence, witnesses
Words and phrases
  a rubro ad nigrum, **8**, 231
  acta jure gestionis, **1**, 419
  actio ex contractu, **18**, 139
  actio non datur non damnificato, **13**, 116
  "actions in response to", **28**, 122-3
  actor incumbit onus probandi, **1**, 209, 420, 464; **18**, 216
  allegans contraria non audiendus est, **1**, 318 n. 17: *see also* Estoppel
  alternativa petitio non est audienda, **6**, 70
  amiable compositeur, **21**, 368
  causa proxima non remota inspicitur, **3**, 249
  communis opinio juris, **2**, 197; **5**, 300; **8**, 387; **10**, 185, 200; **14**, 236
  compensation légale, **21**, 74 n. 25
  consensus ad idem, **24**, 182
  contra proferentem, **1**, 214
  culpa in contrahendo, **3**, 30; **5**, 248
  damnum emergens, **2**, 387 n. 1; **10**, 189; **15**, 248, 268; **21**, 330
  delegata potestas non potest delegari, **27**, 325

dessaisissement de juge, **3**, 177, 182, 187, 195, 196, 330 n. 3
dicta, **4**, 178, 180
dies certus quando, **21**, 64 n. 3
dies incertus quando, **21**, 64 n. 3
ei qui affirmat, non ei qui negat, incumbit probatio, **20**, 266
eiusdem generis, **5**, 3; **23**, 240
ex aequo et bono, **12**, 82; **21**, 368
ex malo jus non oritur, **8**, 444-7
ex parte, **3**, 387
ex proprio motu, **24**, 27
exceptio non adimpleti contractus, **22**, 304, 317-23
exequatur, **6**, 133, 135, 138, 139; **18**, 118, 122, 127, 137, 139, 140, 141, 142, 143, 149 n. 66
expressio unius exclusio alterus est, **5**, 268; **8**, 264; **12**, 59, 78; **13**, 252; **16**, 27, 307
faute quasi-délictuelle, **3**, 30
force majeure: *see* Force majeure
forum non conveniens, **7**, 137; **8**, 266
functus officio, **3**, 177, 182, 187, 195, 196, 330 n. 3
generalia specialibus non derogant, **13**, 88; **14**, 329
gestion d'affaire, **7**, 164
in absentia, **22**, 253
in jure, non remota causa, sed proxima spectatur, **11**, 48
"Iranian properties", **28**, 125-41
juge d'instruction, **2**, 285, 286, 346; **3**, 300; **5**, 54
jus cogens, **15**, 216
jus imperii, **10**, 313; **17**, 264
jus sanguinis, **2**, 181, 184, 185; **5**, 274, 305
jus soli, **2**, 181, 184; **5**, 274, 305
lacunae, **21**, 330
lex est dictamen rationis, **21**, 365
lex loci actus, **21**, 63 n. 2
lex loci contractus, **21**, 63 n. 2
lex non cogit ad impossibilia, **18**, 328
lex specialis, **8**, 378, 428; **21**, 121, 125, 330; **30**, 255
locum tenens, **6**, 6, 72, 239, 240; **7**, 172; **18**, 262
locus regit actum, **21**, 63 n. 2; **22**, 161
locus standi, **7**, 120, 123, 124, 135, 198, 199; **9**, 326-33; **10**, 45-6, 148, 325; **11**, 86, 213, 311-13; **14**, 34; **15**, 195; **16**, 12-16, 300-3, 305, 310-12, 329; **17**,

Words and phrases *(cont.)*
263; **18**, 166, 209; **20**, 266; **21**, 103, 339-40
  lucrum cessans, **2**, 387 n. 1; **15**, 249-51, 258-9, 270, 305; **21**, 330
  mutatis mutandis, **21**, 3, 6
  note en délibéré, **4**, 61
  nullus commodum capere de sua injuria proprio, **6**, 228
  obligatio tertio non contrahitur, **13**, 43
  oeuvres préparatoires, **20**, 247, 276
  onus probandi, **25**, 116
  opinio juris, **21**, 121
  ordre public, **2**, 221; **3**, 14
  pacta sunt servanda, **1**, 114, 210; **9**, 140; **13**, 231-3; **15**, 294 n. 10
  pacta tertiis nec nocent nec prosunt, **13**, 43
  pendente lite, **5**, 113
  période suspect, **22**, 136 n. 4
  persona standi, **5**, 273, 274
  probandit necessitas incumbit illi qui agit, **18**, 325
  procès-verbaux, **2**, 198
  proprio motu, **3**, 298; **5**, 371; **9**, 333; **14**, 61
  quantum meruit: *see* Quantum meruit
  quantum valebat, **4**, 234
  ratione materiae, **5**, 278
  ratione personae, **5**, 278
  ratione temporis, **5**, 278
  rebus sic stantibus: *see* Changed circumstances
  res derelicta, **6**, 173
  res inter alios acta, **13**, 122
  res judicata, **1**, 170, 171, 287; **2**, 311, 371; **4**, 16, 73 n. 1, 233 n. 1; **6**, 227 n. 2; **11**, 141; **12**, 174, 367; **15**, 196; **21**, 295; **27**, 266
  res litigiosae, **27**, 266
  restitutio in integrum, **2**, 386-7; **6**, 157, 170; **8**, 385, 395-8; **10**, 201, 204 n. 39; **15**, 247, 255, 262, 265, 266
  société simple, **21**, 103
  stare decisis, **8**, 141; **9**, 170
  sua sponte, **5**, 146; **6**, 41, 177; **7**, 116; **22**, 107, 299
  sub silentio, **20**, 263, 327
  sui generis, **4**, 116 n. 1
  travaux préparatoires, **20**, 247, 276, 315
  ultra petitio, **13**, 41, 43
  ultra vires, **3**, 125-9, 140-4, 146, 297-301, 302 n. 2, 315, 324; **5**, 335, 336; **6**, 252, 271; **13**, 41, 43; **18**, 48; **21**, 400; **22**, 296
  ut res magis valeat quam pereat, **1**, 292 n. 25; **12**, 46, 68 n. 7, 89; **25**, 258
  venire contra factum proprium, **20**, 155
  verba ambigua accipiuntur contra proferentem, **2**, 211; **5**, 281, 286, 288, 330; **9**, 225, 371, 393-4; **10**, 329, 331